$34.95

The Blackwell Guide to the

Modern Philosophers

Blackwell Philosophy Guides

Series Editor: Steven M. Cahn, City University of New York Graduate School

Written by an international assembly of distinguished philosophers, the *Blackwell Philosophy Guides* create a groundbreaking student resource – a complete critical survey of the central themes and issues of philosophy today. Focusing and advancing key arguments throughout, each essay incorporates essential background material serving to clarify the history and logic of the relevant topic. Accordingly, these volumes will be a valuable resource for a broad range of students and readers, including professional philosophers.

The Blackwell Guide to Epistemology
Edited by John Greco and Ernest Sosa

The Blackwell Guide to Ethical Theory
Edited by Hugh LaFollette

The Blackwell Guide to the Modern Philosophers
Edited by Steven M. Emmanuel

The Blackwell Guide to the Modern Philosophers

From Descartes to Nietzsche

Edited by

Steven M. Emmanuel

First published 2001

2 4 6 8 10 9 7 5 3 1

Blackwell Publishers Inc.
350 Main Street
Malden, Massachusetts 02148
USA

Blackwell Publishers Ltd
108 Cowley Road
Oxford OX4 1JF
UK

Library of Congress Cataloging-in-Publication Data

The Blackwell guide to the modern philosophers : from Descartes to Nietzsche / edited by Steven M. Emmanuel.
p. cm. — (Blackwell philosophy guides)
Includes bibliographical references and index.
ISBN 0-631-21016-4 (hardcover : alk. paper) — ISBN 0-631-21017-2 (pbk. : alk. paper)
1. Philosophers, Modern—Europe. 2. Philosophy, Modern. I. Emmanuel, Steven M. II. Series.

B791 .B53 2000
190—dc21

00-022954

British Library Cataloguing in Publication Data

A CIP catalogue record for this book is available from the British Library.

Typeset in 10 on 13 pt Galliard
by Ace Filmsetting Ltd, Frome, Somerset
Printed in Great Britain by TJ International, Padstow, Cornwall

This book is printed on acid-free paper.

Contents

List of Contributors

Martha Brandt Bolton is Professor of Philosophy at Rutgers, the State University of New Jersey. She has published numerous articles on Locke, including "The Epistemological Status of Ideas: Locke Compared to Arnauld," in *History of Philosophy Quarterly* (1992); and "The Real Molyneux Question and the Basis of Locke's Answer," in *Locke's Philosophy*, ed. G. A. J. Rogers (1994).

Terrell Carver is Reader in Political Theory at the University of Bristol, England. He is the editor of *The Cambridge Companion to Marx* (1996) and author of several book-length studies, including *Marx's Social Theory* (1982); *Marx and Engels: The Intellectual Relationship* (1983); and *A Marx Dictionary* (1987).

N. J. H. Dent is Professor of Philosophy at the University of Birmingham. He is the author of *The Moral Psychology of the Virtues* (1984); *Rousseau: An Introduction to his Psychological, Social and Political Theory* (1988); and *The Rousseau Dictionary* (1992).

Wendy Donner is Associate Professor of Philosophy at Carleton University. She is the author of *The Liberal Self: John Stuart Mill's Moral and Political Philosophy* (1991); "John Stuart Mill's Liberal Feminism," *Philosophical Studies* (1993); and "Utilitarianism," in *The Cambridge Companion to Mill*, ed. John Skorupski (1997).

C. Stephen Evans is Professor of Philosophy at Calvin College. He is the author of *Kierkegaard's Fragments and Postscript: The Religious Philosophy of Johannes Climacus* (1983); and *Passionate Reason: Making Sense of Kierkegaard's Philosophical Fragments* (1992).

Richard Fumerton is Professor of Philosophy at the University of Iowa. He is the author of *Metaepistemology and Skepticism* (1996), as well as numerous articles, including "Inferential Justification and Empiricism," *The Journal of Philosophy* (1976);

"Induction and Reasoning to the Best Explanation," *Philosophy of Science* (1980); and "Externalism and Epistemological Direct Realism," *The Monist* (1998).

Don Garrett is Kenan Distinguished Professor for Teaching Excellence, University of North Carolina at Chapel Hill. He is the editor of *The Cambridge Companion to Spinoza* (1996). His articles include "Spinoza's Theory of Metaphysical Individuation," in *Individuation in Early Modern Philosophy*, eds. Gracia and Barber (1994); "Spinoza's Ethical Theory," in *The Cambridge Companion*; and "Teleological Explanation in Spinoza and Early Modern Rationalism," in *New Essays on the Rationalists*, eds. Huenemann and Gennaro (1998).

Ross Harrison is Professor of Philosophy at King's College, Cambridge University. He is the author of *Bentham* (1985) and *Democracy* (1993). He contributed the introduction to Bentham's *A Fragment on Government*, eds. J. H. Burns and H. L. A. Hart (1988).

Gary Hatfield is Professor of Philosophy at the University of Pennsylvania. His numerous articles on Descartes include "First Philosophy and Natural Philosophy in Descartes," in *Philosophy, Its History and Historiography*, ed. A. J. Holland (1985); "Descartes' Physiology and Its Relation to His Psychology," in *The Cambridge Companion to Descartes*, ed. John Cottingham (1992); and "Reason, Nature, and God in Descartes," in *Essays on the Philosophy and Science of René Descartes* (1993).

Stephen Houlgate is Professor of Philosophy at the University of Warwick. He is the author of *Hegel, Nietzsche and the Criticism of Metaphysics* (1986); *Freedom, Truth and History: An Introduction to Hegel's Philosophy* (1991). He also edited *The Hegel Reader* (1998).

Christopher Janaway is Professor of Philosophy at Birkbeck College, the University of London. He is the author of *Self and World in Schopenhauer's Philosophy* (1989) and *Schopenhauer* (1994). He is also the editor of *Willing and Nothingness: Schopenhauer as Nietzsche's Educator* (1998) and the *Cambridge Companion to Schopenhauer* (1999).

Patricia Kitcher is Professor of Philosophy at Columbia University. She is the author of *Kant's Transcendental Psychology* (1990) and the editor of *Kant's Critique of Pure Reason: Critical Essays* (1998). Her articles on Kant include "Apperception and Epistemic Responsibility," in *Central Themes in Early Modern Philosophy*, eds. Jan Cover and Mark Kulstad (1990); and "Revisiting Kant's Epistemology," *Nous* (1995).

A. P. Martinich is Roy Allison Vaughan Centennial Professor of Philosophy, University of Texas at Austin. His books include *The Two Gods of Leviathan* (1992); *A Hobbes Dictionary* (1995); *Thomas Hobbes* (1997), and *Hobbes: A Biography* (1999).

Steven Nadler is Associate Professor at the University of Wisconsin, Madison. He is the author of *Malebranche and Ideas* (1992) and *Arnauld and the Cartesian Philosophy of Ideas* (1989). He is the editor of *Malebranche: Philosophical Selections* (1992), as well as the forthcoming *Cambridge Companion to Malebranche.*

David Fate Norton is Macdonald Professor of Moral Philosophy at McGill University. He is the author of *David Hume: Common-Sense Moralist, Skeptical Metaphysician* (1982), and the editor of *The Cambridge Companion to Hume* (1993). He is currently working on the first critical edition of Hume's *A Treatise of Human Nature.*

George Pappas is Professor of Philosophy at Ohio State University. His numerous articles on Berkeley include "Berkeley and Immediate Perception," in *Essays on the Philosophy of George Berkeley*, ed. Ernest Sosa (1987); "Epistemology in the Empiricists," *History of Philosophy Quarterly* (1988); and "Berkeley and Skepticism," *Philosophy and Phenomenological Research* (1999). He is the author of a forthcoming book entitled *Berkeley's Thought.*

Donald Rutherford is Associate Professor of Philosophy at the University of California, San Diego. He is the author of *Leibniz and the Rational Order of Nature* (1997). His articles include "Philosophy and Language in Leibniz" and "Metaphysics: The Late Period," both of which appeared in *The Cambridge Companion to Leibniz* (1995).

Richard Schacht is Professor of Philosophy at the University of Illinois, Urbana-Champaign. He is the author of *Nietzsche* (1995) and *Making Sense of Nietzsche: Reflections Timely and Untimely* (1995). He edited *Nietzsche: Selections* (1993); *Nietzsche, Genealogy, Morality: Essays on Nietzsche's "Genealogy of Morals"* (1994); and *Nietzsche: Human, All Too Human* (1996).

Ernest Sosa is Romeo Elton Professor of Natural Theology and Professor of Philosophy at Brown University. He is the editor of *Mill's Utilitarianism*, with James Smith (1969); *Essays on the Philosophy of George Berkeley* (1987); and *A Companion to Epistemology*, with Jonathan Dancy (1996). His articles include "Berkeley's Master Stroke," *Essays on Berkeley: A Tercentennial Celebration*, eds. John Foster and Howard Robinson (1985) and "How to Resolve the Pyrrhonian Problematic: A Lesson from Descartes," *Philosophical Studies* (1996).

James Van Cleve is Professor of Philosophy at Brown University. He is the author of *Problems from Kant* (1999). His articles include "Foundationalism, Epistemic Principles, and the Cartesian Circle," *Philosophical Review* (1979); "Descartes and the Destruction of the Eternal Truths," *Ratio* (1994); and "Reid on the First Principles of Contingent Truths," *Reid Studies* (1999).

Preface

In the introduction to his magisterial *History of English Thought in the Eighteenth Century*, Leslie Stephen observed:

> [W]hen we look beyond the narrow circle of illustrious philosophers, we are impressed with the conviction that other causes are at work besides those which are obvious to the logician. Doctrines vanish without a direct assault; they change in sympathy with a change in apparently remote departments of inquiry; superstitions, apparently suppressed, break out anew in slightly modified shapes; and we discover that a phase of thought, which we had imagined to involve a new departure, is but a superficial modification of an old order of ideas.[1]

An adequate history of philosophical ideas, he went on to argue, must therefore take into account "the social conditions which determined their reception" (19). This ideal of looking at earlier philosophers in the context of their own time and situation was not one that Anglo-American philosophers in the twentieth century were quick to emulate. In a tradition primarily concerned with problems and arguments, studies in the history of philosophy often presented little more than what Bertrand Russell called "the isolated thoughts of remarkable individuals."[2] Russell's own contribution to the field, *A History of Western Philosophy*, published in 1945, was intended to be an exception to this pattern in its conscious attempt to "exhibit philosophy . . . as both an effect and a cause of the character of the various communities in which different systems flourished" (ix). There have been other notable exceptions. But even among the better surveys, in which some care is given to reconstructing the original social, cultural, and intellectual climate, we find that the discussion of the major figures is often confined to the leading ideas and texts, or to those most congenial to the author's own narrative purposes. Historians of modern philosophy, in particular, have been notoriously selective in their coverage of the major writings of the period – especially so in the case of scientific works.

There is, however, a discernible tendency in recent scholarship to reinterpret the great thinkers of the modern period in the context of their own time and in terms of a more comprehensive examination of the range of their thought. One very fine example of this tendency is Stephen Gaukroger's *Descartes: An Intellectual Biography*, which reevaluates Descartes's contributions to epistemology and metaphysics in the light of a close examination of his earlier work in mathematics and natural science, and in particular his commitment to central tenets of Copernican astronomy.[3] Gaukroger convincingly demonstrates that a truly adequate explanation of Descartes's philosophical achievement must take into account specific historical events (for example, the condemnation of Galileo by the Inquisition in 1633), formative intellectual influences both within and outside the traditions of philosophy, and the role of philosophical commentators, who disseminated interpretations of Cartesianism that would affect its reception from the seventeenth century down to the present. He also introduces a further consideration that can be added to those noted by Leslie Stephen in the passage quoted above: the fact that a thinker may deploy "explicitly 'philosophical' modes of argument" in order to "obfuscate rather than elucidate" his true position (14).

This is not to say that the truth of philosophical arguments cannot be evaluated apart from very detailed knowledge of the social and cultural conditions from which they emerged, or apart from the larger story of a philosopher's intellectual progress. When truth is the primary concern, our historical interest may extend only to ascertaining what a philosopher actually said, thereby preparing the way for the work of logical analysis. Somewhat ironically, it was Bertrand Russell who, in the preface to his early critical exposition of Leibniz's thought, championed this "properly philosophical" method of inquiry:

> [I]n such inquiries the philosopher is no longer explained psychologically: he is examined as the advocate of what he holds to be a philosophic body of truth. By what process of development he came to this opinion, though in itself an important and interesting question, is logically irrelevant to the inquiry how far the opinion itself is correct; and among his opinions, when these have been ascertained, it becomes desirable to prune away such as seem inconsistent with his main doctrines, before those doctrines themselves are subjected to a critical scrutiny.[4]

In pedagogical practice, this has long been accepted as the most efficient – even if not the most intellectually satisfying – method for surveying a whole period of philosophical thought within the span of a single semester. But such an approach admittedly does little to help students understand what motivated philosophers to propose the arguments they did, the social and cultural developments to which they were responding. It fails to give students a sense of how ideas are created and transmitted. This shortcoming is all the more acutely apparent when viewed in the light of current scholarship.

No general survey of the modern period will be able to reproduce the depth and detail of scholarly discussion available in book-length studies of individual philosophers. Nevertheless, a better introductory guide to modern philosophy is needed by students and teachers; one that is attuned to the most recent developments in the critical literature. The present work is intended to address precisely that need.

The contributors to this volume provide a genuinely scholarly basis for understanding the development of philosophical thought from Descartes to Nietzsche. Readers who are interested primarily in the major arguments of the modern philosophers will find that these are delineated here in admirably clear and accessible treatments. A chief strength of the volume is that the contributors themselves are specialists who write with an expert knowledge of their thinkers and the issues that currently occupy the attention of scholars in the secondary literature. What is more, they have undertaken to give a more comprehensive account of each philosopher's thought – and of its significance for subsequent debate – than is customary in textbook discussions.

Although the contributors have in every case endeavored to reconstruct the intellectual environment in which their philosophers wrote, they have followed their own judgment in determining the best approach to presenting the material. In some cases, very detailed attention is given to the prevailing social and cultural climate; in others, the emphasis is more toward demonstrating the philosopher's relevance to contemporary debates; and in still others, the discussion concentrates on peculiar difficulties of reading and interpretation. As a totality, the volume presents a richly nuanced study, which will serve as a useful point of entry into the history of philosophical thought in the modern period. For those who are interested in pursuing a more advanced study of the history of modern philosophy, a select bibliography is included at the back of the volume.

Finally, I would like to express my sincere thanks to the contributors for sharing their expertise; to the entire staff at Blackwell for their helpfulness and good humor throughout the project; and to my good friend and colleague Patrick Goold for his sound advice and unfailing support along the way.

Notes

1 Leslie Stephen, *History of English Thought in the Eighteenth Century* (London, 1876), I, p. 3.
2 Bertrand Russell, *A History of Western Philosophy* (New York: Simon & Schuster, 1945), p. ix.
3 Stephen Gaukroger, *Descartes: An Intellectual Biography* (Oxford: Oxford University Press, 1995). Among the very newest titles are Roger Ariew's *Descartes and the Last Scholastics* (Ithaca: Cornell University Press, 1999), Steven Nadler's *Spinoza: A Life* (Cambridge: Cambridge University Press, 1999), and A. P. Martinich's *Hobbes: A Biography* (Cambridge: Cambridge University Press, 1999).
4 Bertrand Russell, *A Critical Exposition of the Philosophy of Leibniz* (London, 1900). Russell's intention here was not to dismiss the "strictly historical inquiry," but rather to add a much-needed philosophical analysis of Leibniz's views to the existing body of secondary literature.

Chapter 1

René Descartes

Gary Hatfield

Descartes is the most notorious of modern philosophers. His philosophical teachings have been so influential that they cannot be avoided, whether one agrees with them or not. The extreme skeptical doubt brought on by the "evil deceiver" can seem easy to dismiss, or hard to shake. Descartes's way out of this skepticism, through the famous phrase "I think, therefore I am," finds many uses in one-line humor. It seems funny that anyone would need to prove that they exist – especially to themselves. His theory that mind and body are independent substances, which is known as "mind–body dualism," has provoked the greatest philosophical response. Few now accept the philosophical theory that mind is a substance independent of body. But Descartes is still much invoked in the philosophy of mind, as hero or villain, by those who admire or disparage his realism about the mental. Some blame him for many modern ills, contending that his dualism caused thinkers to devalue the body and emotions. Others find cause to celebrate his high achievements in mathematics, natural philosophy (or natural science), and metaphysics.

In this chapter we want to get past stereotypes and reputation in order to look at Descartes anew. The real Descartes was an original scientist, mathematician, and metaphysician, who laid the basis for analytic geometry, published the first unified celestial and terrestrial physics, and proposed new and interesting theories of mind, body, and their interaction. These new theories framed Descartes's work on the philosophy and psychology of sense perception and on the role of the body in emotion. In examining Descartes's writings and considering his legacy, we will focus especially on his work in metaphysics and natural philosophy, including the senses and emotions.

1. Descartes's Ambitions

Descartes was a talented youth who came to believe he had a mission in life, to establish a new philosophy. He was born in 1596 in the Poitou region of France, near Tours in the small town of La Haye (subsequently renamed "Descartes").[1] His mother died just over a year later. He lived with his maternal grandmother until entering the newly established Jesuit college at La Flèche, which he attended from 1606 to 1614. The curriculum included grammar, rhetoric, literature, mathematics, logic, natural philosophy, ethics, and metaphysics. The last four areas, which constituted the principal parts of philosophy, drew upon the Aristotelian tradition. In 1616 Descartes received a law degree from the University of Poitiers, where he probably also studied medicine. Two years later, while traveling as a gentleman soldier, he met the Dutch natural philosopher Isaac Beeckman, who rekindled his interest in mathematical approaches to nature. Beeckman encouraged Descartes to explain the properties of material things by thinking of them as composed of small round spheres, or atoms, of matter. Descartes dedicated his first written work to him, the *Compendium on Music* (written in Latin and published posthumously in 1650).

Descartes and Beeckman were alive to the excitement of their time. Nicholas Copernicus's hypothesis that the Earth moves around the Sun had stirred controversy and interest in astronomy. A moving Earth would violate Aristotle's physical principle that all earthly matter naturally strives to reach the center of the universe – a principle which entailed that Earth is unique as a solid globe surrounded by air and water, motionlessly occupying its central position. Galileo Galilei had used the newly invented telescope to observe the heavens, and in 1610 he discovered moons around Jupiter, thereby challenging the uniqueness of Earth. Descartes took part in a celebration of this discovery at La Flèche that same year. Johannes Kepler published new works in mathematical optics in 1604 and 1611, explaining that the lens in the eye forms an image on the retina, and showing how the telescope works. Astronomy and optics had been mathematical sciences since antiquity, but now they were being radically revised. Descartes and Beeckman joined Kepler and Galileo in developing new mathematical approaches to a variety of physical problems. Descartes later became a prominent advocate of reform in science, and his work helped inspire Isaac Newton's physics.[2]

Despite his early penchant for mathematical science, Descartes was uncertain what road in life he should take. In November 1619, while in Germany en route to join the Bavarian army, he had three powerful dreams, which he believed confirmed his quest for a new scientific system. In the year following, he worked intensively on mathematical problems and achieved significant results in geometry (solving cubic and quartic equations using the circle and parabola). He started a book on "universal mathematics" which was to build on these results; however, he interrupted his work for a trip to Italy. Upon returning to Paris in 1625 he was still uncertain of his calling, and he briefly considered taking up a position in civil administration. He soon gave up that idea, and while in Paris from 1625 to 1628 he joined a group of mathematicians and intellectuals that included Marin Mersenne, an advocate of mathematical descriptions of nature. During this time Descartes discovered the sine law of refraction. He returned to his universal mathematics, now conceived as a method for either solving or rejecting as ill-posed all problems conceivable by human beings – whether mathematical or natural scientific – through an algebraic science of quantity. He abandoned this project in 1628, and the unfinished manuscript was published in 1701 (in Latin) as the *Rules for the Direction of the Mind*.

In 1628 and 1629 Descartes reformulated his ambitious intellectual agenda. Late in 1628 he attended a public lecture arranged by the Papal Nuncio in Paris. The lecture was given by a chemist named Chandoux, who criticized Aristotle's natural philosophy and offered instead a chemically based account of nature. The talk was received warmly by the Parisian intellectuals in attendance, except for Descartes. Cardinal Bérulle, an important religious and intellectual figure in Paris, asked Descartes to explain his disapproval. Descartes praised the speaker's rejection of Aristotle's philosophy, but blamed him for offering merely probable opinions in its place. He boasted that he himself possessed a universal method for separating the true from the false with certainty. Bérulle encouraged him to devote himself to bringing the fruits of this method to the world. Descartes devoted the rest of his life to intellectual pursuits, publishing four major books – covering geometry, optics, the physical world as a whole, and metaphysics – and leaving several others unpublished at his death in 1650.

In 1629 Descartes moved to Holland. His first nine months there were devoted to metaphysics. He developed a new approach to knowing God and the soul as immaterial beings, and recorded a fundamental insight into the nature of the eternal truths. Early in 1630 Descartes wrote to his friend Mersenne that contemplation of God and the soul had led him to "discover the foundations of Physics" (AT 1:144).[3] He also told Mersenne that "mathematical truths, which you call eternal, have been established by God and are entirely dependent on him, just as are all his other creations" (AT 1:144–5). By this he meant that the mathematical truths are free creations of God, dependent on God's will, such that God might have willed them otherwise. These remarks will be discussed with Descartes's metaphysical writings.

Descartes was composing a small treatise on metaphysics when he was interrupted in the summer of 1629 by a scientific problem. In April of that year Christopher Scheiner had observed an impressive set of false suns, or parhelia, near Rome. A report was circulated among natural philosophers. When Descartes learned of it, he set immediately to work on explaining this optical phenomenon (which is caused by ice crystals in the upper atmosphere, and not by a solid ring of ice as suggested by Descartes, AT 6:355). He soon felt compelled to expand his project beyond optics and atmospherics. In November he wrote to Mersenne that completion of his work would be delayed about a year, since "instead of explaining a single Phenomenon, I am determined to explain all the Phenomena of nature, that is, the whole of Physics" (AT 1:70). His study of "the whole of Physics" included anatomy and physiology, and during this time he regularly visited the butcher shop to watch animals being slaughtered, and to retrieve parts to take home for dissection (AT 1:263, 523; 2:525). The project developed into Descartes's *World*, which was to have three parts: a treatise on light (which would contain a general physics), a treatise on man (covering human physiology), and a treatise on the soul. After three years of work, he had produced (at least) the first two treatises when he learned of Galileo's condemnation by the Roman Catholic Inquisition (in 1633) for defending the Copernican hypothesis that the Earth moves about the Sun. Since Descartes affirmed the Copernican hypothesis in his physics, he felt compelled to suppress his writings, and even considered burning them (AT 1:270–1). They were published posthumously in 1664 (in French) as *The World, or Treatise on Light* and the *Treatise on Man*.

After the Galileo affair Descartes did not give up his project of reforming the sciences, but he decided to test the reception of his new ideas by offering a sampler. In 1637 he published the *Discourse on the Method* as a preface to three essays, the *Dioptrics*,[4] *Meteorology*, and *Geometry*. Although publication was anonymous, the identity of the author was soon known. Descartes used the *Discourse* to introduce his intended program of scientific work to the public, to sketch some of his metaphysical arguments, and to request funds in support of empirical observations to decide among his own rival hypotheses for explaining various phenomena.

The essays themselves presented his mathematical accomplishments and gave a foretaste of his new physics. The *Meteorology* began from certain "suppositions" or hypotheses, that "the water, earth, air, and all other such bodies that surround us are composed of many small parts of various shapes and sizes, which are never so properly disposed nor so exactly joined together that there do not remain many intervals around them; and that these intervals are not empty but are filled with that extremely subtle matter through the mediation of which, I have said above, the action of light is communicated" (AT 6:233). Descartes's physics (discussed in section 3, below) was founded on the suppositions that all bodies are composed of small parts (which, he explained, are not atoms but are infinitely divisible), that there is no void but that subtle matter fills the interstices of larger bodies, and that causation is communicated by contact among particles. Descartes did not, in the *Discourse* and essays, explicitly reject all other explanatory entities in physics, such as the active principles or "substantial forms" of the scholastics, and the "real qualities" by which they explained color perception; but he did signal that he would not use such notions in his own explanations (AT 6:239). In the *Discourse*, Descartes claimed to be able to "deduce" the first principles of his physics from metaphysics, and to have purposely refrained from doing so in that work (AT 6:76). For now, the corpuscularian principles of his physics would be sustained by being "proven" through effects; that is, he argued that the fact that his principles sufficed to explain a wide variety of phenomena served as strong, if not certain, confirmation for them.

Descartes invited readers to send any objections to his publisher, and soon he found himself defending his physical suppositions, his omission of substantial forms and real qualities, and his metaphysics, including the mind–body distinction. In letters from the late 1630s he remained unwilling to reveal either the entirety of his physics, or its metaphysical foundations. He did, however, defend his claim that his physics was confirmed by its explanatory scope (AT 1:423–4, 563; 2:199), and he promised to publish his metaphysics (AT 2:622).

The promised metaphysical treatise was published in 1641 as the *Meditations on First Philosophy*. As he sent the manuscript to Mersenne in November 1640, he insisted that "the little Metaphysics I am sending you contains all the Principles of my Physics" (AT 3:233). Yet, oddly enough, the *Meditations* contains no extended discussion that can easily be identified as principles of physics. Descartes explained this seeming omission in a subsequent letter to Mersenne (January 28, 1641).

> I will say to you, just between us, that these six Meditations contain all the foundations of my Physics. But, please, you must not say so; for those who favor Aristotle would perhaps have more difficulty in approving them; and I hope that those who will read them will unwittingly become accustomed to my principles, and will recognize the truth, before they notice that my principles destroy those of Aristotle. (AT 3:297–8)

It is difficult to find Descartes's physical principles in the *Meditations* because he purposely obscured their presence. Which leaves it to his readers to find them.

Descartes believed that his *Meditations* was an important work, but he did not recommend that readers should devote constant attention to it. He wrote the *Meditations* in order to reveal the true metaphysics as a basis for investigations into physics, medicine, mechanics, and morals.[5] As he wrote to the Princess Elizabeth of Bohemia in 1643, "just as I believe that it is very necessary to have properly understood, once in a lifetime, the principles of Metaphysics, because they are what gives us knowledge of God and our soul, I also believe that it would be very harmful to occupy one's intellect frequently in meditating upon them, because this would impede it from properly attending to the functions of the imagination and the senses" (AT 3:695). It is the latter functions that are used in the practical guidance of one's actions, and also in the investigations of natural philosophy, beyond the first principles.

Even as he published the *Meditations*, Descartes was hatching a plan to publish his entire philosophy in a form suitable for the schools. In effect, he was hoping to replace the prevailing Aristotelian curriculum with his own, which meant replacing at least the metaphysics and physics. Consequently, in 1644 he published (in Latin) the *Principles of Philosophy* in four parts. The first part reviewed his metaphysics from the *Meditations*. The second revealed the fundamental principles of his physics, including the equation of matter with extension, the denial of a vacuum, and his three comprehensive laws of motion. The third described the formation and motions of the various solar systems, and explained the transmission of light as a result of contact between small spherical particles. The fourth concerned the Earth, its formation, the cause of gravity, and the explanation for various particular phenomena, including the properties of fire, chemical substances, minerals, and the magnet. He had intended to write a fifth and a sixth part, to cover biological phenomena, including plants, animals, and the human animal, but ended up simply appending to Part Four a discussion of the human senses and sensory nerves.

At this juncture Descartes had realized his ambitions in metaphysics and general physics, but he still had not achieved the results he desired in the fields of medicine and morals. He had boasted earlier that he would find a proper health regimen in time to extend his own life by a century (AT 1:507), though as time passed he moderated his claims (AT 2:480, 4:329). In the mid-1640s he returned to his physiological studies (AT 4:329), and once again decided to start from the beginning and cover everything. In 1647–8 he worked on but left unfinished his *Description of the Human Body* (published posthumously in 1664, in French). The final work published in his lifetime, the *Passions of the Soul* (1649, in French), contained Descartes's theory of the emotions and his moral psychology. It was written in response to queries from Princess Elizabeth, who also pressed Descartes on metaphysical questions concerning the mind–body distinction. In 1649 Descartes accepted the invitation of Queen Christina of Sweden to come to Stockholm as a court philosopher. He died of pneumonia early the next year (February 11, 1650). His followers soon published many of his letters (1657–67), containing philosophical, mathematical, and scientific discussions, as well as pharmaceutical and medical advice for his friends. They subsequently published the other posthumous works mentioned herein.

2. The New Metaphysics

The *Meditations on First Philosophy* are a philosophical gem. The body of the *Meditations* runs fewer than 100 pages, but contains subtle arguments that have powerfully engaged its readers from the start. Although much of the material of the *Meditations* was repeated and elaborated in Part One of the *Principles*, the former work remains the reference point for discussion and will guide our examination of Descartes's new metaphysics.[6]

The Meditations as a written work

Part of the success of the *Meditations* comes from Descartes's creativity in casting his philosophical arguments so as to engage individual readers. In crafting his work he adapted methods of argument and exposition from previous culture, drawing on mathematics, medieval philosophy and theology, and religious writings. These factors are of great importance in understanding whence Descartes believed the philosophical force of his work derived.

Descartes intended the *Meditations* to allow individual readers to see for themselves the basic philosophical truths he considered himself to have discovered. As a result, he wrote it according to the "analytic method," or the method of discovery, which he believed was a secret method of the ancient mathematicians (AT 7:155–9). Usually with the analytic method one starts from something familiar or given, and then looks for the principles that serve for its demonstration. Descartes added an extra twist. He started by doubting everything so as to arrive at a first "given" that all readers should be willing to grant as certain. Then he examined this indubitable starting point, until he found its basis. Subsequently, he used this basis as a means to discover yet further first truths. The method was "analytic" in that it allowed the reader to follow along in the discovery of first truths, rather than expecting the reader simply to accept certain axioms or first principles presented by the author.

To further his aim of convincing the widest variety of readers of his new metaphysics, Descartes engaged in another innovation. Medieval scholastic works sometimes took the form of disputations, in which the opinions of various sides, pro and con, were reported on any number of topics. Descartes had engaged in such disputations at La Flèche, but he took this practice another step. He distributed printed versions of the body of the *Meditations* to some of the leading philosophers of his time. They then submitted written objections, which were printed with the *Meditations*, together with Descartes's responses. The objectors represented innovative as well as conservative viewpoints. The innovators included the English philosopher Thomas Hobbes (in France since 1640), the French priest and Epicurean philosopher Pierre Gassendi, and Mersenne himself (who arranged most of the exchanges). The Dutch theologian Johannes Caterus and the French theologian Antoine Arnauld offered objections, and Mersenne organized two sets of objections representing other theologians, philosophers, and geometers (including his own questions). The second edition of the work (published in 1642), included an extensive set of objections from a Jesuit, Pierre Bourdin.[7]

Finally, the form of the work itself is modeled after meditative writings, or spiritual exercises, in the Roman Catholic tradition. Descartes engaged in such exercises at La Flèche. He patterned his meditations in similar literary order, but he cast them as cognitive and epistemic, rather than religious and spiritual, exercises. Meditations were intended to train the meditator's mental faculties. Descartes used the meditative mode to help the reader achieve new cognitive insights. In spiritual exercise one withdrew from the sensory world, contemplated God, and sought to model one's will after a divine will so as to avoid sin. In the *Meditations*, the meditator withdraws from the senses, contemplates his own soul and then the idea of God, and then seeks to regulate his or her will so as to avoid error in judgment. Knowledge of Descartes's use of this literary structure will help the reader understand the concluding remarks of the first four Meditations, when he speaks of training his will to pretend that the world does not exist (AT 7:22), of fixing a result in memory (AT 7:34), of contemplating God (AT 7:52), and of controlling or restraining the will (AT 7:62). Descartes's arguments are intended to train the reader cognitively, and so to produce experiences in readers that go beyond the simple act of reading.[8]

Skepticism and the cogito

Notoriously, in the First Meditation Descartes uses skeptical arguments to call his previous knowledge into doubt. He does this with the aim of ridding himself (and his reader or co- meditator) of previous, often false, beliefs, so as to begin afresh and establish something "firm and lasting in the sciences" (AT 7:17). Since he is seeking something firm and lasting, he will reject any belief that is subject to the least doubt. The skeptical arguments he uses are organized as a kind of internal dialogue, in which one argument is given and then answered, a stronger or more sweeping argument is given and answered, until finally an argument is given that seems unanswerable, at least for the moment. These arguments are not targeted at particular beliefs, one by one, but at the cognitive sources of belief, the senses and reason.

Descartes first has the meditator doubt the senses by noting that they have been deceptive on occasion. An example of such deception, supplied in the Sixth Meditation (AT 7:76), is a square tower that looks round in the distance. Descartes reasons: "occasionally the senses have been found to deceive, and it is prudent never to trust fully those who have misled us even once" (AT 7:18). Should we in general disbelieve anyone who has misled us even once, no matter how trustworthy they have been on other occasions? That depends on what is at stake, and on whether the circumstances tell us when our informant is reliable. What is at stake here is the rejection of any belief that is subject to the least doubt, not for the purposes of everyday life, but as part of a theoretical quest in the sciences (AT 7:22).

Descartes rejects this first argument as a general indictment of the senses. For, he has the meditator reason, even if the senses deceive us about things that are small or far away, surely they can be trusted for things near at hand. So perhaps the senses can serve to provide the desired firm and lasting knowledge. Could we ever be wrong about the presence of the things that we experience right around us? Do we ever have vivid experiences of touching objects right in front of us, when the objects do not exist, or at least are not present? Surely we do. Descartes recalls that we sometimes have dreams in which we experience ourselves as doing all sorts of things that do not really happen, or at least not at the time of the dream. So we can have the experience of seeing things up close, and yet those things are not there. This gives us cause to question, on any given occasion, whether the experience we are having is real, or a dream. But since sensory experience can be deceptive about whole scenes and episodes, perhaps it is always deceptive. And so Descartes has us doubt whether anything from our sensory experience must be accepted as certain (AT 7:20).

He now retreats to the areas of knowledge that were accepted as absolutely certain in the *Rules*, namely, arithmetic and geometry (pure, not applied). Surely these are unshakable. And yet, he remembers the opinion that there is an all-powerful God who created everything there is. Perhaps this God not only deceives him about the entire sensory world, but even in simple matters such as that two and three make five. Or perhaps there is a malevolent demon who causes such deception. Or perhaps there is no God at all, and the human mind is a haphazard product of nature. In any of these cases, Descartes recognizes reasons that are "powerful" and "considered" for suspending his previous opinions (AT 7:21). But he hasn't yet found anything firm and lasting.

At the beginning of the Second Meditation Descartes reviews these doubts. The meditator is now provided the insight that we, who may indeed be deceived about many things, must nonetheless exist as long as we have any thoughts at all. This conclusion was expressed in the *Discourse* as "I think, therefore I am" (AT 6:32). In the *Meditations*, Descartes concludes that "this proposition, 'I am, I exist,' whenever uttered or mentally conceived by me, is necessarily true" (AT 7:25). Because this conclusion takes instances of thinking as its basis, it is called the *cogito* reasoning, for the Latin word meaning "I think." The *cogito*, then, provides the certainty Descartes was hoping to find.[9] He has engaged in this reasoning not because he was worried about whether he existed and felt the need to prove it, but because he was seeking an unshakable truth upon which to build.

Descartes spends the rest of the Second Meditation investigating the "I" of whose existence he is certain. He finds that the "I" is a "thinking thing," and acknowledges that in his present state of uncertainty he does not know whether a thinking thing might not actually be material (AT 7:27). But he is able to discover some things about the "thing that thinks." He finds that it experiences various kinds of thoughts, including doubting, affirming, understanding, willing, desiring, imagining, and (at least seemingly) sensing.[10] Yet, curiously, the "I itself cannot be imagined," in the way that we are able to have sensory images of, or to form "in the imagination" a concrete image (like a picture) of a body. Descartes reports that he is unable to form an image of his mind from a third-person perspective. Does this mean that bodies, which are represented imagistically, are better known? He thinks not. The mind is known by its acts of perception, including primarily certain acts of intellectual perception, or purely mental scrutiny (AT 7:31–4). To demonstrate such acts, he observes that he can mentally grasp the infinite mutability of a piece of wax, despite the fact that the imagination is unable to represent all the possible shapes. In grasping the possibility of an infinity of shapes, pure thought exceeds the capacity of the imagination. In this way, by the end of the Second Meditation, Descartes has revealed what he later will call the "pure intellect."

Clear and distinct perception, and the Cartesian circle

The conclusion that he exists as a thing that thinks is not itself of great interest to Descartes. Rather, he wants to find out how he knows this unshakable truth, so that he can see if other truths can be known in the same way. In the Third Meditation he investigates the basis for this first knowledge. Right away, he finds that "in this first cognition there is nothing other than a clear and distinct perception of that which I am affirming." Which, he reasons, "would not suffice to make me certain of the truth of the matter if it could ever happen that something I perceived so clearly and distinctly were false." One cannot derive certainty from a source that is the least fallible, as we have seen. He therefore concludes, "I seem to be able to set forth as a general rule, that everything I perceive very clearly and distinctly is true" (AT 7:24). Clear and distinct perception is his proposed criterion for discovering the truth.

Many questions might be asked about this criterion. For one, how are we to recognize clear and distinct perceptions? Descartes explains in the Fourth Meditation that they are the ones which compel the will to affirm them as true (AT 7:58–9). But how can we be sure that our will is truly compelled, and is not simply acting out of habit? Descartes has no response here, except to recommend caution, or repeated meditation.

A more immediate question is why Descartes was not able to see from the beginning, even in the First Meditation, that his clear and distinct perceptions were to be trusted. After all, presumably even then clearly and distinctly perceiving that two plus three is five would have compelled his will. But this raises a further question. If two plus three equals five could be doubted in the First Meditation, why wouldn't it be subject to doubt now? Let us take up these questions in order.

Descartes was unable to appeal to clear and distinct perception in the First Meditation because he had reason to believe that most of his readers were unaware of, or had a false interpretation of, the sort of clear and distinct perception he had in mind – namely, intellectual perception independent of the senses. According to the dominant Aristotelian theory of cognition, all cognitive content depends on images that must originate in the senses. One cannot directly conceive of something that has no sensory presence. Aristotelian commentators known to Descartes, such as Francisco Toledo, wrote that the human intellect "cannot naturally possess clear and distinct cognition of immaterial substance," which would include God and the soul.[11] By contrast, Descartes hoped to use his *Meditations* to bring the reader into acquaintance with what he called "pure intellect," and its clear and distinct perceptions of God, the mind or soul, and the essence of matter. Descartes's cognitive exercises are contrived to help the reader discover the proper use of the pure intellect (in connection with the will, as explained in the Fourth Meditation), so that the meditator can go on to discern the first principles of metaphysics.

The second question, about why two plus three equals five should be accepted without doubt now, occurred to Descartes himself. In the fourth paragraph of the Third Meditation he finds himself having to call clear and distinct perception back into doubt. He is caught in a dilemma. When he thinks of simple mathematical truths, or of the *cogito* reasoning, he defiantly declares that he cannot be deceived. But when he recalls the deceiving God hypothesis, it seems he should allow the possibility of error "even in those things I deem to be intuited most evidently with the mind's eye" (AT 7:36). And yet, he also recognizes that the deceiving God hypothesis is just that, a hypothesis. So now the most pressing order of business is to investigate this hypothesis, which he says gives him only a "slight" and "metaphysical" reason for doubting.

This investigation occupies parts of both the Third and Fifth Meditations. Descartes argues in both for the conclusion that God exists and is no deceiver, a conclusion that removes the radical doubt of the deceiving God hypothesis. The trouble is, he appears to use clear and distinct perception in the very arguments he is using to vindicate that criterion of truth. In the Third Meditation, he appeals to what he calls "the natural light" in his argument for the existence of God. The latter argument is quite intricate. It depends on the premise, which each meditator is supposed to accept as self-evident, that we find the idea of an infinite being in our minds (AT 7:40, 45). Descartes then argues that we could not generate the idea of an infinite being ourselves; only an infinite being could create the content of that idea. His argument assumes that the content of an idea requires a cause. Further, it requires that this cause must match the degree of "being" exhibited in the content. As an example, he later suggests that if someone possesses the idea of an intricate machine, the conception of that machine must have a cause – either its present thinker is the inventor, or someone else provided the idea (AT 7:103–4). The idea of God, he claims, contains so much being in its content that only an infinite being could create it. As he asserts in the Third Meditation, it is "manifest by the natural light that there must be at least as much in the efficient and total cause as in the effect of that cause" (AT 7:40) – in this case, at least as much being in the cause of the idea as in its content.

Moving on, in the Fifth Meditation Descartes argues that contemplation of the idea of God reveals existence to be part of God's essence. From this, he concludes that God must exist. But since God is no deceiver, he can be assured that his clear and distinct perceptions are true (AT 7:69–70).

From the start Descartes's readers have accused him of arguing in a circle in using a proof of the existence of God to support the veracity of clear and distinct ideas. Arnauld raises this point in the fourth set of Objections (AT 7:214). The problem is called the "Cartesian Circle." It is not a formal circle; Descartes need not be seen as using the veracity of clear and distinct ideas as a premise in his argument. But he presumably uses clear and distinct perception as a method by which to arrive at the truth, even in the proofs of God's existence; and God's existence is then used to substantiate that method.[12]

There are various ways that Descartes might try to get out of the circle. One would be to claim that in the Third Meditation he did not appeal to clear and distinct perception in his proof, but to the "natural light" of the intellect. If he appeals to the natural light in the arguments used to vindicate clear and distinct perception, and if the natural light is different from clear and distinct perception, there is no manifest circle. But if the natural light is different, we must ask why it should be trusted. In an interesting passage, Descartes maintains that "whatever the natural light shows me – such as that from the fact I was doubting it would follow I exist, and the like – can in no way be doubted, because there can be no other faculty equally trustworthy as this light that could inform me such things are not true" (AT 7:38–9). This passage is interesting in many respects. But of immediate interest is the fact that he gives only the *cogito* reasoning as an example of something known by the natural light. It therefore appears that the natural light is the same as clear and distinct perception, since the latter has previously been identified as the source of the *cogito* reasoning. Consequently, the circle cannot be side-stepped by alleging the independence of the natural light.

We are still left with a problem. Descartes has said that the natural light cannot be doubted, since nothing else could convince him that its deliverances are not true.

But clear and distinct perception is currently under doubt. These two facts are not hard to reconcile if we suppose that the natural light (or clear and distinct perception) can be subject to doubt only if that light itself examines and accepts the grounds for doubt. And that is precisely the question in the Third Meditation: Should the hypothesis of a deceiving God be accepted, or does the natural light instead give us reason to believe in a non-deceiving God?

This last realization, that all grounds for doubt must be examined by the natural light, may help us to consider further the charge of circularity. Perhaps in order to vindicate the natural light, one need not start from nothing and prove it trustworthy. Perhaps one need only remove any reasons that arise for doubting it. This would not prove that the natural light must yield truth, but it would show that we have no reason to doubt what we learn through it. Since we have already accepted, in the second paragraph of the Third Meditation, that the natural light (or clear and distinct perception, since we are equating them) is our primary guide to the truth, we would then be left to follow it.

In the First Meditation Descartes gave two reasons for his radical doubt: a God that deceives, or a naturally defective reason (AT 7:21). In the Third Meditation, he examines the deceiving God hypothesis. He treats the hypothesis as a tenuous reason for doubting the recently extracted criterion of clear and distinct perception. Using the clear and distinct perception of the natural light, he then examines and removes this ground for doubt by finding that we have reason to believe that there is a benevolent God, incapable of deception, rather than a deceiving God. Grounds for doubt must be convincing to have force. Once the deceiving God hypothesis has been found to be ill-founded, the natural light is left unchallenged. The doubt has been removed and the circle of using the natural light to prove its own absolute reliability has not been entered.

In the Fifth Meditation Descartes again appeals to the existence of a benevolent God to remove any question that our origin is defective (AT 7:70). The extreme doubt of the First Meditation arises because he remembers the opinion that "there is an omnipotent God who created me such as I am." God might have created him so he could go wrong. An alternative ground is that there is no God, and that we have arisen from "fate" or "chance" through a continuous causal chain; but, the less powerful his cause, "the more likely it is that I am so imperfect as to be deceived at all times" (AT 7:21). In the Fifth Meditation these doubts are presented as problems that arise for us when we are not having clear and distinct perceptions. They are doubts to be removed through knowledge that God exists and is no deceiver (AT 7:69–70). Are these cases of a merely tenuous doubt? If we indeed cannot be sure of our intellect without knowing our origin, it is hard to see how we could avoid using the natural light to prove the very thing that is supposed to secure its trustworthiness. Perhaps the hypothesis of a deceiving God can be shown to be incoherent. But assuming that the hypothesis of a natural origin is not itself incoherent or problematic, then to remove this doubt the natural light must be used to establish a positive metaphysical thesis, that we were in fact made by a benevolent God. The circle is not avoided.

Nonetheless, Descartes treats the problem of his origin as a merely nagging doubt, and so thinks he has avoided the circle. Why so? Perhaps because at the beginning of the Third Meditation he has extracted his criterion of truth (clear and distinct perception) from the *cogito* reasoning.[13] The strength of this extraction argument must then be weighed against the threat of a defective origin. If the extraction argument is sound, then we need only remove the leftover doubts as a matter of intellectual housekeeping. But if the extraction argument is weak, or if there is a problem in generalizing beyond the *cogito*, then the need remains to certify the natural light through appeal to its origin or maker, and the circle closes.

Mind–body distinctness and union

Now convinced of the trustworthiness of clear and distinct perception and of the existence of mind, in the Fifth and Sixth Meditations Descartes seeks to determine the essence and existence of matter, and the essence of mind. At the beginning of the Fifth Meditation, in a paragraph that is easy to overlook, he has the meditator examine his or her ideas of bodies to see what is clear and distinct in them. Presumably, the result will reveal the "essence of matter," as promised in the title of the Meditation (AT 7:63). By consulting innate ideas given independently of the senses, the meditator discovers that in body extension (in length, breadth, and depth), size, shape, position, and motion can be perceived clearly and distinctly. Although not stated directly at this point, the implication is that the essence of matter consists in geometrical extension.

In the Sixth Meditation Descartes first consolidates his knowledge of the cognitive faculties by distinguishing pure intellect from imagination (as was done preliminarily in the Second Meditation). He then begins again to search for things about which there now need be no doubt. His first metaphysical conclusion is that mind and body are distinct. Recall that in the Second Meditation Descartes had refrained from drawing this conclusion. But now, having bolstered his confidence in clear and distinct perception, and having found that extension is the essence of body, he uses his intellect to discern that mind and body have different essences and can exist apart. He uses his intellect to discern the essence of mind: "from the fact itself that I know I exist, and that in the meantime I notice that nothing else at all pertains to my nature or essence except that I am a thinking thing, I rightly conclude that my essence consists solely in my being a thinking thing" (AT 7:78). It is not completely clear that in this act of "noticing" (through the intellect) what pertains to his essence, he has ruled out everything corporeal. Still, the fact that he asserts that his essence consists solely in thinking suggests that he has. Presumably, he thinks he can do so because the natural light can now be trusted to discern whether body belongs to his essence, whereas in the Second Meditation the criterion of clear and distinct perception via the natural light had not yet been extracted. In any case, in the very next sentence he appeals to clear and distinct perception to sustain a real distinction between mind and body: "because I have, on the one hand, a clear and distinct idea of myself insofar as I am solely a thinking, non-extended thing, and, on the other, a distinct idea of body, insofar as it is solely an extended, non-thinking thing, it is certain that I am really distinct from my body, and can exist without it." Mind and body are perceived by the intellect to have mutually exclusive essences, thinking and non-extended as opposed to non-thinking and extended. Hence, they must be really distinct things – which are, as Descartes explained in the first set of Replies, capable of existing apart as substances, or complete beings (AT 7:120–1).

Descartes proceeds from here to establish two things: the existence of bodies, and the union of mind with a body. He argues that the existence of bodies is the only reasonable cause of the sensory ideas that seem to present bodies to us. If God caused these ideas himself, he would be a deceiver (AT 7:79–80). The second half of the Sixth Meditation is taken up with mind–body union. Sensations and other feelings teach us that we have bodies. Further, "nature also teaches me, by these sensations of pain, hunger, thirst and so on, that I am not merely present to my body as a sailor is present in a ship, but am most closely joined to, and so to speak intermingled with it, to the extent of forming one thing with it" (AT 7:81). As a result of this mind–body union, our sensations inform us of bodily states, including needs (as in hunger or thirst). Other sensations inform us about bodies in our environment. The latter sort of sense perceptions were called into doubt in the First Meditation. Can they be trusted now? That depends on the use. We should not expect sense perception to reveal the natures or essences of the things around us (AT 7:83). But we should trust the senses to inform us of benefits and harms in our immediate environment. The senses can also inform us of properties of things, such as their shapes, for the purposes of natural science (AT 7:80).

Foundations of physics

These are the metaphysical teachings of the *Meditations.* Which of them provide foundations for physics, and destroy the Aristotelian philosophy?

The core principle of Descartes's physics was that body is constituted of extended matter in motion, with no other qualities or active principles adjoined. This principle is advanced in the Fifth and Sixth Meditations. It allowed Descartes to strip the world of Aristotelian substantial forms and real qualities, to be replaced by matter in motion interacting only by contact, with no activity except translation of position (local motion).

Aristotelians could not allow that extension might be the essence of body. Mathematical extension was an accident of body in the Aristotelian scheme; that is, it was something "incidental" or nonessential to body. They held it was a special sort of accident, a "universal accident," or one that all bodies must have. But no body could exist having only extension for its property. Bodies must have a substantial form, which is essential to that kind of body. Such forms were conceived qualitatively. The bare elements, earth, air, fire, and water, were thought of as a combination of "matter" (pure potentiality) and "form" (in this case, a combination of the qualities hot, cold, wet, and dry). "Matter" in this context cannot exist by itself, but only as joined to, or "informed by," a substantial form. Substantial forms served to direct the characteristic activities of each thing, whether animate or inanimate. In virtue of its substantial form, a magnet draws iron. Each substance, each kind of thing in nature, is composed of matter and form. There are active principles in everything.[14]

For Descartes, qualities such as hot or cold, wet or dry, are to be explained as the effect of the size, shape, and motion of minute particles. The properties of individual kinds of things, such as magnets or rabbits, are to be explained by the organization of their parts. But these parts are conceived exclusively in terms of size, shape, position, and motion. In the *Principles* Descartes would propound some laws of motion, alleged to govern all material interactions, and he would explain the source of motion (which lay in God). But the *Meditations* contained the basic foundation of his mechanistic picture of the universe: matter is inert, extended stuff, and nothing else.

Beyond that, the *Meditations* entail a great change in the physics or natural philosophy of mind. Aristotle had taught that mind informs body, that mind or soul is needed to first make a body into a human body. Descartes allowed that mind and body might exist apart. He did hold that it takes both mind and body to make a human being, but the mind does not "inform" and govern the inner activity of the human body. Rather, the activity of the body arises mechanistically from the heat of the heart (as Descartes had taught in the *Discourse*, AT 6:48–56). The soul can direct the body, but only by influencing the motion of the nervous fluids. Further, Descartes rejected the Aristotelian account of sensation, according to which the sensitive power of the soul informs or animates the sense organs and the act of sensation takes place in each organ. According to Descartes, the sense organs and nerves are inert, unfeeling machinery, which can affect the mind only in a small region of the brain (AT 7:86), which he elsewhere identified as the pineal gland or conarion (AT 3:361–2). Instead of sensation arising from active principles in the nerves, sensation arises only from lawful interactions between body and mind. Descartes thus conceived the idea that there are psychophysical laws that govern mind–body interaction.

Finally, the important metaphysical doctrine that the eternal truths are created by God arises only in the Objections and Replies, and not in the body of the *Meditations.* We have seen that in 1630 Descartes told Mersenne that this doctrine was a foundational insight underlying his physics. The doctrine states that God could have created a world with other mathematical rules than ours, so that, for instance, all the radii of a circle are not equal (AT 1:152). We may not be able to conceive such possibilities, since we have to think in accordance with the truths that were created, and those specify equality of the radii (Descartes had no inkling of non-Euclidean geometry). But nonetheless, Descartes held that all the eternal truths (except those of the divine nature itself) are free creations of God's will. These created truths are eternal and unchanging only because God's will is constant.

How can this doctrine serve to support Descartes's physics? One possibility is that it helped him free his physics from certain theological implications. In the scholastic Aristotelian scheme, which had been incorporated into Roman Catholic theology, to know the essence of a thing was by definition to come to understand the absolute limits to God's creative power.[15] Orthodox Aristotelian metaphysicians did not hold that the essences of things, such a rabbit or an oak tree, exists independently of God. But they also did not believe that God can create a rabbit that isn't an animal, or that violates the essence of rabbithood in any other way. On this scheme, the essences are not chosen by God, but they depend on his absolute creative power. He understands the essences by understanding what he can and cannot create. Thus, a natural philosopher who claims to know the essences of things is claiming to have a fundamental knowledge of God's power. Descartes's doctrine of the creation of the eternal truths allows the natural philosopher to claim to know the essences of things without thereby claiming to comprehend the structure or limits of God's creative power. And since it was an article of Catholic faith that God cannot be fully comprehended, Descartes would in this way be able to sidestep theological problems that might arise from his claim to know fully what the essence of matter is.

3. Reconceiving the Natural World

When Descartes went to school, the sciences of nature were split into two groups. Natural philosophy proper, or physics, was conceived as the science of nature in general. It studied the essences of natural things. The domain of nature included the natural elements, and the "mixed bodies" they composed, including minerals, vegetables, animals, and humans. The substantial forms of those bodies were also included, which meant that the human soul was regarded as part of nature. This physics was qualitative, not mathematical, describing the composition and the characteristic activities of things. It divided the world into two regions. The Earth was at the middle of the universe. The stars were conceived as arranged in the surface of a sphere at the outer boundary. The sphere of the moon (a structure that carried the moon around the Earth) divided the two regions. Above the moon were the planets and Sun, an unchanging realm of circular motion. Below the moon was the world of natural change, governed by the substantial forms of the various kinds of bodies. The universe as a whole was a big bubble with a smaller bubble inside it, and the smaller bubble surrounded the Earth.

Alongside physics existed a second group of sciences, the "mixed mathematical" sciences, in which mathematical methods were applied to physical subject matter. These sciences included optics, astronomy, music, and statics. Mixed mathematical sciences could not reveal the essences of things, for, as we have seen, the geometrical or mathematical properties of bodies were regarded as (perhaps universal) accidents. The mathematical sciences of optics and astronomy were highly developed in antiquity and the middle ages, by Hellenistic Greek and then Islamic scientists. But these sciences were thought to describe only some interesting properties of things, not to reveal their substantial being.[16]

When Descartes, under the guidance of Beeckman, studied mathematical approaches to nature, he was working in the tradition of mixed mathematical sciences. In the *Rules* as well he speaks simply of applying mathematics to particular physical problems (AT 10:395), such as discovering the shape of an anaclastic lens (one that refracts parallel rays of light so that they meet in a point). He had not yet achieved his radical new vision of nature. This picture is first expressed a few years later, in the *World*. Descartes now saw the material world as physically unified, containing everywhere the same matter governed by universal laws. While Copernicus and Galileo had rejected the Aristotelian picture that sealed the Earth inside the bubble of the moon and gave it a unique place at the center of the universe, neither author expounded a universal physics to cover both the terrestrial and celestial realms. That is what Descartes did, first in the *World*, then in the *Principles of Philosophy*.[17]

In both of those works Descartes tells a story in which the universe evolves out of a chaos of matter in motion (AT 10:34, 8A:101). The world, he held, is a plenum; it is completely full, there is no empty or void space. Variously sized pieces of matter are everywhere. Some matter is very fine and forms an invisible aether that fills the interstices between larger particles. Within this plenum of particles, some will naturally move around in a closed loop, the path of least resistance. These quasi-circular paths, on a cosmic scale, form vortex motions, like whirlpools. Within the vortices, planets congeal. At the center of each vortex is a star or sun. Outward pressure within the vortex yields light. Vortices surrounding each planet beat down the objects near the surface of the planet, which explains the "gravity" or weight of bodies (AT 10:73–80, 8A:212).

Such was Descartes's grand vision of a unified physics. All causation in the realm of body is by contact between particles of matter. Descartes conceived of three laws governing this matter. The laws were stated in Part Two of the *Principles* (and also in the *World*). The first law is "that each thing, as far as it is able, always continues in the same state; and so when it is once moved, it always continues on" (AT 8A:62). This law describes motion and rest as naturally persisting states of things. The second law is "that all motion, in and of itself, is along a straight line; therefore, those things that move in a circle always tend to move away from the center of the circle they are describing" (AT 8A:63). These two laws are similar to Newton's law of inertia (his first law of motion), although Descartes does not treat changes of direction as requiring the same force as changes in speed (and so does not treat inertial motion as a vector quantity). The third law is "that one body, in colliding with a stronger body, loses none of its own motion; but in colliding with a weaker body, it loses as much of its motion as it transfers to that weaker body" (AT 8A:65). This law is implausible on the face of it, since it suggests that a snooker ball could never move one of the slightly larger balls used in pool, no matter how hard it was driven. Descartes explained away such counterexamples by observing that in our matter-filled environment, the larger body is surrounded by the fluid of the air, which makes it easier to move (AT 8A:70).

These laws of motion are more important for their role in spreading the vision of a law-governed universe than for any technical contribution they made to the analysis of the laws of colliding bodies. Indeed, Descartes himself rarely appealed to these laws, or to the seven rules of impact he claimed to derive from them (at AT 8A:68–70). The only law that receives direct use in the remainder of the *Principles* is the second law, which is invoked to explain the outward tendency of the particles in the cosmic vortices (AT 8A:108, 117, 170). Nonetheless, Descartes's mechanistic picture of the universe required that the interactions of matter be governed in a regular way, and these laws were an attempt to fulfill that requirement.

But what explains the laws themselves? Can they be explained? Newton's laws are typically regarded as explanatorily basic. They are the place where explanation stops. A conceptual revolution occurred when, in post-Newtonian physics, the continued motion of bodies in a straight line no longer required explanation, whereas in the Aristotelian scheme continued motion required a continuous cause.[18] Descartes, too, posited the action of a continuous cause in nature. He conceived of matter itself as totally inert. A piece of matter endowed simply with the property of extension would be powerless to affect anything else. In Descartes's world, only God, angels, and the human mind have active causal power (AT 8A:65). And it is God who acts, at each instant, to preserve bodies in motion in a continuous straight line, and to move them after impact in a manner consistent with the laws of motion. As Descartes put it, God recreates the universe at each instant, with each individual particle placed according to its tendency to motion in the previous instant. This picture has its own problems. Thus, it has been objected that in a particular instant a body can have no tendency to move, since for Descartes motion is the literal transference from one location to another. The force of this objection depends in part on Descartes's notion of an instant, and in particular on whether such instants are merely vanishingly small, or are dimensionless points. In any event, Descartes is committed to the view that God, who (perhaps with angels and the human mind) is the source of all motion in the material world, is able to keep track of the tendencies of particles from instant to instant.[19]

In Descartes's natural philosophy of the material world, the real explanatory work is not done by the laws of motion, but by comparison of complicated natural bodies to machines. Whether in explaining the action of the magnet, or the properties of oil and water, or the actions of animals, Descartes appealed to intricate microstructures to explain how these things act as they do. Thus, he explained magnetism via corkscrew-shaped particles that constantly stream from the poles of the earth (AT 8A:275–310). These streams of microparticles will collide with and turn a magnetic needle – which contains parallel channels threaded to fit the particles – until it is parallel with the flow of particles; the north and south poles of the magnet are differently threaded, as are the streams of particles coming from each terrestrial pole. Descartes explained the viscosity of oil as arising from the branch-like appendages of oil particles, whereas water flows more easily because its particles are eel-shaped (AT 8A:232, 247). All animals bodies, including the human body, are complex machines driven by the heat of the heart, which causes the blood to form a rapidly moving material known as animal spirits. These spirits cause motions in the animal body by being shunted into various tubes and causing the muscles to inflate and contract (AT 11:130–42).

Descartes cast his explanations of the workings of nature in terms of micromechanisms. He recognized that more than one mechanism, each consistent with his general principles, might underlie various phenomena. Experiments would choose among the alternatives. As he wrote in the *Discourse*, he did not know of any other means to decide among competing explanations "except to seek again for some experiments which are such that their results are not the same if one of these explanations is correct, rather than the other" (AT 6:65; also 8A:242).[20]

We have seen above that the human soul was included in physics or natural philosophy by the Aristotelians. Descartes did not specifically say whether he followed this classification, though in *Passions* he did speak of approaching the emotions "as a physicist" (AT 11:326). This does not imply, though, that he was attempting to reduce the passions to purely material processes. Rather, it suggests he considered the laws of mind–body interaction to fall within natural philosophy or physics. In any case, he discussed those laws in the "physical" part of the *Principles* (pt. 4), and his followers, such as Régis, made the classification explicit.[21] In the subsequent sections, we will examine Descartes's physics or natural philosophy of the mind, as found in his theories of the senses and of the passions.

4. Descartes's Theory of the Senses

Descartes's new physics of matter required a radical reconception in the theory of the senses. He replaced the dominant Aristotelian scheme with a thoroughly mechanistic interpretation of sensory qualities and their effect on the sensory nerves. This required also replacing the Aristotelian theory that a "real quality" is transmitted from the object to the sensory soul and is thereby perceived.

Aristotelian "real qualities" are given that name because the qualities we sense are direct representatives, or instances, of a quality in the object. When we see a red tulip, the real quality of redness is transmitted to our senses and received by our sensory soul as a "form without matter." The form of redness is what makes the tulip red; this same form is expressed in the red we experience, in accordance with Aristotle's principle that like is known by like. In between, the form is transmitted "without matter" through the air, into the eye, and down the optic nerve (conceived as a hollow tube). Scholastic Aristotelians worked hard to elaborate this theory, because the notion of a form transmitted through the medium without the matter was difficult to interpret. If the form of red makes the object red, why doesn't it turn the air and the eye red? But the air between the tulip and us does not appear red, and the eye does not turn red when we see a red thing. To explain these facts, the Aristotelians taught that the form in the medium has a special kind of diminished existence, called "intentional being." The form of red in the air and in the eye was called an "intentional species." In effect, the Aristotelians posited such species so that they could square their theoretical commitment to the principle that like knows like (which required that forms from objects be received in the soul) with the observed facts.[22]

In the *Dioptrics*, Descartes indicated that he had no use for the "intentional species that exercise the imagination of the philosophers" (AT 6:85). He replaced the Aristotelian picture with an account in which all of the properties and processes of sensation, up to the point of mind–body interaction, are purely mechanical. That is, he accounted for the red in the object, the transmission of light and color, and the effect of light and color in the nervous system, all in terms of the sizes, shapes, and motions of particles. On Descartes's view, the color in the object consists simply in the geometrical features of its surface, which cause it to put one or another spin on the spherical particles of light. This spin is transmitted to the eye, where it affects the retinal nerves in one way if the object is what we call "blue," and in another way if the object is what we call "red" (AT 6:91–2). These differing effects in the nervous system, when transmitted into the brain, cause differing sensations in the soul, in this case of blue or red. Color in objects, then, is a purely mechanical property that has a purely mechanical effect on our nervous system; this effect is transmitted to the pineal gland, the seat of mind–body interaction, where the mechanical process causes a sensation of red. The experienced red is the content of a sensation; it has only an arbitrary relation, established by God, with the physical property in objects that regularly causes it (AT 6:130–1).

In this way, Descartes was an early advocate of the distinction that Robert Boyle and John Locke later drew between primary and secondary qualities. Primary qualities are the basic physical properties of bodies, here conceived as the size, shape, and motion of particles. Secondary qualities are other properties bodies have in virtue of the effect of their primary qualities on the human sensory system. The particles of bodies really are round or square, small or large. But they are not "really" red in the way they were thought to be by the Aristotelians. Rather, we call bodies "red," and assign them a physical property called "red," because of an effect that the physical property has on us, namely, to cause us to have a red sensation. Although Descartes rejected the Aristotelian "real quality" of redness, he did hold that objects are really red in the sense that they have a property that causes us to experience them as red.

Descartes worked extensively in other areas of visual theory, including the perception of size. Visual theorists had long known that the same sized object subtends a smaller angle at the eye as its distance increases. The Arabic philosopher Alhazen and his European followers argued that we combine our sensation of an object's visual angle with our knowledge or estimate of its distance. If perceivers do this accurately, they can experience an object's true size even as it recedes from them, rather than perceiving it as shrinking (a phenomenon known today as "size constancy"). Descartes held that at least in near space, we do experience objects as having their true sizes. He adopted the traditional explanation, according to which distance is taken into account through an unnoticed act of judgment. Hence, although Descartes equated thought with consciousness, for him that did not mean we actually notice or attend to all of our thoughts. Some thought processes go on unnoticed, perhaps because they are habitual and rapid.[23]

To traditional judgmental accounts of size and distance perception, Descartes added a novel explanation of his own. He argued that when the eyes focus on objects within a moderate range of distance, their axes converge more for near objects, less for far objects. This convergence of the eyes, as well as the accommodation of the eye's lens for distance, is under the control of a purely mechanical brain process. Simultaneously, the mechanical process for near or far distance directly causes the soul to perceive objects as near or far. That is, the very same brain state that causes the nerves to converge the eyes (or accommodate the lens) also gives the soul an idea of distance appropriate to that degree or convergence or accommodation (AT 6:1378, 11:182–3).

Descartes considered that mind and body are, in general, related in lawful ways. We have seen that he considered brain states to be regularly related to sensations of color and perceptions of distance. There must also be a lawful relation between a mental volition to move our limbs and the resultant nervous processes that control the body. In addition, Descartes held that thirst, hunger, and pain result from regularities instituted by God that link sensations to nerve states (AT 7:80–1, 87–9; 8A:316–17). The last work of his life extended this account to the passions or emotions of the soul, or at least to those that depend on the body.

5. Passions of the Soul

In 1645 Princess Elizabeth, who previously had pressed Descartes on the metaphysics of mind–body union (AT 3:661), wrote to him concerning her melancholic state of mind (AT 4:233). The ensuing correspondence led to the last work published by Descartes in his lifetime, the *Passions of the Soul*. The book had three parts. The first concerned the passions in general, and it described Descartes's speculative physiology of the human body in greater detail than any work prior to the posthumous *Treatise on Man*. This part defined the passions, described their general function, and mentioned ways they might be controlled. The second part classified the passions. It contained Descartes's theory that there are six primitive or basic passions: wonder, love, hatred, desire, joy, and sadness (AT 11:380). The third part classified specific passions in relation to the six basic passions, and described the behaviors that accompany them.

Descartes divided human emotions into two sorts, those that depend on the mind alone, such as intellectual joy, and those that the body causes in the mind (AT 11:397). The former are actions of the mind, the latter its passions. Descartes allowed that all effects of the body on the mind, including sensations and imaginings, might be termed "passions" in a general sense; but he restricted the "passions" proper to states of mind that, while caused by the body, are referred to the mind itself (AT 11:349). Joy that has a bodily cause is referred to the mind, and is a "passion of the soul" in the sense intended by the title of the work.

Descartes held that the function of the passions is to "move and dispose the soul to want the things for which they prepare the body" (AT 11:359). His formulation is interesting, because it suggests that the "passion," which must be a state of mind, itself prepares the body. But he means that the same state in the body that causes a passion in the mind simultaneously prepares the body for an appropriate action. Consider the feeling of fear. It arises in the mind from a movement of the animal spirits, that is, from a particular brain state. This brain state might be caused by the presence of a certain object, say, a lion. The very same brain state that causes the mind to feel fear (and so to want to flee) also causes the body to prepare to flee. It does the latter "automatically," so to speak, without intervention from the mind.

Although Descartes is known for reserving intelligent action to mind (AT 6:57–9), here he assigns to purely mechanical processes the sophisticated function of preparing the body to flee. This will seem less surprising if we recall that he considered animals to be purely mechanical devices, without souls or minds (AT 4:573–6, 6:58–9). When a sheep sees a wolf, its response must be accounted for in a purely mechanistic fashion. Human bodies are also wonderful machines. In his view, purely mechanical processes, devoid of mental intervention, produce much of human behavior (AT 11:202). The body automatically responds to many benefits and harms in the environment. For example, it naturally approaches an object of love, as is revealed in Descartes's theory of hugging. When an object of love is near, "we feel some kind of heat around the heart, and a great abundance of blood in the lungs, which makes us open our arms as if to embrace something." The movement of the arms thus far is governed by purely mechanical causes. The state of the body also affects the mind, making it "inclined to join to itself willingly the object presented to it" (AT 4:603). Consequently, the mind will cause the body to close its arms around the beloved.

Descartes did not think that we can alter our passions directly by simple force of will. The passions are caused by the body, and that cause–effect relation cannot be set aside. We can, however, affect our passions by training the body not to react so strongly in some circumstances. Thus, fear is often caused by surprise. But if we exercise forethought and prepare ourselves, we are less likely to be caught unawares (AT 11:463). Nonetheless, once we are afraid we cannot summon up courage simply by willing it. Rather, we must learn to think of things that are joined with the passions we want, and opposed to those we don't want. Thus, to encourage boldness and quell fear, "we must apply ourselves to consider the reasons, objects, or examples which persuade us that the danger is not great; that there is always greater safety in defence than in flight; that we shall gain glory and joy in conquering, whereas we can expect nothing but regret and shame in flight; and the like" (AT 11:363).

Although Descartes equated thought with consciousness and believed that we can know all our own thoughts,[24] he did not suppose that our emotional lives are transparent to us. Indeed, he believed that many of our adult passions arise as a result of connections established in childhood, which we no longer remember and which we only dimly understood (if at all) at the time. In a letter to Pierre Chanut (February 1, 1647) he explained how adult passions could arise from prenatal and childhood associations between passions and bodily functions. He attributed only four of the six passions to the unborn child: joy, love, sadness, and hate. Before birth, these were

> only sensations or very confused thoughts, because the soul was so attached to matter that it could not yet concern itself with anything else except receiving various impressions from it; and even though, some years later, it should begin to have other joys and other loves besides those that depend solely on the good condition and proper nourishment of the body, nonetheless, what is intellectual in its joys or loves has always been accompanied by the first sensations which it had of them, and even by the motions or natural functions that occurred then in the body – so that, insofar as love was, before birth, caused only by proper nutriment which, entering in abundance into the liver, heart and lungs, produced more heat there than usual, it now happens that such heat always accompanies love, even though it always arises from other, very different causes. And if I were not afraid of going on too long, I could show in detail how all the other bodily conditions that occurred with these four passions at the beginning of our life still accompany them. (AT 4:605–6)

The emotional life of the adult is conditioned by the emotional life of the child in relation to its bodily functions. The passions of the adult are open to mental inspection, consonant with Descartes's equation of thought with consciousness. But their causes and childhood connections are not transparent to consciousness. Our current passions are influenced by our emotional history. These effects are recorded in the structure of the brain, and also in mental habits whose origins we cannot now fathom. That the mind is "better known than body" (AT 7:23) cuts both ways here, for the body deeply conditions many mental states. The mind is open to us only through occurrent thoughts; habits of mind are not transparent. But habits of body and mind govern much of our lives, as Descartes well knew.

6. Descartes's Legacy

The perception of Descartes's legacy has changed from century to century. His achievements in mathematics were soon recognized and are still appreciated. In the seventeenth century, although Baruch Spinoza paid great attention to Descartes's metaphysics, the primary focus was on his natural philosophy. His physics was widely taught through the first half of the eighteenth century. As Newtonian physics replaced it, Descartes became known more for his skeptical doubt and his arguments for mind–body dualism. Nonetheless, even in the nineteenth century the Darwinian Thomas H. Huxley could praise him as "a physiologist of the first rank."[25]

Throughout much of the twentieth century Descartes was famous for his method of doubt, his *cogito* reasoning, and his mind–body dualism. In the latter part of that century, philosophers took renewed interest in the cultural context of philosophy. Philosophy has always been engaged with the great intellectual and cultural events of its time. Philosophers now find it helpful to study Descartes's arguments in relation to their original purpose, which was largely to found a new science of nature. Beyond that, philosophers find that his mind–body dualism set an important problem, even if most of them now reject his substance dualism. Some find it compelling to believe, with Descartes, that mental phenomena are real. They may also believe that mental phenomena depend upon, or perhaps are identical with, states of the brain. What seems very difficult, and remains unsolved, is how to understand and explain a mental phenomenon fully and completely by appeal only to the known physical and chemical properties of neural states. How can our experience of red be reduced to electrical and chemical events? This unsolved problem, too, is part of Descartes's legacy.

In the end, Descartes's legacy lies mainly with the many readers who are engaged by his works. Whether one is most strongly drawn to the depth of his metaphysical arguments or to the imaginative speculations of his mechanical philosophy, there is great philosophical pleasure and insight to be won from serious study of Descartes.

Notes

1 Detailed information about Descartes's life and work can be found in Stephen Gaukroger, *Descartes: An Intellectual Biography* (Oxford: Oxford University Press, 1995). Another general work is A. B. Gibson, *Philosophy of Descartes* (London: Methuen, 1932).

2 On the Scientific Revolution and Descartes's part in it, see Richard Westfall, *Construction of Modern Science: Mechanisms and Mechanics* (Cambridge: Cambridge University Press, 1977), A. Rupert Hall, *The Revolution in Science, 1500–1750* (London: Longman, 1983), and Gary Hatfield, "Metaphysics and the New Science," in *Reappraisals of the Scientific Revolution*, eds. David Lindberg and Robert Westman (Cambridge: Cambridge University Press, 1990), pp. 93–166. Descartes's relation to Beeckman is examined in Gaukroger, *Descartes*, ch. 3.

3 The page citations given in the text of this chapter are to the standard edition of Descartes's works, edited by Charles Adam and Paul Tannery (hence, "AT"), *Oeuvres de Descartes*, new edition (Paris: Vrin, 1964–76), which is cited by volume and page number. All translations in this chapter are by its author; they are from the original French in the case of the letters, and from the French or Latin of Descartes's books. The page citations will allow the reader to locate passages in the standard translations, where the pagination of AT is shown in the margins. All of Descartes's philosophical writings, some of the scientific writings, and a selection of letters are translated in *Philosophical Writings of Descartes*, tr. John Cottingham, Robert Stoothoff, Dugald Murdoch, and Anthony Kenny, 3 vols. (Cambridge: Cambridge University Press, 1984–91). The extant parts of Descartes's *World*, and selections from other scientific writings, are in *The World and Other Writings*, tr. Stephen Gaukroger (Cambridge: Cambridge University Press, 1998).

4 The title of this work in French is *La Dioptrique*, which is properly translated as "diopt-

rics," although some translations render it as "optics." The ancient science of dioptrics studied vision through refracted rays, and was normally joined with "optics," or the science of vision through direct rays, and "catoptrics," the science of vision through reflected rays, as in a mirror. In his work entitled *Dioptrics*, Descartes covered all three areas, but the focus was on refracted light, vision aided by lenses, and normal human vision. Descartes may have chosen the title to advertise his important result published therein (the sine law of refraction), as well as his account of lenses (which operate through refraction), including a description of the telescope, which had only recently been invented.

5 This list of the fields of knowledge that metaphysics can support is from the Author's Letter to the French translation of *Descartes's Principles of Philosophy* (AT 9B:14).

6 Works focusing primarily on Descartes's *Meditations* include Edwin M. Curley, *Descartes Against the Skeptics* (Cambridge, Mass.: Harvard University Press, 1978), Bernard Williams, *Descartes, The Project of Pure Inquiry* (London: Penguin, 1978), Margaret D. Wilson, *Descartes* (London: Routledge & Kegan Paul, 1978), and *Articles on Descartes' Meditations*, ed. Amelie Rorty (Berkeley: University of California Press, 1986).

7 Further discussion of the objectors and their objections may be found in *Descartes and His Contemporaries: Meditations, Objections, and Replies*, eds. Roger Ariew and Marjorie Grene (Chicago: University of Chicago Press, 1995). Because of his concern to have his worked deemed consistent with orthodoxy, Descartes had originally intended to send it to "the twenty or thirty most learned Theologians" he could find (AT 2:622).

8 On the *Meditations* as spiritual exercises, see the first three essays in *Articles on Descartes' Meditations*, ed. Rorty.

9 The *cogito* has been the object of much philosophical discussion. For some recent work (which contains further references), see *Essays on the Philosophy and Science of René Descartes*, ed. Stephen Voss (New York: Oxford University Press, 1993), chs. 2–4, and Peter Markie, "The *Cogito* and Its Importance," in *The Cambridge Companion to Descartes*, ed. John Cottingham (Cambridge: Cambridge University Press, 1992), pp. 140–73.

10 Descartes used the Latin word *cogitare*, "to think," and the corresponding French word *penser*, and their related nouns, to cover all states of consciousness. Thus, "thinking" and "thought"included for him not only the usual intellectual contents of thought, but also acts of will, sensations, and pains.

11 Francisco Toledo, *Commentaria una cum quaestionibus in tres libros Aristotelis De anima* (Cologne: Birkmann, 1594), bk. 3, ch. 7, qu. 23. In a letter to Mersenne (October 28, 1640), Descartes remembered several Aristotelian commentators from reading them twenty or more years before, including the commentaries from the University of Coimbra, those of Francisco Toledo and his student, Antonio Rubio, and a textbook written by Eustace of St. Paul (AT 3:185).

12 The literature on the circle is large and contains a variety of positions. Two points of entry into it are Louis E. Loeb, "The Cartesian Circle," in *The Cambridge Companion to Descartes*, ed. Cottingham, pp. 200–35, and Curley, *Descartes Against the Skeptics*, ch. 5.

13 Another possibility is that Descartes was not out to establish absolute truth, but only to produce a firm conviction through internally consistent arguments. For these purposes, he need only convince himself that his grounds for doubt were ill-founded; he would not need to vindicate the truth criterion, because he was not seeking truth. This posi-

tion has been suggested by passages in the second Replies. In one passage Descartes remarks, concerning clear and distinct intellectual perception, "it is also no obstruction if someone feigns that such things appear false to God or an angel, because the evidence of our perception does not allow us to listen to such fictions" (AT 7:146). Harry Frankfurt, in *Demons, Dreamers, and Madmen* (Indianapolis: Bobbs-Merrill, 1970), p. 179, made much of a related passage, in which Descartes rejected allegations of possible "absolute falsity" because the persuasion he felt was absolutely firm (AT 7:145). If Descartes was really concerned with persuasion, not truth, then he must be seen as merely recommending his metaphysics as the most persuasive to human reason, but not as asserting its truth.

14 Some initial acquaintance with the physics of Aristotle as presented in Descartes's time can be gained through the brief selections from the physics of Eustace of St. Paul as printed in *Descartes's Meditations*, eds. Roger Ariew, John Cottingham, and Tom Sorell (Cambridge: Cambridge University Press, 1998), pp. 80–92. Dennis Des Chene, *Physiologia: Natural Philosophy in Late Aristotelian and Cartesian Thought* (Ithaca: Cornell University Press, 1996), provides an extensive overview.

15 The discussion in this paragraph follows Hatfield, "Reason, Nature, and God in Descartes," in *Essays*, ed. Voss, pp. 259–87.

16 In addition to Des Chene, *Physiologia*, information on Aristotelian natural philosophy and the mixed mathematical sciences can be obtained from William A. Wallace, "Traditional Natural Philosophy," in *Cambridge History of Renaissance Philosophy*, ed. Charles B. Schmitt (Cambridge: Cambridge University Press, 1988), pp. 201–35, and Roger Ariew and Alan Gabbey, "Scholastic Background," in *Cambridge History of Seventeenth Century Philosophy*, eds. Michael Ayers and Daniel Garber (Cambridge: Cambridge University Press, 1998), pp. 425–53. On medieval natural philosophy and mathematical science, see *Science in the Middle Ages*, ed. David Lindberg (Chicago: University of Chicago Press, 1978).

17 On Descartes's part in the development of a new outlook in natural philosophy (and so, ultimately, natural science), see Daniel Garber, "Descartes' Physics," in *The Cambridge Companion to Descartes*, ed. Cottingham, pp. 286–334, Gaukroger, *Descartes*, Hall, *Revolution in Science*, and Hatfield, "Metaphysics and the New Science," pp. 111–17.

18 Newton himself regarded continuous motion as the product of an inertial force, during at least some of the time he was developing his physics; see Alan Gabbey, "Force and Inertia in the Seventeenth Century," in *Descartes: Philosophy, Mathematics and Physics*, ed. Stephen Gaukroger (Sussex: Harvester Press, 1980), pp. 230–320 on pp. 272–86 (Gabbey's article also examines the similarities and differences between Descartes's and Newton's laws). In any case, later Newtonians conceived of inertial motion as basic, requiring no continuing force.

19 On God as the agency behind motion, see Gary Hatfield, "Force (God) in Descartes' Physics," in *Descartes*, ed. John Cottingham (Oxford: Oxford University Press, 1998), pp. 281–310. On the notion of the instant in Descartes, see Daniel Garber, *Descartes' Metaphysical Physics* (Chicago: University of Chicago Press, 1992), pp. 266–73.

20 On Descartes's philosophy of science, see Desmond M. Clarke, *Descartes' Philosophy of Science* (University Park: Pennsylvania State University Press, 1982).

21 Pierre Sylvain Régis (1632–1707), *Systême de philosophie: contenant la logique, metaphysique, physique & morale*, 7 vols. (Lyon: Anisson, Posuel & Rigaud, 1691), "Physique," bk. 8, pt. 2, ch. 1, art. 7 (5:347): "the brain acts on the soul in a special

way, which consists in God having resolved to produce sensations in the soul in accordance with the laws of the union every time there are certain movements in the brain. From which it follows that, in this respect, these movements can and should be considered the true physical and natural causes of the sensations."

22 On scholastic theories of sense perception, see Gary Hatfield, "The Cognitive Faculties," in *Cambridge History of Seventeenth Century Philosophy*, eds. Ayers and Garber, pp. 953–1002, on pp. 954–9, and Alison Simmons, "Explaining Sense Perception: A Scholastic Challenge," *Philosophical Studies*, 73 (1994), pp. 257–75.

23 Descartes, *Dioptrics*, AT 6:138–40; *Meditations*, Sixth Replies, AT 7:437–8. On the perceptual theories of Alhazen and Descartes, see Gary Hatfield and William Epstein, "The Sensory Core and the Medieval Foundations of Early Modern Perceptual Theory," *Isis*, 70 (1979), pp. 363–84.

24 *Meditations*, Fourth Replies: "there can be nothing in the mind, insofar as it is a thinking thing, of which it is not conscious" (AT 7:246).

25 Thomas Henry Huxley, *Science and Culture* (New York: Appleton, 1884), p. 208.

Chapter 2

Thomas Hobbes

A. P. Martinich

Thomas Hobbes, along with Descartes, is one of the two great founders of modern philosophy. He, a decade older than the Frenchman, began writing philosophy later, because from 1608, when he graduated from Magdalen Hall, Oxford, to about 1630, when he began serious scientific investigations, his time was largely taken up by the quotidian duties of his employers, chiefly the wealthy Cavendish family of Derbyshire, for whom he served variously as tutor, companion, secretary, and sometime financial adviser. The time he had for intellectual pursuits was devoted to humanistic studies. His first significant publication, a translation of Thucydides' history, *The Peloponnesian Wars* (1629), coincides with the end of what is sometimes known as his humanistic period.

Hobbes's scientific and philosophical interests – the two disciplines were not sharply distinguished at the time – began in large part because of his association with a cousin of his employer, William Cavendish, the future Duke of Newcastle, who supported a group of English scientists and promoted correspondence with Continental ones. Also, during a trip to the Continent between 1634 and 1636, Hobbes met the ailing and imprisoned Galileo and became acquainted with some of the age's most famous French scientists and philosophers, who gathered at the residence of Marin Mersenne, an intellectual broker for such luminaries as Descartes and Pierre Gassendi. During this period, Hobbes became enamored of the rigor of geometry and its possible application to all scientific and philosophical problems.

Much of Hobbes's earliest scientific interests were motivated by Descartes's work, and he would criticize Descartes in print from the late 1630s until Descartes died in 1650. Both men were concerned about methodology. Because scholastic philosophy obviously had a defective method, nascent modern science, which aimed to supersede it, needed an explicit statement of the proper way to study reality. Since most people were roughly equal in intelligence, according to both philosophers, what made some people stand out intellectually from others was the way they conducted their thinking. Both philosophers also agreed that mathematics, in particular geometry, was the key to productive thinking. Finally, both philosophers related methodological issues to problems in optics because of the realization, largely due to Galileo, that, contrary to appearances, properties such as color are not genuinely part of the physical world. Hobbes's "Optica" was published in Mersenne's *Universae geometriae synopsis* (pp. 567–89); and many of his works on geometry were published, especially late in life. For his part, Descartes devoted two or the three appendices of his *Discourse on the Method of Rightly Conducting the Mind* to optics and geometry. The nature of geometry became one of the most contested areas between the two philosophers. Descartes invented analytic geometry, which applied algebra to geometry. The new geometry in effect reduced geometry to arithmetic. Hobbes never appreciated the power of algebra and resented the promotion of arithmetic over geometry. He thought that geometry was superior to arithmetic and that Euclidean geometry, supplemented with the theoretical underpinnings of his materialism, gave the only true picture of reality. Traditionally, arithmetic was understood to deal with discrete quantities; geometry with continuous quantity, and Hobbes thought that reality, which is nothing but matter, was continuous. Although Hobbes was cautious enough not to assert that a vacuum was impossible, he thought that no one had ever proved its existence (DCo 26.2–4).[1] In the 1650s and 1660s, he conducted an acerbic debate over just this point with Robert Boyle, who believed he had created a vacuum by pumping air out of a glass jar.

For Hobbes, an uncompromising materialist, even geometrical objects are bodies. Points are bodies of which only their position is used in reasoning, their length, width, and breadth being ignored. (Points do not even have to be small. In astronomical calculations, the earth can be considered a point.) Lines are bodies, of which only their length is used in reasoning, their width and breadth being ignored. Plane and solid figures are similar, *mutatis mutandis.*

Hobbes and Descartes began commenting on each other's work when Hobbes wrote a commentary on the latter's *Discourse on the Method of Rightly Conducting the Mind.* Mersenne was impressed while Descartes was outraged by it: "I [Descartes] was very surprised by the fact that . . . [Hobbes] seems to stray from the truth in every single claim he advances" (C, p. 57). Hobbes was equally unimpressed with Descartes. About the Frenchman's view that air particles are like small trees, Hobbes said that it was "scarcely that of a sane man."

Mersenne sent Hobbes a pre-publication copy of Descartes's *Meditations* in early 1641. Hobbes's objections, which were published as the third of the six sets appended to the original edition of the *Meditations*, and Descartes's reply, constitute one of the stellar examples of philosophers talking past each other. Concerning skepticism, Hobbes thought that Descartes could have used the proposition, "I walk; therefore, I am" to as much purpose as the *cogito.* He seems to be unaware that Descartes's premise needs to be indubitable as much as true. The crucial aspect of Descartes's solution that Hobbes rejects is the search for a criterion. Descartes thought that clear and distinct ideas were the criterion. Hobbes, like everyone other than Descartes, realized that there was no way to distinguish between the genuinely clear and distinct ideas and the ones that just seemed to someone to be so. Further, every criterion is subject to the question: Why is that the criterion? Hobbes says "it is clear enough that there is no criterion enabling us to distinguish our dreams from the waking state and from veridical sensations" ("Third Set of Objections," in *The Philosophical Writings of Descartes*, vol. 2, p. 121). People simply count those experiences that cohere nicely as waking experiences, and those lacking that coherence as dreams. This remark, however, is not Hobbes's solution to the skeptical challenge. For that, Hobbes had in fact two solutions, neither of which appear in his "Objections."

The first involves the nature of definitions: they are true in virtue of being stipulated by the definer. Anyone who defines a term has the authority to do so in any way he wishes; so the definitions cannot be false. This constitutes a solution to the problem of skepticism, because, as we shall see below, Hobbes thought that genuine knowledge (science) consists only of definitions and their consequences. Moreover, since the definitions are for the sake of the scientist himself, there is no issue of the definition being misunderstood by a hearer (DCo 6.11). The second solution is a kind of generalization of the first. The only way to settle a dispute in any area is to designate a supreme authority. For Hobbes, this is ultimately the sovereign, who has the authority to settle disputes in every area. More will be said about this in our discussion of Hobbes's political philosophy.

It did not take long for Descartes to refuse to receive any further communications from Hobbes. They met only once, did not get on together, and never met again. In large part they hated each other because they were so close in disposition and aspiration. Both were self-centered, glory-seeking, and intent on being the first to give a satisfactory mechanical account of the physical world. So the metaphysical difference between them, Descartes's dualism and Hobbes's materialism, is less important than generally thought. A more difficult matter concerns their epistemology. Descartes is a rationalist; but whether Hobbes is a rationalist or empiricist depends upon how those terms are defined. If a rationalist is one who believes that scientific propositions are necessarily true, then Hobbes is a rationalist, because for him science consists of definitions and their logical consequences. But he is an empiricist, too, if an empiricist is one who believes that all knowledge begins with sense experience and that the basic terms of science refer to sense objects (DCo 25.1). So Hobbes holds the nonstandard view that the basic propositions of science consist of empirical terms formulated in definitions and hence necessarily true. He is a term empiricist and an analytic rationalist.

For Hobbes, the canonical or logical form for scientific propositions is conditional or hypothetical, even when the usual grammatical form is subject predicate. For example, the proposition, "All human beings are rational animals" is logically of the form

> If something is a human being, then it is a rational, animal body.

And it asserts an entailment relation between the antecedent and the consequent (DCo 3.11). Ideally, a scientific proposition asserts how an object may be generated, for example,

> If something is a circle, then it can be generated by fixing a point and drawing around it a closed curved line all the points of which are equidistant from it.

Neither of these sample propositions asserts the existence of anything; so neither is empirically refutable; yet each is anchored to the world through its terms, which are empirical. Some of these views may have been derived from ancient Stoic logicians.[2]

One reason that Hobbes wanted science to be necessarily true was that he was a determinist. (A determinist is a person who believes that all things and all events are necessarily the way they are, because the laws of nature, which are fixed and inviolable, determine that there is only one way for them to be.) Hobbes was in fact confused about necessity. He thought that because the world was necessarily the way it is, scientific propositions had to be analytically true or true by definition. However, determinism is compatible with the view that all scientific truths are contingent propositions; that is, their negations are not contradictory. In other words, Hobbes conflated logical necessity and metaphysical necessity (DCo 3.10–11, 10.5, *Of Liberty and Necessity* in *English Works*, ed. Molesworth, p. 276, *Questions Concerning Liberty, Necessity, and Chance* in *English Works*, pp. 195, 222).

Hobbes's desire to identify logical and metaphysical necessity was linked to another deep concern of his. He believed in the unity of science. He thought that the only real things are bodies in motion. Human beings, like animals and to a lesser extent plants, are merely highly complex systems of moving bodies. And, finally, political systems are ultimately highly complex systems of human beings. Consequently, if one began with full knowledge of (the initial speed and direction of) the smallest bodies and the laws of nature, then one could presumably deduce the whole course of the world, including the actions of human beings; and thus also the origin and fates of governments. To proceed in this way is to reason "synthetically" in the argot of Renaissance and early modern thinkers: one is building up science by reasoning from causes to effects. Alternatively, one could reason "analytically," to use the same argot, that is, to begin with effects and reason (conjecturally) to their causes: one is breaking down objects into their component parts. In fact, there is an asymmetry in these two methods. Synthetic reasoning begins with possible causes and deduces possible effects. In contrast, analytic reasoning begins with actual effects and conjectures possible causes for them. Hobbes captured this asymmetry when he defined philosophy as the knowledge of appearances that is acquired by correct reasoning from "some possible production or generation" of the possible effects [synthetic reasoning] or "from the knowledge we have of the effects" to some actual or possible cause of them (DCo 6.1; cf. DCo 1.2; DH 10.4–5). The element of conjecture or guesswork in science may seem to contradict the earlier claim that all scientific propositions are necessarily true; but it does not. Scientific propositions are necessary in virtue of their logical structure; the conjectural element attaches to the process of discovering what propositions to use as explanations. Since there can be more than one way for an effect to be caused, the scientific propositions accounting for an effect may be necessarily true, but not factually or historically correct. For example, an actual circle might have been generated either by being drawn with a compass or by being imprinted by a circular stamp. It is indifferent to science which way it actually occurred. What science asserts is that if this figure was generated in a certain way, then it is a circle; or alternatively, if this is a circle, then it could have been generated in such and such a way.

Since he thought that philosophy studied three basic kinds of objects (bodies, human beings, and governments), Hobbes divided his system into three "sections" and published them, out of chronological order, as *De Corpore* (1655), *De Homine* (1658), and *De Cive* (1642, second edition 1647). How could Hobbes have published the third section first if science is a unity? The answer is that there is a difference between the logical relationship of entailment that links propositions of physics to propositions of anthropology to propositions of political philosophy and the epistemic links between human beings and some of the propositions of these sciences. In particular, it is possible for people to know the basic propositions of political philosophy independently of some of the basic propositions of physics and anthropology. Consequently, political philosophy can be done before the other two.

Our purposes are best served if we explain the rest of Hobbes's philosophy in the logical order he intended for them: physics, anthropology, politics. Hobbes presented his complete physics in *De Corpore.* However, that book does not get around to presenting the physics ("Physics or the Phenomena of Nature") until the last of the four parts. Part One is titled "Computation or Logic." Part Two is "The First Grounds of Philosophy." Part Three is "On the Proportions of Motions and Magnitudes."

"Computation or Logic," as explicated by Hobbes, should be construed broadly. In addition to a simplified and nominalistic version of Aristotelian syllogistic reasoning, logic for him includes a philosophy of language, a theory of scientific method, and a geometry. The Aristotelian logic can be passed over. It is underpinned by an inadequate philosophy of language. According to Hobbes, words have two basic uses. The historically earliest and logically primary one is to serve a person as a token to help him or her remember an idea. For some reason, Hobbes thinks that it is easier to remember an idea, say, red, by keeping what he calls an arbitrary "mark", say, "red," in memory. When one wants to think of something red, one conjures up the word "red." The historically later and logically derivative use of names is to serve as signs to other people of our own ideas. Anticipating Frege, Hobbes maintained that in order to function as signs, words have to be part of a sentence; individual words are not signs. Communication then is the speaker's act of getting a hearer to think of the same idea as the speaker by means of the sentence uttered. For example, a speaker wanting a hearer to think that a certain cat is on a certain mat will say "The cat is on the mat." If the hearer thinks of that idea because of the speaker's utterance, then communication has occurred. Hobbes's theory is a paradigmatic case of the kind of "private language" theory that Ludwig Wittgenstein demolished in *Philosophical Investigations.* To mention only one problem: communication requires that people at least sometimes know when they have succeeded. But if ideas, in the sense of privately viewed and exclusively possessed entities, are the things that are meant, then neither speaker nor hearer could ever know when communication was successful. It is no good to say that one could determine what the other person was thinking by paying attention to her behavior, because one could never discover the appropriate correlation between the person's behavior and her ideas, if one never had access to her ideas.

We have been talking about words as signs of ideas. They also name objects. The proper name "Fido," for example, is the name of one particular dog. (Philosophers typically ignore or explain away the fact that thousands of objects have the same proper name.) Hobbes's views about the objects named by common names are determined by his nominalism, the doctrine that only individual objects exist. The only thing universal, according to him, is a name (DCo 2.9). ("Noun" means the same as "name.") What he means is that a name, such as "dog," is a universal because it is the name of many individual dogs.

Hobbes's materialistic nominalism causes some trouble for his theory of names. He avers that "future" is a name even though the future does not exist; "impossible" is a name even though what it names cannot exist; and "nothing" is a name even though it cannot be the name of anything. He asserts these views but does not explain them beyond indicating that these non-entities are useful fictions (DCo 2.6).

His materialistic nominalism also influences his view of the nature of reasoning. It is nothing but computation in the sense of adding and subtracting (DCo 1.2). Typically what is added or subtracted are names; for example, the names "rational," "animate," and "body" added together sum as "human being"; "rational" subtracted from "human being" has "animal" as its remainder. Hobbes then explains the validity and invalidity of categorical syllogisms respectively as the correct or incorrect adding or subtracting of names. This latter idea is actually defensible.[3] As long as the types of things are the same, anything can be added or subtracted from anything else: "body to body, motion to motion, degree to degree of quality, action to action, conception to conception, proportion to proportion, speech to speech, name to name" (DCo 1.3).

Part Two of *De Corpore* explicates some important physical, philosophical, and geometrical concepts. Space is "the phantasm [sense image] of a thing existing without the mind simply." Place is "a space which is completely filled or occupied by a body" (DCo 6.5). Time is the phantasm of before and after in motion. A body is something coextensive with space and not dependent on human thought (DCo 8.1). An accident [property] is a power of a body to cause a conception in an animal (DCo. 8.2). Motion is the continual relinquishing of one place and acquiring of another (DCo 8.10). A cause is the collection of the accidents of all the agents and patients which necessarily produce an effect (DCo 6.10, 9.3). A more contemporary way of putting this would be that a cause is the set of conditions sufficient to produce an effect.

Part Three, "Proportions of Motions and Magnitudes," is a combination of geometry and physics. For Hobbes, motion is the cause of everything and consequently the cause of geometrical objects. Taking the idea of a point as basic, he says that "a line is made from the motion of a point, a surface from the motion of a line," and so on (DCo 6.6). To understand what a circle is, one must know what kind of motion makes it. Because geometry has already been rendered scientific by "Euclid, Archimedes, and Appollonius," Hobbes restricts his discussion to his own discoveries. This part contains one of his notorious attempts to square the circle, that is, an attempt to prove that, for any given circle, a square of identical area can be constructed, using only a straight stick and a compass. Since the impossibility of this project was proved only in the nineteenth century, it was not obvious that Hobbes was tilting at a geometrical windmill. What was unfortunate was that he stubbornly refused to see or was unable to see the validity of the numerous criticisms that were directed against his proofs.

Also in this section, Hobbes discusses one of his key ideas of physics, that of "endeavor" ("*conatus*"), a concept that was picked up by Spinoza and Leibniz. An endeavor, according to one definition, is a motion smaller than any motion that can be measured (DCo 15.2).[4] Endeavors, then, are relative to a system of measurement. If a foot is the smallest unit of measurement, then a motion across one inch or even eleven inches would be an endeavor. If, however, an inch is the smallest unit, then those motions across one or eleven inches would not be endeavors, but motions of a quarter or a half inch would be. Since points for him have length, width, and breadth (which are ignored in doing proofs), he sometimes says that an endeavor is "a motion made through the length of a point" (DCo 15.2). Also, since the smallest unit of measurement is usually at the limit of human perceptual powers, Hobbes sometimes defines an endeavor imprecisely as an imperceptibly small motion. Because someone might object to the idea of invisibly small motions, Hobbes gives a proof of their existence. Space, like matter, is infinitely divisible. Take the smallest perceptible space. Divide it in half. Although this space is not perceptible, it must be possible for a body to traverse it. Such a motion is an endeavor (L 6.1). Hobbes uses the concept of an endeavor to define other physical concepts. For example, resistance is the endeavor of one body against another body that is in motion; and pressure is the endeavor of one object against another (DCo 15.2, 22.1).

Endeavor is also the key concept in his psychology. An appetite is an endeavor towards an object; and aversion is an endeavor away from an object. Love, hate, contempt, good, evil, and every other emotion is ultimately defined in terms of appetites and aversions and hence ultimately in terms of endeavors. Finally, an act of willing is in fact nothing but the last desire an agent has before acting. Since desires are appetites, and appetites are endeavors, acts of will are endeavors (DH 11.1–3).

An interlude is appropriate here. Hobbes's doctrine that to know something is to know what kind of motion made it has a consequence that undermines his threefold sectioning of philosophy; for it follows that knowledge of human cognition is nothing but knowledge of what motion "makes a thing to be seen or heard" (DCo 6.6). So cognitive science is part of geometry or physics for Hobbes: "Thus those who study natural philosophy study in vain unless they take their principles of inquiry from geometry" (DCo 6.6). And in fact, he discusses his central psychological concept, "endeavor" ("*conatus*") in the third part of *De Corpore* and sensation in the fourth part. (He argues that sensation is part of Physics because physics is preeminently the science of "phenomena or appearances" and these occur exclusively in sentient beings (DCo 25.1).) Moreover, he would devote about half of *De Homine*, which should explain what is distinctive about human beings, to optics, which properly belongs in *De Corpore*. Thus it makes more sense to divide science into two sections: natural science, of which anthropology is a part, and artificial science, which explains politics; and in fact the division of science in *Leviathan* reflects this view. One consequence of this dyadic division is that both ethics and "the science of just and unjust," not to mention logic, poetry, and rhetoric, become part of "Natural Philosophy" (L 9.4).

At this point, we should begin presenting Hobbes's views about what he expressly claims to be the second of the three sections of philosophy, namely, the nature of human beings. Of course, we actually began this presentation two paragraphs ago by explaining what an endeavor is. And, since Hobbes discusses sensation in *De Corpore* as much as *De Homine*, not to mention *Leviathan*, we are continuing with an explanation of his physics as much as his anthropology.

For most contemporary philosophers of a materialistic or naturalistic bent, the mystery of sensation is the existence of what is now referred to as qualia: that brute experience of the world as colored, sounding, odiferous, and textured. Scientists from Galileo, Descartes, and Hobbes, down to our own day, have argued that qualia are not part of the world in itself, but only exist as our way of experiencing the world. Most philosophers are bothered, if not awestruck, by the facticity of qualitative experience. Hobbes was not. He sanguinely asserts that sensations are nothing but complex tiny motions in animals (endeavors), which motions are caused by external bodies acting on sense organs, which in turn act on internal parts of the body: "sense is some internal motion in the sentient" (DCo 25.2). He is equally sanguine about using the term "phantasm" for these motions, even though that is the scholastic equivalent of "qualia."

The difference between sensation and imagination is the presence and absence, respectively, of the object causing the internal motion. That is, imagination is "decaying sense" (DCo 25.7). What is most important about this latter definition is what it suggests about Hobbes's project in psychology. Imagination is sense; senses are complex endeavors; and endeavors are tiny motions. His project is completely reductive. Seemingly higher-level types of cognition, such as memory, thinking, believing, understanding, and speaking, are analyzed as variations on sensation and hence reducible to motions. The analogous procedure is followed for analyzing emotions, as we already indicated. All emotions, such as love, fear, and hope, are analyzed in terms of appetite, aversion, and sometimes a form of cognition; and these three things were analyzed as endeavors, and endeavors are small motions (DCo 25.13). Ideally, the analyses of these concepts should have been given in physical terms: physico-chemical explanations. But he can be forgiven his conceptual analyses because science was nowhere near sufficiently advanced to provide such. Neuroscientists today are filling in the details of Hobbes's philosophy.

One of the things that seems to be eliminated in a scientific view of mankind is free will. And so it is in Hobbes's philosophy, although he keeps both freedom and will. Freedom is unconstrained activity. An undammed river, a wandering animal, and a person doing what she wants are all completely free, according to Hobbes. "Will" he defines as the last appetite or desire before acting (DCo 25.13). But there is no such thing as a faculty of will, and instances of will are not free, because acts of will are not chosen; they are caused by other physical events, and the will itself is just a causal factor in bodily action.

After an introductory biographical note, we can turn to Hobbes's political philosophy. In late 1640, with the English Civil War impending, Hobbes left England for France, "the first of those who fled," as he said in his autobiography. In 1642, his first great political work was published anonymously and in a limited edition, *De Cive* [*On the Citizen*]. In 1647 a second edition with explanatory notes was published in a large print run. At the age of 59, he had achieved a substantial reputation. In 1651, he returned to England just prior to the publication of his *magnum opus, Leviathan.* Most of it was similar to what he had already written in *De Cive.*

To grossly simplify the issues behind the English Civil War, some supporters of the king thought that the sovereign's authority has to be absolute; and some opponents of the king thought that ultimate political theory has to reside in the citizens. And it would appear that these two positions are impossible to reconcile. Not for the only time, Hobbes tried to do the impossible. For him, all political authority springs from individual people. The people choose whether they will be governed by a democracy, aristocracy, or monarchy. But whichever form is chosen, the government, called "the sovereign," is absolute. That is, the government has a monopoly on political power and has the authority to regulate any area of human life.[5] Hobbes abhorred the idea of a division of powers. Such a division was tantamount to civil war, because each component of government would compete with each other for control.

Hobbes's project then was to show (i) how governments come into existence; (ii) what makes them legitimate; and (iii) what their powers are. Concerning (i), there are two great traditions in political philosophy. One that maintains that government is natural, of which Aristotle is the foremost representative; and one that denies it, such as the Epicureans. Hobbes belongs to this latter tradition. He maintains that governments are artificial constructs and that human beings are not naturally fit for society. For Hobbes, it is easy enough to think of human beings as being human and not living under any government at all, that is, "the state of nature."

The state of nature functions in a thought experiment.[6] Think of human beings as they would be if there were no government at all. In such a condition, according to Hobbes, everyone would be equal in the following sense. Each would have the ability to kill any other person. Even the weakest and stupidest person has enough sense and strength to wait for the strongest and smartest person to fall asleep, creep up to the person, and then kill him. Hobbes is often counted as an early liberal political theorist because he asserts the natural equality of all people. But it is important to realize that he considers this equality to be a source for the wretchedness of the state of nature. A decent life requires the kind of inequality introduced by government.

The equal ability of each person to kill anyone else is the most important kind because the basic psychological principle according to Hobbes is that everyone desires to preserve his own life.[7] This principle itself follows from a more basic proposition: Whatever is desired is good, or everyone desires his own good (DH 11.4–6). This has been called "tautological egoism" since Hobbes propounds it as a definition. (Everyone desires life because that is a necessary condition for all other desires.) Hobbes sometimes construes his egoistic principle as meaning that everyone desires only what benefits himself. He thinks he needs this latter principle, psychological egoism, in order to explain purely natural human behavior.

In the state of nature, everyone would have a right to preserve herself ("the right of nature"). Put another way, there are no laws that could constrain behavior. Given that everyone has to decide for herself what the best means are for surviving, it follows, according to Hobbes, that everyone has a right to everything.[8] This means that it is inevitable that people will sometimes compete for the same objects. This is one cause of war. Further, this potential competition will make each person suspicious and distrustful of everyone else; and each person will also know that everyone else is suspicious of her. This is a second cause of war and exacerbates the first. Finally, there are some people who simply are not willing to be treated as equals and will demand glory for themselves even by force. This is a third cause of war. In short, human life in the state of nature is "solitary, poor, nasty, brutish and short" (L 14.8, 14.9).

Salvation from the dangerous natural condition can come about only by the creation of something that can protect each person from her fellows. Moreover, because it is something that humans construct themselves and because it is analogous to an animal in that it has goals, can make decisions, can act, and so on, Hobbes calls this thing an artificial animal, namely, "Leviathan." Hobbes takes the name from a primeval monster in the Book of Job, which was called "king of all the children of pride" (L 28.27). (Traditionally, the original sin was thought to be due to pride, that is, taking credit for something that is not the result of one's own merits.) Leviathan is a "mortal god, to which we owe, under the immortal God, our peace and defense" (L 17.13).

How exactly does Leviathan, the government, get constructed? The answer to this is in effect the answer to (ii). The first thing that Hobbes needs are laws of nature. A law of nature, as he defines it, "is a precept or general rule, found out by reason, by which a man is forbidden to do that which is destructive of his life, or takes away the means of preserving the same, and to omit that by which he thinks it may be best preserved" (L 15.3). Because the correct understanding of this definition is perhaps the most acerbically controverted point in Hobbesian scholarship, I shall tread lightly here. Hobbes distinguishes between two kinds of precepts: commands and counsels. A counsel is a precept that has the good of the addressee as its goal, for example "I recommend (advise, suggest) that you eat healthy food and exercise regularly." A command is a precept that has the good of the speaker as its goal. What Hobbes means is that when a command is given the addressee has an obligation to do what the speaker wants, and Hobbes believes that whatever a person wants (desires) is good. Further, a command can be issued only by someone in authority. But who is the authority that commands the laws of nature? Sometimes Hobbes says or implies that God commands them. But in other places, he says or implies that humans know nothing about God, and that the laws of nature are not really laws but only counsels. If this latter interpretation is correct, then Hobbes's philosophy has a serious problem. His misnamed "laws of nature" are merely counsels, that is, prudential maxims. And in this case, it is not clear whether he has an ethical theory at all, according to most scholars, who think that moral precepts have a bindingness and force that is absent from prudential maxims. Moreover, if the laws of nature are supposed to provide prudential advice for self-preservation, then there seem to be cases where prudence would dictate not following the laws of nature. But this consequence does not square with the standard view that morality is not subordinate to prudence.

According to one interpretation, Hobbes's laws of nature are really laws because they are commanded by reason. This interpretation has the problem of explaining how reason, which is merely calculation, could command anything. Also, according to Hobbes, a command can be issued only by someone in authority, and authority requires overwhelming power to back it up. Reason has no such power.[9]

Whether Hobbes thought that reason commands anything or not, it certainly is his view that the laws of nature are at least discovered by reason.

The content of the laws of nature is circumscribed by the requirement that they dictate a course of action that enhances the chances of self-preservation. This element of the definition is crucial for the following reason. From the definition of a law of nature, Hobbes deduces the specific laws of nature by inferring what is necessary for self-preservation. Without this specific content, reason would have no way of proceeding.

Although Hobbes is not explicit about how his laws of nature follow from the definition, it is plausible that his proofs are all instances of *reductio ad absurdum*. For example, to prove the first law, "Every man ought to endeavor peace, as far as he has hope of obtaining it" (L 15.4), suppose that it is not true. Then every man remains in the state of war and thereby jeopardizes his life. But this contradicts the definition of the law of nature. Therefore, every man should endeavor peace, as far as he has hope of obtaining it.

This first law of nature is the first half ("branch") of what Hobbes calls "The precept or general rule of reason" in *Leviathan* (L 15.4). The second half is another precept (but not a law), namely, the right of nature, which states that if peace is unobtainable, then one may use "all the helps and advantages of war" to stay alive. (In *De Cive*, this second "branch" had been part of the first law of nature (DC 2.2).)

The second law of nature, namely, that for the sake of peace and his own life, a person is to be willing, to the extent that others are, to lay down his right to all things, can also be proved with a *reductio* argument. Suppose a person is unwilling to lay down his right to all things. Then he does not desire peace. But this contradicts the first law of nature. Therefore, a person should be willing to lay down his right to all things.

There is an ambiguity in this law. Does laying down one's right to all things mean that one lays down every right or that one lays down only some rights? Hobbes trades on the ambiguity. Sometimes he says the latter, as when he says that there are "some rights, which no man can be understood by any words or other signs to have abandoned or transferred," such as not resisting a life-threatening assault, because, according to Hobbes, such an action "cannot be understood to aim thereby at any good" to the person himself (L 15.8). So the right to life is an inalienable right for Hobbes.[10] He exploits this interpretation to make his theory palatable to citizens. Concerning the other meaning of the second law, Hobbes sometimes writes as if a person gives up every right when she joins a government (L 17.13). He wants to suggest this in order to make his case for absolute sovereignty plausible. More will be said about this below.

The third law of nature, "men perform their covenants," is easy enough to deduce. If people do not keep their covenants, then they will incite war, which contradicts the first law of nature. But there is more to this law than meets the eye. Covenant is one of the central concepts of Hobbes's political theory. A covenant, for him, is a contract that involves some future action on the part of one of the people making it. The most important covenant that people enter into is the one they make with a group of other people to form a government. Because Hobbes holds this view, he holds a "social contract theory." According to his version, people in the state of nature, aiming at peace, lay down their right to all things and thereby create a sovereign, who has the collective power of all the citizens, to fulfill the aims of that covenant, namely, their peace and security.

The sovereign thereby created cannot be legitimately opposed by his subjects for two reasons. One is that in making the contract they have authorized him to act for them, the other is that they have alienated their rights to him; in neither case does a subject have a right to complain (DH 15.3). These two reasons are at least in tension with each other and are arguably contradictory. Nonetheless that Hobbes holds them is clear from the formula that he proposes as capturing the essence of sovereign-making: "I authorize and give up my right of governing myself to this man or to this assembly of men . . . and authorize all his actions" (L 17.13). Authorization and alienation ("give up my right") are in tension because authorizing someone requires that one retain rights to the matter, while alienating a right means that one loses that right. The tension in Hobbes's thought is one that reappears in much casual talk about governments: one the one hand "we are the government"; on the other hand, "the government is superior to and controls us." The short answer then to question (ii) above, is that subjects agreed to have their sovereign act for them and to govern them.

That brings us to (iii). Hobbes, as we said, thought that sovereignty by definition was absolute. The sovereign has all the political power and has authority over every aspect of life. In *Behemoth*, his history of the English Civil War, Hobbes says that a son has the obligation to kill his own father if commanded to do so by the sovereign. According to him, if any restrictions are put on the scope or depth of the sovereign's political power, then the stability of the government is undermined. In other words, the concept of limited sovereignty, the view supported by most educated Englishmen of the time, is self-contradictory and hence absurd. Hobbes enjoyed giving his opponents short shrift.

A large part of *De Cive* and about half of *Leviathan* are concerned with religion. Modern science introduced a worldview that was clearly inconsistent with the biblical cosmology and apparently inconsistent with revealed religion. The choices for a modern person were to abandon revealed religion or to reinterpret it. Religion was too ingrained for most people to abandon it. That left reinterpretation. Galileo provided a bumper sticker solution: "Religion does not teach how the heavens go but how to go to heaven." Hobbes attempted a comprehensive reinterpretation. Religion, he said, was the fear of invisible powers, either imagined by people or taught. True religion was religion that correctly described these powers. Superstition – and almost all religions are superstitious – is religion that is not permitted by the authorities.. He asserted that religion is law, and since the sovereign makes laws, the religion of a land is the religion of the sovereign. His critics immediately recognized that Hobbes's view entailed that religion is relative. Further, by his definition, Roman Catholicism was superstition in England, but not in Spain; and Christianity was superstition in ancient Rome and modern Turkey. Hobbes caught holy hell for these deflating definitions. But he taught even more threatening doctrines about revelation, prophets, and miracles.

The key to understanding Hobbes's views here is to distinguish between metaphysics (the study of the most basic things that exist) and epistemology (the study of the scope and limits of human knowledge). Hobbes, piously enough, asserted that revelation has occurred, that miracles have happened (but no longer do), and that there have been true prophets. These claims belong to metaphysics. But he then undercut them with some epistemological claims. It is impossible to know when revelation occurs, when a miracle occurs, or who is a true prophet, until it is too late for a prophet to do any good. Let's consider these seriatim.

There are two kinds of revelation, direct and indirect. Indirect revelation occurs when some person P_1 is told by another person P_2 that God has spoken to P_2. Since there is no way for P_1 to determine rationally whether P_2 is telling the truth or not, beliefs about revelation cannot count as knowledge. Direct revelation is no better. People often believe that God talks to them in dreams. But, as Hobbes pointed out, to say that God appeared to me in a dream means the same as that I dreamed that God appeared to me. Since the latter has no evidential value, neither does the former. And it is no good to object that some people believe that God appears to them when they are awake; for some people believe that they are awake when they are in fact asleep, even during broad daylight; and what is more likely, that the person is unwittingly asleep or that God appeared to them? The same conclusion follows: there can be no knowledge of revelations.

One could trust revelations if one could identify true prophets. But, alas, this is difficult to do during the life of the prophet. Hobbes quotes incidents from the Bible that prove that prophets are often mistaken in their predictions, often lie, and sometimes deceive each other. Even God says that prophets are liars. Of course, true prophets can be identified, but only after their predictions have been borne out. But by the time that has happened, it is too late for them to be any help. Almost all of the prophets who are praised in the Bible were honored only posthumously. When they were alive, they were roundly condemned or ignored.

One could identify a true prophet during his lifetime if one could identify miracles, since God uses miracles as signs of His prophets. A miracle, Hobbes says, is (a) an "admirable" work of (b) God, (c) done for the making manifest to his elect, (d) "the mission of an extraordinary Minister for their salvation" (L 37.1, 37.7). An admirable work is one that occurs rarely and has no conceivable natural explanation at the time it occurs. Concerning (a), the first rainbow, the one seen by Noah after the Deluge, was a miracle. But rainbows cannot be miracles for us both because they occur too frequently and because we now understand their physics. Concerning (b), Hobbes does not want any human being to acquire any authority as a consequence of being a miracle-worker. Concerning (c), as a Calvinist, Hobbes believed that Jesus died only for the elect; so they are the only proper audience for a miracle. Concerning (d), miracles cannot be idle acts of wonderment; they need a relevant salvific purpose. The most important consequences of Hobbes's analysis are that the more science progresses, the narrower the range of possible miraculous phenomena, and to claim to see a miracle is to admit one's ignorance of natural causes.

The foundation for revelation, prophets, and miracles, then, is not knowledge but faith, and faith is trust in another person. The proper person to trust in a commonwealth is the sovereign since he is the one that people have authorized to act for them. Consequently, religion is law and relative to a state. These religious views, as well as some of his political ones, turned most clerics and laymen against Hobbes. Some tried to have charges brought against him in parliament in the 1660s. But these efforts failed. His views were not quite outrageous enough – he affirmed his orthodoxy and attended Anglican services. His personal life was beyond reproach – people believed that atheism caused immorality. And he had friends in high places – he was a friend and former tutor of the king, Charles II.

During his last years, Hobbes returned to some of the humanistic delights of his youth. He produced translations of Homer's *Odyssey* and *Iliad* that went into several editions. Eventually, he retired from the hustle and bustle of London to the estates of the family that gave him his first job after graduation from Magdalen Hall, Oxford, the Cavendishes of Devonshire. Upon his death on December 4, 1679, he was buried under a black marble slab within St. John the Baptist Church, Ault Hucknall.

Soon after his death, his philosophy was transmogrified into a caricature, Hobbism, a term used to designate any vaguely materialistic and atheistic system or any philosophy one disapproved of. By the middle of the eighteenth century, Hobbes was largely ignored, only to have his reputation among Anglo-American philosophers resurrected in the last quarter of the twentieth century as one of the great philosophers of all time.

Notes

1 I use the following abbreviations:

C = *Correspondence*, ed. Noel Malcolm (Oxford: Oxford University Press, 1994)
DC = *De Cive*
DCo = *De Corpore*
DH = *De Homine*
L = *Leviathan*

Unless otherwise noted, Hobbes's works are referred to by chapter and paragraph, e.g. "L 14.2" refers to Leviathan, chapter 14, paragraph 2.

2 Hobbes's philosophy coincides with or is very similar to Stoic philosophy on a number of issues. In addition to the form of scientific propositions, both believe in divine providence, were determinists, deny free will, and believe that cognitions include an emotional coloring that comes from an action of the heart. It is not clear how direct the influence was.

3 Fred Sommers, "The Calculus of Terms," *Mind* 79 (1970), pp. 1–39.

4 Hobbes says that an endeavor is a motion smaller than can be measured in space or time. This makes his view problematic in ways that cannot be discussed here. For our discussion, I will pretend that endeavors are measured only spatially.

5 Most theorists thought that democracies accorded more freedom to their citizens than monarchies; but Hobbes scoffed at the idea. How much liberty the people have is determined by the individual sovereign, whatever form that takes.

6 It is a concept that can be realized in three situations: in the condition of primitive peoples, in civil war, and in international relations.

7 Scholars argue over whether Hobbes thinks that this principle is ever violated; see Sharon Lloyd, *Ideals as Interests in Hobbes's Leviathan* (Cambridge: Cambridge University Press, 1992).

8 In fact, this conclusion follows simply from the proposition that there are no laws, since only laws take away rights. But Hobbes never argues in this simpler way.

9 Some, if not all, of these interpretive options, could have been avoided if in his definition Hobbes had used the active form, "X forbids," rather than the passive voice, "a man is forbidden." In general, the passive voice should be avoided unless there is good reason to use it, for example, in this sentence, which focuses on "the passive voice."

10 Further, he holds that whoever wills the end wills the means and that one can never be sure what one might need to preserve his life. These views seem to entail that one can never give up one's right to anything; unfortunately this contradicts the second law of nature.

Chapter 3

Benedict de Spinoza

Don Garrett

The thought of Benedict (Baruch) de Spinoza constitutes a genuine philosophical system; that is, it provides deeply interrelated answers to a full range of philosophical questions in metaphysics, philosophy of mind, epistemology, philosophy of physical science, philosophy of psychology, ethics, political theory, and philosophy of religion. His work is profound, original, and often strikingly modern; but in order to understand its formulation, it is essential to have some understanding of his life and of the distinctive historical and cultural perspective that he occupied.

1. Life, Writings, and Context

In 1632 – the same year in which Galileo published his *Dialogue Concerning the Two Chief World Systems* and thereby provoked the Catholic Church to put him on trial for heresy – Spinoza was born to a moderately prosperous merchant family in the Jewish community of Amsterdam. Most members of that community were, like Spinoza's own family, descended from Spanish and Portuguese Jews who had either fled from or been expelled by the Inquisition. This rather cosmopolitan community sought to rediscover its Jewish heritage in the Netherlands, which had recently achieved its independence from Spain and now offered a degree of religious freedom. Accordingly, Spinoza received a religious education that included Hebrew, the Torah and the Talmud, and important medieval Jewish thinkers such as Moses Maimonides. In addition, he soon discovered the philosophy of Descartes – who himself had moved to the Netherlands four years before Spinoza's birth in order to write in relative freedom and solitude, remaining there until he joined Queen Christina's court in Sweden in 1649. Between 1652 and 1654, Spinoza studied Latin (the language in which he wrote for publication) and Cartesian philosophy in the school of the Cartesian Francis van den Ende. At least partly to avoid being associated with potentially heretical views – such as the doctrine that God is corporeal and the denial of personal immortality – the Jewish community excommunicated the no longer observant Spinoza in 1656. Upon his excommunication, Spinoza changed his first name from "Baruch" to its Latin equivalent "Benedict" and relocated just outside Amsterdam.

In 1660, he moved near Leiden, where he supported himself by grinding lenses and by tutoring students of the nearby university. There he worked on his never-completed *Treatise on the Emendation of the Intellect* and on his *Short Treatise on God, Man, and His Well-Being*. The latter work, an early treatment of the main topics of his later *Ethics*, was discovered – in the form of a Dutch manuscript translation – and published only in the nineteenth century. His first work to appear in print was *Descartes's Principles of Philosophy*. Written in an axiomatized format in which numbered propositions are demonstrated by appeal to axioms, definitions, and previous propositions, it provides a presentation and exposition of Part One, Part Two, and an initial portion of Part Three of René Descartes's four-part *Principles of Philosophy*; it also includes some unaxiomatized background material called "Metaphysical Thoughts." Published in 1663, this work had developed – with the encouragement of his loyal circle of friends, many of them Christians of the nondogmatic Collegiant sect – from Spinoza's axiomatization for a tutorial student of Part Two of the *Principles of Philosophy*. It helped to establish Spinoza's reputation as an interpreter of Descartes's metaphysical and natural philosophy.

In the same year, Spinoza moved to the outskirts of The Hague, where he remained in communication with his Amsterdam-centered circle of friends and also with such important scientific figures as Henry Oldenburg (the secretary of the British Royal Society) and the Dutch mathematician and physicist Christiaan Huygens. In 1670, he published his *Theological-Political Treatise* concerning the interpretation of scripture and the role of religion in the state. The book was written partly in response to the murder by an angry mob of the De Witt brothers, leaders of the republican party in the Netherlands. Always cautious about disseminating his more controversial views too widely, Spinoza published the book anonymously and with a false imprint of "Hamburg." In 1673 he declined a proffered chair at the University of Heidelberg, partly on the grounds that it would interfere with his study and partly on the grounds that he might not be able to honor the invitation's expressed presumption that he would not use his promised freedom of expression to "disturb the established religion."

Spinoza's masterpiece, and by far the most complete statement of his philosophical system, is the *Ethics* (*Ethica Ordine Geometrico demonstrata*, or *Ethics Demonstrated in Geometrical Order*). This work consists of five parts, all in axiomatized form, beginning with metaphysics and epistemology, and leading through psychology to ethics and the way to blessedness. He traveled to Amsterdam in 1675 to see to the book's publication, only to change his mind for reasons of prudence. The following year, he received a two-week visit from Leibniz (returning to the continent from a trip to England). Leibniz, who had originally corresponded with him years earlier on a question of optics, was both attracted and repelled by Spinozism, and regarded it as a significant intellectual rival to his own philosophy. Spinoza died of respiratory disease, likely caused or exacerbated by the inhalation of glass dust in his work, in 1677. His friends saw to the publication of his *Opera posthuma*, which included the *Ethics*, the unfinished *Treatise on the Emendation of the Intellect*, an unfinished *Political Treatise*, a *Hebrew Grammar*, and *Correspondence*.

The philosophical tasks that Spinoza undertook during his short lifetime were set for him in some measure by the time and place in which he lived. Throughout western Europe, the new science that followed in the wake of the Copernican Revolution was undermining the traditional scholastic philosophy derived from Aristotle and Christian church teachings. This new science was mechanistic and quantitative in spirit, and seemed to leave no room for the older conception in which the nature and behavior of bodies was explained through their possession of distinctive substantial forms and natural ends. Thus, one problem that Spinoza faced was that of providing a new metaphysical understanding of the ontological structure of the universe that would incorporate and render intelligible the new mechanistic science. Related to this was the crucial problem of explaining the place of mentality in general and of human minds in particular in relation to this world of physical mechanism. With revolutionary changes in conceptions of the natural world and the place of human beings within it naturally came new questions about the nature of human knowledge and the proper method to follow in understanding both the physical world and the human mind itself.

Spinoza's concerns, however, were not limited to metaphysics, philosophy of mind, epistemology, philosophy of physical science, and philosophy of psychology. In his conception of philosophy, all of these topics gain their ultimate value from the contribution that an understanding of them can make to a good human life. Thus, he was particularly concerned to employ his more metaphysical and epistemological results to shed light on how human beings should live their lives, what they should pursue, how they can control their dangerous passions, and even how the modern state should be organized in order to promote human flourishing. Particularly important to the well-being of the well- ordered state is the role played by popular religion; and it is largely for this reason that Spinoza devoted intensive effort to the proper interpretation of the Bible. The significance of religion is not, however, by any means limited to its role in the state. On the contrary, stimulated no doubt in part by the ongoing conflict between science and Christianity – which he of course viewed from the distinctive perspective of an excommunicated Jew – he radically reconceived the nature of God, God's relation to human beings, and human beings' relation to God. Spinoza's identification of God with Nature is among the most striking and distinctive aspects of his philosophy; his radical displacement of revelation and ritual by philosophy and science is among its most modern.

2. Metaphysics

The fundamental categories of Spinoza's ontology are "substance," "attribute," and "mode." He defines "substance" at the outset of the *Ethics* as "what is in itself and is conceived through itself; that is, that whose concept does not require the concept of another thing, from which it must be formed" (1d3).[1] The dual nature of this definition, which employs the parallel notions of being "in itself" and being "conceived through itself," reflects his fundamental commitment to the view that whatever is true of things themselves is reflected in the ideas of those things. Descartes would have agreed with Spinoza that a substance is "in itself," meaning by this that it has qualities or "modes" (for example, a particular size, shape, and color) without itself being the quality of any other thing. Evidently led by the reflection that such qualities are dependent for their existence on the things of which they are qualities in a way in which those things are not dependent on their qualities, Descartes defines a substance as something that is not dependent on any other thing for its existence. A consequence of this Cartesian definition, however, is that Descartes must acknowledge that only God is a substance in the strongest and strictest sense, since only God is *entirely* independent of *anything* else for his existence; other things, such as bodies and human minds, are substances only in a weaker sense, for they depend for their continued existence, in Descartes's view, on God's concurrence. Spinoza, in contrast, uses the term "substance" univocally. For him, the requirement that a substance be absolutely in itself and conceived through itself entails that a substance must be absolutely the sole cause of its own existence. This is because things are conceived through their causes (1a4), so that if anything else caused a substance, the substance would be conceived through that cause and hence not through itself. But a thing can be *self-caused* only if its existence derives from its own essence (1d1) rather than from any external thing; and since a thing is properly conceived by conceiving its essence (2d), it follows that a substance is a thing whose existence cannot be denied by anyone who forms a proper concept of its nature. Furthermore, it may be noted, since an adequate definition captures the essence of a thing (as Spinoza repeatedly emphasizes), only something whose existence follows from its definition alone – so that its existence can be demonstrated *a priori* – can be a substance. Since bodies and human minds lack this characteristic, instead deriving their being as well as many of their qualities from external causes, they cannot be substances in Spinoza's sense.

Spinoza defines an "attribute" as "what the intellect perceives of a substance, as constituting its essence." This concept of an "attribute" derives, in part, from Descartes's concept of a "principal attribute." For Descartes, every ordinary quality, or "mode," of a substance is in some way a modification (or, one might say, a determination or specification) of this principal attribute. While a Cartesian substance may undergo change of its particular modes, it cannot undergo a change of its principal attribute, for the principal attribute constitutes what the substance essentially is. According to Descartes, a substance cannot be without its principal attribute, and whatever has a given principal attribute is a substance of the kind constituted by that principal attribute. In his view, there are two kinds of created substances, each with its own principal attribute: bodies having extension – that is, physical/spatial/dimensional character – as their principal attribute (and thus having, for example, particular sizes, figures, and motions among their modes); and minds having thought as their principal attribute (and thus having, for example, acts of conceiving, affirming, doubting, desiring, and willing among their modes). While Spinoza agrees that extension and thought are each attributes that constitute the nature of a substance – and so correspond, thus far, to Descartes's conception of "principal" attributes – he denies that bodies and human minds are themselves substances, and he denies that a substance need be limited to having a single attribute. On the contrary, the more reality or (equivalently, for Spinoza) perfection a substance has, the more such attributes it will have (1p9). God, the most real and most perfect being, can therefore be defined as the substance who has infinite (that is, an unlimited array of, or all possible) attributes, each of which is necessarily infinite (unlimited) within its own realm (d6). Since the existence of God necessarily follows from this definition, according to Spinoza (1p11d), God necessarily exists. This God exists as a thinking substance (1p1), as previous philosophers had maintained, but also and equally as an extended (that is, physical, or corporeal) substance (1p15s and 2p2), and as a substance of other infinite attributes unknown to human minds as well. Each divine attribute may thus be thought of as a fundamental *way of being* for God, each constituting the *essence* of God insofar as God is considered as existing in that particular way.

Spinoza defines a "mode" as "the affection [i.e., the modification, or quality] of a substance, or that which is in another through which it is also conceived." Every mode of a substance is thus a particular modification of an attribute of that substance. Since every mode is *in* and *conceived through* the substance of which it is a mode, it must also be entirely *caused* by the substance of which it is a mode; thus, all causation is the self-determination and self-expression of a substance. Every mode is either an "infinite mode" or a "finite mode," depending on the way in which it is produced and the scope of its existence. Infinite modes follow, either immediately or mediately (that is, either directly or through one or more other infinite modes), from the "absolute" nature of the attribute of which they are modes (1p21d and 1p22d); in consequence, they are permanent and pervasive features or aspects of an entire attribute, such as, for example, general features corresponding to the general laws of nature governing extension or thought. Although finite modes also follow from the nature of the attribute of which they are modes, they do not follow simply from the "absolute" nature of those attributes but require the existence of other finite modes as well (1p28); hence, they introduce temporally and locally limited variety within an attribute. The causation of finite modes by other finite modes in no way violates the thesis that all modes are caused by the substance of which they are modes, because causation *through* its modes is simply one way in which a substance can express or exert its own causal power.

Because all causation is the self-determination and self-expression of a substance, there could be no causal interaction between Spinozistic substances even if there could be a plurality of substances. In fact, however, Spinoza famously holds that there is and can only be one substance, which he calls "*Deus, sive Natura*" – that is, "God or Nature" (where the use of "or" has the force of "in other words"). He argues that God is the *only* substance on the grounds that substances cannot share an attribute (1p5) and God – the substance of all attributes – necessarily exists; God thereby forestalls the possibility of any other substance (1p14d). This denial that substances can share an attribute is distinctively Spinozistic; Descartes, for example, supposed that human minds were individual substances (albeit in the weaker sense of the term "substance") all sharing the attribute of thought. Spinoza rejects the sharing of attributes on the grounds that it would be impossible to distinguish two different substances within the realm of a single attribute. For two such substances could not be distinguished by a difference of modes of that attribute unless the difference of modes could be conceived through a difference in the attributes through which those modes must be conceived; but if one seeks to base the distinction of two substances within the realm of an attribute on a *difference* in the relevant attribute, then one grants that the two substances are not sharing the *same* attribute after all (1p5d). Spinoza's doctrine that there is only one substance is sometimes called "monism" or (to distinguish it from the doctrine of plurality of attributes that he endorses) "substance monism."

If God is the only substance, then what are the ordinary bodies and minds that common sense regards as substances? Spinoza's answer is forthright: they are finite modes of God, local and temporary expressions of the divine nature. Finite modes are limited expressions of God's attributes; for example, a particular body is constituted by a "fixed pattern" or "fixed ratio" of motion and rest occurring within the attribute of extension (definition following 2p13s), and a particular mind is the idea representing the actual existence of such a persisting pattern (2p13). Nevertheless, Spinoza does not deny that bodies and minds are things, or at least thing-like, as well. On the contrary, just as God is *absolutely* in itself and conceived through itself, certain finite modes – which Spinoza also calls "singular things" – are *to a finite and limited extent* "in themselves." Each singular thing, in his view, has its own essence and its own modes; and the more causal power a singular thing has – that is, the more it has an essence or nature of its own, from which effects follow – the more *in itself* that thing is, and the more able it is to sustain itself in continued existence through its own power (3p6). (This self-sustaining activity is, of course, compatible with its having an external cause for its *origination* in existence.) Although singular things are not substances, they thus *model* in a finite and limited way the absolute nature of the one genuine substance of which they are modes and whose power they utilize and express.

3. Philosophy of Mind

As both an extended substance and a thinking substance, Spinoza's God has *modes* of extension and *modes* of thought. Furthermore, because "the order and connection of ideas is the same as the order and connection of things" (2p7, derived from 1a4), there is an isomorphism between these attributes: for each mode of extension, there is a corresponding mode of thought which is the idea of that mode of extension. In fact, Spinoza goes further – each mode of extension is *identical* with the idea that is its corresponding mode of thought (2p7s). God as an extended thing is expressed through a system in which modes cause other modes through their respective shares of God's infinite physical (or, one might also say, dynamic) power; and God as a thinking thing is expressed through a system in which the *ideas* of those modes cause one another through their respective shares of God's infinite thinking (or, one might also say, logical) power. That is, just as God's existence is expressed in different ways of being, so God's power is expressed in different ways of being. These ways in which God's existence and power are expressed are each self-contained and self-sufficient: facts about the world of extension are explained completely and exclusively by God's extended nature, and facts about the world of thought are explained completely and exclusively by God's thinking nature. There is no possibility that this causal independence of the attributes could have resulted in a world of thought that is *not* isomorphic with the world of extension, for everything that occurs does so through the utter necessity of the divine nature (1p16, 1p29, 1p33): just as there is only one possible way that the world of extension could be, so there is only one possible way – a parallel way – in which a world of extension could possibly be conceived in the attribute of thought.

This conception of the relation between the attributes of extension and thought provides Spinoza with a distinctive solution to the problem – so acutely felt both by Descartes's followers and by his critics – of explaining the relation between the human mind and the human body. First, Spinoza argues that a given human mind is just the idea of that human being's body (2p13) – that is, it is the mode of thought that is identical with that human body and which has that human body as its object. Although he does not deny that the human mind contains ideas that represent things other than the human body, these ideas do so, on his conception, only through first representing some aspect of the human body to which those other things are related. Because the human mind and the human body are thus *the very same mode* of God, each expressed and conceived through a different attribute of God, there is no question of how they can be related as distinct substances, or indeed as *distinct* things of any kind. Furthermore, because the attributes of extension and thought are each causally self-contained, there is no question of bodily events *causing* mental events or vice versa. Every physical event in the body, insofar as it is a physical event, is caused by other physical things exclusively. But every physical event is also identical with a mental event; and that mental event, insofar as it is a mental event, is caused by other mental things exclusively. Spinoza thus holds a form of the *mind–body identity* theory concerning human beings. But for him, this identity is merely a particular instance of a far more pervasive feature of the universe, one according to which not only each animal body but each non-organic body as well has an idea (though it may be sufficiently weak and rudimentary that it need not be called a "mind") that stands to that body in the same general relation as that in which a human mind stands to a human body. As he puts it, all individuals "are animate" but "to different degrees." This view is based not on any supposition that mentality is required to explain the behavior of inanimate bodies – for even in the case of human beings, the attribute of thought plays no role in the proper explanation of the behavior of extended bodies – but is based rather on the thesis that God is an infinitely thinking thing, so that whatever is expressed in extension is also expressed in thought. Just as all of the individual bodies in the universe compose an infinite extended individual that is in God (2p13s), so too the ideas of those things – including human minds – are parts of the all-inclusive idea that is God's infinite intellect (2p11c). But although the human body is part of an infinite extended individual and the human mind is part of God's infinite intellect, for Spinoza, it is not correct to say that human beings are parts of God. For these infinite things are themselves only infinite modes of God. At least in the sense in which parts are logically prior to the wholes that they compose and are potentially separable from those wholes, God itself has no *parts* – only infinite and finite modes.

4. Epistemology

Spinoza's epistemology, like his metaphysics, exhibits many illuminating contrasts with the views of Descartes. One of these contrasts concerns the two philosophers' respective conceptions of the method by which knowledge is to be discovered. One of Descartes's chief methodological goals is what may be called "methodological caution" – that is, the avoidance of "hasty and precipitate judgments." In order to achieve methodological caution, Descartes recommends what is sometimes called "methodological doubt." His philosophical method proposes that an inquirer should begin by setting out to doubt whatever can be doubted; for only what is indubitable – that is, cannot be doubted – is entitled to be accepted as certain knowledge. In the service of methodological doubt, in turn, the Cartesian inquirer pursues what may be called "methodological skepticism" – the endeavor to discover and render credible the strongest possible grounds for doubt. Because truth consists, for Descartes, in an agreement between ideas and the states of affairs they represent, and because there are strong initial grounds for skepticism concerning things outside the inquirer's mind, Descartes seeks an internal property of ideas themselves that can serve as a *criterion* for their truth. After first demonstrating that God exists and is not a deceiver, Descartes takes himself to have rendered "whatever is perceived clearly and distinctly is true" indubitable, thereby entitling himself to accept the clarity and distinctness of ideas as a criterion of their truth.

Spinoza agrees that methodological caution is a worthy aim, but he denies that methodological doubt (and hence methodological skepticism) is the best way to achieve it. Doubt, as he explains in his *Treatise on the Emendation of the Intellect*, arises exclusively from acquiring ideas in the wrong order. More specifically, it arises when the mind understands enough to see that one idea has some relation to another idea but lacks the causal knowledge to grasp exactly how the two ideas are properly related. For example, if one knows enough about sense perception to know that perceptions of distance have sometimes been misleading, but without knowing enough about the causal origin of a particular sense perception of the sun, then one will doubt whether the sun really stands at just the distance at which it appears. The proper order of inquiry, for Spinoza, is to begin with adequate ideas of causes and to derive ideas of the effects from them. When this is done consistently, doubts never arise. Thus, for example, whereas Descartes doubts for most of his *Meditations* whether or not he has a body, the question of the existence of the human body does not arise in Spinoza's *Ethics* until the point (in Part Two) at which he is prepared to demonstrate the relation between the human mind and human body as a result of understanding the causes of each. As this illustrates, doubt, for Spinoza, is not something first to be induced and then to be refuted; rather, it is something always to be avoided by following the proper order. If this is done, no doubts can be successfully raised, since any doubt suggested about the truth of a piece of knowledge will already be seen to be unfounded in light of the inquirer's already-clear grasp of the truth of that piece of knowledge.

The perception of truth is, for Spinoza, unmediated by any *criterion* of truth of all, as he emphasizes in the *Treatise on the Emendation of the Intellect*, and hence it is unmediated by any criterion whose reliability might itself be called into question. He agrees with Descartes that clear and distinct ideas are true; but unlike Descartes, he does not see the clarity and distinctness of ideas – or as he usually prefers to say, their "adequacy" – as a property distinct from their truth itself. True ideas do agree with their objects (1a6), but at the same time their truth also involves the internal characteristic of *adequacy*: "By adequate idea I understand an idea which, insofar as it is considered in itself, without relation to an object, has all the properties, or intrinsic denominations of a true idea" (2d4). Thus, whereas Descartes *argued* that there is an internal characteristic that is possessed by all and only true ideas (that is, ideas constituting genuine knowledge), Spinoza's definition of "adequacy" simply takes this for granted. His metaphysics suggests why he thinks he can legitimately do so. Because every idea is identical with its object, a thing and the idea of that thing are the very same mode of God considered in two different ways; and hence, the *internal* adequacy of an idea and the complete *correspondence* between an idea and its object can be regarded as the very same *feature* of that idea, considered in those same two ways. It may also be supposed that the adequacy of an idea lies in its representing its object with sufficient distinctness and coherence to show that what it represents is genuinely possible; for the doctrine that there is only one possible way in which the world could have been entails that whatever is genuinely possible is also actual.

Of course, to say that the *agreement* of *true* ideas with their objects can be explained through the *identity* which *all* ideas have with their objects raises the question of how any ideas can ever fail to be true. On Spinoza's conception of falsehood, however, it is not a positive characteristic of ideas, but rather a kind of privation or "mutilation." Because things must be understood through their causes, an idea of a thing that does not include knowledge of its cause is incomplete and partial. Every idea of a thing, *as that idea exists in God's infinite intellect*, exists in the context of ideas of that thing's causes, and is complete, adequate, and true. As some of these ideas exist in human minds, in contrast, they are without the context of the related ideas through which their full understanding depends, and hence *as they exist in the human mind* they are inadequate and incomplete – that is, false.

For Spinoza, the distinction between those ideas that are complete and adequate in the human mind and those that are not corresponds to the distinction – also emphasized by Descartes and Leibniz – between ideas that are conceived by (or in) the intellect and those that are conceived by (or in) the imagination, respectively. Ideas of the imagination are images of a sensory character (in a broad sense that includes visual, auditory, and other kinds of externally and internally derived sensory impressions). Sense experience itself is classified as a form of *imagination* for Spinoza – not because the objects that it represents are unreal, but because it presents those objects in *images*, which do not themselves provide a full, or intellectual, understanding of their causes. Imagination also includes the recollection or rearrangement of the content of such images of experience through memory, dreaming, and thinking with images. The intellect, in contrast, is not fundamentally imagistic and constitutes a higher kind of understanding through ideas that are themselves adequate.

Spinoza distinguishes (2p40s2) three kinds of knowledge (or, better, three kinds of cognition – the Latin is *cognitio*). "Knowledge of the first kind," which he also calls "imagination," is the lowest kind of knowledge. It includes knowledge from report or testimony (either written or spoken) and mere unregulated sense experience or generalizations of sense experience. "Knowledge of the second kind," which he also calls "reason," derives from "common notions" and "adequate knowledge of the properties of things." "Common notions" are aspects or ways in which all things of a given kind agree and which are present "equally in the part and in the whole." Because they are aspects of things that can be found complete in each part as well as in the whole, these general aspects or features of things cannot be grasped only partially and so must be grasped adequately if they are grasped at all. The "properties" of a thing, in Spinoza's technical sense of that term, are qualities of a thing that follow from the thing's essence but do not themselves constitute its essence; since a thing cannot exist without its essence, it also cannot exist without its properties, which follow from it. (Properties may thus be distinguished from mere accidental qualities, which a thing may lose.) "Knowledge of the third kind," which he also calls "intuitive knowledge" (*scientia intuitiva*), proceeds "from the formal essence of certain attributes of God to the adequate knowledge of the essence of things." Knowledge of this highest kind, then, involves knowing things in the proper order, by conceiving essences through their causes.

By way of explanation, Spinoza offers an example of something known in each of these ways. For the numbers 1, 2, and 3, the fourth proportional (that is, the number such that 3 stands to it in the same proportion in which 1 stands to 2) is 6. If one knows this merely by remembering what was asserted by one's teachers (report) or by experimenting with the proportions of simple numbers until one happens on a rule for finding the fourth proportional that seems to work for those examples (unregulated experience), then one has *knowledge of the first kind*. If, however, one understands Euclid's demonstration that a general property of all proportions is that the product of the means (the second and third numbers) is equal to the product of the extremes (the first and fourth), then one can determine from this general property that the proportion of 1 to 2 is the same as that of 3 to 6 by *the second kind of knowledge*. But if one grasps, as it were, the very essence of the proportion of 1 to 2, so that one can simply see that the proportion of 3 to 6 is the same proportion, then one has *knowledge of the third kind*. According to Spinoza, the second and third kinds of knowledge each provide *adequate* knowledge, and each is a function of the intellect. Knowing things through the third kind of knowledge is preferable, however, because it more closely follows the proper order of inferring effects from a complete knowledge of their causes; knowledge of the second kind allows us to conceive only enough of the essences and causes of things to be certain that a given property is present. Whereas knowledge of the second kind shows with certainty *that* something is true, knowledge of the third kind shows precisely *why* it must be true.

5. Philosophy of Physical Science

Spinoza is deeply committed to the view that there is a necessitating cause for every state of affairs, so that there is no such thing as chance and no such thing as a brute, unexplainable fact. This commitment is evident in the initial axioms of the *Ethics*, which require that everything must be conceivable (1a2), that things must be conceived through their causes (1a4), and that causes must necessitate their effects (1a3). Spinozistic causes need not precede their effects temporally, however. Thus, God is eternally self-caused and self-causing, because God's very essence entails God's existence, so that God exists and acts eternally from the necessity of its own nature alone. Furthermore, all of God's modes – that is, everything else that exists – follow necessarily from the nature of God (that is, from God's attributes), through which they must also be conceived. For this reason, a sufficiently powerful intellect can deduce not only God's existence but a complete description of the universe, including the laws of nature that must govern it, from the idea of God. In fact, the infinite intellect of God itself is just such a powerful intellect and consists of just such a deduction.

Although carrying out such a detailed deduction is of course far beyond human powers, Spinoza holds that it is nevertheless within the scope of human intellect to grasp many fundamental and pervasive features of the universe as causal consequences of the divine attributes of extension and of thought. He ascribes adequate ideas of the attributes of thought and extension themselves, at least, to all human beings (2p45 and 2p46), on the grounds that such ideas are required in order to have any ideas of modes of those attributes. His confidence in the power of the intellect to reveal pervasive laws or other features of the operations of nature through the power of ideas conceived in the intellect leads him naturally to give priority in scientific investigations to high-level theoretical reasoning rather than to empirical observation. Although he certainly does not reject experience as useless – in addition to recognizing its obvious role in guiding everyday practice, he also appeals to it to confirm doctrines derived in other ways – he nevertheless emphasizes that mere sense experience is inconclusive and does not alone provide knowledge of the essences of things; when unregulated and uninformed by the intellect, it is merely knowledge of the first kind.

Spinoza's substance monism entails that the extended or material universe cannot consist of a number of distinct substances. On the contrary, there can only be one extended substance, and this substance must be God itself. (This does not imply, of course, that God has a body; for bodies are finite and bounded modes of extension, whereas God is an infinite extended thing.) One problem posed by Cartesian physics was that of how to count extended substances. Descartes denied extension to God on the grounds that its divisibility was incompatible with divine perfection. Although he sometimes hinted that the physical universe as a whole constituted the only extended substance, Descartes's usual policy was to grant the status of substances to all individual bodies in the natural world. This policy had the consequence that extended substances have other extended substances as parts, and those substances have other substances as parts, through indefinitely many divisions. Yet the dependence of wholes on the parts of which they are composed called into question the appropriateness of according substantiality to these compound bodies. Spinoza's metaphysics resolves this problem by denying that bodies (which are finite by definition) are substances at all. He avoids both the seemingly nondivine imperfection of a divisible substance and mathematical paradoxes concerning the infinite divisibility of extended substance by denying that the one extended substance is, insofar as it is substance, divisible at all. Although extension may seem divisible as we conceive it in the imagination, when it is conceived by the intellect this appearance vanishes. As truly perceived by the intellect, the one extended substance is a single continuous thing, no region of which can possibly be separated from the rest. As such, it has no genuine parts (1p23, 1p13, 1p15s).

Spinoza appears to hold that local variation occurs within the one extended substance through the differential distribution of quantities of the dual-natured force of "motion-and-rest." Individual bodies, on this account, are patterns of distributions of motion and rest that have at least some tendency or power to persist through an indefinite duration until destroyed by some external cause (2p13s, 3p6). The location of these patterns, it may be inferred, changes more rapidly with increases in "motion," and less rapidly with increases in the complementary quantity of "rest." The existence of individual bodies with different natures can thus be understood through the different possible patterns of motion and rest, and the fundamental laws governing the physical realm may be understood as mechanical – that is, concerned with interactions of motion and rest among bodies – in just the way required by the new science.

Although there is only one extended substance, these finite modes of that substance constitute thing-like entities whose natures or essences can be investigated, and which, insofar as they tend to persist, exert some power – power which is a share of the divine power – to persevere in their own being. Indeed, to understand the essence of such a thing *is* just to understand how it operates and exerts causal power to persevere in its own being as a distinctive pattern of motion and rest. In fact, Spinoza's conception of singular things as finite approximations to a genuine substance accommodates and reconciles two competing paradigms of natural science, and it does so at two different levels. Natural science prior to the seventeenth century was most often conceived as the understanding of the *essences of things.* During the seventeenth century, this older conception was gradually giving way to a new conception of natural science as the understanding of *natural laws.* Although Spinoza clearly takes the highest object of knowledge to be the divine essence, to understand this essence – as it is constituted by infinitely many divine attributes, of which we grasp only extension and thought – involves understanding the most general laws of those attributes. In the case of extension, these are what we would call the laws of physics. In treating individual things as finite approximations to substance, Spinoza is able to treat them as quasi-independent objects of conception (that is, objects of explanation and understanding) and as quasi-independent centers of causal activity as well. In order for singular things play this role, however, they must have their own essences through which their own properties can be understood. Thus, the instantiation of various limited essences permits the existence of various special sciences concerned with the understanding those essences. The understanding of the essences of particular things and of particular kinds of things, in turn, involves understanding what Spinoza conceives of as "laws" governing the nature of specific kinds of things, laws which are the subjects of more specialized disciplines. These laws explain the behavior of individuals and species – although they must, of course, be understood ultimately as applications of the more general laws of the attributes themselves.

6. Philosophy of Psychology

Each finite thing, for Spinoza, exerts some power to persevere in its existence; if it did not, it would not qualify as a particular thing. In fact, all of a thing's own proper power is power to persevere in existence (3p7d). Spinoza's Latin term for this striving is "conatus." Conatus is physical, insofar as it is conceived as belonging to a mode of extension. But each mode of extension is identical with a mode of thought; and hence conatus is mental as well as physical. Although all singular things have some conatus, some singular things are (i) sufficiently complex that their power for self-preservation can undergo significant increases and decreases and (ii) capable of forming and retaining images of external things, towards which this striving can become directed. For these beings – human beings and also many animals – their conatus provides the basis for a psychology of the emotions.

Spinoza's psychology distinguishes three basic emotions. "Desire" is conatus itself, insofar as it becomes directed onto the attainment of some particular conceived end or object (3p9s). "Joy" (or pleasure) is a passage to a state of greater perfection, or greater power to act. (3p11s). "Sadness" (or pain) is a passage to a state of lesser perfection, or lesser power to act. Other emotions are defined in terms of these, as they appear in particular situations or combinations. Thus, "love" is joy with the accompanying idea of an external cause, and "hate" is sadness with the accompanying idea of an external cause (3p14s). In keeping with his conception of scientific method, Spinoza seeks to deduce the nature and effects of a wide variety of human emotions from his axioms, definitions, and previously demonstrated propositions, without formal appeal to any empirical observations other than two extremely general empirical postulates: that human minds can undergo changes increasing or decreasing their power of action, and that human minds can form images of things.

A crucial distinction for Spinoza is that between "activity" and "passivity." Something is active when it is the adequate cause of some effect – that is, when an effect can be understood entirely through it (3d3 and 3d2). Something is passive when it is the inadequate cause of some effect – that is, when the effect must be understood through something else as well. Human beings *act* when they pursue their own genuine advantage – understood as self-preservation – with adequate knowledge through their own conatus, or power. Emotions that are induced in human beings by external causes are called "passions," because human beings are passive with respect to them. For example, through the agency of personal or impersonal external causes, a human being's desire – which is by nature directed at what is beneficial or advantageous – may be misdirected onto an object that is not genuinely beneficial. Joy and sadness, love and hate, may equally be induced by external causes. Because passions are not necessarily conducive to one's own true advantage, they are dangerous, and one of the most important aims of philosophy is to provide a measure of control over the passions. In addition to passions, however, there are also emotions of desire and joy that are *active* – that is, that result from the human being's own proper power and activity. Such emotions include the desire for knowledge, the joy of understanding and – ultimately – the intellectual love of God that brings blessedness and the highest satisfaction or peace of mind.

7. Ethics

Although popular religion often presents ethical precepts in the guise of dictates of an external authority, a deeper philosophical analysis shows, Spinoza holds, that ethical precepts are practical dictates of one's own reason. When one reasons, one forms adequate ideas concerning human life and what is conducive to one's advantage – that is, to persevering in one's being. Because each person endeavors to persevere in his or her being, this very *knowledge* is, at the same time, also a *desire* to do or have that which is most advantageous. In this way, those who act ethically are acting under "the guidance of reason." The joy that popular religion offers as an externally bestowed reward for virtuous action is, in reality, the inevitable mental consequence of virtuous action. Spinozistic ethics is demonstrated by showing what is truly to one's advantage; this knowledge, for those who attain it, will be internally motivating, just as virtuous action itself is internally rewarding.

Spinoza characterizes what he regards as virtuous character and action through his description of an ethical model or ideal, that of the "free man" (5p67–5p73). Freedom cannot consist in action that is causally undetermined, for Spinoza, since everything is equally necessitated. Rather, freedom lies in being determined to act by one's own nature rather than by external causes (1d7). Only God is absolutely free in this sense (1p17c2); no human being can be entirely unaffected by external causes (4d). Nevertheless, human beings can achieve a finite *measure* of freedom to the extent that they pursue their own advantage through their own conatus without being overcome or disturbed by passions. To increase one's freedom in this sense, and thereby to come closer to the ideal of the "free man," is to be better able to pursue one's advantage. Hence, whatever enables us to come closer to this ideal may be classified as "good." For although human beings generally use the term "good" simply for whatever they happen to desire, Spinoza proposes that the term be used instead to signify "what we certainly know to be useful to us" (4d1). Since the mind is entirely active when its adequate ideas give rise to other adequate ideas, and since the most perfect object of conception is God, it follows that "knowledge of God is the mind's greatest good" (4p28). It should be observed however, that all knowledge is, in one way or another, knowledge of God; for whatever is, is in God and must be conceived through God (1p15).

Although ethical motivation is inevitably and undeniably grounded in considerations of one's own advantage for Spinoza, his practical precepts are less selfish than this fact might lead one to suppose. There are two related reasons for this. First, he regards human cooperation and friendship as extremely beneficial even for the pursuit of mundane and limited goods, such as food, shelter, and the conveniences of life that are a precondition for philosophical study. Hence, he places high value on whatever is conducive to good social relations. Second, he regards human cooperation and friendship as especially important for attaining the highest good, which is the understanding of God. The good of understanding and loving God through adequate ideas is entirely noncompetitive: that is, one person's achieving it or acquiring it does not leave less of it for others (4p36). On the contrary, knowledge and love of God are far more easily attained in community with co-inquirers. For these reasons, Spinoza distinguishes two species of virtuous desires: "tenacity," which is "the Desire by which each one strives, solely from the dictate of reason, to preserve his being," and "nobility," which is "the Desire by which each one strives, solely from the dictate of reason, to aid other men and join them to him in friendship" (3p59s).

It is fair to say that Spinoza's ethics is, among other things, an ethics of mental health. That is, its aim is to increase the mental and emotional health of human beings through the replacement of disturbing passions with peace of mind. One notable example of this concerns what Spinoza calls "favor" and "indignation." "Favor" is love toward one who has benefited another, whereas "indignation" is hate toward one who has done evil to another. Favor can be in accordance with reason, for human being can be the active causes of benefits to others (4p51). Indignation, however, as a kind of sadness, is evil (4p51s); and when we understand that those who do evil are not the adequate causes of their own actions, but that they are instead overcome by external causes, we will no longer hate them. Thus, reason leads the Spinozist to love those who do good, without experiencing the disturbance of hating those who do evil.

Although Spinoza endorses some ethical doctrines characteristic of Christianity, such as the doctrine that one should "repay the other's hate, anger, and disdain toward him with love" (4p46), he rejects others. For example, he characterizes pity, repentance, and humility as evils rather than as virtues (4p50, 4p53, and 4p54), because they are species of sadness: while the virtuous man comes to others' assistance when needed, forms an accurate conception of his own powers, and seeks to avoid repeating mistakes, he does so without pity, humility, or repentance.

8. Political Theory

Because of the protection and the opportunities for cooperative action it provides, citizenship in a state is of great value to those who are guided by reason (4p73). Spinoza's conception of rights is similar in some ways to that of Thomas Hobbes. For Spinoza, each person's – and each thing's – right is coextensive with its power. The state serves to protect individuals from one another and to facilitate cooperation. It does this by restricting each subject's power and hence each subject's right. But whereas Hobbes conceives of subjects surrendering all rights to the sovereign, other than the right to resist death, Spinoza emphasizes in the final chapters of the *Theological-Political Treatise* that any actual state's ability to restrict the power and hence the rights of its subjects is limited; subjects will necessarily retain their determination to pursue their own advantage, in the light of the incentives and disincentives created by the state, in whatever way they most desire. The power, and hence the right, of the state is therefore never absolute. In fact, the state itself is clearly a kind of particular or singular thing, with its own conatus. Like a human being, it best preserves itself not when it exercises all of the powers that it may have, but rather when it exercises them wisely. Thus, although the state may have the power to establish a religion and to control the speech (though not the thought) of its subjects, it acts most wisely when it allows freedom of religion and of speech. Popular religion, in particular, constitutes a danger to the state, because it sets up authorities other than those of the state itself. This danger is best controlled not by establishing a state religion, whose functionaries will challenge the authority of the state itself, but rather by allowing freedom of religion. This prevents any one religion from becoming too powerful and also forces religions to compete with one another for adherents. This competition should encourage religions to downplay their harshest elements.

9. Philosophy of Religion

In order to address both the dangers and the opportunities posed by the prevalence within European states of biblical religion, Spinoza devotes considerable effort in the earlier chapters of *Theological-Political Treatise* to the interpretation of the Bible. His approach to interpreting the Bible is to bring as much historical and linguistic knowledge to bear on the text as possible, and then, in the light of this knowledge, to determine the meaning of the text from the text itself. This means, in particular, that no presuppositions concerning what the Bible *should* say or *must* say should be employed. When it is interpreted in this way, Spinoza holds, the Bible reveals that the different prophets believed many different things and that each conceived God in his own way, according to his own experience and temperament. However, he argues, the Bible itself does not teach any particular piece of theological doctrine or dogma as required for salvation. Rather – and this is the politically beneficial message that Spinoza's scriptural interpretation seeks above all else to establish – the Bible itself affirms that the only things required for salvation are charity towards one's neighbor and obedience to the state. Whatever beliefs individuals may find helpful for achieving these goals are therefore permissible from the standpoint of Biblical religion.

Popular religion is thus concerned not with the truth of doctrines about God, but with their practical efficacy. Philosophy, however, *is* concerned with the truth about God, and Spinoza's own revolutionary understanding of God is developed in the *Ethics*. In many ways, his God coincides with the God of the western theological tradition: God is absolutely infinite and absolutely perfect, eternal, all-powerful and all-knowing, the first cause and source of all things, existing necessarily from his own nature or essence alone, indivisible, and even the source of blessedness as the object of eternal intellectual love. But while Spinoza's God is an infinite thinking thing, it is equally an infinite extended thing. God is not the creator of a natural world distinct from himself; on the contrary, God *is* Nature itself. God is not a person and has no desires or purposes; nothing is either good or evil for God, and God does not literally love human beings. God acts not to achieve some end, whether for human beings or for itself, but simply because each of infinitely many effects follows necessarily from the divine nature itself.

Because God is Nature, all scientific understanding of nature is knowledge of God, for Spinoza. Because this adequate knowledge brings joy, accompanied by the idea of God as its cause, human beings can enjoy an intellectual love of God. Furthermore, to the extent that human beings have adequate intellectual knowledge, eternal ideas, which have always been in the infinite intellect of God, become part of their own minds as well. To this extent, those who achieve genuine understanding have a greater "part of their minds that is eternal" (5p23); this eternal part is, in fact, the intellect itself (5p40c). Thus, through the pursuit of scientific understanding, human beings can enjoy an intellectual love of God that is eternal. This kind of "immortality" is not personal, for it involves no memory or sensation, and no identity as a distinct individual after death. Rather, it consists in actively participating, during one's lifetime, in an intellectual understanding of the eternal that brings peace of mind. Because it carries the mind outside the confines of its own specific and limited perspective in the universe, this understanding renders death less harmful and thoughts of death less disturbing (5p38). It thereby provides, Spinoza thinks, a way in which those who achieve genuine eternal understanding succeed best of all in "persevering in their being" – even if the duration of their lives is, as Spinoza's own life was, all too brief.

Notes

1 References to elements of Spinoza's *Ethics* follow the standard format explained in Jonathan Bennett's *A Study of Spinoza's Ethics* (Indianapolis: Hackett, 1984): the initial number indicates the Part of the *Ethics*; "a" abbreviates "Axiom"; "p" abbreviates "Proposition"; "s" abbreviates "Scholium" ("note" in some English translations); "c" abbreviates "Corollary"; and "d" abbreviates either "Definition" or "Demonstration," depending on whether it immediately follows a *Part* number or a *Proposition* number. All translations from Spinoza's works are taken from *The Collected Works of Spinoza*, vol. I, edited and translated by Edwin Curley (Princeton: Princeton University Press, 1985).

Chapter 4

Nicolas Malebranche

Steven Nadler

When Descartes died in 1650, some of his most vehement opponents – and there were many – must have hoped that that would be the end of Cartesian philosophy as well. Little did they suspect that Cartesianism would be the dominant philosophical paradigm for the rest of the century. In France, the most important Cartesian – perhaps, in fact, the most important philosopher – of this period was a Catholic priest from a prominent and well-connected family in Paris. When, in 1660, the young Nicolas Malebranche turned down the offer of a canonry at the Cathedral of Notre Dame de Paris and chose instead to join the Oratory, an Augustinian order founded by Cardinal Bérulle, who had been a good friend of Descartes, his intellectual fate was sealed. The rest of Malebranche's life would be devoted to synthesizing the thought of his two philosophical and spiritual mentors, St. Augustine and Descartes, into a grand system that, while piously fortifying the doctrines of the Catholic tradition, would incorporate and develop the insights and power of the new mechanistic science.

During his four years under the tutelage of the Oratory's instructors, Malebranche immersed himself in the writings of the Bishop of Hippo, along with the usual studies in Bible and ecclesiastical history. He did not actually read any of Descartes's works, however, until 1664 when, strolling along the banks of the Seine, he happened upon a copy of Descartes's *Treatise on Man* in a bookstall. The event was life-changing. Malebranche's earliest biographer tells us that the joy of becoming acquainted with so many discoveries "caused him such palpitations of the heart that he had to stop reading in order to recover his breath."[1] Malebranche devoted the next ten years of his life to studying mathematics and philosophy, especially of the Cartesian variety. He was particularly taken by Descartes's critique of the Aristotelian philosophy that he had, in his earlier studies at a Jesuit college, found so stultifying and sterile.

Those ten years of study culminated in the publication in 1674–5 of *The Search After Truth*, Malebranche's most important work and a philosophical masterpiece in its own right.[2] It is a wide-ranging treatise that deals with questions of knowledge, metaphysics, physics, sense-physiology, methodology, and philosophical theology. Malebranche's stated goal in the *Search* is to investigate the sources of human error and to direct us toward the clear and distinct perception of truth – truth about ourselves, about the world around us, and about God. He is ultimately concerned to demonstrate the essential and active role of God in every aspect – material, cognitive, and moral – of the world, but without undermining the new science's commitment to mechanistic modes of explanation of natural phenomena. The *Search* was Malebranche's first and most ambitious work, and contains early but solidly-argued presentations of his three most famous doctrines: the vision in God, occasionalism, and his theodicy. All of these doctrines received further and more developed treatment in his later writings, especially the *Treatise on Nature and Grace* (1680) and the *Dialogues on Metaphysics and Religion* (1688).[3]

1. The Vision in God

Nearly all philosophers in the seventeenth century agreed that human perception and knowledge is mediated by immaterial representations immediately present to the mind, which after Descartes came generally to be called "ideas." There was much debate, however, regarding the origin and ontological status of these representative beings: What *are* ideas? How do they become present to the mind? Are they mental or mind-independent? Are they *acts* of the mind or the *objects* of its acts?[4] Malebranche's doctrine of the vision in God was the most unorthodox theory of ideas in the period, and his answers to these questions embroiled him in a number of philosophically important controversies. He looked back to the Christian-Platonic and Augustinian model, according to which ideas proper are archetypes or essences in the divine understanding. Human beings have access to these ideas, which serve as the ground of all eternal truths, through an ongoing process of illumination that informs their cognitive powers.

Malebranche orients his discussion of ideas and knowledge in the *Search* around the problem of error, particularly the errors that arise when we base our judgments upon the testimony of the senses and the imagination, rather than reason and understanding. He relies in his analysis of error on what is probably the most comprehensive and systematic account of the physiology of sense and imagination in the seventeenth century. Based upon a detailed investigation into the structure of the eye and the geometry of optics, he argues that vision does not present to us the extension of external bodies as it is in itself, but rather only as it is in relation to our body. All we ever see of a body's dimensions is a relative perspective. Malebranche describes the eye as a kind of "natural spectacles," and examines the ways in which the material images that they convey into the brain (and thus the sensory images that these stimulate in the soul) are typically affected by the distance between the eyes, the different humors in the eyes, the shape of the crystalline lens and its distance from the retina, and other variable factors. The difference between sensation and imagination is due simply to the fact that in imagination the tiny fibers in the center of the brain are agitated not by impressions made by external objects on the exterior surface of the nerves, but by the flow of the animal spirits initiated by the soul itself. These animal spirits are easily affected by the changing state of the body and by external things, as well as by "moral" causes (prejudices, "conditions of living"). Thus, the imagination, in addition to our senses, represents a second important source of the differences between minds and how things are represented to them. Malebranche's goal in highlighting the ways in which the senses and the imagination "lead us into error" is to warn us not to allow their images to serve as a basis for judgement about the truth of things. We should rely, rather, on the testimony of reason and the perfect evidence of clear and distinct ideas.[5]

Malebranche's account of ideas is grounded in the basic ontological framework of Cartesian dualism that was so essential to the new mechanistic science. Mind, or thinking substance, is unextended thought, and has absolutely nothing in common with matter, defined as extension or spatiality. A material body has only the mathematical properties of shape, size, divisibility, and mobility. All other sensible qualities – color, heat, cold, taste, odor, etc. – are really only sensations in the mind, mental modifications occasioned by external material objects. While such sensations may indicate to us the presence of bodies to our own body – and thus warn us about what may be harmful or helpful to our physical well-being – they cannot provide us with clear and distinct knowledge of those bodies. Sensations can directly inform us only of what is presently taking place in our own minds; they have no representational value with respect to the external world. Malebranche claims, however, that in addition to our own inner sensations, we have access to certain "representative beings [êtres représentatifs]," ideas. Ideas, unlike qualitative sensory states, have a clear and distinct representational content – generally of a quantitative nature – and provide us with unambiguous, complete, and adequate knowledge about objects and their properties. The idea of a square, for example, presents with perfect evidence all the information needed for full knowledge of the geometric properties of squares. On the other hand, the heat that one feels when near a fire is simply an obscure sensation that reveals nothing about the nature of fire itself in its material (extended) reality. Malebranche's ideas are, in effect, pure concepts, and their content has no sensory component whatsoever. They just are the logical essences of things or kinds. Malebranche's epistemological distinction between ideas and sensations derives from Descartes's distinction between clear and distinct ideas and obscure and confused ideas, and roughly corresponds to the distinction made famous by the English chemist Robert Boyle and the philosopher John Locke between ideas of primary qualities and ideas of secondary qualities.

An important and peculiar feature of Malebranche's theory, however, is that this epistemological difference between ideas and sensations has its foundation in an ontological difference. While sensations are mental, that is, properties or modifications of an individual human mind, ideas are not. Representative ideas are "present to the mind," but they are not modifications of the mind's substance. (This, in fact, is what allows them to represent to the mind extended or material reality.) Rather –

and here is Malebranche's stunning innovation – ideas are in God, and finite minds have access to them because God wills to reveal them to those minds, all of which exist in a perpetual union with God. That ideas do not belong to the mind becomes clear from the fact that some of our ideas are infinite, and it is impossible for a finite mind to have an infinite property or modification. Likewise, our ideas are all general – they only become particular or specific when combined with some sensory components – and a particular substance such as the human mind cannot have a modification that is general.

Ideas function in all of the mind's cognitive activities; most importantly, in conception and perception. In conception, the mind apprehends a pure idea by itself, without any sensations to "color" or particularize the experience (for example, conceiving a geometric circle). Ideas are also present in sense perception, but accompanied by various sensory elements. Thus, when we perceive the sun, our "intellection" of the pure idea of a geometric circle is accompanied by color and heat sensations. Malebranche intends his theory of ideas, at least in part, to account for the cognitive elements in perception that distinguish it from mere sensory awareness. True perceptual acquaintance is "informed" by ideas, and thereby necessarily has a conceptual or epistemic component.

Malebranche offers two kinds of argument to demonstrate that representative ideas are required for knowledge and perception. First, he argues that there is generally an unbridgeable distance between the mind and its external objects. He sometimes appears to mean this literally, and to be relying on the fact that the mind is not locally present to the bodies it knows and sees, and that in cognition it is neither the case that objects travel to the mind nor that the mind leaves the body to "travel across the great spaces" that separate it from its objects.[6] His more considered intention, however, is probably to draw our attention to the metaphysical (and not the physical) gulf that separates mind from matter. Bodies, being extended, cannot be united with and thus present to the unextended mind in the way required for direct cognitive acquaintance. Thus, what is required are intermediary entities that can both represent extended bodies and be immediately present to the mind: ideas.

Second, it is often the case that we have a perceptual experience of an object when in fact the object itself does not actually exist (for example, in hallucinations and dreams). But Malebranche insists upon the truth of the principle of intentionality, or the claim that every perception must be object-directed ("to perceive is to perceive something"). As Malebranche understands this principle, every perception must be the direct and immediate apprehension of some really present object. As the illusory cases illustrate, however, the intentional objects of the mind cannot be really existing material bodies; for if they were, we could never have perceptual experiences of objects that do not exist. Thus, it must be that we directly apprehend ideas, nonmaterial representations, even though sometimes there is no external body corresponding to the idea.[7]

Malebranche then argues that the ideas that function in human perception and knowledge are simply God's ideas, the eternal essences and archetypes in the divine understanding; or, in Malebranche's own words, "that we see all things in God." In the *Search*, Malebranche relies mainly on an argument from elimination to establish this bold claim. He shows how all other accounts of the source of our ideas – the Aristotelian-Scholastic and Epicurean doctrines (with external bodies literally sending material resemblances of themselves to the mind), various Cartesian theories (innatism, self-production by the soul) – are untenable, thus leaving the vision in God as the only viable alternative.[8] But in this work and elsewhere, he also marshals more positive considerations in support of his doctrine. His account, he insists, is simpler than any other hypothesis, hence more worthy of God's ways. It also best fosters a proper and pious sense of our ontological and epistemological dependence upon our creator: we, as knowers, are not self-sufficient, no more than we as beings are self-sufficient substances. In a number of "Elucidations" appended to the *Search*, Malebranche's argument takes a more Augustinian turn. For St. Augustine, what we see in God are eternal and immutable truths. Truth is, by its nature, changeless, universal, and uncreated. Moreover, truth is higher than and common to many minds. Thus, it can be nowhere but in the divine reason, in God himself (in Augustine's words, truth *is* God). For Malebranche, too, truth is necessarily universal, immutable, and infinite. But the truths we know just are relations between ideas. Thus, the ideas themselves must be universal, immutable, and infinite. And such ideas can be found only in an immutable, infinite understanding, that is, in God.[9] The vision in God, in Malebranche's eyes, is the only possible explanation for our common knowledge of necessary truths: we are all similarly united with one universal, infinite Reason, in which we perceive the same ideas.

Malebranche's doctrine of the vision in God is motivated, then, not just by the problem of how we perceive bodies in the external world – a rather Cartesian concern – but primarily by the Augustinian problem of how we have knowledge of eternal truths. And behind it all lies Malebranche's deep-seated fear of the dangers of skepticism. The vision in God represents, for Malebranche, the strongest and most effective counter-skeptical strategy available. First, we can be sure that the ideas we apprehend in sense-perception really do represent bodies in the world because these ideas just are the archetypes that served and directed God in creating those bodies. Thus, they cannot fail to reveal the nature of extended things as they are in themselves. On the other hand, if ideas were, as many Cartesians insisted, merely fleeting and subjective modifications of the soul, there would be no justification for believing that what they represent about bodies in the world really characterizes those bodies. Second, any skeptical worries about the necessity, universality, and objectivity of mathematical and moral knowledge are forestalled by showing that the ideas upon which such knowledge is based are mind-independent (nonsubjective) realities accessible to all knowers in a universal and infallible Reason.

To be sure, there are many relevant questions that the vision-in-God doctrine cannot, and was not intended to, answer. For example, while the ideas we apprehend in God inform us as to the essences of things, they cannot provide any evidence about the existence of things. Certainty in this regard can only come through a combination of faith (in God's revelation that he created a material world) and sensory experience. This is not to say that Malebranche is a skeptic or a fideist when it comes to the existence of the external world. Although he claims that we cannot have purely rational and demonstrative certainty about the existence of a world of things, we still have no good reasons to doubt of it, as well as a natural and reliable propensity to believe in it. Nor does the vision in God provide us with a clear and distinct idea of the soul, which would make possible a science of the soul that is as certain as our science of bodies (physics) based on the idea of body. Our knowledge of the soul is limited to the testimony of *sentiment intérieur*, to what we actually experience introspectively in consciousness. Malebranche thus rejects Descartes's claim that we know the soul as well as (or even better than) the body.

The vision in God is a systematic attempt to combine the doctrine of divine illumination that Malebranche found in St. Augustine with a somewhat deviant Cartesian metaphysics and philosophy of mind. The theory is deeply Augustinian in inspiration, but is geared also to answer certain epistemological questions that only really get raised in the seventeenth century, particularly in the light of the mechanistic science's elimination of all qualitative sensory characteristics (color, taste, heat, etc.) from bodies and its reduction of the material world to the purely mathematical properties of extension.

As Malebranche's contemporary critics were quick to point out, the doctrine was fraught with ambiguity and inconsistency. For example, if there is a single, immutable idea in God for each object or kind of object he creates, then how is it that we perceive change and motion in extended things? Malebranche, in the "Elucidations," denies that he ever meant that there is a plurality of individual, discrete ideas in God. He insists that there is in God an "infinite intelligible extension," and that by applying our minds to this extension in different ways we apprehend representations of different extended bodies.[10] Moreover, Malebranche appears to accept the categories of Cartesian dualism as exhaustive and exclusive: everything is either a mind or a body or a property of one or the other. But what are ideas? They are not material, but neither are they minds or properties of minds (while ideas are in the divine understanding, Malebranche insists that they are not modifications of the divine substance). In what sense, then, are they "in" God and "present to" our minds?

Simon Foucher, Malebranche's first (and perhaps least comprehending) critic, focused on this latter point. If ideas are spiritual, but are not substances, then they must be modifications of some spiritual substance. Malebranche denies that they are, but then what else can they be? And if they are not *façons d'être* of our minds, then they must be as external to our minds as anything else, and thus not "present" to the mind in the manner required for direct cognition. Foucher was also concerned about how immaterial ideas could possibly represent and make known material bodies that they do not, according to Malebranche's dualism, resemble.[11] This was not a problem for Malebranche alone. One of the primary difficulties facing Cartesian dualists in the seventeenth century was to explicate how ideas could *represent* bodies when mind and matter were alleged to be so radically different from each other.

Malebranche's most well-known and harshest critic was the Jansenist theologian and Cartesian philosopher Antoine Arnauld. Arnauld argues that the whole notion of ideas as representative beings that are distinct from the mind's perceptions and which are in fact the mind's objects in perception and conception is false and even incoherent. Ideas, Arnauld insists, are mental acts – what he calls *perceptions* – that represent objects to the mind but are not themselves distinct objects. He claims that Malebranche's theory, far from explaining how we perceive bodies external to us, actually demonstrates that we never perceive such bodies, and that the mind is surrounded by a divine "palace of ideas" beyond which it has no cognitive access. Arnauld also focused his attack on Malebranche's doctrine of the infinite intelligible extension, and wondered how Malebranche can avoid the charge of materialism, of having placed extension really in God and thus making God himself extended.[12]

This latter point is taken up in Spinozistic terms by Dortuous de Mairan, a young man whom Malebranche had once tutored. De Mairan was impressed by Spinoza, and he challenged Malebranche both to refute Spinoza's arguments and to show how the relationship between the infinite intelligible extension in God and the material extension of bodies differs from the substance/mode relationship that for Spinoza characterizes the relationship between infinite extension and particular bodies.[13]

The extended polemics with Foucher, Arnauld, and de Mairan constitute only a few of the many controversies in which Malebranche engaged over his theory of ideas. There were, in the period, few doctrines as maligned and ridiculed (and perhaps misunderstood) as the vision in God.

2. Occasionalism

Just as the doctrine of the vision in God demonstrates the epistemological dependence that we as knowers have upon God, so the causal doctrine of occasionalism demonstrates the ontological dependence that we and all beings have upon God. Nothing, according to this doctrine, exists or happens in the universe that is not a direct and immediate effect of the divine will. Although occasionalism has its ancestry in medieval theories of causation and divine omnipotence, especially the voluntarist tradition, as well as in Descartes's metaphysics; and while there were others before Malebranche who were, to one degree or another, occasionalists; Malebranche was truly the first to argue for a thoroughgoing version of occasionalism in a rigorous and systematic manner.

The essential claim of occasionalism is that all finite created entities are absolutely devoid of causal efficacy and that God is the only true causal agent. Bodies do not cause effects in other bodies or in minds, and minds do not cause effects in bodies or even within themselves. God is directly, immediately, and solely responsible for bringing about all phenomena. When a needle pricks the skin, the physical event is merely an occasion for God to cause the appropriate mental state (pain); a volition in the soul to raise an arm or to think of something is only an occasion for God to cause the arm to rise or the idea to be present to the mind; and the impact of one billiard ball upon another is an occasion for God to move the second ball. In all three contexts – mind–body, body–body, and mind alone – God's ubiquitous causal activity proceeds in accordance with certain general laws, and (except in the case of miracles) he acts only when the requisite material or psychic conditions obtain.

Far from being an *ad hoc* solution to a Cartesian mind–body problem, as it has traditionally been portrayed, occasionalism is argued for by Malebranche (and others) from general philosophical considerations of the nature of causal relations, from an analysis of the Cartesian concept of matter, and, perhaps most importantly, from theological premises about the essential ontological relationship between an omnipotent God and the created world that he sustains in existence.[14]

Malebranche's first argument that there are no real causal powers in finite created substances and that God is the sole causal agent focuses on the motion of bodies. He begins with the causal principle that in order for one thing, *A* (which can be a substance or a state of being of a substance), to count as the cause of another thing, *B*, there must be a necessary connection between the existence of *A* and the existence of *B*. "A true cause as I understand it is one such that the mind perceives a necessary connection [liaison nécessaire] between it and its effects."[15] But we can find no such connection between any two physical events, nor between any human mental event and a corresponding physical event. It is always possible to conceive, without contradiction, that the one event occurs without the other. For example, it is certainly conceivable that one wills to raise one's arm but the arm does not rise. "When we examine our idea of all finite minds, we do not see any necessary connection between their will and the motion of any body whatsoever. On the contrary, we see that there is none and that there can be none."[16] When we consider God, however, as an infinitely perfect being, we see that there *is* such a necessary connection between the divine will and the motion of bodies, since it is logically impossible, hence inconceivable that an omnipotent God should will to move a body and it does not move; such is the nature of omnipotence. God, therefore, is the only true cause of the motion of bodies.

Malebranche's second argument is based on the "inconceivability" that any natural cause, any finite mind or material body, should have "a force, a power, an efficacy to produce anything."[17] First, the idea of body – that is, the clear and distinct idea of extension – represents it as having only one property: the entirely passive faculty of "receiving various figures and various movements."[18] It certainly does not represent body as having any active power. Here Malebranche is drawing out the ramifications of Descartes's conception of matter: a Cartesian material body, *qua* pure extension, is essentially passive and inert, and devoid of any motive force. In fact, such a force or power is perceived as *incompatible* with the notion of extension, since it cannot be reduced to or explained in terms of relations of shape, divisibility, and distance. Thus, bodies cannot *act*, whether on minds or other bodies. Second, whatever minimal knowledge I have of my soul does not involve the perception of any power, whether to move the body or even to produce its own ideas. All I perceive through inner consciousness is an actual volition to move my arm upwards, and all I notice in my body is that my arm subsequently rises. But I do not perceive, either by inner consciousness or by reason, any power on the part of the soul by means of which it might effect this motion. It is in this sense that "those who maintain that creatures have force and power in themselves advance what they do not clearly perceive."[19] Indeed, according to Malebranche, I perceive a general incompatibility between the idea of a created finite being and such a power or productive faculty. Only in my idea of the will of an infinite being do I clearly and distinctly recognize any element of power whatsoever.

The third argument is based on a supposedly intuitive premise which (echoing an argument for occasionalism introduced by the Flemish philosopher Arnold Geulincx) sets an epistemic condition on the notion of "cause": in order to count as the cause of an effect, a thing must know how (*savoir*) to bring about that effect. Malebranche then appeals to the evident fact that this condition is not satisfied by our minds in order to show that we do not, in fact, cause those motions that we consider voluntary: "There is no man who knows what must be done to move one of his fingers by means of animal spirits." This same condition rules out not only the mind's causal activity upon the body, but also the mind's ability to produce its own ideas. It also rules out, *a fortiori*, the possession of causal efficacy by bodies.[20]

Malebranche's most sweeping argument against real causal interaction between created beings appeals to God's role as creator and sustainer of the universe. The argument – which has its roots in both medieval and Cartesian doctrines of divine sustenance – purports to show that it is an "absolute contradiction" that anything besides God should move a body. God's activity is required not only to create the world, but, since creatures are absolutely dependent on God, to sustain it in existence as well. Indeed, for God there is no essential difference between creation and sustenance. "If the world subsists, it is because God continues to will that the world exist. On the part of God, the conservation of the creatures is simply their continued creation."[21] When God conserves/recreates a body, he must conserve/recreate it not in abstraction, but in some particular place and in some specific relation of distance to other bodies. If God conserves it in the same relative place from moment to moment, it remains at rest; if God conserves it successively in different places, it is in motion. But this means that God is and can be the *only* cause of motion. "The moving force of a body, then, is simply the efficacy of the volition of God who conserves it successively in different places . . . Hence, bodies cannot move one another, and their encounter or impact is only an occasional cause of the distribution of their motions."[22] And finite minds are no more causes of motion than bodies are.

Thus, God is the direct and efficacious cause of every event in nature; finite beings are only "secondary" or "occasional" causes. Malebranche empties the created world of any "natures" or powers or forms – most of all, the occult qualities of the Scholastic philosophy – and traces all laws and causality back to the will of God. His doctrine can thus be seen as an extreme development within a voluntarist tradition that extends from certain medieval Arabic and Christian thinkers – many of whom, like al-Ghazali, attacked the Aristotelian theory of nature in the name of safeguarding God's omnipotence – up through Descartes.

This does not mean that for Malebranche natural philosophy has been reduced to a single theocratic claim. At the level of physics proper, the task of the scientist is still to uncover regularities in nature and formulate the laws that govern the correlations between events. The scientific program of the mechanical philosophy, to which Malebranche enthusiastically subscribes, remains the same: to discover the hidden mechanisms that underlie observed phenomena and to frame explanations by referring to secondary causes described solely in terms of matter and motion. What Malebranche's occasionalism provides are the metaphysical foundations of Cartesian physics. Motion, the primary explanatory element in the new science, must ultimately be grounded in something higher than the passive, inert extension of Cartesian bodies; it needs a causal ground in an active power or force. Because a body consists in extension alone, motive force cannot be an inherent property of bodies. Malebranche accordingly – and his account seems to be a logical extension of the role Descartes gives to God as the "universal and primary cause of motion" – places the locus of force in the will of God. Bodies behave the way they do because that is how God ordinarily moves them around, following the laws of nature he has established.

Malebranche did, in fact, use his metaphysics of motion to modify some details of Descartes's physics, particularly the rules governing bodily impact. This led to an extended debate with Leibniz over the laws of motion. In the *Search*, Malebranche insists, contrary to Descartes, that bodies at rest do not have a force to remain at rest (unlike bodies in motion, which have a force to remain in motion). This conclusion follows directly from his occasionalist account of motion: although God does need to will positively to put a body in motion, he does not need to apply any force to keep it at rest; all he need do is will that it continue to exist, that is, recreate it in the same relative place. Thus, the tiniest body in motion will contain more force than the rest of the largest body. And this, if true, means that three of Descartes's seven rules of impact are wrong.[23] Leibniz, in his general critique of Cartesian physics, praises Malebranche for recognizing Descartes's errors. He insists, however, that because Malebranche was still wedded to Descartes's conservation law (where what is conserved in nature is quantity of motion (mass × speed), rather than the quantity of force (mass × the square of velocity) that Leibniz proposed), Malebranche has failed to see that *all* except the first of Descartes's rules, along with the new rules he had substituted for the ones he rejected, were wrong. In 1692, Malebranche published his *On the laws of the communication of motions*, in which he concedes that Leibniz is right about the rules themselves but continues to maintain the old conservation law. It was not until a letter to Leibniz in 1699 and the 1700 edition of the *Search* that Malebranche admits that Descartes's conservation law is false.

3. Ethics

For Malebranche, God's ubiquitous causal activity did not eliminate freedom of the will in human beings. God is the direct source of an invincible inclination or "natural motion" in the soul towards good in general. We cannot not will to be happy, and we necessarily love what we "clearly know and vividly feel" to be good. But it is in our power to allow or to refuse to allow this general determination towards good given to us by God to rest upon one or another of the particular things we believe to be good. All minds, he notes, love God "by the necessity of their nature," and if they love anything else, it is by a free choice of their will. We sin when, rather than directing the will by a clear and distinct perception of the supreme good to the love of God, we allow it to be directed away from God towards the pleasing but false goods presented to us by our senses.[24]

In his *Treatise on morality*, Malebranche elaborates on just what this love of God involves and provides a fuller account of our ethical duties.[25] Within God, there lies an immutable order or law, which God consults when acting. This order is constituted by what Malebranche calls "relations of perfection," which in turn entail a hierarchy of value among beings. Order dictates, for example, that a beast is more perfect, hence more worthy or "estimable" than a rock, and a human being more perfect and worthy than a beast. A human being is thus to be treated with more consideration than a horse. Through our "union with the eternal word, with universal reason" we can have rational knowledge of order. Our duty, then, consists in "submitting ourselves to God's law, and in following order." We ought, like God, to regulate our actions and esteem by consulting it. In this way, "there is a true and a false, a just and an unjust" that is binding upon *all* intelligent beings. Malebranche insists that our principal duty and our "fundamental and universal virtue" is to love order and obey its precepts.

4. Philosophical Theology

Malebranche's occasionalism takes on even greater importance in the context of his theodicy, or justification of God's ways in the realms of nature and grace. In his *Treatise on Nature and Grace*, Malebranche undertakes the task of explaining how God's omnipotence, benevolence, and perfection can be reconciled with the persistence of evil and imperfections in the natural world (including human suffering and sin) and with the apparent unfairness and inefficiency in the distribution of divine grace and everlasting happiness.

Our concept of God tells us that God is infinitely wise, good, powerful, and perfect. And yet the world which God has created certainly appears to us to be quite imperfect in its details and full of disorders of every variety. As Theodore, Malebranche's spokesman in the *Dialogues on Metaphysics*, exclaims, "The Universe then is the most perfect that God can make? But really! So many monsters, so many disorders, the great number of impious men – does all this contribute to the perfection of the universe?"[26] Aristes, his interlocutor, is led thereby to wonder about either the efficacy of God's will or the benevolence of God's intentions: either God could not accomplish his plan to create the best (which would call into question God's omnipotence) or he did not wish to create the best in the first place (which would call into question God's goodness).

The resolution of this conundrum, as presented in both the *Dialogues* and the *Treatise on Nature and Grace*, is to be found in the consideration not just of the particular, superficial, and obvious details of the universe, but also of the means undertaken to achieve and sustain the whole. God, according to Malebranche, when creating looks not only to the final result of the creative act (that is, to the goodness and perfection of the world *per se*), but also to his work or ways of operation. And the activity or means most expressive of God's nature are of maximum simplicity, uniformity, fecundity, and universality. God does not accomplish by complex means that which can be accomplished by simple means; and God does not execute with many particular volitions that which can be executed by a few general volitions. This holds true even if it means that the world created by God could be spared some imperfections were God to compromise the simplicity and generality of his operations. Thus, the perfection of the world in its details as a product is completely relative to the mode of activity that is most worthy of God. God might increase the absolute perfection of the world, perhaps by decreasing the number of defects or evils therein through specifically tailored actions. God might, for example, make special efforts to keep the rain from falling on anything but fertile and inseminated soil. But this would entail greater complexity in the divine ways and constant departures from the general laws of nature established at creation.

Thus, the world that God has created is the one out of the infinitely many possible worlds that best reconciles perfection of design with simplicity and generality of means of production and conservation. By a number of "particular volitions [volontés particulières]" – volitions that are *ad hoc* and not occasioned by some prior event in accordance with some law of nature – God could correct deformities of birth, keep fruit from rotting on trees, prevent physical disasters about to occur by the regular course of the laws of nature, and forestall sin and wickedness. But, Malebranche insists, "we must be careful not to require constant miracles from God, nor to attribute them to him at every moment."[27] God, in other words, acts only by "general volitions [volontés générales]" – volitions that are in accordance with some law and whose operation is occasioned by a prior event, as dictated by that law – and the most simple ways ("les voies les plus simples"), and never by particular volitions.

The solution to the problem of evil, then, is found in the simplicity and uniformity of God's causal conduct in the world, in the generality of the divine will. Similar considerations apply to the problem of grace. A benevolent God wills, with what Malebranche calls a "simple volition," that sinners convert and that all human beings should be saved. But clearly not all humans are saved; many souls are lost to damnation. And not all those who are saved appear to be worthy of salvation or ready to receive grace. The anomaly is again explained by the generality of God's volitions. The distribution of grace is governed by certain general laws willed by God. The occasional causes responsible for the actual distribution of grace in accordance with those laws are the thoughts and desires in the human soul of Jesus Christ. Because Jesus *qua* human has finite cognitive capacities, he cannot at any given time attend to all the relevant facts about the agent upon whom grace is to be bestowed – for example, whether they are ready to make the best use of it – or actually think of all who deserve to be saved. Thus, as with the distribution of evil and imperfection in the natural world, God *allows* grace to be distributed unevenly and even inequitably by the laws of grace in combination with the occasional causes that activate them.

It was the *Treatise on Nature and Grace*, with its claim that God wills to save *all* humans and the implication that God's volitions are not always efficacious (since not everyone is saved), that initially aroused Arnauld's ire and occasioned his attack on Malebranche's whole system. For Arnauld, as a Jansenist, was committed first and foremost to a strong doctrine of predestination and to the efficacy of divine volitions, particularly in the matter of grace. If God wills that someone is saved – and not all people are so blessed – then that person is saved.

5. Influence

Malebranche's influence in the seventeenth and eighteenth centuries was significant, but subtle and often unacknowledged. There is no question that his contemporaries recognized him as *the* major representative of the Cartesian system, however unorthodox his Cartesianism may have been. Leibniz's arguments against "the Cartesians," for example, are often directed at Malebranche. And yet, despite his criticisms of occasionalism, Leibniz was himself impressed by Malebranche's discussion of causation and critique of interaction between substances. And Leibniz's own theodicy and solution to the problem of evil was clearly influenced by what he read in Malebranche. Like Malebranche, Leibniz insists that God in creation chooses from an infinity of possible worlds, and that God pays particular attention not just to the created theater itself, but especially to its relationship with the laws of nature and grace. Malebranche considers the laws as separate from "the world," and gives them a higher value. He grants that the world God created may not be, absolutely speaking, the best of all possible worlds, but it is the best that can be done given the absolute simplicity of means God employs. Leibniz, on the other hand, considers the laws and the universe they govern together as "the world," and insists that the combination *is* the best world overall. But they both believe that evil and sin occur because God *allows* them to occur as a result of the ordinary course of nature as governed by the laws God has chosen. They agree that God could diminish the visible imperfections of the created world, but only by violating the simplicity of the divine ways (as Malebranche would put it), or by detracting from the *overall* optimality of the world (as Leibniz would say). Leibniz even goes so far as to suggest to Malebranche that, in the end, their accounts are the same, although Malebranche disagrees.

Malebranche's influence extended across the English Channel as well.[28] Despite Berkeley's rather surprising claim that "there are no principles more fundamentally opposite than his [Malebranche's] and mine,"[29] there are obvious echoes of Malebranche's doctrines in Berkeley's works (as testified by the accusations of Berkeley's contemporaries that he was himself a "Malebranchist"). Berkeley does not draw either an ontological or an epistemological distinction between ideas and sensations, as Malebranche does. Sensory states and perceptions of so-called primary qualities are all equally "ideas." But Berkeley's ideas, like Malebranche's ideas, are not modifications of the human mind. Although they are "present" to the mind, they are, in an important sense, independent of and external to it: they continue to exist even when not perceived by any finite spirit. What makes this persistence possible is that ideas, for Berkeley, are also in the mind of God, "an infinite spirit who contains and supports" the world of ideas. Similarly, with respect to causation, Berkeley denies that our ideas of bodies provide us with any notion of causal power or efficacy. Berkeley is not a complete occasionalist. He departs from Malebranche's doctrine to the extent that he grants real causal power to the human soul. Still, like Malebranche, Berkeley insists that the ordinary course of natural phenomena, the regularities and correspondences in our ideas of external things (or at least those ideas that do not depend on our own will), are the direct result of the causal activity of the will of a governing spirit, that is, God.

Hume was more forthcoming in acknowledging his debt to Malebranche in his conclusions about causality. Some of his well-known demonstrations showing that causal reasoning lacks philosophical justification seem to come right out of Malebranche's arguments for occasionalism in the *Search*. He was also, at the same time, one of Malebranche's more rigorous early modern critics.

Hume asks whether our idea of body provides us with a legitimate notion of causal power. Like Malebranche, he concludes that it does not: "There is no part of matter, that does ever, by its sensible qualities, discover any power or energy, or give us ground to imagine, that it could produce any thing, or be followed by any other object, which we could denominate its effect."[30] Moreover, and unlike Berkeley, both Malebranche and Hume deny that we can acquire any idea of causal power from introspection, from attending to the soul's operations.

Malebranche and Hume also stress the centrality of the concept of necessary connection to our understanding of causation. More importantly, both of them deny that the requisite necessity can be discovered, either by reason or by experience, between any things in nature. Hume argues, like Malebranche, that reason will never discover a necessary connection between two discrete objects or events on the grounds that one can always conceive, without contradiction, the one without the other. The conception of no thing, taken by itself, implies or even indicates the existence of anything else; and if two things are really separate, then no matter how many times we have apprehended or thought of them together, we can always imagine the one to exist but not the other. Nor does experience, either of a single instance of one event following another or of multiple instances (what Hume calls "constant conjunction"), offer greater help here. Malebranche insists that all that we can ever truly discover by our senses is that one event follows the other, but not that the one has the power or force to produce the other. We certainly do not experience any necessary or causal connection between them. Similarly, Hume argues that when we closely examine what it is we apprehend when we experience one object following another, either once or many times, we find only that the two are "contiguous in time and place, and that the object we call cause precedes the other we call effect."[31]

The crucial difference between the two thinkers, however, is that Malebranche then proceeds to show that we do discover a necessary connection between the will of God and any event willed by God, while Hume goes to great lengths to refute such a claim. In fact, Hume turns Malebranche's own arguments for occasionalism against the doctrine itself, insisting that any consistent application of them should lead to the conclusion that we have no more justification for thinking of God as a necessitating cause than anything else. Just as it is always possible to conceive of any one thing without thinking of any other thing, so is it possible to imagine both that God wills something and that that thing does not occur; to insist otherwise is simply to beg the question. Moreover, because we have never had an experience of power (or, in Humean terms, because we lack an *impression* of power), Hume insists that "we have no idea of a being endow'd with any power, much less of one endow'd with infinite power."[32]

While there were a small number of "Malebranchists" in England and on the Continent – John Norris, for example – Malebranche's immediate legacy lay more in his contributions to the internal development of Cartesian philosophy and science before their demise by the end of the seventeenth century. If he influenced other major philosophers of the early modern period, it was more a matter either of their finding in his doctrines or arguments convenient instruments for their own devices (as Leibniz, Berkeley, and Hume did), or of their using his system in a negative way to distance themselves from his "enthusiasm," much as many thinkers used Spinoza to distance themselves from his "freethinking atheism."

Notes

1 Père Yves André, *La vie du R. P. Malebranche, prêtre de l'Oratoire* (Paris, 1886; Geneva: Slatkine Reprints, 1970).

2 *De la recherche de la vérité*, in volumes 1–3 of the *Oeuvres complètes de Malebranche*, ed. André Robinet, 20 vols. (Paris: J. Vrin, 1958–67; henceforth referred to as OC). The standard English translation of the work is *The Search After Truth*, tr. Thomas M. Lennon and Paul J. Olscamp (Columbus: Ohio State University Press, 1980; reissued by Cambridge University Press in 1997; henceforth referred to as LO).

3 *Traité de la nature et de la grace* (vol. 5 of OC) and *Entretiens sur la métaphysique et sur la religion* (vol. 12). I refer the reader to the translation of the *Entretiens* by Nicholas Jolley and David Scott, *Dialogues on Metaphysics and on Religion* (New York: Cambridge University Press, 1997; henceforth referred to as D).
4 For a general discussion of these issues about ideas, see Robert McRae, "'Idea' as a Philosophical Term in the 17th Century," *Journal of the History of Ideas* 26 (1965), pp. 175–84; and John Yolton, *Perceptual Acquaintance from Descartes to Reid* (Minneapolis: University of Minnesota Press, 1984). For more particular studies, see Nicholas Jolley, *The Light of the Soul: Theories of Ideas in Leibniz, Malebranche and Descartes* (Oxford: Clarendon Press, 1990); and Steven Nadler, *Arnauld and the Cartesian Philosophy of Ideas* (Princeton: Princeton University Press, 1989), and *Malebranche and Ideas* (Oxford: Oxford University Press, 1992).
5 See Books 1 and 2 of the *Search.*
6 *Search* I.14, OC 1:156, LO 67; *Search* III.2.i, OC 1:413–14, LO 217.
7 See, for example, his response to a letter from Arnauld, OC 9:910.
8 *Search,* III.2.1–6, OC 1:413–47; LO 217–35.
9 *Elucidations to the Search After Truth,* 10.
10 *Elucidations to the Search After Truth,* 10.
11 Foucher made his initial objections in his *Critique de la recherche de la vérité,* first published in 1675.
12 The Arnauld–Malebranche debate, one of the most philosophically interesting episodes in seventeenth-century philosophy, began with Arnauld's publication in 1683 of *Des vrayes et des fausses idées,* in which he attacked Malebranche's theory of ideas.
13 For de Mairan's correspondence with Malebranche, see OC 19.
14 This point is argued at greater length by Thomas Lennon, "Occasionalism and the Cartesian Metaphysic of Motion," *Canadian Journal of Philosophy,* supplementary volume 1 (1974), pp. 29–43; and Steven Nadler, "Occasionalism and the Mind–Body Problem," *Oxford Studies in the History of Philosophy,* vol. 2: *Studies in Seventeenth-Century European Philosophy* (Oxford: Oxford University Press, 1997), pp. 75–95.
15 *Search* VI.2.iii, OC 2:316; LO 450.
16 *Search* VI.2.iii, OC 2:313; LO 448.
17 *Search,* Elucidation 15, OC 3:204; LO 658.
18 *Dialogues* VII.1–2, OC 12:148–51; D 105–7.
19 *Search,* Elucidation 15, OC 3:204; LO 658.
20 See *Search* VI.2.iii, OC 2:315; LO 449–50.
21 *Dialogues* VII.7, OC 12:157; D 112–13.
22 *Dialogues* VII.11, OC 12:161]en]2; D 117.
23 See *Search* VI.2.ix.
24 See, for example, *Search* IV.1.
25 *Traité de morale,* OC 11.
26 *Dialogues* IX.9, OC 12:211; D 114–15.
27 *Treatise on Nature and Grace* I.21, OC 5:34.
28 While it would be difficult to argue that Locke was influenced by Malebranche in any significant way, he did devote some time to criticizing Malebranche's theory of ideas. The reader may want to look at "An Examination of P. Malebranche's Opinion of Seeing All Things in God," in *The Works of John Locke,* 10 vols. (London: Tegg, 1823), vol. 9.

29 *Three Dialogues Between Hylas and Philonous*, Dialogue 2.
30 *An Enquiry Concerning Human Understanding*, eds. L. A. Selby-Bigge and P. H. Nidditch (Oxford: Oxford University Press, 1975), p. 63.
31 *A Treatise of Human Nature*, eds. L. A. Selby-Bigge and P. H. Nidditch (Oxford: Oxford University Press, 1978), I.3.14, p. 155.
32 *Treatise* I.4.5, p. 248.

Chapter 5

G. W. Leibniz

Donald Rutherford

Gottfried Wilhelm Leibniz was born in Leipzig in 1646. With the exception of four formative years in Paris (1672–76) and a year's journey through Italy (1689–90), he spent his life in German lands, the greatest part of it during his forty-year employment as librarian, legal adviser, and court historian to the dukes of Brunswick-Lüneberg. Leibniz died in Hanover in 1716.[1]

Leibniz is renowned for the range of his accomplishments. He was a brilliant mathematician who vied with Isaac Newton for honor as inventor of the differential and integral calculus.[2] He made seminal contributions to the science of dynamics, comparative philology, and historiography. On the practical side, he was instrumental in founding scientific societies in Berlin and Vienna, and worked tirelessly on behalf of a reunion of the Protestant and Catholic churches. Throughout his life, Leibniz sought to promote the discovery and dissemination of new knowledge and the reconciliation of religious and political differences, in the interest of the greater good of humanity.

Lying behind all of these activities was a comprehensive philosophical position. Leibniz's philosophy is marked by two dominant characteristics. He is first and foremost a metaphysical thinker who expresses complete confidence in the ability of human reason to comprehend the underlying nature of reality. Drawing a sharp distinction between appearance and reality, Leibniz allies himself most closely with the philosophy of Plato; in this way his position becomes an important stepping stone to Kant's *Critique of Pure Reason* and the doctrine of transcendental idealism. The second defining feature of Leibniz's philosophy is its synthetic spirit. In contrast to other major figures of the early modern period, Leibniz did not argue for the necessity of overthrowing the legacy of ancient philosophy. Although influenced by the writings of Descartes, Gassendi, Hobbes, and Spinoza, Leibniz had serious reservations about many of their views. Of particular concern to him was the thesis that nature can be fully understood in terms of the properties of matter alone, operating according to the laws of efficient causation. While allowing the appropriateness of the "mechanical philosophy" as an account of the phenomena of sense experience, Leibniz believed that such an account falls short of a complete explanation of nature. In opposition to the growing tide of modern thought, he argued that there are fundamental metaphysical questions – about the origin of the universe, of life, sensation and reason, of the laws of nature and the principles of morality – that can only be answered by drawing on the resources of ancient philosophy. Leibniz did not conclude from this that the development of modern philosophy was a mistake, or that it ought to be abandoned in favor of a return to the ancients, but that the true philosophy must unite the best insights of the ancients and the moderns – giving no allegiance to one particular school over another. Consistent with his larger project of reconciliation, Leibniz held that in philosophy, as much as in religion or politics, the way forward was found by overcoming sectarian differences. "I have tried to uncover and unite the truth buried and scattered under the opinions of all the different philosophical sects," he writes in a late letter, "and I believe I have added something of my own which takes a few steps forward. . . . I have found that most of the sects are right in a good part of what they propose, but not so much in what they deny."[3]

The study of Leibniz's philosophy is complicated by the fact that he wrote no full-scale treatise in which he explains and defends his doctrines. The two philosophical books Leibniz composed, the *New Essays on Human Understanding* (1704) and the *Theodicy* (1710), are both polemical works, which introduce his views selectively while responding to the claims of other thinkers. For the rest, we are left with a small collection of published essays, spanning some fifty years, and a huge mass of unpublished writings and philosophical correspondences. Many of Leibniz's best-known and most important works fall into the latter class: the *Discourse on Metaphysics* (1686), the *Monadology* (1714), the correspondences with Arnauld, De Volder, Des Bosses, and Clarke. Regrettably, none offer a definitive statement of his philosophy. In virtue of the brevity and particular focus of each work, we must inevitably turn to others to check and supplement our understanding of Leibniz's views, building stepwise a full picture of his philosophy. The very description of this method, however, also suggests its limitations. Leibniz possessed a quick and wide-ranging mind, which took delight in thinking through problems for their own sake. His philosophical corpus reflects his incessant movement from one set of issues, concerns, and correspondents to another, with only secondary consideration given to whether what he said today was exactly the same as what he said yesterday, let alone a decade before.

Although Leibniz gave no definitive formulation of his philosophy, a single set of principles guides his thinking from beginning to end. If the body of his philosophy is a living one that grows and develops, these principles are the skeleton upon which the flesh hangs; while the shape of the body changes, it retains a similar structure, supported by a framework of fixed principles. To understand Leibniz's philosophy, we must begin with these principles, considering with care their content, the source of their certainty, and their relation to the rest of his thought.

1. First Principles

In the *Monadology*, Leibniz famously asserts what he calls the "two great principles" of all our reasoning:

> *that of contradiction*, in virtue of which we judge that which involves a contradiction to be false, and that which is opposed or contradictory to the false to be true. And *that of sufficient reason*, by virtue of which we consider that we can find no true or existent fact, no true assertion, without there being a sufficient reason why it is thus and not otherwise, although most of the time these reasons cannot be known to us. (secs. 31–2)[4]

Aristotle maintained that the principle of contradiction cannot be coherently denied, since any attempt to argue for its falsity would presuppose its truth. Leibniz seems to have believed something similar in the case of his "two great principles." In an appendix to the *Theodicy*, he suggests that both principles "are contained in the definition of the true and the false."[5] The claim is plausible in the case of the principle of contradiction. On any account, it is integral to an understanding of truth that a proposition and its negation cannot both be true simultaneously, or equivalently, that their joint assertion must be false. In the same way, Leibniz believed that most basic "primary truths" are statements of identity ("A is A") in which the same term is asserted of itself, for the denial of such truths produces a self-evident contradiction (AG 30–1).

Leibniz's claim is less obvious in the case of the principle of sufficient reason. How does the demand that there be a *reason* for all that is true or existent follow from the very definition of "truth"? The plausibility of this claim rests on what has come to be called Leibniz's "predicate-in-subject principle," or his conceptual containment theory of truth. According to Leibniz, the truth of any subject–predicate proposition is based on the containment of the concept expressed by its predicate in the concept expressed by its subject.[6] Thus, to pick a simple example, the truth of the proposition "Horses are animals" is based on the fact that the concept *animal* is contained in the concept *horse*, or that anything understood to be a horse also must be understood to be an animal. Given this, there is a close relationship between the predicate-in-subject principle and the principle of sufficient reason. If the former states a necessary and sufficient condition for the truth of any proposition, then for any true proposition there is a determinate reason why it is true, namely, the containment of the concept of its predicate in the concept of its subject. The precision of this idea greatly impressed Leibniz and informed the presentation of his philosophy. During the 1680s, the period of the *Discourse on Metaphysics* and the correspondence with Arnauld, Leibniz maintained that many of the central doctrines of his philosophy, including the theory of preestablished harmony, follow from this one basic idea.[7]

The influential commentaries of Bertrand Russell and Louis Couturat, both published in the first years of the twentieth century, took up this theme and defended in different ways the thesis that Leibniz's metaphysics could be accounted for as consequence of his logic, broadly understood to include the predicate-in-subject principle.[8] For Russell and Couturat, the main problem faced by this theory – one recognized by Leibniz – concerns its treatment of contingent propositions, particularly those asserting the existence and contingent properties of individuals. As a theory of truth, the account is most compelling in the case of definitional truths, or those asserting essential properties of their subjects (for example, "Horses are animals"). Here it reveals the necessity of such propositions, the fact that they must be true, given the content of their terms. It is just this, though, that threatens the theory in the case of contingent propositions, such as "G. W. Leibniz was born in Leipzig on July 1, 1646." If the same reasoning is to hold, the truth of this proposition must depend upon the containment of the concept of the predicate "born in Leipzig on July 1, 1646" in the concept of the individual Leibniz. Leibniz strongly supports this conclusion, maintaining that for each actual or possible individual substance, there is a "complete concept" which contains all and only those predicates (past, present, and future) that can be asserted of that individual. The obvious drawback of this claim is that it leaves him on the verge of concluding that everything that is true of any actual or possible individual, including the fact that it exists, is true of it necessarily. This conclusion, however, is one that Leibniz rejects, for it contradicts core commitments of his theology: that the world and its constituents are a contingent creation of God, and that the free acts of human beings, for which they bear responsibility, presuppose their contingency. Leibniz explores several strategies for dealing with these problems. The one that bears most directly on his theory of truth draws the distinction between necessary and contingent truths on the basis of whether their truth can be demonstrated through a finite analysis of the subject, as in the proposition "Horses are animals," or whether such an analysis would continue indefinitely, an end never being reached, although the predicate would nonetheless be contained within the subject and would be known to be so by God.[9]

Another critical issue raised by the interpretations of Couturat and Russell is whether Leibniz's two great principles are in a strict sense foundational to his system and, if so, whether the foundation they supply is a logical one. On both counts, skepticism is warranted. The principles of contradiction and sufficient reason are foundational in the sense that they are as deeply held as any part of Leibniz's philosophy and many of his other views rely on them. It is a mistake, however, to think of them as providing an axiomatic basis for the rest of his system. While Leibniz himself experiments with deducing key commitments of his metaphysics from the predicate-in-subject principle, such a deduction glosses over many implicit assumptions about, for example, the proper understanding of God, substance, and causation, which are essential in determining the content of his philosophy.

Among the most important of these assumptions are theological ones. For Leibniz, neither the principle of contradiction nor the principle of sufficient reason are fully intelligible as philosophical principles without their relationship to the divine understanding and will. While Leibniz maintains that the truth of any proposition depends upon the containment of its predicate in its subject, he also claims that the reality of truth as such, as well as of possibility and necessity, require that these be grounded in ideas of the divine understanding. Thus, the ultimate basis for truth (either necessary or contingent) is not that the appropriate relation exists among the ideas of any human mind but that it exists among the ideas of *God's* mind.[10] Similarly, Leibniz maintains that logical possibility would be a fiction were there not a ground in God's ideas for the reality of such possibilities as ways the world could be.[11]

The connection to theology is at least as intricate in the case of the principle of sufficient reason. In an unpublished fragment, Leibniz remarks, "One of my great principles is that nothing happens without a reason. This is a philosophical principle. However, at bottom it is nothing other than the admission of divine wisdom, although I do not speak of that at first."[12] Here Leibniz acknowledges that in the case of contingent propositions, the principle of sufficient reason presupposes what some have called the "principle of perfection" (or "principle of the best"), namely, God's wise choice of the best possible outcome. A complete explanation of why an individual has a particular contingent property ultimately must take into account God's volition to unite that property with that individual.[13] A similar theological cast is given to another key principle, that of the identity of indiscernibles, which underwrites Leibniz's critique of such entities as material atoms and absolute space.[14] According to the principle of the identity of indiscernibles, any two numerically non-identical individuals must be distinguished by some quality that one possesses and the other lacks. The weight of this principle is that numerical distinctness is not a brute fact about the world; there cannot be two individuals qualitatively alike in all respects. If we ask why this is so, Leibniz's deepest, nonquestion-begging answer is that under the imagined scenario even God would have no basis for determining whether there was one individual or two, for everything true of the one also would be true of the other. Thus, assuming God creates only what he completely understands, he will not create two indiscernible individuals.

In many contexts Leibniz's employment of the principle of sufficient reason turns on an implicit appeal to what God would choose to create, assuming that his will is inclined to choose the greatest good and is guided by perfect understanding. These are substantive claims about the divine nature that could be contested. Suppose it is denied that God's will is constrained in these ways. Then there might be facts about the world that have no further reason save that God has willed them. Leibniz's rejection of this possibility – his insistence that there always must be an intelligible reason why the world is the way it is – rests on theological commitments that transcend any particular theory of truth. Our next step, therefore, is to look more closely at Leibniz's understanding of God and of God's relation to the created world.

2. God and Creation

Leibniz's philosophy is best known for the striking claim that the world we inhabit is the best of all possible worlds. This is the centerpiece of his "theodicy," or doctrine of the justice of God, which defends the world and all it contains as a creation worthy of a supremely perfect being.

Leibniz's theodicy responds, at the most basic level, to two age-old questions: What is the ultimate reason for the world's existence? And, why does there exist this world, containing so much evil and human suffering, rather than any other possible world? In response to the first question, Leibniz begins from the fact that the world does exist, and asks what could account for this. Presupposed again is the principle of sufficient reason.[15] Leibniz observes that no set of events within the world can explain its existence, for there is no necessity internal to the world, nothing which entails that the world *must* exist. Thus, there must be an external (or "extramundane") reason for the world's existence. To complete the explanation in a way consistent with the principle of sufficient reason, this external reason must contain the ground of its own existence, a property that belongs only to God.[16]

Leibniz's reasoning is a version of the traditional cosmological argument, which argues for God's existence in an *a posteriori* manner, beginning from the existence of the world. As he writes in the *Theodicy*, "without God there would not even have been a reason for existence, and still less for any particular existence of things" (sec. 187; H 245). Leibniz also holds, though, that it is possible to give an *a priori* proof of God's existence, utilizing the traditional ontological argument. He insists, however, that Descartes's version of the ontological argument must be emended. In the fifth of his *Meditations* Descartes maintains that the essence of a supremely perfect being entails its existence, since any being that lacked existence would be less than supremely perfect. Leibniz agrees with the spirit of Descartes's reasoning but claims that it fails to prove its conclusion, unless it is first demonstrated that a supremely perfect being is *possible*. Leibniz endeavors to do this, thus completing the ontological argument, by showing the compatibility in a single subject of all positive absolute "perfections" (or forms of reality), among which he includes God's infinite power, wisdom, and goodness.[17]

Supposing that a necessary being exists and that this being, God, contains the ground of the existence of all finite things, what accounts for God's creating this particular world rather than any other possible world? This brings us to the second question, which bears directly on the problem of evil. Why, for example, should God have chosen to create a world so full of human suffering, that brought about by natural events and by the evil actions of other human beings? Leibniz's theodicy revolves around giving an answer to this question, one which would succeed in demonstrating the justice of God's creation. This requires showing that God has acted in the best possible manner, realizing a world of which no greater can be conceived.

To establish this, Leibniz argues, creation must be understood as the product of God's wise choice. This entails making certain assumptions about the nature of the world and of God's agency. As already noted, the world is not necessary in itself; there are other ways the world could have been, other possible worlds, and some external cause is required to bring one of these worlds into existence. The cause of the world's existence is God, yet here Leibniz insists on an important distinction.

Mindful of Spinoza's attack on the Judeo-Christian doctrine of creation, Leibniz maintains that the world does not follow from God with an absolute necessity but only with a "moral necessity" that is contingent upon God's free choice to create this world rather than any other possible world. In distinguishing his philosophy from Spinoza's, Leibniz is above all concerned to defend a conception of God as an intelligent agent who chooses to create the best world, and not simply a brute power that necessitates the world's existence. At the same time, however, he is anxious to distinguish his account from those that ascribe some element of arbitrariness to God's choice, or hold that God acts freely only if there is no reason that determines God to one action rather than another. Leibniz asserts, on the contrary, that it is essential to the freedom of an intelligent being that it chooses what it understands to be the greatest good.[18]

According to Leibniz, it is certain that God will choose to create the best possible world; however, this certainty does not amount to a strict or metaphysical necessity. This is because creation is determined by *choice*, in which reasons (here the relative perfection of possible worlds) "incline without necessitating." Other worlds remain "possible in themselves" insofar as they have a ground in the divine understanding as ideas of how the world could be. Having a perfectly good will, God is most strongly inclined to choose the best possible world, and God understands with perfect intelligence which world is the best. However, because God's choice of the best does not render other worlds *impossible*, the existence of this world is a contingent fact, consistent with God's exercise of free will. Summing up his position in the *Monadology*, Leibniz writes:

> Since there is an infinity of possible universes in God's ideas, and since only one of them can exist, there must be a sufficient reason for God's choice, a reason which determines him towards one thing rather than another. And this reason can only be found in *fitness*, or in the degree of perfection that these worlds contain, each world having the right to claim existence in proportion to the perfection it contains. And this is the cause of the existence of the best, which wisdom makes known to God, which his goodness makes him choose, and which his power makes him produce. (secs. 53–5; AG 220)

The identification of the actual world as the best of all possible worlds serves to confirm the justice of God's creation. By itself, however, it falls short of a full answer to the problem of evil, for along with the perfection of this world, God seems to bring about considerable imperfection, including the suffering of human beings. Isn't this evil something for which God bears responsibility: a fault which undermines the assertion of his justice and serves as a legitimate basis for our dissatisfaction with creation?

Leibniz's answer to this question is complex, involving several closely related doctrines. He argues, first, that God does not have a positive will for evil. The divine will, like any will, is an inclination for the good. At most, therefore, it can be said that God *permits* evil as an unavoidable aspect of any created world. To insist that God create a world without evil or imperfection would be to demand that God create something that was, like himself, wholly perfect, which is to say, uncreated and the source of its own existence – an obvious contradiction. In creating the world, then, God has willed the existence of the greatest possible perfection, and this has inevitably brought with it a minimal degree of imperfection or evil.

But does this world really contain only the minimal amount of evil? The defense of this point takes us deep into Leibniz's metaphysics, revealing a shortcoming of many presentations of his doctrine of the best of all possible worlds. Within his theodicy, Leibniz distinguishes three types of goodness and three correlative types of evil. *Metaphysical* goodness is simply perfection or reality – the being of God and of all created things; metaphysical evil is the absence of perfection or reality. *Physical* goodness is the pleasure of sentient beings; physical evil, their pain. *Moral* goodness, finally, is the disposition of rational beings to act in a virtuous manner; and moral evil, their disposition to act in a wicked manner.[19] Leibniz assigns a fundamental role to metaphysical goodness, for it is this which God immediately brings into existence. Understood metaphysically, evil is simply a *lack* of this goodness or perfection; hence it is nothing that has been created by God and nothing for which God is causally responsible. Metaphysical evil is the limitation, or imperfection, inherent in the nature of any finite being, and as such it is part of the eternal essence of that being as understood by God. Should God choose to create that thing, he permits its imperfection to exist as part of the best world; yet God's causation is limited to its metaphysical goodness.

The primacy of the metaphysical standpoint for Leibniz gives us an important hold on how to understand the idea of the best of all possible worlds. Most basically, Leibniz conceives of God as disposed to realize the world of greatest metaphysical goodness or perfection, which he does by creating the greatest variety of beings united by the "most fitting" order. This simultaneously leads to the world of greatest *harmony*, which Leibniz defines as "unity in variety." The thesis of a maximization of perfection and harmony is fundamental to Leibniz's conception of the best possible world and brings with it a straightforward answer to the problem of evil: in maximizing metaphysical goodness, God has by that very fact minimized metaphysical evil. Having realized as much perfection as can be realized in the world, God has acted justly.[20]

Yet few would find this a fully satisfying resolution of the problem of evil. In the first place, is it entirely obvious that this is the world of great perfection and harmony? Leibniz arrives at this conclusion by speculating about the kind of world a supremely perfect being would choose to create. But is this consistent with our experience? Here again it is necessary to stress the connection between Leibniz's theodicy and his metaphysics. Like Plato, Leibniz believed that our senses offer only a partial and confused view of reality. To appreciate how this is the world of greatest perfection and harmony, we must rely on reason, which allows us to form an intellectual understanding of reality as it is known by God. As Leibniz intimates in a passage from a summary of his *Theodicy*, he reserves this task for metaphysical theories such as his system of preestablished harmony:

> The infinite wisdom of the Almighty allied with his boundless goodness has brought it about that nothing better could have been created, everything taken into account, than what God has created. As a consequence all things are in perfect harmony and conspire in the most beautiful way: the formal causes or souls with the material causes or bodies, the efficient or natural causes with the final or moral causes, and the realm of grace with the realm of nature. Whenever, therefore, some detail of the world of God appears to us reprehensible, we should judge that we do not know enough about it and that according to the wise who would understand it, nothing better could even be desired. (S 123–4)

A second and more pressing objection concerns the plight of human beings. Even if it can be established that we inhabit the world of greatest perfection and harmony, what relevance does this have for the problem of moral evil and undeserved human suffering? In fathoming Leibniz's answer to this question it is crucial to note, first, the dependence of physical and moral goodness on metaphysical goodness. Leibniz defines pleasure as the "perception of perfection," in oneself or another (MP 146–7). Thus, one necessarily enjoys greater physical goodness to the extent that one perceives greater metaphysical goodness. Moral goodness, on the other hand, is dependent on the perfection of the will, or its degree of metaphysical goodness. But the will, we have seen, is subordinate to the intellect: the will is naturally inclined to choose what the intellect judges to be good. Thus, the moral goodness of a will is proportional to its capacity to apprehend the good, or to the perfection of the understanding. The upshot is that Leibniz embraces the Socratic view that no person ever knowingly does wrong. In general, "evil is like darkness, and not only ignorance but also error and malice consist formally in a certain kind of privation" (*Theodicy*, sec. 32; H 142). Both the wicked person and the person misled by sensual pleasures owe their misdeeds, and their consequent unhappiness, to a deficient knowledge of the good. Correspondingly, an individual will enjoy greater virtue and happiness to the extent that he or she is endowed with greater perfection (a more perfect intellect and will). It does not obviously follow from this that the world with the greatest total perfection is one in which the happiness of human beings is maximized, or that virtue by itself guarantees happiness. Leibniz is committed to both of these claims, but for the moment we must leave them undefended. We will return to them at the end of this chapter.

The topic of creation raises one final important issue. As we have seen, Leibniz maintains that God is the cause of the metaphysical goodness or perfection of created things but not of their metaphysical evil or imperfection. God's contribution to the existence of finite things, however, does not end with the original act of creation. In common with the mainstream of Christian theology, Leibniz holds that God also is responsible for the *conservation* of created things:

> [W]hen it is said that the creature depends upon God in so far as it exists and in so far as it acts, and even that conservation is a continual creation, this is true in that God gives ever to the creature and produces continually all that in it is positive, good and perfect, every perfect gift coming from the Father of lights. (*Theodicy*, sec. 31; H 141)

As Leibniz makes clear in this passage, created things depend upon God not only for their existence but also for their actions, in which God "concurs," "in so far as these actions have some degree of perfection, which must always come from God" (S 115).

To assert the continual dependence of created things on God is to uphold God's majesty, to acknowledge that in relation to God created things are, as it were, nothing. Beneath this expression of piety, though, there lies the threat of a dangerous impiety. If God is causally responsible for everything positive in the actions of created things, do created things really act at all? Might it not be more accurate to say that whatever happens in the world happens as a result of God's action? Malebranche, in his doctrine of occasionalism, embraced this view, affirming that God is the only real cause of change in the world, while at the same time claiming that finite things possess a separate, created existence. Spinoza, on the other hand, drew the more radical conclusion that if finite things remain dependent upon God for their existence and actions, then, in truth, they are not separate substances at all but merely modifications of the one infinite substance, God.

Leibniz walks a fine line in distinguishing his position from those of Malebranche and Spinoza. A well-known passage from the *Monadology* echoes the *Theodicy's* image of God as the "Father of lights," from which all created things "are generated, so to speak, by continual outflashings [*fulgurations*] of the divinity from moment to moment" (sec. 47; AG 219). Yet Leibniz is aware of the dangers inherent in such ways of speaking, how they are liable to lead to the conclusion that finite things are not separate beings created by God, but merely "diffusions" or "emanations" of God's own being. While Leibniz freely employs emanationist imagery, in his late writings he explicitly rejects the doctrine of emanationism:

> The existence of actual things depends upon God . . . since all things have been freely created by God and are maintained in existence by him. There is a sound doctrine which teaches that divine conservation is a continued creation – comparable to the rays continually emitted by the sun – although created things do not emanate from the divine essence or emanate necessarily. (S 115)[21]

The challenge for Leibniz is to explain exactly *how* finite things can remain dependent upon God, while at the same time retaining a separate existence. His solution of this problem is a clarification of the nature of *substance*, the basic form of existence created by God. What Malebranche failed to perceive, in Leibniz's view, was that if created substances are to enjoy an existence separate from God, they must be endowed with an enduring *force*, by which they can sustain their existence through a succession of states. If substances lacked such a force, "it would follow that no created substance, no soul would remain numerically the same, and thus, nothing would be conserved by God, and consequently everything would merely be certain vanishing or unstable modifications and phantasms, so to speak, of one permanent divine substance" (AG 160). The inevitable consequence of Malebranche's occasionalism, therefore, is Spinoza's monism. Leibniz believed he could avoid this fate by claiming that the substances created by God are active beings with the capacity to endure through changes of which they themselves are the causes. This is consistent with the doctrine of divine conservation, in Leibniz's view, since what God maintains in existence is an enduring force having a certain degree of perfection. God concurs in its actions insofar as he conserves the existence of the force itself.

3. Substance and the Kingdom of Nature

The world God creates, then, is a world of substances. As the most basic type of created being, substance has certain essential characteristics. Most importantly, it must be capable of initiating change and of retaining an identity through change. The paradigm of this type of being, for Leibniz, is a soul or "substantial form." Unlike material things, a soul has an intrinsic unity that is not dependent on the arrangement of external parts (of which it has none); hence it is capable of remaining the same through change. Similarly, unlike mere matter, the soul is able to initiate change by virtue of its power of will or appetite. Finally, Leibniz highlights the soul's capacity for perception: its ability to represent the multifarious detail of the universe within the unity of its nature. Throughout his career, one of Leibniz's main philosophical goals is to develop a general theory of nature grounded in these essential properties of substance.[22]

In writings from the 1680s, Leibniz distinguishes substance as a being whose nature is defined by a "complete concept." In section 8 of the *Discourse on Metaphysics*, he writes:

> the nature of an individual substance or of a complete being is to have a notion so complete that it is sufficient to contain and to allow us to deduce from it all the predicates of the subject to which this notion is attributed. . . . God, seeing Alexander's individual notion or haecceity, sees in it at the same time the basis and reason for all the predicates which can be said truly of him, for example, that he vanquished Darius and Porus; [God] even knows *a priori* (and not by experience) whether he died a natural death or whether he was poisoned, something we can know only through history. (AG 41)

Leibniz presents this definition as a consequence of his predicate-in-subject principle: the concept of an individual substance must contain whatever is true of that substance, that is, concepts of all of its predicates – past, present, and future. The above quotation shows that there is also an important theological dimension to the definition. A complete concept is identified with God's knowledge of a substance, which, given his omniscience, includes everything true of it. Leibniz is not simply making a point about divine knowledge, however. Because God creates things exactly as he conceives them, the definition amounts to a claim about what it is to *be* a substance, namely, that substance is an individual whose *nature* is complete. Elaborating his example of Alexander in section 8 of the *Discourse*, Leibniz concludes:

> [W]hen we consider carefully the connection of things, we can say that from all time in Alexander's soul there are vestiges of everything that has happened to him and marks of everything that will happen to him and even traces of everything that happens in the universe, even though God alone could recognize them all. (AG 41)

The doctrine of "marks" and "traces" is the most perplexing part of Leibniz's theory of substance. At a general level, it reflects his commitment to the thesis that in this and every possible world "all is connected" (*Theodicy*, sec. 9; H 128). In the case of substance, this thesis translates into two separate but closely related claims, one concerning causation, the other perception. First, for any substance, there is an intrinsic connection among its successive states. As Leibniz is fond of remarking, each substance is "pregnant with its future," by which he means that it has the power to bring about changes in its own states, which are naturally connected by virtue of following from the same causal principle.[23] Second, Leibniz holds that each substance is endowed with a type of perception, and that there is an intrinsic connection among the contents of its perceptions and those of every other substance: a substance's perceptual states contain "marks" of all its past and future states and "traces" of the perceptual states of every other substance, although these marks and traces are such that only God can reliably relate the different perceptions to each other. Leibniz ascribes these marks and traces to the fact that, as a finite exemplar of God's infinite perfection, every created substance is "confusedly omniscient." As he explains in section 9 of the *Discourse*:

> every substance bears in some way the character of God's infinite wisdom and omnipotence and imitates him as much as it is capable. For it expresses, however confusedly, everything that happens in the universe, whether past, present, or future – and this has some resemblance to an infinite perception or knowledge. (AG 42)

The concept of "expression" plays a critical role in Leibniz's account of the perceptual relations among substances. In a letter to Arnauld, he gives one of his fullest explanations of this notion:

> One thing expresses another, in my usage, when there is a constant and regular relation between what can be said about one and about the other. It is in this way that a projection in perspective expresses a geometric figure. Expression is common to all forms and is a genus of which natural perception, animal feeling, and intellectual knowledge are species. In natural perception and feeling it suffices that what is divisible and material and is found dispersed among several beings should be expressed or represented in a single indivisible being or in a substance which is endowed with a true unity. The possibility of such a representation of several things in one cannot be doubted, since our soul provides us with an example of it. (L 339)

A careful reading of this passage shows that Leibniz uses the term "expression" in two distinct senses. His favorite example of expression is a geometrical projection, in which there is a one-to-one mapping between the points on two curves. In this case, expression implies a relation between two separate sets of entities. When Leibniz applies the term to the faculty of perception, however, he equates expression with an act of mental representation: in perception, what is "divisible and material" is "expressed or represented in a single indivisible being." Although this could be taken to imply a relation between the perceiver and an external world, this is not how Leibniz understands it. The material things expressed in perception are merely *phenomena*. A substance expresses the universe not by directly representing external things but by being created as a unique perspective on a "universal system of phenomena":

> [A]s God turns the universal system of phenomena which he has seen fit to produce in order to manifest his glory, on all sides and in all ways, so to speak, and examines every aspect of the world in every possible manner, there is no relation which escapes his omniscience, and there thus results from each perspective of the universe, as it is seen from a certain position, a substance which expresses the universe in conformity to that perspective, if God sees fit to render his thought effective and to produce that substance. (L 311–12)

Leibniz's account of substance is closely bound up with the attempt to comprehend God's plan for creation. Basic to this plan, he believes, is a system of "universal harmony," formed through the creation of a variety of substances connected through their perceptions of a common universe of phenomena. Universal harmony follows, in Leibniz's philosophy, from the conjunction of three doctrines: completeness, universal expression, and connection. According to Leibniz, each substance expresses a universe of changing phenomena, which it brings about as a result of the completeness of its nature. As he writes in section 14 of the *Discourse*,

> each substance is like a world apart, independent of all other things, except for God; thus all our phenomena, that is, all the things that can ever happen to us, are only consequences of our being. . . . [W]hat happens to each is solely a consequence of its complete idea or notion alone, since this idea already contains all its predicates or events and expresses the whole universe. (AG 47)

In principle, God could have created any substance by itself and it still would have expressed the same phenomena. However, because God desires to create a *world* of substances (and not just any world but the best of all possible worlds), it is necessary that he create a plurality of *connected* substances, for without any connection, it would be just as accurate to say that God had created many worlds rather than one.[24] This connection is realized in the fact that, although each substance is the source of all its own perceptions, substances express the same universe of phenomena. Thus, although they differ qualitatively, the perceptions of different substances "mutually correspond," in much the same way as "several spectators believe that they are seeing the same thing and agree among themselves about it, even though each sees and speaks in accordance with his view" (AG 47).[25] God's strategy for maximizing the perfection of the world is implicit in the description of this scheme.

Understood metaphysically, the best of all possible worlds is the world in which there exists the greatest variety of harmonious perceivers, each individually realizing as much perfection as possible.[26]

The doctrine of universal harmony remains a central component of Leibniz's philosophy until the end of his life. In later writings, however, he ceases to stress the close connection between this doctrine and the complete-concept theory. Under the influence of his work in dynamics, Leibniz emphasizes instead the notion of force, or power, as the key to understanding the nature of substance:

> The concept of *forces* or *powers* . . . brings the strongest light to bear on our understanding of the true concept of *substance*. Active force differs from the mere power familiar to the Schools, for the active power or faculty of the Scholastics is nothing but a proximate possibility of acting, which needs an external excitation or stimulus, as it were, to be transferred into action. Active force, by contrast, contains a certain act or entelechy and is thus midway between the faculty of acting and the act itself and involves conatus. It is thus carried into action by itself and needs no help but only the removal of an impediment. . . . I say that this power of acting inheres in all substance and that some action always arises from it. (L 433)

Leibniz conceives of substance as having more than a capacity or potential to act; rather, it is an active force or "entelechy," from which some change always follows. As before, this change is limited to a substance's internal states and is determined by its own actions. Thus, although Leibniz sets aside the terminology of a "complete concept," he retains the assumption that each substance has a fully determinate nature. This is encapsulated in the thesis that for every substance there is a "law of the series," which dictates the sequence of its states.[27] The endurance, or temporal identity, of the substance is explained by the fact that this law is realized as a "primitive force," from which follows a unique succession of states, each one leading to the next.[28] Defending this view in a letter to De Volder, Leibniz writes:

> The succeeding substance will be considered the same as the preceding as long as the same law of the series or of simple continuous transition persists, which makes us believe in the same subject of change, or the monad. The fact that a certain law persists which involves all of the future states of that which we conceive to be the same – this is the very fact, I say, which constitutes the enduring substance. (L 535)

Leibniz leaves no doubt that these "primitive forces" are the attributes of unextended, soul-like substances. In an earlier letter to De Volder, he declares: "I regard substance itself, being endowed with primitive active and passive power, as an indivisible or perfect monad – like the ego, or something similar to it" (L 529–30). Here he employs his technical term for a substance possessing a "true unity": a *monad*. In the late essay that has become the most popular statement of his philosophy, the *Monadology*, Leibniz defines the monad as "nothing but a simple substance that enters into composites – simple, that is, without parts" (sec. 1).[29] Because of its simplicity, he argues, a monad can only "begin by creation and end by annihilation, whereas composites begin or end through their parts" (sec. 6). For the same reason, there is "no way of explaining how a monad can be altered or changed internally by some other creature"; nothing can pass in or out of monads, for they have "no windows through which something can enter or leave" (sec. 7). Despite their simplicity, however, Leibniz insists that monads must have some internal qualities, in terms of which they undergo change and are distinguished as individuals (secs. 8–9). Furthermore, the monad itself must involve a principle of change, "since no external cause can influence it internally" (sec. 11).

Leibniz limits a monad's qualities, or "intrinsic denominations," to its varying *perceptions* and *appetitions.* He defines perception as the representation of a multitude in the unity or simple substance (sec. 14). A monad's appetitions, on the other hand, are the momentaneous actions "of the internal principle which brings about the change or passage from one perception to another" (sec. 15). Both types of quality mark the monad as essentially soul-like. Indeed, Leibniz writes, "if we wish to call *soul* everything that has *perceptions* and *appetites* . . . then all simple substances or created monads can be called souls" (sec. 18). Yet he adds an important qualification to this. Although some monads are conscious of their perceptions (as in the sensations and thoughts of human beings), perception does not presuppose consciousness. Some monads are conscious of none of their perceptions; and all monads are unconscious of the vast majority of their perceptions. This is because, as we have seen, every created substance is confusedly omniscient:

> [S]ince the nature of the monad is representative, nothing can limit it to represent only a part of things. However, it is true that this representation is only confused as to the detail of the whole universe, and can only be distinct for a small portion of things. . . . Monads are limited, not as to their objects, but with respect to the modifications of their knowledge of them. Monads all go confusedly to infinity, to the whole; but they are limited and differentiated by the degrees of their distinct perceptions. (sec. 60)

A monad's appetitions take the form of strivings for greater perfection, or a greater proportion of distinct perceptions.[30] Every monad, therefore, operates according to the laws of final causation (or teleology): it acts for the sake of what it perceives to be the greatest good. The success of these endeavors is conditioned by the distinctness of a monad's perceptions, which limit its capacity to discriminate greater and lesser goodness. This striving proceeds continuously and without influence from external things. As "entelechies," Leibniz writes, monads have a sufficiency that makes them the sources of their actions, and, so to speak, incorporeal automata" (sec. 18).

In late writings, Leibniz advances the provocative thesis that, understood most fundamentally, reality consists solely of monads and their properties of perception and appetition.[31] These monads all differ from each other in their degrees of perfection, or the extent to which they instantiate the divine perfections of power, knowledge, and will (sec. 48). Among the highest monads are the rational minds of human beings. Lesser monads include the souls of animals, which lack reason but possess sensation, feeling, and memory. The lowest "bare" monads lack even these faculties; their qualities are limited to the basic operations of perception and appetition. An obvious question, which to this point we have left aside, is the status of bodies in this theory. Are bodies, as earlier suggested, merely phenomena, the mind-dependent objects of monadic perception, or do they possess a more substantial existence?

In the period of the *Discourse of Metaphysics* and the correspondence with Arnauld, Leibniz seems to have taken seriously the possibility that in addition to soul-like substances there might also exist *corporeal* substances. These would not be, as Descartes held, purely extended things. By itself, an extended thing lacks the properties of unity and activity essential to a substance. Leibniz instead follows Aristotle in conceiving of corporeal substance as a "hylomorphic" being, in which matter is activated by an immaterial soul or form. The paradigm of such substances are living organisms such as human beings, dogs, and plants. In the case of such creatures, it is natural to think of the mass of the body as animated by a soul-like principle which determines both the identity of the creature through change and its characteristic motion or activity.

Vestiges of the hylomorphic theory remain prominent in Leibniz's later account of substance. They are found at two distinct theoretical levels. First, Leibniz insists that, in contrast to God who is wholly active, every created monad possesses both a primitive active and primitive passive power, the latter of which he designates its "primary matter." Primary matter is understood abstractly as the principle of limitation inherent in the nature of any created being. Leibniz identifies it with a monad's confused perceptions. A monad's primitive active and passive powers are inseparable; they are two aspects of a single entity. By virtue of its active power, a monad strives continuously for the good, or greater perfection; by virtue of its passive power, or confused perceptions, it is limited in what it is able to attain of the good.

In addition to this union of active and passive powers, or form and primary matter, Leibniz maintains that no monad is ever without an organic body (sec. 71). Just as the human soul is the soul *of* a particular body, so all monads have an organic body which they represent as *theirs*.[32] The difficulty is to explain exactly what this body is and how it is related to the soul or monad. One possibility is that a monad's body is nothing more than a special set of phenomena. Leibniz holds that it is characteristic of the perceptions of any substance that it represents the universe from the point of view of a body, whose states it expresses more distinctly than the states of other bodies (sec. 62). This is a primitive feature of our own experience – all things being equal, we represent changes in our own body more immediately and vividly than changes in other bodies – and Leibniz extends this feature to the perceptual content of all monads. There is also, however, a deeper motivation for the view. Leibniz recognizes that it is only possible to define the sort of harmony that makes a set of monads members of a single world *if* it is possible to define their relations with respect to the "universal system of phenomena" that all express. For this, every monad must express itself as having a spatiotemporal position relative to that of every other monad, and this it can do only if it is associated with a body.[33] Significantly, these expressive relations can be defined without any commitment to the substantiality of monads' bodies. All that is required is that every monad represents itself as an embodied creature and that it thereby acquires a position with respect to every other monad within the universe of phenomena.

While this type of phenomenalism forms an important strand in Leibniz's thinking, it does not exhaust his metaphysics. Instead, he consistently maintains that a monad not only represents itself as an embodied creature, but that it *has* a body, which is an actual mass, or "secondary matter," distinct from the perceiving monad or soul. The best known part of Leibniz's theory of the soul–body relationship is his "system of preestablished harmony," first published in the 1695 paper "A New System of the Nature and Communication of Substances" (AG 138–45). Leibniz advanced his "new system" as a response to what he saw as irreparable problems in the Cartesian account of the mind–body relationship. When Descartes proposed his account of the human being as composed of two kinds of substance, mind and body, he assumed that these two substances interact causally: stimulation of sensory organs produces sensations in the mind and volition initiates motion in the body. However, Descartes was unable to explain how two such different kinds of substance *could* interact. At this point, Leibniz remarks, "Descartes had given up the game" (AG 143). It was left to Malebranche to offer a plausible Cartesian account of mind–body communication. Since, according to occasionalism, God is the only real cause of change in the world, there is no special mystery about how the mind and body are able to interact. To say that the mind and body are "occasional causes" of each others' effects is just to say that there are lawlike correlations between their states, or that certain states of one substance are "occasions" for God to bring about changes in the state of the other.

We have seen that Leibniz has general reasons associated with the doctrine of divine conservation and the nature of substance for rejecting Malebranche's occasionalism. In the case of the mind–body relationship, however, he lays greatest emphasis on occasionalism's failure to account for the wisdom God has exercised in creation. A world in which God was required to perform "perpetual miracles," bringing about changes in the states of the mind and the body, would not be a world worthy of God's wisdom. A much better world, in Leibniz's view, would be one in which the natures of created things were sufficient to bring about all of their own effects, thus relieving God of the necessity of intervening in the course of nature. Leibniz believes he has discovered the design of this world in his system of preestablished harmony. According to his account, the mind and the body do not interact; nor does God bring about changes in one in response to changes in the other. Instead, God has created the mind and the body such that each brings about the appropriate changes in itself through laws intrinsic to its nature. The mind brings about changes in its states through laws of appetite, or final causation; the body undergoes changes in its states in accordance with the laws of physics, or efficient causation. The crucial claim of the system of preestablished harmony is that within a single human being God has arranged that these changes occur in perfect synchrony, such that changes in the state of the mind *appear* to bring about changes in the state of the body and vice versa.

Leibniz goes on to develop his system of preestablished harmony as a general theory of nature. Extrapolating from the mind–body relationship, he maintains that nature as a whole is composed of souls (or monads) paired with organic bodies, each operating according to its own laws. Thus, there is realized a global harmony between two autonomous "kingdoms" – that of final causes and that of efficient causes (sec. 79). Rather than competing with his theory of monads, this picture of nature completes the theory and shows how it is realized within the best of all possible worlds. To demonstrate this requires one further step in the analysis of the concept of body. The system of preestablished harmony is a corollary of Leibniz's general account of substance as a "complete" being – one with a nature sufficient to determine all its own states. The soul, we know, is a paradigmatic Leibnizian substance. By itself, however, the body is not a substance. In Leibniz's view, the body of a living creature is an *aggregate* composed of an infinity of smaller bodies, each endowed with its own soul or "dominant monad" (sec. 70). As a composite of smaller creatures to infinity, a body lacks the intrinsic unity of a substance. Thus, the central thesis of preestablished harmony – the causal self-sufficiency of substance – can only apply indirectly in the case of bodies. For bodies to satisfy the conditions of preestablished harmony, they must be constituted from soul-like substances. As Leibniz elaborates his view, any portion of matter is composed of a multitude of living creatures, each consisting of a monad plus an organic body (secs. 66–7). As these bodies and all of their parts are formed in exactly the same way, in the limit the bodies of monads consist of nothing but more monads:

> [A]n organic body, like every other body, is merely an aggregate of animals or other things which are living and therefore organic, or finally of small objects or masses; but these also are finally resolved into living things, from which it is evident that all bodies are finally resolved into living things, and that what, in the analysis of substances, exist ultimately are simple substances – namely souls, or, if you prefer a more general term, *monads*, which are without parts. (MP 175)[34]

In Leibniz's final theory, both the reality and causal activity of bodies are ascribed to the fact that bodies are infinite pluralities of monads. As they are represented by finite minds, these monads appear as extended things that act in accordance with the laws of physics. With the help of the intellect, however, we are able to understand these bodies for what they really are: unextended monads.[35] Thus, Leibniz is able to preserve the thesis that, from the most fundamental point of view, reality consists solely of monads, although he supplements this with the claim that in the best of all possible worlds every monad is dominant with respect to an infinity of lesser monads, which it represents as its body.[36]

4. Rational Beings and the Kingdom of Grace

Although all monads possess the same basic properties of perception and appetition, the minds of human beings (and more elevated angelic creatures) are distinguished by their capacity for reason, or "the knowledge of eternal and necessary truths" (sec. 29). Leibniz ascribes this capacity to the fact that the mental representations of minds include an immediate awareness (or "apperception") of their own nature. This awareness consists of

> reflective acts, which enable us to think of that which is called 'I' and enable us to consider that this or that is in us. And thus, in thinking of ourself, we think of being, of substance, of the simple and of the composite, of the immaterial and of God himself, by conceiving that that which is limited in us is limitless in him. And these reflective acts furnish the principal objects of our reasonings. (sec. 30)

The capacity for reason creates a significant divide between minds and other monads. Through the knowledge they are able to form of mathematics and metaphysics, minds acquire a new perspective on the world. Whereas monads in general are limited to expressing the universal system of phenomena, minds in addition possess intellectual knowledge that expresses the content of God's understanding. In Leibniz's words, they are "images of the divinity itself, or of the author of nature, capable of knowing the system of the universe, and of imitating something of it through their schematic representations of it, each mind being like a little divinity in its own realm" (sec. 83).

Along with this knowledge comes a moral identity that other monads also lack. By virtue of their knowledge, Leibniz argues, minds are "capable of entering into a kind of society with God," who in relation to them is "not only what an inventor is to his machine (as God is in relation to the other creatures) but also what a prince is to his subjects, and even what a father is to his children" (sec. 84). Because rational beings are able to understand the fundamental laws of justice, they are able to appreciate the rightness of God's plan for creation (the goal of Leibniz's theodicy) and to act on the same principles in their dealings with other rational beings. United with each other and with their creator through the common bonds of justice, rational beings form "a moral world within the natural world" (sec. 86). Following Augustine, Leibniz designates this "moral world" as the "city of God," or "the most perfect possible state under the most perfect of monarchs" (sec. 85).

The realization of the "city of God," a world in which rational beings live and act according to the principles of justice, represents the crowning achievement of creation. "The glory of God truly consists in this city," Leibniz writes, "for he would have none if his greatness and goodness were not known and admired by minds" (sec. 86). Yet Leibniz is clear that the city of God is an achievement that must be won through the efforts of rational beings, and that innumerable obstacles stand in the way of its realization. Here, finally, we return to the problem of evil. In Leibniz's view, the fact that the city of God is "the highest and most divine of God's works" does not imply that God has created human beings so that they may enjoy unlimited virtue and happiness. Although the city of God is the most glorious of God's works, it is not the principal goal of creation (*Theodicy*, sec. 118; H 188). That is to produce the greatest possible perfection, which is achieved by producing the greatest variety of creatures ordered in the most fitting manner. The priority of this goal entails that God may create rational beings whose degrees of perfection limit their ability to act virtuously, and that he may even sacrifice the happiness of rational beings for the sake of the perfection of the whole. Although the explosion of a volcano or the flourishing of a bacterium may cut short the happiness of a human being, these may be legitimate means to achieving the greatest total perfection.

No human being, therefore, can count on the best of all possible worlds being an earthly paradise. Nevertheless, Leibniz believes that we have good reason to maintain an optimistic attitude toward the fate of humanity. In addition to the general providence that governs the world as a whole, God exercises a special justice with respect to minds. Although rational beings do not always act in a virtuous manner, the laws of justice dictate that no virtuous person should suffer in spite of their virtue and no wicked person should profit from their crimes. Consequently, whenever an imbalance occurs between virtue and happiness, justice demands that a correction be made. Leibniz's principal claim concerning this justice is that it is carried out through the mechanism of nature itself:

> God the architect pleases in every respect God the legislator, and, as a result, sins must carry their penalty with them by the order of nature, and even in virtue of the mechanical structure of things. Similarly, noble actions will receive their rewards through mechanical means with regard to bodies, even though this cannot, and must not, always happen immediately. (sec. 89)

Along with the harmony between the two "natural kingdoms" of efficient causes and final causes, therefore, there is realized a final harmony between the "physical kingdom of nature" and the "moral kingdom of grace" (sec. 87).

Leibniz is committed to the proposition that the world of greatest perfection is also the world of greatest happiness and virtue (AG 210). Conscious of the extent to which human beings lack these qualities, he does not claim that the world at present contains all the happiness that it could contain. The defining characteristic of the best of all possible worlds, instead, is that there is the potential for unlimited improvement in the human condition, which Leibniz argues is intrinsically better than a static state of contentment. As he writes in the *Principles of Nature and Grace*, "our happiness will never consist, and must never consist, in complete joy, in which nothing is left to desire, and which would dull our mind, but must consist in a perpetual progress to new pleasures and new perfections" (AG 213). Stirred by the discoveries of the scientific revolution, Leibniz is convinced that opportunities for greater knowledge and technological advancement are limitless, and that these in turn will lead to greater happiness and, ultimately, moral improvement. The latter, however, cannot be seen as a consequence of scientific and technological progress alone. Rather, moral progress presupposes that we understand these accomplishments in relation to God's design of the best of all possible worlds. Acknowledging the justice God has exercised in creation, we must endeavor to exhibit the same justice in our own actions, finding our greatest happiness in the contemplation of the perfection of the world and the contributions we are able to make to it. Only when we see ourselves as citizens of the city of God, acting on the timeless decrees of divine justice, will we enjoy the full fruits of creation (sec. 90).

Notes

1 For further biographical details, see Roger Ariew, "G. W. Leibniz, Life and Works," in *The Cambridge Companion to Philosophy*, ed. Nicholas Jolley (Cambridge: Cambridge University Press, 1995). A briefer account can be found in my article "Gottfried Wilhelm Leibniz," in *The Columbia History of Western Philosophy*, ed. Richard Popkin (New York: Columbia University Press, 1999), pp. 396–404.

2 See Donald Rutherford, "The Newton–Leibniz Controversy," in *The Columbia History of Western Philosophy*, pp. 430–7.

3 G. W. Leibniz, *Philosophical Papers and Letters*, tr. Leroy E. Loemker (Dordrecht: Reidel, 1969), pp. 654–5. Subsequent citations of this volume are abbreviated L followed by page number(s).

4 G. W. Leibniz, *Philosophical Essays*, tr. Roger Ariew and Daniel Garber (Indianapolis: Hackett, 1989), p. 217. Subsequent citations of this volume are abbreviated AG followed by page number(s).

5 G. W. Leibniz, *Theodicy*, tr. E. M. Huggard (La Salle: Open Court, 1985), p. 419. Subsequent citations of this volume are abbreviated H followed by page number(s).

6 To Arnauld, Leibniz writes: "in every true affirmative proposition, whether necessary or contingent, universal or particular, the notion of the predicate is in some way contained in that of the subject. *Praedicatum inest subjecto*; otherwise I do not know what truth is" (L 337). See also *Discourse on Metaphysics*, sec. 8 (AG 41).

7 See *Discourse on Metaphysics*, sec. 9 (AG 41–2) and his remarks on Arnauld's first letter, which responded to Leibniz's summary of the *Discourse* (AG 76).

8 Bertrand Russell, *A Critical Exposition of the Philosophy of Leibniz* (1900); Louis Couturat, *La Logique de Leibniz* (Paris: Félix Alcan, 1901).

9 Controversy continues over whether Leibniz's infinite analysis theory can adequately explain the basis of contingent truth. In his correspondence with Arnauld, Leibniz maintains that in contingent propositions the connection between the subject and predicate terms is "intrinsic" but not necessary, since it depends upon God's "free decrees and acts." See AG 76; L 336–7. For recent discussions of this topic, see Sleigh, *Leibniz and Arnauld* (New Haven: Yale University Press, 1990), ch. 4 and Adams, *Leibniz: Determinist, Theist, Idealist* (Oxford: Oxford University Press, 1994), ch. 1.

10 See *New Essays on Human Understanding*, tr. Peter Remnant and Jonathan Bennett (Cambridge: Cambridge University Press, 1981), p. 397. Subsequent citations of this volume are abbreviated RB followed by page number(s).

11 "The very *possibility* of things, when they do not actually exist, has a reality grounded in the divine existence: for if God should not exist, there would be no possibility, and possible things are from eternity in the ideas of the divine intellect." *Causa Dei*, sec. 8, in G. W. Leibniz, *Monadology and Other Philosophical Essays*, tr. Paul Schrecker and Anne Martin Schrecker (Indianapolis: Bobbs-Merrill, 1965), p. 115. Subsequent citations of this volume are abbreviated S followed by page number(s). See also *Theodicy*, sec. 184 (H 243–4); *Monadology*, secs. 43–4 (AG 218); and the discussion in Adams,

Leibniz: Determinist, Theist, Idealist, ch. 7.

12 *Die Leibniz-Handschriften der Königlichen Öffentlichen Bibliothek zu Hannover*, ed. Eduard Bodemann (Hannover, 1889; repr. Hildesheim: Olms, 1966), p. 58.

13 This is obvious in the case of actual individuals, for God's decision to create this world provides the ultimate reason for the existence of any substance and its properties. But it is also true for any possible individual, since, according to Leibniz, the contingent properties of such individuals presuppose certain free decrees of God, which determine the particular order of their world: "[T]he possibilities of individuals or of contingent truths contain in their concept the possibility of their causes, that is, of the free decrees of God in which they differ from the possibilities of species or eternal truths, which depend upon God's understanding alone without presupposing his will. . . . I conceive that there was an infinite number of possible ways of creating the world according to the different plans that God could form, and that each possible world depends upon . . . certain primary free decrees (conceived as possible) or laws of the general order of that possible universe to which they are suited and whose concept they determine, as well as the concepts of all the individual substances which must enter into this same universe." *The Leibniz–Arnauld Correspondence*, tr. H. T. Mason (Manchester: Manchester University Press, 1967), pp. 56–7. Subsequent citations of this volume are abbreviated M followed by page number(s).

14 See e.g. the preface to the *New Essays* (AG 297).

15 See the opening of his unpublished *Resumé of Metaphysics*: "There is a reason in Nature why something exists rather than nothing. This is a consequence of the great principle that nothing happens without a reason, and also that there must be a reason why this thing exists rather than another." G. W. Leibniz, *Philosophical Writings*, tr. M. Morris and G. H. R. Parkinson (London: Everyman, 1973), p. 145. Subsequent citations of this volume are abbreviated MP followed by page number(s).

16 For succinct presentations of this argument, see *On the Ultimate Origination of Things* (AG 149–50) and *Monadology*, secs. 36–8, 45 (AG 217–18).

17 This conclusion is summarized in *Monadology*, sec. 45 (AG 218). For a detailed discussion of Leibniz's treatment of the ontological argument, see Adams, *Leibniz: Determinist, Theist, Idealist*, chs. 5 and 6.

18 See *Theodicy*, sec. 22 (H 136–7) and sec. 367 (H 345); "Observations of the Book Concerning 'The Origin of Evil'," secs 1–3 (H 405–8)

19 *Theodicy*, sec. 21 (H 136).

20 For a fuller account of these issues, see Rutherford, *Leibniz and the Rational Order of Nature* (Cambridge: Cambridge University Press, 1997), chs. 1–2.

21 By contrast, compare his earlier *Discourse on Metaphysics*: "[I]t is very evident that created substances depend upon God, who preserves them and who even produces them continually by a kind of emanation, just as we produce our thoughts" (sec. 14; AG 46).

22 For a complete account of Leibniz's doctrine of substance and its relation to his theory of nature, see Rutherford, *Leibniz and the Rational Order of Nature*, chs. 6–10.

23 *Monadology*, sec. 22 (AG 216).

24 In a published reply to the criticisms of Pierre Bayle, Leibniz writes: "God could give to each substance its own phenomena independently of those of others, but in this way he would have made as many worlds without connection, so to speak, as there are substances" (L 493).

25 Significantly, the "mutual correspondence" or "harmony" of perceptions also counts as

a species of expression, understood as "a constant and regular relation between what can be said about one and about the other." Leibniz uses the term in this sense, which more closely approximates his example of a geometrical projection, when he writes to Arnauld: "This expression takes place everywhere, because every substance sympathizes with all the others and receives a proportional change corresponding to the slightest change that occurs in the whole world" (L 339). See also *Monadology*, sec. 59 (AG 220).

26 *Monadology*, sec. 57–8 (AG 220).

27 "In my opinion it is the nature of created substance to change continually following a certain order which leads it spontaneously . . . through all the states which it encounters, in such a way that he who sees all things sees all its past and future states in its present. And this law of order . . . constitutes the individuality of each particular substance" (L 493).

28 "Derivative force is itself the present state when it tends toward or preinvolves a following state, as every present is great with the future. But that which persists, insofar as it involves all cases, contains primitive force, so that primitive force is the law of the series, as it were, while derivative force is the determinate value which distinguishes some term in the series" (L 533).

29 Where no title is indicated parenthetical citations refer to sections of the *Monadology*. All quotations are from the translation of Ariew and Garber (AG 213–25).

30 *Principles of Nature and Grace*, sec. 13 (AG 211).

31 See, for example, AG 181–2, 185, 189, 227, 319.

32 See *Theodicy*, "Preliminary Discourse," sec. 10 (H 80), and sec. 130 (H 202).

33 See *New Essays*, II, xv, 11 (RB 155).

34 Cf. AG 147.

35 "It is necessary to consider that matter, understood as a *complete being* . . . is only an aggregate of things, or what results from it, and that every *real aggregate* presupposes *simple substances* or *real unities*; and if one bears in mind what constitutes the nature of these real unities – that is, *perception* and its series of states – one is transported into another world, so to speak; from having existed entirely amongst the *phenomena of the senses*, one comes to occupy the *intelligible world of substances*. And this knowledge of the inner nature of matter shows well enough what it is naturally capable of." *New Essays*, IV, iii, 6 (RB 378–9).

36 See *Principles of Nature and Grace*, sec. 3 (AG 207).

Chapter 6

John Locke

Martha Brandt Bolton

Because John Locke's father fought for the Puritan cause, his son was admitted to the leading school in England. The son went on to Oxford, where he successfully completed the course of study, but reported finding little of value in the curriculum. Interested in medicine, he grew familiar with innovative mechanist treatises on natural philosophy by Descartes, Gassendi, and Boyle. It was during this period that, meeting with five or six friends, Locke formed the project of investigating human understanding. As he recalls in his letter to the reader of the *Essay*, difficulties quickly brought their discussion to an impasse, which made him think that "before we set our selves upon Enquiries of that Nature, it was necessary to examine our own Abilitys, and see, what Objects our Understandings were, or were not fitted to deal with" (E 7:14–33).[1] We have two drafts of a treatise on human understanding from the year 1671, and one considerably longer draft from 1685, but the published version did not appear until late 1689–90.

In the meantime, Locke was swept up in dramatic events that ensued after he joined the staff of Anthony Ashley Cooper (later Earl of Shaftesbury). Cooper ranked high among advisers to the newly restored king, but as the monarch's allegiance to France remained firm while French intolerance of Protestants surged, and relations with Parliament deteriorated, Cooper helped instigate a plot to depose the British king. Scholars believe Locke's famous tract, later published as *Second Treatise of Civil Government*, was intended as a defense of the planned revolution. In fact, it never occurred. The plot was discovered, Cooper immediately fled Britain for his life, and Locke took refuge in Holland within the year. While in exile, he turned again to his work on human understanding. When he returned in 1690, William and Mary, sovereigns of tolerant Holland, had been installed as monarchs of Britain. Now unemployed, Locke assumed duties within the new government and became a trusted adviser to the king. He revised five successive editions of the *Essay* before his death in 1704, and twice defended it from attack for undermining religion and morality. His main literary projects during this time were tracts on education and matters touching religion, including

The Reasonableness of Christianity, which advocates minimal articles of the Christian faith.[2]

The *Second Treatise* is a powerful argument for the social contract theory of political obligation and authority, which had significant influence on the political theories of the American and French revolutions. Thomas Jefferson hung Locke's portrait in his study at Monticello. Since the eighteenth century, the treatise has repeatedly been cited in defense of individual freedom although recent libertarians have found its defense somewhat limited. His essays on toleration and education were important in Enlightenment thought. But the broad cultural significance of the *Essay Concerning Human Understanding* is even more pervasive. A work with great popular appeal, it nevertheless deals systematically with the spectrum of difficult issues at the core of modern philosophical thought. I have chosen to focus on it in this chapter.

1. The Overall Project of the *Essay*

Locke hopes, in the Introduction, that readers will find the *Essay* useful in the pursuit of truth. We are portrayed as naturally inclined to seek the truth. Endowed, as humans are, with the faculty of understanding, we are expected to use it. Since we cannot avoid having opinions about how to conduct our lives, this is foremost among questions we need to examine (I, i, 5, 6). But rational creatures have a more general obligation regarding belief and disbelief. As far as circumstances allow, each individual ought to form opinions on the basis of her own examination of evidence, rather than taking them on trust from some supposed authority. It is demeaning "to live lazily on scraps of begg'd Opinions" (E 6; also I, iv, 23; 100–1).[3] Why did Locke think the *Essay* might be helpful to us in conducting our capacity for understanding?

The book aims "to search out the *Bounds* between Opinion and Knowledge," and the "Measures [by which] . . . we ought to regulate our Assent" when we lack certainty (I, i, 3). Human understanding comprises all our cognitive abilities: sense perception, reflection, memory, judgment, reasoning, imagining, and so on. But it was not as if others in the seventeenth century, and before, had not proposed theories of knowledge in the context of psychological theory. Consider Descartes, for example. In *Meditations*, he urges that indubitably certain knowledge is the product of intellect, a faculty capable of clear and distinct perception, which he sharply distinguishes from sense and imagination. Unlike the senses, pure intellect has innate ideas and it can exist and operate completely separated from matter and the senses. In taking a psychologically grounded approach to the nature of knowledge, Locke was by no means unique.

Still he defines his subject a little differently than his predecessors did. He will not "meddle with the Physical Consideration of the Mind" – that is, causal questions. And he proposes to use the "Historical, plain method," that is, to trace the development of cognitive faculties from infancy on (I, i, 2). His subject is perception, knowledge, and judgment insofar as they are conscious processes, which are more or less coherent or rational. To discover them, we are to reflect on what we do ourselves and observe how others speak and act (I, iv, 25; 103:5–11). This reflects the experimental orientation of the recently founded British Royal Society to which Locke belonged.

The significance of this method lies also in the fact that seventeenth-century authors had produced widely discrepant reports of human cognitive abilities. Descartes and Malebranche, among others, claimed we have the ability to comprehend abstract entities, essences, and ideal objects which cannot exist in the material, sensible world. They taught that cognition of such things grounds scientific knowledge in mathematics, physics, and morals.[4] Hobbes, in contrast, held that we have no abstract or universal conceptions, but instead have only the ability to use general names. The dispute was regarded as sensitive. Some charged materialists like Hobbes with degrading human nature, while Hobbes thought the others were driven by superstition. A catalogue of human cognitive abilities was subject to scrutiny in light of controversial issues.

Locke bases his account on nothing but experiences readily available to all. He chides the Cartesians: by insisting that the mind is always consciously thinking, they make people question whether they have properly functioning minds (II, i, 19; 115:26–116:15). Better to admit ignorance of our essential nature than insist on a doctrine that strikes most people as dubious. Human understanding, on his theory, is stripped of mystery.

His examination culminates, in Book IV, by identifying a significant domain in which we can secure knowledge and certainty, as well as considerable scope for reasonable judgment. These positive results confirm that our natural faculties suffice for certainty about what concerns us most: the means to enhance our comfort and convenience and the principles of morality (I, i, 5; 45; also IV, xii, 11; IV, xxi). But on the negative side, "the vast ocean of *Being* . . . [is not] the undoubted Possession of our Understandings" (I, i, 7). While Book IV proposes measures to increase the scope of our knowledge, it also identifies impassable barriers.

Book I of the *Essay* attacks the doctrine of innate knowledge and ideas in versions widely accepted in Locke's time. The account of knowledge, its scope and limits, is deferred to Book IV. Locke wants first to examine the materials from which we assemble the assertions, or propositions, we know. These "materials of Reason and Knowledge" are "Ideas" (for example, II, i, 1–2; 104). Book II urges, against the innatists, that all our ideas are extracted from experience; Locke is an empiricist about ideas. Along the way, the various sorts of ideas we have are reviewed.

Book III deals with the signification of words. It was necessary to clarify how words are related to ideas before tackling the grounds of our knowledge of propositional truths, since it is only by expressing propositions verbally that we can discuss them. Locke contends that many philosophers have an erroneous theory of how the general names in a sentence like "Man is an animal" signify things. The point affects what is required for knowledge of the true propositions sentences express. Moreover the mistake in theory of language licenses abuses that create confusion, but nonetheless "pass for erudition." Locke aims to expose this pernicious pretense. Here he gives voice to a view of the purpose of philosophy in the new era of modern theoretical science. Not one of the "Master-Builders" of physics or chemistry, he works as an "Under-Labourer . . . clearing the rubbish that lies in the way of knowledge" (9:34–10:26).

All is in place in Book IV for the theory of human knowledge and its limits. In outline, the account of what distinguishes knowledge from mere opinion goes like this. Consider, for example, the proposition expressed by "A triangle is a three-sided figure." The proposition is composed of the ideas immediately signified by the words that compose the sentence – the ideas expressed by "triangle" and "three-sided figure." To entertain the proposition is to perform a mental act of "joining" the ideas, an act expressed by "is." Once you perform this act, you know the proposition is true if you find evidential basis for uniting the ideas as you have. Locke describes this as "perception of the connexion and agreement, or disagreement and repugnancy of [the] ideas" (IV, i, 2). In the case of our example, evidence of the connection comes from the ideas themselves. They make the proposition true. No one could entertain the proposition and fail to understand its truth. Locke calls this self-evidence, or "intuitive knowledge." With some other propositions, evidence is not immediate in this way, but comes from a series of intermediate ideas that connect the two that compose a proposition, for example, "The sum of the angles of a triangle equal two right angles" (see IV, i, 1–7). In this case, knowledge is "demonstrative." On Locke's theory, you know a proposition if you perceive its evident truth, either immediately or by intermediary ideas. Perception of this sort is an act in which understanding is achieved rather like seeing something to be the case with your eyes (for example, IV, ii, 1).[5] Locke recognizes a third sort of knowledge, sense perception of particular things; we will say more about it in section 6. So far, we have just an overview of the *Essay* and how each of the four books has a part in it.

2. Ideas: Immediate Objects of Awareness

At every stage, Locke speaks of ideas. Ideas are also central in Descartes's philosophy, and that of most other prominent philosophers of the seventeenth century. But although Locke accepted a general picture of what ideas are, he developed it in quite an original way. This helps to explain many of his disagreements with other early moderns.

For Locke, ideas are "immediate objects" of perception (II, viii, 7; 134:17; IV, xxi, 4; 721:3–5) or "Object[s] of the Understanding" (I, i, 8; 47:30). They are within us, in the sense that they depend on our awareness of them. Notice that, nevertheless, Locke does not deny that thought and perception normally reach beyond ideas. He does not deny that the objects of thought and perception exist, independently of us, in the world (for example, I, i, 3). By being immediately aware of ideas, we become aware of other things and events.

Unlike with Descartes, Locke's ideas are entirely inseparable from the mind's awareness of them.[6] As object of awareness, an idea exists only if the mind is aware of it and even then it is nothing but what the mind takes it to be: "'Tis the first Act of the Mind, . . . to perceive its *Ideas*, and so far as it perceives them to know each what it is, and thereby also to perceive their difference, and that one is not another" (IV, i, 4). It is true that he sometimes says ideas "exist in the mind" and he refers to them as "objects," but all he means is that we are, or can be, immediately aware of ideas when the occasion arises (II, x, 2).

It is obvious, he seems to think, that we need ideas in order to know other things (for example, IV, iv, 3). This point is made explicitly in the end: "For since the Things, the Mind contemplates, are none of them, besides it self, present to the Understanding, 'tis necessary that something else, as a Sign or Representation of the thing it considers, should be present to it: And these are *Ideas*" (IV, xxi, 4:720–1). Ideas are "present" in two ways: they are dependent on the mind and they can be brought to awareness when occasion demands. External things, such as a horse, are not present in the first way, but why not the second? Couldn't a mind think of a horse without immediate awareness of an internal entity that represents it? This issue was disputed throughout the modern period, and the need for some sort of internal representations that fix objects of thought continues to be debated nowadays. Locke's position probably comes from his anti-innatism coupled with his theory of sense perception. It is not controversial that when you perceive a horse, it causes some sort of effect on your sensory system. According to Locke, it causes sensory ideas, sensations that signify or represent their external cause. Later on when you think of the horse in its absence, Locke supposes, you bring back to mind these ideas which represent the horse. He extends the model. You direct thought to an object never encountered in experience by immediate awareness of an idea that represents it – this time one constructed from ideas supplied by experience.

This seems a plausible view of what occurs during sense perception (to focus on that, for the present). But recent critics, perhaps reacting to the twentieth-century theory of sense data, question whether perception of outer objects is mediated by sensations. Instead some urge that objects cause preconscious psychological effects that eventually result in direct awareness of and judgment about outer objects and their sensible qualities. But to Locke, it is obvious that perception involves sensation, as well as judgment about external things. When you stroke a cat, on his view, you feel sensations of softness and warmth because of which you take the cat to be soft and warm. Nowadays the dispute over whether perception is mediated by sensations is left mainly to empirical psychology. There are at least two important questions about Locke's position.[7] What sort of signs or representations are sensory ideas supposed to be? How do they lead to judgments about outer things?

More will be said about the first question in section 7 (below) on representation and reality. As for the second, Locke says nothing explicit about the complete act of sense perception: how immediate awareness of ideas enables judgments about external things. This omission is one fact, among others, that led some to make the "veil of ideas" charge. We immediately perceive ideas, but they are in us, so how do we know things outside us?

In one version, the charge is that we are trapped, because we cannot even form an idea that represents an "external" object that is more than a mere collection of our own sensations or sense impressions. This charge was made by Berkeley and elaborated by Hume,[8] but it assumes a view of ideas rather different from Locke's. As we will see, he is best understood as holding that sensory ideas have an essential representative character, in that they essentially make it seem as if there are outer objects. In contrast, his empiricist successors explicitly maintain that sensory ideas (Hume's impressions) are not representations, but mere sensations. In a different version of the "veil," it is granted that we have ideas of external things, but the charge is that immediate awareness of ideas fails to provide any assurance that they exist.[9] We will consider in section 9 (below) how Locke defends his claim that we have sensory knowledge of the real existence of particular things.

Ideas are the "materials" of all sorts of cognitive activity, not just sense perception, but also theoretical reasoning, deliberating, day-dreaming, etc. Much of Books I and II are concerned with laying out Locke's distinctive views on several questions: whether ideas are acquired from experience, how ideas represent, and what they represent.

3. Against Innate Knowledge

The view that we are created with innate knowledge of the principles of morality and the theoretical sciences was urged by many early modern philosophers. It was widely disseminated in popular tracts and sometimes taught from the pulpit. Locke was wary of the authoritarian uses to which the doctrine might be put (see I, iv, 24). But he mainly doubted its truth. He mounted a reasoned attack on it. He begins with speculative (logical or scientific) principles, taking as an example the logical principle of identity, "whatever is, is." Moral principles are postponed to the following chapter.

One issue is how to understand the claim that a principle is innately "stamped on the mind." Locke begins with a crude response: innate propositions are "constant Impressions, which the Souls of Men receive in their first Beings," and as a consequence, these propositions are "agreed upon by all Mankind" (I, ii, 2). Children and idiots suffice to refute this. But most innatists have a more tenable view. Leibniz, in *New Essays concerning Human Understanding*, pointed out that there is nothing mysterious in the fact that a mind possesses ideas during intervals when it is not aware of them. Locke, himself, says ideas are "stored in memory." In a dispositional sense, a mind "has" an idea if it is able to be aware of it given the right context. According to Leibniz and many others, what is innate are dispositions to bring certain propositions to mind.[10]

Locke attacks this version of innatism, too. If the doctrine that a maxim is innate has any importance, he argues, it must come to something more than the claim that humans have the capacity to assent to the maxim. Otherwise the dispute will be over nothing (I, ii, 5; 50). How, then, do Locke and dispositional innatists disagree?

Locke contends that we construct the logical maxim from materials supplied by experience. First we perceive particular things by sense; then we form general ideas by abstraction from similar particulars, proceeding from less to more general ideas by further abstraction (see I, ii, 15–16). The idea of being, or "what is," is among the very most general. So a child will not assent to the principle of identity until well along in her cognitive development; she will assent first to many less general identical propositions, for example, "Sweet is sweet." In contrast, Locke's opponents maintain that the maxim is available to the mind without this sort of constructive work. We are innately disposed to bring the maxim fully formed into explicit awareness although, as they insist, the right context is needed for this. Locke demands to be told what this context is; perhaps an innatist might say, a child's attaining the "use of reason." But according to Locke, this conflicts with what we observe about the order in which children assent to various propositions (I, ii, 6–14 and 17–18). He is right that the issue has to be settled empirically, but he had little detailed evidence about the development of cognitive skills. Innatism (or nativism) remains a controversial issue in current linguistics and psychology.

Beyond this question, however, Locke argues that innatism is useless as a theory of knowledge, or the rational ground of assent. He grants there is "universal assent," if that means that all humans assent to the logical maxims "at first hearing and understanding their Terms" (I, ii, 17–23). For this to happen, a person must frame the maxim, and anyone who entertained the proposition "Whatever is, is" could not help but perceive its truth. It is intuitively known. As Locke urges in Book IV, the fact that the maxim is self-evident is the rational ground for affirming it.[11] As far as theory of knowledge is concerned, then, there is nothing for innatism to explain.

In the seventeenth century, the most common form of innatism concerned moral principles; indeed, it was often supposed that they are so innately ingrained as to be self-evident. But if they were self-evident, then everyone who understands them would assent to them, as we have just seen. On the contrary, Locke argues, all too often people question moral rules and openly flaunt them. In fact, "there cannot any one moral Rule be propos'd, whereof a Man may not justly demand a Reason" (I, iii, 4; 68). Examples of moral rules are that we ought to be charitable or act justly. Locke does not doubt that such rules can be demonstrated. His argument is that we need reasons before we assent to them; that means we assent to them because of reasoning, which in turn implies that they are not innate. This argument can be questioned. Leibniz challenged the assumption that nothing learned by a process of reasoning is innate.[12] But perhaps the most glaring weakness in Locke's position is that he never showed just how to demonstrate a moral rule.

4. Ideas Acquired from Experience

Locke's theory of the origin of ideas concerns ideas in the sense of dispositions. The question how a mind gets its idea of *x* is the question how it gets its ability to consider, conceive, or otherwise think of *x*. The main thesis of Book II is that all ideas we have, all our abilities to think of specific things, can be acquired from experience. Locke assumes that if ideas can be acquired from experience, then it would be pointlessly redundant if they were innate (see I, ii, 1).

Experience takes two forms: "Our Observation emply'd either about *external, sensible Objects; or about the internal Operations of our Minds, perceived and reflected on by ourselves*" (II, i, 2). The first is perception by the five senses. The second is reflection which makes us aware of our own thinking, perceiving, doubting, willing, and the like. Locke contends: "In all that great Extent wherein the mind wanders, in those remote Speculations, it may seem to be elevated with, it stirs not one jot beyond those *Ideas*, which *Sense* or *Reflection*, have offered for its Contemplation" (II, i, 24; 118:14–17). To make this more precise, Locke draws several distinctions among ideas.

Ideas are either simple or compound (II, ii). Simple ideas are "not distinguishable into different *Ideas*" (II, ii, 1; 119:20). The claim is that a mind has a simple idea *F* only if it has encountered an *F* (something that is *F*) in experience. Once it has some simple ideas, the mind makes new complex ideas by "repeating, comparing, and uniting" the ones it has (II, ii, 1–2). In this way, we enhance our repertoire of ideas by our own efforts. Compound ideas are either ideas of substances, modes or relations, and we will consider some of their differences in section 7.

Some simple ideas come from the senses alone: sweet, bitter, motion, extension; others, from refection alone: perceiving, judging, doubting, willing; still others, from both sense and reflection: pleasure, pain, power, unity, being. If this is correct, it has implications for what our ideas of power, being, and unity are – what we express by the words "being" and "unity," or how we conceive these things. For Locke, the simple idea of being is a finite being. The simple idea of number is a unit and we form an incomplete idea of infinity by projecting repetitions of that idea (II, xvii, 8). The idea of God is constructed by expanding ideas derived from observing our own (limited) powers of thought and volition (II, xxiii, 35–6). Compare Descartes, who claims we have a simple innate idea of an infinitely perfect being. He grounds the ontological argument for the existence of God on this idea, whereas Locke held that argument to be unsound.[13]

Locke urges a naturalistic, and in some ways deflationary, account of our whole stock of ideas. This underlies many of his disagreements with the doctrines of other early moderns with strongly Platonist views. He disagrees with Descartes over whether we have an idea of the *shape* of a chiliagon.[14] We will see this deflationary tendency is at work in Locke's agnosticism about substance, as compared to Descartes's dogmatic theory of the structure of substances and their essences.[15]

The final division of ideas is into particular and general. According to nearly all early modern philosophers, things that exist in the world are entirely particular, so experience in itself yields ideas of nothing but particular things. But clearly we are able to think of kinds of things, for example dogs, and to entertain general propositions, "A dog is a mammal." Ideas by which we represent kinds were often held to be innate. But according to Locke, general ideas are formed from ideas of particular things by the mental operation of abstraction. To have a general idea is, here again, to be able to bring the idea to mind when occasion demands. Typically this is accompanied by knowing the name of the kind. And Locke tacitly assumes it involves further abilities, to identify instances of the kind, recognize truths about it and make inferences.[16]

No doubt Locke tends to think of general ideas as images (see, for example, II, xxix, 14). By "image" I mean a mental reconstruction of a sensory appearance (visual, tactual, auditory, etc.); to have the image of a square, think what it's like to see or touch a square. But the view that all general ideas are images faces a difficulty.

The problem had been identified by Gassendi, who also rejected innate ideas. He said that we start out representing kinds of things by sensory images, either by a collection of images of different things in the kind or by a single image. But neither technique is adequate, because the collection will inevitably be incomplete and it is impossible to form a single image that represents, say, all men. Any image of a man will depict features, perhaps being short and middle aged, that do not belong to all men. Nonetheless, he noted, we do conceive what it is to be a man, which pertains to all men.[17] Gassendi eventually concluded that we have a faculty whose operations depend on images but reach beyond them to knowledge of abstract natures suggested by what images depict. But he did little to explain how cognition of abstract entities is constructed from the products of sense and imagination.

The problem could be handled differently. Berkeley, writing after Locke, insisted that an image can represent only what it resembles, but noted that the resemblance need not be complete. He proposed that we make, say, the general idea of a triangle by perceiving a particular triangle, focusing on a certain aspect of it and deciding to use it to represent all and only things that resemble it in that aspect.[18] In this way, you could use a particular isosceles triangle to represent all isosceles triangles, or all triangles, or all closed plane figures – depending on what you choose as the basis of resemblance. Locke may have held something like this theory of general ideas and, if he supposed all general ideas are images, it is likely he did.

Many passages that describe the process of abstraction can be read as implicitly urging either view: images or abstract entities (see III, iii, 7:411; II, xi, 9; III, iii, 8–9). One passage, however, seems to decide against the view that all general ideas are images, according to Locke – IV, vii, 9. Berkeley singled it out for attack. It says the general idea of a triangle is something that is neither oblique nor rectangular, but nonetheless represents things that are oblique and those that are rectangular. No image could do that. It seems likely, then, that although Locke tended to think of general ideas of images, he supposed that, with "pain and skill," we form ideas with intelligible content.[19]

5. The Natural World: Primary and Secondary Qualities

In Book II, Locke urges two doctrines about things in the natural world that are represented by our ideas: qualities and substances. He is working against the background of the seventeenth-century mechanist movement in physical theory. Broadly put, the theory is that the corporeal world consists of nothing but matter and its modifications, so all corporeal events are to be explained in these terms. Modifications of matter include extension, impenetrability (or solidity), figure, size, and motion, although there was some uncertainty about forces, or the causes of motion, such as impulse, inertia, and the resistance some associated with solidity. An important mechanist tenet is that matter is a substance. That is, matter has modifications and underlies change; it needs nothing else in order to exist, and it is basic in physical explanation. This contradicted established scholastic-Aristotelian metaphysics, which taught that substances, that is, things basic in this way, are a union of matter and immaterial form, in which form plays the more important role. To mechanists, these "forms" were, for purposes of physics, useless and incomprehensible.

Mechanists disagreed over atomic and plenum theories of matter, but united behind a mereological theme: composite material things are identified with wholes composed of material parts, the parts being more basic. This implies that modifications of the parts – extension, size, shape, solidity, motion (or tendency to motion) – fully account for the modifications of the whole. Another tenet is that a body's state of motion or rest is changed by another body only by impact. So the arrangement, (tendency to) motion, size, and shape of extended solid parts execute the operations of bodies they constitute – as in machines, like a clock. The hypothesis was that bodies big enough to be perceived by sense consist of singly insensible particles, whose mechanical interactions explain what happens at the perceivable level.

Locke admired the program: "the corpuscularian Hypothesis . . . [goes] farthest in an intelligible Explication of the Qualities of Bodies." But he added it was not "his business to decide among hypotheses" (IV, iii, 16; 547:29–548:2). What he doubted especially was the tenet that all bodily interaction is due to collision. Newton's physics, published in 1687, showed that bodies have gravitational powers that operate at a distance in some way we do not conceive.[20] And he had other reservations about the explanatory adequacy of mechanism (see section 10). Still some tenets of the mechanist theory, such as that matter (without form) is a substance, are assumed in his metaphysical views.

The doctrine of primary and secondary qualities is certainly attuned to mechanism. It has two parts: first, a metaphysical distinction between two sorts of qualities that belong to bodies and, second, a distinction between how the ideas caused by these qualities compare with their causes.

A quality is a "Power to produce any *Idea* in our mind"; the powers of a snowball to produce ideas of white, cold, and round are qualities of the snowball. At this point, Locke confesses he sometimes speaks of ideas as being *in things*, but in such cases he means to refer to *qualities* in things that cause those ideas in us (134:24–6). Keep this correction in mind, because he does this repeatedly.

Qualities are of two main sorts. (1) Primary qualities are "utterly inseparable from the Body, in what estate soever it be," whether it is big enough to perceive or too small to be sensible by itself (II, viii, 9). These are extension, solidity, motion, figure, size, also position and number. To be sure, when a particle is divided, the parts do not have the size and shape of the original whole; but they will have some size and shape of their own. (2) Secondary qualities "are nothing in Objects themselves, but Powers to produce various Sensations in us," which they do by their primary qualities, for instance, bulk, figure, texture, and motion of their insensible parts. These qualities are colors, sounds, tastes, smells, warmth, and the like. Locke does not mean to deny that a sensible body divided into sensible parts has, say, some color or other. The point is that singly insensible particles, being insensible, have no color or other such qualities. Since secondary qualities are "nothing but" powers to cause ideas, primary qualities must be something in addition. What, in addition?

It is important to realize that when Locke says that primary qualities are "powers," he means they are causes. Power, he explains, is a source of action (see II, xxii, 10, 11; II, xxi, 4); and having said that all qualities are powers, he refers to primary qualities as "the exciting Causes of all our various Sensations from Bodies" (II, xxxi, 2; 376:18–19; also see II, iv, 1). It is natural to express this notion by the phrase "power *which* causes such-such." But Locke also uses the word "power" to refer to an ability, or disposition – a power *to* produce some effect. A secondary quality is a disposition, a power to cause specific sorts of ideas, which belongs to a body because it has insensible parts whose primary qualities jointly produce ideas of that sort.

In addition, primary qualities cause a variety of further effects. In bodies of perceivable size, they cause sensory ideas of solidity, extension, shape, size, and motion. Moreover the primary qualities are involved in the mutual interaction of bodies. In this connection, the most important primary qualities are solidity and motion. Solidity is "an insurmountable Force" that "hinders the approach of two Bodies, when they are moving one towards another" (II, iv, 1; 123:7–9). Bodies exert "mutual impulse" because of it (II, iv, 5; 126:13–15). Solidity and motion (or impulse) are mainly responsible for what happens when bodies collide, according to the mechanist way of thinking. The remaining primary qualities – figure, number, size – can be defined in geometrical or mathematical terms. But as modifications of solid extended things, they have physical consequences, since they determine some aspects of what bodies do when they come into contact.

Secondary qualities are dispositions defined in terms of effects in sentient creatures. The quality red is a body's disposition to cause red sensations by the primary qualities of its inner structure. Since secondary qualities are defined by these causal relations, their existence depends on that of animals with eyes, ears, and sensory systems which are affected in the specified ways. This is not true of primary qualities:

> The particular *bulk, figure, and motion of the parts of Fire, or Snow, are really in them*, whether any ones Senses perceive them or no: and therefore they may be called *real Qualities*... [but] [L]et not the Eyes see Light, or Colours, nor the Ears hear Sounds; let the Palate not Taste, nor the Nose Smell, and all Colours, Tastes, Odors, and Sounds, as they are such particular *Ideas*, vanish and cease, and are reduced to the Causes, *i.e.* Bulk, Figure, and Motion of Parts. (II, viii, 17)

Take sentient creatures out of the world and secondary qualities would disappear. Neither red sensations nor the bodily quality red would exist; and the inner structures distinguished because they cause red sensations would no longer be distinguished as a kind. But the primary qualities would remain and continue to operate in a world without perceivers.

Locke goes on to say that this metaphysical distinction has consequences for perceptual representation: "*Ideas of primary Qualities* of Bodies, *are Resemblances* of them," but this is not the case with ideas produced by secondary qualities. "There are in the Bodies, we denominate from them, only a Power to produce those Sensations in us: And what is Sweet, Blue, or Warm in *Idea*, is but the certain Bulk, Figure, and Motion of the insensible Parts in the Bodies themselves, which we call so" (II, viii, 15; 137:12–17). Sensations of warmth are like pains, Locke urges: a fire causes both of them in us and there is nothing *in the fire* that resembles either one. Now pains are sensations, which no one takes to be images (or resemblances) of things that cause them. In the same way, Locke urges, ideas of warmth, sweetness, and whiteness are sensations, but not images of the physical structures that cause them. Here Locke seems tacitly to assume the mechanist theory of causes.[21] The claim is equally plausible in light of modern physics and the chemistry of color, sound, flavor, and aroma. Colors, tastes, sounds, and odors as we sense them do not *resemble* their physical causes.

But although this seems plausible, it assumes that sweetness, blueness, etc. are sensations in us. As we have said, the view that sense perception involves immediate awareness of sensations is controversial. A different view currently popular is that what we are aware of when we see, smell, and taste are physical structures, not inner sensations. To be sure, colors, odors, tastes do not seem to look, smell, and taste like what is described in physical chemistry. But, it can be argued, this does not settle the issue over direct sensory awareness of these structures.

This issue about direct perception affects the other half of Locke's thesis, too, that we perceive figure, motion, solidity, and so on by sensing images that depict them. A different objection is that Locke's primary qualities have no special role in contemporary physics. Even so, however, the fact remains that in practice, we simply assume that the world is populated by extended, solid, moving bodies with different sizes and shapes. We do not doubt this would be the case whether or not there were sentient creatures to perceive them. This common-sense belief seems to count in Locke's favor, but it is challenged by Berkeley and Hume.[22] Can you conceive things with extension, size, and shape without supposing that color, warmth, coldness, or some other *sensed* quality occupies the extension?

6. The Natural World: Substances and Substratum

We have compound ideas of substances, modes, and relations (II, xii). Here are some examples of substances: body, spirit, gold, lead, magnet, horse, man. Locke says ideas of substances are "taken to represent distinct particular things subsisting by themselves." They are compound ideas that include, first, ideas of a number of qualities – in the idea of gold, ideas of yellow, weight, malleability, solubility in *aqua regia*, etc. – and, second, the "confused and obscure idea of Substance" (or substratum) (II, xxii, 6). I will shortly come to the confused and obscure part. As the examples indicate, substances are identified by their qualities, or causal powers. Such things constitute the natural world. When Locke refers to them as "substances" that "subsist by themselves," he implies that they are the primary objects investigated in natural science. This way of characterizing the constituents of nature, which dominates seventeenth-century philosophy, was inherited from Aristotle.

To help understand the way substances "subsist by themselves," first consider what Locke says about modes. Here his examples include justice, murder, a dozen, wrestling, beauty. Modes are "complex *ideas*, which . . . contain not in them the supposition of subsisting by themselves, but are considered as Dependences on, or Affections of Substances" (II, xii, 4; 165:1–4). It is obvious that these entities depend upon substances. There can be no murder without humans that commit it, no dance without a dancer, no dozen without eggs, or the like, to be counted. The things Locke classes as substances – humans, horses, gold, and so on – do not depend on other things in *this* way.

Philosophers going back to Aristotle recognized that the structure that enables a substance to have this sort of independent existence requires explanation. Mechanists, we have said, rejected the scholastic-Aristotelian theory of form and matter, so they proposed various alternatives. Descartes, for instance, said that our innate ideas exhibit conceptual connections which indicate the structure of substances, and also identify their essences.[23] Locke bases his view on what we infer from information provided by our senses – meager as it is.

In experience, we notice that a certain number of sensible qualities "go constantly together" which we "presume to belong to one thing." For example, you might observe a certain figure, weight, exceptional hardness, and sparkle appearing repeatedly in the same place at the same time. Naturally you suppose these qualities belong to the same thing, say, a diamond. How do we conceive a thing that has many qualities? Locke says: "not imagining how these simple *Ideas* [*sic*] can subsist by themselves, we . . . suppose some *Substratum,* wherein they do subsist, and from which they do result, which therefore we call *Substance*" (II, xxiii, 1; 295:13–15).[24]

This supposition is quite reasonable, on Locke's view.[25] No quality can subsist on its own; there can be no color or hardness without something that is colored and hard. Qualities belong to a larger structure comprising some hidden constituent, and the complete structure subsists by itself. The complete substance does not depend on anything in the way qualities depend on a constituent hidden within it, nor in the way modes depend upon complete substances. What Locke wants to stress, against Descartes and others, is that we know virtually nothing about this inner structure. All we have is an obscure idea of an "unknown substance," or "substratum," a "Supposition of he knows not what support of . . . Qualities" (295:19–20).[26]

In Locke's words, qualities "result" from substratum and it is the "cause of their union" (295:16; 298:14). This is extremely vague, but the inherence relation is illustrated by this:

> If anyone should be asked, what is the subject wherein Colour and Weight inheres, he would have nothing to say, but the solid extended parts: And if he were demanded, what is it, that that Solidity and Extension inhere in, he [could only reply] . . . something, he knew not what. (II, xxiii, 2)

It would make sense to say that color and weight "inhere in" solid extended parts. According to mechanist theory, color and weight are qualities that belong to a compound body because of its solid extended parts. The parts are the structure within the compound that endows it with its color and weight – provided other bodies and creatures with eyes exist. This is apparently what Locke means by saying qualities "result" from an inner structure which is the "cause of their union" – the substratum endows the substance with its various causal powers.

Why, then, do solidity and extension require something in which to inhere? The best response seems to be this.[27] One could hardly suppose that a particle is endowed with all of its qualities because of its solidity and extension alone. It is easy to see why. Solidity and extension, insofar as Locke understands them, do not account for all the qualities particles have. He points out that we do not understand how "solid parts . . . cohere together to make Extension" (II, xxiii, 23; 308:15–16); he makes no pretense of fully understanding what solidity is (II, iv, 1, 3, 6), or how motion is communicated among bodies, let alone how particles cause ideas in us (IV, iii, 29; 559:34–560:1). So Locke infers there is something more basic within particles because of which they manifest solidity, cohesion, and other causal powers although we do not know what it is.

One might question whether anything could count, for Locke, as an informative account of substratum. If any specific attributes were proposed, wouldn't we always think there is something in which those attributes inhere? (see especially II, xxiii, 3; 297:5–9). We would, if we did not understand how those attributes could be sufficient for bodies to have all the qualities we know they do. Locke is skeptical that we will attain a state of complete understanding (see section 10 below). But if we did, then we would know there is no further unknown substratum on which those attributes depend.

When Locke turns to specific kinds of material substances, such as diamond, horse, loadstone, he mentions both an inner constitution and an unknown substratum. The qualities distinctive of diamonds are "supposed to flow from the particular internal Constitution, or unknown Essence of that Substance" (II, xxiii, 3; 296:24–5). Here he agrees with the mechanist view that inner constitutions, or real essences, consist of insensible particles. Different kinds of composite material substances – iron, lead, horse, oak – consist of particles differently organized and these inner constitutions endow composites with their observable qualities. At a deeper level, however, there is a substratum that endows material particles with their qualities.

We have reflective awareness of thinking, willing, perceiving, and so on. These operations, too, cannot exist without something that performs them, and so we infer they inhere in a substratum although we know nothing more about it. Locke vigorously attacks the dogmatic materialist doctrine that all substances are corporeal, including spirits, or minds. Hobbes, for example, argued for this claiming that we cannot even conceive a noncorporeal substance. Locke points to operations of bodies just as difficult for us to conceive as are the operations of minds. And in both cases, substratum is entirely unknown: "If we would enquire farther into their Nature, Causes, and Manner, we perceive not the Nature of Extension, clearer than we do of Thinking" (II, xxiii, 29; 312:24–6). So it is just as easy – or difficult – to conceive that thinking substance is immaterial as to conceive that its operations arise entirely from matter. Later Locke uses the same line of reasoning to attack Descartes's dogmatic thesis that thinking substances are immaterial (see IV, iii, 6; 540:22–543:30).

7. Ideas: Representation and Reality

Let's return to a question raised earlier: how do ideas serve as "signs or representations" of other things? The issue has a special urgency for Locke, because he says we are immediately aware only of ideas. But it is a type of question important in philosophy of language and mind: what is the representative content of psychological states?

Several crucial chapters are devoted to the reality, adequacy, and truth of ideas (II, xxx, xxxi; IV, iv). They explain conditions in which ideas represent things that are genuinely real. Simple ideas, we have seen, are the fundamental representative entities, and all other ideas represent because of these simple components. We posed the question in section 2: in sense perception, how do ideas represent things in the world?

There is one basic way. Simple ideas are regularly caused in us by qualities of corresponding sorts, which they represent:

> these several Appearances, being designed to be the Marks, whereby we are to know, and distinguish Things, which we have to do with; our *Ideas* do as well serve us to that purpose . . . whether they be only constant Effects, or else exact Resemblances of something in the things themselves; the reality lying in that steady correspondence, they have with the distinct Constitutions of real Beings . . . (II, xxx, 2; 372:26–373:6; also see II, xxxi, 2)

Clearly this assumes sensory ideas are caused by the different constitutions of external objects. One question, from section 2, is what entitles Locke to this assumption. But for now, I want to call attention to something else suggested by this passage: when we receive simple ideas of sense, we *take* them to have external causes distinguished by the sorts of ideas they cause. All simple ideas of sensation have this rudimentary representative character. Some also resemble their causes (see II, viii, 15).

It is fair to ask how simple ideas come to be taken as signs of external causal powers. Is it essential to simple ideas that they be taken this way or is it contingent? Of course Locke is officially opposed to any view to the effect that sensory ideas are judged by means of innate ideas or conceptual abilities.

This is the point of his answer to Molyneux's question (II, ix, 8). A newly sighted man could *not* immediately say which of his visual sensations represents a cube and which a globe. This answer puzzles many readers. Locke endorsed it, because he assumed that sight alone provides sensations of color and light. The man would receive no visual representations of figure, just color and light.[28] Lacking innate ideas, he would need experience to discover that patterns of color and light indicate the shapes of objects at various distances from the eyes. Because "the several variations [of Space, Figure, and Motion] change the appearances of its proper Object, *viz.* Light and Colors, we bring ourselves by use, to judge of the one by the other" (II, ix, 9; 146:30–2). Grown people typically do make these judgments without even noticing. Now it is easy to see how a mind acquires ideas of the figures of objects by which to make judgments based on visual sensations. It gets them by touch. There could be no similar explanation of how a mind learns to judge its tactual sensations (compare II, ix, 9). We have no other sense modality by which to acquire ideas of figure. For similar reasons, it seems Locke could not explain how we come to understand that simple ideas have external causes, if there are no sensory ideas that are originally and essentially taken that way.

He could approach the problem by saying that simple sensory ideas have intensional representative character.[29] Things have "intensional" content, if they make it seem *as if* something is the case; the world may, or may not, actually be as represented. For example, pictures have intensional content. Locke might hold that all simple sensory ideas are sensed as if they have external causes. But could this view be reconciled with his doctrine that ideas caused by secondary qualities do not resemble their causes? Certainly he denies that sensations of warmth, color, and the like are images of their causes; on the contrary, they are like pains. Pains are sensations and we are not at all inclined to think they, or anything like them, belong to inanimate objects. But this is not to say that pains altogether lack intensional character. Descartes observed that pains are typically felt as being in some part of one's body; this appearance may be false, as when amputees continue to feel pains as being in their lost limbs.[30] When Locke compares feelings of warmth to pains, he may well mean that both are felt *as* sensations located in some part of one's body. He could plausibly say, at the same time, that feelings of warmth are felt as coming from a source located outside the body in a certain direction. It is difficult to see what other position is open to Locke in view of his rejection of innate ideas.[31]

Turning from simple to compound ideas, Locke describes the representative function of ideas of substances and mixed modes. (Relations are tacitly subsumed under modes in the relevant chapters.) There ideas are constructed by us, so there is a special worry about whether they represent anything real.[32] Real ideas, Locke says, have "a Foundation in Nature" or "conformity with that reality of Being, to which they are tacitly referr'd, as to their Archetypes" (II, xxx, 1; 372:12–14). On his elegant theory, ideas of substances and ideas of modes refer to what exists in very different ways.

On the one hand, ideas of substances are "made all of them in reference to Things existing without us, and intended to be Representations of Substances, as they really are" (II, xxx, 5; 374:15–17). The reason we bother to form ideas of gold, iron, or horse is that we take them to be basic in nature, as discussed above. So in making them, we aim very strictly to pattern them on things that exist in the world. Should someone concoct an idea consisting of sensible qualities, plus the idea of substratum, when in fact there is nothing that has those qualities, the idea would be used as a representation of something that actually exists, but the representation would not be real. The idea of a mermaid, and (probably) the Loch Ness monster, are "fantastical," not "real." But even if the idea of a substance is real, it is inevitably inadequate. Although a chemist has an idea of gold more complete and accurate than that of a jeweler, the chemist is far from knowing all causal powers of the metal. Nor does she know the inner constitution which gives rise to those powers, but at best has only a hypothesis about it; not to mention the ultimate substratum.

Ideas of modes, on the other hand, represent reality by a different device. They are "voluntary Collections of simple *Ideas*, which the Mind puts together, without reference to any real Archetypes, or standing Patterns" (II, xxxi, 3; 376:22–4); "voluntary," in the sense that our intentions place no constraints on how we construct them, other than internal consistency of the representation. The point is that nature does not mark them out as unitary traits, activities, or events. Fencing, running, beauty, testiness, parricide, even justice are culturally or socially delineated;[33] nothing in nature sets those movements, physical aspects, or ways of behaving apart from the flow of movements and mass of physical or mental features of things, on Locke's view. The habits and interests of individuals, groups, or societies govern ideas of modes. Since they are made by us for our own purposes, they cannot help being real and adequate as long as they are internally consistent.

Substances pose a special problem for Locke's theory of representation, because, as he insists, we do not know the real essences, or inner constitutions, on which different sensible qualities depend. Scholastics maintained that kinds of substances are distinguished by real essences, and that each essence gives rise to a collection of strict "properties" that belong to all and *only* members of a kind. They made no pretense of knowing essences, except for the species man (rational animal), but nonetheless they held that we classify substances into kinds determined by such essences. Locke opposes both points. He attacks the presumption that essences marked by strict sets of "properties" divide specimens in nature (for example, III, iii, 15–17; III, vi, 8–20). And to Locke, it is absurd to suppose we have an idea of a real essence if we are ignorant of marks that distinguish it (II, xxxi, 6; 378:34–379:3; also III, vi, 9, 18–19). How, then, can we have ideas that represent substantial kinds? His solution is to relativize real essences. We base our ideas on what we know, groups of qualities observed to go together, and use them to demarcate real essences (for example, II, xxiii, 3–6; III, iii, 17–18; III, vi, 6–7).

Ideas of modes pose a different challenge, because they are central to the nonnatural sciences. To review them "would be to make a Dictionary of the greatest part of the Words made use of in Divinity, Ethicks, Law, and Politicks, and several other Sciences" (II, xxii, 12; 294:34–5).[34] The problem is that mixed modes are things that do not, or may not, exist – justice, beauty, and the like. Innate knowledge is, in effect, cognitive access to ideal entities that do not exist in the actual world. Locke has no use for that. Far from having ideal archetypes, he declares our ideas of mixed modes "are themselves Archetypes" (II, xxx, 4). That is, our ideas define the entities they represent. It follows that we cannot fail to know the real essences of modal kinds (III, iii, 15–16, 18; III, v). This is the basis – perhaps unsatisfactory – for Locke's account of how we attain systematic knowledge in morals, political theory, and so on.

8. Individuation and Identity

The mechanist hypothesis that sensible bodies are wholes composed of insensible particles is background for Locke's account of individuation and identity over time. The question what makes one individual horse, say, numerically different from all other horses was a traditional metaphysical issue. For Locke, the "principle of individuation" is this: no two individual substances of the same kind can exist in the same place at the same time (II, xxvii, 1; 328:14–15). We have, he says, ideas of three kinds of substances: God, finite immaterial intelligences, bodies. (He is not insisting that finite minds are immaterial substances, but just explaining how they are individuated in case they are.) It soon becomes clear he means that no two *simple* substances of the same kind can exist in the same place at the same time (II, xxviii, 2).

A simple material substance is an atom. It is individuated by the time and place at which it begins to exist. Locke maintains that the same atom endures provided there is some atom at every position in a continuous spatial-temporal path that begins with this initial position (II, xxvii, 3; 330:7–13). The identity condition for a mass, or assembly of atoms, follows naturally. It continues to exist as long as its constituent atoms are collected together, but if even one atom is gained or lost it is destroyed.

But for living things, "their Identity depends not on a Mass, or the same Particles; but on something else" (330:21–2). An oak grows, is pruned, and grows some more; the particles that compose it come and go, and yet it is still the same tree. Of course it is not the same in terms of its qualities, but it is the same individual tree. An oak is a succession of different masses of particles. Nonetheless in Locke's view, "it continues to be the same Plant, as long as it partakes of the same Life" (331:5–7). As long as there is a continuous succession of particles with a "like continued

Organization, conformable to that sort of Plants," the same life is passed from one to the next and the same plant continues to exist. When its particles cease to be organized in the way that sustains vital functions, the tree dies and the oak ceases to exist. A "dead oak" is not strictly an oak.

The same goes for the identity of animals, such as horses and humans (leaving aside the controversial question of an immaterial soul). We hold now that living things are composed of cells that are continually sloughed off and replaced. Locke's account of what it is for the same plant or animal to endure remains viable nowadays.

A human being is one thing, and a person another, according to Locke. Persons, too, have diachronic identity. As a person, you have existed for a number of years, changing in many ways, but still the same individual self. Personal history is centrally important for assigning moral responsibility in this life, and especially hereafter, in Locke's view (see, for example, II, xxvii, 13, 18). He defines a person quite carefully: "a thinking intelligent Being, that has reason and reflection, and can consider it self as it self, the same thinking thing in different times and places" (II, xxvii, 9; 335:10–14). With this in view, he proposes that a person, conscious of self at one time, is identical to the person who performed a certain act at an earlier time just in case "consciousness can be extended backwards to that Action" (335:25–6). In other words, you are the person who performed a certain act that did occur in the past if and only if you can remember doing it. This is not to say that you do remember it or that you could easily do so, but just that you can be brought to recall it, perhaps by extraordinary means (see II, xxvii, 26).

Locke distinguishes three things: a person, who is the self of consciousness; a human being, who is a living organism; a thinking substance, comprising thoughts and a substratum in which they inhere. His contention is that it is possible, as far as we know, that the same person might have a series of different human bodies, as in the story of the prince infused into the body of a cobbler boy. For similar reasons, it is in principle possible that two persons, or "two distinct incommunicable consciousnesses," could act in turns in the same man, as in the case where the man, Socrates, is one person by day and another person by night (II, xxvii, 23).

The same reasoning pertains to the substance that gives rise to the thoughts that a person is aware of at different times, even supposing that substance is immaterial. This is a radical claim: it is possible, as far as we know, that the thoughts one person has over a period of time might occur in a succession of different immaterial substances, the person's memory abilities being transferred intact from one to the next. By the same token, one substance might produce the thoughts that belong to a number of different persons, each denied access to the consciousness of the others (see II, xxvii, 13–14). Shockingly unorthodox as this is, it serves to insulate personal identity and accountability – here and hereafter – from doubts about the immaterial soul. On Locke's account, personal identity is compatible with any outcome regarding the nature of thinking substances.

Above all, persons bear moral responsibility, deserve moral praise and blame. Locke's motivating thought is that a person cannot justly be held accountable for some action he is entirely unable to recognize as his own. That would be tantamount to being "created miserable" (347:5), or punished without desert. This is not to deny that a person can lie about what he remembers. The fact that we cannot tell for sure whether he is lying explains why a man is held accountable for what he did when drunk (II, xvii, 20). Human justice is dispensed with imperfect knowledge, but Locke is speaking of true justice.

There is undeniable appeal to the view that personal survival consists in continuity of psychological traits and abilities, rather than bodily or substantial continuity. Teletransportation is fiction, but not obviously absurd. Versions of Lockean theory have been defended recently. But several difficulties are raised against Locke. The objection that we forget many of our actions is blunted by stressing that identity demands just the capacity to remember. Also, Locke points out, the undeniable fact that a *man's* memories can be obliterated, say, by disease does not prove that a *person* can survive loss of mnemonic ability (II, xxvii, 19). An early objection associated with Thomas Reid charges the theory with violating the logic of identity.[35] Suppose a youth robs an orchard, becomes a young officer who captures the enemy's standard, and is later promoted to general; imagine the young officer remembers stealing apples, the general remembers taking the standard, but the general cannot under any stimulus recall raiding the orchard. On Locke's theory, the young person is identical to the person at early-career, who is identical to the person in late-career, but the young person is not identical to the one in late-career; transitivity of identity fails. But Locke might have been willing to accept this. He would not deny that the *man* who stole apples is identical to the man who retires as a general.

Recent empirical research on autobiographical memory suggests a different objection. Whereas Locke makes personal identity depend on memory of particular events, it seems a person's actual view of her past is a simplified reconstruction that runs together many particular occurrences. Personal memories are continually being created and revised, and in ways that tend to sustain one's self-image.[36] If this is correct, it confirms Locke's notion that one's sense of self is closely tied to personal memory. But it casts doubt on his thesis that the sense of self fixes moral responsibility.

9. Knowledge of the Existence of Particular Things

In section 2, we raised the question how we can be certain of the existence of external objects that cause our sensory ideas, according to Locke. This comes under the heading "Real Existence," in Locke's classification of propositions, or ways ideas "agree or disagree" (IV, i). Each of us has intuitive knowledge that "I exist" is true. Locke offers an argument, based on the existence of contingent things, for the existence of God (IV, ix and x).

But how do we know that other particular things exist on the basis of our senses? In fact, Locke says this is not as certain as intuitive and demonstrative knowledge although it is certain nonetheless (IV, ii, 7). A question is raised about the existence of things perceived by sense, "because Men may have such *Ideas* in their Minds, when no such Thing exists . . . But yet here, I think, we are provided with an Evidence that puts us past doubting" (IV, ii, 14; 537:13–15; IV, xi, 3; 631:14–17). We have assurance on the point and, more important, there is no *reason* to question it.

What assures us of the existence of things is their acting upon us: "'Tis therefore the actual receiving of *Ideas* from without, that . . . makes us know, that something doth exist at that time without us, which causes that *Idea* in us" (IV, vi, 2; 630:25–8). Locke does not suppose we infer the existence of external objects on evidence supplied by ideas. Normally perceptual judgments do not take the form of conclusions (see IV, xi, 2).

But doubts are raised about such judgments on the ground that sometimes we have sensory ideas when there is nothing external causing them. This is no reason to doubt, according to Locke. He correctly observes that, in practice, we have little difficulty distinguishing ideas that occur in dreams or memory from those that are caused from without (IV, ii, 14). He ends with the tart observation: "Where all is but Dream, Reasoning and Arguments are of no use" (537:25). For all its breeziness, this remark calls attention to the fact that asking a question pragmatically implies the possibility of a coherent answer; if a question puts that in doubt, its reasonableness is implicated. Locke concludes that our certainty of the existence of external things that cause our ideas "goes beyond bare probability . . . [and] passes under the name of Knowledge" (IV, ii, 14; 537:5–7).

This may seem a meager response to skepticism about the external world. But it deploys a cogent strategy that can be seen by comparing it to Descartes's use of skepticism. In *Meditation* I, Descartes doubts the existence of bodies perceived by sense because we sometimes dream. Notice that this fact alone is no reason to doubt our senses in general; for that, one needs to add that we cannot tell, in a particular case, whether we are dreaming or not. But, as Locke observes, we can tell, and Descartes agrees with that later on.[37] As further basis for doubt, Descartes proposes the evil genius hypothesis: as far as he knows (at that stage), all his sensory states are caused by an evil genius, not by bodies, as he is inclined to believe. Because this challenges the reliability of our sensory faculty, all beliefs based on the senses are under suspicion. Descartes discharges the doubt by (purportedly) using his faculty of intellect to prove the existence of a nondeceiving God and eventually using that to show the evil genius is not possible after all.[38] Intellect is a faculty distinct from and independent of the sensory faculty, Descartes contends. The point is that no challenge to the overall reliability of a cognitive faculty can be met by using that same faculty, not without circularity. In fact, some critics suspect Descartes of circular reasoning at one stage. If the "metaphysical doubt" in *Meditation* III, based on the hypothesis of a deceiving god, is meant to question the truthfulness of intellect, as the authors of some of the "Objections" supposed, then Descartes could not remove it without using his intellect.[39] That would be like someone trying to assure us that his memory is reliable by saying he remembers his doctor telling him so.

Locke steers clear of this trap by resisting suggestions to the effect that our sensory faculty *needs* any defense. The most important point is that there is no ground on which to suspect the general reliability of our senses. We can, after all, tell the difference between dreams, illusions, and reliable sensory judgments. So all that is left of skepticism is a purely theoretical question: but how do you *know* there isn't an evil genius, or that the faculty of sense is reliable? Locke's wry remark brings out the unreasonableness of asking for "proof." This is skillful enough. Yet it may leave one unsatisfied, because Locke does little to allay the suspicion that we need an answer to the (unanswerable) theoretical question in order to be warranted in trusting our sensory faculty.

10. Barriers to Natural Science

For all his stress on experience and alliance with mechanism, Locke was not optimistic about advancing knowledge in the natural sciences. Part of the reason is that he sets a very high standard for knowledge. Intuitive and demonstrative knowledge require evidence consisting of the perception of conceptual connections; and sensory knowledge extends only to the existence of objects with powers to cause the sensory ideas we actually have (see IV, xi, 9). Modern physics, for instance, falls short of these standards. Beyond that, he gives a more specific argument for strict limits to what we can discover about nature, that is, about substances and their powers.

His main skeptical case in point is the immateriality of the mind. There can be no doubt that we think and that this operation is performed by a substance. Nor can we doubt that we have a body, whose powers belong to a substance. But, Locke argues, we cannot know whether the material substance of our bodies is, or is not, the substance that thinks (IV, iii, 6). We may suppose our bodies are "Systems of Matter fitly disposed" to receive "sense, perception, and thought"; alternatively, we may believe our bodies are "joined and fixed" to immaterial substances that execute our powers of thought. Either way, we find something incomprehensible. On the first view, matter gives rise to thought, whereas on the second, particles cause sensations in immaterial substances; both are inconceivable to us. As we have said, the issue was sensitive. If the soul is, in fact, immaterial, it is naturally able to survive death and bodily destruction, If not, life after death and resurrection are foreign to the nature of the soul and entirely miraculous. Locke contends, however, that neither religion nor morality is at risk over this issue.

An the natural world more generally, there are barriers to our knowing the collections of qualities that "co-exist in the same substance." Is all gold malleable, that is, do all bodies that have the qualities represented in the idea of gold also have malleability? Of course this is no issue, if the idea of gold already includes the idea of malleability. Then the proposition is known, but trifling (IV, vi, 9; IV, viii). It may well be that every sample of gold we have tested exhibits malleability. But because many instances will not have been examined, these results do not prove the general claim. Two considerations stand in the way of our knowing the qualities that always co-exist in the same body. First, we do not know the "Root they spring from, not knowing what size, figure, and texture of Parts they are, on which depend and from which result those Qualities which make our complex *Idea* of Gold" (IV, iii, 11; 545:1–3). There is a second "more incurable part of Ignorance," namely, "there is no discoverable connection between any *secondary Quality, and those primary Qualities* that it depends on" (IV, iii, 12; 545:10–15). So if we knew specific inner constitutions, we could discover no "necessary connection" among the secondary qualities that belong to samples of gold.

With aids like the microscope, we might overcome the first barrier. If we knew the inner constitutions of gold and *aqua regia*, we might predict ahead of time that the one is a solvent for the other. Primary qualities are causes and we know how they interact, Locke supposes (see IV, iii, 25; 556:5–21). Lacking access to inner constitutions, however, our assurance of the qualities that always co-exist in the same compound body reaches no farther than our experiences of particular cases (IV, iii, 24–7, 9–10, 16).

Turning to the more incurable ignorance, Locke assumes external bodies produce sensations of colors, sounds, etc. But it is not easy to imagine that *this* is a mechanical process: "These mechanical Affections of Bodies, having no affinity at all with those *Ideas*, they produce in us, . . . we can have no distinct knowledge of such Operations beyond our Experience" (IV, iii, 28; 558:31–559:4). Now this lack of affinity might be only superficial; there is no apparent affinity between opium and the state of somnolence, yet it was widely supposed that the drug causes sleep by purely mechanical means. However, if minds are immaterial substances, as Locke thinks likely, the lack of affinity is real.[40] No immaterial substance could have solidity and extension, which are required for mechanical interaction. So the sort of information about inner constitutions that stands a chance of allowing us to have genuine knowledge of *interbodily* powers that always co-exist in the same body would not enable us to know about the co-existence of psychophysical powers. Locke concludes: "we can go no farther than particular Experience informs us of matter of fact, and by Analogy to guess what Effects the like Bodies are, upon other tryals, like to produce. But as to a perfect *Science* of natural Bodies, (not to mention spiritual Beings,) . . . I conclude it lost labour to seek after it" (IV, iii, 29; 560:27–9). Progress in understanding nature depends on painstaking experiments to determine the qualities that are regularly found together in the same things (see IV, xii, 8–13).

11. Conclusion

A close reader will find Locke's reasoning has much more subtlety than this brief discussion conveys, and even a casual reader will find he applies it to many important topics not mentioned here. I will close with a few broad remarks about the general significance of the *Essay*. During Locke's lifetime, it was greatly admired by some, but vehemently attacked by others for its unorthodox stands on innate morality, knowledge of substance, theory of personal identity, and above all agnosticism about thinking matter. In the eighteenth century, however, the *Essay* was widely applauded for its stand on these same topics. It was especially admired for inculcating the view that, as creatures endowed with understanding, we should accept no proposition without using our own faculties to determine its certain or probable truth. Beyond that, the reading public was fascinated by a "natural history" of human understanding, its development and education, its foibles, susceptibilities, and means of improvement. Acquaintance with the *Essay* was shared by readers of both sexes and all stations of life throughout Britain, France, the whole of Europe, and in America.[41] During the nineteenth century, Locke's influence was eclipsed by Kantian, and more radical, forms of idealism. But in the twentieth century, the *Essay* has come to be regarded as the classic modern attempt to combine empiricism about ideas and realism about the natural world. Recent philosophical thinking is influenced in several ways directly traceable to the *Essay*, including: theories of personal identity and personal survival based on continuity of psychological traits, and debate over colors, and the like, as we sense them and their physical bases.

Notes

1 Quotations and citations are taken from *An Essay Concerning Human Understanding*, ed. P. H. Nidditch (Oxford: Clarendon Press, 1975). Passages in the main text are identified first by book, chapter, and section; or by page and line. Passages outside the main text are identified just by page and line, prefaced with the abbreviation "E." There is a useful glossary at the back of the Nidditch volume.

2 For more biographical information, see J. R. Milton, "Locke's Life and Times," in the *Cambridge Companion to Locke*, ed. Vere Chappell (Cambridge: Cambridge University Press, 1994), pp. 5–25.

3 On what is "obligatory" or "suitable" for creatures with our cognitive abilities, see IV, xvii, 24, also I, iv, 22–34.

4 In the early modern period, the term "science" retained connotations of Aristotelian demonstrative science, that is, roughly knowledge of the basic principles in an area of study, necessarily true principles that mention the ultimate causes, or "essences," of things studied by the science, from which other general propositions about them are deduced and explained. The term was not reserved for natural or empirical sciences.

5 Locke also recognizes a dispositional state of knowledge consisting of the ability to remember having performed such an act (IV, i, 9). Descartes also identifies knowledge with an act of maximally perspicuous perception and a dispositional ability; see "Second Replies," CSM II, 100; AT VII, 140.

6 See *Meditation* V (CSM II, 44; AT 63–4).

7 One might ask what sort of dependent metaphysical status ideas have, for example, mental acts or objects with mind-dependent existence (see Descartes, Preface to *Medi-*

tations, CSM II, 7; AT VII, 8). There is some evidence Locke regarded this as the sort of "physical consideration" with which he did not want to meddle; see *Remarks upon Mr. Norris' Books, Works*, 11th edn. (London: T. Davison, 1812), 9 vols., X, 248.

8 See Berkeley, *Principles of Human Knowledge*, Pt. I, secs. 3, 8, 16–17, 23–4, and so on; Hume, *Treatise of Human Nature*, Bk. I, Pt. IV, sec. II.

9 See Berkeley, *Principles*, Pt. I, sec. 18; he was not the first to make this charge against Locke.

10 Leibniz, *New Essays concerning Human Understanding*, tr. P. Remnant and J. Bennett (Cambridge: Cambridge University Press, 1996), esp. pp. 77–9.

11 The reference at 58:7–8 to what he will "shew hereafter" anticipates the discussion of intuitive knowledge in IV, ii, 2; also IV, vii, 4.

12 See Leibniz, *New Essays*, p. 85.

13 See IV, x, 7; also "Deus," an essay found in Locke's papers, edited by Peter King, *The Life and Letters of John Locke* (London, 1884; Garland reprint 1984), pp. 3–6. On Descartes's defense of the simplicity of the idea, see "First Objections," CSM II, 72; AT VII, 99–100 and "First Replies," CSM II, 83–4; AT 117–18.

14 Compare *Essay*, II, xxix, 14 and *Meditation* VI; CSM II, 51; AT VII, 72.

15 Descartes, *Principles*, Pt. I, nos. 60–2 (CSM I, 213–15; AT VIII A, 28–30).

16 This is implicit in the argument against innate ideas of identity, etc. in I, iv.

17 Gassendi, *Institutio Logica*, tr. Howard Jones (Assen: Van Gorcum, 1981), Pt. I, cans. 4–8, pp. 86–92).

18 Berkeley, *Principles of Human Knowledge*, Intro., sec. 12, 15–16.

19 But see Michael Ayers' *Locke* (London: Routledge, 1991), vol. I, ch. 5 for a different view on the question.

20 Locke expressed this opinion in his second letter to Stillingfleet, *Works*, IV, 464–5.

21 According to the scholastic theory of "sensible species," we normally see, for instance, the quality red when looking at an apple, because we receive in our senses a quality that is, at least in kind, the same as the quality red that exists in the apple. Mechanists explain the causes of perception differently.

22 See Berkeley, *Principles*, Pt. I, sec. 10; Hume, *Treatise*, Bk. I, Pt. IV, sec. IV.

23 See *Principles*, I, 60–3; compare *Essay*, I, iv, 18.

24 Locke uses "idea of substance" to refer both to ideas of complete substances, such as gold or horse, and to a constituent of those ideas, the idea of substratum in which the qualities of gold or a horse inhere. It is not unusual for both scholastics and early moderns to speak of the "substance of a substance," meaning roughly that constituent of a complete substance that makes it a substance, that is, something that subsists by itself.

25 In his first letter to Stillingfleet, Locke says the existence of qualities by themselves is "inconsistent" and "the mind perceives their necessary connection with inherence or being supported" (*Works*, IV, 21).

26 Locke exploits our ignorance of the nature of substance in defending his "container" theory of space, II, xiii, 18–20.

27 Commentators have interpreted Locke's position on the substratum in different ways; see, for example, articles by Michael Ayers, Jonathan Bennett, and the present author in *Locke*, ed. Vere Chappell. For a longer discussion, see Michael Ayers, *Locke* (London: Routledge, 1991), vol. II, chs, 3 (London: Routledge, 1991) 5.

28 The view was familiar to Locke and Molyneux from the theory of geometrical optics developed by Witelo, Kepler, and others. See by the present author, "The Real Molyneux

Question and the Basis of Locke's Answer" in *Locke's Philosophy*, ed. G. A. J. Rogers (Oxford: Clarendon Press, 1994), pp. 75–100.

29 Locke initially says that a simple idea contains "one uniform Appearance, or Conception in the mind, and is not distinguishable into different *Ideas*" (II, ii, 1; 119:19–20). But not long after, he admits that all simple ideas "include some kind of relation" and notes, among other examples, that "sensible Qualities, as Colours and Smells . . . [are] . . . but the *powers* of different Bodies, in relation to our Perception, *etc.*" II, xxi, 2 (234:19, 24–60).

30 *Meditation* VI; CSM II, 53; AT VII, 77.

31 This does not settle all questions about whether Locke is a consistent anti-innatist or just what his anti-innatism involves.

32 Also see IV, iv.

33 This can be said of moral entities, on Locke's view of them, inasmuch as God and creatures form a sort of community.

34 Mathematics deals with simple, rather than mixed, modes; see remarks about the idea of a triangle, II, xxxi, 3; also II, xii, 4–5 and II, xiii.

35 *Essays on the Intellectual Powers of Man* (1785), ch. 6. Reid was not the first to raise an objection of this sort.

36 See Marya Schechtman, "The Truth About Memory," *Philosophical Psychology* 7 (1994), pp. 3–20.

37 *Mediation* IV, CSM II, 61–2; AT VII, 89–90.

38 *Meditation* VI, CSM II, 54–5; AT VII, 79–80.

39 See "Objections," CSM II, 89 and 150; AT VII, 125 and 214; and "Replies," CSM II, 100–1 and 171–2; AT VII, 140–1 and 246.

40 In his first letter to Stillingfleet, *Works*, IV, 33, Locke says it is probable that the mind is an immaterial substance referring to his demonstration of the immateriality of God (IV, x). He hints at this in IV, iii, 6 (542:2–6) and II, xxvii, 13 (338:19–21).

41 See Kenneth MacLean, *John Locke and English Literature in the Eighteenth Century* (New Haven: Yale University Press, 1936; Garland reprint, 1984).

Chapter 7

George Berkeley

George Pappas

George Berkeley was born in Kilkenny, Ireland in 1685 and took his BA at Trinity College, Dublin in 1704 when he was nineteen. He became a fellow at Trinity in 1707, and in the same year took religious orders. At about the same time, and continuing well into 1708, Berkeley kept a private notebook in which he worked out his views on vision, science, mathematics, and metaphysics. This notebook was first published in 1871, and is now known as the *Philosophical Commentaries*. It contains nearly 900 numbered entries of varying length. There followed in short order Berkeley's main works, first on vision in the *Essay towards a New Theory of Vision* (1709), then on metaphysics in the *Principles of Human Knowledge* (1710), and finally the *Three Dialogues Between Hylas and Philonous* (1713).

The *Principles* was conceived as a work in three parts, and Berkeley wrote all or most of the second part, only to lose the manuscript en route from Italy. He wrote the short monograph *De Motu* in 1721, and submitted it for a prize competition (he did not win). While in Newport, Rhode Island, starting in 1728, Berkeley wrote *Alciphron*, a work in the philosophy of religion which was published in 1734. He had journeyed to the New World bent on establishing a college in Bermuda, but crown funds were never provided, and he returned to Britain. Berkeley became Bishop of Cloyne in Ireland, and spent most of the remainder of his life at that post.

Berkeley's other main works include *The Analyst* and the *Defense of Freethinking in Mathematics* (1735). These are works in the philosophy of mathematics, and include Berkeley's criticisms of mathematical practices and theories current in his day. About a decade later he published *Siris* (1744), which is a curious mixture of Platonistic metaphysics and a defense of the medicinal virtues of tar-water. He died in 1753 at Oxford where he was visiting his son.

Berkeley's earliest works, the *New Theory of Vision*, *Principles of Human Knowledge*, and *Three Dialogues*, all published in a span of just four years, secured for him an important place in both the history of psychology and the history of philosophy. His theory of vision, which stressed the extent to which and manner in which visual perception of distance is learned, was a leading contender in the field down through the nineteenth century. Some of its leading ideas, especially that of the manner in which perception by means of one sense serves to "suggest" perceptions one will or might receive by another sense, greatly influenced later philosophers such as Thomas Reid. Further, the metaphysical and epistemological theories expressed in the *Principles* and *Three Dialogues* helped shape empiricist philosophy down nearly to the present day. For these reasons, in what follows attention will be directed mainly towards these early works.

1. Visual Perception

Berkeley's first major published work, the *Essay towards a New Theory of Vision* (1709), is a study in the psychology of perception. As such it is mainly a contribution to science, though it has major philosophical presuppositions and implications as well. The primary focus of the book is on how we see distance and things at a distance, and with how we see or visually estimate the actual location and magnitude of things placed at a distance from ourselves.

Berkeley takes over from others a definition of distance from an observer to an object seen: distance, he says (*New Theory*, sec. 2), is a line extending endwise from the eye of the observer to the viewed object. So thought of, distance is not immediately seen, because the line projects just one point, corresponding to one end of the line, into the "fund" of the eye or retina. Still, distance is in some sense seen, even if not immediately seen, and it is one job of a theory of distance perception to explain how this works. One theory which was then current held that in binocular vision light rays reflected from the distant objects enter the eyes and make angles at an imaginary line, which extends from the pupil of one eye to that of the other. It is presumed that the observer knows the length of this pupil-to-pupil line, and that she is immediately aware of the angles formed by the incoming light rays and this line. Then, by a kind of natural geometry the observer merely calculates the altitude of the triangle formed by the light rays and the pupil-to-pupil line, and that is the distance from the observer to the object. The geometrical calculation is thought of as "natural" because it is regarded as something one can accomplish without any training in geometry. Everyone visually estimates distance in this manner, at least for objects which are not remote, by calculating, whether they are mathematically literate or not.

Against this geometrical theory, Berkeley lodges two main objections. In the first he denies that the observer is immediately aware of either the incoming light rays or the angles they form at the pupil-to-pupil line. He says:

> it is evident that no idea which is not itself perceived can be the means of perceiving any other idea. If I do not perceive the redness or paleness of a man's face themselves, it is impossible I should perceive by them the passions which are in his mind. . . . those angles and lines are not themselves perceived by sight, it follows from sect. 10 that the mind doth not by them judge of the distance of objects. (*New Theory*, secs. 10 & 13)

This passage both sets the objection and tells us something about the important concept of immediate perception, a concept which is importantly deployed in Berkeley's later writing. As the passage indicates, perception is immediate when it is not dependent on some other perception. We can illustrate by considering an example. Suppose you are visiting Washington DC and you are looking at the Washington Monument from a distance of a hundred feet. Imagine, too, that there is a very dense fog which surrounds the monument and pervades the space between you and the monument. In this case, your seeing the monument depends on your also seeing the fog; you would not see the monument, in these circumstances, were you not to see the fog. So, Berkeley would say that you are not immediately seeing the monument; rather, your perception of the monument is mediate or indirect. In this case, however, something is immediately seen, namely the fog. Perception of it is not similarly dependent on seeing the monument.

We can now see the full import of the objection. The geometrical theory agrees that distance is not immediately seen. Hence, given the definition of immediate perception, if distance is seen at all, then it is seen in a way that depends on some other perception. But within the theory the only other perception on which seeing distance might depend is one's awareness of the light rays and the angles they form at the line between the eyes. But, Berkeley claims, these rays and angles are not things one is immediately aware of, and so it follows that a key element of the geometrical theory is false.[1]

A second objection to the geometrical theory is that it allows that a person may visually estimate distance without previous experience of objects at a distance, or without learning. His reason for claiming this is that the geometrical calculations one makes depend merely on necessary connections between the measure of the interior angles and the length of the base of a triangle. This is the triangle formed by the pupil-to-pupil line (the base) and the incoming light rays, each emanating from a single point on the distant object. Given the knowledge of the length of the base and the degree of the interior angles, the triangle's altitude follows of necessity. But it is clear that some experience is necessary before one becomes adept at visual estimation of distance, and so the geometrical theory is implausible.

Berkeley's alternative to the geometrical theory tries to explain what sort of experience is needed. He holds that one learns to associate certain sensations or ideas with others. One learns that the distinctness or confusion of the visual appearance, the feelings one receives when the eyes turn in different directions side to side and up and down, and the sensations which attend the straining of the eyes, all acting together serve to suggest distance. They do this by suggesting the tactile sensations or ideas one would receive were one actually to traverse the distance between one's current position and the distant object. Learning to estimate distance visually, then, involves learning how visual ideas happen to correlate with various nonvisual ideas, especially tactile ones. Different correlations of this sort line up with different distances, something one gradually becomes accustomed to over time. For example, the visual ideas gained when viewing a barn from a distance of fifty feet, together with the sensations gotten from eye movement and strain, correlate with the tactile ideas one would acquire were one to walk to the barn. Knowing or predicting what the latter would be, and how many tactile sensations would be received, is knowing the distance to the barn from one's present position.

Berkeley gives a similar account of visually estimating the situation (location) of distant objects and of estimating their magnitude. He infers from the theory two very important consequences. He infers, first, that a person born blind and then later given sight by a surgical procedure would not be able to tell by sight alone the distances of objects, nor their location, magnitude nor shape. Such a person would not be able to tell by sight the difference in shape between a cube and sphere both placed beyond his reach, and neither could he tell how far distant they were. He says of such a person:

> The objects intromitted by sight would seem to him (as in truth they are) no other than a new set of thoughts or sensations, each whereof is as near to him as the perceptions of pain or pleasure, or the most inward passions of his soul. For our judging objects perceived by sight to be at any distance, or without the mind, is . . . intirely the effect of experience, which one in those circumstances could not yet have attained to. (*New Theory*, sec. 41)[2]

A second result which Berkeley infers from his theory is that the ideas of sight and touch are heterogeneous. By this he means that each idea of sight is numerically and specifically distinct from each idea of touch. No idea of sight is numerically identical to an idea of touch, and neither is it even the same ***kind*** of thing; visual and tactile ideas are different in kind or type. This twofold heterogeneity thesis is directly opposed to a view held by Locke, namely, that some ideas are common to both sight and touch. Here we find a major philosophical thesis, that of heterogeneity, being taken by Berkeley as implied by his scientific theory of distance perception. However, this result and the opposition to Locke is not the full story. For Berkeley seems to have held that the heterogeneity thesis makes Locke's famous distinction between primary and secondary qualities dubious. He says that

> It hath been a prevailing opinion and undoubted principle among mathematicians and philosophers that there were certain ideas common to both senses: whence arose the distinction of primary and secondary qualities. But I think it hath been demonstrated that there is no such thing as a common object, as an idea, or kind of idea perceived both by sight and touch. (*Theory of Vision Vindicated*, sec. 15)

The phrase "whence arose" can be interpreted in different ways, but its most likely meaning is that the thesis of ideas which are common to sight and touch provides some evidence for the distinction between primary and secondary qualities. In that case, the heterogeneity thesis would weaken the support for the latter distinction, perhaps to the point of leaving the primary–secondary distinction without a secure foundation. Berkeley's scientific theory of distance perception may thus be seen, through its implied heterogeneity thesis, to have major philosophical implications.[3]

Berkeley's theory of visual distance perception is in the empiricist tradition, which holds that distance perception is something one learns to do from repeated experience. The geometrical theory, by contrast, is mainly in the nativist tradition, which allows that distance perception can be accomplished without much or even any learning, so long as one can do the natural geometry required. The empiricist tradition has largely held sway since Berkeley's time, and his own specific theory was the received view for nearly two centuries.[4]

2. Philosophical Works

Berkeley's properly philosophical writing began with the *Treatise on the Principles of Human Knowledge*, published in 1710. He felt that this work was little understood, and so he recast its main themes three years later in *Three Dialogues Between Hylas and Philonous.* These two works are pretty much coincident in doctrine, though they differ in thematic stress, and so will be treated as one.[5]

Locke had said in Book III of the *Essay* that some ideas are abstract, and that such abstract ideas are needed to adequately explain certain facts about language, as well as to be the immediate referents of general terms. Berkeley felt that nearly all of what Locke had taught about abstract ideas was in error, and so opened the *Principles* with a sustained criticism of Locke's position.

One form of abstract idea is the idea of a single, determinate sensible quality. A person may see a surface which is both red and square shaped, and thus receive an idea of red color and square shape. The red color, of course, is a red of some specific shade. To form the abstract idea of red color, abstracted from the square shape, one either separates the red color in idea from the shape, or one separately attends to the red color in idea without attending to the shape. The result is an abstract idea of a determinate shade of red color. More general forms of abstract ideas would be those of color alone, or of a person as opposed to an idea of a particular person. Both would be formed by noticing commonalities in the ideas of many particulars. For example, one might observe many differently colored objects and notice that they are all alike insofar as they all have some color. Then by leaving out what is peculiar to the several ideas one has of these colored objects and retaining what is common, one reaches the abstract idea of mere color, or of color in general. A similar process would apply in the case of the idea of a person. One forms in observation the ideas of many different particular persons, leaves out of these ideas what is peculiar to each, retains what is common, and so achieves the abstract general idea of person.

Berkeley maintained that the abstract idea of determinate color is impossible because one cannot successfully carry out the process of abstraction; and the abstract general ideas of, for example, color and person cannot be had because they themselves are impossible objects. Of the former, Berkeley argued that one cannot separate in thought (in idea) what cannot be separated in reality. As there cannot be, in reality, an object with just color but no shape, then color and shape cannot be separated in reality. It follows, he claims, that such qualities cannot be separated in idea either, and so one cannot have an abstract idea of a single quality, such as a determinate red of some shade. He says, "I deny that I can abstract one from another, or conceive separately, those qualities which it is impossible should exist so separated" (*Principles*, Introduction, sec. 10).

No object can have a color but no specific color, any more than an object can have a shape but no specific shape. Neither can a person be neither tall nor short, but no particular height; neither fat nor thin, but no particular weight. Berkeley claims that the same holds for ideas. So, the general idea of color would have to be an idea which has some color but no particular color, which is impossible. Or it would have to be an idea of a thing which has color but no specific color, which is likewise impossible. Similarly with the abstract general idea of a person. It would have to be an idea of a person with no determinate features, and it is impossible that there be such a person. Hence, Berkeley concludes that it is also impossible for us to have an abstract general idea of a person. Similar arguments would apply to the abstract general idea of any other quality (for example, shape) and any other body (for example, dog or tree).

Locke's view that abstract ideas, including general ones, are needed to explain certain features of language is also rejected. General terms such as "color" or "person" may immediately signify particular and wholly determinate ideas so long as one uses those particular ideas to represent or stand for many different resembling things. So one may have an idea of a specific person, for example, Mrs. Grundy, and one may use this idea to stand for many different similarly aged women. The idea itself need not be abstracted or general in order for this representative function to be discharged. A person would learn general terms in a language by learning that they correctly apply to a range of resembling things, and not by learning that they apply to abstract general ideas.

There is no doubt that Berkeley's worries about abstract ideas are motivated by his broadly nominalist sympathies. He holds that everything that exists, in reality and in thought or idea, is wholly particular; nothing which exists is really general. He also aims to correct Locke's view of language, which had been used to prop up the doctrine of abstract ideas. The further fact that there is no sustained discussion of abstract ideas later on in either the *Principles* or the *Dialogues* would naturally lead one to the conclusion that abstract ideas are connected, for Berkeley, just to the concerns he has with nominalism and language. However, this natural interpretation is not how Berkeley himself conceived of abstract ideas. On the contrary, he held that the question of abstract ideas is intimately bound up with nearly all of the further metaphysical points which he defends. He says:

> It will not be amiss to add, that the doctrine of *abstract ideas* hath had no small share in rendering those sciences intricate and obscure, which are particularly conversant about spiritual things. Men have imagined they could frame abstract notions of the powers and acts of the mind, and consider them prescinded, as well from the mind or spirit it self, as from their respective objects and effects. Hence a great number of dark

> and ambiguous terms presumed to stand for abstract notions, have been introduced into metaphysics and morality, and from these have grown infinite distractions and disputes amongst the learned. (*Principles*, no. 143)

Included in these distractions and disputes, Berkeley puts the debates about the infinite divisibility of matter, the notions of absolute space and time found in Newtonian physics, the thesis that objects have an absolute existence distinct from being perceived, the denial of the heterogeneity thesis, and the question of skepticism regarding the external world. We can illustrate one of these important connections with the heterogeneity thesis.

In *New Theory* (no. 122), Berkeley notes that the thesis that some ideas are common to sight and touch is supported by the doctrine of abstract ideas, in particular by the claim that there is an abstract idea of extension in general. The doctrine of ideas common to sight and touch, if true, would refute the heterogeneity thesis and that, in turn, would threaten Berkeley's theory of distance perception. Accordingly, Berkeley finds it important in *New Theory* no. 123 to deny that there is any abstract general idea of extension. Rejection of abstract ideas of this sort is needed, for otherwise key elements in philosophy stand open to direct refutation. A similar point may be made about the Lockean thesis that objects exist independently of all perception. In *Principles* no. 5 Berkeley indicates that this Lockean position is supported by the doctrine of abstract ideas in this way: if there are abstract ideas, then the Lockean thesis is true. In turn, this would undermine Berkeley's famous doctrine of *esse is percipi*, that is, the doctrine that objects and their qualities exist if and only if they are perceived. Hence, he needs to reject abstract ideas if he is successfully to ward off refutation of this key element of his metaphysics.

One further connection is that between abstract ideas and skepticism about physical objects and their qualities. One chief aim of the *Dialogues* is to undermine those doctrines which underwrite and provide support for skepticism, and among the doctrines which provide this evidence according to him is that of abstract ideas. The claim that there are abstract ideas is thus taken either to imply or strongly to support skepticism about objects. By rejecting abstract ideas, therefore, Berkeley feels that he has swept away one of the strongest reasons in favor of thinking that skepticism is correct. In these three connections, to the heterogeneity thesis, to the thesis of *esse is percipi*, and to skepticism, we see that for Berkeley the doctrine of abstract ideas is of fundamental importance to his philosophy, quite beyond his concerns with nominalism and language.[6]

Berkeley's criticisms of other doctrines held by Locke and others are also important and useful for understanding some of his positive ideas. He takes Locke to have held the representative realist theory of perception, and to have accepted the distinction between primary and secondary qualities. The representative theory holds that objects, which exist independently of perception, are perceived only indirectly, by means of the ideas one experiences immediately. Experiences of these ideas are caused by the objects, but the objects are not immediately perceived. Further, some of the experienced ideas represent the objects; these are the ideas of primary qualities which represent the objects by resembling real primary qualities in the objects. All of these doctrines are criticized in the opening sections of the *Principles*, and the criticisms are repeated in the *Dialogues*.

Berkeley contends that the resemblance relation between some ideas and qualities in objects cannot hold. On the contrary, he says in *Principles* no. 8, "an idea can be like nothing but an idea." Resemblance, then, if Berkeley is right, can hold only between one idea and another; indeed, he would doubtless say only between one idea and another of the same sense, as in one visual idea resembling another. This criticism, however, has no effect on a nonrepresentative realist theory of perception. Accordingly, Berkeley indicates in *Principles* nos. 18–20 that all indirect realist theories of perception lead to skepticism about objects. If any such theory of perception is correct, then objects are never immediately perceived at all; instead, it is merely the ideas we have which are immediately perceived. Hence, any knowledge we have of objects would have to be inferred from knowledge gained about the ideas then experienced. An inference here would have to be either a deductive inference, from statements about currently experienced ideas to some statement about an object, or some inductive inference. Statements about ideas, however, do not logically imply any statement about an object, so deduction is not an option.

The inductive inference needed to bridge the gap would most likely be an explanatory-causal one. That there are objects with various features best explains the ideas which we have on various occasions, and so the hypothesis that there are such objects is justified and known on the basis of this explanatory inference. Berkeley considers this option, and argues that it fails because it presumes that there is causal interaction between an external physical object and the minds of percipients. A mind, however, Berkeley takes to be a nonmaterial substance, and each of the philosophers he regards as advocates of the representative realist theory (Locke, Malebranche, probably Descartes) all accept the same view of the nature of minds. Hence, they are not in a good position to avail themselves of an explanatory inductive inference from ideas to objects, and so against their positions Berkeley's argument has some weight.

Berkeley is also suspicious of the distinction between primary and secondary qualities. However, in attacking this distinction it is not enough merely to note that ideas cannot resemble qualities in objects. The distinction between primary and secondary qualities can be held independently of the resemblance thesis. Berkeley does have an alternative argument, one which is related to the argument which uses the no separation principle against abstract ideas. He notes (*Principles* sec. 10) that the sensible qualities we attribute to objects are inseparable from one another. One cannot separate a shape (a primary quality) from a color (a secondary quality) in an object, leaving an object with just shape but no color. This is a logical point as Berkeley sees it; the separation is not logically possible. He infers from this argument that the primary qualities are "located" only within the mind, because that is the "location" of the secondary qualities, a conclusion which betrays his own account of the sensible qualities. However, Berkeley's real point is that what holds for the primary qualities holds as well for the secondary. So, if one thinks that the primary qualities are inseparable from bodies, as defenders of the primary–secondary distinction maintain, then Berkeley's argument would show that the secondary qualities enjoy the same status, and such a result vitiates the primary–secondary distinction. His argument on this point stands on its own, independently of the criticism of the claimed resemblance between ideas and some qualities in bodies.

All of the philosophers Berkeley criticizes held the thesis of metaphysical realism, viz., the view that objects exist independently of all perception, and some also held that objects consist in or are made up by a material substratum in which various qualities inhere. Berkeley argues at some length against both of these positions. He finds the relation of inherence especially perplexing and mysterious, so much so that the notion of a material substratum which somehow supports qualities is meaningless.[7] Moreover, material substrata would be entities which exist independently of perception, as would physical objects as conceived by the representative realist. Berkeley argues, to the contrary, that everything which is not itself a perceiver exists when and only when it is perceived. This is the famous thesis of *esse is percipi* or to be is to be perceived, as it applies to nonperceiving things. He concludes that even if the concept of material substrata makes sense, there are no such entities; and by the same reasoning in favor of the *esse is percipi* thesis, he concludes that metaphysical realism is false.

The argument by which the falsity of metaphysical realism is supposed to be reached has come to be called "the master argument."[8] Berkeley asks whether it is possible to conceive a sensible object existing unperceived. For him a sensible object is any sensible quality or a physical object. He notes that in the attempt to engage in this conception, one must have some ideas of the object, a general point which follows from the theory of ideas. However, he argues, in conceiving these ideas one is thereby perceiving the object, and so one has failed to conceive it existing unperceived. The attempt to perform this conception is self-defeating. Berkeley concludes from this that sensible objects cannot exist unperceived. He generally puts this point by saying that all sensible objects exist only in the mind, or negatively but equivalently, sensible objects do not exist without the mind. He does not mean, of course, that sensible things such as chairs and trees are literally in someone's mind. He means, rather, that they exist if and only if they are perceived by a mind.

Now this argument, even if successful, does not show that material substrata do not exist. The argument, after all, applies just to sensible objects, and material substrata in themselves are in principle not perceivable. Nevertheless, Berkeley can and does argue that the thesis that objects consist in sensible qualities inhering in a material substratum contradicts the *esse is percipi* thesis, inasmuch as the latter implies that sensible qualities exist in and only in the mind, and material substrata surely do not exist in the mind. He says:

> But why should we trouble ourselves any farther, in discussing this material *substratum* or support of figure and motion, and other sensible qualities? Does it not suppose they have an existence without the mind? And is this not a direct repugnancy, and altogether inconceivable? (*Principles*, no. 17; see also no. 73)

One could say, perhaps, that it is possible that a bare material substratum exists, devoid of all qualities which it supports, but it is difficult to see what reason there might be for supposing this. The point of adverting to material substrata was to find a support for the several qualities. So Berkeley is on firm ground in concluding that there is no material substratum, once the truth of the *esse is percipi* thesis is granted.

Berkeley's alternative view of the nature of sensible objects has two elements. First, he holds that each sensible quality is an idea; and second, he claims that each physical object is a "collection" or group of sensible qualities. The latter are not "held together" by all inhering in some material substratum; the collection of qualities is just identified with the object. If each sensible quality is an idea, however, Berkeley's view reduces to the phenomenalist thesis that each physical object is really identical to a "collection" or group of ideas. The claim that each sensible quality is an idea was merely assumed in the *Principles*, and Berkeley seems to have realized that this was a strategic error on his part. In the *Three Dialogues* he corrects this error by devoting a good portion of the first dialogue to arguments designed to show that sensible qualities are just ideas. Berkeley says comparatively little about what he means by the term "collection" in this context. What he does say indicates that he thinks of ideas which recur in the same patterns as part of what it is to be a collection of ideas. One sequence or pattern of ideas which repeats over time in normal circumstances constitutes a certain object; another repeatable sequence or pattern of ideas in normal circumstances makes up another. This seems to be what he means when he says that

> The ideas of sense are more strong, lively, and distinct than those of the imagination; they have likewise a steadiness, order, and coherence, and are not excited at random, as those which are the effects of human wills often are, but in a regular train or series, the admirable connexion whereof sufficiently testifies the wisdom and benevolence of its Author. Now the set rules or established methods, wherein the mind we depend on excites in us the ideas of sense, are called the *Laws of Nature*: and these we learn by experience, which teaches us that such and such ideas are attended with such and such other ideas, in the ordinary course of things. (*Principles*, no. 30; emphasis in original)

The *esse is percipi* thesis requires that each sensible object is actually perceived. It is clear that Berkeley thinks that sensible objects exist even when no humans perceive them. He says:

> I must be very particular in explaining w^{t} is meant by things existing in Houses, chambers, fields, caves etc w^{n} not perceiv'd as well as w^{n} perceiv'd. & show how the Vulgar notion agrees with mine when we narrowly inspect into the meaning & definition of the word Existence wch is no simple idea distinct from perceiving & being perceiv'd. (*Philosophical Commentaries*, no. 408, in *Works*, vol. 1, pp. 52–3)

In cases like these, when nobody perceives the objects inside a house or chamber, those objects nonetheless continue to exist. Berkeley also says that such objects would be perceived if some humans were to come by to perceive them. However, this truth about what would be perceived under certain conditions does not constitute the existence of the objects; to exist they must actually be perceived. Thus Berkeley resorts to God as the perceiver. God perceives all things at all times, and so actually perceives sensible things when no human is on hand to do so.

This comment about God's perceptions tells us something important about how Berkeley understands the position of the metaphysical realist. In saying, as the latter does, that objects exist independently of all perception, the term "independently" has to be taken to have broad scope. That is, it is to be understood to mean independently of any perception by any person and even independently of being perceived by God. Berkeley refers to such a view as the thesis that objects have an absolute, independent existence, which thus means that objects would exist even if there were no perceptions by any thing capable of perceiving, even God. This is the view that Berkeley opposes with the *esse is percipi* thesis.

This thesis, however, is in conflict with the position Berkeley had taken just one year earlier in the *New Theory of Vision*. In the latter, as we have noted, one learns to estimate distance visually by learning to correlate the visual ideas with the tangible ideas one would get under certain circumstances, including those tangible ideas one would get by walking over to the distant object. This way of thinking, however, presumes that there is an object at a distance that one can approach by walking, and so presumes that objects exist without the mind, or unperceived. Berkeley concedes this point (*Principles* no. 44); in his theory of visual distance perception he did make this assumption. However, he denies the inconsistency, on two grounds: first, he says that he made the assumption of tactile objects existing unperceived in the theory of vision as a matter of strategy only; it was easier to work out the theory with this assumption than without. Second, Berkeley claims that he could have worked out the theory of vision on the assumption of the *esse is percipi* thesis, and so the inconsistency is apparent only. Both these points are made in a single passage:

> That the proper objects of sight neither exist without the mind, nor are the images of external things, was shewn even in that treatise. Though throughout the same, the contrary be supposed true of tangible objects: not that to suppose that vulgar error, was necessary for establishing the notion therein laid down; but because it was beside my purpose to examine and refute it in a discourse concerning *vision*. (*Principles* no. 44; emphasis Berkeley's)

Representative realists agree with Berkeley that in all perception one immediately perceives ideas. Realists further claim that our experiences of these ideas are produced by causal interaction with independently existing physical objects. Berkeley is blocked from this position, partly because he holds that physical objects are not independently existing things, as we have noted, but also for another reason. He holds that each sensible idea is "visibly inert," by which he means that each idea can be perceived to be causally inactive. Ideas are not themselves causes, though of course they are effects. In the case of some ideas, those of the imagination, we are the causes of the ideas we have. Berkeley feels there needs to be a similar cause of the ideas of sense, a personal cause. Presuming that persons do not cause any ideas of sense, whether their own or those of another, Berkeley is led to the view that these ideas are caused by God. The theory of causation he thus embraces is that of *agent causation*, which differs from the usual way of thinking of causation as a relation between events.

When God causes ideas of sense, it is persons who are the recipients of these items. A person's body Berkeley will regard as a collection of ideas, as with any other physical object. No collection of ideas, he urges, is a perceiver of ideas. Hence, he takes perceivers who are persons to be spirits, or mental substances. These are simple mental substances or minds in the Cartesian sense, which are essentially active beings, engaging in acts such as understanding, willing, imagining, and thinking. Berkeley contrasts these spirits with ideas:

> besides all that endless variety of ideas or objects of knowledge, there is likewise something which knows or perceives them, and exercises divers operations, as willing, imagining, remembering about them. This perceiving, active being is what I call *mind, spirit, soul* or *my self*. By which words I do not denote any one of my ideas, but a thing entirely distinct from them, wherein they exist, or, which is the same thing, whereby they are perceived. (*Principles*, no. 2; emphasis in original)

But with this account of mind or self, a potential problem arises.

Berkeley rejects *material* substance, or substratum, as we have seen, and it might be wondered whether he is consistent to accept *mental* substance. Minds or mental substances have ideas in them, by way of perception, and we might think that this is no more than ideas inhering in minds, despite the fact that Berkeley debunks the notion of inherence in the case of material substance. Further, Berkeley agrees that we do not have ideas of minds, not even our own minds, and so minds may seem unknowable, and not the sorts of things Berkeley is in a position to countenance.

Berkeley recognizes these objections and confronts them. First, he denies that ideas said to be in minds inhere in them. At one point he writes:

> it may perhaps be objected, that if extension and figure exist only in the mind, it follows that the mind is extended and figured; since extension is a mode or attribute, which (to speak with the Schools) is predicated of the subject in which it exists. I answer, those qualities are in the mind only as they are perceived by it, that is, not by way of *mode* or *attribute*, but only by way of *idea*. (*Principles*, no. 49, emphasis in original)

Inherence is the relation which, in the Aristotelian tradition, underwrites predication. Where the quality redness inheres in a material substance, then something, namely the object consisting of the substance and that quality, is said to be red. Thus if an idea of red inhered in a mind, it would make the mind a red thing. This is what Berkeley is denying in the passage just quoted. Ideas are in the mind only in the sense that they are perceived by the mind, not by way of inherence. This is one fundamental disanalogy between material and mental substance.

Another disanalogy concerns knowledge. Though Berkeley agrees that both sorts of substance are imperceivable, he holds that this leads to unknowability only in the case of material substance. Material substance is unknowable because we are in principle unable to have ideas of such things. Mental substance, Berkeley says, is knowable despite our having no ideas of it, because we can engage in *reflex acts.* By this he means that whenever one engages in a perceptual act, or has any other ideas such as those of imagination or of thinking, one can also train one's awareness on to *what* is engaging in those perceptual or cognitive activities and this active thing is the self or mind. The awareness one then has, the reflex act, is not mediated by ideas, and so the awareness of the self is direct or immediate. However, as it is not mediated by ideas it is not a form of perception. Instead, in a reflex act one is aware *that* the mind is engaging in some cognitive act, and it is this awareness that the mind is so engaged that yields knowledge of the mind on that occasion. Indeed, Berkeley holds that this knowledge is immediate or, as he puts it, intuitive, not based on other bits of knowledge. This, he feels, is an important *epistemic* disanalogy between material and mental substance.[9]

We have seen thus far that Berkeley's philosophy allows for spirits. These are of two sorts: finite spirits, which are persons, and one infinite spirit or God. There are also ideas of sense, imagination, and memory, taken singly or in groups. Some groups of ideas of sense, we have noted, Berkeley takes to be physical objects; these are collections of ideas in which ideas which recur in regular patterns are grouped. Aside from the various acts in which minds engage, these are the bare elements of Berkeley's metaphysics. It is an austere idealist metaphysical picture: austere because of the few types of entities it accepts; and idealist in virtue of acceptance of the *esse is percipi* thesis, the specific collections account of objects which takes ideas as the elements of the collections, and the thesis that minds are nonmaterial, spiritual substances.

3. Perception and Knowledge

One alternative to a representative realist theory of perception, and to any nonrepresentative version of indirect realism, would be *direct* realism. Such a theory would hold that it is physical objects themselves which are typically immediately perceived; perception of objects is not mediated by perception of ideas. Berkeley cannot hold this theory; indeed, it is a theory which is virtually unthought of until Thomas Reid toward the end of the eighteenth century. The reason Berkeley cannot hold direct realism, of course, is that Berkeley is not a metaphysical realist about the existence and nature of objects. Nevertheless, he does hold, or try to hold, a theory of perception which comes close to direct realism without embracing metaphysical realism.

With the representative realist, Berkeley accepts the theory of ideas. Hence, he agrees that in every perception, some ideas are immediately perceived. However, as Berkeley thinks that physical objects are just collections of ideas, he thus feels entitled to hold as well that physical objects are immediately perceived. This is the main perceptual component of direct realism, and it is on this point that the latter theory and Berkeley's coincide. One passage which shows that this is Berkeley's position comes from the *Three Dialogues*:

> Wood, stones, fire, water, flesh, iron, and the like things, which I name and discourse of, are things that I know. And I should not have known them, but that I perceived them by my senses; and things perceived by the senses are immediately perceived. (*Works*, vol. 2, p. 230)

Another passage written years later makes the same point; it occurs in a letter from Berkeley to the American philosopher Samuel Johnson:

> I see no difficulty in conceiving a change of state, such as is vulgarly called Death, as well without as with material substance. It is sufficient for that purpose that we allow sensible bodies, *i.e.*, such as are immediately perceived by sight and touch. (*Works*, vol. 2, p. 282)

While these passages help to show that Berkeley said he accepted the view that objects are immediately perceived, one might wonder whether he can consistently hold this position so long as he also holds the theory of ideas.[10] To see that he can, we need to reconsider his collections theory of objects along with his views on perception.

Suppose that a person immediately perceives some group of ideas at a given time, and imagine further that all of the members of this group are elements of the collection of ideas which make up or constitute some physical object, perhaps a chair. Then Berkeley can hold that *by* immediately perceiving the group of ideas, all of which are elements of the collection which *is* the chair, then that person also immediately perceives the chair. One analogy might be the case of seeing a brick wall. By seeing some of the bricks which make up the wall, one thereby sees the wall. One need not see every brick in the wall in order to see the wall by seeing some of its bricks. Similarly with Berkeley's account: one need not immediately perceive every idea in the collection which is the chair in order immediately to see the chair by immediately perceiving some of the constituent ideas in the collection.

This example of the bricks in the wall is merely an analogy, but it is inexact. The bricks are parts of the wall, while the ideas which are constituents in a collection are not parts of the object. A better example would thus be one in which a person sees some whole – say a division of marching troops – by seeing some constituent elements of it which are not parts, such as some of the troops in the division. By seeing some, but not all, of these troop constituents, one thereby sees the division. This example exploits the relation of member-to-larger-whole which is more closely analogous to Berkeley's collections account of objects, and shows more narrowly how Berkeley can claim that objects are immediately perceived when one immediately perceives some of their constituents.

It is to be stressed that what is given here is an interpretation. Berkeley does not actually say that one immediately perceives an object *by* immediately perceiving some of the constituent ideas which make up the collection identical to the object. What he says explicitly is everything else in the interpretation: the theory of ideas, the collections account of objects, and the thesis that objects are often immediately perceived. The claim that objects are immediately perceived by immediately perceiving some elements making up the object is the added interpretive element, but it is a justified addition, since it, and it seems only it, enables Berkeley to reach his overall conclusion that objects are immediately perceived.[11]

In order for Berkeley to say that physical objects are immediately perceived, he must use the term "immediately perceives" in a narrow way. It must be understood as essentially a non-epistemic concept, in the sense that immediately perceiving something does not imply that one gains knowledge or a justified belief about that thing. We can see this easily by supposing that "Person P immediately perceives object O" means something like "P acquires knowledge of O." Reverting to our example of the brick wall, from the fact that person P acquires knowledge of a group of bricks, which he would do if he immediately perceived the bricks given this meaning equivalence, it does not follow that P acquires any knowledge of a wall, even though the bricks are parts of the wall. He may know what bricks are, acquire knowledge of bricks that are part of a wall, but fail to know that it is a wall there because he lacks the concept of a wall. The relevant inference will break down when the relevant term is epistemic in this way. But we have seen that Berkeley needs to be able to say that one immediately perceives an object by immediately perceiving some of the elements which make up the collection which is the object. For this inference to succeed, Berkeley's concept of immediate perception must be non-epistemic.[12]

However, we should not conclude from this that immediately perceiving a thing has no relation to gaining knowledge of that thing. By immediately perceiving a thing, one may thereby acquire knowledge of that thing as a result. One may acquire knowledge of a chair by immediate perception of that chair. This is Berkeley's view, and he goes to some length to contrast his view of knowledge gained in perception with the views he finds in the representative realist. In fact, on the question of knowledge, Berkeley goes even further, claiming that on his account one often acquires immediate (intuitive) and certain knowledge of objects as a result of immediately perceiving them.

The notion of immediate, intuitive knowledge derives from Locke. He first defines knowledge: "*Knowledge* then seems to me to be nothing but *the perception of the connexion and agreement, or disagreement and repugnancy of any of our Ideas.* In this alone it consists" (*Essay*, IV, i, 1; emphasis Locke's). In terms of this definition, Locke then defines intuitive knowledge:

> if we will reflect on our own ways of Thinking, we shall find, that sometimes the Mind perceives the Agreement or Disagreement of two *Ideas* immediately by themselves, without the intervention of any other: And this, I think, we may call *Intuitive Knowledge*. (*Essay*, IV, ii, 1; emphasis Locke's)

The immediacy of intuitive knowledge, then, is that it is knowledge which is not dependent on other knowledge. In one of Locke's examples, one knows intuitively that white is not black, and one does this directly without the intervention of (dependency on) any other idea or knowledge.

Locke himself was unwilling to maintain that we have intuitive knowledge of objects. But in the *Commentaries*, Berkeley claims that we do have intuitive knowledge of objects and not merely of ideas. Two passages show this to be so:

> We have intuitive Knowledge of the Existence of other things besides our selves & even praecedaneous to the Knowledge of our own Existence, in that we must have Ideas or else we cannot think. (*Philosophical Commentaries*, no. 547, in *Works*, vol. 1, p. 69)
>
> I am the farthest from Scepticism of any man. I know with an intuitive knowledge the existence of other things as well as my own soul. This is w^{t} Locke nor scarce any other Thinking Philosopher will pretend to. (ibid., no. 563; p. 70)

To see that by the term "other things" Berkeley is referring to physical objects, we may consider this passage:

> we see philosophers distrust their senses, and doubt of the existence of heaven and earth, of everything they see and feel, even of their own bodies. And after all their labour and struggle of thought, they are forced to own, we cannot attain to any self-evident or demonstrative knowledge of the existence of sensible things. But all this doubtfulness which so bewilders and confounds the mind, and makes philosophy ridiculous in the eyes of the world, vanishes, if we annex a meaning to our words, and do not amuse ourselves with the terms *absolute, external, exist,* and such like, signifying I know not what. (*Principles*, no. 88)

These passages show that Berkeley accepts the position that physical objects are things about which we have immediate, intuitive knowledge. He also indicates that this is knowledge we can have *because* objects are immediately perceived. He says:

> I see this cherry, I feel it, taste it: and I am sure nothing cannot be seen or felt or tasted; it is therefore real. Take away the sensations of softness, moisture, redness, tartness, and you take away the cherry . . . a cherry, I say, is nothing but a congeries of sensible impressions or ideas perceived by the various senses . . . When I see, and feel, and taste, in sundry matters, I am sure the cherry exists or is real. (*Works*, vol. 2, p. 249)

Here Berkeley is speaking of certainty rather than intuitive knowledge, but I doubt that this matters. Certain knowledge which is not demonstrative, Berkeley would hold, is intuitive knowledge. Moreover, this passage does not outright mention *immediate* perception, but just instances of perception with no qualification. Still, I think we can be reasonably confident that Berkeley is referring to immediate perception of the cherry, because in cases where *mediate* perception is at issue, he uniformly puts in the qualifying term "mediate." The default position, so to speak, is that Berkeley means immediate perception when he uses the term "perceives" and related terms (for example, "sees," "feels") without a qualifier. With these points clarified, we can read the passage as claiming that we often gain intuitive knowledge of objects as a result of immediately perceiving them.[13]

Berkeley also claims that we have *certain* knowledge of objects as a result of immediately perceiving them. The last-quoted passage suggests this, as do these:

> if by *material substance* is meant only sensible body, that which is seen and felt (and the unphilosophical part of the world, I dare say, mean no more) then I am more certain of matter's existence than you or any other philosopher pretend to be . . . I do therefore assert, that I am as certain as of my own being that there are bodies or corporeal substances. (*Works*, pp. 237–8)
>
> N.B. I am more for reality than any other Philosophers, they make a thousand doubts & know not certainly but we may be deceiv'd. I assert the direct contrary. (*Philosophical Commentaries*, no. 517)

In the first passage Berkeley is speaking through Philonous, and contrasting his epistemic view with that of Hylas, who stands for the representative realist. In both passages, Berkeley's tone is boastful, claiming a kind of superiority of his theory over that of the realist. This tone may be misplaced and unwarranted, however, because Berkeley does not mean by "certain" what his predecessors had meant. For Descartes, for instance, a belief counts as certain when one cannot be mistaken in that belief, or when one cannot doubt or have grounds for doubting that belief. This is not what Berkeley means by the term, however; he has a weakened concept of certainty. For him, a belief counts as certain when one has no *actual* grounds for doubting it, and so many beliefs about objects will count as certain on that understanding of the term. Indeed, on such a weakened concept of certainty, it is not clear why Descartes or Locke could not also plausibly claim that some of our beliefs about objects qualify as certain.

The empiricists generally, and Berkeley in particular, have all been taken to hold a certain theory of knowledge which we would nowadays say is *foundationalist*. On the empiricist version of this theory, it is said, the basic knowledge on which all else rests is immediate (intuitive) knowledge of ideas; and all nonbasic knowledge, including that of objects, if there is any, is derived in some manner from the basic knowledge of ideas. Whatever may be said of the merits of this account for Locke or Hume, it does not correctly describe Berkeley's position. We have already seen two reasons why this is so. First, Berkeley holds that we have immediate, intuitive knowledge of the self as a result not of the experience of ideas but as the result of engaging in reflex acts. Second, Berkeley claims that we have immediate, intuitive knowledge of physical objects, as lately described. Neither of these two types of knowledge is derived from more basic knowledge of ideas. Hence, if Berkeley is a foundationalist at all about knowledge, what is to count as basic knowledge will have to be considerably augmented over merely knowledge of ideas.

4. Skepticism and Common Sense

In the *Three Dialogues* more so than in other works, Berkeley stresses that he aims to vanquish skepticism, and to defend common sense. He has in mind skepticism about the physical world, the sort of view which says that we do not have knowledge of objects, either in perception or by any other manner. He indicates that four doctrines of his opponents actually lead to skepticism, in the sense either of entailing it or at least strongly supporting it. These doctrines are the thesis that there are abstract ideas, the thesis that objects consist in material substance with inherent qualities, the thesis of metaphysical realism, and the representative realist theory of perception.[14] However, none of the first three claims nor their conjunction actually leads to skepticism directly. This is because each of these theses taken alone is consistent with direct realism concerning the perception of objects. On that theory objects are immediately perceived, and we know that Berkeley takes immediate perception of objects to suffice for intuitive knowledge of those same objects. The same may be said of the conjunction of these three theses: that conjunction is also consistent with direct realism. Berkeley's point in claiming that these theses lead to skepticism is a little more complex. The thesis of abstract ideas and the thesis of material substance each imply that metaphysical realism is correct, and this taken together with the theory of ideas implies that some form of indirect realism is true. The form which most concerns Berkeley is representative realism. It is this which leads to skepticism; the other doctrines lead to skepticism only indirectly and via coupling with the theory of ideas and the tacit dismissal of direct realism as a serious option.

Berkeley says that he aims to vanquish skepticism. This may mean just refuting those doctrines which he says lead to skepticism, an enterprise we have already charted above. This would have the effect of sweeping away some of the ground for skepticism, maybe even all of the ground for it. However, it would not refute skepticism itself; refuting or falsifying the support for a doctrine is not generally sufficient for falsification of the doctrine. But Berkeley does want to do that, and not merely undermine the support for skepticism. He says:

> If the principles, which I here endeavor to propagate, are admitted for true; the consequences which, I think, evidently flow from thence, are, that atheism and scepticism will be utterly destroyed, many intricate points made plain, great difficulties solved, several useless parts of science retrenched, speculation reduced to practice, and men reduced from paradox to common sense. (Preface to *Dialogues*, in *Works*, vol. 2, p. 168)

Berkeley seems to think that merely by establishing the *esse is percipi* thesis he has thereby refuted skepticism. He writes:

> I can as well doubt of my own being, as of the being of those things which I actually perceive by my senses: it being a manifest contradiction, that any sensible object should

> be immediately perceived by sight or touch, and at the same time have no existence in Nature, since the very existence of an unthinking thing consists in being perceived. (*Principles*, no. 88)

Establishing the *esse is percipi* thesis, of course, entails the falsity of metaphysical realism, and thus undermines something which indirectly leads to skepticism. But the *esse is percipi* thesis does not, by itself, refute skepticism.[15] In order to establish that we have knowledge of objects, Berkeley needs to establish that objects are immediately perceived, and we have seen that to do this, he needs to adopt the collection thesis about objects, and the thesis that by immediately perceiving some of the constituents in the relevant collections, one thereby immediately perceives the object. Lacking the immediate perception of objects, Berkeley would be no better off than the representative realist when it comes to skepticism.

The refutation of skepticism is one element in Berkeley's attempted defense of common sense. On the interpretation given here, skepticism is refuted by allowing for (1) immediate perception of objects, and (2) immediate, intuitive knowledge of objects. Both of these statements are regarded by Berkeley as parts of common sense. But they are not all there is to common sense, of course, and the defense of common sense goes beyond the refutation of skepticism. He makes extravagant claims in regard to common sense; perhaps the most extreme is when he says in the *Philosophical Commentaries* that he "side[s] in all things with the Mob" (no. 405). It is clear that this is an overstatement. After all, the *esse is percipi* thesis is hardly a part of common sense,[16] and neither is the doctrine of agent causation. So, Berkeley has to be understood to maintain that his philosophy fares better with regard to common sense than does any of the competition. The simplest way to understand this idea is to think of Berkeley's philosophy being consistent with a greater number of propositions of common sense than any competing philosophical system, such as that defended by Locke or Descartes. Berkeley claims that he wins such a competition, but if he does, it is doubtful that the margin of victory is very great.

Imagine that Berkeley *does* win such a competition; why should this make any difference to the overall plausibility or acceptability of *his philosophy* versus the competitors? There is no doubt that Berkeley thinks that victory in this competition makes some difference, for he has Philonous say at the end of the *Three Dialogues*:

> After all, is there any thing remaining to be done? You may remember you promised to embrace that opinion, which upon examination should appear most agreeable to common sense, and remote from *scepticism*. This by your own confession is that which denies matter, or the absolute existence of corporeal things. (*Works*, vol. 2, p. 259)

This passage makes it seem that degree of agreement or consistency with the propositions of common sense is the decisive factor militating in favor of one philosophical theory as against another. However, this is not actually the role that agreement with common sense plays for Berkeley. The last quoted passage comes on the heels of a long discussion of the factors which are used to decide for one philosophical theory versus another. These factors include the degree to which the theory explains certain truths in science, the degree to which the theory agrees with what are taken as received truths in religion, and the degree to which the theory solves outstanding philosophical problems without raising new problems of its own. Degree of agreement with common sense is just one factor among all of these other factors. It is just one more piece of evidence to be included and assessed in determining whether Berkeley's theory is more plausible, overall, than its major competition. Degree of agreement with common sense can also be used to break a tie, when all else between competing philosophical theories is equal. But this tie-breaking role does not elevate agreement with common sense to any more weighty status in deciding between philosophical theories.

Notes

1 Berkeley's confidence that one is not immediately aware of the light rays and angles is supported by his belief that if one is in some mental state, then one is aware that one is in that state. So, if one were in the state of being immediately aware of rays and angles, then one would be aware of being in that state. As Berkeley himself is not aware that he is ever in such states, he feels confident in concluding that he is not immediately aware of the rays and angles. Of course, he is not making merely a biographical point; he is confident that what is true of him is true of everyone else, too. The argument appears in sections 12 and 19.

2 The question of whether the newly sighted person could tell shapes by sight alone was perhaps first posed, famously, by William Molyneux in correspondence with Locke. Molyneux's question, reported by Locke in the *Essay Concerning Human Understanding* at II, ix, 8, was answered by both Locke and Berkeley in the negative. In 1728 the surgeon William Cheselden reported a boy who had been born blind and later given sight, and his report indicates that the boy could not tell by sight alone whether an object before him was a cube or a sphere. Berkeley took the Cheselden report to be some confirmation of his theory. He says: "Thus, by fact and experiment, those points of the theory which seem the most remote from common apprehension were not a little confirmed, many years after I had been led into the discovery of them by reasoning" (from the *Theory of Vision Vindicated and Explained*, sec. 71, in *The Works of George Berkeley*, eds. A. A. Luce and E. E. Jessop (Edinburgh: Thomas Nelson, 1948–57), vol. 1, p. 276).

3 The matter of the thesis of common ideas supporting the primary–secondary distinction is discussed in Margaret Atherton, *Berkeley's Revolution in Vision* (Ithaca: Cornell University Press, 1991), pp. 174–5, and pursued further in connection with Berkeley's rejection of abstract ideas in George Pappas, *Berkeley's Thought* (Ithaca: Cornell University Press, forthcoming), ch. 4.

4 Berkeley's theory was discussed critically by the psychologist T. G. R. Bower in his *Development in Infancy* (San Francisco: Freeman, 1974). It has been most fully discussed by the philosopher Margaret Atherton in *Berkeley's Revolution in Vision*.

5 The *Dialogues* stresses Berkeley's concerns with skepticism and defending common sense in ways not highlighted in the *Principles*, but does not contain a sustained discussion of abstract ideas of the sort one finds in the Introduction to the latter work.

6 Hume felt that Berkeley's attack on abstract ideas was an achievement of great importance. In a note on his own discussion of this topic, Hume says: "I look upon this [Berkeley's attack on abstraction] to be one of the greatest and most valuable discoveries that has been made of late years in the republic of letters." The passage is in Hume's *A Treatise of Human Nature*, 2nd edn., ed. P. Nidditch (Oxford: Clarendon Press, 1978), p. 17.

7 In the first of the *Three Dialogues* Berkeley discusses through Hylas, the spokesperson of his opponents, the idea that material substratum is spread under and thus supports several qualities, in the way that the foundation of a garage is spread under and supports the structure. This cannot be what is intended by inherence, however, for anything spread under another has some extension, and the material substratum which is said to support qualities supposedly, taken in itself, has no qualities. See *Works*, vol. 2, pp. 197–8.

8 The master argument occurs first at *Principles* 22–4, and is repeated in the first of the *Dialogues*, in *Works*, vol. 2, pp. 200–1. The master argument is not the only one Berkeley offers for the *esse is percipi* thesis, but it seems to be the main one. The term "master argument" derives from André Gallois, "Berkeley's Master Argument," *Philosophical Review* 83 (1974), pp. 55–69. The usual criticism of the argument as Berkeley develops it is that he confuses conceiving a sensible thing with perceiving that thing.

9 For further discussion of immediate knowledge of the self, in both Locke and Berkeley, see G. Pappas, "Epistemology in the Empiricists," *History of Philosophy Quarterly* 15 (July, 1988), pp. 285–302.

10 Additional textual support for this contention may be found in Pappas, *Berkeley's Thought*, ch. 6.

11 G. Pappas, "Berkeley and Immediate Perception," in *Essays on the Philosophy of George Berkeley*, ed. E. Sosa (Dordrecht: Reidel, 1987), and more fully in Pappas, *Berkeley's Thought*, ch. 6. See, too, Kenneth Winkler, *Berkeley: An Interpretation* (Oxford: Clarendon Press, 1989), pp. 155–60. For an opposing view, see George Pitcher, "Berkeley and the Perception of Objects," *Journal of the History of Philosophy*, vol. 24, (1986), pp. 99–105.

12 If Berkeley's concept of immediate perception were what Russell once thought of as acquaintance, the inferences would succeed. Acquaintance is knowing a thing, rather than knowing some proposition about a thing. But it is doubtful that Berkeleyan immediate perception is the same as Russellian acquaintance.

13 One does not always acquire intuitive knowledge of objects by immediately perceiving them. This may not happen when one is inattentive, for example, or when one simply does not have the concepts necessary to acquire knowledge in that context, as in the case of very small children.

14 For the first of these claims see the introduction to the *Principles*, sec. 6, as well as *Principles* no. 97 and *De Motu* 43; for the second claim, see the first of the *Three Dialogues*, in *Works*, vol. 2, p. 172; for the third, see *Principles* no. 88, and for the fourth see above and *Principles* nos. 8 and 18–20.

15 For further details, see my "Berkeley and Scepticism," *Philosophy and Phenomenological Research* 59 (March, 1999), pp. 144–8.

16 Berkeley tries to make the *esse is percipi* thesis seem commonsensical, when he says we should ask the gardener (a representative of common sense) why he believes that some object exists and the gardener will answer "because I see it." However, this is an epistemic point; what the gardener answers gives merely his *reason* for believing that the object is there. It does nothing to show that what it *is* for the object then to exist is for it to be perceived. The point is made in *Three Dialogues*, in *Works*, vol. 2, p. 234.

Chapter 8

David Hume

David Fate Norton

Much of what David Hume said about a broad range of philosophical issues remains of great importance today. In the first volume of his first work, *A Treatise of Human Nature*, a work in which he articulates a new "science of human nature," Hume focuses on an interrelated set of issues in epistemology, metaphysics, and philosophical psychology. More particularly, he explains how it is that we form such important conceptions as cause and effect, external objects, and personal identity. At the same time, he offers an equally important account of how or why we believe in the objects of these conceptions: of why we believe that events or things are causally related, that there are enduring external objects and enduring selves. In the second volume of the *Treatise*, Hume expands his account of human psychology, focusing on the origin and role of the passions and the nature of human freedom. In the third and final volume of this work he explores the origins and nature of morality. In later works he returned to many of these issues and also made substantial contributions to our understanding of political theory, aesthetics, economics, and philosophy of religion. He also wrote an influential six-volume *History of England*.[1]

1. Life and Writings

Hume was born in Edinburgh, Scotland's capital, on April 26, 1711. The years of his youth were divided between that city and Ninewells, his family's small landholding at Chirnside, a village near the border with England. Little is known about Hume's childhood. His father died when he was two; his mother thereafter devoted herself to her three children. Hume began studies at the University of Edinburgh in 1723 and continued there through the spring of 1726, when he would have been fifteen. After leaving university he apparently made a desultory effort at learning law, but soon enough was devoting all his efforts to philosophy, and especially to the work that eventually became his *Treatise of Human Nature*. In 1734, discouraged by his inability to present his views in satisfactory form, he tried the more active life of a merchant's assistant. Within months he abandoned this experiment and traveled to France, where he remained for three years and at last finished an acceptable first draft of his long philosophical work. In September 1737 he settled in London. In January 1739 the first two volumes of the *Treatise* were published and Hume returned to Edinburgh. In late 1740 he published the third and final volume of the *Treatise*. Two volumes of his essays (*Essays, Moral and Political*) appeared in 1741–2.

To support himself during the next fifteen years Hume took positions first as companion to a mad nobleman, then as aide-de-camp and later secretary to a British general, and finally as Keeper of the Advocates Library in Edinburgh. During this period he published *An Enquiry concerning Human Understanding* (1748),[2] a revised and expanded version of *Essays, Moral and Political* (1748), *An Enquiry concerning the Principles of Morals* (1751), *Political Discourses* (1752), the first two volumes of *The History of England* (1754, 1757), and a volume of essays, *Four Dissertations* (1757), that included his *Natural History of Religion*. By the mid-1750s Hume was financially independent because of the success of his writings, but after he had completed the final two volumes of his *History of England* (1762), he accepted two further public service appointments: from 1763 to 1765 he was at first Secretary, then Chargé d'affaires to the British Embassy in Paris, and in 1767–8 he was Undersecretary of State (Northern Affairs) in the British government. He then retired to Edinburgh for the last time, and lived there until his death in 1776. In his will Hume left instructions for the publication of his longest work on the philosophy of religion, *Dialogues concerning Natural Religion*; this work appeared in 1778.

2. Experience and its Limits

We lack a detailed account of Hume's early reading and education, but it is clear that he had a thorough grounding in classical authors, especially Cicero and the major Latin poets. In college he would also have studied a wide range of topics in moral philosophy: logic, including theory of knowledge and philosophy of mind; metaphysics and natural religion; morals and the theory of the passions.[3] He also studied elementary mathematics and world history and followed a course of lectures and experiments in natural philosophy (such sciences as mechanics and hydraulics, for example) organized around the writings of Robert Boyle, whose use of the experimental method obviously impressed Hume. Hume also joined a private library that gave him access to a wide range of books on the sciences then studied.[4]

Hume came away from these studies with serious reservations about the state of philosophy. The moral philosophy of the ancients, he concluded, was defective because, like ancient natural philosophy, it had been too speculative, depending "more upon Invention than Experience." In putting together their theories of virtue and happiness, its authors had failed to give adequate attention to human nature, "upon which every moral Conclusion must depend." Hume found modern philosophy, in some respects, to be even worse. In his notes on his reading he complained that modern philosophers, because they had emphasized reason at the expense of feeling, had not treated ethics as well as the ancient philosophers had.[5] As he summed up the situation in the Introduction to the *Treatise*, even ordinary people know that the philosophical enterprise is not going well. Even they can see that philosophy is characterized by tedious debate and ill-founded assertiveness (Intro. 2; SBN xiii–xiv).[6]

To remedy this situation – to give philosophy a new and viable form – Hume calls on philosophers to follow a new method. In the Introduction to the *Treatise*, itself an attempt "to introduce the experimental Method of Reasoning into Moral Subjects," Hume argues that the moral sciences must also make use of the observational and experimental method championed by Francis Bacon and used so effectively by such scientists as Galileo, Boyle, and Newton. Hume himself aims to develop a new science of human nature which is to be the foundation for all the other moral sciences (for logic, politics, morals, and natural religion, for example). But, just as this science of human nature is "the only solid foundation" for these other sciences, so too are "experience and observation," the only "solid foundation" for his new science of human nature (Intro. 4–7; SBN xv–xvii).

This foundational commitment to experience and observation is a unifying feature of Hume's philosophy. In a brief *Abstract* of the *Treatise* Hume describes himself as promising to "draw no conclusions but where he is authorized by experience" (Abs. 2; SBN 646). In *An Enquiry concerning Human Understanding* he argues that it would be useless to try to understand any event, any cause or effect, "without the assistance of observation and experience," and explicitly extends this commitment to mental events (EHU 4.11, 7.10, 18). In his *Enquiry concerning the Principles of Morals* he says that we can expect success in our efforts to understand "the foundation of ethics" only "by following the experimental method, and deducing general maxims from a comparison of particular instances" (EPM 1.10). In "Of the Original Contract," an essay first published in 1748, Hume tells us that "A small degree of experience and observation suffices to teach us, that society cannot possibly be maintained without the authority of magistrates," and that, moreover, the "observation of [certain] general and obvious interests is the source of all allegiance, and of that moral obligation, which we attribute to it" (para. 35; M 480). "Of the Standard of Taste," first published in 1756, tells us that it is obvious that the "rules of composition" are nothing more than "general observations, concerning what has been universally found to please in all countries and in all ages," and that in this regard their "foundation is the same with that of all the practical sciences, [namely] experience" (para. 9; M 231).[7]

To appreciate fully the force of Hume's remarks, we must keep in mind that they carry with them an unspoken but deep distrust of the *a priori* reasoning that characterizes the philosophy of the Cartesians. At other times Hume is explicit about the limitations of our faculty of reason and the shortcomings of those philosophical systems that give it priority. He pointedly notes that, although we all believe that every event or object has a cause, there are no valid arguments establishing this conclusion. And, although we all believe in enduring, external objects, reason cannot establish that such objects exist, and even if it could, would be of no use to that vast population of people and animals who, without the use of a single argument, believe such objects to exist. Although reason may help us determine how to achieve some desired goal, it has by itself absolutely no motivating force. Although we all make moral distinctions – we take some acts or persons to be virtuous or good, others to be vicious or morally wrong – it is a special kind of feeling, not reason, that makes this possible. It is this distrust of *a priori* reasoning, coupled with the commitment to experience and observation, that makes it appropriate to think of Hume as an empiricist.

What is often missed, however, are Hume's strictures on experience and observation. It may well be legitimate to classify Hume as an empiricist, but he is by no means an uncritical champion of empiricism. In fact, his commitment to experience and observation is qualified in at least five substantial ways:

A. Experience has intrinsic limitations. In our quest to understand human nature, for example, we may follow experience as far as it will take us, but we will still remain ignorant of the most fundamental or ultimate features of our nature. As Hume puts it at the beginning of the *Treatise*, we may try to make our conclusions as general or as universal as possible by "explaining all effects from the simplest and fewest causes," but because we know that experience has limitations, we must remember that any theory that claims to have discovered "the ultimate original qualities of human nature, ought at first to be rejected as presumptuous and chimerical" (Intro. 8; SBN xvii).

B. Moral philosophy cannot make its experiments "purposely [and] with premeditation" in the way that natural science can. Such artificial or laboratory-like experiments would disturb and distort the phenomena under examination. For this reason, the science of human nature must find its experimental data through "a cautious observation of human life, and take them as they appear in the common course of the world, by men's behaviour in company, in affairs, and in their pleasures." Hume is not, however, discouraged by this limitation. "Where experiments of this kind are judiciously collected and compared," he goes on to say, "we may hope to establish on them a science, which will not be inferior in certainty, and will be much superior in utility to any other of human comprehension" (Intro. 10; SBN xix).

C. Hume, as much as any of the Cartesians, insists that all sensory experience is indirect. We do not experience objects themselves. We experience only, in the language of Descartes and Locke, *ideas* or what we suppose to be mental representations of objects. Hume uses a slightly different language, but is firmly committed to this view. Near the beginning of the *Treatise* he reports that it is "universally allow'd by philosophers, and is besides pretty obvious of itself, that nothing is ever really present [to] the mind but its perceptions or impressions and ideas, and that external objects become known to us only by those perceptions they occasion." Hume repeats this claim in each book of the *Treatise*, in the *Abstract*, and in the *Enquiry concerning Human Understanding*.[8]

D. Given the fact that we experience only "perceptions" and further facts about the nature of our perceptions, Hume concludes that our deep and ineradicable belief in the existence of external objects is not ultimately due to the senses. The senses may play a role in the process that brings about this belief, but the senses operating alone would be unable to produce this fundamental belief. Moreover, the senses operating alone would be unable to account for our belief in causal connections or personal identity.

E. Experience is not the source of certain of our fundamental passions. Locke had argued that there are no innate ideas, and had made this conclusion one of the defining features of what we now call empiricism. Locke, according to Hume, was both confused and mistaken. Locke used the term *idea* too broadly and thus failed to distinguish, as he ought to have done, between two kinds of perceptions, impressions (original perceptions) and ideas (derivative perceptions). If we make this needed distinction we see that, while it may be true to say that there are no innate *ideas*, it is false to say that there are no innate *impressions*. As Hume puts it, it is clear that some of "our stronger perceptions or impressions are innate, and that natural affection, love of virtue, resentment, and all the other passions, arise immediately from nature" (Abs. 6; SBN 648–9).

As we will see, these perceived limitations of experience profoundly shape Hume's arguments and conclusions.

3. Skepticism and Belief

In the two and a half centuries since he began to publish his views, Hume has been routinely portrayed as a destructive skeptic whose principal achievement was to show that the empiricism of Locke and Berkeley, when taken to its logical conclusion, results in the denial of the reality of causes, objects, enduring selves, human freedom, and objective values; and who, moreover, was entirely satisfied with this radically skeptical result. There is a substantial irony in this assessment. It was Hume's immediate predecessors who had come, collectively, to the very skeptical impasse that he is said to have created, while Hume, although an avowed skeptic of one sort, sought to get beyond this impasse.

Hume's study of philosophy had convinced him that such important philosophers as Malebranche, Locke, Bayle, and Berkeley had already taken traditional metaphysics and epistemology to their skeptical conclusions. In the early modern period, it was these philosophers, not Hume, who first argued that philosophy is unable to provide us with reliable accounts of the real natures and relations of things. It was Malebranche, a leading Cartesian, who had argued that there are no true causes in nature, that our natural faculties are unable to establish that there is a material world, and that we know even less about ourselves than we do about nature. It was Locke who had concluded that our knowledge of substances, whether material or immaterial, reduces to a vague *something, I know not what.* It was Bayle who had argued that every conceivable theory of space and time, and every philosophical system, is incoherent. It was Berkeley who had denied the existence of material objects. In the realm of ethics and politics, it was Hobbes and Mandeville who had denied that there is any substantive basis for the moral distinctions we routinely make.

Granted, some of these arguments were mitigated by further considerations and commitments. Malebranche, for example, hypothesized that the activity of the Deity accounts for what we take to be natural causes and effects, and that the existence of the material world is established by (but only by) the revealed word of God. Locke's intent was more likely practical than skeptical; he wished, that is, to divert attention from fruitless metaphysical quarrels to more useful pursuits. Berkeley denied the existence of material objects in the hope of overturning skepticism and materialism. But the fact remains: Hume's predecessors were, intentionally or otherwise, deeply skeptical about the *philosophical* grounds of our most basic beliefs.

Hume clearly believed that human knowledge is limited in both scope and depth, and that philosophers' claims to know ultimate reality are shot through with error and pretension. He had, however, no need to establish this obvious point. Well aware of the pervasive if often implicit skepticism of his predecessors, Hume concluded that the most important remaining task of philosophy, indeed, perhaps the only plausible remaining task, was to show how, given the apparent triumph of skepticism, we get on with our lives, including both our intellectual and our moral lives. In contrast to his predecessors, Hume undertook to account for the fact that, although nothing is ever present to the mind but perceptions, humans not only have ideas of these entities, but also that we naturally or instinctively believe them to have a real and substantial existence outside the mind.

4. The Elements of Hume's Philosophy

In Part 1 of the *Treatise* Hume describes what he calls the "elements" of his philosophy. These elements, *perceptions* in one of two forms, *impressions* or *ideas*, are the only things "present to the mind," the only immediate objects of thought. Impressions are generally the more forceful or lively of our perceptions; they are also causally prior to the ideas that represent them. Ideas complement impressions insofar as they are said to be "faint images" of and causally dependent on impressions. Hume describes impressions as "all our sensations, passions and emotions, as they make their first appearance in the soul" or mind, and then distinguishes two kinds, *impressions of sensation* and *impressions of reflection.*[9]

Impressions of sensation, he says, arise "in the soul originally, from unknown causes." This is virtually all that the *Treatise* is ever to tell us about the origin of these impressions. The fact that Hume talks about *impressions of sensation*, or even about *sensations*, should not mislead us. How sensations arise and what their causes may be are not Hume's concern. He says that the study of our sensations is the work of anatomists and natural philosophers, not of moral philosophers such as himself. Consequently, he never offers a theory of perception. That is, he never attempts to explain how external objects (assuming there are such objects) affect our sense organs and thus become causes of what are called impressions of sensation, nor does he make any attempt to prove that there is or is not an external or material world. Indeed, at one point he says that, so far as his philosophical aims are concerned, knowing the source of our sensations is unimportant. Whatever their ultimate source, our impressions and ideas relate and cohere in ways that leave us with an ineradicable belief in causes and objects. As we will see, Hume does provide us with a detailed explanation of how it is we come to believe in external objects, but we must recognize at the outset that this is an explanation of belief, not of perception.[10]

Impressions of reflection are what Hume calls *secondary impressions*, thus distinguishing them from the impressions of sensation (the *original impressions*) with which experience typically begins. This is not to suggest that impressions of sensation are of more importance than impressions of reflection (they are not), but only to emphasize that the latter impressions are "deriv'd in a great measure from our ideas." We feel such original impressions as heat or cold, thirst or hunger, or those impressions that give us pleasure or pain. Of these impressions we then form ideas, and these ideas give rise to new and different secondary impressions. For example: I remember – I have an idea of – the intense facial pain I felt while walking into yesterday's bitterly cold wind. This idea of pain gives rise to a feeling of aversion, a disinclination, as it were, to avoid facing such a wind again. This new feeling, the feeling of aversion, is an impression of reflection.

Hume begins by suggesting that ideas are fainter or less intense than impressions, and that both ideas and impressions may be either simple or complex.[11] He goes on to argue that the real and fundamental difference between impressions and ideas is that the latter are causally dependent on the former.[12] The "first principle . . . in the science of human nature," he says, is that "all our simple ideas proceed, either mediately or immediately, from their correspondent [resembling] impressions." This important conclusion is supported by two facts. First, simple impressions and ideas are regularly found in resembling pairs; that is, it is typically the case that for each simple impression (the pain of a pinprick, say) there is an associated and resembling simple idea (a recollection of this pain).[13] Such a "constant conjunction" convinces Hume that the relationship between such resembling perceptions is a close one. Second, those who are unable to experience a given simple impression are unable to form an idea of that phenomenon. Those who have never eaten a pineapple (never had the impression of a pineapple) cannot form an idea of the taste of that fruit, while those lacking a particular sense organ are unable to form ideas of the qualities (color or sound, for example) associated with that organ (1.1.1.4–12; SBN 3–7).

The elements of Hume's philosophy include also the relations between our many and varied perceptions. He distinguishes two kinds of relation, natural and philosophical. The three *natural* relations, *resemblance*, *contiguity*, and *causation*, are in fact three forms or principles of natural association. If, for example, we see a portrait, its *resemblance* to the person portrayed may well involuntarily lead us to think of that person. If we think of the door to our home, an idea of the *contiguous* door frame and walls may involuntarily arise in the mind. If we perceive a particular *effect* (if we look out the window and see that, although the sky is cloudless blue, everything in sight is soaking wet), we may well think of the *cause* of that effect, namely, an earlier rain. In each of these cases there is said to be an "associating quality" that connects two ideas in such a way that the experience of either idea "naturally introduces the other" (1.1.5.1; SBN 13). Hume suggests that such naturally occurring associations are of great importance because they are "the only links that bind the parts of the universe together, or connect us with any person or object exterior to ourselves . . . they are really *to us* the cement of the universe, and all the operations of the mind must, in a great measure, depend on them." He also suggests that if anything entitled him to be thought of as an innovator it was the use he had made of these natural associations. The human imagination, he notes, is free to join or separate ideas so as to make up virtually any combination it wishes. Nonetheless, this freedom of the imagination is limited by the fact that "there is a secret tie or union among particular ideas, which causes the mind to conjoin them more frequently together, and makes the one, upon its appearance, introduce the other" (Abs. 35; SBN 661–2; see also 1.1.4.6; SBN 12–13).

As we have seen, Hume argued that we have the ability to place any two ideas together, and then to ask in what respect(s) they are related. When we do this, we produce what he calls "the ideas of *philosophical* relation." He distinguishes seven such relations. Think, for example, of two apparently unrelated subjects never before compared together. Think of the ancient landmass known as Pangea and the Eurodollar. We can ask whether our ideas of these subjects (1) *resemble* one another, or if they are (2) *identical*, (3) *contrary*, or (4) *contiguous*. We can also ask how they relate with respect to (5) *proportions of quantity* or (6) *degrees of any quality*. And we can even ask if the breakup of Pangea was in fact (7) the *cause* or *effect* of the Eurodollar. As it happens, this particular set of comparisons provides no significant insight into the subjects compared, but it does illustrate the extent to which we are free to explore possible relationships between any subjects or ideas whatsoever, including those that may never before have been thought of together. In calling such comparisons *philosophical relations* Hume was perhaps suggesting that just such imaginative comparisons are an essential component of the philosophical enterprise.[14]

5. Fundamental Ideas and Beliefs

In the first book of his *Treatise* Hume attempts to show how the elements just described work together to produce our *ideas* of causal connection, external existence, and personal identity, matters in which we believe and on which "life and action entirely depend."[15]

Causation: Hume is often said to have denied that there is physical necessity and that we have any idea of necessary connection. This interpretation is significantly mistaken. Hume had been convinced by the Cartesians, and especially by Malebranche, that neither the senses nor reason can establish that one object (a cause) is connected together with another object (an effect) in such a way that the presence of the one necessarily entails the existence of the other. Hume's own analysis of what we suppose to be experiences of cause and effect reveals only three perceptible features: (1) objects taken to be causally related are contiguous in time and space; (2) objects taken to be causes are prior to those taken to be effects; and (3) objects taken to be causally related have been constantly associated in this way. These are the only perceptible features of such putative causal connections. And yet there seems to be more to the matter. "There is," he says, "a NECESSARY CONNEXION to be taken into consideration" (1.3.2.5–11; SBN 75–7).

It is our *idea* of necessary connection that must be explained. Despite our demonstrated inability to see or prove that there are necessary causal connections, we continue to think and act as if we had knowledge of such connections. We act, for example, as though the future will necessarily resemble the past, and "wou'd appear ridiculous" if we were to say "that 'tis only probable the sun will rise to-morrow, or that all men must dye" (1.3.11.1; SBN 124). To explain this phenomenon Hume asks us to imagine what life would have been like for Adam, suddenly brought to life in the midst of the world and in "the full vigour of understanding." Adam would have been unable to make even the simplest predictions about the future behavior of objects. He would not have been able to predict that one moving billiard ball, striking a second, would cause the second to move (Abs. 11–13; SBN 650–1). And yet we, endowed with the same faculties, can not only make, but are unable to resist making, this and countless other such predictions.

What is the difference between ourselves and this putative Adam? Experience. We have experienced the constant conjunction (the invariant succession of paired objects or events) of particular causes and effects and, although our experience never includes even a glimpse of a causal connection, it does arouse in us an expectation that a particular event (a "cause") will be followed by another event (an "effect") previously and constantly associated with it. Regularities of experience give rise to these feelings, and thus determine the mind to transfer its attention from a present impression to the idea of an absent but associated object. *The idea of necessary connection is copied from these feelings* (1.3.14.14–23; SBN 162–6). The idea has its foundation in the mind and is projected onto the world, but there is nonetheless such an idea. That there is an objective physical necessity to which this idea corresponds is an untestable hypothesis, nor would demonstrating that such necessary connections had held in the past guarantee that they will hold in the future. From these considerations we see that Hume does not explicitly and dogmatically deny that there are real causal connections. We have no experience of such necessary connections and hence can be, at best, skeptical or agnostical about their existence. But there is an idea of necessary connection, and we ordinarily and naturally *believe* that reality corresponds to this idea. Hume's skepticism about causes comes down to his claim that our idea of necessary connection is derived from a feeling, and hence leaves us able to suppose that our belief in causal connections, however natural, may be mistaken.

Hume's account of our *belief* in future effects or absent causes – of the process of mind that enables us to *plan effectively* – is a part of this same explanation. Such belief involves an idea or conception of the entity believed in, but is clearly different from mere conception without belief. This difference cannot be explained by supposing that some further idea, an idea of belief itself, is present when we believe, but absent when we merely conceive. There is no such idea. Moreover, given the mind's ability to freely join together any two ideas, if such an idea were available we by an act of will could, contrary to experience, combine the idea of belief with any other idea, and by so doing cause ourselves to believe anything. Consequently, Hume concludes that belief can only be a "different MANNER of conceiving an object"; it is a livelier, firmer, more vivid and intense conception. Belief in "matter of fact or existence" – the belief that because some event or object is now being experienced, some other event or object either has existed or will exist – is brought about by the same experience that gives us the idea of necessary connection. When some *A* and some *B* have been associated together in such a way that *A*s are taken to be the causes of *B*s, a new *impression* of one of these objects or events automatically gives rise to the *idea* of the other. This experience has, moreover, the effect of transferring the force or liveliness of the impression to the associated idea, thereby causing this idea to be believed or to take on the lively character of an impression (T 1.3.7, Abs. 17–22; SBN 94–8, 652–4).

External Existence: That there are external objects, objects, that is, that continue to exist when they are not perceived and that are distinct from and external to the mind and its perceptions is, Hume says, something "we must take for granted." We can reasonably ask, however, why we believe that there are such objects. This is in effect to ask which of three faculties, the *senses*, *reason*, or the *imagination*, produces our belief in these objects (1.4.2.1–2; SBN 187–8).

Hume argues that neither the senses nor reason can account for the fact that we have an idea of external objects. Such objects are taken to have continuous existence over relatively long periods of time, while our sensory impressions are either routinely interrupted or exist for relatively short periods of time. Neither can reason be the source of our belief in external existence. The vast majority of humans believe in external objects despite the fact that they have not so much as heard of the arguments by which philosophers (Descartes, for example) attempt to prove that such objects exist. Consequently, it must be the imagination, the only remaining faculty of the mind, that is responsible for our idea of, and belief in, external objects.

The imagination achieves this important result because some of our sense impressions, although interrupted or short-lived, manifest a notable degree of *constancy* and *coherence*. I look from my window and have an impression of a mountain, of trees, and of buildings. I look again a moment, a day, a year later, and these same items, in the same relationship to each other, appear again. Such *constancy* is a unique feature of those impressions "whose objects are suppos'd to have an external existence." This constancy is, however, imperfect. The trees that I see from my window regularly undergo noticeable changes. So, too, although more slowly, do the buildings and even the mountain itself appear to change. But through all these changes my impressions of these items preserve a *coherence* that contributes to my belief in the continuity of objects. One impression may be only similar to the preceding one, but the difference is so small that I take the two impressions to be identical. Or, if the difference between two impressions is still greater, it may nonetheless follow a pattern like that of previously experienced items. Returning to his room after an hour's absence, Hume finds that his fire has changed. Before he left it was a cheerful blaze; when he returns it is no more than a few weakly glowing embers. But, having observed fires before, he is satisfied that the two states, despite their differences, are consistent with the burning of a single log. Impressions change, but they change in familiar and patterned ways that lead us to suppose that certain sets of significantly different impressions have a single, external, and continuing source.

Constancy and coherence of this sort enable the imagination, working involuntarily and unnoticed, to lead us to believe that these sets of perceptions are produced by independently existing objects, and to attribute to these objects a degree of continuity unmatched by the perceptions that trigger our belief in them. These effects Hume explains by comparing the imagination to a boat that, once put in motion and given direction, continues on its course even when the oars are at rest. Because many individual impressions and ideas are experienced together in patterned ways, the imagination is, as it were, set on a course. Then, even when the pattern is disrupted, it continues on that course. When the pattern is disrupted (when some objects are not now experienced or available to be experienced) the imagination goes on thinking about these objects, or at least remaining ready to think about them. The mere sound of a squeaking hinge gives us an idea of the door to which the hinge is attached. The idea of the door is linked to that of a hall, to a stairs, to an entire house and garden, to a street, a town, a country, to a continent surrounded by the ocean. My present perception of the mountain in the distance is so like my past perceptions (preserved as ideas in the memory) of mountains in the distance that I fail even to think of these as different perceptions. As a result, I form the idea of a single, continuous mountain. In addition, the force and vivacity of my present impression of that mountain is transferred to this idea, causing the idea to feel like an impression. When this happens, and despite the fact that the relevant perceptions are either distinct from one another or fleeting, I involuntarily *believe* in an independent and continuously existing object. In short, because of the behind-the-scenes work of the imagination, we naturally believe the world is populated with objects having an independent and continuing existence.

In the *Treatise* Hume initiates his discussion of external existence with the claim that it is pointless to ask if there are external objects because the existence of these objects must be taken for granted. He closes this discussion on a more skeptical note, saying he is disinclined to trust either his senses or his imagination. Having argued that belief in external objects arises only because of certain features of the imagination (its tendency to continue a course once begun), and certain features of perceptions (their coherence and constancy), he now notes that these features fail to provide unassailable grounds for that belief. Insofar as there is apparently no one who does not, most of the time, have an implicit faith in the existence of objects, philosophical questions about external existence can be dismissed as pointless. On the other hand, careful reflection on the question of external existence produces skeptical doubt and, moreover, although such doubt is always of brief duration, it is "a malady" that can never be completely cured. In the *Enquiry concerning Human Understanding* Hume argues that the question of the existence of external objects is a factual question, but a factual question that can never be given a definitive answer. Nothing, we have learned, is ever present to the mind but impressions and ideas. It follows, then, that we are never in a position to know if any of these perceptions represent or are caused by objects external to the mind – we have no direct experience of external objects and hence cannot know that they do or do not exist. This is in one important sense only a theoretical skepticism, for all of us naturally believe that external objects exist. As we will see, however, the recognition that our knowledge is limited in this fundamental way is one aspect of the form of skepticism Hume defends.

Personal Identity: Hume's account of the origin of our idea of personal identity, our idea of an enduring self, is meant to parallel his account of the idea of external existence. Several of his predecessors had argued that we have direct and intuitive access to our essential, enduring self, thus suggesting that any *idea* we have of such a self could be traced to what Hume would call an impression of it. Hume shows that these views are mistaken. In *Treatise* 1.4.5 he argues that we have no direct impression of an immaterial substance that unites our perceptions and that claims about the make-up of such a substance are unintelligible. In *Treatise* 1.4.6 he argues that our idea of our self cannot be copied from a direct impression of the self because there is no such impression. When we turn our attention inward, trying to catch a glimpse of some simple self or mind that underlies and unifies our diverse experience, we encounter only a succession of perceptions, never such a simple self or mind. As far as our experience is concerned, we are each of us nothing more than "a bundle or collection of different perceptions, which succeed each other with an inconceivable rapidity, and are in a perpetual flux and movement." Our perceptions vary from moment to moment; our thoughts are even more variable; there is no aspect of the mind that remains unchanged. So far as our experience is concerned, the mind is at most "a kind of theatre" wherein perceptions "pass, re-pass, glide away, and mingle in an infinite variety of postures and situations" lacking both the simplicity and the identity philosophers have claimed to find there.[16]

We do not, Hume finds, come by our idea of personal identity in the way that earlier philosophers had claimed. And yet we do have such an idea. How, then, do we come to have this idea? What factors give us our deep-seated inclination to suppose that our successive perceptions are related to a single, underlying identity or self, and to suppose that this self maintains, as Hume put it, "an invariable and uninterrupted existence thro' the whole course of our lives?" (1.4.6.5; SBN 253).

The answer to this philosophically pressing question lies in a correct understanding of how the mind works in matters relating to identity. In such matters our minds commonly make a substantial mistake. Although our ideas of *identity* (of a single object completely invariant throughout some given number of moments of time) and of *diversity* (of several different objects experienced one after the other) are significantly different from, even contrary to, one another, we commonly confuse these two ideas with one another. We take things that are in fact distinct to be identical. We do this because certain acts of the mind resemble one another and because these *resembling acts* come to be thought of as *resembling perceptions.* This confusion is then further compounded. We also come to imagine that our nonresembling perceptions, just as much as our resembling ones, are united by some underlying entity. We imagine or "feign" that "some new and unintelligible principle" or entity – a self, a soul, a substance, or at least something "unknown and mysterious" – somehow holds together or unites the diverse acts and perceptions that constitute our experience of our minds (1.4.6.6; SBN 253–4).

The process just described should not be thought of as an elaborate form of conscious pretending. On the contrary, it is unconscious, automatic, and, for all practical purposes, universal. We each of us naturally enough say of ourselves that we are one person, thus suggesting that our multiple perceptions are united or connected by something that provides a "real bond." It is only after philosophical analysis that we come to realize that our perceptions are distinct existences, each different, distinguishable, and separable from every other perception. This analysis makes us realize that there is no real bond between perceptions, and that we feel such a bond only because of the effects of the associating principles, resemblance, contiguity, and causation. That is, these associating principles so relate our perceptions to one another that we seem to feel a real bond between them even though they are entirely distinct and separable. Much as a determination of the mind or a feeling of expectation is the source of the idea of necessary connection, so is what Hume calls a "smooth and uninterrupted progress of the thought along a train of connected ideas" the source of the idea of the self. In his terms the idea of an identical self is one of the several important "fictions" the mind naturally produces. This idea has a source (it is derived from specifiable impressions), but on inspection we find that the relevant impressions bear little resemblance to the idea they engender. Identity is clearly not one of their features: "identity is nothing really belonging to these different perceptions, and uniting them together." Identity is, rather, a quality which we attribute to these perceptions "because of the union of their ideas in the imagination, when we reflect upon them" (1.4.6.16; SBN 259–60).

In an Appendix to the third volume of the *Treatise* Hume tells us that he is no longer satisfied with the account of the origin of the idea of the self found in 1.4.6, and doubtful about his ability to find a satisfactory one. He is, he says, still satisfied with his basic principles – that every idea is derived from an impression, for example. He is also satisfied that just as we "*have no idea of external substance, distinct from the ideas of particular qualities*," so do we see "*that we have no notion of* [internal or mental substance], *distinct from the particular perceptions*" (App. 11–19). But, he says, he now finds a serious defect in his account of how we come to think of our perceptions as bound together in "a real simplicity and identity." He is convinced, on the one hand, that if "perceptions are distinct existences, [then] they form a whole only by being connected together." He is also convinced, on the other hand, that "no connexions among distinct existences are ever discoverable by human understanding" (App. 20). Moreover, he cannot now see how to reconcile these two insights or "principles," nor is he prepared to renounce either as false. The notion of personal identity arises from reflection on the way in which the past perceptions of the mind naturally introduce one another, but Hume is no longer able "to explain the principles, that unite our successive perceptions in our thought or consciousness" or to discover any satisfactory theory of personal identity (App. 21). Candidly admitting that this issue is too difficult for him to solve, he holds out the hope that someone else may find a solution to it.

Moral Theory: Hume's moral theory encompasses substantial discussions of a wide range of overlapping topics. Of these, this essay focuses on four: the passions and their role in motivating behavior; the will, freedom, and necessity; the origin and nature of moral distinctions; and the kinds of virtue and the origin of political society. At the outset we should note that morality for Hume is an entirely human affair founded on stable features of human nature and the circumstances of human life, and that his discussion shows how these features and circumstances have, over time, given rise to morality.

6. The Passions and their Role

Hume distinguishes two fundamentally different kinds of passion: Some of our passions arise "from a natural impulse or instinct, which is perfectly unaccountable." These include the desire to see enemies punished and friends happy, hunger and thirst, and sexual appetite. Such passions produce pleasure and pain and thus are aptly called *productive* passions (THN 2.3.9.8; SBN 439). The remaining passions are impressions of reflection that arise, in specifiable circumstances, as responses to pain and pleasure and thus are aptly called *responsive* passions.

Productive Passions: When Hume says that we cannot account for the natural instincts that give rise to the productive passions he means only to emphasize that we cannot explain *why* we have these natural instincts or impulses. About *how* these passions work significant things can be said. We can describe and explain, for example, how custom, time, and distance affect such passions. We can also see that these instincts provide deep-seated and apparently universal motivations for human actions, and that some of them (our instinctive but limited generosity and our interest in the activities of others, for example) play a significant role in our lives as moral agents. Hume tells us, for example, that love between the sexes arises from the conjunction of three different passions. These include a responsive passion, "the pleasing sensation arising from beauty," and two productive passions, "the bodily appetite for generation [sexual appetite]; and a generous kindness" or desire for the happiness of our friends. These three passions work together, with beauty and the pleasure arising from beauty enhancing and even exciting both sexual appetite and benevolence (THN 2.2.11; SBN 394–6). Consider also Hume's explanation of that "love of truth, which was the first source" of the philosophical investigations he is pursuing. This passion, he says, is excited by some intellectual activities, but not by others. He then compares intellectual curiosity to the "insatiable desire" some have to know "the actions and circumstances of their neighbours" and suggests that each of these apparently distinctive desires derives ultimately from something "implanted in human nature." Moreover, Hume says that both forms of this curiosity contribute positively to human well-being (THN 2.3.10; SBN 228–54).

Responsive Passions: The responsive passions are impressions of reflection that arise in response to pain and pleasure. Hume divides these into two types, *direct* and *indirect*. Direct passions are those that arise directly from pain and pleasure; desire, aversion, grief, and fear are examples of such passions. Indirect passions are those that arise from pain and pleasure in conjunction with other qualities; pride, humility, love, and hatred are examples.

Hume's discussion of these passions is extensive. His goal is to extend his science of human nature by providing an explanation of the formation and operation of these passions, an explanation that treats them as perceptions – as elements of the mind – and not as physical effects. Consequently, his explanation relies entirely on features of the mind to provide what he called an "altogether . . . new and extraordinary" account of the passions (Abs. 30). These features include our tendency to associate ideas and impressions and also our ability to communicate feelings to one another directly (by means of *sympathy*), and they work together in a variety of ways to cause the feelings that constitute certain passions. Suppose, for example, I witness my brother acting in a clearly virtuous manner. According to Hume I will have an immediate (an unreflective and unmediated) feeling of pleasure in response to the action I am witnessing. Then, because of an association of ideas and impressions, I feel *love* or *esteem*, a distinct passion, for my brother. Three other passions, pride, humility, and hatred, are explained in this relatively straightforward way. In addition, a subset of these four passions may be mixed together to form one of eight *compound passions* (benevolence, anger, pity, malice, envy, respect, contempt, and love between the sexes) that Hume discusses.

The Role of the Passions: The details of Hume's account of the passions are likely to seem strange to us, but we can readily appreciate his goals. He wanted, first, to provide an explanation that is both economical (based, that is, on the fewest possible explanatory principles) and consistent with the rest of his science of human nature. This means he had to explain the passions without relying on speculative physiology. Many of his early modern predecessors (Descartes and Malebranche, for example) had accounted for the passions by means of elaborate but unconfirmed appeals to "animal spirits."[17] Hume, committed to the principle that nothing is ever present to the mind but impressions and ideas, and also fully aware that there neither is nor could be experimental evidence of such spirits, takes the responsive passions to be perceptions – to be nothing more than reflective or secondary impressions that derive from previously experienced impressions and ideas.

Hume also sought to rescue the passions from the negative assessments of many of his predecessors. From ancient times to the eighteenth century the passions had been routinely characterized as irrational, inexplicable, and unnatural elements which, given their head, undermine and enslave reason, the essential and defining characteristic of humans. Moreover, many of Hume's predecessors maintained that the human will is influenced by both reason and the passions. In marked contrast to these views, Hume supposes the passions to be an integral and legitimate part of human nature, and a part that is to be explained observationally in the same way that other perceptions (ideas and beliefs, for example) are explained. While arguing that reason alone can never directly influence the will, he explicitly rejects three related claims: that reason should direct the will; that reason can dispute with the passions over the direction of the will; and that we are virtuous only to the extent that our choices and actions conform to the direction of reason.

According to Hume, there are two kinds of reasoning, demonstrative and probable. Although both of these can contribute to our efforts to attain what we seek, neither kind of reasoning can by itself motivate us to seek any given end. Demonstrative reasoning enables us to determine, for example, the total of our bills, but it cannot motivate us to pay these. Probable reasoning enables us to determine how any given end is to be obtained, but, while information of this kind is likely to affect our subsequent choices and actions, knowing which actions will produce which effects is not in itself enough to motivate us to undertake those actions in order to produce those effects. "It can never in the least concern us to know," Hume says, "that such objects are causes, and such others effects, if both the causes and effects be indifferent to us." Unless we have a prior interest in those causes and effects, we will make no use of the related information (THN 2.3.3.3; SBN 413–14).

This analysis prepares the ground for what Hume calls a "somewhat extraordinary" pronouncement, namely, that "Reason is, and ought only to be the slave of the passions, and can never pretend to any other office than to serve and obey them." The discoveries of reason, he has argued, never in themselves either produce or prevent the desires and volitions that lead to action. Notwithstanding the widespread talk about the war between reason and passion, reason and passion never come into direct conflict because they have substantially different roles to play. The passions alone determine our choices, while reason can only inform us about the relations of ideas or the connections between matters of fact. Moreover, so far as Hume is concerned, the fact that reason has only this subsidiary role to play is neither inappropriate nor lamentable. Thus he concludes that reason not only is, but also ought to be governed by the passions. Note, however, that Hume goes on to emphasize that reason does play a substantial role in determining what our passions will be. If one of our passions, some desire, for example, is founded on a mistaken belief that certain objects exist, or on a mistaken assessment of objects that do exist, it is reason that would inform us of these mistakes. When it has done so, we can expect the desire we previously felt to be altered or even extinguished. As Hume says, "The moment we perceive the falsehood of any supposition, or the insufficiency of any means our passions yield to our reason without any opposition" (THN 2.3.3.4–7; SBN 414–17).

7. The Will, Freedom, and Necessity

Although Hume avoided involvement in traditional puzzles about the correct definition of the will, he twice addressed the "long disputed question concerning *liberty and necessity.*" Earlier philosophers had in the course of an extensive debate focused on the will as a faculty that either does or does not have an undetermined liberty or freedom to choose or reject anything presented to it.

On one side of the issue were those who embraced what can be called a libertarian or indifferentist point of view: the view that the will is free in the sense that it is undetermined by anything but its own choice and thus has *liberty of indifference.* These libertarians did not deny that there are external forces or motives and that these necessarily determine the choices and actions of all those creatures (animals, most notably) that lack freedom of the will. But libertarians did insist that the human will has the ability to remain completely indifferent to these influences and is thus able, however strong the influences may be, to retain its freedom in the form of an uninfluenced power of choice. They insisted, in other words, that the human will is capable of uncaused actions or choices.

On the other side of the issue were those who maintained that all choices of the human will are influenced in such a way that each such choice is the effect of some cause, and thus that any talk of uncaused choices is fundamentally unintelligible. These writers typically argued that while humans have a form of freedom, this freedom amounts only to the ability to act in accordance with our volitions, volitions which are themselves influenced by our intellectual faculties or passions. Hume aligns himself with this second group by saying that human freedom extends no further than *liberty of spontaneity*, or freedom from coercion and physical constraint.

Hume challenges the libertarian claim that the will may be entirely indifferent to external influence and thus is a faculty from which uncaused actions or choices may issue. He begins by noting that all parties in this dispute agree that, because events in the physical world are connected together causally, there is no liberty or freedom in physical nature. Given agreement on this issue, the only question remaining concerns actions of the mind. Are they subject to this same kind of necessity or can they be free of necessity?

To answer this question, Hume reminds us that our idea of causal necessity does not arise from sensory experience of a direct link between an object called a cause and some other object called the effect of that cause. Neither does it derive from some form of rational insight, an insight that reveals to us from the "essence of bodies" just how they are necessarily connected together. Rather, it is only after we have experienced two objects in constant conjunction that we form the idea that they are causally related, and we do so then only because the constant conjunction has produced "a determination of the mind to pass from one object to its usual attendant" (THN 2.3.1.4; SBN 400). In other words, we find ourselves entirely willing to say that physical nature is subject to necessity even though physical objects or events said to be causally related are perceived to be connected by nothing more than the relations of contiguity, succession, and constant conjunction. Consequently, if we find that these are precisely the relations holding in the moral domain we should be equally ready to grant that this same necessity characterizes this domain.

Hume surveys the moral world and finds that these same relations do hold in it. Motive, on the one hand, and volitions and actions, on the other, are just as regularly and constantly conjoined as a wide range of phenomena in the natural world. "No union," he says, "can be more constant and certain, than that of some actions with some motives and characters" (THN 2.3.1.12; SBN 404). Of course, human behavior may sometimes seem capricious, but the uncertainty or unpredictability of the moral world is no greater than that routinely observed in the physical world. The fact to notice is that the experience of irregularities in the natural world never leads us to give up our belief that physical events are determined by causes. A perfect uniformity of experience provides greater evidence and a higher probability than does less uniform experience, but, however mixed our experience, we never conclude that the actions of bodies are uncaused and the work of mere chance. We simply conclude that some events, some outcomes, are more probable than others, and express the hope that further experience will enable us to discover causes that are presently unknown.

We respond in the same way to experience of the moral world. A perfect uniformity of moral experience provides greater evidence than does less uniform experience, but, however mixed this experience may be, we never conclude that human actions, including acts of the will, are free in the sense of being uncaused or undetermined. Suppose for the sake of argument that the will is a distinct power of the mind. Now, if motives of type *A* (a particular kind of desire, for example) are always followed by actions of type *B* (an action of the will of the kind that results in the satisfaction of the desire specified), then we have, in Hume's terms, a *proof* that *A*-type motives cause *B*-type actions. If our experience is somewhat less uniform, we will be content to say that it is only *probable* that *A*-type motives cause *B*-type actions. If our experience lacks regularity or pattern, we will be content to say that we do not know what kinds of motive cause *B*-type actions, but this uncertainty will not leave us ready to say, nor will it force us to say, that these actions of the will are uncaused. We will not be able to say what the cause is, and we may even doubt our ability to find out what it is, but we will have no grounds for concluding that the choices of the will were uncaused.

Hume further supports his view by pointing out that what is called *moral evi-*

dence (that is, causal inferences based on the regular conjunctions of motives and actions) is widely and regularly mixed with *natural evidence* (that is, causal inferences based on the regular conjunctions of objects) to form a linked set of causal connections: A "prisoner, who has neither money nor interest, discovers the impossibility of his escape, as well from the obstinacy of the gaoler, as from the walls and bars with which he is surrounded; and in all attempts for his freedom chooses rather to work upon the stone and iron of the one, than upon the inflexible nature of the other" (THN 2.3.1.17; SBN 406). All things considered, then, we find no good reasons to think that, so far as necessity is concerned, the moral world is different from the physical world. Our idea of necessity is derived from the experience of objects or events found to be contiguous, successive, and constantly conjoined. The events of the moral world are in this respect no different from those of the physical world. The events of both worlds fall into patterns that give rise to the idea of necessary connection and consequently, whatever the libertarians may claim, each act of the will, each choice, must be supposed to have a cause.

8. The Origin and Nature of Moral Distinctions

Hume takes it as given that we make meaningful moral distinctions. He thought it appropriate, for example, to describe Brutus as virtuous and Nero as vicious, and noted that we competently use a wide-ranging moral vocabulary that includes such terms as *virtue*, *vice*, *motive*, *duty*, *laudable*, *blameable*, *benevolence*, and *justice*. In the *Treatise* Hume focuses on the origin of these distinctions. In the *Enquiry concerning the Principles of Morals* he pursues the same end indirectly by focusing on those qualities of mind that constitute what he calls "PERSONAL MERIT" (THN 3.2.2.2, 3.3.1.11; SBN 500, 579; EPM 1.10).

There had recently been, Hume tells us, an attention-getting controversy about the foundations of morality. The debate was over the correct answer to the question, are "*moral distinctions . . . founded on natural and original principles, or* [do they] *arise from interest and education?*" Those who chose the second of these alternatives and traced the distinction between virtue and vice to self-interest and education had claimed that morality is founded merely on the pain or pleasure that arises from considerations of self-interest and thus is entirely a matter of convention with "no foundation in nature." Those who argued that moral distinctions are founded on natural and original principles had claimed that morality is not merely a matter of self-interest and convention but "something real, essential, and founded on nature" (THN 2.1.7.2–5; SBN 295–6). Hume's account of the foundations of morality incorporates elements of both of these alternatives. He argues that some virtues derive from self-interest and are appropriately described as conventional or "artificial," while others derive directly from essential features of human nature and are appropriately described as "natural." Hume is careful, however, to distance himself from the moral skepticism of those (Hobbes and Mandeville, for example) who argue that moral assessments are really nothing more than expressions of self-interest and convention. He is equally careful to distance himself from those (Ralph Cudworth and Samuel Clarke, for example) who claim that moral distinctions are founded on *a priori* and eternal principles and relations made known to us by reason. Hume chose instead to adapt the moral sense theory that had been most fully articulated by his older contemporary, Francis Hutcheson. According to this theory, morality and moral distinctions derive from those features of human nature that cause us to approve benevolent motives and actions, and to disapprove harmful ones.[18]

The first problem Hume sets for his moral theory is that of explaining how virtues are distinguished from their complementary vices. His answer is constrained by his commitment to the view that nothing is ever present to the mind but impressions and ideas. Given this commitment, he need only determine whether we distinguish between virtue and vice by means of ideas or impressions. A lengthy argument shows that the distinction is not made by means of ideas. Hume argues, for example, that the ideas of virtue and vice do not derive, as the rationalists would have us think, from the relations of ideas. Such relations are too general or wide-ranging to account for the moral assessments we make. He also points out that virtue and vice are not known by means of impressions of sensation. Even the most careful observation of a vicious act (a case of willful murder, for example) shows us that moral qualities (vice and virtue) produce no sensory impressions of virtue and vice. As we have learned that all ideas are derived from impressions, it follows that the idea of virtue is not a copy of such an impression, nor can we, he adds, derive our moral ideas (those of duty, for example) from nonmoral ones (THN 3.1; SBN 455–70).

Hume next undertakes to show that virtue and vice are known by means of certain impressions of reflection, the moral sentiments. He argues that virtue produces in those who observe it a feeling of pleasure, an agreeable sentiment or feeling that he typically calls *approbation*, while vice, in contrast, produces in those who observe it a feeling of pain, a disagreeable sentiment called *disapprobation*. Consequently, virtue and vice may be known by these sentiments: "virtue is distinguish'd by the pleasure, and vice by the pain, that any action, sentiment or character" produces in those who observe it (3.1.2.11; see also 3.3.1.30). Hume sees, however, that clarification is needed. Many things produce pleasure and pain and yet are not taken to be virtuous or vicious. He provides this clarification by noting that the moral sentiments are distinctive feelings. They are "*particular* pains or pleasures." If, he contends, we can explain how it is that we come to feel these unique sentiments, we will have understood moral distinctions themselves. If we call a motive or action virtuous or vicious "because its view causes a pleasure or uneasiness of a particular kind," then, by accounting for the origin of that distinctive pleasure or uneasiness, we will "explain the vice or virtue" that causes them (3.1.2.3).

The desired explanation incorporates several important claims. (1) There are many different kinds of pleasure and pain. The pleasure produced by good music is different from that produced by good wine. Similarly, the kind of pleasure produced by moral qualities is different from those produced by other personal qualities. (2) Moral qualities are found only in persons. It is only certain relatively durable qualities of mind (intentions, motives, or character traits) that give rise to the moral sentiments. Actions, although they serve as signs of these moral qualities, are neither virtuous nor vicious. Actions *per se* are morally neutral. (3) The moral sentiments arise only in distinctive circumstances. These unique sentiments are felt only when we abstract from or ignore our own self-interest. The behavior of an enemy may cause us substantial pain, but if we consider this behavior impartially it may produce approbation, thus leading us to judge this enemy to be honorable and virtuous (THN 3.2.1.2–8, 3.3.1.3–5, 2.2.3.3–8, 2.3.2.6–7; SBN 470–4, 574–5, 348–51, 410–12).

Let us now, adopting Hume's perspective, review the behavior of some individual. To ensure that our self-interest is not involved, let us choose a historical figure, Marcus Brutus, the man now best remembered for his part in the assassination of his friend, Julius Caesar. Hume takes Brutus to have been a virtuous person. He does so because, although Brutus is seen to have taken part in the assassination of his friend, his underlying motive was not personal gain, but the preservation of the Roman republic. We, when we attend to this behavior (not only the relevant act, but also the motive, the quality of mind, that led to it), feel the distinctive pleasure of approbation and, in consequence of this feeling, judge Brutus to have been virtuous. If, to take a second example, we review the behavior of Nero, observing the substantial harm he did to many individuals and of the motives underlying his behavior, we feel the distinctive pain of disapprobation and judge Nero to have been vicious. It is important to notice that, while all such moral assessments make use of what we now typically describe as a *subjective* component (a feeling) in the observer, they are responses to features of agents (certain qualities of mind) that are *objective* insofar as they are entirely distinct from the observer making the assessment.

9. The Kinds of Virtue and the Origin of Political Society

As we have seen, Hume supposed that there are two kinds of virtue. There is a set of virtues (generosity and humaneness are examples) that are an essential part of human nature and that invariably accompany human experience. These he calls the *natural virtues.* There is another set of virtues (justice, promise-keeping, allegiance, and chastity are examples) that, although they derive from and are consistent with human nature, are conventions, the product of human contrivance. These he calls the *artificial virtues.*

Of the natural virtues we can say that (a) they are original or inherent features of human nature; (b) these inherent features are specific natural passions that have always motivated specific kinds of human behavior; (c) these motivating passions produce good on each occasion of their operation; (d) these passions produce positive sentiments of moral approval whenever they are observed to motivate the behaviour of another human.

In contrast, we can say of the artificial virtues that (a) they are not natural and inherent features of human nature; (b) they have not always motivated or influenced human behaviour – they were unknown to humans living in their first, uncivilized state; and (c), although their uniform practice appears to be absolutely necessary to the public good, this practice may on any given occasion be contrary to both individual and public good (THN 3.3.1.13; SBN 580). In such cases, the relevant virtuous acts produce only weak sentiments of approbation. More generally, the artificial virtues, although they *derive* ultimately from inherent features of human nature, and particularly from self-interest as it has been modified by a wide variety of contingent circumstances and necessities, have developed over the course of time in response to just such circumstances and necessities. In their original condition, Hume argues, humans had no need for the artificial virtues because their natural virtues or dispositions were adequate to maintain order in small, kinship-based units. But, as human society became larger and more complex, circumstances changed (some material goods became scarce, for example), and these changes led to conflicts within or between the existing social units, conflicts that the natural virtues were unable to resolve. As a consequence, new moral conventions – the artificial virtues – were gradually developed.

Hume's account of the development of the artificial virtues is also his account of the origins of political society. The most fundamental of these virtues is justice.[19] He argues that humans in their original, uncultivated state would neither have needed rules concerned with the distribution of property nor even been able to think of such rules and their attendant obligations. Before there was property (before, that is, there was need to associate specific external goods with specific individuals), rules governing such associations could not have been conceived. Having reached this important conclusion, Hume goes on to describe how the conventions of justice developed.

Of all animals, individual humans appear to have the fewest natural advantages in proportion to their needs and desires. Individually, humans are weak, inept, and in constant danger of losing whatever material goods they have gathered together. Only by joining forces could these deficiencies be remedied; only by forming societies (convention-governed social units) could humans add substantially to their strength, abilities, and security. Such societies were unknown to our remote ancestors but, fortunately, their development depended upon an ineradicable feature of human nature: sexual appetite. Societies were not a part of our moral beginnings, but they emerged naturally enough as a consequence of the socialization that begins with sexual appetite and leads to the family, itself a social group (but not, in Hume's view, a convention-governed one). This initial socialization eventually led some of our ancestors to realize that disputes over external goods were the leading source of conflict among them, that it would be in the interest of each individual to reduce these conflicts, and that this end could be achieved by conventions stabilizing the possession of these goods. In other words, the unreflective self-interest that characterizes the morally primitive state and that prevents the development of society was gradually restrained and redirected. This reflective or enlightened self-interest produced conventions (in Hume's terms, the rules of justice) having to do with property.

But how does it happen, Hume goes on to ask, that we treat the observance or neglect of property conventions deriving from self-interest, even reflective self-interest, as *moral* matters? How are we to explain the fact that we feel a "*moral* obligation" to be just or that we feel one of the distinctive moral sentiments in response to observed acts of justice and injustice? Hume's answer to this question is complex. He sees the development of the virtue of justice as a three-stage process. Stage 1 was humanity's original or "wild uncultivated state," the stage prior to the development of the conventions of justice. In stage 2 the conventions that define and protect property were developed (3.2.2.23–4). In time the societies made possible by these conventions grew significantly larger. As a result, it became more difficult for individuals to see how their private interest was being served by adherence to the conventions that had developed. As a result, some individuals began to disregard these conventions – they began to act unjustly, perhaps without even noticing that they were doing so. Others, however, did notice when these conventions were violated and they themselves were thereby harmed. Moreover, even when such unjust actions were remote and thus did not harm those who only observed them from a distance, these observers still disapproved such actions. They did so, according to Hume, because they found such unjust behavior "prejudicial to human society, and pernicious to every one that approache[d] the person guilty of it" (3.2.2.24). What in stage 2 was a self-regarding concern with the conventions of justice became in stage 3 an other-regarding concern that these conventions be followed.

Hume traces this further development to two deep-seated features of human nature. The first is our tendency to establish general rules and to maintain these rules with an inflexibility that can withstand even the pressures of self-interest. The second is sympathy, that inherent principle of communication that enables observers to feel the pleasures and pains produced in others affected by just or unjust acts that have no direct bearing on these observers. Once the conventions of justice are established, actions that conform to or transgress these conventions are "*naturally* attended with a strong sentiment of morals," a result, Hume says, owing to the fact that sympathy connects us with "the interests of society" (3.3.1.12).

Promise-keeping: Hume also argues that in humanity's original condition there were no promises or contracts. It was only as some of our ancestors found that they as individuals needed the help of other individuals, and for that purpose needed also a means of securing future relations (particularly those having to do with external goods), that the concept and the practice of promising arose. That is, humans began to make simple contracts with one another: If you'll help me with my harvest today, then I'll help you with yours tomorrow. As in time this practice became commonplace and clearly understood, individuals involved in it came to feel (again because of the effects of sympathy) the distinctive moral sentiments in response to the keeping or breaking of promises. It is important to note that Hume was satisfied that promises and contracts developed only after the conventions of justice had given societies their basic form. Consequently, although he agreed that governments are formed to protect the interests of the governed, he was critical of those (Hobbes and Locke, for example) who had argued that all political societies are founded on a contract or covenant (THN 3.2.5; SBN 516–25).

Allegiance: Our sense of loyalty or allegiance to a form of government or a particular head of government is another artificial virtue. Because our remote ancestors found rule-governed societies necessary to their well-being, conventions constituting justice and promises were developed and practiced. It was then found that our deep-seated tendency to put short-term interests before long-term ones threatened the existence and well-being of these needed societies. To rectify this situation, governments were contrived, usually tacitly, to ensure that justice was done and contracts honored. In time members of these societies began to feel that they *ought* to obey and be loyal to their ruler or state. It was at first enlightened self-interest that produced this sense of obligation. Later, because of the effect of sympathy, the distinctive moral sentiments were felt in response to actions showing or failing to show allegiance. Thus it is that we take disloyal or treasonous actions to be vicious or morally wrong (THN 3.2.7–8; SBN 534–49).

Chastity and modesty: Hume also maintains that chastity and the parallel virtue of modesty are contrivances developed for the good of society. He argues that the traditional family is dependent upon the commitment of the male to this unit, that the connection between a male and his children is not as obvious as that between a female and those same children, and that only if a male can be assured that he has fathered a particular child will he feel the parental bond that motivates him to contribute to the care of that child. It was in order to produce this bond and assurance that chastity came to be expected of women. If a woman restricts herself to sexual activity with her husband, then a link, a conventional or artificial link, is created between her children and her husband. When that link is strong, the husband can be expected to contribute to the care of these children. The parallel virtue of modesty has been developed and inculcated because it reinforces this important link. The woman who not only is rigorously faithful to her husband, but also always appears to be chaste is said to strengthen the grounds for believing that her children are also her husband's children. As a result, the conventions to which women are expected to conform have come to encompass matters having little or no connection with sexual activity. It was also only a matter of time until sympathy brought us to feel the distinctive moral sentiments in response to chaste or unchaste behavior (THN 3.2.12; SBN 570–3).

10. Philosophy of Religion

In Hume's earliest works religious themes are notable for their absence. The *Treatise* and early essays are unusual for their time insofar as they offer wide-ranging explanations of profound topics without a single appeal to supernatural principles. When in later works Hume does take up religious issues, his arguments and conclusions thoroughly justify his reputation as a religious skeptic. *An Enquiry concerning Human Understanding* includes two of his most provocative forays into the philosophy of religion, "Of Miracles" and "Of a particular Providence and of a future State," while *The Natural History of Religion* was denounced as atheistic even before it was published. His widely read *Dialogues concerning Natural Religion*, published two years after his death, cemented his reputation as a religious skeptic.

These works challenge the value of religious belief and attempt to curb its excesses by undertaking to show that it derives from sources or causes about which we ought to be deeply suspicious. In "Of Miracles" Hume argues that belief in miracles, a kind of putative fact used to justify a commitment to certain creeds, can never provide the secure foundation such creeds require. He sees that these commitments are typically maintained with a mind-numbing tenacity and a disruptive intolerance toward contrary views. To counter these objectionable commitments, he argues that the widely held view that miracles are violations of a law of nature is incoherent; that the evidence for even the most likely miracle will always be counterbalanced by the evidence establishing the law of nature which the miracle allegedly violates; and that the evidence supporting any given miracle is necessarily suspect. His argument leaves open the possibility that violations of the laws of nature may have occurred, but shows that the logical and evidential grounds for a *belief* in any given miracle or set of miracles are much weaker than the religious suppose. There are and always will be those who believe that miracles have occurred, but Hume's analysis shows that such beliefs will never have the force of evidence needed to justify the arrogance and intolerance that characterizes so many of the religious.

"Of a particular Providence and a future State" (supplemented by the *Dialogues concerning Natural Religion*) has a similar effect. Philosophers and theologians of the eighteenth century commonly argued that the well-ordered universe in which we find ourselves can only be the effect of a supremely intelligent first cause, the Deity. On the basis of this conclusion, these individuals went on to claim that each aspect of this divine creation is well-designed to fulfil some beneficial end, and then to assert that these further effects reveal the Deity to be, among other things, benevolent and concerned for humanity's well being. Hume shows that the conclusions of this line of reasoning (the *argument from design*, as it is known) go well beyond the available evidence. The pleasant and well-designed features of the world are balanced by a good measure of the unpleasant and the plainly botched. In addition, our belief in causal connections depends on the experience of constant conjunctions; these cause the vivacity of a present impression to be transferred to the idea (the idea of an absent cause or effect) associated with it, and leave us believing in that idea. But in this case the effect to be explained, the universe, is unique, and its cause unknown. Consequently, we cannot possibly have experiential grounds for any precise claims about this cause. On experiential grounds the most we can say is that there is a massive, mixed effect, and, as we have through experience come to believe that effects have causes commensurate to them, that this effect probably does have a commensurately large and mixed cause. Furthermore, as the effect is remotely like the products of human manufacture, we can say "*that the cause or causes of order in the universe probably bear some remote analogy to human intelligence*" (*Dialogue* 12). There is indeed an inference to be drawn from the unique effect in question (the universe) to the cause of that effect, but this inference provides no foundation for any sectarian claim or even the mildest forms of intolerance.

The *Natural History of Religion* focuses on the question of "the origin of religion in human nature." Hume asks, that is, what features of human nature account for the widespread (but not universal belief) in invisible and intelligent power(s). He delivers a thoroughly deflationary and naturalistic answer: religious belief does not derive from any universal and fundamental principle of human nature, but from second-order features whose operation "may easily be perverted . . . [or] altogether prevented." Moreover, it is the darker, less salubrious features of our nature that take the principal parts in this story. Primitive peoples found nature not an orderly whole produced by a beneficent designer, but arbitrary and fearsome, and, motivated by their own ignorance and fear, they came to think of the activities of nature as the effect of a multitude of petty powers – gods – that could, through worship, be influenced to improve the lives of those who engaged in this worship. In the course of time, these same fears and perceptions transformed polytheism into monotheism, the view that a single, omnipotent being created and still controls the world and all that transpires in it. From this conclusion Hume goes on to argue that monotheism, seemingly the more sophisticated position, is in fact *morally* retrograde, for, once having established itself, monotheism tends naturally toward zeal and intolerance, encourages certain demeaning, "monkish virtues," and proves itself a danger to society because it is a source of violent and immoral acts directed against those found to hold other views. In contrast, polytheism is tolerant of diversity and encourages genuine virtues that improve humankind. The important point here, however, is that all religious belief appears to derive from fear and ignorance, and, moreover, to foster the continued development of these undesirable characteristics.

11. Skepticism Revisited

Hume's skepticism, like his empiricism, is significantly limited. He did not suggest, as some skeptics had, that philosophy itself is doomed to failure. On the contrary, noting that his philosophical predecessors had left their subject in disrepute, Hume sought to reform philosophy by keeping it within the bounds of experience. He also, as we have seen, offered a comprehensive account of human nature and human experience, and some parts of this account (the discussion of morals, for example) suggest that we can have reliable knowledge of some aspects of experience. Nonetheless, for a number of reasons, Hume is fairly described as a skeptic:

A. He is, as we have seen, openly critical of claims or arguments widely believed to justify religious belief. Moreover, he offers a thoroughly naturalistic account of such belief.

B. He is satisfied that, because of our intrinsic limitations, not one of our sciences, not even the "science of human nature" to which he devoted himself in the *Treatise*, is able to discover ultimate principles. Consequently, he counsels us to be satisfied with this state of affairs because doing so will help us curb our tendency to suppose that we have discovered entirely "certain principles" when in fact we have only managed to produce "conjectures and hypotheses" (THN Intro. 9–10; SBN xvii–xix).

C. This ignorance about ultimate principles is accompanied by an unusual kind of agnosticism about the objects of many fundamental beliefs. As we have seen, Hume attempts to explain why we believe in such things as necessary causal connections and enduring objects. But the actual existence of each of these things is, he also says, a question of fact that we are unable to answer. Do we believe in causal connections and objects? We do, and we do so with great assurance. Are there, really, causal connections? Are there, really, enduring objects? In all honesty, we must say that we do not know the answer to these questions (see, for example, EHU 12.9).

D. In the *Treatise* Hume calls himself a skeptic. In the *Abstract* he says that the philosophy of Book 1 of the *Treatise* is "very skeptical." In Section 5 of the *Enquiry concerning Human Understanding* he expresses his admiration for the "Academical philosophy" or what we now call Academic Skepticism.[20] This species of philosophy, he says, protects those who adopt it from the arrogance, pretension, and credulity that characterize other forms of philosophy. The academic skeptic, noting the dangers of hasty and dogmatic judgment, emphasizes continually the advantages of "doubt and suspence of judgment . . . of confining to very narrow bounds the enquiries of the understanding, and of renouncing all speculations which lie not within the limits of common life and practice" (5.1). In Section 12 of the same work Hume defends and explains the form of skepticism he endorses. In doing so he distinguishes his position from the incoherent "antecedent skepticism" associated with Descartes and from the shallow "consequent skepticism" he attributes to the Pyrrhonians. Although these other forms of skepticism remind us that our faculties are unreliable and hence are of some value, both are unlivable not least because they each in their own way require us to suspend our common-sense beliefs (our belief in causes or enduring objects, for example). In contrast, Hume outlines a skepticism which he believes to be consistent, livable, and of significance. This skepticism recognizes that we cannot suspend our common-sense beliefs. It also recognizes that many of our philosophical or religious beliefs are deeply entrenched in the human experience. In the face of these psychological realities Hume shows us how to moderate our beliefs. He shows us first that neither reason nor the senses provide an adequate foundation for some of our most important common-sense beliefs (see, for examples, section 5 above). He then goes on to show that deeply entrenched philosophical and religious views are equally unfounded (see, for examples, section 9 above). The two findings are linked: if "we cannot give a satisfactory reason, why we believe, after a thousand experiments, that a stone will fall, or fire burn; can we ever satisfy ourselves concerning any determination, which we may form, with regard to the origin of worlds, and the situation of nature, from, and to eternity?" (EHU 12.25).

The form of skepticism that Hume endorses constitutes a philosophical method. This method calls for us to challenge our beliefs, even those beliefs that appear most natural or are most cherished. We are actively to *doubt*: we are to attend to the counter-evidence and counter-arguments; we are to avoid precipitate decisions on the issues before us; we are to take note of the inherent limitations on our faculties; we are to confine our enquiries to those subjects of which we have had, or can yet have, experience. Hume recommends doubting in this way because such doubt can be expected to diminish our blind biases in favor of our own views and against those who disagree with us (12.24; SBN 161). Such voluntary doubt, although it may never extinguish any given belief, may nonetheless prevent our belief from rising to the height of dogmatic and intolerant certainty. Philo, one of the characters in the *Dialogues concerning Natural Religion*, puts it this way: "if a man has accustomed himself to skeptical considerations on the uncertainty and narrow limits of reason, he will not entirely forget them when he turns his reflection on other subjects; but in all his philosophical principles and reasoning, I dare not say, in his common conduct, he will be found different from those, who either never formed any opinions in the case, or have entertained sentiments more favourable to human reason" (Part 12). The "mitigated skepticism" that Hume defends results in mitigated belief and tolerance for the views of others.

12. Conclusion

At the beginning of this essay I said that many of Hume's philosophical insights remain of importance today. In the course of the essay we have identified some of these insights. Hume saw, for example, that empiricism and skepticism, two philosophical perspectives with which he had pronounced sympathies, are subject to important limitations. The senses alone, he argues, are unable to provide adequate grounds for our ideas of causal power or of external objects. Nor is unaided introspection able to provide grounds for the idea of our self. These skeptical findings are, however, balanced by detailed accounts of how we come to have these ideas and, moreover, to form, unconsciously, deep-seated beliefs in what they represent. Hume also saw that our emotional life can be explained without reliance on speculative physiology and that our passions and emotions contribute positively to our well-being; that all our choices are part of a causal sequence, and indeed must be if we are to be held morally responsible for our actions; that our moral assessments, while probably not applicable to whatever higher beings there may be, are founded on human nature and human experience and are both adequate and reliable for human purposes. More generally, and even more importantly, Hume saw that all our disputes are best carried out in a spirit of moderation. The wise, he saw, proportion their belief to the evidence (EHU 10). Because the evidence for claims about the world around us – especially claims about the moral, religious, and social world – must necessarily remain incomplete, the wise will retain some suspicion about all such claims, and especially about their own.

Notes

1 In this relatively brief essay on Hume's work it has not been possible to discuss his views on aesthetics, economics, and history. For helpful discussions of these topics as well as others that are addressed in this essay, see the relevant essays in *The Cambridge Companion to Hume*, ed. D. F. Norton (Cambridge: Cambridge University Press, 1993).

2 Originally titled *Philosophical Essays concerning Human Understanding.*

3 In Hume's time philosophy had two distinctive branches. One, natural philosophy, included those subjects we now think of as the physical and natural sciences. The other, moral philosophy, focused on humans or human activity and included those subjects we would think of as the core of philosophy (theory of knowledge, metaphysics, and ethics, for example), as well as such subjects as psychology, political science, sociology, economics, and aesthetics (to use our terms), and important aspects of the study of religion.

4 On Hume's knowledge of the science of his time, and of Boyle in particular, see Michael Barfoot, "Hume and the Culture of Science in the Early Eighteenth Century," in *Oxford Studies in the History of Philosophy*, ed. M. A. Stewart (Oxford: Clarendon Press, 1990), pp. 151–90. To locate further studies on the many aspects of Hume discussed in this essay, see Roland Hall, *50 Years of Hume Scholarship* (Edinburgh: Edinburgh University Press, 1978), and Roland Hall and, later, William E. Morris, "The Hume Literature . . .," *Hume Studies*, vols. 4–7, 10–11, 13–14, 20–?.

5 See "Hume's Early Memoranda," ed. E. C. Mossner, *Journal of the History of Ideas* 12 (1948), p. 517.

6 The *Treatise* is cited from *A Treatise of Human Nature*, eds. D. F. and M. J. Norton, in the Oxford Philosophical Texts series (Oxford: Oxford University Press, 2000), with references also given to the edition (designated SBN) prepared by L. A. Selby-Bigge and P. H. Nidditch (Oxford: Clarendon Press, 1978). The reference here is to Hume's Introduction to the *Treatise*, paragraph 2, and to the corresponding pages in SBN. A reference of the form (1.1.4.6–7; SBN 13–14) is to Book 1, Part 1, section 4, paragraphs 6 and 7 of the *Treatise* and to the corresponding page numbers in the Selby-Bigge/Nidditch edition. A reference of the form "Abs. 2; SBN 646" refers to para. 2 and a corresponding page number of *An Abstract of*... *"A Treatise of Human Nature"*, para. 2. This work is included in both the Norton/Norton and Selby-Bigge/Nidditch editions of the *Treatise.* A reference of the form "EHU 4.11a"; refers to sec. 4, para. 11 of *An Enquiry concerning Human Understanding*, ed. T. L. Beauchamp, Oxford Philosophical Texts (Oxford: Oxford University Press, 1999). A reference of the form "EPM 1.10" refers to sec. 1, para. 10 of *An Enquiry concerning the Principles of Morals*, ed. T. L. Beauchamp, Oxford Philosophical Texts (Oxford: Oxford University Press, 1998). References to Hume's essays are to paragraph numbers, with the corresponding page numbers of *Essays Moral, Political, and Literary*, ed. E. G. Miller, rev. edn. (Indianapolis: Liberty Classics, 1987). References to the *Dialogues concerning Natural Religion* are to

the Parts of that work.

7 Hume's primarily historical works are by their very nature observational. In his *Natural History of Religion* he attempts to discover "the origin of religion in human nature" by extrapolating from present facts (religion and human nature as they are at present) and the historical record of the beginnings and development of religion. The explanation is constrained within the limits of observable, natural phenomena; no supernatural beings or principles are appealed to or presupposed. His *History of England* is an attempt to provide an impartial history, one that records the *development* of British political institutions and practices, treating these not as derivations from preexisting principles, but as the hard-won and still developing products of centuries of experience and observation.

8 THN 1.2.6.7; SBN 67. See also THN 1.4.2.21, 47, 2.2.2.22, 3.1.1.2; SBN 197, 212, 343, 454; Abs. 5 (SBN 647); EHU 12.9.

9 Most passions are impressions of reflection; see section 6 below.

10 THN 1.1.2.1, 2.1.1.2, 1.3.5.2; SBN 7–8, 275–6, 84. Although Hume wanted nothing to do with a physical anatomy attempting to explain sensation, he does repeatedly describe himself as engaged in *an anatomy of human nature* (see THN 1.4.6.23, 3.3.6.6, SBN 263, 620–1; *The Letters of David Hume*, ed. J. Y. T. Greig, 2 vols. (Oxford: Clarendon Press, 1932), 1: 32–3).

11 Simple perceptions, those of particular colors or tastes, for example, "admit of no distinction nor separation" (1.1.1.2; SBN 2). These perceptions are basic and unanalyzable. In contrast, complex perceptions, impressions, or ideas of Paris, for example, can be analyzed or divided into constituent parts.

12 As Hume proceeds he grants that some ideas may be as intense as, and function like, impressions. The first book of the *Treatise* may be seen as an effort to explain how some ideas come to have the intensity and force or effect of impressions – how, that is, these ideas come to be *believed.*

13 Hume's speculation about how one might form the idea of a previously unexperienced shade of blue (THN 1.1.1.10–11; SBN 5–7) shows that some simple ideas may not be derived from exactly resembling simple impressions. But he finds the example to show that even this apparently anomalous idea of blue is ultimately derived from simple impressions (from impressions of the gradated set of blues most like it), and thus he concludes that all simple ideas derive, either directly or indirectly, from simple impressions.

14 THN 1.1.3.4, 1.1.4.1, 1.1.5; SBN 10–11, 13–15. Note that three relations, resemblance, contiguity, and causation, may be either natural (the result of an involuntary associating quality) or philosophical (the result of a voluntary act of the mind).

15 Abs. 4; SBN 647. Hume also explains the origin of our ideas of space and time, but we have not space here to review this explanation.

16 THN 1.4.6.4; SBN 252–3. Hume warns against letting the comparison with a theatre mislead us: "They are the successive perceptions only, that constitute the mind; nor have we the most distant notion of the place, where these scenes are represented, or of the materials, of which it is compos'd."

17 Animal spirits were supposed to be an extremely fine, movable fluid found in the brain and nerves, and to serve as a means of sensation and movement.

18 For a fuller description of the philosophical background to Hume's moral theory, see D. F. Norton, "Hume, Human Nature, and the Foundations of Morality," in the *The Cambridge Companion to Hume*, pp. 149–58.

19 In Hume's account, the rules of justice have to do only with external goods or property

(see THN 2.1.10.1, 3.2.2.7; SBN 309–19, 487–8). This does not mean that he had no concern for the many other issues that we would suppose to be matters of justice and injustice. It only means he supposes these issues to fall within the scope of other virtues and vices. Thus, for example, a failure to respond to another person's suffering would be inhumane, while the failure to show respect for another person would be a vicious form of pride.

20 This form of skepticism is so named because it was first articulated (in the third century BC) at the Academy earlier founded by Plato.

Chapter 9

Thomas Reid

Ernest Sosa and James Van Cleve

Thomas Reid (1710–96) was the founder of the Scottish common-sense school of philosophy.[1] He was an acute critic of Hume and is known especially for his trenchant opposition to the Way of Ideas. His views exerted a good deal of influence until the mid-nineteenth century or so, when they began to be eclipsed by absolute idealism, pragmatism, and other philosophical movements, but they are the subject of renewed interest in the present day.

After being educated at Marischal College in Aberdeen, Reid served for 15 years as a parish minister in nearby New Machar. In 1752 he was appointed professor at King's College in Aberdeen, where he taught mathematics, physics, and philosophy. In 1764 he published his first major work, *An Inquiry into the Human Mind on the Principles of Common Sense*, in which he systematically outlined how we arrive at knowledge by means of the various senses and gave his reasons for opposing the reigning theory of ideas as intermediaries in all knowledge. In the same year he accepted the chair in moral philosophy at Glasgow, recently vacated by Adam Smith. He lectured there for 16 more years, resigning in 1780 to prepare his last two major works: *Essays on the Intellectual Powers of Man* (1785), devoted to the contribution of perception, memory, reason, and other cognitive powers to human knowledge, and *Essays on the Active Powers of Man* (1788), devoted to the nature of action, will, freedom, and morality.[2]

This chapter provides brief accounts of Reid's positions on various important issues of modern philosophy: the Way of Ideas, sensation and perception, nativism, primary and secondary qualities, and conception and intentionality. A much longer concluding section discusses in greater detail what is perhaps most famous and distinctive in Reid's philosophy: his defense of a philosophy of common sense in terms of a set of epistemic principles with a distinctive status, set against any deliverances of reason, intuitive or inferential.

1. Critique of the Way of Ideas

Almost alone among the great modern philosophers, Reid espoused a direct realist theory of perception. He repudiated the Way of Ideas–the assumption that what is immediately present to the mind is never an external thing, but only an internal image, impression, representation, or (to use the most common eighteenth-century term) idea. Ideas were conceived of as mental entities that existed only as long as there was awareness of them. Some proponents of the theory of ideas (such as Descartes and Locke) were realists, conceiving of physical objects as mind-independent things that cause ideas to arise in us. Others (such as Berkeley) were idealists, repudiating the existence of a world outside the mind and believing that the things we call physical objects are simply bundles of ideas. In either case, the theory of ideas cuts us off from direct perception of the external world – either because there is no external world to be perceived or because our perception of it is indirect – not strictly perception at all, but inference based on what we do perceive, namely, ideas.

Reid makes at least three important points against the theory of ideas. First, the arguments in favor of the theory are weak and without cogency; second, the theory does nothing to explain how perception is possible; third, the theory stands in the way of our knowing or even being able to conceive of the physical world.

One of the arguments for ideas Reid criticizes is the "no action at a distance" argument, which may be put as follows (see EIP 2.14):

1 Nothing can act or be acted upon where it is not.
2 When we perceive objects, we act upon them or they upon us.
3 Therefore, we perceive only those objects that are right where we are, smack up against our minds – presumably, ideas.

Reid's response to this argument is somewhat surprising by present-day lights. He challenges its second premise, denying that in perception there need be any "acting" of perceiver on percipient or vice versa, which puts him at odds with contemporary causal theories of perception and intentionality more generally. But another response to the argument would have been available to Reid. Even for its proponents, the first premise is plausible only if understood as saying that nothing can act *immediately* where it is not. The lighting of a fuse here can cause the explosion of a keg way over there, provided there is an intervening series of contiguous causal links. With the first premise restated in this way, the second premise must also be restated in order for the conclusion to follow: when we perceive objects, we act upon them or they upon us *immediately*. Reid could have rejected the revised version of the second premise without denying the need for a causal connection between perceiver and percipient altogether.

Another argument for ideas Reid criticizes is a version of the argument from perceptual relativity. Hume had observed that the "universal and primary opinion of all men" that they perceive external objects directly is "destroyed by the slightest philosophy." In section XII of the *Inquiry Concerning Human Understanding*, he offers the following as a specimen: "The table, which we see, seems to diminish as we remove further from it; but the real table, which exists independent of us, suffers no alteration. It was therefore nothing but its image which was present to the mind." Recast somewhat, Hume's slight bit of philosophy takes the form of the following syllogism:

1 What I see diminishes in magnitude as I retreat from it.
2 The table itself does not diminish in magnitude as I retreat from it.
3 Therefore, what I see is not the table itself (but only an image or idea).

Reid proposes that Hume's premises are true only if we restate them as follows (see EIP 2.14, p. 224ff):

1 What I see diminishes in *apparent* magnitude as I retreat from it.
2 The table itself does not diminish in *real* magnitude as I retreat from it.
3 Therefore, what I see is not the table (but only an image or idea).

Here Reid is appropriating for his own purposes Berkeley's distinction between real (or tangible) and apparent (or visible) magnitude. As Reid develops the distinction, the real magnitude of an object (for example, the edge of a table) is an intrinsic property of it, measured in inches or feet, whereas the apparent magnitude of an object is a relation between the object and a perceiver, measured by the angle the object subtends at the eye. It is easy to see that apparent magnitude varies with the distance between object and perceiver (objects subtending smaller angles when further away) while real magnitude does not. Once we record these facts correctly as in Reid's version of the syllogism, we see that the argument commits the fallacy of two middle terms. (Of course, Reid must resist any temptation to analyze the dyadic relation of appearing so large into a triadic relation involving the object, the observer, and an idea or sense datum with a certain real magnitude.)

Reid's second point against the hypothesis of ideas is that "ideas do not make any of the operations of the mind to be better understood" (EIP 2.14; p. 229). They are supposed to explain how we manage to perceive or apprehend what is distant, what is past, and what does not exist at all, but in fact they are no help in this regard. Ideas are of no use in explaining the intentionality or aboutness of mental operations because such explanations inevitably presuppose intentionality. In the first place, ideas can represent objects for us only if the ideas are interpreted (like the symbols in a book) as standing for the objects, but that presupposes precisely the ability of the interpreter to have the object in mind.[3] In the second place, ideas themselves must be made objects of perception or some kind of awareness, but that again presupposes intentionality:

> It is as difficult to conceive how the mind perceives images in the brain, as, how it perceives things more distant. If any man will shew how the mind may perceive images in the brain, I will undertake to shew how it may perceive the most distant objects: for

> if we give eyes to the mind, to perceive what is transacted at home in its dark chamber, why may we not make these eyes a little longer-sighted? (Inq. 6.12, p. 121)

Reid's third point against the theory of ideas is that it has led philosophers into conclusions shockingly at odds with common sense (see EIP 2.14, pp. 230–2). If we do not simply see external objects, it becomes necessary to prove their existence by arguments, but the arguments philosophers have offered to this end are all problematic. Thus, if we start down the way of ideas, we are in danger of losing the material world. Hume developed the consequences of the theory of ideas even further, showing that the mind itself must be reduced to a series of ideas. Reid tells us that though he once subscribed to the theory himself, Hume's philosophy convinced him (by making its inevitable consequences manifest) that it must be rejected.

2. Sensation and Perception

To Reid we owe the now familiar distinction between sensation and perception – operations of the mind that are often conflated, but distinguishable if we pay attention:

> Thus, *I feel a pain; I see a tree*: the first denoteth a sensation, the last a perception. The grammatical analysis of both expressions is the same: for both consist of an active verb and an object. But, if we attend to the things signified by these expressions, we shall find, that in the first, the distinction between the act and the object is not real but grammatical; in the second, the distinction is not only grammatical but real.
>
> The form of the expression, *I feel pain*, might seem to imply, that the feeling is something distinct from the pain felt; yet, in reality, there is no distinction. As *thinking a thought* is an expression which could signify no more than *thinking*, *so feeling a pain* signifies no more than *being pained*. What we have said of pain is applicable to every other mere sensation. (Inq. 6.20, pp. 167–8)

When I see a tree, there is an object (the tree itself) apart from my act of seeing, but when I have a sensation, there is no object apart from the act of sensing. Is that because an act of sensing has itself for its object, or because it has no object at all? Although Reid's language sometimes suggests the former option, his proposal that *being pained* is the model for all sensation suggests the latter. If we take Reid in the latter way to hold that sensation is objectless, he is a precursor of adverbial theories of sensation: to have a sensation of red is not to be the subject of an act directed upon a red item as its object, but is simply to sense in a certain way, "redly" as the adverbial theory styles it. If sensing required its own special objects, the argument from perceptual relativity for the way of ideas could be reinstated. The mountain that looks blue from a distance and green from close up would do so by generating first blue and then green sensory objects in my mind, and these special objects would displace the mountain itself as my immediate objects.

Although sensations do not have objects, they can become objects for us, in the sense that we can know through proper attention what sorts of sensations we are having. Reid's views about our epistemic relation to our sensations involve a delicate balancing act: if we attend carefully to our sensations, we can know perfectly what they are like; yet they commonly pass unnoticed, serving as mere cues or signs from which our minds leap instantly to other things that they signify. Our apprehension of that which sensations signify is *perception.*

Reid's characterization of perception always involves three elements – conception, belief, and immediacy:

> If, therefore, we attend to that act of our mind which we call the perception of an external object of sense, we shall find in it these three things. *First*, Some conception or notion of the object perceived. *Secondly*, A strong and irresistible conviction and belief of its present existence. And, *thirdly*, That this conviction and belief are immediate, and not the effect of reasoning. (EIP 2.5, pp. 111–12; see also Inq. 6.20, p. 168)

Note that this definition makes no mention of sensation. Although Reid says that sensation generally serves as the trigger for the conception and belief involved in perception, the intentionality or object-directedness of perception is carried by the conception. Moreover, Reid thinks it possible that perception should occur in the absence of sensation, and that there is one variety of human perception that actually does occur without any characteristic sensation – namely, the perception of visible form. Reid thus de-emphasizes the role of sensation in perception in a way that some contemporary theorists (for example, Gibson) would applaud. By the same token, however, his threefold definition may strike others as leaving out precisely that by which a genuine perception of the snake in my path is distinguished from the conception and immediate belief in it I may form merely as the result of my friend's warning. Here Reid's views may gain in plausibility if we reckon his "conception" as more akin to Russellian acquaintance than to Kantian subsumption under concepts (as urged by Wolterstorff).

3. Nativism

Though generally classified as one of the British Empiricists, there is one important point on which Reid is not an empiricist at all, but a nativist. He believes that we have a number of important conceptions, including those of external extended objects and of the self as a subject of mental operations, that are not abstracted from sensation. Negatively, his doctrine is that a being endowed with sensations and rational powers alone would never be able to form any conception of extension. There is no "internal" connection between any sensation and anything extended – no resemblance between them nor any connection discernible by reason. Reid supports this contention with a thought experiment he calls his *experimentum crucis*

(Inq. 5.6 and 5.7, pp. 65–72). He asks us to imagine a being furnished with a progressively richer array of sensations, beginning with the prick of a pin, advancing to more complex sensations such as the pressure of a blunt object against its body, and culminating with the sensations accompanying the motion of its limbs. He asks at each step in the series whether the sensations in question would suffice to give anyone a conception of extension, and his answer is no. Positively, Reid's doctrine is that the conception of extension is innate, not in the sense that we have it from birth, but in the sense that it is triggered in us by certain sensations from which it could never have been abstracted. We are enabled to form the conception of extended things only because we are innately programed to do so. "That our sensations of touch indicate something external, extended, figured, hard or soft, is not a deduction of reason, but a natural principle" (Inq. 5.7, p. 72).

Reid's nativism is part of his defense of common sense; it is meant as an antidote to skepticism about the material world. But exactly how is it an antidote? Here it is useful to distinguish two varieties of skepticism: the epistemological skepticism of Hume, who says we cannot *know* that there are material objects distinct from our impressions, and the more radical skepticism of Berkeley, who says we cannot even *conceive* of a material world lying beyond our sensations. It may be debated whether Reid's nativism has any relevance against the epistemological variety of skepticism. How would showing the nonsensory origin of certain conceptions do anything to demonstrate the warrantedness of our belief in their objects? To a thinker like Kant, showing that certain conceptions are non-empirical only exacerbates the question of their legitimacy and raises the demand for what Kant called a "transcendental deduction" of them. But however this debate is resolved, it does seem that Reid at least has an answer to the skeptic who says we cannot so much as conceive of a world beyond our sensations. He attributes to Berkeley the following argument (Inq. 5.8, p. 75):

1 We can have no conception of anything but what either resembles or is deducible from our sensations.
2 Nothing resembles or is deducible from sensations but other sensations.
3 Therefore, we can have no conception of anything but sensations.

Reid thinks the second premise is quite correct, and he credits Berkeley with having made it evident. But he thinks the first premise and the conclusion are false. "That we have clear and distinct conceptions of extension, figure, motion, and other attributes of body, which are neither sensations, nor like any sensation, is a fact of which we may be as certain, as that we have sensations" (Inq. 5.8, p. 76).

4. Primary and Secondary Qualities

Reid endorses a version of Locke's distinction between primary and secondary qualities. He thinks that some of Locke's teachings on this topic are wrong – in particular, he thinks there is no resemblance between any primary quality and any idea or sensation in our minds. But there is something to the distinction nonetheless:

> [T]here appears to me to be a real foundation for the distinction; and it is this – that our senses give us a direct and a distinct notion of the primary qualities, and inform us what they are in themselves. But of the secondary qualities, our senses give us only a relative and obscure notion. They inform us only, that they are qualities that affect us in a certain manner, that is, produce in us a certain sensation; but as to what they are in themselves, our senses leave us in the dark. (EIP 2.17, p. 252)

Our conception of the squareness of a body is direct: in knowing that a body is square, we know something about how it is intrinsically. By contrast, our conception of the redness of a body is not direct, but relative: in knowing a body to be red, we know only that it is so constituted as to produce a certain kind of sensation in us, not how the body is intrinsically or in itself.

The import of Reid's views on secondary qualities may be brought out by contrasting them with three doctrines that oppose them in different ways. First, there is the naive realism that would place sensuous heat or color in external objects. Reid thinks this view is an error that hardly anyone commits, even though philosophers often attribute it to the vulgar. Common sense, Reid thinks, ascribes to objects not sensuous heat or color, but only some quality that causes sensations of heat or color in us. Second, there is the view of Mill and Putnam that *all* properties we ascribe to objects are really secondary qualities – in other words, that we never know how objects are intrinsically, but only what sensations or other responses they elicit in us. Reid thinks to the contrary that in knowing an object to be hard or square, we know how it is intrinsically. Third, there is the view of Smart and Sellars that we conceive of our own sensations only by reference to qualities of bodies ("it's like what happens when you look at a ripe tomato"). Reid would say that Smart and Sellars have it backwards: we do have a direct conception of our own sensations, and we conceive of secondary qualities by reference to them.

5. Conception and Intentionality

Reid holds that all the operations of our minds but sensation have objects distinct from themselves. "[H]e that conceives, must conceive something" (EIP 4.1, p. 405), and the same goes for perception, memory, and other acts of the mind. Reid appears to think that such object-directedness or intentionality is a primitive feature that is not to be reduced to anything else. Moreover, in some cases our acts of mind have objects that do not exist. He notes that conception has one property that "essentially distinguishes it from every other power of the mind; and it is, that it is not employed solely about things which have existence" (EIP 4.1, p. 404).

On these points Reid is sometimes seen as a precursor of Brentano and Meinong

– of Brentano insofar as he holds that intentionality is an irreducible feature of mental acts and of Meinong insofar as he holds that a mental act can have an object that does not exist. Meinong's doctrine – that there can be cognitive relations to the utterly nonexistent, from which it follows that a thing need not exist in order to stand in relations – strikes many as intolerably paradoxical. Yet Reid makes it look like one more piece of common sense, or at any rate, a consequence of two pieces of common sense (EIP 4.1, p. 405):

1 I can conceive of a centaur.
2 No centaur exists.
3 Therefore, I can conceive of what does not exist.

Some would object that this argument does not really force us to accept relations to the nonexistent, since conceiving need not be understood as a relation. It could perhaps be understood in an adverbial way, as with sensation, in which case the first premise should be reconstrued as

1′ I conceive centaur-ly.

Yet this suggestion faces a hurdle. One who resists the overall soundness of the argument 1–3 can nonetheless recognize that on its face, the argument is logically valid. But once we replace 1 by its suggested substitute and the conclusion by some parallel construction, the resulting argument is no longer logically valid. Proponents of adverbial alternatives to Meinongism owe us a way of regimenting arguments like 1–3 that account for their validity.

Those who view Reid as a proto-Meinongian sometimes enlist this side of his views as one more weapon against the way of ideas (see Cummins). Suppose that perception itself (in virtue of having conception as its carrier of intentionality) can have objects that do not exist. Then one can account for familiar cases of illusion (for example, the second candle that appears when one presses one's eyeball) by positing nonexistent material objects of perception rather than the existent mental objects that go with the theory of ideas.

6. Causation and Freedom

As noted above, Reid thinks we have many conceptions, such as that of a self or subject of mental operations, that we could not have on Humean principles. Among them is the conception of active power, or real efficacy in bringing about changes. He thinks we obtain a clear conception of such power when we are conscious of our own activity in bringing something about by an act of will.

Active power is exercised only by agents or substances, not by events, so in the strictest sense of causation, only agents are causes for Reid. When we speak of one event causing another, Reid tells us, it would be more proper to speak of events related by lawful sequence or a relation of sign and thing signified.

That we sometimes act freely (or that we possess "moral liberty") is, according to Reid, a natural conviction, comparable to our belief in a material world, that we are justified in accepting because it is part of our constitution to do so. He rejects accounts of moral liberty, such as those of Hume and Hobbes, that seek to make it compatible with determinism. Thus he would reject the suggestion that I did *A* freely if I did *A* as a result of willing to do it and would have done otherwise if I had willed otherwise. In a universe in which my willing was itself the end of a causal chain tracing back to dinosaur days, the conditions of this definition might be satisfied, yet I would not, according to Reid, have acted freely. It is a further requirement of liberty that my willing not have been determined by antecedent events in that way. But that is not to say that my willing must be random or uncaused – in a case of free action, it is caused by *me*, the agent. In this way Reid brings his theory of agent causation into his account of liberty, attempting to escape the dilemma that has determinism as one horn and arbitrary uncaused acts of will as the other. Reid believes that every event has a cause, but he holds that the cause of an event need not be another event – it may be an agent.

Agent causation theories of human action inspired by Reid were advocated for a time by Chisholm and Taylor and are now undergoing something of a revival. They offer a tantalizing glimmer of hope for resolving old problems, yet face formidable problems of their own. If I am the cause of my willing to do *A*, mustn't there be such an event as my causing the willing? If so, what is the cause of *that* event? If it is *nothing*, we have fallen back on the randomness horn and violated Reid's professed belief that every event has a cause. If it is a *further event*, we are back on the horn of determinism. If it is the *agent*, we have taken the first step of a regress in which I am the cause of my willing *A*, the cause of my causing of my willing *A*, and so on *ad infinitum*.

7. Moral Philosophy

Reid is often considered to be a member of the moral sense school of philosophy, insofar as he holds that moral notions and moral determinations are the product of a moral faculty or sense. He insists, however, that the employment of the term 'sense' is accurate only with the proviso that a sense can deliver judgments as well as feelings. In opposition to Hume, he holds that "moral approbation implies a real judgment" (EAP 5.X, p. 457), capable of being true or false, and is not merely the expression of feeling (though his criticisms sometimes convert the supposedly noncognitivist view he is attacking into a subjectivist form of cognitivism). In further opposition to Hume, he holds that reason is not merely the slave of the passions, but has a real role to play in the selection of ultimate ends of action.

Reid also opposes the kind of view that most often today goes under the rubric of moral sense theory – the view that moral properties are analogous to secondary qualities, as in the suggestion that for an action to be right is for it to arouse favorable moral emotion in those who contemplate it. Reid protests that such accounts abolish the necessity of moral principles – it is necessary, according to him, that actions of certain types are right, but contingent that they produce whatever effects they do in those who contemplate them. On the whole, Reid's views probably bear less resemblance to moral sense theories than they do to the intuitionism of G. E. Moore, whom he may well have influenced. Much of what Reid says about *right* anticipates what Moore said about *good*: that it is indefinable, that we understand what it is by an original power of the mind, and that our moral faculty provides us with first principles about which types of acts are right and which wrong.

8. First Principles: An Epistemology of Common Sense

Contingent First Principles

Knowledge of one's own mind, of the external world, and of other minds; knowledge gained inductively, or conveyed through memory, or through testimony – all such knowledge rests for Reid on his "first principles," including his "First Principles of Contingent Truths":

1 That if one is conscious that *p*, then it is true that *p*.
3 That if one distinctly remembers that *p*, then it is true that *p*.
5 That if one distinctly perceives by one's senses that *p*, then it is true that *p*.
9 That certain features of the countenance, sounds of the voice, and gestures of the body, indicate certain thoughts and dispositions of the mind.
10 That there is a certain regard due to the human testimony in matters of fact.
12 That, in the phenomena of nature, what is to be, will probably be like to what has been in similar circumstances.[4]

These are numbered here by their place in Reid's list, with the first changed from a principle about what exists to one about what is true, and aligned thus with the others. Lest we trivialize the first three principles, we must not give their antecedents a "success" reading; on the contrary, "conscious" is there elliptical for "ostensibly conscious," "remembers" for "ostensibly remembers," and "perceives" for "ostensibly perceives." Finally, for Reid the scope of "ostensibly conscious" is restricted to one's own ostensibly present mental states, the faculty involved being that of *introspective* consciousness ("reflection," he would say).

A philosopher of Common Sense, Reid has this to say about sense: that in "common language sense always implies judgment. A man of sense is a man of judgment. Good sense is good judgment. Nonsense is what is evidently contrary to right judgment. Common sense is that degree of judgment which is common to men with whom we can converse and transact business" (EIP 6.2; p. 557). Otherwise put, "sense, in its most common, and therefore its most proper meaning, signifies *judgment*, though philosophers often use it in another meaning. From this it is natural to think, that common sense should mean common judgment; and so it really does" (EIP 6.2; p. 560).

What exactly does Reid mean by common sense? Does he mean a shared faculty or a shared set of believed propositions? Although the answer is "mostly the latter," Reid does occasionally mean faculties, rather than beliefs, as the relevant items commonly shared. This ambiguity is most apparent where Reid takes up the reliability of our belief-forming faculties. He speaks there of "principles of common sense," a faculty itself sometimes qualifying as a "principle" though in other passages the relevant "principle" seems rather a proposition about that faculty, one generally taken for granted: that it is a reliable faculty. Yet elsewhere other "principles of common sense" say nothing of any faculty or its reliability. Putting this exegetical issue aside, we concentrate for now on principles as propositions, including those concerning faculty reliability listed above as "first principles." We shall return to faculties in due course.

Although on the present interpretation principles such as Reid's fifth (and others) escape triviality, they still succumb to falsity. What we ostensibly perceive fails to correspond without exception to external reality. Fortunately we need claim, not infallibility, but only high enough probability, allowing principle 5 to take a less assertive form: "That if one distinctly perceives by one's senses that *p*, then *most probably* it is true that *p*."

Two other problems for Reid's proposed list of Principles are not so easily dispatched:

Problem 1 Such principles as stated seem abstract enough to escape the notice of most people. It seems absurd to suppose that ordinarily they are so much as considered, much less irresistibly and immediately believed from the dawn of our intelligence.

Problem 2 In any case it is hard to see how we could justify belief in them without vicious circularity: we surely need to exercise our memory, perception, and reason in constructing the supportive arguments required for such justification. How could we arrive at the conclusion that memory, perception, and reason are reliable faculties through any such reasoning without viciously presupposing the reliability of our faculties in that very reasoning?

The following hopes to illuminate both Reid's epistemology and also the issues themselves.

Beliefs and implicit commitments

Adherence to a principle can be explicit and theoretical or implicit and practical: either through conscious acceptance or through subconscious commitment. In either case one is required to believe instances of the consequent when aware of instances of the antecedent, and to do so in virtue of some psychological state of one's own. For example, it will not suffice that some external agency make one believe instances of the consequent upon one's becoming aware of instances of the antecedent, an agency that acts haphazardly, instance by separate instance, only *its* agency enabling our continued conformity to the principle. This would not show one's own implicit and practical commitment to the principle: mere conformity owed to such external agency does not manifest true commitment, not even implicit commitment.

Prejudice is betrayed not just through conscious belief that members of a certain group are inferior, but also through one's systematic and deliberate treatment as inferior of those known to one as members of that group, this even despite one's protestations to the contrary. Through one's treatment of such people one may manifest one's "belief" that they are inferior, even if, when asked directly and explicitly, one sincerely and vigorously denies that they are. Actions speak louder than words.

Whether the operative psychological state is called "belief" is not so important. The crucial question is whether such states are operative in one's psychology, whatever they may be called, whether states of "belief" or of "commitment" or "adherence" to principles. The point is that such states can powerfully affect one's cognitive dynamics, what one comes to believe in various circumstances given what else one already believes, what one gives up, and so on; and also one's psychological dynamics more broadly: what desires one acquires or relinquishes, and so on.

Some such commitments are habits, as Hume emphasized, but others seem innate, as they did to Reid. Learning can surely change our cognitive habits or commitments, however, as when diminishing acuity leads one to narrow the scope within which to trust one's senses, accepting their deliverances at face value. Such revision may be principled, through principles themselves evaluable epistemically as are beliefs.

The knowledge of normal, adult humans is thus metaperspectival to some degree. The knowledge of lower animals or infants, and even some mature human knowledge, is graced with little reflection. (Still it is interesting to explore what is required for such unreflective knowledge, especially if it may be seen to underlie even our most reflective knowledge.) In any case, adult humans do have a rich epistemic perspective, even if its contained commitments remain implicit, mostly beyond our capacity to articulate. When explicit, moreover, such commitments tend to rise only to a Moorean common-sense level, below the sophistication of any Cartesian epistemology supernaturalized, or any Quinean epistemology naturalized.

Exceeding our capacity to verbalize is not distinctive of our epistemic perspective, anyhow, since much of our nontrivial knowledge, even at the animal level, far outstrips our vocabulary. How friends look, how dishes taste, etc. – this barely scratches the surface of the mute knowledge manifest in behavior systematically dependent on relevant input cues. We know the look of our friend, which guides our greeting behavior; we know the typical heft of a billiard ball, that of a tennis ball, and that of a ping-pong ball, even when unable to estimate that heft in pounds or ounces, perhaps unable even to "imagine" such specific degrees of heft with any assurance. Nevertheless, the experienced heft will reveal whether it feels right, whether it is that proper to such an object, which enables us to behave accordingly.

While unable to articulate a certain mode of belief acquisition or sustenance, we may yet grasp it well enough to enable appropriate responses as it starts to fail us through diminished powers or environmental change. Corrective responses may hence be driven by yet deeper "beliefs" about how to respond. Just as inarticulable knowledge of a face can help guide our conduct, so inarticulate and even inarticulable knowledge can guide belief management. What is more, and moving up a level, such knowledge of how to acquire and sustain beliefs might guide corrective responses when faculties begin to falter.

The main points above concerning our metaperspective would remain, anyhow, even if we denied the title of "belief" to the more purely habit-like "commitments" in our framework of attitudes, including those constitutive of our epistemic metaperspective. These commitments would still be psychological states with "content." A commitment that carried one from belief that *Fa* to belief that *Ga* might be ascribed the subjunctive-conditional content that ($Fa \rightarrow Ga$), for example, or perhaps the content: (For all x, $Fx \rightarrow Gx$) – each such commitment comprising, or at least yielding, the disposition to believe *Ga* when one believed *Fa* (both commitments perhaps coexisting in one's mind at the relevant time, hierarchically ordered). Assigning it that content would seem appropriate since our assessment of such a commitment would depend on whether the corresponding content was true. Thus a habit of moving from the belief that a picked-out item is *F* to a belief that it is *G* might be criticized if items thus picked out (in the relevant circumstances) are *not* such that they would be *G* if *F*.

That is one sort of normativity to which such commitments are subject (as are beliefs). But normativity is also involved in further evaluation of how epistemically worthy it is to host that habit. Two dimensions are here relevant: one of aptness, and one of justification or rationality. Habits are inapt if acquired or sustained in ways unconnected with the truth of the beliefs they instill. Habits are unreasonable or irrational, moreover, when acquired or sustained arbitrarily or superstitiously. So, here again, dimensions of assessment are shared by ordinary beliefs and by such habits or other implicit commitments.

The point is this: much if not the whole of our epistemic structure of true, apt, justified "belief" that is non-accidentally true, unGettiered, etc., is applicable to these further psychological states – to these implicit commitments, including the innate – just as they are to the most explicit and central beliefs. Some implicit commitments are not verbalizable, nor, perhaps, are they even conscious, and they may even lie beyond our imagistic capacities. But, as we have seen, this also applies to ordinary belief.

Our epistemological curiosity and categories seem therefore applicable to the underlying commitments anyway – and that is now our main point. We cannot depend just on habits that happen to be reliable no matter how they got there or stay in place. Once this is clear, it seems a harmless verbal simplification to view such commitments as "beliefs" of a sort, especially given how similar they are to ordinary beliefs that subconsciously guide our conduct.

Reid seems often to be simplifying thus when he speaks of our "believing" his common-sense first principles.

However, a subject's cognitive structure, including its epistemic perspective, might be mixed, containing elements that vary variously. In particular, it might contain both (a) fully articulable scientific or theological beliefs, as well as (b) highly implicit and inarticulable ones. What is important is that its component psychological states be evaluable epistemically in the usual ways, which includes both a dimension of aptness and one of justification or rationality. What is distinctive of the metaperspectival component of any such cognitive structure is that its elements are about or "about" the body of beliefs upon which, at least in part, the perspective takes a "view."

No essential disagreement would now divide us (or Reid) from anyone granting our need to postulate such implicit commitments, and to assess them through epistemic categories and standards identical or analogous to those used in assessing beliefs.

A general proposition might be accepted subconsciously even while denied consciously, as when someone is clearly prejudiced, his sincere protestations to the contrary notwithstanding. Does the subject then believe, all things considered, or not? Better just to distinguish the states, allowing conscious explicit affirmation – or even *conscious belief* – to coexist with subconscious, implicit disbelief, detrimental as this may be to the unity of that mind. Do you really know that the members of the target race are your equals and not inferior, given your sincere, well-founded, conscious profession to that effect? Even if you are granted some grade of knowledge on that account, it will be knowledge at best degraded by your implicit and action-guiding "belief" to the contrary.

Whether the implicit states are called "beliefs" or not, they are in any case states of implicit adherence to "principles," or "commitments" that one holds. And some are presumably held *on the inferential basis* of others. Thus one may hold the implicit belief, about someone one perceives to be a member of the target race, that he in particular is inferior, based on a more general implicit prejudice that members of that race generally are inferior. So the epistemic status of some implicit commitments will depend on the epistemic status of other commitments whence they are validly derived.

Accordingly, we might well inquire into the epistemic structure of our relevant body of psychological states, including not only our consciously explicit beliefs, but also our subconsciously implicit commitments, and even our sensory experiences.[5] And here looms the Pyrrhonian problematic, with its three familiar options: foundations, circle, and regress.

Suppose we opt for foundations. Can the foundations be exhausted by the taking of the given? What is thus taken would now include both necessary truths known by *a priori* intuition and contingent truths known through introspection of one's salient current states of consciousness, along with *cogito*-like propositions (*cogito* itself, for example, and also *sum*). How now can we know our various cognitive faculties to be as reliable as we ordinarily take them to be?

It might be thought we could do so by appeal to the foundational inputs delivered by these very faculties. Consider the intuitive, perceptual, introspective, and memorial inputs that they deliver. These might now enable a picture of our own nature, of the world around us, and of how the two are systematically related, on which we could base our trust in the reliability of the very faculties that deliver those inputs.

However, in accepting those deliverances of our faculties we already rely on a commitment that those very faculties are indeed reliable. Arbitrarily accepted inputs will yield no adequate input knowledge to underwrite the relevant picture. Faculties of perception in particular involve commitment to accept inputs of certain general sorts. Consider such a faculty or subfaculty: for example, vision, or color vision, etc., beyond just perception in general. By entailing the delivery of certain sorts of beliefs in certain correlated general conditions, it may hence bundle built-in implicit commitments to accept certain beliefs based on awareness of certain circumstances.[6] That causes a problem for the foundationalism that would have us infer a belief in the reliability of a faculty such as perception from the deliverances of that faculty (among others). After all, a commitment to the reliability of such deliverances is already required for the proper operation of the faculty. So the commitment must be there already and cannot without vicious circularity be supposed to obtain its epistemic status from any such inductive inference. Therefore, a question remains as to how such commitments could gain their required status. Absent such status, surely, the deliverances of the correlated "faculty" would be worth little, and could not provide inputs inductively yielding conclusions with derived epistemic worth.

There seems no alternative to granting foundational status to some such general commitments built into one's possession of a cognitive faculty. So these, some at least, must attain their epistemic worth independently of being inferred inductively. And it is here that evolution, or Divine Providence, may have its place.

We turn accordingly to Problem 2: How can belief in the Principles be justified without vicious circularity?

How are the principles justified?

One possibility is that the principles be each a normative principle of evidence in its own right, a fundamental principle specifying conditions within which a belief would be justified, and from which it would derive justification. As a proposal in epistemology this has the drawback that the relevant principles would have to be a multitude with no apparent unity.[7] As a proposed interpretation of Reid, it would also detach the principles as principles of evidence from two of the features that Reid seems most intent on attributing to them: namely, first that they reflect or constitute our believing as we do (indeed innately and irresistibly, all of us who are relevantly sound), and *second* that they are true or approximately true principles, according to which if we believe in certain ways in certain circumstances we will be right, we will believe *with truth.*

Granted, if we interpret the principles as normative principles of evidence, we may avoid vicious circularity in deriving them from beliefs acquired by *falling under* those very principles. And it must be granted further that in places Reid seems committed to the view that the various sorts of evidential sources specified by these principles do yield normative status (justification or the like) for the resultant beliefs. Nevertheless, these important advantages must be weighed against drawbacks already noted. And inevitably it will be asked whether some alternative account might not provide both a more plausible reading of Reid and a better substantive epistemology in its own right. Any such account would need to provide a way to arrive at justified belief in the principles without circularity and without detaching them from the attachments insisted upon by Reid: to truth, at least approximate truth, and to irresistible "belief."[8] And of course it would also need to be compatible with the passages according to which the sources cited by the principles do yield (or help yield) epistemic justification for the beliefs that derive from them.

An important concept of justification involves evaluation of the subject as someone separable from her contingently given environment. Of course not only agents and subjects are assessable as justified or not. Actions and beliefs are, too, and more fundamentally so. One is assessable as justified *in acting or believing a certain way.* Nevertheless, the evaluation of particular acts might imply an indirect evaluation of the agent or subject herself. A tennis shot may count as accurate or not, which will imply only a minimal comment on the shotmaker. That same shot may also be assessed as skillful or not, however, which does substantially involve some evaluation of the agent by indirection.

Abstracting from the circumstances, anyhow, at least insofar as the agent does not bear responsibility for them, some evaluations of belief focus on the believer herself, on her relevant constitution and her rational procedure. Such evaluations take into account only factors internal to the mind of the subject, not only beliefs but also experiences. Evaluations of a belief as justified or not hence take into account proceedings downstream from experience. Only if such proceedings manifest cognitive virtue are the outcome beliefs justified. And how do we assess whether such a procedure does or does not manifest the sort of virtue that helps make its output belief justified, and even a case of knowledge? No alternative seems more plausible for the determination of *epistemic* or *cognitive* virtue than that of truth-conduciveness. *Understanding* will matter too, however: knowing the whys and wherefores, especially on important issues pregnant with explanatory (and predictive) payoff. And such understanding is intimately connected with coherence, since the explanatory interrelationship among our beliefs is bound to function as a, or even the, main component of epistemically efficacious coherence.

Commitment to principles as inference patterns: How are these justified?

Jungle guides, farming peasants, and experienced sailors embody practical lore that they cannot articulate. A certain gestalt look of the environment will prompt practically appropriate inferences: that a storm is coming, say, even if the knowledge embodied must remain inarticulate: the knowledge that when the sea and the heavens look a certain way, a storm is likely brewing. Acceptance of the fact that when things look that way, we can expect such an outcome, may nonetheless be revealed by repeated expectation of the outcome in situation after situation when things in fact do look that way. While accepting something of the form "When things look *F* they are likely to turn *G*" our subjects' acceptance is manifest not through conscious articulation, but only through a pattern of "inferences."

And we come finally to the question "What might justify commitment to such an inference pattern?" Sundry things could do so; for example, "the fact that the pattern fits one's experience and is accepted in part at least because of that." That's one way to block the threatening regress. Another way is simpler: namely, that we be innately hard-wired for that inference pattern, by God or Nature, so that it may justifiedly guide our reasoning. And this it may do even independently of whether the environment jibes with our specific cognitive makeup when we make that inference. The inference is still "justified" in any case, since it is the sort of inference that it is appropriate for us to make downstream from experience, regardless of the etiology of that experience or the nature of the environment, and thus regardless of how "apt" the belief may be relative to the environment within which it is acquired or sustained. So long as in our world it is a normally successful pattern, and it is no accident that we have acquired and sustain the commitment to its use (through God or evolution) with sensitivity to its validity, we may evaluate ourselves individually as "justified" in the beliefs acquired or sustained by means of that pattern, and evaluate the beliefs (the believings) themselves as thus justified on that basis.[9]

Note finally how, compatibly with this approach, we might still enjoy such (internal) justification even when victims of the Evil Demon. For, in considering whether we are thus justified, we evaluate ourselves and our proceedings *downstream from experience*, and such proceedings are evaluable positively even if they unfold in a demonic world, so long as the basis for evaluation is how likely it is that their like would put us in touch with the truth *in the environment wherein the evaluation is rendered*. After all, the environment that provides the basis for the evaluation is not the Demon world but the actual world inhabited by the evaluators who are considering, as a hypothetical case, the case of such a victim.[10]

Principles and circularity

Reid joins the crowd accusing Descartes of vicious circularity (EIP 6.5; p. 631):

> Des Cartes certainly made a false step . . . ; for having suggested this doubt among others, that whatever evidence he might have from his consciousness, his senses, his memory, or his reason; yet possibly some malignant being had given him those faculties on purpose to impose upon him; and therefore, that they are not to be trusted without a proper voucher: to remove this doubt, he endeavours to prove the being of a Deity who is no deceiver; whence he concludes, that the faculties he had given him are true and worthy to be trusted.

It is strange that so acute a reasoner did not perceive that in this reasoning there is evidently a begging of the question.

In assessing this disagreement between Descartes and Reid it will be helpful first to reflect in general on what it is that makes circular reasoning vicious, when it is vicious, though we have room for little more than a fragmentary sketch.[11]

Reasoning is related epistemically to knowledge in two ways, corresponding to two sorts of knowledge, the reflective and the unreflective. The latter, "animal" knowledge, is concerned with the acquisition and sustenance of apt, reliable belief, whereas the former requires the belief to be placed also in a perspective within which it may be seen as apt.

Animal knowledge repels circularity for reasons that do not concern reflective knowledge. Beliefs about matters beyond the subject's skin, in particular, must be acquired through mechanisms connecting that belief with how it is out in the world. Essential circularity unsuits a stretch of reasoning for making that connection unaided, vitiating it as provider of animal knowledge. When reasoning circles back on itself essentially, it fails to connect its conclusion aptly with the world so as to make it a viable candidate for knowledge. What is distinctive of reflective knowledge is unbothered by such detachment, however, since reflective knowledge, while building on animal knowledge, goes beyond it precisely through integration in a more coherent framework. This it achieves via an epistemic perspective within which the object-level animal beliefs may be seen as reliably based, and thus transmuted into reflective knowledge.

Several are the ways to acquire our Reidian or other principles: through training or schooling, for example, or by noticing correlations then buttressed through deliberate testing. Alternatively, one might just pick them up through life experience, or through appropriate testimony. Some (especially the Reidian) may even turn out to be just innate mechanisms triggered in the way language acquisition is said to be triggered while vastly underdetermined by available evidence. Our experience-trusting habits of thought, where in normal circumstances we take our shape and color appearances at face value, seem largely of this sort.

Reasoning will yield animal knowledge only if it holds up with truth, aptness, and justification at every lemma on which it relies essentially in connecting its conclusion with relevant external reality. This is bound to depend on ultimate premises owed to some sort of perception, aided perhaps by memory. At this level circularity is plausibly prohibited, since circles of reasoning will fail properly to connect any conclusion with the world beyond the circle.

That is, however, compatible with one's being subject to no such prohibition when the objective is knowledge that will be reflective and not just animal. Having grasped how it is around us through connections involving the perception/memory/reasoning required for animal knowledge, further reasoning on that basis may enhance our conscious integration and explanatory coherence, lending epistemic virtue to our beliefs. There is no more vice in this circular procedure than in a case of visually-apparent-sprinkling/circles-in-puddles/pitter-patter-on-the-window-panes/car-wipers-wiping/umbrellas-up/felt-drops-on-one's-bare-arms/recalled-forecast, etc. There is nothing wrong with accepting various subarguments in such a case concurrently, believing the conclusion of each partly on the basis of the other beliefs used as premises. It would of course be bad to hold those subarguments concurrently *absent any connection with the relevant externalia*. Even when one holds the lot of them concurrently interlocked, however, *this does not imply that one holds them so detached.* (And a special, rational form of viciousness spoils attempts to reach conclusions about the contingent world around us through reasoning detached not only from the world beyond but even from those states and beliefs required as peripheral intermediaries for the desired connection with the world. Prominent among these states are the experiential states whose job it is precisely to mediate in that way between our contingent beliefs about the world around us and the world that they are about. Much circular reasoning would be defective in just that way.)

By using our various faculties and subfaculties, including those constituted by certain habits or other inferential patterns, we may reach a consciously reflective worldview distinguished by two features from the largely implicit framework that precedes it. Call that earlier framework of implicit commitments and other beliefs "framework FI." Call the later explicit worldview "framework FE." Two epistemically significant features may distinguish FE from FI: (a) that the earlier implicit "beliefs" are now explicit, and (b) that such consciousness-raising enables greater cognitive coherence, with member beliefs now more tightly integrated with other component beliefs, now explicitly seen to be interrelated.

Reid does have a worldview according to which we can rationally acquiesce in the use of our God-given faculties that yield the beliefs and the very concepts by which we thrive individually and collectively. How can he regard himself as epistemically justified in believing that these faculties are God-given and accordingly truth-conducive? Is not his reasoning bound to be just as viciously circular here as Descartes's reasoning is alleged to be?

There is I believe a way out for Reid. Ironically it is akin to Descartes's own way, or so one may plausibly suggest. The way out is to distinguish between *scientia* and *cognitio*, as does Descartes, between reflective and unreflective (animal) knowledge. It is viciously circular to reach the Reidian worldview via reasoning that includes claims concerning faculty reliability – that is, the various commitments constitutive of the operative faculties and subfaculties – while these very commitments also comprise the worldview thus arrived at. This is viciously circular if we conceive of the commitments/beliefs arrived at as identical with the commitments from which they are derived as conclusions. On behalf of Reid we may now respond that the conclusions we reach are conscious, explicit beliefs, constitutive of an explicit, articulated worldview; and these are not quite the same as our implicit intellectual-conduct-guiding commitments, no matter how closely related they may be, and indeed even should they turn out to share the very same contents.[12]

Still: How are such principles justified?

Still the question remains: How can those implicit commitments be justified, if their contents are general, contingent propositions? How can such a proposition be justified foundationally or immediately, as a "self-evident" universal or probabilistic truth? How can we sensibly allow ourselves justification for believing such a truth from the armchair, absent proper empirical inquiry into our actual contingent surroundings?

On behalf of Reid, I answer: What would make us justified is that we proceed in an epistemically appropriate and desirable way, given the aims of systematic acquisition and retention of truth (especially truth that gives understanding), and that we do so not by accident, but in a way that derives from our nature and the nature of things, which makes us non-accidentally sensitive precisely to the "validity" of the inferential patterns constitutive of those faculties and their bundled implicit commitments. Now this last could be detailed more specifically in various ways, the two main competing options involving respectively (a) Divine Providence, and (b) natural evolution; either one would serve present epistemological purposes. Reid clearly took the first (as did Descartes). But, however the story is detailed at that level, the fact remains: humans are a certain way by nature, a way that, given our normal environment, furthers our epistemic aims of attaining truth and understanding, and does so with non-accidental sensitivity to the truth, including the subjunctive truth constitutive of the validity of our inferential patterns. So we can be assessed for whether our inbuilt mechanisms are operating correctly even if, unfortunately, we are in an abnormal environment relative to which those very mechanisms operate so as to take us away from truth and understanding. The main point is now straightforward: namely, that the mechanisms in question might include, and according to Reid do include, taking our sense experience at face value, and gaining access to the states of mind of our neighbors through beliefs instinctively prompted by the external, behavioral signs of such states. *Et cetera.*

Thus may we attain justification for the use of our basic faculties, for our "belief" in or implicit commitment to the various "first principles," adherence to which in practice is constitutive of such faculties. And this justification would remain even for victims of a Cartesian evil demon. Reasoning from such implicit commitments may eventually yield conscious awareness of your faculties and subfaculties, of their nature and how they fit you for cognitive success in your relevant normal environment. To a greater or lesser extent this would constitute a worldview that underwrites, with coherent understanding, your use of those faculties. Moreover, such conscious awareness of your intellectual makeup (your nature and second nature) might also aid its gradual improvement, as when you no longer take the sun to be (strictly) rising, no longer take the oar to be bent, no longer take the Muller–Lyer lines to be incongruent, and so on. You might no longer accept deliverances which earlier, however briefly or long, had been admitted without question.

Is that vicious? No more so here than it was for Descartes. Who could object to the use of our faculties resulting in such a worldview with its attendant coherence and yield of understanding? How plausible, surely, that the individual component beliefs should also gain epistemically by now being part of a more comprehensively coherent and explanatory establishment. When we judge them better justified, our assessment is relational, true enough, and indirectly dependent on intellectual surroundings involving the believer's operative cognitive virtue. But that is no more strange than is the evaluation of the archer's shot as skillful, which remains an evaluation of the shot itself, even if an indirect one dependent on factors involving the surroundings, and most of all the archer's operative skill.

Notes

1 "First Principles: An Epistemology of Common Sense," the section comprising the second half of the chapter, is by Sosa, the earlier sections by Van Cleve.

2 Page references will be given in the text to the following editions of Reid's works: *An Inquiry into the Human Mind on the Principles of Common Sense*, ed. Derek Brookes (Edinburgh: Edinburgh University Press, 1996), abbreviated as Inq.; *Essays on the Intellectual Powers of Man*, ed. Baruch Brody (Cambridge, Mass.: MIT Press, 1969), abbreviated as EIP; and *Essays on the Active Powers of the Human Mind*, ed. Baruch Brody (Cambridge, Mass.: MIT Press, 1969), abbreviated as EAP. For the benefit of readers who do not have these editions at hand, references will also include chapter and section numbers from the *Inquiry* and essay and chapter numbers from the *Essays*.

3 This point is developed by Keith Lehrer, *Thomas Reid* (London: Routledge, 1989), at pp. 13–14. In Reid's own writings it is perhaps most explicit in *The Philosophical Orations of Thomas Reid*, ed. D. D. Todd (Carbondale, Ill.: Southern Illinois University Press, 1989), p. 62.

4 *Essays on the Intellectual Powers of Man*, Essay VI, ch. V, pp. 614–43. Such principles are thought by Reid to be irresistibly believed from an early age, some even from birth, or at least to be such that belief in them is triggered very early, absent any reasoning properly so-called, and certainly absent any conscious reasoning, whether deductive or inductive.

5 Sensory experiences may plausibly be assigned content even when they do not give rise to belief, as when it looks to one as if the pencil in the water is bent. The visual experience is here correctly characterizable in terms of such propositional content, even when one has no temptation to actually believe, consciously or subconsciously, that the pencil before one is really bent.

6 This can even be applied to Reid's faculty of introspection or reflection, whose deliverances would be states of being ostensibly conscious or aware that one is in such and such a mental state. But it is unclear to what extent it may apply to the case of memory. Reid unfortunately does not distinguish personal, experiential memory (which can be viewed as analogous to external perception) from retentive memory (which cannot be so viewed, in important respects). Reid fails to recognize important differences between these cognitive subfaculties. Thus while perceptual belief can be viewed as derived from perceptual experience with corresponding content (from "it looks as if here's something white and round," as experiential premise, to "here's something white and round," as belief conclusion), there is nothing like this in retentive memory, which simply preserves a belief across time.

7 Reid is aware of this sort of issue: "I confess that, although I have, as I think, a distinct notion of the different kinds of evidence . . . yet I am not able to find any common nature to which they may all be reduced" (EIP 2.20; p. 291).

8 As the case of the bent pencil exemplifies, what is irresistibly "believed" is not the consequent instance of our belief-managing underlying commitment, but rather the underlying commitment itself, probabilistic and implicit as it remains: the "belief," namely, that is *constituted* by our irresistible disposition to believe that a thing is bent, when in normal circumstances we are presented with a certain appearance of something bent. The probabilistic character of the content reflects the fact that we do allow exceptions, as with the bent pencil.

9 But we must be clear that "validity" here is broader than just formal, logical validity, and includes also the kind of subjunctive validity that underwrites inferring that x is G from the perceived fact that it is F, a subjunctive validity that amounts to it being the case that anything that (in the relevant environment) were F would also be G. Even if ours is not the only sense one could reasonably assign to philosophers' terminology of "epistemic justification," moreover, it does seem one interesting such sense.

10 Consider our implicit belief in Reid's principles and the like, or the habits and other implicit commitments that guide our intellectual conduct. These are perhaps not "downstream from experience," and seem exceptions to our claim that assessments of epistemic justification are indirectly assessments of cognitive structures, mechanisms, and proceedings downstream from experience; but in any case much the same reasoning as above would still apply also to the evaluation of our implicit, Reidian belief-guiding commitments, which would still be intrinsic to the subject, and separable from the vagaries of her environment.

11 Reid often supports one's harboring the first principles constitutive of various faculties, and argues that we may trust these simply because they come from God. But how does he obtain epistemic justification for believing that they are so derived? How in the end could he here avoid the sort of circularity that he finds in Descartes?

12 But the defense of Reid here would survive even if one granted that the "beliefs" at the end of the reasoning are indeed the same after all as the "beliefs" that serve as inputs to that reasoning. One could still defend such reasoning, so long as it results in conclusion beliefs that are somehow significantly *changed* from how they were as premises of that reasoning: for example, if the result is an explicitly conscious and integrated system of beliefs, this may be a valuable result of such "reasoning" despite the fact that the inputs to it involved the very beliefs, in implicit subconscious mode, that are now consciously integrated. This may still reasonably be regarded as a cognitively valuable result, adding some measure of cognitive virtue to the resulting beliefs.

Chapter 10

Jean-Jacques Rousseau

N. J. H. Dent

Rousseau retains his place in the canon of great modern philosophers in view of one work above all, *The Social Contract*, published in 1762. This continues to be regarded as one of the classic essays in political philosophy, taking its place alongside Plato's *Republic*, Machiavelli's *The Prince*, Hobbes's *Leviathan*, Hegel's *Philosophy of Right*, and other works which will find their way into any reading list of treatises central to this subject. Rousseau was an exceptionally vivid and forceful writer, and some of his remarks have become very widely known, perhaps most famously his statement "Man is born free; and everywhere he is in chains" (SC I, 1, 165; OC III, 351).[1]

My principal purpose here will be to offer an interpretation and assessment of what I take to be the key themes and theses Rousseau presents in SC. It is however misleading and unhelpful, I believe, to approach this work as if it were an isolated masterpiece that can effectively be understood and evaluated in independence of considering some of his other writings, for a number of reasons. First, as Rousseau himself says in the Foreword to SC, "This little treatise is part of a longer work, which I began years ago without realizing my limitations, and long since abandoned" (SC 164; OC III, 349). Thus, although SC appeared alongside other works of Rousseau's intellectual maturity (*Émile*, 1762, and *La Nouvelle Héloïse*, 1761), we can and should expect it to contain ideas which reflect earlier stages of his thinking and which may require supplementation with reference to later material.

Secondly, SC is not really fully self-contained as a piece of discussion and argument, in the sense that it does not contain within itself all the ideas and material necessary to its being well understood. It becomes harder, not easier, to grasp Rousseau's leading concerns if we look at it apart from the arguments of the *Discourse on Inequality* (of 1755) in particular, but also of the *Discourse on Political Economy* (also of 1755) and *Émile*. The DPE contains what may be regarded as first sketches of some key themes of SC; and we find in E Book 5 (458–67; OC IV, 836–48) what is in effect a short summary of SC.[2] We have reason, therefore, to take it that we may extend and consolidate the reading we make of SC with reference to the ideas in these works. In any event, this is how I shall approach the material of SC and the justice of doing so will be borne out (or not) by the interpretation that issues.

Before beginning this principal discussion, I shall give a brief overview of Rousseau's writings and of the shape of his philosophical output. Although some musical composition, and short essays on musical and educational topics, precede it, Rousseau's first significant piece of writing is his *Discourse on the Sciences and the Arts*, published in 1750. This is often referred to as his *First Discourse*, the *Second Discourse* being the *Discourse on the Origin of Inequality* and the *Third Discourse* being the *Discourse on Political Economy*, referred to already. The *First Discourse* was Rousseau's winning entry for a prize essay on a topic set by the Academy of Dijon, namely "Has the restoration of the arts and sciences had a purifying effect upon morals?" Rousseau recounts that when he saw this question he was so overcome by ideas that he became dazed, had to interrupt his journey, and discovered at that moment his destiny as a creative thinker.[3] In this essay Rousseau broaches many themes, albeit in a crude and limited way, which pervade the whole of his social and political thinking. He argues that the craving for invidious distinction, the rage of singularity, has twisted the practice of the arts and sciences from their true ends, the pursuit of knowledge and service to the public good. Instead, personal celebrity and winning applause become the leading objectives of men of learning and they deform their activities accordingly.

Rousseau himself won some celebrity and applause for this essay, and could well have found his way to a career as a man of letters or artistic figure, particularly in view of the success of his one major opera, *Le Devin du Village*, which followed a couple of years later. However, Rousseau renounced all favor from the Court, and salon distinction, and returned to his criticisms of contemporary society and political structures. In 1755 he published his most substantial and important discourse, the *Second Discourse* (DI), in which central elements in his thinking are fully expounded for the first time. (This was also written in response to a prize essay question, but Rousseau did not win this time.) I shall consider DI in some detail below. Around this time, he began work on his *Essay on the Origin of Languages* (a work left uncompleted), in which he puts forward important ideas about the causes of different linguistic formations and about the social and political significance of language and musical structures. Also in 1755, Rousseau's article on "Political Economy" appeared in volume 5 of Diderot and d'Alembert's *Encyclopédie*; this was republished in 1758 as the *Discourse on Political Economy.* (Rousseau additionally contributed many articles on musical topics to the *Encyclopédie*, around 200 in all. These formed the basis for his *Dictionary of Music*, published in 1767.)

I said above that DPE contains first sketches of some key themes of SC, and it is evident that when, in 1756, Rousseau withdrew decisively from the cultural milieu of central Paris to work in the cottage he was loaned at Montmorency, he was devoting a lot of his time to trying to carry forward his *magnum opus* on political institutions which he had first conceived while secretary to the French Ambassador in Venice in 1743. It is the "fragments . . . extracted" from this work that went to make up the text of SC once he had finally abandoned this bigger project (around 1759). But this was Rousseau's most creative and brilliant period, and two others of his major works were written at this time. First was *La Nouvelle Héloïse*, an epistolary novel of illicit passion and spiritual redemption (published, with great success, in 1761); and second was *Émile* (or: *On Education*) which Rousseau regarded – as I believe should we – as his most important work. This appeared in 1762, just a few weeks after the publication of SC, and it was E rather than SC which attracted the more attention, and condemnation, at that time. There are also a number of smaller pieces dating from the period 1756–60: the *Letter to Voltaire on Providence*; the *Moral Letters*, written for Sophie d'Houdetot, the inspiration for the character of Julie in his novel; and Rousseau's impressive *Letter to M. D'Alembert on the Theater*, in which he attacks the socially and morally deleterious effects of plays and of attendance at the theater, in a manner often reminiscent of Plato's condemnation of poetry and poets in the *Republic*.

One of the principal reasons for the condemnation of E arose out of the long passage in Book 4 where Rousseau presents his most extensive account of his religious ideas (through the character of a Vicar of Savoyard). His ideas were found subversive and intolerable by the Catholic Church, and Rousseau was forced to flee France, in June 1762, to escape possible imprisonment. Some very unsettled years followed. He wrote at some length in self-defense against the condemnation of his work his *Letter to Christophe de Beaumont, Archbishop of Paris* (published 1763); and when, for other reasons, he was also criticized by J.-R. Tronchin, attorney-general of Geneva, he wrote his extensive *Letters Written from the Mountain* (1764) to rebut these criticisms. But the output of these later years is best remembered for his great works of autobiography and apologia. Most important of these is *The Confessions*. Rousseau began work on this around 1764, although it was not finally published until after his death. Work on the *Confessions* is prefigured in his *Letters to Malesherbes* of 1762; and there is in addition his remarkable work of self-analysis and self-explanation, *Rousseau Judge of Jean-Jacques*, completed in 1776 (again published posthumously). Rousseau suffered intermittent bouts of mental illness from 1765 onwards (he was disposed to paranoia throughout much of his adult life), but a curious accident in 1776, when he was knocked down by a large dog, appears to have dispelled his distress of mind and his last work, *The Reveries of a Solitary Walker*, an album of personal reflections and recollections, has an extraordinary calm and lucidity.

Along with this extensive output, Rousseau also prepared his *Dictionary of Music* (referred to above) and some writings on botany (for which he had a passion). However, he had not lost sight of his political concerns entirely. He began, in 1764, his *Project for a Constitution for Corsica* (left unfinished) in response to an approach by an agent of the leader of the Corsican rebels, an approach prompted by Rousseau's favorable remarks about that country in SC (II, 10, 203; OC III, 391). And, in 1772, he wrote his substantial essay, *Considerations on the Government of Poland*, also in response to a personal approach. These two works provide a very interesting insight into how Rousseau saw some of the theoretical notions he presents in SC having application to particular peoples in specific historical circumstances (Compare SC II, 11; OC III, 391ff).

Even this very brief and selective outline of Rousseau's output shows both how very wide and diverse were the expressions of his genius, but also how restricted this output is in terms of the core topics of philosophical inquiry, at least as these are conceived of nowadays. Aside from his central achievement in political and social philosophy, and allied concerns with morality and moral psychology, his works on education, music, and language, and his novel and major autobiographical works, would not ordinarily be taken to be part of someone's philosophical achievement. He had very little to say on issues of epistemology, of any developed kind; and made only some small contributions to metaphysics and philosophy of religion (principally in the *Creed of a Savoyard Vicar* alluded to earlier). Although his *Essay on the Origin of Languages* is still studied, its dominant concerns stand rather to one side in relation to contemporary work in the philosophy of language, as do his psychological investigations (central to *Émile*) in relation to current thinking in the philosophy of mind. And his reflections on aesthetics are quite limited notwithstanding his extensive writings on musical topics. If we compare him with, say, Hume or Kant, whose lives and works were in different ways touched by Rousseau's, we do not find in him someone with a comprehensive system which encompasses almost all aspects of philosophical inquiry. Rousseau is, one might say, a one-track thinker. But this is not to belittle his achievement, only to characterize the kind of achievement it is.

1. Rousseau's Leading Concerns

With what problematic did Rousseau see himself as engaging in his central works of social and political philosophy? Most immediately evident is, perhaps, his hostility to all forms of human oppression, of the poor by the rich, of the peasant by the nobility, of the weak by the strong. Rousseau saw patterns of dominance and subjugation as incarnated in virtually all social structures and processes around him, and set himself not only to diagnose the sources, character, and consequences of these patterns, in society in general and in the psychology of the individual, but also to try to identify what kind of society, polity, and individual would emerge, or be disclosed, if such patterns were removed or, rather, were never established in the first place.

It is common enough to depict Rousseau as a leading figure of the Enlightenment, albeit a somewhat idiosyncratic figure, inasmuch as he shared with others of his time a concern with the "liberation of the individual," with liberation from the power and control of the established Church, liberation from long-established forms of social hierarchy, liberation from forms of political rule in relation to which the vast majority of people could be nothing other than oppressed or obedient subjects, liberation from the idea that there were natural orders of men, the lowly and the high-born, from one's position in which there could be no escape. And, as far as it goes, there is justice in representing Rousseau in this way.

However, it is important to be careful in how one deploys this frame of account. It should not lead one to think that Rousseau, or anyone, had ready-to-hand a fully formulated and understood conception of the character, powers, or significance of this "individual" who is emancipated in all these various ways. We do better, I believe, to see Rousseau as trying to *fashion* the notions by which human beings can begin to make sense of themselves in this new situation rather than as setting down some comprehensively formed theory which provides a finished and decisive conception of what it is to be one of these "individuals" set loose from the social circumstances of their birth, only accidentally the member of any religious community, and so on. I emphasize this because it appears to be very readily assumed, in assessments of Rousseau's ideas, that just because thinking in these terms has become very familiar to us it must have been so for him. But I believe he had the harder task of trying to work out a way of understanding how things would stand if viewed in these terms, necessarily without a clear sense in advance of where the investigation would lead.

More specifically, we could say that Rousseau was playing a part in fashioning the idea of an "autonomous" individual (an idea which was, of course, given much more direct, and influential, attention by Kant). But if we do so, we need to be sure we don't invest in the idea of "autonomy" powers and capacities which are in themselves controversial, and then use them as a benchmark by which to criticize Rousseau's account. An autonomous person, certainly, is not subordinate to the rule of another, he is self-ruling; he is not bound to answer to a lord or master, he has the right to make up his mind. But does this mean he is bound by no rule, no order at all? That his own will and decision, unregulated by any criteria of judgment but what strikes him as fitting, has final authority on all questions? Such was certainly not Rousseau's view; he would have regarded such a figure as inheriting all the characteristics of an imperious despot and not at all as the honorable and estimable creature who should emerge from the dissolution of the social and political structures of power and control. One (somewhat florid) quotation bears this out plainly:

> Liberty is a food easy to eat, but hard to digest; it takes very strong stomachs to stand it. I laugh at those debased peoples who, allowing themselves to be stirred up by rebels, dare to speak of liberty without having the slightest idea of its meaning, and who, with their hearts full of all the servile vices, imagine that, in order to be free, it is enough to be insubordinate. O proud and holy liberty! If those poor people could only know thee, if they realised at what price thou art won and preserved; if they felt how much more austere are thy laws than the yoke of tyrants is heavy . . . (GP VI, 186; OC III, 974)

This makes it quite plain that, for Rousseau, liberty has its "laws," and thus that a free man will, in that freedom, be governed by law, too. (This is, of course, also true in Kant's account of autonomy.) I shall, in what follows, try to clarify Rousseau's notions of moral and civil liberty as the modes of rule-governed agency appropriate to moral beings and to citizens. What needs to be emphasized is that there is no idea here of freedom as involving the absence of all rule and regulation of any kind whatsoever. If this is found a shortcoming, it needs to be asked whether an idea of freedom as involving such absence is the idea of a valuable and desirable condition for us to enjoy. It is not obvious that it is.

I have structured my account of central themes in Rousseau's thinking around the trio of notions which – whatever Rousseau's own role in making it so may have been – came to occupy such a central part in the ideology of the French Revolution. The importance of equality and liberty to him have already been indicated; the question of fraternity will be addressed in due course. It will be seen to play a key role in making the realization of equality and liberty possible, as well as incorporating intrinsic values of its own. I begin by looking at Rousseau's discussion of equality – or, more properly in the first instance, of inequality.

2. Inequality and Equality

Rousseau's fullest discussion of inequality (one of his most brilliant discussions overall) is – not surprisingly – in the *Discourse on the Origin of Inequality*, of 1755. I shall give a brief account and analysis of the main themes of this essay, and try to offer an assessment of their overall significance to his thinking.

Right at the start, Rousseau distinguishes "natural or physical" inequalities from "moral or political" inequalities (DI 44; OC III, 131). The former comprise differences of "age, health, bodily strength, and the qualities of the mind or of the soul"; the latter comprise "different privileges which some men enjoy to the prejudice of others; such as being more rich, more honored, more powerful, or even in a position to exact obedience." Rousseau is much the more interested in these latter inequalities.

A brief clarification of his idea of moral or political inequality is desirable since his own explanation is too narrow and slanted even for his own purposes. The notion of a "moral inequality" depends on the idea that we each have certain titles, rights, privileges, duties, requirements upon us which govern (what is regarded as) the proper and due way for us to conduct ourselves in relation to each other in terms of our behavior, expectations etc. Thus there is a moral inequality – of a not necessarily prejudicial kind – between a parent and child, or between a teacher and pupil, just as much as there is, prejudicially, between a lord and peasant. We need this more generic notion of "moral inequality" to be able to explain effectively what lies at the center of the significance of moral *equality* for Rousseau, as we shall see.

Rousseau's essay seeks not only to explain the character and consequences of moral and political inequalities but also their origin, so he begins by considering a time when they were absent from men's experience. He proceeds in a moderately sophisticated way not presenting "historical truths, but only . . . conditional and hypothetical reasonings, rather calculated to explain the nature of things, than to ascertain their actual origin" (DI, 45; OC III, 132–3). (He doesn't, in fact, entertain alternative hypotheses and try to show that his provides the best explanation.) In this context, he presents his famous account of the "noble savage":

> His soul, which nothing disturbs, is wholly wrapped up in the feeling of its present existence, without any idea of the future, however near at hand; while his projects, as limited as his views, hardly extend to the close of day. (DI 56; OC III, 144)

In the state of nature, men live almost entirely as isolated beings, coming together only occasionally out of sexual impulse or to meet some temporary common need. Other human beings are scarcely recognized as such:

> They maintained no kind of intercourse with one another, and were consequently strangers to vanity, deference, esteem and contempt; they had not the least idea of "mine" and "thine", and no true conception of justice; they looked upon every violence . . . rather as an injury that might easily be repaired than as a crime that ought to be punished. (DI 69; OC III, 157)

The "savage's" psychological constitution comprised, centrally, the motive of *amour de soi*, an instinctive concern for self-preservation, and a disposition towards pity or compassion ("a natural repugnance at seeing any other sensible being, and particularly any of our own species, suffer pain or death"; DI 41; OC III, 126).[4] *Amour de soi* becomes elaborated beyond this original form, however, in view of man's capacity for free will (his "liberty to acquiesce [in] or resist" an impulse) and of his "perfectibility" ("faculty of self-improvement"; DI 54; OC III, 142). Humans learn how their environment works and adjust their behavior accordingly. (Rousseau does not see our perfectibility as an unalloyed asset; in leading us to widen our understanding and broaden our scope, it can as much contribute to our misfortune as to our betterment.)

How, then, did this state of innocence and tranquillity get left behind? In the discussion of the *Discourse*, Rousseau all but argues that the processes by which we come to be fully human – recognizing and interacting with others of our kind – are at one and the same time processes which irretrievably damage us and deform our lives. I shall question later on whether this is his final view, but it is certainly visible in his treatment here.[5] Rousseau suggests that, gradually, people came to live more settled lives and to interact more regularly and systematically with each other. This change of circumstance brings with it profound changes in the character of persons and their mode of agency, in the structures of feeling, attitude, relationship that they have. In particular, a different kind of self-concern comes into play, *amour-propre* (DI 66 note; OC III, 219 Note XV).

There is no precise English equivalent of this term, which has in some measure been incorporated into the language. It is quite often translated as "vanity" or as "pride," but neither of these quite match the role and significance of *amour-propre* as Rousseau explains this. He suggests two ways in which this more settled life engenders transformations in the character of our self-concern, the manner in which we have regard to ourselves, different from that involved in *amour de soi*. First, sexual jealousy comes into play. In place of the casual couplings of the state of nature, one partner wishes to make a possessive claim on the other, to exclude all other people from consideration, to demand that (s)he have the only place in the other's attention and activity.[6] Rights and privileges over others are asserted; but also, holding a special place in another's regard comes to be crucial. A complex, partly aggressive, relationship of control and anxious demand for regard is established between people making them dependent upon each other in debilitating ways.

Rousseau however spends more time looking at a second type of development. People, he argues, come to seek distinction and regard more generally:

> Each one began to consider the rest, and to wish to be considered in turn; and thus a value came to be attached to public esteem. Whoever sang or danced best, whoever was the handsomest, the strongest, the most dextrous, or the most eloquent, came to be of most consideration; and this was the first step towards inequality, and at the same time towards vice. From these first distinctions arose on the one side vanity and contempt and on the other side shame and envy . . . As soon as men began to value one another, and the idea of consideration had got a footing in the mind, every one put in his claim to it, and it became impossible to refuse it to any with impunity. Hence arose the first obligations of civility even among savages; and every intended injury became an affront; because, besides the hurt which might result from it, the party injured was certain to find in it a contempt for his person, which was often more insupportable than the hurt itself. (DI, 81–2; OC III 169–70)

What is in view here, is, as I have said, a radical change in self-understanding, understanding of the significance of others, and of the character and footing of relationships between people. To use a more modern terminology, people come to have a "being-for-others."[7] The figure one cuts in others' eyes, the regard one can command from them, the precedence one enjoys – all these, and more, come into play and utterly change the mode of self-conception, leading in time to a displacement of the simpler concerns of *amour de soi*.[8] *Amour-propre*, as thus far presented, directs us not just to seek the good regard and esteem of others but contains two further elements. First, it directs us to seek *preferential* regard, so that I enjoy precedence, superiority over other people in the deference and consideration I receive, which I come to regard as my entitlement and its neglect as an affront to me. Secondly, my enjoyment of this dominant position comes to be for me the key, even the exclusive, element in what makes my life a rewarding and worthwhile one in my eyes, and what makes me a worthwhile and estimable person.[9]

These two elements have important ramifications. The first leads to incessant malicious competition between people, to secure the first place. Bound up with this is the need to have, or to put on a show of having, those attributes which are apt to secure a deferential response from others. Indeed, what these attributes may be takes on a curious and sinister character, for they need have and often will have no other significance at all than that of enforcing an invidious distinction in deferential regard between one person and another, so that my distinction consists in nothing other than someone else's lack of it. (See, particularly, DI 101, 107; OC III 189; 202, Note IX.) It is not as if one is, say, a better runner than other people, this being a genuinely meritorious distinction which attracts differential admiration and esteem.[10] It is rather that the enjoyment of differential esteem is the sole point, and the quest for that so to say invents discriminatory features in order to be able to judge that one is better because others can be regarded as inferior, contemptible, no-hopers. At various places, Rousseau calls these factitious, fashion or (mere) opinion attributes, presented as if they were genuine merits but actually only markers in an aggressive competition.

Rousseau depicts here a vision of society and human relationships that borders on the hellish. Human beings are quite absorbed by an aggressive competition for domination, measured in terms of the subjugation of other people in reference to attainments devoid of any other significance than the (supposed) pleasures of the scope for contempt they afford:

> Civilized man . . . is always moving, sweating, toiling, and racking his brains to find still more laborious occupations . . . He pays court to men in power, whom he hates, and to the wealthy, whom he despises; he stops at nothing to have the honour of serving them; he is not ashamed to value himself on his own meanness and their protection; and, proud of his slavery, he speaks with disdain of those, who have not the honour of sharing it. What a sight would the perplexing and envied labours of a European minister of state present to the eyes of a Caribbean! . . . for him to see into the motives of all this solicitude the words "power" and "reputation" would have to bear some meaning in his mind; he would have to know that there are men who set a value on the opinion of the rest of the world; who can be made happy and satisfied with themselves rather on the testimony of other people than on their own . . . in the midst of so much philosophy, humanity, and civilization, and of such sublime codes of morality, we have nothing to show for ourselves but a frivolous and deceitful appearance, honour without virtue, reason without wisdom, and pleasure without happiness. (DI 104–5; OC III, 192–3)

It is plain that inequality between people is the very essence of this mode of life. Writ large, consolidated and institutionalized, it becomes the overall organizing principle of society.

One may, of course, assess the significance of these ideas in many ways. I should here like to emphasize that not only do these inequalities involve great evils in themselves – the denigration and humiliation of countless people – but they also impact very directly on human liberty. (Rousseau's leading concerns interlock in many ways.) That this is so in the case of those who are socially "inferior" is obvious – they will be oppressed in innumerable ways by those in ascendancy over them as well as by the social and political structures that codify and enforce these inequalities.[11] It is, however, also true of those who enjoy power and dominance, according to Rousseau. For they are subject to the judgment of others for the sense of their own worth, for their lives to have meaning and worth.[12] This "enslavement" is not confined to control of outward behavior alone. It shapes the aims and values which configure the individual's sense of self. A "false" self, fashioned by the dictates of the need to achieve social domination, replaces any self-determined goals which might have meaning and value in terms of a cogent and defensible account of human fulfillment.

As noted earlier, Rousseau concentrates much more on the nature and consequences of inequality than of equality in the *Discourse*. What can we infer, in fact, about his views on equality? He declares himself opposed to a "rigorous equality," arguing that distinction and favor "according to the actual service done to the State" can and should be given to men.[13] On the other hand, I think we can say that there is a basic, inviolable level of equal common regard and recognition that everyone alike is owed, according to Rousseau, for without that the abjection and humiliation of some would still remain, in clear opposition to the primary emphasis of his criticisms of inequality. Detail as to what this would amount to is lacking, however, and I shall return to the issue when I consider aspects of the argument of SC.

In considering the arguments of the *Discourse*, I have generally proceeded as if Rousseau is presenting us with a fairly definite either/or position. Either we remain as isolated beings in the state of nature, and are thus exempt from the demands of *amour-propre*, and all that brings with it; or we become members of society, civilized men, and lose ourselves and lives to the aggressive competition for precedence that social interaction appears to entail. However, I have hinted once or twice that it is not obvious that this is Rousseau's only, or most developed, view about the implications of socialization for the individual. Indeed, even in the pages of the *Discourse* itself there are suggestions that Rousseau held there could be a "just mean" between "the indolence of the primitive state" and the "petulant activity of our *amour-propre*," which mean, he says, "must have been the happiest and most stable of epochs," the "real youth of the world" (DI, 82–3; OC III, 171).

It is possible to read the phrase "petulant activity of our *amour-propre*" as meaning that the activity of our *amour-propre* is as such and necessarily "petulant." But that does not appear to be borne our by Rousseau's discussion in these pages.[14] It is not until property is introduced that the first germs of inequality present in primitive society begin to multiply and produce the large-scale ills that I have been examining – or so Rousseau appears to say. But whatever the niceties of the interpretation of this passage, I want to take from them the idea that it is possible that *amour-propre* need not be, in and of itself, "petulant" in its activity but may and can form an essential element in the basis of human relationships in society, playing a positive role. I certainly believe that it does so in Rousseau's further discussions of related issues in *Émile*, and it is to an assessment of these I now turn.

3. Aspects of *Émile*

Émile is a complex and many-stranded work, and the one which Rousseau regarded as his best achievement in which he succeeded, he felt, in setting out his best ideas most effectively. The book presents challenging ideas about education and learning, psychology, religion, morality, sex, marriage, women, politics, and many other matters. I shall be, here, very selective in what I take from it, concentrating on the issue of whether *amour-propre* is given a different account from that generally – though, as I suggested, not universally – to be found in the *Second Discourse.*

I have stressed that *amour-propre* as presented in the *Second Discourse* is pervaded by aggression. The desire for distinction, consideration, deference operates in a context in which others are apprehended as competitors, out to do one down, who need to be engaged in a challenging, combative, and domineering way. This is precisely the representation of the character and attitudes of other people, and of the terms of one's relation to them, that is intrinsic to an aggressively hostile outlook (and quite largely without regard to whether other people are *actually* like this).[15] I believe it is very significant that Rousseau pays very close attention, in the formation of the representative child's (Émile's) development, to his tendency to aggression and the consolidation of the sense of all human dealings as a contention for dominance over a malign other.[16]

Rousseau is very emphatic that the intensification and consolidation of aggressive attitudes and patterns of relationship is very damaging not only to those who are at the receiving end (so to say) but also to the aggressive agent. Most of what were, in the *Second Discourse*, identified as the ill effects of *amour-propre* emerge in the discussion in *Émile* as the ill effects of the structures of aggressive encounter. With this in view, it is possible to argue that it is not *amour-propre* as such, but *amour-propre* coupled with aggression, that is predominantly responsible for the ills that attend it. I think we can usefully make a distinction between *amour-propre* in its "normal" form and its "inflamed" form to register this difference, and I suggest Rousseau's thinking is this.

Amour-propre in its normal form is a desire for recognition, acknowledgment and respect from other people, recognition that one is a fellow human whose ideas, wishes, beliefs merit attention and consideration on at least a level footing with anyone else. One might say that *amour-propre* is the desire to have one's moral dignity as a human being acknowledged, the desire for a form of basic, unconditional, and absolute regard which registers and incorporates one as an equal member of the human community with a voice and a significance.

It is perfectly proper to describe such a desire as a desire for "consideration," the key term in Rousseau's first discussion of *amour-propre* in the *Second Discourse.* But what is crucial is that this "consideration" is not, as such, invidious, requiring preference before others, found only in another's despite. It is perfectly possible that all alike should enjoy it, in equal measure. One could go further, and argue that the consideration one receives from another only comprises a recognition and affirmation of one's human worth if it is consideration from those whose regard and respect counts for something in one's own estimation, those to whom one oneself affords consideration. So reciprocity of equal regard and respect is not simply compatible with the objectives of the *amour-propre* of each person, it is, arguably, required by these.[17]

Such matters take on a very different aspect, however, if through an aggressive construction of the character of human encounter it is felt that recognition and acknowledgment can only be secured from another in the face of threat and by a contention of will. Then it will appear necessary to achieve ascendancy over them, to dominate them, on pain else of their domination and subjection of you. But such a relation could never, in fact, deliver what is sought from it: sure unconditional consideration in the forum of human transactions. Also, there is a self-defeating aspect to the whole pattern; the deference and consideration one might extract on these terms will be from those one despises and denigrates, from those who, by one's own estimate, amount to nothing. It will, thus, be void of significance. To be otherwise, one must accord weight and value to the judgment of others, which is what, in aggressive encounter, one is determined not to do. But suchlike inconsistencies are typical of an aggressive reading of human transactions.

The possibility of what I referred to above as the reciprocity of equal regard and respect proper to "normal" *amour-propre* is strengthened if in place of human relations structured by aggression those shaped by pity or compassion come to be fundamental to human dealings. Rousseau takes up his very brief comments on pity in the *Second Discourse*, referred to earlier, and expands and develops them very extensively in the discussions in *Émile* (particularly in Book 4, 220–55; OC IV, 502–51). His view is, to put it with great brevity, that through our capacity for pity we register and respond to the humanity of another person in relation to the most common and pervasive of all human predicaments, that of suffering pain. In such a context all matters of privilege, status, power, dominance are stripped away, and our common vulnerability and weakness becomes salient. Our compassionate response incorporates another's need into the circle of our immediate concern, and – in Rousseau's view – such a response is naturally apt to be met with a return of gratitude, an affirmation of the value of the help given and of the provider of that help. In this case a bond of mutual care and esteem can grow, one rooted in a universal human experience, and in this context *amour-propre* – which takes us beyond the dynamics of emotional interaction to the establishment of entitlements and claims – can much more readily assume its normal character rather than its inflamed, aggressive, form.

If this is an appropriate reading of Rousseau's principal themes here, then a number of points arise. First, we get a clearer sense of what sort of basic equality Rousseau thought it desirable for humans to enjoy, just that equality of recognition and regard which acknowledgment of another as a suffering creature worthy of care in their need involves. This is the recognition of others as making a moral claim on us, a recognition bound up with our own participation with them in human community (as, ourselves, bearers of moral titles). Such equality is, of course, perfectly compatible with many differences of status and privilege, providing these never displace this foundational level of absolute regard owed by all to all.

Secondly, we see better how acceptance of that equality is strengthened through the development of bonds of mutual care and affection which grow out of experience of a universal human predicament. A sense of human solidarity both helps to create, but is in turn sustained by, the relations of reciprocal moral regard. It is, I think, possible to argue that, for Rousseau, the moral equality of all human beings stands in relation to the common experience of suffering as the civil equality of members of a state stands in relation to their fraternal experience of a shared history, culture, and destiny. I shall return to this in a moment.

Finally, we may consider what conception of the human individual, situated in society, is emerging from this. Such individuals regard themselves as worthy of regard and respect from those they engage with and, at the same time, acknowledge the respect owed to those people too, not as an imposed demand or moral command but as the principle intrinsic to their own self-understanding and position. It will be clear that for such persons to act freely, without check or impediment on their will, necessarily involves their acknowledgment of a principle of moral equality since that is the inherent character of their will. There is no question, in this conception of the liberated individual, of the exercise of a will wholly without regulation and order; but neither is that regulation something imposed as a constraint. Rather it is the order incorporated in the very character of the will of a moral being as such.[18] The fundamental importance of this point to Rousseau's thinking will become apparent when we turn to the basic elements of his reasoning in the *Social Contract*. Before doing so, however, I want to look a little more at the issue of fraternity, alluded to just above.

4. Fraternity

For the remainder of this essay I shall focus on core themes in Rousseau's political philosophy which, I argued at the start, are clarified by consideration of the issues I have examined thus far. To facilitate the transition to this, it is worth considering Rousseau's ideas about the nature and role of fraternity, a sense of brotherhood, in his thinking about the civil community.

Rousseau was very decidedly of the opinion that without some quite powerful and pervasive unity of sentiment, sense of common life, and shared destiny, the possibility of the formation and maintenance of a just and humane civil community would be very limited. Precepts of reason, of natural law, prescribing fair and equal treatment may, in themselves, be true and justified. But, he held, their truth would scarcely be understood, and even less would they be embraced and become the living principle of people's outlook and actions, unless there was already in people's outlook and attitudes some felt bond of shared life. (I considered, in the previous section, a parallel line of thought concerning compassion and the requirements of moral duty.)

We can readily enough see the force of Rousseau's thought here if we look briefly at smaller scale human unions, such as those of the family or of friendship.[19] Friends and family members certainly have rights and duties in relation to each other, but at the very least the willingness to embrace these duties would be much reduced unless there were a strong sense of involvement in the well-being and life of the other parties in the relationship. And when there is that sense of involvement, although the duties remain, they are not perceived and responded to as such, as if restraints needed to curb harmful conduct or demands needed to prompt beneficial conduct, but are carried out as the natural expression of the affection which unites people. To put it crudely, the duties of friendship and family members largely comprise a codification of what such people would, as such, be wanting to do for the others involved anyway.

What lies at the root of this is what one might call an "enlargement" of the sense of self, and the interests of the self, to incorporate the well-being and flourishing of others as components of what one seeks and wishes for in order for one's own life to be well. Any sharp, clear-cut, distinction between "mine" and "thine" is eroded, in the sense that I embrace the concerns of (some) others as being as immediately significant, valuable, and compelling as those which impinge on me considered as a being entirely separate and apart.[20]

It is with such instances in mind, I suggest, that Rousseau considers the conditions necessary to the formation and maintenance of a just and humane society, the conditions necessary to enable citizens to value and embrace the "burden" of respecting, honoring, and cherishing the need and good of all their fellows alike. What, in his view, takes the place of the spontaneous affection of friendship, the shared life of the family, is the sense of patriotism, the sense of shared rootedness in and belonging to a homeland, with the fortunes of which and of all those who have like roots, one's own good fortune and well-being is bound up as a constitutive element.

Rousseau considers this theme in many places, but perhaps the clearest statement of his view is given at DPE 135ff (OC III, 259ff).[21] There he writes:

> If . . . they [men] were early accustomed to regard their individuality only in relation to the body of the State, and to be aware, so to speak, of their own existence merely as a part of that of the State, they might at length come to identify themselves in some degree with this greater whole, to feel themselves members of their country, and to love it with that exquisite feeling which no isolated person has save for himself . . . Not only does philosophy demonstrate the possibility of taking steps in these new directions; history furnishes us with a thousand striking examples. If they are so rare among us moderns, it is because nobody troubles himself whether citizens exist or not, and still less does anybody think of attending to the matter soon enough to make them.

We shall see, later on, that it is the principal role of the Legislator, in Rousseau's political theory in the *Social Contract*, to engender this sense of identification with the greater whole, when that is not already present and vivid in people's lives (see SC II, 7; OC III 381ff).

We are, today, perhaps more aware of the drawbacks of patriotism, of the aggressive sectionalism it often gives rise to. But it would be hasty to dismiss Rousseau's thinking here out of hand since he is addressing what, under any circumstances, must be a key concern of any theory of the state, namely how and why members of it can be brought to find the responsibilities and commitments they necessarily undertake for each other in the state to be something they find valuable, and shall fulfill willingly. The force of law alone – even supposing just laws would be passed in a context of mutual hostility or indifference – is inadequate; it leads only to resentment or the desire to evade its reach unless there is some appreciation of its ends, and that means some appreciation of the good in a just and equal treatment of all alike even though that places considerable burdens on each individual. To neglect, or merely to take for granted, the conditions for fashioning and strengthening that appreciation is to threaten the very existence of the civil community as anything more than a forum of competitive interest, from which people are unable to escape.[22]

It is time now to pull these various threads of argument together and to try to show, as promised at the start, that we gain better access to and a clearer understanding of Rousseau's central ideas in the *Social Contract* by seeing this work as informed by the ideas in these other writings of his. All I can do in this context is select some key elements in SC and try to show how their clarity is enhanced and the cogency strengthened by seeing them as building on material considered thus far.

5. Key Elements of the Social Contract

At the heart of Rousseau's political theory in SC is his account of the composition, functioning, and role of the sovereign body. The sovereign body, in any state, is that body which has final authority to determine what shall and shall not be done by all members of that state, though it may delegate the exercise of some of its powers and functions. Its principal function is to devise and promulgate the laws which bind all those who are part of the civil community, and it follows that it is necessarily of the greatest significance for the well-being of all in the community that the sovereign body should be constituted satisfactorily and discharge its functions in a proper manner. Rousseau writes of the sovereign as follows:

> This public person [collective body] . . . formed by the union of all other persons, formerly took the name of *city*, and now takes that of *Republic* or *politic body*; it is called by its members *State* when passive, *Sovereign* when active, and *Power* when compared with others like itself. Those who are associated in it take collectively the name of *people*, and severally are called *citizens*, as sharing in the sovereign authority, and *subjects*, as being under the laws of the state. (SC I, 6; 175; OC III, 361–2)

A few pages later he goes on:

> Laws are, properly speaking, only the conditions of civil association. The people, being subject to the laws, ought to be their author: the conditions of the society ought to be regulated solely by those who come together to form it. (SC II, 6, 193; OC III, 380)

Laws, which declare what shall or shall not be done, can be understood as the expression of a will that directs this or that. On this understanding, the sovereign has a will, and the will of the sovereign body when it is legitimately and properly declared is called by Rousseau the general will. (There can be declarations of the will of the sovereign body which express only factional or sectional interests; such declarations do not express the general will and any requirement thus arrived at which may be promulgated as lawful is not legitimate, in Rousseau's view. (See e.g. SC III, 2 and II, 3; OC III, 400ff and 371ff.)

I shall return to the character of the general will in a moment, but it is useful to consider straightaway Rousseau's account of the composition of that collective body which is the sovereign. As we have seen, Rousseau holds that the sovereign should be composed of all the people who are subject to the law (presumably there would be an age qualification, but I am not aware that Rousseau anywhere specifies this). Why is this? One reason is contained in the passage quoted just above, that the conditions of society ought to be regulated by those who form it. But we are in a position to see a deeper, or further, reason also. For by participation, *qua* citizen, in the actions of the sovereign each person enjoys recognition and honor as someone whose opinions and voice have weight and force on a par with those of anyone else. No one is merely subject to the will or judgment of another, brushed aside as a servile or insignificant nullity fit only to be imposed upon. By this, therefore, the central demands of the *amour-propre* of each person are met in that their standing as a significant figure in the community is incorporated into the very structure of the supreme authority in that community.

Of course, no individual persons will consider themselves only as citizens; they will also retain a particular or individual interest (see SC I, 6, 177; OC III, 363). And, from that point of view, they may well prefer that their particular will should have a more dominant or wider scope, resenting the requirement to give weight and place to the interests of others as equal alongside their own. But we know from prior discussion that that preference, for superiority and dominance, cannot lead to personal happiness nor indeed to the meeting of the demands of the individual's *amour-propre*. It is, thus, really an illusion to suppose that what one might prefer in this way from one's individual perspective is preferable. To assume the character of a citizen will be in fact to meet more comprehensively and successfully one's *individual* desires. These don't need to be set aside or suppressed; rather – or such is Rousseau's view – they find in this way their fulfillment. Becoming a citizen is a completion of the individual's project; not the substitution of another one. (There is no suggestion here, on Rousseau's part, that individuals will, in some sense, lose their separate identity in the State and become like worker ants or some such thing. For citizenship only engages with the general conditions of civil association; there will remain very much else that is private and personal to each.) (See SC II, 4, 186; OC III, 372–3.)

Nor should the requirement to pay honor to the like right of all to participate in the functions of sovereignty be regarded as a limitation on liberty, again for reasons considered earlier. For acceptance of that requirement will be the natural expression of what one wishes to do as a moral being, understanding oneself as a bearer of rights and titles united with others likewise understood. It is only by treating the individual or particular will as if it were paramount here that there can appear to be a loss of liberty. But if that is given paramount place then it leads to its own despite. And, once we take in the factors surrounding the issue of fraternity, the sense will be reinforced that respecting and honoring the good of all alike is a proper component of the realization one's own good.

What then is the general will? How does the people, active as members of the sovereign, determine its will in a way that is going to be legitimate and appropriate, such that it shall be general in character and object? The question breaks down into two elements. First, it requires us to say more precisely in what it is that the "generalness" of the general will consists, what it is for a will to have that character. Secondly, it requires us to say by what method or process the people can arrive at specifically what a will with that character would determine. Regarding the generalness of the "object" of the general will, the matter is plain enough, that it must issue in "general conventions"; the law "considers subjects *en masse* and actions in the abstract, and never a particular person or action" (SC II, 6, 192; OC III, 379). To elucidate the generalness of its character is more problematic, but I suggest a key remark to understanding this is to be found in SC II, 4, 187 (OC III, 373), where Rousseau says "the general will, to be really such, must be general in its object as well as its essence; that it must both come from all and apply to all" (the French reads, strictly, "come from all *in order to* apply to all," which surely conveys Rousseau's meaning better).

The key phrase here is that it must "come from all." I suggest that we should understand this to mean that each and every member of the sovereign, each and every citizen, should have the same, good reason to subscribe to, assent to, a proposal which is put forward as a prospective law. Or, if some have better reasons for assent than others, no one must have less than adequate reason to assent, where adequate reason must encompass not only the protection of their own person and goods (see SC I, 6, 174; OC III, 360), but also their incorporation and role as an active member of the sovereign body whose voice carries the same force and weight as anyone else's. (See also SC II, 9, 204; OC III 391–2.) I stress the need to have the same, or never less than adequate, *reason* for assent, rather than the mere fact of giving assent, since, as Rousseau himself stresses (see particularly SC II, 6, 193; OC III, 380), individuals, as well as a whole people, can be ignorant, confused, deluded, or misled over what it assents to as good ("The individuals see the good they reject; the public wills the good it does not see"). Of course, this raises a host of problems, not least over who is in a position to judge whether or not adequate reason for assent is present, but it would require a whole further essay to consider these properly. My claim here is only that this is Rousseau's view of the matter, not to undertake a full defense of his view.

If this is right, it means that any actually obtaining procedure of voting, or other method for determining members' assent to a proposal, will not necessarily be a reliable method for identifying a declaration of a genuinely general will. Although Rousseau says quite a lot about voting procedures (at, for example, SC II 3, 185; OC III, 371; SC IV, 2; OC III, 439ff), it is clear that these are idealized procedures, which concern what a well-advised person *would* assent to, not what actual, short-sighted, confused, and possibly ill-intentioned people *do* agree to. We should not conclude from this, however, that we can make no progress whatever in identifying what the general will would be, since unless there were some pretty widely shared and commonly understood ideas of what people needed for protection of their person and goods, and for their incorporation into the sovereign, then the very possibility of establishing a civil community at all would scarcely exist. (See SC II, 1, 182; OC III, 368.)

Rousseau says, at SC II, 11, 204 (OC III, 391) that the objective of every system of legislation is liberty and equality. We can see plainly how the general will, as the legislative will, procures equality; the liberty it procures is not, of course, the liberty of an individual to do just as he pleases (as discussed earlier) but the liberty proper to a moral being and citizen where to act under the requirements of respect for the good and standing of others is the inherent constitutive principle of action.

In SC II, 3 (OC III, 371), Rousseau distinguishes the general will from the will of all, which is "no more than a sum of particular wills," whilst arguing that we can discover the general will from the will of all by "taking away" from these same wills the "pluses and minuses that cancel one another," and the general will remains as "the sum of the differences." This passage has caused much difficulty of interpretation. I would suggest that among the clearest assessments of Rousseau's meaning is to be found in this passage from Kant:

> the *republican* constitution is the only one which does complete justice to the rights of man. But it is also the most difficult to establish . . . since men, with their self-seeking inclinations, would be incapable of adhering to a constitution of so sublime a nature. But in fact, nature comes to the aid of the universal and rational human will, . . . and makes use of precisely those self-seeking inclinations in order to do so. It only remains for men to create a good organisation for the state . . . and to arrange it in such a way that their self-seeking energies are opposed to one another, each thereby neutralizing or eliminating the destructive effects of the rest. And as far as reason is concerned, the result is the same as if man's selfish tendencies were non-existent, so that man, even if he is not morally good in himself, is nevertheless compelled to be a good citizen.[23]

And more to the same effect. Kant even says that this problem can be solved "by a nation of devils (so long as they possess understanding)."

There are two further matters I should like to comment on briefly, before concluding. The first concerns the nature and role of the Legislator (see SC II, 7; OC III, 381ff) in Rousseau's argument. I have alluded to this matter before (above, section 4), and we should in fact be well prepared to understand Rousseau's principal intent in this matter. The Legislator is someone of "superior intelligence," aware of "all the passions of men without experiencing them," independent of the need of men for his happiness, but yet interested in ours, and so on. What then is his role? It is to try to bring it about that there is "a people" who can have a general will. A mere multitude, an aggregate of persons not an association (see SC I, 5,

173; OC III, 359), is not aware of the vital necessity to them of the social tie, the bond of living union between them; they are apt to be confined to the vision and sentiments of their "physical and independent existence" and will not understand, let alone respond to, the need to recognize the liberty and equality of all and make that the principle of their own life. Rousseau has elsewhere, as we saw, sufficiently explained the importance of the fraternal bond and, when he considers the significance of the Legislator I suggest that it is precisely this issue which is under consideration again.

It may be objected that such a figure is utterly unrealistic and that, therefore, Rousseau is left with nothing to say about how a bond of union between persons, sufficient to make them a people, can be established and maintained. I would suggest that this is not so. In all but the theoretically limiting case – where the task of state formation starts from nothing, so to say – the functions of the legislator are in fact carried by the customs, history, habits of a people which provide the beginnings of a sense of common union which legislation refines and reinforces (see SC II, 10, 203; II, 12, 206–7; OC III, 390–1; 394).[24]

The second matter concerns being "forced to be free" (SC I, 7, 177; OC III, 364). Rousseau writes:

> In order that the social compact may not be an empty formula, it tacitly includes the undertaking, which alone can give force to the rest, that whoever refuses to obey the general will shall be compelled to do so by the whole body. This means nothing less than that he will be forced to be free; for this is the condition which, by giving each citizen to his country, secures him against all personal dependence.

Scarcely any remark of Rousseau's has attracted more unfavorable comment. Yet I think Rousseau's meaning here is by no means as sinister as it has been made out to be. The key lies in his elucidation concerning being secured "against all personal dependence." What submission to the general will requires of a person is that he acknowledges the standing of all others within the civil community as equals, in the ways I have tried to clarify. I have also tried to show how that acknowledgment should not be viewed as a constraint upon action, but rather as the principle of action intrinsic to one's character as a moral being and citizen, the assumption of which "character" should not be seen as the circumscription of the needs and wants one has as a "naturally independent" being (to use Rousseau's own phrase) but as providing their proper completion. It is in this way one acquires freedom by submission to the general will.

On the other side, we should reflect that those who decline to obey the general will are, by this, seeking some unequal advantage for themselves over others. But, as we have seen at length in earlier discussion, such "advantage" is, in Rousseau's estimation, quite illusory and the immediate and indirect effects of seeking it procure a greater bondage and servitude than it might be thought is being avoided.

It is surprising, moreover, that Rousseau should be so generally criticized on this point. A recognition and respect for certain fundamental human equalities is a key element in all modern liberal democracies. Are we then to suppose that all members of such polities should regard their freedom as being profoundly limited by this? If so, why then do they submit to it? In fact, of course, it is usually presented as some kind of requirement of universal practical reason, and hence as being a principle of moral agency, and not a curb on that. But that is in effect Rousseau's position, too, though he would argue for it in somewhat different terms. Here, as elsewhere, his fault is, perhaps, that of seeing things more deeply and clearly and saying rather plainly what he sees, rather than that of saying things that are indefensible.

I have, quite evidently, not touched upon very many things that Rousseau discusses, and illuminates, in the argument of SC. What I have tried to do is concentrate upon what I have called the "key elements" of his thinking about the character of a civil community, and to show how these are rooted in and are clarified by his treatment of these issues in others of his works. Rousseau provides us with what is, I believe, a remarkably highly integrated and systematic vision of man in society, and one which is of no mere antiquarian interest but which poses questions and offers insights which still have great vitality today.

Notes

1 References to, and abbreviations of, Rousseau's texts are as follows: *A Discourse on the Origin of Inequality* (DI), in Jean-Jacques Rousseau, *The Social Contract and Discourses*, tr. G. D. H. Cole; revised and augmented by J. H. Brumfitt and J. C. Hall (London: Dent, 1973). *A Discourse on Political Economy* (DPE), in Cole/Brumfitt/Hall. *The Social Contract* (SC), in Cole/Brumfitt/Hall. *Considerations on the Government of Poland* (GP), in Rousseau, *Political Writings*, tr. and ed. F. Watkins (Edinburgh: Nelson, 1953). *Émile* (or: On Education) (E), tr. with intro. and notes by Allan Bloom (New York: Basic Books, 1979). *Oeuvres Complètes* (OC), J.-J. Rousseau, *Oeuvres Complètes*, eds. B. Gagnebin and M. Raymond (Paris: Bibliothèque de la Pléiade, Éditions Gallimard, 5 vols., 1959–97). References to the English editions used are followed by references to the *Oeuvres Complètes*, giving volume and page number. References to the English edition of SC used give the Book, chapter and, where relevant, page number.

2 This short summary is also printed in Cole/Brumfitt/Hall, pp. 300–10.

3 See *Letters to Malesherbes*, Second Letter, in *Citizen of Geneva*, tr. and ed. C. W. Hendel (Oxford, 1937); OC I, 1135–6; *The Confessions*, Book 8, tr. J. M. Cohen (Harmondsworth: Penguin, 1954), pp. 327–8; OC I, 351–2.

4 Rousseau considers pity further in DI (67–8; OC III, 155–7), and also at length and in detail in E, 4, 220ff (OC IV, 502ff). I consider this latter material very briefly in section 4, below. See also Dent, *Rousseau* (Oxford: Blackwell, 1988), ch. 4.

5 I consider this view in "An Integral Part of His Species . . . ?" in *Jean-Jacques Rousseau and the Sources of the Self*, ed. T. O'Hagan (Aldershot: Avebury, 1997), pp. 25–37, esp. p. 31.

6 Rousseau discusses jealousy further in E V, 429–31; OC IV, 796–8.

7 But compare E I, 41; OC IV, 251.

8 Kant writes, in a passage clearly inspired by Rousseau, as follows:

> The predisposition to humanity can be brought under the general title of a self-love which is physical and yet *compares* . . . Out of this self-love springs the inclination *to acquire worth in the opinion of others.* This is originally a desire merely for *equality*, to allow no one superiority above oneself, bound up with a constant care lest others strive to attain such superiority; but from this arises gradually the unjustifiable craving to win it for oneself over others. Upon this twin stem of *jealousy* and *rivalry* may be grafted the very great vices of secret and open animosity . . . vices, however, which really do not sprout from nature as their root; rather they are inclinations, aroused in us by the anxious endeavours of others to attain a hated superiority over us.

See *Religion within the Limits of Reason Alone*, Bk. 1, sec. 1, tr. T. M. Greene and H. Hudson (New York: Harper & Row, 1960).

9 See DI 66 Note 2 (OC III, 219–20, Note XV); and DI 104 (OC III, 193), where Rousseau writes:

> he [a Caribbean] would have to know that there are men who set a value on the opinion of the rest of the world; who can be made happy and satisfied with themselves rather on the testimony of other people than on their own . . . social man . . . only knows how to live in the opinion of others, so that he seems to receive the consciousness of his own existence merely from the judgement of others concerning him.

10 See the episode about running in E, II, 141–2 (OC IV, 393–4); and compare the important remarks at E IV, 339 (OC IV, 670–1).

11 See Rousseau's discussion of what sometimes gets referred to as the "false" social contract at DI 88ff (OC III, 176ff).

12 See DI 86 (OC III 174–5), and note 9 above; also E II, 83; OC IV, 308–9.

13 See DI, 100 note (OC III, 222, Note XIX); and compare e.g. SC II, 6, 192; III, 11, 204 (OC III 379; 391–2).

14 Compare Note 7 to the translation of DI in *Rousseau's Political Writings*, eds. A. Ritter and J. Conaway Bondanella, tr. J. Conaway Bondanella (New York: W. W. Norton, 1988), p. 39.

15 My thinking about these issues has been much influenced by Wollheim. See particularly R. Wollheim, *The Thread of Life* (Cambridge: Cambridge University Press, 1984), ch. 7, "From Voices to Values: The Growth of the Moral Sense."

16 See, out of many comparable passages, E I, 48; 65–6; II, 87–8 (OC IV, 261; 286–7; 314–15); and Allan Bloom's "Introduction" to *Émile.*

17 See the passage from Kant, quoted in note 8 above.

18 I have tried to develop this assessment of Rousseau's thinking more fully in my *Rousseau.* See particularly ch. 4 secs. 5, 8 (e.g. p. 150), and ch. 5 secs. 4, 5.

19 See Rousseau's own reference to the family in this connection: E 5, 362–3; OC IV, 699–700.

20 Compare E IV, 222–3 (OC IV, 506). This whole issue is considered and developed at length by Schopenhauer, in *On the Basis of Morality*, who was much influenced by Rousseau. And see Aristotle, *Nicomachean Ethics*, 1166a30: "the good man . . . is related to his friend as to himself (for his friend is another self)."

21 There is much relevant material in his *Considerations on the Government of Poland* and in the *Letter to M. d'Alembert on the Theatre.* This element in Rousseau's thinking is

discussed in A. Cohler, *Rousseau and Nationalism* (New York: Basic Books, 1970).

22 Rousseau discusses this very vividly in a chapter in the Geneva Manuscript of SC, usually referred to as "The General Society of the Human Race." See Cole/Brumfitt/Hall, pp. 155–162; OC III, 281–9.

23 See Kant, *Perpetual Peace*, First Supplement, in Kant, *Political Writings*, ed. H. Reiss, tr. H. B. Nisbet (Cambridge: Cambridge University Press, 1992), pp. 112–13.

24 I develop this theme in the entry on the "legislator" in my *A Rousseau Dictionary* (Oxford: Blackwell, 1992), pp. 144–7.

Chapter 11

Immanuel Kant

Patricia Kitcher

As befits a philosopher who believed that human beings must be understood largely in abstraction from their physical attributes, Kant's life, insofar as it is worth telling, was entirely a life of the mind. He was born (1724) and died (1804) in the same town, Königsberg, East Prussia. He had neither wife nor children. He spent his entire university career teaching at the institution (Königsberg) where he was educated.

In contrast to his limited geographical confines, Kant's intellectual interests ranged over most parts of the (then) known world of ideas. He made seminal contributions to epistemology, ethics, political philosophy, and aesthetics. Along with his predecessor and frequent target, David Hume, he attempted a major realignment of the entire discipline of philosophy away from metaphysics. Hume and Kant also changed the face of academic religion. Although Kant tried to sequester himself from political affairs, his efforts to bring enlightenment to religion earned him a rebuke from his (unenlightened) monarch, Frederick William II.

1. The Unity of Reason

The global sweep of Kant's intellectual endeavors was principled. It rested on the central distinctive tenet of his philosophy, transcendental idealism. Transcendental idealism is a subtle, many-faceted doctrine, but its core is the idea that the human mind is creative, not merely receptive and reactive. On Kant's view, human beings could acquire neither knowledge nor moral wisdom simply by taking in information about the passing show of objects and human events through their various senses. For morality and knowledge to be possible, human mental faculties had to be active in interpreting sensory data and in judging moral rightness.

Kant believed that the human faculties of perception, feeling, conception, judgment, and reason displayed a systematic or organic unity. The actions of these faculties make sense only in relation to their contributions to the whole. In the *Critique of Judgment*, he explained that philosophy had to possess systematic unity, because the human cognitive faculties that partially shaped knowledge and action were systematically unified.

For Kant, the "shaping power" (to borrow Coleridge's apt phrase)[1] of the human mind unified the branches of knowledge. His interest in various disciplines was driven by his desire to find additional evidence for his central thesis. He wanted to establish that, at least in terms of their fundamental principles, all scientific disciplines rested on core assumptions that reflected the way that our minds work to produce knowledge. The unity of the mind also unified thought and action. He insisted that it was the same reason that enabled us to make sense of sensory data in scientific theories that guided our moral deliberation and created our political institutions.

For Kant, not only thought and action, but also art and science were intimately bound up with the creative activities of the human faculties. He argued that we take pleasure in art, precisely because our encounters with works of art provide intimations of the strength and harmony of the human faculties, the very faculties needed to understand the natural world and to create a rational social world of our own design.

2. The Limits of Knowledge

To understand the details of Kant's system of philosophy, we should begin, as he did, with *The Critique of Pure Reason*. The "*First Critique*" focuses on a number of interrelated problems in epistemology and metaphysics. In epistemology, Kant considered such perennial questions as: What are the sources of knowledge, sensory evidence and/or innate ideas? What are the scope and limits of human knowledge? He also asked such standard metaphysical questions as: What is the nature of reality? Was the universe created by God? What is the relation between free will and causal determinism? To appreciate his highly original approach to these issues, it is helpful to situate his work in its historical context, both in philosophy and in the world of ideas more generally.

Background

Kant's philosophy can be understood only in light of the pressing philosophical questions raised by the Scientific Revolution. The hallmark of the "new science" was succinctly captured in Galileo's dictum that "the book of nature is written in the language of mathematics." To take a striking example, according to Newton's second law, the force operating on a body is precisely equal to its mass multiplied by its acceleration ($F = ma$). This law, and mathematical science more generally, are so familiar to us now that it is hard to recapture the sense of puzzlement that ought to accompany such a startling result. Why should these three physical quantities, force, mass, and acceleration, be related to each other according to a precise mathematical formula?

Given standard views of the status of mathematical claims, the puzzle becomes even more intractable. According to the philosophy of mathematics in Kant's day, mathematics is something like an elaborate game. Theorems of geometry are acceptable, because they can be derived from Euclid's axioms, and Euclid's axioms are acceptable, because they present definitions of geometrical terms. To take one of Kant's examples, why is there exactly one straight line connecting any two points? On the standard view, the answer must be either that this claim follows from other axioms, or that it is acceptable itself because of the ways we define "straight," "point," and/or "line." If that is the correct explanation of why mathematical statements are accepted, because of the way we define our terms, then it seems utterly mysterious how mathematical equations could precisely capture real relations among physical quantities.

The laws of classical mechanics raised another serious epistemological problem. How could we ever know that *all* bodies obey Newton's three laws of motion? How could we know that *all* bodies have the property that they attract each other with a gravitational force proportional to their masses and inversely proportional to the square of their distance from each other? Newton's evidence for his laws could only be the observation of a small number of cases (the motions of the six known planets, plus the moon). What about the other celestial and earthly bodies that were claimed to obey this law?

If the laws of mathematics and science seemed incomprehensible on standard accounts, the situation was no better with what Descartes called the "eternal truths" of philosophy. These would include such basic principles of reasoning as the law of noncontradiction, "nothing can both be and not be at the same time" or the law of identity, "$a = a$". According to Descartes, such principles were usable in human reasoning, because God made them true and then implanted them in each human mind. Kant's great predecessor, Gottfried Wilhelm Leibniz, recoiled at the idea that the laws of thinking might depend on God's free choice – as if God could simply have chosen to make "$a \neq a$" instead!

Where do the "eternal truths" come from and why are they valid? For some, like Leibniz, principles such as the law of noncontradiction and the *ex nihilo* principle (nothing comes out of nothing) were self-evidently true. Neither sensory evidence nor Divine origin was necessary to establish the credentials of such basic principles. As soon as any person thought carefully about the law stating that the same claim cannot be both true and false at the same time, then he or she must recognize that the law is valid.

When some of Kant's other predecessors turned their attention to fundamental principles of philosophy, however, they came to the opposite conclusion, at least for some cases. Most famously, when Hume examined the *ex nihilo* principle, he found no reason to accept that "nothing can come out of nothing" or, expressing the principle positively, that "everything must have a cause." By his lights, the belief that "every event must have a cause" and the related belief that "the same cause has the same effect" were popular opinions that were accepted simply because they were widely held.

In *A Treatise on Human Nature*, Hume launched a ferocious attack on the legitimacy of using causal concepts, an attack whose force is still felt today. Lest anyone doubt the general nature of his criticism, Hume concluded his *Inquiry Concerning Human Knowledge* (which Kant owned in German translation) with a suggestion that any book of metaphysics – indeed any book at all that was neither mathematics, nor based firmly on experiment and evidence – should be burned!

Kant's project

Given this background, it is no mystery why Kant believed that epistemology had to address three key questions (B 15–18):[2]

How is mathematics possible?
How is natural science possible?
How is metaphysics possible (as a science)?

He regarded these puzzles as variations on a single theme, because each discipline made claims that were universal in form.

[In all cases] the shortest distance between two points is a straight line.
All bodies attract each other with gravitational force.
All events have causes.

Further, the claims of mathematics, natural science, and metaphysics all seemed to have the same force: they were not merely true, but "necessary." Although the notion of "necessity" is complex and controversial, one common meaning is that a "necessary" claim could not be false. Even if evidence were offered against the claim, the evidence would be rejected rather than the claim.

Since the status of the claims of mathematics, science, and particularly metaphysics, was questionable, Kant tried to show that we were justified in accepting them. His attitude towards science and mathematics was complex. Although scientists and mathematicians were rightly regarded as making major advances in knowledge, the inadequacies of previous explanations of how it was possible to offer universal and necessary claims required a fresh attack on the problem.

Kant's novel approach grew out of his appreciation of the weaknesses of previous attempts. From the work of Hume (among others) he recognized that universal and necessary claims in mathematics, science, or metaphysics could not be justified by appeal to empirical evidence. Sensory experience could only tell us what had been the case (all observed samples of gold have an atomic weight of 79). It could never tell us that past regularities will always hold (all samples of gold have an atomic weight of 79) or that such regularities are necessary (no stuff with an atomic weight other than 79 will be accepted as gold). The impossibility of finding empirical evidence in favor of universal and necessary claims did not bother Hume, because he happily forswore the "eternal truths" of metaphysics. In Kant's eyes, Hume's rejection of necessary and universal truths in general would have been brought up short, had he not accepted the standard view of mathematics. Hume could preserve the laws of mathematics, because he took them to be a matter of definition.

In terminology that Kant did much to introduce, Hume regarded the truths of mathematics as "analytic" (A 6/B 10ff). Consider again the geometrical proposition that the shortest distance between two points is a straight line. On the standard view Hume espoused, this claim would either be a stipulative definition of "distance" or it would be derivable from other stipulative definitions. Once the definitions were substituted into the original claim, the predicate concept ("straight line") would be revealed as contained in the subject concept ("the straight line between two points"). With the substitutions made, it is clear that the proposition must be accepted, because it asserts nothing more than that a straight line is a straight line.

Kant agreed with Hume (and many others) that if a universal and necessary claim is analytic, then that would be sufficient to justify it. But he rejected the view that mathematics was just a matter of the definitions. More broadly, he rejected the notion that interesting claims could be established by appealing to definitions. The fatal flaw in this approach is that *any* claim can be turned into an analytic claim, simply by adjusting the subject concept so that it contains the predicate concept.[3] Such a maneuver is as useless as it is easy. If you try to prove that "All *A*'s are *B*'s" by defining *A* in such a way that it includes *B*, say $A = B + X$, then that simply invites the question of whether that newly defined concept is appropriate for describing reality. And to show that, it would be necessary to establish that all those objects that have the attribute (or attributes) indicated by *X* also have attribute *B*. Thus, it would be necessary to show that "All *X*'s are *B*'s" and no progress would have been made.

As a contrast to "analytic," Kant introduced the term "synthetic" to describe those claims where the predicate concept is not contained in the subject concept. His position – unusual in the history of the subject – was that mathematical claims were synthetic. In stark contrast to much of twentieth-century "analytic" philosophy, he also maintained that the basic principles of philosophy were synthetic.

Kant believed that his Empiricist predecessors could not solve the problem of mathematics (or science) in ways that were acceptable by their own scruples. Sensory evidence could never be adequate to justify universal and necessary claims and justifying the universal and necessary claims of mathematics on the grounds that they were analytic made the success of mathematical science incomprehensible. In Kant's view, his Rationalist predecessors fared no better. They assumed the "lazy hypothesis" that key concepts and logical principles were innate, having been Divinely implanted in the human mind to harmonize perfectly with the laws chosen by God to govern the universe.

Despite the legendary obscurity of Kant's prose, he was clear about the alternative to Empiricism and Rationalism that he was going to explore. In the opening paragraphs of the Introduction to the *Critique of Pure Reason*, he explained:

> There is no doubt that all our cognition begins with experience . . . But even though all our cognition commences **with** experience, nevertheless, it does not for that reason all originate **from** experience. *For it might well be that our empirical cognition itself is a composite of what we receive through impressions and of what our own cognitive faculties give up out of themselves (merely induced by sensory impressions)* . . . (B 1; my italics)

The possibility Kant raised, which he spent much of the *First Critique* exploring, was that even so-called "empirical" cognition is and must be a *conjoint* product of the contributions of objects, through the sensory impressions they cause in us, and the contributions of our faculties in sorting and combining the materials brought in through the senses.

Having raised the possibility of two sources of cognition, Kant introduced a pair of contrastive terms, *a priori* and *a posteriori* cognition:

> One calls such **cognitions** [i.e. what our cognitive faculties give up out of themselves] **a priori**, and distinguishes them from the **empirical** [ones], which have their sources *a posteriori*, namely in experience. (B 2)

The possibility of two sources of cognition, *a posteriori* cognition from sensory impressions and *a priori* cognitions from the activities of the mind set in motion by the receipt of sensory impressions (B 1), raised an immediate question. How is the "fundamental material" provided by the senses to be distinguished from that which the mind provides out of itself?

Given his historical context, Kant had no trouble in finding sure signs or "marks" by which *a priori* cognitions could be unfailingly separated from *a posteriori* ones. Since sensory experience could not be the basis of either necessary or universal claims, if a claim has those characteristics (which themselves always go together), then it must be *a priori* (B 3–4). Mathematics and science provided examples of universal and necessary claims, so it was reasonable to assume that human beings were in possession of *a priori* cognition. Kant regarded the claims of mathematics, metaphysics, and science as synthetic. Thus he formulated the central epistemological problem of the *First Critique* as that of explaining how synthetic *a priori* judgments were possible. With some grasp of his technical terminology, this problem can be made more explicit. How are the nonstipulative, and so synthetic, universal, and necessary, and so not *a posteriori* from sensory impressions, but *a priori* from the mind, cognitions exemplified in mathematics, science, and (perhaps) metaphysics, possible?

As Kant recoiled at the suggestion that the status of mathematics, science, or metaphysics could plausibly be explained by either human definitions or Divine decrees, it is natural for his readers to wonder how he thought he could justify universal and necessary claims by appealing to the activities of the mind upon the receipt of sensory data. Our minds engage in many fanciful flights of imagination and thought that would be poor bases for knowledge claims. Kant had something far more restrictive in mind, and again introduced a special term to clarify his purpose: "transcendental." "Transcendental" philosophy is the investigation of those cognitions that are *a priori*, coming from the activities of the mind, and *that are necessary conditions for any cognition at all.* Although certain cognitions arise from the activities of the mind itself, they would be neither arbitrary or dispensable – *if* Kant can show that they arise from activities of the mind that are essential for any cognition.

A central claim of the *Critique of Pure Reason* is that any cognition must ultimately be based on two factors, the receipt of data through various senses (which he collectively referred to as the faculty of "sensibility") and the classification of that data through concepts of the understanding (A 50/B 74ff). In contemporary terminology, he maintained that any cognition must be based on perception and conception. Thus transcendental epistemology divided naturally into two sub-inquiries:

Sensory Perception	Conceptual Classification
Are any aspects **both**	Are any aspects **both**
A priori from the mind?	*A priori* from the mind?
Necessary for any cognition?	Necessary for any cognition?

These inquiries are taken up in the first two of the principal divisions of the *Critique of Pure Reason*, the Transcendental Aesthetic and the Transcendental Analytic.

Kant compared his highly original approach to knowledge to the Copernican revolution in astronomy. Just as Copernicus was able to make sense of celestial phenomena only by changing perspective, by considering whether the spectator (on earth) revolved around the sun, rather than the reverse, Kant believed that we could understand cognition only by making a fundamental shift in perspective. Rather than assume that our knowledge conformed to objects, we should explore the possibility that the objects of our knowledge conform to our cognition (B xvii).

Although the notion of objects "conforming" to our cognition can seem backwards, we are now in a position to see what he meant. The objects of cognition must "conform to" or

> agree with [the *a priori*] . . . condition of sensibility, because only through it can they appear, i.e. be empirically intuited [perceived] and given . . . [and also agree with] *a priori* concepts [which are] necessary conditions under which something can be . . . thought as an object. [In that case] all empirical cognition is necessarily in accord with such concepts, since without their presupposition nothing is possible as an **object of experience**. (A 93/ B 125–6)

Suppose that perception is possible only because incoming sensory data are organized in certain ways by the perceptual system. Suppose further that classification under concepts is possible only because perceptual (and other) properties of objects are organized in certain ways by a further faculty (which Kant sometimes calls "understanding," sometimes "reason"). It would follow that any perceived and conceptualized objects would display both universal perceptual and universal conceptual properties.

Perception, mathematics, and mathematical science

Kant presented "Transcendental Aesthetic" as the "science of all principles of *a priori* sensibility" (A 21/B 35). It would study those elements of perception that were both *a priori* and necessary conditions for cognition. To locate his quarry, Kant first had to "isolate" those aspects of cognition that were perceptual as opposed to conceptual. Then he had to isolate those elements of perception that did not come from sensory impressions (A 22/B 36). Although he did not announce this project, he immediately took up the task of arguing that certain *a priori* elements of sensibility were not optional, but required for any cognition. By the time he finished this remarkable section, however, he offered a solution to the puzzle about mathematics already considered and a solution to the long-standing debate about the nature of space and time that had been vigorously contested by Newton, Leibniz, and their followers.

As further preamble, Kant announced what his results would be. The *a priori* principles of sensibility are space and time. Somewhat oddly, he began his detailed arguments about space and time by asserting that they are *a priori* representations: "Space is not an empirical concept that has be derived from outer experience" (A 23/B 38); "Time is not an empirical concept that can be derived from any kind of experience" (A 30/B 46). Commentators have tried to determine the considerations that entitled him to make (or to believe he could make) these key claims.

One possibility is that although our sensations come in a particular temporal order – I see lightening and then I hear thunder – the order of the sensations is not another sensation. Similarly, although I can see the moon above the horizon, I do not see three things, the moon, the horizon, and "above," but only two. How do I represent these things as standing in a particular spatial relation? In further prefatory remarks, Kant described that which permits the ordering of sensations as the "form of intuition." He suggested that the form of intuitions must be *a priori* not *a posteriori*, presumably because he believed that the order of sensations was not a further sensation (A 20/B 34).

There seems a fairly obvious problem with this suggestion, at least as it pertains to space. Our representations of relative spatial position (above, below, to the left of, between) depend on the positions of objects in the world. Indeed, our sense organs are well designed to register such relations. The spatial position of the moon "above" the horizon, will be registered in the relative positions of the images of these items on the retina. (Because the lens of the eye inverts the image, the moon will be on the bottom of the retinal image, the horizon on the top.) Given these well-known facts about the visual system, it would be odd for Kant to regard the faculty of sensibility as the *source* of the representation of relative spatial position. The case of time is less clear, because it is not well understood how we are able to represent events in temporal relations.

Perhaps Kant had something else in mind as the background for his claim about the apriority of spatial properties. By the time he was writing, it was widely recognized that although the retina could register such two-dimensional properties as "above" and "to the left of," the eye could not take in information about the third dimension, distance, in any direct fashion. The problem was formulated clearly by Dr. William Molyneux:

> For *distance* of itself, is not to be perceived; for 'tis a line (or a length) presented to our eye with its end toward us, which must therefore be only a *point*, and that is invisible.[4]

It is not possible to register the distance of an object directly on the retina, because the first point along any line of sight occludes all other points on that line of sight. To see distance directly, it would be necessary to register the distance between the first point viewed and some later point.

Both Descartes and Berkeley had offered famous theories to explain how we are able to "see" depth, even though it does not register on the organ of vision. Here, at least, was a spatial property that is, and was widely recognized to be, unable to be registered in sensory impressions. Whether the debates of his predecessors over perceiving the third dimension or a general problem with sensing relations (as opposed to items related) lay at the base of Kant's thinking, he obviously believed that he had good reasons for regarding spatial and temporal properties of sensory representations as *a priori*. I have presented some plausible historical and factual candidates for those reasons, because his claims about the apriority of temporal and particularly spatial representations have sometimes been claimed to be as groundless.[5]

These background considerations also provide some means of dealing with an obvious objection. If the spatial and temporal properties of perceived objects are *a priori*, then why are some objects perceived as spheres, others as cubes? Do the sensory data play no role here at all? Are these representations simply arbitrary?

Lorne Falkenstein has recently provided a way of thinking about the *a priori* "forms of intuition [perception]," as Kant calls space and time, that addresses this crucial question.[6] Suppose these forms are understood as "orders of sensations." On Falkenstein's view, it would be the organization of the retina, for example, that accounted for our representing the moon as above the horizon. The orders would not be arbitrary, but grounded in the constitution of our sense organs.

If we consider the issue of 3-D perception, another possibility suggests itself. As our retinal image is a planar projection of the objects we encounter through sight, our perception of objects in 3-D space can be understood as a "reverse" projection (a 3-D interpretation) of the 2-D retinal image. Although many different 3-D interpretations are possible for any given 2-D figure, many more are ruled out, for the reverse projection must be able to be projected back onto the 2-D retinal image.

The advantage of both models is that they honor two key constraints. They do justice to Kant's insistence that some features of the sensory perception go beyond anything that is directly sensed; yet they avoid the charge that these additional features, created by the mind, are simply arbitrary. Although we have considered only sensory perception, the problem just raised is pervasive. Kant's general position was that cognition was a joint product of *a priori* and *a posteriori* elements. How do these two elements relate? If the *a priori* elements he claimed to be essential to cognition were totally ungrounded in empirical data or in anything else, then his theory would make cognition both arbitrary and incomprehensible. How do various *a priori* forms get attached to particular *a posteriori* contents? If this question cannot be given a plausible answer, Kant's theory is doomed.

At this point, we have considered only Kant's grounds (or possible grounds) for regarding space and time as *a priori*. In order to complete his case for their "transcendental" status, he needed to show that representations of spatial and temporal relations were necessary conditions for all cognition. The basic line of reasoning can be captured in a few claims. To have any cognition, it must be possible to distinguish between the way things are and the way they merely seem. Even to perceive an object, there must be some way to sort out real perception of an object from illusion. How could the is/seems distinction ever be made, however, in the absence of a spatio-temporal framework against which the careers of individual objects can be tracked?

Consider, for example, Macbeth's vision of a dagger. He knew that he was hallucinating, because when he tried to touch the dagger, he felt nothing. Had he felt for the dagger in a different place or several hours later, his failure to feel metal would not have suggested illusion. Thus, it seems that distinguishing between appearance and reality requires, at a minimum, a spatio-temporal framework for keeping track of objects. But should Kant's strong claim that *any* cognition *must* involve the representation of spatio-temporal position be accepted on the basis of particular cases? At first glance, the conclusion seems unwarranted. Even if it is possible to see how very helpful it was for Macbeth to have a spatio-temporal framework in his case, how can anecdotal considerations establish Kant's sweeping claim that there are *no* other means for achieving cognition, or drawing the is/seems distinction?

The current view is that such "transcendental" arguments about the necessary (and *a priori*) status of certain representational elements in cognition is that they are best understood as laying down a challenge. It is clear from ordinary examples that information about spatio-temporal position is crucial in drawing an is/seems distinction. If there is some *other* way to draw this distinction, then the burden is on Kant's opponent to show how.

Suppose, as Kant did, that he had shown that space and time are *a priori* "forms of intuition" that are required for all sensory perception. Important questions would remain. What is the nature of the space (or time) that is contributed by the faculty of sensibility to sensory representations? At this point, it will be helpful to return to the synthetic *a priori* propositions whose problematic status provided much of the impetus for the investigations of the *Critique*. Kant believed that he could satisfactorily resolve both issues, because he saw them as intimately related. Like many commentators, I will consider only the simpler case of space.

Assume that the definitions and theorems of Euclidean Geometry are synthetic and necessary and universal. Any actual plane or solid figure must be describable by Euclid's principles. How is this possible? Such a claim could not be established either by stipulative definition or by exhaustive checking. Now suppose that the *a priori* form of human sensory perception is *Euclidean* space. It would follow that the solid and plane figures we encounter in sensory perception would one and all conform to Euclidean Geometry.

Despite its ingenious character, Kant's solution to the status of mathematical propositions has not been widely accepted. Like his predecessors, Kant's successors have largely remained committed to the view that mathematics is analytic and see no problem to be solved. Recent work by Michael Friedman has argued that Kant was probably right that the mathematics of his time was synthetic.[7] In the absence of adequate definitions of key notions such as "continuity," mathematical practice was to establish theorems via the construction of figures. Further, if these proofs by construction were acceptable, then that would imply that human perceptual space was Euclidean. We could construct the needed figures only if that were true.

The difficulty is that although such proofs were accepted, they were not adequate as proofs. The central difficulty, both for proving the theorems and for establishing the Euclidean character of perceptual space, was that there is no way to tell by inspection whether a figure is Euclidean. We could never tell by looking that a line between two points was either continuous (in the mathematical sense defined in the nineteenth century) or straight.[8]

Thus, even if mathematics is synthetic, Kant's attempt to show the inevitability of Euclidean Geometry by appeal to the necessary spatial form of intuition falls short. He may still be right that our spatial representations are necessary for cognition and *a priori*, so that there is a particular form of human intuition. He might even be right that that form is Euclidean, but his attempt to establish this result through linking mathematical proof to spatial perception was unsuccessful.

Kant believed that he could extract a further and very important result from his science of *a priori* sensibility, namely, a solution to the debate over the nature of space and time. Newton and his followers had maintained that space and time existed independently of the objects in them. In opposition, Leibniz and his followers regarded space and time merely as a system of relative spatial and temporal positions extracted from our experience with objects.

Kant had entered the Newton–Leibniz debate about space and time early in his career. In the *First Critique*, he tried again to resolve this major intellectual controversy. He began from the plausible view that all cognition rests on perception and inferences from perception guided by scientific laws and theories. Thus, there were exactly two sources for our knowledge of space and time, perception and science. Whether Newtonian science established the existence of Newtonian space was, however, precisely the point at issue in the debate with the Leibnizeans. Now consider

Kant's results about our spatial and temporal representations. If he is right, then the source of these representations cannot be an independent *or* relational space or time, whether or not such things exist or could exist. Hence, he concluded that *what we represent* as space is nothing but our own form of intuition, and that questions about the existence or character of some real space or time in addition to our spatial and temporal representations were beyond the reach of our cognitive powers.

Kant's contention that he could put an end to these lengthy debates depended on his plausible assumption that Newtonian science was correct. With the fall of classical mechanics and its replacement by the theory of relativity, the "newer" science has provided important evidence about previously unsuspected features of the spatial and temporal character of the physical universe.

Logic – natural, school, and "transcendental"

The second major division of the *Critique of Pure Reason* is the Transcendental Analytic. After the investigation of the *a priori* features of perception that were necessary for cognition, the topic shifts to conceptual classification. Kant understood the distinction between sensibility and understanding (perception and conception) as bound up with another fundamental distinction, that between receiving information and sorting and combining that information.

In opposition to the Empiricists, Kant argued that cognition was possible only because the understanding combines information "spontaneously," according to its own rules. On the Empiricist account, the senses take in information, which then becomes "associated" into complex concepts and judgments according to the patterns in the sensory data. The complex concept of an apple, for example, would be formed by the constant association of the round shape, red color, and distinctive taste and smell of apples in sensory experience. Constant association of these properties in sensory experience produces associations of them in the mind, the concept of an apple, the judgment "apples are red," and so forth.

By contrast, Kant believed that concepts and judgments required spontaneous combination according to the mind's own rules. *A priori* concepts would be those concepts that were produced by the rules governing the mind's combining activities, *insofar as those activities were necessary conditions for the production of any concepts and judgments whatsoever.* Since cognition requires concepts as well as perception, these activities and the concepts they construct would be necessary for all cognition.

It is natural to wonder how Kant thought he could fathom such necessary activities and *a priori* concepts. His answer in the *First Critique*, logic, can be better understood by looking briefly at his *Logic Lectures.* This work was compiled from Kant's notes by Benjamin Jäsche. The lectures began by defining "logic" as the "science of the necessary laws of the understanding and reason in general, or what is the same, of the form of thought in general" (Ak. IX:13.) As this definition implies, Kant's conception of logic was much closer to the "Port Royal Logicians," who understood logic as the "art of thinking," than to modern conceptions of logic in terms of proof and model theories.

Kant had no doubt that (like all things in nature) the faculty of understanding "is bound in its action to rules" (Ak. IX:11), so he believed that the laws of logic were there to be found. To uncover them, it was necessary to begin with "natural" as opposed to "school" logic. Natural logic was a compendium of inferences ordinarily accepted as valid. The task of "school" logic was threefold. First the implicit rules by which we draw inferences had to be formulated as explicit rules. From cases such as "All men are mortal," "Socrates is a man," therefore "Socrates is mortal," logicians abstracted the rule of "categorical inference" (Ak. IX:122–3): All *A*'s are *B*, *x* is an *A*, therefore *x* is a *B*. Next, any features of these laws that derived from objects (and their properties) had to be eliminated. For example, even though it is possible to infer from the fact that an object is released near the earth's surface to the fact that it will fall, that inference depends on knowledge about objects: they have mass, they are subject to gravitational forces. By contrast, rules such as categorical inference apply to all objects, including nonphysical and imaginary "objects": If all unicorns have horns and Albert is a unicorn, then Albert has a horn. Finally, the remaining rules would be checked for consistency and redundancy. Kant believed that when the abstracting and reducing were completed, what remained were rules that were necessary for any thought at all.

The *Logic Lectures* address two serious questions about this enterprise. Logic should be normative, a codification of the rules of *good* thinking. If the starting point is the inferences people ordinarily make, won't logic be merely descriptive? Second, how is "school" logic possible? We have no faculties to bring to the task of evaluating and systematizing the rules of logic except understanding and reason. Yet, there is something paradoxical about using the understanding, with its rules, to seek knowledge of the rules of understanding itself (Ak. XVI:28).

Kant believed that logic could be normative (prescriptive), because he thought it was possible to learn the "correct use of the understanding . . . in which it agrees with itself" (Ak. IX:14). A putative principle would be tested to determine whether it yielded invalid conclusions or contradicted other established principles of logic. Such testing could be done only by the human understanding, either individually or publicly in a community. There were no other options. Appeals to the decrees of the Divine understanding were useless and appeals to definitions question-begging (because they presupposed the appropriateness of the definitions). The difficulty with appealing to sensory evidence is one we have encountered before. No amount of sensory evidence could show that *every* use of categorical inference yields a valid argument.

Although Kant appreciated the paradox of using the understanding to determine the laws of the understanding, it did not drive him to skepticism. Even Descartes, who had made free use of skeptical arguments to undermine the testimony of the senses, drew the line at the suggestion that people might be lacking in reason and so incapable of knowledge. Kant was a great proponent of the Enlightenment, whose guiding insight he summed up in the motto: think for yourself (Ak. VIII:35). As the ultimate court of appeal for morality, politics, art, religion, and science was individual and collective human reason, so too with logic and epistemology – even though their subject-matters were the laws of human reason and understanding.

The *First Critique* presupposes "school" logic. Kant's project of "transcendental logic" was a related enterprise. Suppose that we have a system of logic, displaying all the patterns of valid argument in a perspicuous and parsimonious way. How can logic ever be used in thinking? As with mathematics, Kant did not regard logic as a game, utterly divorced from the task of achieving knowledge of the world. How then could it be applied to sensory data to produce cognition?[9]

To understand the overarching goal of the Transcendental Analytic, it is necessary to understand the connection Kant saw between transcendental logic and the project of showing that certain *a priori* concepts were necessary for cognition. (He called these special concepts "categories.") The Empiricists had cast reasonable doubt on the legitimacy of using any concept in an empirical knowledge claim whose origin could not be traced to the senses. Kant modeled his celebrated "transcendental deduction" of the categories on legal deductions. As in the legal case, the general strategy was to defend a claim of legitimacy by tracing it back to its origins and revealing the origins as adequate to confer legitimacy.[10] In the case of the categories, this involved tracing concepts such as "cause" and "substance" back to combining operations of the understanding that were necessary in order to apply the laws of logic to objects of cognition. Thus would the categories be revealed as legitimate in a very special sense: they were non-arbitrary and indispensable, because unless sensory evidence was interpreted through these concepts, the laws of logic could not be applied to objects of cognition and there would be no thinking about objects at all.

Kant's account is relentlessly abstract and it will make his position clearer to think more concretely about the problem. Consider again, the categorical argument form: All *A*'s are *B*'s, *x* is an *A*, therefore *x* is a *B*. This form can produce cognition, the knowledge that *x* is a *B*, only if there is some way to be in a cognitive relation to an object *x*, which enables us to know or even believe that *x* is an *A*, or that *x* is both an *A* and a *B*. The first problem is to single out objects.

Kant has a wonderful discussion of what it takes for something to be such an *x*, an object of representations. The object is that which "checks our representations from being random or haphazard" (A 104). Put positively, different representations can be understood as representations of the same object only if they display consistency and coherence. Although true, Kant's claim would be vacuous unless he could spell out conditions for determining consistency and coherence. The central argument of the Transcendental Analytic is that those conditions are captured by the categories, in particular the category of cause (and effect) and substance (and "accident" ("property" in contemporary terminology)).

Consider again Macbeth's dagger. Macbeth recognized that he was hallucinating, because he could not feel a dagger in the spot where he saw one. Instead of a dagger, suppose that Macbeth believed that he had seen a perfectly round smoke-ring. In that case, what should he conclude if could feel nothing or if he looked back a couple of seconds later and saw it no more? Given our understanding of the nature of certain kinds of things and the causal relations among them, there is an obvious difference between the case of the untouchable, disappearing dagger and the case of the untouchable, disappearing smoke-ring. Smoke-rings are not tangible and are quickly dissipated by air currents. Daggers are more robust.

This is Kant's claim: as a spatio-temporal framework is necessary for sorting hallucinations from perceivings of real objects, so too is a framework of beliefs about various kinds of substances and their properties, and the causal relations among them. The forms of intuition make cognition possible by organizing sensory data into a unified system of spatial and temporal relations; categories of the understanding such as cause and substance make cognition possible by combining sensory representations into a unified system of relations among substances and their properties, causes and their effects. Although the Empiricists were right that neither the concept of a substance nor that of a cause can be traced to sensory experience, these concepts are nonetheless legitimate, because unless we interpreted sensory data as data about causally interacting substances, we could not determine when we are representing real objects. In eliminating causal beliefs, the Empiricists would unwittingly eliminate a necessary condition for any cognition of objects, including empirical observation of them.

Kant claimed to combine the insights of Rationalism and Empiricism. In support of Empiricism, he denied that any particular causal relations or substances could be determined *a priori*. His position was that the human faculty of understanding actively sought substances and causes in the sensory data. With new evidence, crude beliefs about what kinds of things there were and the causal relations among them would be replaced by ever more sophisticated ones. But Rationalists were right about the need for causes and substances, because any background system of belief adequate to distinguish objects from illusions must represent objects of cognition as particular kinds of things that causally interact in particular ways. It is this conception of cognition that stands behind Kant's intentionally shocking statement of transcendental idealism: "the understanding is itself the source of the laws [or lawfulness] of nature" (A 127).

The details of Kant's defense of the concept of "cause" in "reply" to Hume is offered in an important section of the Transcendental Analytic, the "Second Analogy of Experience."[11] Both Kant's overall approach of a "transcendental deduction" of the categories and the specific argumentative moves made in Second Analogy have generated enormous controversy. From the Empiricist side, it is natural to question whether the principles or beliefs by which we separate objects from illusions cannot themselves be acquired from experience. Further, even if these principles have to be causal, perhaps Hume and Kant were simply mistaken in believing that causal laws could not be extracted from sensory evidence.

Or perhaps Kant was wrong in maintaining that empirical objects and events were comprehensible only if interpreted in terms of causally interacting substances. At least on some interpretations, theories of quantum mechanics imply that there are noncausal, but still comprehensible events. Further, even if Kant was right about the necessity of *a priori* elements, such as causes and substances, for cognition, how do *a posteriori* sensory data fit into this *a priori* framework? (Given a stream of sensory data, how does the understanding determine what are the causes and what are the effects, what are the substances and what are the properties of substances?)

All these questions, and more, have been raised about Kant's theory. Still, at the moment, it is unclear what frameworks *other than* causally interacting kinds of things in space and time might suffice for a distinction between object and illusion, and unclear whether it is possible to provide an empirical derivation for causal laws. On the other hand, it is also far from obvious how to unite *a priori* and *a posteriori* elements of cognition.

Beyond his novel defense of the categories, Kant's efforts in the Transcendental Analytic had another important goal. Descartes had taken the first principle of philosophy to be the existence of a thinking self: "I think, therefore I am." Hume famously denied any knowledge of a continuing self. Kant entered this debate from his unique epistemological perspective. Hume was right in denying that the existence of a thinker was self-evident or evident upon mental inspection. It is only by considering the necessary conditions for cognition (or morality) that it becomes clear why a continuing subject must exist (A 107). If cognition requires perceptions and concepts, and indeed the combination of much information into a complex spatio-temporal, causal-substantival account of the natural world, then a very large number of perceptions and thoughts (plus the faculties needed to combine incoming information into cognition) must belong to one mind. Philosophical evidence for the thinking self is indirect, but conclusive, because a creative subject consisting of key faculties and manifold perceptions is necessary for cognition.

The ideals of reason

The third major division of the *First Critique*, the Transcendental Dialectic, was intended to present Kant's negative conclusions about the futility of metaphysics. It would be the "critique of pure reason." However, recent work has suggested that parts of the Dialectic (most importantly, the Appendix to the Ideal of Reason) offer further positive conclusions. Before turning to Kant's attack on metaphysics and the vices of reason, we should first consider its virtues.

Although Kant's terminology was somewhat fluid (hence my alternation between "understanding" and "reason" above), the Dialectic presents reason as a new faculty, separate from understanding. Reason is the faculty of inference, and this faculty combines the beliefs of the understanding into a *system* of knowledge.

In particular, Kant argued that the test of truth for a putative causal law was its ability to be part of a system or hierarchy of laws, where laws governing the behavior of a particular class of objects were brought under ever more general laws (A 647/ B 675). For example, to show that applying heat *causes* ice to melt, it would be insufficient to observe that the application of heat was always followed by the melting of ice. Scientists also consider (and need to consider) how this putative causal law fits with accepted laws about the behavior of heated solids.

Although the task of showing how cognition was possible should already be complete, the Transcendental Dialectic returns to a thorny problem that Kant originally raised in the Transcendental Deduction (A 100). What would happen if natural phenomena and hence sensory data were so unstable and so diverse that it was impossible to form concepts? Suppose that gold were sometimes yellow, sometimes black, sometimes shiny, sometimes dull, or suppose that objects had no properties in common. We could form no concepts and no object could be thought.

Kant realized that no capacities of *our minds* could prevent this epistemic catastrophe. Instead we can only hope, or expect, that nature will be fathomable by us – that there will be sufficient stability and commonality of properties, and enough systematic interconnections among laws to permit cognition. Putting the best face on the situation, Kant described this expectation as a "demand" of reason.

Although some systematic unity of nature is necessary for the discovery of causal laws, Kant noted an important difference between the cases. Cognition was impossible in the absence of some crude or refined causal law validating an event or object as real. No cause meant no cognition. By contrast, even though scientists can advance their theories only by assuming or "projecting" the systematic order of nature (A 647/B 675), a *complete* "system of nature" cannot be found. It is merely a "regulative ideal" guiding research.

Reason and metaphysics

The principal task of the Transcendental Dialectic is to reveal metaphysics as the product of misunderstanding the ideal character of the systematizing principles of reason. Despite their great utility for science, the tendencies of reason to seek ever deeper, more systematic explanations leads to metaphysical questions that are beyond our abilities to answer.

Take any event, the Lisbon earthquake of 1755 for example. To explain this catastrophe, it is necessary to appeal to general laws about the movements of large land masses and to particular facts about the conditions around Portugal in the eighteenth century. More generally, any event must be explained in terms of general laws and particular facts. But whenever any fact is used, it is always possible to inquire how that fact came to be, which leads to more laws and further facts. In the case of laws, if earth masses move in regular ways, then reason naturally seeks more basic laws about the composition of matter and the forces to which matter is subject to explain the regular motions, a quest that leads eventually to metaphysical questions about the basic constituents of the universe.

In the search for further facts, we inevitably proceed back through time to ever earlier events, thus raising the metaphysical question of whether there is some first event. On Kant's view, such questions are as fruitless as they are inevitable. Although science advances by seeking further explanations, metaphysical hypotheses such as the familiar claim that God is the First Cause of the universe block further detailed study and engender endless controversy. Kant's hope was that once we understand the source of metaphysics, in the relentless seeking of our own faculties of reason, then we would not be tempted to think that there must be answers to questions about first causes and ultimate constituents.

Besides these issues, Kant also considered Rationalist speculations about the nature of the soul in the Paralogisms (faulty syllogisms) chapter of the Dialectic. He tried to show that the attempt to demonstrate the immortality of the soul by appeal to the capacities needed for knowledge were complete failures. Cognition required a continuing thinker, not an indestructible one. Kant summed up his attack on metaphysics with the observation that the three cardinal propositions of metaphysics, the existence of God, the freedom of the will, and the immorality of the soul, were undecidable by human reason, because they could not be discovered in the progress of science, nor could they be revealed as necessary for cognition (A 799/B 827).

This was not, however, the end of metaphysics for Kant. In the preface to the *Critique of Pure Reason*, he characterized his goal as one of limiting knowledge to make room for faith. For Kant, and many thinkers who have followed him, the proper grounds for belief in God and an afterlife were not the abstruse (and inconsistent) proofs of metaphysics, but faith. In his case, it will turn out that belief in God and salvation depend on our hopes for Divine justice.

Free will was importantly different for Kant. For reasons we will see, he believed that people engaged in moral deliberations had to believe that they were free to do what they thought was right. His discussion of free will and determinism in the Third Antinomy [conflict] section of the Dialectic was intended to show that transcendental idealism did not rule out practical faith in free will, even as it denied that it could be established by science or philosophy.

The Third Antinomy thus formed a bridge from Kant's theoretical philosophy to his deep concerns with "practical philosophy" – "ethics" in contemporary terminology. To understand his claim that transcendental epistemology left sufficient "room" for practical freedom, we should consider his own estimation of what his epistemological labors had established.

The limits of cognition: phenomena vs. noumena

After presenting most of his positive theory of cognition, Kant took stock of what he had shown. Even empirical cognition required not just sensory data, but *a priori* contributions from the mind. To borrow his well-known example from the Second Analogy: If we represent a ship as moving downstream, then we must represent it as traversing a 3-D space in a determinate time, and as moved along by a property of the stream, the current. The object of cognitive experience, the moving ship, "conforms" to our cognition, because it can be an object of cognition for us only because spatial, temporal, and causal and substantival interpretations can be put on the sensory data. If the argument of the Second Analogy is accepted (a big "if"), then it follows not that all events are caused, but that all events *of which we can have any cognition* are caused.

Kant's arguments about cognition thus vindicate some metaphysical claims, but only in a limited way. He stressed how limited his conclusions were. The restriction "of which we can have cognition" cannot be lifted. We can make no claims about objects apart from our cognition, and we cannot determine whether the objects we do cognize are as we cognize them to be, if we abstract from our cognition. If we can know objects only through the sensory data they cause in us, then there is no other route to the objects that would confirm or deny that they are as our interpretations of the sensory data take them to be.

To make the restriction "of which we can have cognition" evident, Kant characterized the objects of cognition as "phenomenal." The natural world described by science would be "merely" phenomenal, because although science allows us to explain and predict the behavior of the objects we cognize, it has no resources for disclosing the properties of the world independently of our cognition. As a contrast to "phenomenal," Kant introduced the term "noumenal" to capture the idea of objects considered in independence of our cognition.[12]

Unfortunately, the distinction between phenomena and noumena has led to endless confusions about Kant's thesis of transcendental idealism. By some accounts, he preserved knowledge of mathematics, science, and some elements of metaphysics by having these disciplines characterize a made-up world of phenomena, while denying any knowledge of the real world of noumena. That was not Kant's position. As a 3-D interpretation of a 2-D projection is an interpretation of that planar figure – which could be projected back onto the 2-D figure – he understood causal and substantival beliefs as necessary and non-arbitrary interpretations of the sensory data we receive. Scientific knowledge was not reduced to fiction, but revealed as dependent on both sensory data and the activities of the mind needed to make sense of those data.

Science can interpret the world only through a system of causal laws. But once we understand the source of determinism, in the activities of the mind needed to sort out sensory data, it is open to moral agents to hope that our actions (regarded apart from cognition) do not belong to a chain of causes beyond our control. Such "free" (meaning "uncaused") acts would be incomprehensible, but not impossible.

3. The Commands of Morality

Beyond the link provided by the problem of free will, Kant's theoretical and practical philosophies are united by a common approach. As the creative faculties of the mind were crucial in producing cognition, it is the mind's own creative reason that occupies the central role in Kant's account of morality.

Background

As Kant was reflecting on the fundamental principles of morality, there were three available choices for the grounds of moral or right action: religion, the state, and human psychology. A long-standing view was that God decreed the morally correct actions. To Kant's Enlightenment mentality, this approach was anathema. In practice, following the decrees "of God" meant following the priests and so making one's own moral reasoning subservient to that of an outside authority.

If the authority of religion made an inappropriate foundation for right conduct, then the authority of the state was an even less plausible source. More serious options were the proposals of several British moralists for locating the foundations of morality in human interests and/or sentiments. Thomas Hobbes and his followers regarded morality as the natural consequence of enlightened self-interest. For Francis Hutcheson and David Hume, morality rested on sentiments, in particular, sympathy and benevolence. On this approach, the science of morality would study those actions that naturally inspire admiration or loathing, and those that naturally arise from sympathy and benevolence. This study led both Hutcheson and Hume to propose the rudiments of a moral calculus, since the actions that inspired the greatest approbation turned out to be the ones that produced the greatest good for the greatest number.

Although Kant's moral thinking was partly guided by his reasons for rejecting the preceding options, he found positive inspiration in the ideas of Jean-Jacques Rousseau. Kant accepted Rousseau's radical suggestion that the authority of priests and princes was unnecessary for moral guidance for citizens, because each human being was capable of determining right actions for himself. He also offered his own distinctive solution to Rousseau's conundrum: How can people be free yet bound by common laws? Kant explained that freedom under law was possible, because human reason had its own principles for determining right action. In acting and "obeying" laws, people would be self-determining just so long as statutory laws agreed with the principles of their own reason. Using Kant's preferred terminology, human beings were "autonomous" or self-determining in the moral realm and should be in the political realm as well.

Common morality and its foundations

Kant presented his influential moral theory in two books, the widely read *Groundwork of the Metaphysics of Morals* (1785) and the intended companion to the *First Critique*, *The Critique of Practical Reason* (1788). To a fuller picture of his moral (and political) philosophy, it is also helpful to look at his later discussions in *Religion within the Limits of Reason Alone* (1793) and *The Metaphysics of Morals* (1797).

Kant's method in the *Groundwork* reflects his doctrine. He begins with the common moral understanding of ordinary people and tries to follow that guiding thread to discover the possible foundations of morality. Kant believed that all would agree that the only unqualifiedly good thing is a good will or good intentions. Despite the suggestions of his proto-utilitarian predecessors, the happiness that follows from an action is not a reliable guide to its goodness. Well-intended actions can lead to disaster for reasons totally independent of the agent; in some circumstances, malevolent efforts can go awry in such a way as to produce good results.

The result of the first topic of the *Groundwork*, that the only good thing is a good will, leads directly to the second. What is it that makes the will good? Kant's method is "casuistry" – looking at telling cases to criticize plausible proposals and, ultimately, to reveal the true foundations. This discussion presents one of his least popular theses, that what makes a will good is that the action proceeded from the motive of duty. Kant's first example is clear enough. A grocer who gives his customers fair measure only because cheating would be bad for business deserves no moral credit. But Kant goes further and maintains in the clearest language that even an action done from kindness or sympathy has no true moral worth.

Barbara Herman has recently argued that we can understand Kant's objections to motives such as sympathy, if we consider his elaboration of the situation.[13] Suppose the sympathetic person, who formerly found great satisfaction in helping others, has now become morose. Had his previous actions been guided by duty (whatever other incentives, such as sympathy, were available), then he would still have that motive available, and those in need of his kindness would still receive it. Further, some individuals, who are most in need of kindness, are unsympathetic as people. Kant's reasonable objections are that sympathy is too unreliable and too partial a basis for moral action.

At this point, Kant took himself to have shown that a moral action must be done from the motive of duty and that the worth of a moral action cannot lie in its consequences. What can a moral principle be like that incorporates neither expected results nor any particular desires or sentiments (which Kant lumps together as "inclinations")? In an argumentative move that commentators have tried to make more explicit, he inferred that such a principle can only involve the conformity of an action to law as such. Using then standard terminology, he described people as acting on the basis of "maxims," rules for action, such as "be honest" or "look out for yourself." If morality involves conformity to law as such, he concluded that there must be exactly one moral principle: **"Act only according to that maxim that you could at the same time will to be a universal law"** (Ak. IV:421). Because of its grammatical form, this principle is called the "categorical imperative" (henceforth "CI"). Since it is the highest principle of morality, to which all particular maxims are subject, this principle is also called the "moral law."

Kant was quick to note that, in everyday moral reasoning, people do not think of matters at this level of abstraction. He compared himself to Socrates in merely getting people to see clearly how they have been reasoning morally all along. To confirm the correctness of the CI and also clarify how it operates, he offered a series of examples, two of which are especially helpful. Consider the case of lying to secure a loan. It is not possible to will a law, "anyone who wants a loan lies," because the practice of lending is built on trust in repayment. Such a maxim would annihilate itself when willed as a universal law. Now consider the case of a rich person who could help those who are struggling. Such a person *could* will the maxim "no help for those in need of help" as a universal law. There would be no contradiction, but Kant maintained that a rational person could not *will* such a law. Even great riches cannot guarantee that a person will never be in need of some type of assistance. So willing a ban on aid would be irrational, because the person would both want aid and ban it.

Having made the beliefs that are implicit in our actions and attitudes explicit, Kant turned in the second section of the *Groundwork* to philosophical explanations of morality. He found a common flaw in available theories. They all tried to extract moral principles *a posteriori* from experience, from, for example, noticing a regular correlation between human sentiments such as kindness or benevolence and morally good actions. His objection was that such a connection could never explain moral obligation. If kind intentions fade for some reason, then it would make no sense to regard the person as morally obligated. But ordinary moral thinking does not disqualify a person from the moral realm of rights or duties, because he or she has fallen on hard times (materially or spiritually). Whatever the foundation of morality is, it must persist as long as moral personality persists.

Kant drew attention to a surprising fact. Although everything in nature acts according to laws, only a being with reason can act according to the concept of law. To see his point, consider the difference between the nine planets of the solar system and the nine players on a baseball team. The planets "follow" Kepler's laws only metaphorically. Their behavior can be described by the laws. But baseball players follow the rule "three outs per inning" by having an idea of the rule, counting the outs, and then conforming their behavior to the rule. Unlike the planets, ballplayers can err, because their rule-following is based on their cognitive appreciation of rules and evidence.

With the ability to act according to the concept of law, any rational being could follow the categorical imperative, performing only those actions whose maxims could be willed to be universal laws. But if an empirical foundation for morality has trouble explaining the persistence of moral obligation in the absence of particular sentiments or inclinations, a Rationalist account has the opposite problem. Since a rational being tests maxims through the CI and acts on the results, moral obligation would disappear, because such a being would *always* act correctly. Kant conceded that moral obligation makes no sense for a perfectly rational being, a being guided solely by reason.

How can moral obligation be understood? In a way, the problem faced by both Kant and his Empiricist opponents is unsurprising. Both wish to locate morality in human beings, in either their interests or sentiments, or in their reason. But morality must be prescriptive, explaining not what people do, but what they *ought* to do. Where the Empiricist tried to explain the gap between the commands of morality and actual performance by appealing to a conflict between different sorts of desires or sentiments, Kant appealed to a conflict between reason and inclination. The moral law does not describe, but prescribe, because even though people know what is right, sometimes they make exceptions for themselves. Even though, by considering the CI or some equivalent (what if everybody did this?), I know that the practice of lying to secure a loan is unacceptable, I may do it anyway. Whatever means I choose to evade the moral conclusion, Kant's point is that the moral "ought" arises because we have reason to enable us to evaluate the morality of a proposed course of action, and inclination, particularly self-love, to oppose moral duty.

It will be useful to take stock at this point. Kant has a solution to the problem of locating morality within human beings and still explaining how it might involve an ought. Morality rests on the capacity to think of individual cases as instances of general maxims and to act according to the concept of law. Since inclinations can always oppose, the resulting moral principle is not "I will not lie," but "I should not lie." He has also avoided the inadequate *a posteriori* foundations for morality proposed by his predecessors. Human beings lacking the capacity to formulate and follow moral maxims would not just be incapable of moral action, they would be inappropriate objects of praise and blame, rights[14] and duties.

The metaphysical foundations of morality

Despite these advances, Kant recognized that serious problems remained. Even if he is right that morality is a matter of acting on maxims that conform to the moral law, and doing so from the motive of duty (that is, because the maxims conform), can we grasp how this is possible? Our ordinary moral views also imply that moral praise and blame are appropriate only for actions that the agent "freely" performs, in some sense of that term. The final (third) section of the *Groundwork* returned to the difficult issue of free will.

Kant thought that, at a minimum, free action had to be free from "alien" causes, causes "outside" of the agent. Unfortunately, external compulsion is just one form of alien cause. If at the moment of action, my thoughts are determined by the larger and smaller social worlds in which I grew up, for example, then "alien" causes would still be at work. From the other side, Kant recognized that free actions could not be random. They must be caused by something in the agent that was not itself caused by an alien cause. What might such a cause be like?

Kant argued that the problems of alien and random causes could be avoided only if a free action were caused by the agent's conformity to the principle of law itself, that is, by the categorical imperative. Thus free actions were exactly the actions produced by the categorical imperative. But this move both failed to advance the argument and raised additional problems. If a free will acts according to the moral law, then it is hard to see how anyone could freely do a *wrong* action. Further, even if free actions would be actions produced by the CI, that does not show how free, CI-inspired, action is possible. Kant could not simply beg the question against the British moralists who maintained that action could be motivated only by desire or inclination.

In later works, Kant tried to address some of the defects in the final section of the *Groundwork*. In *Religion within the Limits of Reason Alone*, he distinguished between a faculty of practical reason, which always follows the moral law, and a faculty of "choice" which decides between reason and inclinations based on self-love. Morality requires the capacity to make this choice. But can such a capacity be established? Suppose I tell a lie. As Kant well realized, it is very hard to show that although I did not follow the moral law, I *could* have.

The *Critique of Practical Reason* also tries to improve on the argument of the *Groundwork*. Building on those results, Kant proclaimed a "fact of reason," the fact that, when human beings confront a moral choice, their deliberations always rely on some clear and articulate, or possibly crude and inchoate, version of the moral law. That is the fact. It is a fact *of reason*, because a moral imperative cannot be extracted from sensory evidence. It arises from reason's capacity to formulate and act on general principles which can oppose inclinations.

Moral skeptics rightly complain that Kant has begged the question against them. However, he never intended to *prove* that people engaged in moral deliberation. The goal was to understand how moral deliberation might make sense. What were its presuppositions and were they true?

Since the categorical imperative requires us not to act on maxims that we cannot universalize, we must be able to make our behavior conform to rules such as "don't lie." That capacity is evident in such uncontroversial cases as playing by the rules of games. But perhaps his predecessors were correct that some sort of incentive is always required for action. In the *Second Critique*, Kant argued that an incentive to act on the moral law is always available and that it involves no alien cause. Appealing again to ordinary moral experience, he suggested that the moral law engenders a feeling of respect. When we contemplate what we intend to do, and compare it with what we should do, we feel the unworthiness of our self-interested motives as opposed to the ideal proposed by the CI. His claim is not that we always act out of respect for the moral law, but only that we always feel it. Thus, even if action requires some incentive, morality would be possible, if actions are done out of a feeling of respect for the moral law.

At this point, Kant has done about all that he can to establish the possibility of morality. As he acknowledged, however, deep problems linger about how to understand the possibility of free will and moral responsibility. In a well-known passage, he laid out the difficulties with great candor and force (Ak. V:96). Consider the options for a causal determinist. Either the determinist believes that all actions are caused by outside forces or that some are caused by something internal, some inclination. With causation, once the inclination is present, the action will follow. Further, since the inclination itself must be caused, once *its* cause was present, the inclination would follow (and then the action). The unavoidable difficulty is that, on the assumption of determinism, what an agent will do at "the moment of decision and action" is determined by factors that are in the past – and hence not in his or her control.

To escape these catastrophic implications, Kant made a bold and controversial move. He saw only one way out of the problem of determinism. In the *First Critique* he had argued that, although we must understand the natural world in terms of causes, determinism is our interpretation of sensory data. Since we can never know whether the world apart from our cognition is determined, we can find room for freedom in the possibility that it is not.

Perhaps Kant was right that the belief that free will and determinism are compatible thrives only by a lack of intellectual candor, but his means of "saving" free will raises serious problems. To see the trouble within his own system, consider whether our faculty of reason is or is not law-governed. He assumed that it was in the *Logic Lectures*. In the *First Critique* itself, he explained the practice of science by making the same assumption about reason that he had made about the other cognitive faculties of sensibility and understanding: the operation of all these faculties is uniform across people and across time. If these faculties did not operate in the same way in different people at different times, then these putative cognizers would be incapable of cognition.

If reason operates in a lawful way, however, then once the facts of a case have been presented, the CI should always give the same result (as Kant plainly expected across different people). But if the inclination of respect for the moral law also displays the lawfulness that Kant's epistemological theory presupposes in human faculties, then it is hard to understand how an agent is free at the moment of action on his own theory. Different agents may have different degrees of respect for the moral law, but for an agent at a time, the background of moral training, the strength of inclinations, and the operation of his or her capacities would be constant. If exactly the same moral facts present themselves, how could different acts result? As noted, the systematic character of Kant's views derives in large part from his belief in the unity of reason. The tension between the demands put on a theory of reason by epistemology and those that arise through considerations of ethics go to the heart of the "Critical" system of philosophy.

Further, Kant's ethical theory itself seems pulled in opposing directions. Suppose that human beings engage in moral deliberation, see for themselves the rightness of an action, and do the action because they have understood its rightness. They would be moved by their own faculties of reason and within Kant's moral and theoretical philosophy, it is hard to understand how people might be alienated from their own rational faculties. Are people then free in the moment of decision? At this point, two of Kant's competing insights into morality seem in hopeless opposition. People would be free in the sense of being autonomous, acting only on the basis of their own understanding of the situation; but assuming that reason is law-governed, they could do no other.

Although Kant labored to find adequate metaphysical foundations for morality, his transcendental idealist solution – we cannot know that, apart from cognition, our actions are determined – is currently the least well-respected part of his moral philosophy. Despite its metaphysical shortcomings, however, many philosophers have found the central ideas of Kant's analyses of morality extremely plausible, particularly its emphasis on autonomy. The formulation of the moral law presented above ("Act only according to that maxim that you could at the same time will to be a universal law") has received the most attention, but it was only one of three offered in the *Groundwork*.

A second way to make the principle underlying moral deliberations explicit stressed the importance of thinking about others directly. Rather than weighing maxims by considering what would happen if everybody followed the maxim, it came to the same thing to ask whether a proposed action would treat "humanity in your own person and in that of another as an end and never only as a means" (Ak. IV:429). More briefly, the "principle of humanity" requires us to consider whether an intended action respects the projects and opinions of others.

Whether or not people do respect each other, they ought to, Kant believed. As a rational being, capable of acting on the moral law, each person has a peculiar dignity, is *worthy* of respect, because he or she is a potential source for creating a moral realm. Since human beings can act according to the concept of law, they have the capacity to bring into being a second nature in which the needy are helped, the strong restrained, the good rewarded, and the wicked punished (unlike the amoral world of nature where resources and afflictions are distributed arbitrarily). It is the fact that human beings are themselves the sources of morality and the potential creators of a moral realm that is the basis of their special worth and dignity.

The conception of people as the foundation of a just state leads to the third formulation of the moral law: "act according to the maxims of a law-giving member of a possible realm of ends [persons]," that is, a realm where each person has a will that is law-giving and bound by its own laws (Ak. IV:439). Through the writings of John Rawls (in particular *A Theory of Justice*), Kant's "lawgiver in a kingdom of ends" formulation has exerted considerable influence on debates in ethics and political philosophy over the last 25 years.[15] In Rawls's view, the moral law, particularly in its third formulation, embodies the principles that free and equal persons would choose in order to express their nature as free and equal persons. In his words: "Kant's main aim is to deepen and to justify Rousseau's idea that liberty is acting in accordance with a law that we give to ourselves. And this leads not to a morality of austere command but to an ethic of mutual respect and self-esteem."[16]

4. Civilization and Politics

Kant described the first formulation of the CI as purely "formal," because it lacked any specific "content." As a result, his ethical theory has often been criticized as empty and unworkable. For example, if a maxim passes the test of being able to be universalized, how can a rational agent determine whether he or she would will the universal practice? As we have seen, however, even in the *Groundwork,* Kant appealed to facts about what might be called "the human" condition, to explain why it is a duty to help the needy (even a rich person will need some aid from others). In his anthropology lectures (*Anthropology from a Pragmatic Point of View*, 1797) and his long-promised *Metaphysics of Morals* (1797), he supplied many of the details needed to make his moral system workable.

Pragmatic anthropology

Although Kant lectured on anthropology for many years, his interpreters have wondered how to fit this material into the Critical system. Given his resolute claim in both the *Groundwork* and the *Second Critique* that moral principles must be *a priori*, it seems that anthropology could provide no assistance to moral theory or practice. Further, he was explicit in his philosophy of science (*The Metaphysical Foundations of Natural Science*, 1786) that any true science was mathematical, and that psychology could not even count as a experimental discipline, roughly because psychological variables could not be studied separately. The best that could be hoped for from psychology (and presumably anthropology) was "historical, systematic description" (Ak. IV:471). If anthropology is merely a nonrigorous description of empirical facts, how could it have an important role in Kant's ethics, whose principles were *a priori*?

An obvious suggestion is that Kant's moral or practical philosophy parallels his theoretical philosophy in requiring both *a priori* and *a posteriori* elements. As knowledge requires interpreting sensory data in terms of relations of cause and effect – and particular data to interpret – perhaps morality requires formal, *a priori* principles, which operate on the maxims, goals, and desires that particular human beings actually have in particular natural and social conditions.

Suppose, for example, that you are in a situation where it would be useful to lie to secure a loan. You have no assets and bankers will not give loans without collateral. Before you can act, you must have a certain amount of what Kant calls "worldly wisdom" about how bankers operate, what kind of story they are likely to find plausible, and the like. With that real world knowledge, you know what you are proposing and can formulate an appropriate maxim to be tested through the moral law. Worldly wisdom, and worldly plans and desires, are necessary for morality, because without them the moral law would have no field on which to operate.

All moral agents must have sufficient understanding of their fellow human beings to formulate maxims that can be tested by the CI. But Kant urged the study of anthropology as a discipline, because it could be enable people to improve their own faculties and to increase their understanding of themselves and their situation: "pragmatic knowledge [anthropology] of humanity aims at what people make, or can or should make, of themselves as freely acting beings" (Ak. VII:119). Given his endorsement of anthropology, the long-standing view that he had no time for nonmathematical disciplines needs revising.

Kant may have also believed that the study of social institutions was particularly important in light of Rousseau's scathing analysis of how social inequality corrupts human nature in *The Discourse on the Origin and Foundation of Inequality among Men* (1761). The degrading way that people are treated leads them to act badly, and a failure to appreciate the true source of the bad behavior may create the sort of confusion between cause and effect that led Aristotle to claim that servitude was just, because some people are "naturally" servile. Given the fact of reason, that when people engage in moral deliberation, they are always in a position to see that humanity is deserving of respect in all persons, Kant did not believe that anthropological investigations were necessary for moral action. As a practical matter, however, education could help remove some of the confusions that made disrespectful behavior seem reasonable.

Politics

The *Metaphysics of Morals* contains two parts, the "Doctrine of Right," and the "Doctrine of Virtue." In this work, the interplay between Kant's moral philosophy and his political ideas is complex. Unlike political theorists such as Machiavelli, he believed that political philosophy was constrained by morality; but the division between rights and virtues indicates his recognition of important differences.

In moral action, the intent of the agent is critical, but no state has a right to compel people to act correctly for moral reasons. The state cannot, and should not attempt to, control the way people think, either through education or state-imposed religious or moral training. Kant's deep commitment to autonomy required no reinforcement on this point, but the terrifying and ridiculous spectacle of Robespierre's attempt to enforce a republic of virtue on France may have led him to be especially explicit: "since man is a morally free being, when it is a matter of the incentive (the inner determination of the will), the concept of duty can contain nothing other than **self-restraint** . . . for it is only in this way that freedom can be reconciled with necessity" (Ak. VI:379–80). Even if it could be done, controlling my inclinations (in addition to my actions) by external rewards and punishments would make it impossible for me to do my duty solely from the motive of duty, effectively nullifying the possibility of virtuous action.

The Doctrine of Virtue offers a stark contrast to the foundational, and so abstract, *Groundwork* and *Second Critique*. Drawing on his knowledge of the human condition and society, Kant argued for particular virtues of self-improvement, including the duty not to be servile, and particular duties to others, including the duty to help the needy. He offered an illuminating contrast between this duty and the duty to repay a loan, two of his key examples in the *Groundwork*. In the case of repayment, a debtor can act correctly only by returning the full amount of the loan; but the duty to help the needy cannot prescribe so particular an action. Kant well understood that the degree of obligation depended on individual circumstances concerning other obligations and other sources of aid (Ak. VI:390).

The Doctrine of Right is about those rights that would be compatible with the fundamental principle of the moral law: any right I claim for myself must be possible as a right granted to all. Not surprisingly, there is only one basic right for Kant – freedom. But the principle of universalizability has a further, important implication. Equality under the law is guaranteed, because any law must apply to all.

Like other tracts in the Western political tradition, the Doctrine of Right focuses on social contracts and private property. The basic insight of the "social contract" tradition, that a state is legitimate because it is the result of a contract freely entered into by equal citizens, agreed very well with Kant's idea of autonomy (which it probably helped to inspire). But he did not regard the original social contract as anything like a historical event. A state is legitimate if people *would* so contract. Further, Kant believed that people should contract for a state, because only in that condition can their rights as free, equal, and independent persons be recognized. Since he took the social contract to be a moral imperative, he avoided the convoluted reasoning that justified a state by reference to the essential nastiness of human nature (Hobbes) or the need to protect property (Locke).

If Kant's moral philosophy is criticized for being too abstract, his political philosophy is often attacked for the opposite failing. He was too realistic and hence too conservative. Given the general good of having a state, and the great difficulty of change, revolution is always prohibited. For Kant, violence and mayhem are never justifiable means for remedying a state's failure to grant appropriate rights to citizens. As Rawls and others have noted, however, that does not mean that he would oppose civil disobedience or nonviolent resistance. The culmination of Kant's political system is offered in a slender, but widely read tract, *Towards a Perpetual Peace* (1795). There he argued that war will be inevitable unless states emulate people and band together in a league of nations which can ensure by force the freedom of each from the attacks of others.

5. Art and Nature

The last of the three critiques, *The Critique of Judgment* (1790), is concerned with two topics that seem, at first glance, to be unrelated to each other and to anything that has come before – aesthetic judgments and teleological judgments (judgments about purposes). To understand the unity of Kant's system and to evaluate its strengths and weaknesses, it is important to consider how he saw these studies as filling in troublesome gaps left in his accounts of cognition and morality.

In what respects are Kant's accounts of cognition and morality incomplete? In the Transcendental Dialectic of the *First Critique*, Kant recognized that a fundamental condition for the possibility of knowledge was that sensory data be regular, indeed that they be interpretable as belonging to a systematic order of nature. He also recognized that no capacity of ours could supply this need. We approach nature with the presumption that it will have an order discernible by our faculties. But that can only be a presumption.

In some ways, things are worse with morality. At least we know that we have been capable of cognition in the past, but there are no indisputable cases of morally good behavior. Kant noted the impossibility of establishing the purity of any motive. Even those actions that accord with duty may proceed from ulterior motives; even the agent cannot be sure that the action did not proceed from self-love, perhaps a desire to appear noble in the eyes of the world. Hence, although we know a great deal about the necessary conditions for morality, and about the presence of capacities that satisfy those necessary conditions, we can never point to a single example of behavior produced by the moral law, either directly, or out of a feeling of respect for the moral law (Ak. IV:407).

Towards the end of the *First Critique* (A 805/B 833), Kant explained that there were three fundamental questions of philosophy:

What can I know?
What ought I to do?
What can I hope for?

The *First Critique* tried to answer the first question; the *Second Critique* the second. Since these accounts were incomplete, the role of the *Third Critique* is to supply an answer to the last question. Why is it reasonable for us to hope for knowledge of the natural world and to hope that morality is not merely possible but actual?

It is natural to wonder what these issues have to do with art and the theory of art (aesthetics). Kant's predecessors in aesthetics often linked art and morality.[17] One of the fathers of modern aesthetics, Lord Shaftesbury, maintained that the special sense by which we immediately appreciate the beautiful in art was identical to what he took to be the foundation of morality, the "moral sense." Another seminal figure in aesthetics, Francis Hutcheson, resisted this assimilation. He stressed the idea that our reaction to works of art was "disinterested." Unlike a beautiful house, whose appeal rests in part on the use one might make of it, the pleasure we take in fine art is independent of any further use (beyond experiencing it). Pressing this line more consistently than Shaftesbury, Hutcheson maintained that our aesthetic sense was independent not just of personal, but even of moral, interests.

In the Transcendental Aesthetic, Kant had rejected the idea of aesthetics as a critique of taste. Since taste was a matter of what people did and did not like, it could have no *a priori* principles and could not be a science (except in his special sense where "aesthetics" was the "science of sensibility.") By the time he came to write the Critique of Aesthetic Judgment, he had changed his mind. In the First Introduction to the *Critique of Judgment* and, more briefly, in the second version of the introduction that was published with the book, he offered systematic reasons for thinking that judging, too, must have *a priori* principles, that is, its own rules for operating, regardless of the sensory input.

Kant characterized "judgment" as the faculty of applying the rules of reason and the concepts of the understanding. Judgment would be required for cognition and for morality. In the Transcendental Dialectic, he had made two key observations. The faculty of [determinative] judgment that applies concepts presupposes a faculty of [reflective] judgment that makes concepts. Or, looked at from the point of view of reason, in order to reason about something, for example, to infer that Socrates is mortal, because all men are mortal, we must be able to find a major premise (such as "all men are mortal") from which the conclusion that Socrates is mortal may be derived. It follows that we need some faculty (or set of faculties) that seeks higher premises (or principles) and higher concepts. How might such a faculty proceed?

Kant argues that the faculty of judgment must presuppose that higher premises and higher concepts are there to be found, that the natural world is orderly in ways that we can grasp. In the Introductions to the *Critique of Judgment*, the "demand" of reason from the Transcendental Dialectic, that nature be systematically organized in a way that is useful for our faculties, is presented in a slightly different guise, as a principle for reflective judgment. Reflective judgment must operate on the assumption that nature is "purposive" for judgment, that is, systematic in ways that we are able to discover.

To appreciate the novel connection that Kant saw between reflective judgment and art, we need to turn to the perplexities of aesthetic judgment. Kant believed three claims: aesthetic judgment is a based on feeling; aesthetic judgment is disinterested; aesthetic judgment claims universality. As we have seen, the first two views were common, though not universal, at the time that he was writing. What he meant by the final claim is that if I judge a painting, perhaps Leonardo da Vinci's *Madonna of the Rocks* (1506 version, London), to be beautiful, then I expect that anyone will be able to get some sense of its beauty. Unlike taste in food, Kant believed that taste in art had a certain level of objectivity. Perhaps you prefer modern art, or even resent religious paintings, still it seems that you could be brought to have some appreciation of this painting. Even if you do not respond immediately, I could point to features of the painting, such as the balance of the composition, the grace of the lines, the subtlety of the coloration, and so on that would enable you to appreciate its beauty at least to some degree.

Although aesthetic judgments depend on feeling, they claim universality. I do not claim that Leonardo's painting is beautiful *to me*, but simply that it is beautiful. Further, the objectivity of judgments of taste is not conceptual. I can point to aspects of the painting, but I cannot appeal to any canons of art – principles from which it would follow that the *Madonna of the Rocks* is beautiful. How then can aesthetic judgments claim objectivity, in the sense of being valid for all, if they depend on feelings produced by experiencing particular works of art whose beauty-making features cannot be codified?

Kant's solution to the odd status of aesthetic judgments was to link this problem to that of reflective judgment. He maintained that the pleasure we take in works of art is a consciousness of the free but harmonious play of our faculties. Although beautiful works of art can be brought under no concept and have no purpose, moral or otherwise, in experiencing them we are aware of a nonconceptual unity in diversity. Hence in experiencing them we are conscious of natural objects or representations of objects as suitable to our faculties and our faculties as mutually harmonious or "purposive." If that is the source of pleasure in art, an awareness of works of art as purposive for our faculties, then that would explain why we can expect others to concur that a work is beautiful, since human beings are (and are understood to be) alike in their basic cognitive faculties. Hence, we can expect others to find a work beautiful on the basis of a particular sensory reaction, the feeling of pleasure it causes in them, because of the feeling it causes in us.

Like many in the eighteenth century, Kant divided works of art into the beautiful and the sublime. If beautiful works of nature and art were balanced and harmonious, sublime objects were terrifying, the difference, roughly, between a sunset and a hurricane. As he did so often, Kant reversed the usual way of understanding the fascination of the sublime. Among others, Joseph Addison (editor of the *Spectator*) explained the appeal of the sublime in terms of natural human appreciation for the overwhelming force of the Supreme Being.[18] Kant had quite another idea. We take pleasure in the sublime, because it reveals the tremendous force of reason in the moral law, a force so strong that it commands respect and can overwhelm the normal images of the senses. This produces pleasure not by demonstrating the mutual harmony or purposiveness of our faculties, but by revealing the power of reason.

Beyond firmly establishing the idea that the pleasure in art is and must be disinterested (evident in the "art for art's sake" movement of the nineteenth century) and the Romantic image of the human mind as the source of awe and wonder in the creation, Kant also presented an influential theory of genius. The genius does not imitate nature, but does nature one better, by creating a beautiful representation of unpleasant and even awful aspects of nature, without artifice or dishonesty, but in a way that the spectator finds natural.

In the second part of the *Third Critique*, the Critique of Teleological Judgment, Kant took up a vexing problem in scientific explanation. On the Newtonian paradigm, science explains by appealing to exceptionless laws, which enable us to predict future states of the world by reference to present state and the dynamic forces operating on it. For example, if we note the position of the moon in the sky one night, and determine the gravitational forces operating on it, then we can predict where it will be the next night. But not all explanation in science fits this pattern. In the case of organisms, scientific insight comes not through understanding the forces operating on different parts, but by seeing the parts in terms of their mutual relations in the functioning of the whole. The motion of the heart explains the circulation of the blood, its rhythm, momentum, and so forth. Without a circulatory system, however, the heart would have nothing to do. The motion of the heart explains how blood circulates, but its capacity to circulate blood explains why we have a heart. Because the Greek for purpose or end is "telos," explaining aspects of the organic world by reference to the function or purpose of various organs is usually characterized as "teleological" explanation.

Kant believed that science had to use teleological explanation to assume that each part of a creature had a function, that nothing was gratuitous. This principle, just like the principle that nothing happens by chance, was fundamental to scientific reasoning. But how could these principles be reconciled? His solution to this "antinomy" (conflict) – all explanation is mechanical vs. some explanation by mechanism cannot account for obvious features of the organic world – followed the lines of the Dialectic of the *First Critique*. These two assumptions must be thought of as regulative principles, governing the practice of science and the search for explanations. They cannot be understood as literally true, without contradiction. The two principles are not, however, equal. The law of universal (mechanical) causation is a necessary condition for the possibility of any cognition at all; perhaps it is just a peculiarity of us that we can make sense of organisms only by trying to understand the functions of the parts.

Kant knew there was a standard means of explaining the existence of "natural purposes," organisms in which each part was suitable for the others. The heart and circulatory system would be mutually supporting, because they were the result of a Divine plan or design. Although he did not anticipate Darwin's brilliant solution to the puzzle of teleological explanation, that good design is produced by random mutations that give rise to differences in organisms, differences that are "selected" for survival by natural forces of food supply and predation, he firmly resisted appeals to the supernatural. We destroy the system of nature by trying to solve the problems of science by "mixing in something that does not belong to physics at all, namely, a supernatural cause" (Ak: V:383).

6. Enlightened Religion

In Kant's view, attempts to use "natural purposes" as evidence for the existence of God were as bad for religion as they were for science. The Dialectic of the *Critique of Pure Reason* had offered a subtle logical analysis of the flaws of standard proofs for the existence of God. As he noted there, the only one of those arguments that had ever persuaded laypeople (as opposed to metaphysicians) was the argument from design. At the end of the *Third Critique*, he returned to the task of "limiting reason to make room for faith." In fact, no logical subtlety is required to see that the argument from design is hopeless. As Hume had argued in *The Dialogues Concerning Natural Religion*, how can an all-perfect Creator be inferred from a flawed creation? Worse still, given the moral arbitrariness of nature, an honest inference from the phenomena would not lead to the hypothesis of a just God.

How does the other half of the dictum – faith in God – find any role in Kant's system? Like so much else in his philosophy, Kant's view of the relations among natural science, morality, and religion, reversed standard approaches. Appeals to God had no place in science at all. Nor could moral knowledge depend on appeals to Divine commands. Each person is able to determine right and wrong for himself or herself. Still, Kant thought that belief in God and an afterlife played a role in furthering moral behavior. Since the wicked often seem to flourish, while the good are visited by adversity, it is easy to lose heart that moral deliberation can ever bring about a just society. Perhaps the forces of desire always overwhelm the moral law, so that seemingly moral action is nothing but disguised selfishness. Belief in God and an afterlife are not necessary for morality, so Atheism is no excuse for immorality.

As a practical matter, however, belief in God and an afterlife may provide much needed hope that the moral law can be efficacious and that even those who are unlucky in this life may someday receive their true desserts.

Beyond criticizing alleged "proofs" for the existence of God, Kant was scathing on standard religious practices. He described prayers asking for some boon to the supplicant as superstitious delusions that betrayed an obvious lack of faith in God's wisdom. He regarded the ritual recitation of half-understood creeds as an offense to freedom of thought. Worse still, prayers of adoration, which praise the Lord at the expense of the believer's respect for humanity in his own person, directly weaken the effect of the moral law. Kant saved his sternest condemnation for those who destroyed human life in the name of religion. To take a human life – which your own conscience clearly informs you is wrong – on the basis of some wobbly chain of inference from a long-ago Divine revelation filtered through generations of the "priestcraft," is to act unconscionably.

For Kant, the point of acting morally was not to serve God. Rather, the belief in God served moral purposes. His faith had nothing to do with discerning the unfathomable nature or will of God. Knowledge was impossible here. Conversely, our knowledge of the moral law made room for a uniquely Enlightenment view of religious moral faith. As he explained in a letter: "'moral faith' . . . is the consoling hope . . . of trusting that if we do all the good that is within our power, divine help will bring it to completion" (Ak. X:178). Kant's "faith" in God was a fervent expression of the hope that the moral purposes that human reason discerned so clearly could be realized.

Notes

1 From "Dejection."

2 Kant published two versions of the *Critique of Pure Reason*. References to it will be in the text, with the usual "A" and "B" indications of the 1781 and 1787 editions. Quotations will be my translations, although I have consulted the translations of Norman Kemp Smith (New York: St. Martin's, 1968), Werner Pluhar (Indianapolis: Hackett, 1996), and Guyer and Wood (New York: Cambridge University Press, 1998). I follow Guyer and Wood's convention of indicating emphasis (which Kant usually marked by exaggerated spacing) with boldface. All references to Kant's works, other than the *Critique of Pure Reason*, will be to *Kants gesammelte Schriften, Akademie Ausgabe*, edited by the *Königlichen Preussischen Akademie der Wissenschaften*, 29 vols. (Berlin and Leipzig: Walter de Gruyter and predecessors, 1902–), and will be cited in the text by giving the volume and page numbers after "Ak." for "*Akademie.*" Most translators use the *Akademie* edition pagination in their margins, so the Ak. references should make it easy to find a passage in whatever translation is consulted.

Ak. IV:
Groundwork of the Metaphysics of Morals, 1785.
J. Paton, tr. (1949). New York: Harper and Row.
Foundations [alternative tr. of "Groundwork"] *of the Metaphysics of Morals*, 1785. Lewis

White Beck, tr. (1959), Indianapolis: Bobbs-Merrill.

Metaphysical Foundations of Natural Science, 1786.
James Ellington, tr. (1970). Indianapolis: Bobbs-Merrill.

Ak. V:
Critique of Practical Reason, 1788.
Mary Gregor, tr. (1997). New York: Cambridge University Press.

Critique of Judgment, 1790.
Werner Pluhar, tr. (1987). Indianapolis: Hackett.

Ak. VI:
Religion within the Bounds of Reason Alone, 1793.
Theodore H. Greene, tr. (1960). New York: Harper and Row.

Metaphysics of Morals, 1797.
Mary Gregor, tr. (1991). New York: Cambridge University Press.

Ak. VII:
Anthropology from a Pragmatic Point of View, 1798.
Mary Gregor, tr. (1974). The Hague: Martinus Nijhoff.

Ak. VIII:
"What is Enlightenment," in the Lewis White Beck translation of *Foundations of Metaphysics of Morals* (see above).

Ak. IX:
Lectures on Logic, 1800.
Michael Young, tr. and ed. (1992). New York: Cambridge University Press.

Ak. X:
Philosophical Correspondence 1759–99 [partial], Arnolf Zweig, tr. (1967). Chicago: University of Chicago Press.

3 In a review written by his ally J. G. Schulze with his approval (Ak. XX:408).
4 *Dioptrika Nova*, 1692, quoted in Nicholas Pastore, *Selective History of Theories of Visual Perception, 1650–1950* (Oxford: Oxford University Press, 1971), p. 68.
5 For example by Norman Kemp Smith in *A Commentary to Kant's Critique of Pure Reason* (New York: Humanities Press, 1962), p. 101.
6 *Kant's Intuitionism* (Toronto: University of Toronto Press, 1995).
7 "Kant's Theory of Geometry," *The Philosophical Review* 94 (1985), pp. 455–506.
8 See Charles Parsons, "Infinity and Kant's Conception of the 'Possibility of Experience,'" *The Philosophical Review* 73 (1964), pp. 182–97.
9 Although "transcendental logic" concerns the conditions under which logic could ever be applied to objects of experience, it differs from "applied logic." Kant understood "applied logic" as the study of how our logical capacities operated in particular conditions, such as a weak memory, a lively imagination, or various mental habits (A 53/B 77).
10 See Dieter Henrich, "Kant's Notion of a Deduction and the Methodological Background of the *First Critique*," in *Kant's Transcendental Deductions*, ed. Eckart Förster (Stanford: Stanford University Press, 1989), pp. 29–46.

11 The most comprehensive treatment of the Second Analogy is ch. 10 of Paul Guyer's *Kant and the Claims of Knowledge* (Cambridge: Cambridge University Press, 1987).

12 This way of understanding the phenomenal–noumenal distinction was developed and defended by Gerold Prauss in *Kant und das Problem der Dinge an sich* (Bonn: Bouvier Verlag Herbert Grundmann, 1977).

13 *The Practice of Moral Judgment* (Cambridge, Mass.: Harvard University Press, 1993).

14 Kant need not deny that a severely mentally disabled person has any rights; his point would be only that such a person could not have a right of self-determination, could not be morally autonomous.

15 John Rawls, *A Theory of Justice* (Cambridge, Mass.: Harvard University Press, 1971).

16 Ibid., p. 256.

17 My discussion in this section draws on the work of Paul Guyer, particularly *Kant and the Experience of Freedom* (Cambridge: Cambridge University Press, 1993).

18 Cited in Guyer, *Kant and the Experience of Freedom*, p. 240.

Chapter 12

Jeremy Bentham

Ross Harrison

Most great philosophers have clearly identifiable works which form the central object of study when considering their thought. With Bentham it is more difficult. There are, indeed, two works which are normally taken to be his principal contribution, the *Fragment on Government* of 1776 and the *Introduction to the Principles of Morals and Legislation* of 1789.[1] Both the *Introduction* and the *Fragment* are undoubtedly major works. They also have the advantage that Bentham himself saw them through the press. However, Bentham lived and wrote for a long time and both these works occur relatively early in it. After writing the *Introduction* (the main body of which was finished and printed in 1780, some nine years before it was published) Bentham went on writing for another fifty years. Also it was writing, rather than publishing, which was the center of this life. The material, if it was published at all, was published by others, often after his death.

As their titles suggest, the published *Fragment* and *Introduction* were each only parts of much larger projects. The *Fragment* was a fragment of a much larger study Bentham had planned and substantially written of the leading contemporary jurisprudential writer, William Blackstone. The *Introduction* was the introduction to a rationally organized penal code, much of which Bentham had again drafted. Furthermore the reason he delayed nearly a decade in publishing the *Introduction* was that he had become entangled in a "metaphysical maze." The profound work he then wrote which resolved this maze lay unpublished until this century, when it appeared as *Of Laws in General*.[2]

Bentham's main writings on central philosophical topics, such as ontology, logic, and language, were also not published until after his death, when they were included in volume 8 of Bentham's *Collected Works*, edited by John Bowring in 1843.[3] However some of it did appear in his lifetime, being used in footnotes in the *Fragment* and as an appendix to Bentham's plan for a school, which he called *Chrestomathia*.[4]

The editors who published his writings in his lifetime, hacking coherence out of large piles of manuscripts, had a more dynamic idea of the functions of an editor than modern equivalents. Some of the responsibility for the form in which the writings appear is theirs, yet this is the work which made Bentham known. The chief ornament here is the *Traites de legislation civile et penale*, which contains his *Civil Code*, *Penal Code*, and *Indirect Legislation* writings. This material does relate fairly closely to Bentham's manuscripts, but Bentham gave its editor, Dumont, almost no help with it. It is more readable than the tortured prose of the late Bentham; by making Bentham readable, Dumont made Bentham read. Finally, in this century, a new collected edition has been appearing. Apart from *Of Laws in General* it has particularly concentrated on Bentham's late writings in which he was working out his constitutional code.

It will be seen from this rapid survey that there are difficulties in handling Bentham material, although reference will be made in what follows to all the various kinds which have been mentioned. It will also be apparent that the central theme of Bentham's work is law. This started with his birth. He was born in 1748, the son and grandson of lawyers. He was destined by his father to be a great practitioner of law, wealthy and successful. However, as soon as he started studying the law, the young Jeremy Bentham revolted against the current condition of English law. He felt that it was full of fiction and absurdity. He said that he found "the various rights and duties of the various classes of mankind jumbled together into one immense and unsorted heap." So, instead of studying law as it was, he turned to law as it might be. He turned to sorting it out, to explaining and criticizing it. Instead of making a fortune out of it he wrote profound and critical studies, both about it and also about anything with which it could conceivably be connected. When he died, in 1832, he was surrounded by 70,000 sheets of manuscript.

Although Bentham described himself as a "hermit," and lived very simply for much of his life, he was not just a writer. He wanted to do things by writing. He wanted to change his world. He was also what was called at the time a projector. The chief and most famous of these projects was Bentham's plan for an ideal prison, the panopticon, which was to be built in a circular form so that the warder in the center could keep all the prisoners under continuous surveillance. (Or, at least, so that they could think that he was doing so; the warder spider in the center of the panopticon web was to be hidden from his prisoners.) This "mill for grinding rogues honest" started just as a bright idea and a published set of letters. However at precisely the time that Dumont was struggling with his manuscripts, Bentham gave up the hermit life of writing and instead threw himself into trying to get the project approved and built. His plan was that he was going to run it himself and take the profits. He lobbied the government, bought the steel, nearly bankrupted himself. He was often within a signature of success. However in the end the whole project failed. After a nearly 20-year battle, Bentham did not get government approval. Instead he was compensated and retired to the country to write his profound studies of logic and meaning; as well as having a more realistic, if bitter, idea of the nature of government.

Bentham had many other projects, or bright ideas: trains of carts; frozen peas in winter; a Panama canal; interest-bearing currency; poor houses; schools. Visionary as these were, nothing came of them in his time. So also for many other sensible suggestions in law and government: a free press; registration of real property; abolition of cock fighting; abolition of religious tests; virtual universal suffrage; compensation for criminal injury; and so on. These were for a future age. Instead what Bentham left as his monument were the worked out theoretical ideas which lay behind such proposed practice, or projects.

The central principle here is the principle of utility, or the greatest happiness principle. Thus he starts his first main work, the *Fragment*, with the statement of the "fundamental axiom, *it is the greatest happiness of the greatest number that is the measure of right and wrong.*" The *Introduction* starts with a chapter entitled "Of the Principle of Utility." The great work of Bentham's last years, his *Constitutional Code*, declares that "of this constitution, the all- comprehensive object, or end in view, is, from first to last, the greatest happiness of the greatest number."[5] The prose may get more complex but the central principle is quite steady over his long life. The variation between "happiness" and "utility" in these formulations is not significant. Later on Bentham said that he had used the word "utility" because of Hume and that he preferred to call it "the greatest happiness principle." Yet the word "utility" has stuck, not just for him, but also up to the present. Bentham was the chief of the classical utilitarians.

Although Bentham preferred "happiness" to "utility" late in his life, we have just seen that the first formulation is in terms of "happiness" (although he also talks in the *Fragment* of "the Principle of Utility"). It does not matter. Many terms can be used, but Bentham is quite explicit that they come in this context to the same thing. He makes this quite clear when he formally defines utility in the *Introduction.* He there says that "by utility is meant that property in any object, whereby it tends to produce benefit, advantage, pleasure, good, or happiness," immediately noting that "all this in the present case comes to the same thing" (I, 3). He then similarly notes that the corresponding negative terms "mischief, pain, evil, unhappiness" also come to the same thing. In other words, whether he talks in terms of pleasure and pain or in terms of happiness or in terms of utility, he is making exactly the same points. The maximization of utility, of happiness, of pleasure, are for Bentham merely three equivalent ways of describing the proper end of all actions.

This is the clear central principle of Bentham's work, the bright star which guides the whole journey. Yet if we are to understand Bentham we also have to realize the central importance for him of another idea he took from Hume. This is the distinction between *is* and *ought.* As we now look back at Bentham, through the mists produced by J. S. Mill's infamous proof of utility and by claims made at the beginning of the twentieth century about "naturalistic" fallacies, we may have an idea that people like Bentham got their values (their principle of utility) from claims about the nature of people as seekers of happiness. Yet for Bentham, claims about what we should do are quite distinct from claims about what we are actually like. For Bentham there is no deduction of values from facts, nor is there any confusion between them.

This vital distinction between *is* and *ought* can first be seen in *Fragment on Gov-*

ernment where Bentham distinguishes between someone talking about the law as an "expositor" and someone talking as a "censor." He says in the Preface, "To the province of the *Expositor* it belongs to explain to us what, as he supposes, the Law *is*: to that of the *Censor*, to observe what he thinks it *ought to be*." He notes that the Expositor is a citizen of a particular country; the Censor "ought to be the citizen of the world." In other words one thing we can do is say how the law actually is. This will vary by country according to the different historical ways in which they have constructed their laws. However, these laws can also be criticized (or "censored"). As well as how the law is, there is also how the law ought to be. This will rely on principles of value, independent of country.

If we turn to the start of Bentham's next major work, the *Introduction*, we get the same distinction. Here, though, being slightly more wrapped up, it has confused people. Bentham begins his main text, grandly and rather rhetorically, by proclaiming that "Nature has placed mankind under the governance of two sovereign masters, *pain* and *pleasure*" (I, 1). Pain and pleasure drive the whole Bentham machine. We shall meet them again. However, if we read this opening carelessly we may think we detect some move by which values are meant to emerge from "nature"; from natural facts about people being pleasure seekers and pain avoiders. But this is not what Bentham says. How he actually goes on is: "It is for them alone to point out what we ought to do, as well as to determine what we shall do." So, again, we clearly have both an *ought* and also an *is* (here "ought" and "shall"). Pain and pleasure come into the Benthamite operation in a double role, determining both the *ought* and also the *is*. The next sentence continues the theme. It says: "On the one hand the standard of right and wrong, on the other the chain of causes and effects, are fastened to their throne." Again, two carefully distinguished things. We have a standard of right and wrong. This is the principle of utility, Bentham's master normative principle, which we have already met and seen to be understood in terms of pains and pleasures. Yet as well as this we also have descriptive science, a study of causes and effects. Again pains and pleasures come in, only now in an explanatory role. They explain the causes of action, why people do what they do.

This fundamental point has been established by taking quotations from prominent positions in Bentham's two main early books. It occurs throughout his work. The distinction is not only prominent but also fundamental in understanding Bentham's thought. Without it no sense can be made of his central recommendations or his practical projects. For whether he is designing a prison or a school; or setting out the principles of punishment; or framing the whole structure of the ideal state; the central idea is the same. This is to take people as they actually are and put them in a structure whereby they will do what they ought to do.

For this Bentham needs two principles. He needs a fundamental normative principle, saying what ought to happen, so that he can know what he is aiming at. This is the principle of utility. He also needs a fundamental descriptive principle, setting out the character of the raw material, so he knows what he is working with. This, for Bentham, is that people are self-interested. He thinks that, in general, they seek their own pleasures and avoid pain. Bentham then takes this raw material, that is, people as they actually are, and constructs the prison, or state, or penal code, or whatever, so that these self-interested people will do what they ought to do. He calls this the "Duty and Interest junction principle." For example, when discussing management of poor houses (another of his projects) he notes, "No means to be omitted that can contribute to strengthen the junction between *interest* and *duty*, in the instance of the person entrusted with the management: – i.e. to make it in each man's *interest* to observe on every occasion that conduct which it is his *duty* to observe."[6] To join interest and duty we need an account of both; and also an understanding of how to put them together.

Neither of these separate principles, nor the project of their combination, was original to Bentham. He found them in the people he started reading when he became dissatisfied with his study of law and wanted to work on its improvement, in particular the French writer Helvetius and the Italian jurisprudential thinker Beccaria. Beccaria indeed had already enunciated the famous formula, promoting, as it is put in the 1767 English translation, the greatest happiness of the greatest number (in the original Italian "la massima felicita divisa nel maggior numero"). Helvetius had already talked of connecting the personal with the general interest. Bentham had no intention of disguising such debts. His importance rests not on the invention of the principles but on their defense and on the care with which he worked out their combination. Indeed, the more people agreed with the basic principles, the better and easier for Bentham. The principle of utility was something which he could pluck out of the surrounding Enlightenment air. As we saw, it is declared in the *Fragment* to be an "axiom"; something anyone who considered should be able to accept or presuppose. It is what Bentham does with the axiom which is important. What he does, to return to the first paragraph of the first chapter of the *Introduction*, is "to rear the fabric of felicity by the hands of reason and of law." Felicity (happiness; pleasure and not pain) is the end, the goal. But what has to be worked out by reason, the means involved in reaching this end, is a perfect system of government and of law.

The other part of Bentham's genius, and the part which makes him particularly interesting for philosophers, is that he could not use anything without both brooding deeply about its nature and also seeking to improve it. So he did not only use the principle of utility, ready for him in the Enlightenment air. He also sought to understand it and ground it; to give it a meaning and a justification. So also for law. Law was not just an instrument to be used (in the way that it was by Helvetius and Beccaria); it was also something to be understood. Therefore Bentham gives an analysis of everything he uses, and in so doing reaches powerful and original insights into the nature of law and language; value and government. It is this powerful analytical ability which makes him a great philosopher.

When Bentham started to clarify the law, he thought that this would principally involve him defining his terms and so giving a meaning to the various legal expressions. Here again he thought that the basic principles he needed could be plucked from the surrounding Enlightenment air, this time from Locke. In Locke, and following him Hume, ideas are clarified by being connected with their perceptual base. Both Locke and Hume distinguish between simple and complex ideas. Simple ideas can only be understood if we have had the corresponding perceptions (what Hume calls "impressions"); but we can understand complex ideas of things we have not experienced, such as golden mountains. These are compounded out of simple ideas. Bentham keeps the link to perceptible entities in clarification. Yet "exposition," as he calls it, contains for him not only definition but also a new technique which he calls "paraphrasis." He was driven to this new technique because he soon realized that the terms with which he had to work in the law, terms like *right*, *duty*, *power*, *obligation*, and so on, were neither directly perceptible nor complexes of perceptibles (simple or complex ideas).

The central idea involved in Bentham's solution of this problem is to stop working at the level of individual terms and move instead to the level of complete sentences. We take the problematic term, for example "obligation," and place it in a sentence; for example "everyone is under an obligation not to assault me." This sentence is then replaced with another sentence which, as Bentham puts it, has the same import; for example "anyone assaulting me is liable to be punished." With punishment we reach the idea of threatened, or possible, pain. Pain for Bentham is a perceptible entity; or, as he occasionally puts it, a simple idea. It is something we can experience directly and hence something we can understand. As he puts it in the preface to the *Fragment*, "*pain* and *pleasure* at least, are words which a man has no need, we may hope, to go to a Lawyer to know the meaning of." No more legal obfuscation. No more use of terms like *rights* without understanding their meaning. Instead we have clarification and perceptible good sense. Bentham connects the terms to which he cannot give direct meaning with possible perception, and so with sense. Pain, which we saw entering into its central position at the start of the *Introduction*, is again doing the central work. "Take away pleasures and pains," as Bentham put it in a work called *The Springs of Action*, and *duty*, *obligation*, and so on "are so many empty sounds." As he puts it in the footnote to the *Fragment* in which he first publicly introduces the idea of paraphrasis, "without the notion of punishment (that is of *pain* annexed to an act . . .) no notion can we have of either *right* or *duty*," noting also that "the idea belonging to the word *pain* is a simple one" (V, 6n).

To give a meaning in this way is quite different from connecting the term with a perceptual image, and is shown by Bentham to be different. He also gives examples of such a connection with images. For example, for *obligation* he talks of the image of someone under a heavy load. Different again is the etymology of the term, although this can also provide an image (here it is being bound; tied up; held by a ligature). Bentham knows about these. He calls these processes "archetypation." He also knows that they are clearly different from paraphrasis. These connections with images say something about the words, but they do not give its "import," or meaning. By contrast, paraphrasis gives the meaning. With paraphrasis terms do not need to be given images but sentences have to be related to sentences which can directly be understood in perceptual terms.

Concentrating on this type of analysis and on the primacy of the sentence (rather than term) as the unit of significance makes Bentham a clear forerunner of twentieth-century theorists of meaning. In his *Essay on Language* (one of the works published posthumously in the Bowring edition of the *Collected Works*), he says "it was in the form of entire propositions that when first uttered, discourse was uttered," noting that terms "are the work of abstraction."[7] In other words, we start, both historically and analytically, with the sentence (or proposition) rather than the term. The former is the complete thought; we start with it and then abstract its elements. He then gives a telling analogy saying that "words were but so many fragments" of propositions "as afterwards *in written discourse* letters were of words." No one thinks of discovering the meaning of a word by first finding the meaning of the individual letters of which it is composed. Neither should we think that the significance of sentences can be decomposed into the prior and independent significance of the words with which the sentence is composed.

This is the technique, but Bentham also puts the technique to work. He gives an account of the fundamental legal terms, particularly *right* and *duty*. These are the examples he considers in the footnote to the *Fragment*. The *Fragment* is a criticism of Blackstone, and Blackstone talks a lot about rights and duties. Bentham wants to bring out that what Blackstone says is confused and without meaning. However he also wants to show in this footnote that such terms can be given a meaning. As we have seen, he gives a meaning to *obligation* by connecting it with the possibility of punishment (pain). So also for the closely related notion of *duty*. Someone is under a duty to do something when he is liable to be punished for not doing that thing.

This leaves rights. Bentham analyses rights in terms of duties and so punishment. As he puts it here in this *Fragment* footnote, skipping a stage, "what you have a right to have me made to do . . . is that which I am liable, according to law . . . to be *punished* for not doing." So, in Bentham's analysis, sentences about rights can be replaced by sentences about duties. Someone's right is explained in terms of someone else's duty. The specific nature or content of the right can only be discovered by looking at the nature or content of the duty. In turn, someone has a duty when they are liable to be punished by law. Finally, there is a law when some one or some group (the "sovereign") to whom people have a habit of obedience has threatened punishment (pain) for not doing a particular kind of action.

So rights for Bentham are benefits. They are the benefits secured by duties. My right not to be attacked in the street, from which I benefit, is secured by the duty on you and everyone else not to attack me. (That is, you and they are threatened by law with punishment for so doing.) So, in the fuller analysis Bentham went on to in *Of Laws in General*, he first says that in every law there is the party under the duty, "the person or persons who are exposed at least to suffer by it" (VI, 4). He then notes that "there must also be some person or persons who are favoured by it: meaning a person on whom it is the *intention* at least of the legislator to confer a benefit" (VI, 5). After noting the possibility of "self-regarding offences" where the person under the duty and the person to be benefited are the same, he notes that in the normal case that "every legal command by imposing a duty on one party . . . confers a right to services on another" (VI, 8).

This is all from the unpublished work Bentham wrote when he was working his way out of the "metaphysical maze" into which he had fallen. In it he works out a "logic of the will" which matches the more traditional "logic of the understanding" (as he says, a field unknown to Aristotle). This new logic is all built up from the idea of command and negation. We start with a kind of action. This can be commanded in what Bentham calls a "command." Alternatively, its negation can be commanded. This Bentham calls a "prohibition." We then have the negations of these two. (That is, from the original action kind, *p*, we reach *not commanded that p* and *not commanded that not p*.) These Bentham calls a "noncommand" and a "permission." These four possibilities can, as Bentham says, be fitted into relations of dependency and contradiction. For example, a command implies a permission, and a prohibition is incompatible with a permission. However, this is only the start. His account typically gets even more complex as he investigates the different routes by which these situations can arise.

Nor is this just an exercise in abstract logic; although, typically, once Bentham had started with it he produced a highly original, thorough, and well worked-out account. Bentham was trying to solve the specific problem which led him into the "metaphysical maze." This was the problem of the relation of the penal and the civil law. On Bentham's theory all law is command. Yet the civil law (treating, for example, contracts and property) does not seem to contain commands. Bentham's solution is that there is no ultimate distinction between civil and penal law. He holds that any complete law can be broken into two parts, a command bit and an expository part. The expository part explains or otherwise fills up blanks in the commands.

Therefore at the heart of property law for Bentham are simple commands that you are not to take and use things that are not yours. At the heart of all contract law is the command that you should keep your agreements. But the question of what these commands particularly oblige you to do has to be filled in, like blanks on a check. The legislator can fill in what counts as good title, or property. This shows in detail what the requirement not to steal obliges you to. You yourself, when you make a contract, fill in the blanks as to what your particular obligations are. But unless this expository (or applicative) matter has a command behind it, it will not be law. So all law has an aspect of the penal law. In all law there are obligations; there are offenses; there are commands; punishment is threatened for disobedience.

Bentham also manipulates this same complex structure of commands and permissions to give an account of (legal) powers. If I can make a contract, this is a power. If I am the property holder, I have power over the property. If a group legitimately engages in subordinate legislation, then it has the power to establish bye-laws. In all cases of powers, Bentham reaches an understanding of power by the way of the legislator giving someone (or a group) permission exempting them from a normal obligation not to do something. (It will be remembered that permission has been analyzed as the denial of prohibition.) Thus, normally, people are prohibited from entering land and using things. However this prohibition is countermanded for the owners, giving them permission to do so. To give permission is to give power over the land or movable property. Similarly normally people may not seize others, hit, or confine them. This is prohibited. However the prohibition may be canceled for specific kinds of people, such as parents or schoolmasters, hence giving them permission to do these things; and by giving them permission, gives them power. Similarly the local authority gains legislative power, by gaining permission to fine people for not keeping its bylaws; and so on. Power, a kind or right (a right to rights, as Bentham puts it at one point) is again analyzed in terms of obligation; the will of the legislator; the possibility of punishment.

All the raw material of this legal analysis (rights, duties, powers, property, and so on), all the things on which Bentham lavished his care in *Of Laws in General*, are called by him, there and elsewhere, "fictitious entities." As such they are distinguished by him from what he calls "fabulous entities" (or sometimes "non-entities"). These latter do not exist; in no sense have they any reality. Examples given by Bentham are ghosts, the Devil, or the golden mountain. By contrast what he calls "fictitious entities" do have a sort of truth or existence. They have what he calls a "verbal reality." More specifically, the truth or reality they have is discovered by the paraphrastic analysis. This connects these fictitious entities with "real" entities. (More accurately, it connects sentences about fictitious entities with sentences about perceptibles.) The kind of fictitious entity is discovered by its kind of connection with a real entity. In (the posthumously published) *Of Ontology*, Bentham divides the fictitious entities into various kinds, classes, or "orders." Fictitious entities of the first order are "matter," "form," "shape"; of the second order "quality," "relation," "motion"; and so on.

As Bentham observes in this essay, he is not claiming that all the entities there are can be divided into two kinds, the real ones and the fictitious ones. This would be like saying that some things, the fictional ones, both existed and also did not exist. Rather, his claim is that we should think of the division as a division in language; a division between names. When we see substantives in language, we expect entities. We take them to be the names of entities. However, some of these names, such as "property" or "duty" (or "space" or "quality"), do not name real perceptible entities. They are names of fictional entities. It is therefore, as Bentham puts it in *Of Ontology*, "to language then – to language alone – it is that fictitious entities owe their existence, their impossible, yet indispensable existence."[8] Notice "indispensable" here: we cannot get on without such language.

Elsewhere he talks of the names of fictitious entities being a sort of paper currency (paper currency in Bentham's day was backed by the possibility of exchanging it for gold). That is, we can use it perfectly well (it circulates freely enough), but the value it has is given by the possibility of conversion into a language about real entities (the gold). Otherwise Bentham would just be in a confusion or muddle, holding fictitious entities to be both "indispensable" and "impossible." Here as elsewhere paraphrasis provides the way out. It shows what truth there is in statements about fictional entities. When we say that Jones is under a duty to pay, we are using the fictitious term *duty*, albeit a term indispensable in understanding the law. However, although a fictitious term, it is not mere noise. It is not mere talk about a non-entity. When we say this about Jones we are (indirectly) saying something true about the world, in a way we would not be if we said that Jones had a golden mountain. This truth (about pain and punishment) is revealed by paraphrasis. Similarly if we say that the ball has the quality of redness. We are (indirectly) saying that the ball is red. This is something true about the world; even though a quality is merely a fictitious entity.

As we have seen, a centerpiece of such analysis is to make sense of rights. Rights are fictitious entities. Yet they have in law indispensable existence. They have "verbal reality." Now, from the time Bentham was writing up to the present people have got excited about rights. While he was writing there were famous declarations about rights. In the year Bentham published the *Fragment*, the Americans justified their revolution with the claim that it was a "self-evident" truth that people were created with "certain unalienable rights." In the year Bentham published the *Introduction* it was the turn of the French. They had their revolution. They justified it with a declaration of rights. These declared rights are rights prior to and independent of government; rights of man; rights true for all times and all places ("inalienable"). They are taken to be natural rights, rights following from the "law of nature."

"A great multitude of people are continually talking of the Law of Nature" Bentham wrote in the *Introduction* (II, 14n). At end of the work he criticized one of the American declarations of rights. However, his chief and most virulent criticism was of the French *Declaration of Rights*, which he tore apart article by article. This is in a work which appeared in French translation in his lifetime but only in English after his death. It is usually called by Dumont's title *Anarchical Fallacies* (although Bentham once offered it for publication under the title "pestilential nonsense unmasked"). Bentham wants to show that the French invocation of rights is anarchical in effect. He also wants to show that it is nonsense; that it is without meaning. In a famous phrase in it he says that the French *Declaration* is "nonsense on stilts."

Bentham holds this because he thinks that natural rights are mere fictions. They are not real. What people call natural rights Bentham thinks are not rights at all, but, instead, reasons for having rights. Real rights for him are legal rights. So natural rights are merely reasons for having legal rights. For example, a supposed natural right to property means that there is a reason why there should be legal property rights. It is a reason why the sovereign, the government, should threaten people with punishment for interfering with particular bits of land or objects. By such threats they declare these bits to be "property." There are good reasons for having property, for having legal rights. But, as Bentham puts it in *Anarchical Fallacies*, "reasons for wishing there were such things as rights, are not rights; . . . want is not supply; hunger is not bread."[9]

The basic confusion Bentham sees here takes us back to the distinction emphasized at the beginning, between *is* and *ought*, or between the expository and the censorial stances. We can find out that there actually are rights in a particular country and give an exposition of them. We can also be censorial, thinking that there should be rights. But we should not confuse the two. Yet this is precisely what invokers of rights (and natural lawyers more generally) are accused of doing by Bentham.

For Bentham there are no natural property rights. So we cannot construct an argument, as in Locke, saying that we should have a government to defend our natural property rights. Nor can we object to taxation on the basis that it removes our (natural) property. For Bentham property is the child of law. Government makes property, hence there can be no objections of this kind to taxation. (Any objection to taxation, as to anything else, must be based on utility: people's happiness is suffering because of taxation.) Similarly for contract. It is pointless, as Locke tried and Blackstone repeated, to found government on contract. For, as Bentham says, "contracts come from government, not government from contracts."

The lack of such resources for Bentham does not mean that he cannot provide an argument for government and also for its limits. He can, in fact, do both. In both cases he uses utility. It is not because we have rights that there should be government to protect them. Rather, it is because we do not have rights that there should be government. For rights are good things. They are benefits (benefits secured by law). With rights we have more of what we want. With them we have more happiness. With them we have more utility. So there ought to be rights (security; property; contractual rights; and so on). But we only get rights with government. So we ought to have government.

This does not mean that we automatically have to do anything any particular government says. Rights were traditionally invoked, as in a Lockean contract-style argument, to set limits to government. However, again this is unmeaning for Bentham. Talking of the original contract, while criticizing Blackstone in the *Fragment*, he says that the "indestructible prerogatives of mankind have no need to be supported upon the sandy foundation of a fiction" (I, 36). That way is merely fiction. But instead of fiction we have a more secure basis, utility. Utility supports the goodness of government. Yet it also gives its limits. Some governments diminish happiness instead of increasing it. With them the benefits of rights are bought at too dear a rate. They are not really providing rights or declaring and enforcing useful duties. In such cases rebellion is justified. Obedience is justified, as Bentham puts it in the *Fragment*, only "*so long as the probable mischiefs of obedience are less than the probable mischiefs of resistance*" (I, 43).

Now, however, it looks as if there is a problem in Bentham's overall account. For we saw that Bentham called all the fundamental terms which he used in his great analysis of the law names of fictional entities. We saw that he called legal rights fictional; yet also held these fictions to be both necessary and acceptable. Now we have just seen natural law and natural rights described by Bentham as fictional. Yet Bentham thinks that it follows from this that they are unacceptable and ought to be unmasked and extirpated. However, we now seem to have both good fictions and bad ones, which raises the problem of how Bentham can distinguish between them. Analogously there is the problem of why Bentham's strictures against the law of nature do not also apply against the principle of utility. Indeed at one point in the *Introduction* he says that "it may be convenient, for the purposes of discourse, to imagine a kind of law or dictate, called a law or dictate of utility" (I, 8). Yet, if the principle of utility is conveniently imaginable, why not the law of nature? After all,

all rights for Bentham are no more than conveniently imaginable for the purposes of discourse.

To answer this charge and defend Bentham we have to say more about the principle of utility. We saw that Bentham defined utility in terms of happiness, and happiness in terms of pleasure and pain. Just as pain gives meaning to punishment, and so to rights and duties, so also it gives meaning to Bentham's fundamental evaluative principle, the principle of utility. Bentham again clarifies his fundamental terms by means of an analysis. We start with the most general terms of evaluation, such as *good* and *bad*. The significance of these terms is endlessly disputed. So Bentham's aim is to clarify them by giving them a more precise meaning. *Good* is therefore to be understood in terms of benefit or advantage; what is good for someone is what benefits them. But benefit can in turn be explained. It is what tends to produce pleasure or reduce pain.

This, however, is not by itself enough for Bentham to distinguish between the principle of utility and natural law; or between good and bad fictions. He also needs a defense of his foundational principle and at the end of the same chapter of the *Introduction* he provides one. His central point is that only utility (pleasure and pain) gives determinate meaning to ethical terms. He lumps alternative sources of value (intuition, God, right reason, moral sense) under the labels "principle of sympathy and antipathy" or "principle of caprice." According to Bentham, on all of these alternatives something is held to be right merely because its promoter says that it is right. It is what he called ipse-dixitism: the mere idea that saying that something is right makes it so. But now comes Bentham's argument against all these principles. Since people say different things, with ipse-dixitism they can only achieve cacophony. All we have is mere caprice; and morals become merely noise.

In the *Fragment*, Bentham defends the principle of utility against rivals by saying that "the footing" on which it "rests every dispute is that of matter of fact; that is future fact – the probability of certain future contingencies" (IV, 39). In other words, the principle of utility allows scientific-style determination of the facts. These facts are future contingencies, so they involve the calculation (or guessing) of probabilities; the probable happiness that may accrue from various alternative courses of action. We may get it wrong; but it is not meaningless. We know what we are doing. We can communicate publicly. We know on what the issue rests. As Bentham puts it there, people "would at any rate see clearly and explicitly the point on which the *dis*agreement turned."

This is not to say that the principle of utility is a factual principle. It is not. It invokes a value. However, the point is that if we invoke this value, the issue will then turn on fact. This way it is determinable. It has meaning. It can be handled. Otherwise, as Bentham puts it here, we have mere "scolding and childish altercation."

So the principle of utility has meaning; its rivals do not. What then of the problem of distinguishing between good and bad fictions? To resolve this we need to return to Bentham's analysis of the law. For Bentham a legal right may be a fictional entity, but the analysis shows how it connects with real ones. The point that Bentham wants to make about natural rights is that they cannot be connected with real entities in this way. Rights involve duties, and duties involve the command of someone or some group. However, with natural law there is no commanding person or group; hence there are no natural duties; hence natural rights do not even have a "verbal reality."

So Bentham wishes to make discussion and disagreement about evaluative questions in the end discussion and disagreement about matters of fact. However this will only work if there are facts about the pleasures and pains which accrue from different kinds of actions. Utilitarian decision is only possible if such supposed facts about pleasure and pain are calculable and comparable. Such calculation is also needed for the Benthamite psychology and overall project, which, it will be remembered, is to take people as they are and put them in the situation in which they are motivated to do as they ought.

So, for example, in a properly designed penal code, such as the one to which the *Introduction* was meant to be an introduction, punishments will be annexed to certain kinds of actions thereby making them offenses (contrary to duty). For this to work it has to be determined not only what should count as offenses but also what are the correct amounts and kinds of punishment. The assumption is that self-interested people, desiring to avoid punishment, will not do those things which the legislator does not desire them to do. In other words, following their interest, they will be deterred by the threat of punishment from not doing their duty. However, to know the right kind and level of punishment we have to know the deterrent effects of different kinds and amounts of threatened pains. So the legislator (or Bentham) can only design the code if they can know general facts about the effects on happiness of kinds and amounts of punishment. Therefore they need a psychology which permits calculation of interest and happiness.

Utilitarianism, Bentham's value theory, is notoriously connected in popular reputation with such calculations. In fact Bentham himself did not talk of a "felicific calculus," and the attribution to him of such terms depends more on Dumont's use of expressions like "moral calculus" when introducing his work than it does on Bentham himself. However, as was seen in the *Fragment* extract just quoted, he did claim that the application of the principle of utility rested on the assessment of future contingencies. In the *Introduction* he responded to the challenge that criminals, led by passion, did not calculate with the claim, "men calculate, some with less exactness, indeed, some with more; but all men calculate" (XIV, 28).

Bentham has a chapter called "value" in the *Introduction*. In it he lays out how to measure the value of a pleasure or a pain. He lists seven "circumstances" to consider: intensity, duration, certainty, propinquity, fecundity, purity, and extent. "Propinquity" means how close it is in time. "Fecundity" and "purity" describe its relations to other pleasures and pains (a pleasure is "fecund" if it leads to many other pleasures; pure if unmixed with pain). "Extent" means the number of people involved in it. This is a somewhat strange list, containing, it would seem, several unnecessary elements. If calculation, say of the greatest happiness of a people, is to be made at all, it can be presumed that each person's happiness is calculated and then these are summed to get the total happiness. Similarly if we are considering a single person's happiness, then it seems that we can take the separate pleasures and pains and sum them. But if this is so, talking of fecundity, purity, and extent seems an unnecessarily cumbersome way of saying that we should look at all the pleasures and pains involved.

This still leaves us with intensity, duration, certainty, and propinquity. Even with the same certainty and closeness (for example while having them) pleasures are notoriously of many different kinds. It is not clear that they can be compared in terms of intensity; let alone the positive values of pleasure be calibrated against the negative value of pain. Even Bentham in fact doubted their commensurability. He objects, for example, to the English assumption that everything can be valued in terms of money, saying that no satisfaction of this kind can be provided for someone offended in his honor. Comparing the pain of pecuniary loss with the pleasure of giving vent to ill-will in *Of Laws in General*, he notes "it is plain that between quantities so incommensurate there is no striking a sure balance" (XVII, 12).

In fact for all this talk of calculation, where we would most expect calculation in Bentham, in the "value" chapter in the *Introduction*, we instead get a list of "circumstances" which affect value. This is entirely characteristic of Bentham. Again and again he makes lists of things that need to be considered. He is a supreme classifier. Thus the longest chapter in the *Introduction* is a complete "division of offences," or catalogue of crimes. Before then the *Introduction* considers such things as motives, dispositions, circumstances influencing sensibility, exactly the psychology which we have seen that the theory needs. But in each case Bentham lists the various kinds of factors involved; the various possible "circumstances" (and the chapter called "circumstances influencing sensibility" is much longer than the one on value).

In other words, scientist as he is in fact and intention, Bentham is much more of a qualitative than a quantitative scientist. The sciences he admired, botany and chemistry, were (at this time) of this nature. So we can overdo talk of calculation; or the precision possible for a legislator. He can know some general truths, such as that men do not seek to be slaves, and that they will, if they can, avoid pain. But he cannot work with complete precision in calculation.

There is another kind of problem in the value chapter of the *Introduction* which is that for Bentham value has to serve in a double capacity. It has to enable us to consider the rights or wrongs of actions by means of an estimation of their effect on the general happiness. However, it also has to enable us to predict people's actions so we know how they can be deterred, or otherwise motivated into doing what they ought.

With respect to pleasure and pain, Bentham, at the beginning of this chapter, talks of "their force, which is again, in another point of view, their value." This assumes that measurement of their force upon people (the chain of causes and effects) is the same as measurement of their value (the rightness or wrongness). However this is to assume that how things appear to someone with respect to their interests is the same as how their interests actually are. It assumes, that is, that people cannot mistake their interest. It is the apparent interest which motivates; gives the force. It is the real interest which gives the value. The two may diverge, and Bentham cannot just assume that if he captures one of them he has also thereby captured the other.

A good example where this may make a difference for Bentham is with propinquity. Remember that he distinguishes it from certainty. So here we are talking about pure time preference, the claim that a pain close in time is more important than a later equally certain pain. Now people clearly do discount the future in this way. Bentham points out at the end of this chapter that the value of land is universally understood to vary according to "the nearness or remoteness of the time at which . . . it is to come into possession" (IV, 8). The prevailing real interest rate is standardly taken as such a measure of discount (and is mentioned elsewhere by Bentham).

However, although such discounting of the future may measure what seems to be in people's interest, and so enable us to predict or explain how they act, it may not be what is really in their interest. Later utilitarians such as Sidgwick, for example, argued that mere time should make no difference to value. Bentham himself thought that people did not save as much as they should, which implies that he thought that they undervalued their future pleasures and pains.

Propinquity is an example of where the "force," which shows how people actually do value, arguably comes apart from the real value, or how they ought to value. The legislator needs to know both. Of course the legislator's point of view is different from a single acting individual. The legislator has to look at everyone "whose interest is considered"; single individuals just look at themselves. But, as well as this difference, the legislator has to do more than add up how it seems from the point of view of each individual. In the *Introduction* Bentham emphasizes that it is important to distinguish carefully between "the motive or cause, which, by operating on the mind of an individual, is productive of any act" and "the ground or reason which warrants a legislator in regarding that act with an eye of approbation" (II, 19). We have reasons and we have causes. We have the *ought* and we have the *is*. We have value and we also have motive.

One important piece of psychology which Bentham worked out between the printing and the publication of the *Introduction* was what he called his "axioms of mental pathology." When he eventually published the *Introduction* he added a preface and says that the axioms ought to have been included in preference to several of his already printed chapters. They were in fact first included by Dumont in the 1802 *Traites*. Here Bentham brings out what has subsequently been called the diminishing marginal utility of a good, such as wealth. He points out that such goods are positively correlated with utility, so that, as he puts it "he who has the most wealth has the most happiness." However, he then notes that "the excess in happiness of the richer will not be so great as the excess of his wealth" (*Civil Code*, ch. 6). In other words, each successive equal increment of wealth does not produce an equal increment of happiness. (It will be noted, however, that the way that

Bentham puts it here assumes comparability between different people; something which has frequently been contested.)

The importance of this is that it prevents Bentham (or anyone agreeing with him on this) from using money as a measure of utility and so solving in this way the comparative values of various pleasures and pains. For the value of a particular quantity of money depends upon how much money they already have. This is also why Bentham frequently says it is worse to lose than not to gain; a unit of wealth going down is worth more than the same unit going up.

The axioms of mental pathology are used by Bentham to derive an important intermediate goal of good government. This is equality. It follows straightforwardly from diminishing marginal utility, as Bentham points out. For since a particular unit of wealth (or any other good) adds less utility to someone who already has a lot than to someone who has less, more utility will be gained from giving any additional unit to those who have less. That is (on the same assumption that people's utilities can be compared) equalizing supply of a good will produce most utility.

Equality is one of what Bentham calls the subordinate ends of legislation in the *Civil Code*. The other three are subsistence, abundance, and security. Bentham held consistently to these four subordinate ends thereafter. They are important both for the general idea of a subordinate end and also for what these particular ends are. With respect to the general idea, we should notice that his promotion of subordinate ends means that Bentham does not intend everything to be calculated directly by first principles. In the legal and political area about which he is writing he is what would nowadays be called an indirect utilitarian.

This comes about in an obvious way in the construction of the penal code where laws, or rules, are devised by the legislator. The legislator chooses the rules which best promote the general happiness, and in so doing imposes duties on the population. However, the reason why individuals are under and observe their duties is that they are threatened with punishment if they do not. That is, the legislator's motivation in producing the duty is different from the motivation of the individual in observing it. Or, in more modern terms, it is indirect utilitarianism, in that the utilitarian reasons for having the rules are quite distinct for an individual's reasons for observing them.

This is one example of indirect utilitarianism in Bentham. However in the *Civil Code* with his use of subordinate ends of legislation, the indirectness cuts in at a deeper level. For now even the legislator no longer needs directly to consult utility. Just as a list of various general motivating factors are laid out in the *Introduction* to remind the legislator what to look for, so here we have a list of subordinate evaluative goals. Instead of directly consulting the principle of utility, the legislator can instead consult these subordinate ends. In so doing the legislator gains a more specific sense of which rights to produce and protect.

With the subordinate ends we again have a list. So we again have the problem about how the relative importance of the elements is to be assessed when they conflict. However, this time Bentham does provide a partial ranking. Subsistence is more important than abundance and security is more important than equality. So, although the legislator should aim to increase the general wealth (abundance), and so by the first mental pathology axiom the general happiness, this is less important than making sure that people do not starve (subsistence). The money that buys food gives more utility than the money that buys fine wine.

With respect to security and equality, security is similarly ranked above equality. So although, other things being equal, greater equality promotes greater utility, equality will not promote greater utility if it is purchased at the cost of security. "Security" is a category that includes security of person and goods. As Bentham puts it, it is the only one of these subsidiary ends that connects the present with the future. Security protects expectations; and utility is maximized if expectations are protected. Hence the law, providing the secondary end of security, provides and protects property. By doing so it protects people's expectations with respect to, and control over, land and goods. By securing the person, people's expectations of free movement, and hence liberty, are similarly protected. In effect security plays part of the role in Bentham's thought that liberty plays in the work of other thinkers.

Real liberty, which for Bentham is the absence of restraint and constraint, is always reduced by law. However in cutting into our liberty by imposing duties on us, the law provides a different kind of liberty, security from attack by others. This security is for Bentham the more valuable kind of liberty; the kind he calls "legal liberty." As he puts it in the *Civil Code*, liberty is "a branch of security."

The idea that government only provides goods for us by also producing harms is an important one in Bentham. It also applies to punishment. Bentham is always quite clear that punishment is in itself a harm. As he puts it in the *Introduction*, "all punishment is mischief: all punishment in itself is evil" (XIII, 1). It can only be justified on the principle of utility, therefore, if a greater good comes from it; that is, that the harm done by the punishment is outweighed by the greater good it provides. This is so if the harms produced by punishment are less than the harms that would be done by the acts that it successfully deters (rape; murder; theft; and so on). This is the kind of calculation that the wise legislator has to try and make when deciding on what to punish and how much. Any punishment for its own sake is to be avoided; and Bentham regarded several kinds of action standardly punished as cases "unmeet" for punishment. Even if it is used, it should always be the least amount that will achieve its object. Also, as Bentham points out, it is the "apparent punishment" (that is, the deterrent effect) which does all the good, while the "real punishment" does all the harm.

Use of punishment is use of what Bentham calls the "political sanction." In his early work, such as the *Introduction*, he lists four sanctions. Later he increased the number to five by adding what he called the "sympathetic sanction"; the fact that people are moved by sympathy for others. The other three sanctions are the "moral," or force of public opinion; the "religious"; and the "physical" (which is the fear of the natural physical consequences of action, such as pain for falling down). In principle, the legislator could use any of these sanctions to achieve the goal of the greatest happiness, and in his writings on *Indirect Legislation* Bentham discusses how the legislator can develop and use the moral sanction. However, he is always clear that the principal sanction is the political; that is, the use of legal punishment to deter. Punishment is the great engine which drives the rest of the works.

We have seen how this punishment provides rights and security. But as Bentham's work progressed he came to appreciate more and more a kind of security which he had ignored at first. This is what he calls security against misrule. Otherwise put, he came to appreciate the importance of a constitutional code. People had not only to be secured against each other. They also had to be secured against the great power of government. So government itself had to be controlled; a system of sanctions and incentives had to be organized so that government also would aim at the general happiness.

The legislator, who frequently appears in Bentham's expositions, also has to be understood and controlled. The duty and interest junction principle has to be applied to the governors as well as to the governed. The perfect state has to be constructed so that it is the interest of every official to do their duty. The system Bentham worked out for this was a system of representative democracy. In this the representatives are subject to the sanction of annual election and are also under continuous scrutiny from what Bentham calls the "public opinion tribunal."

Bentham himself moved from urging ruling monarchs to put his proposals into effect to urging the institution of democracy, with a vote for anyone who could read. In both cases he was looking for a power to remove absurdity and abuse and to put his proposals into effect. However, the use of democracy (rather than supposed enlightened monarchs) makes more sense from a utilitarian point of view. For the end to be achieved is, as always, the greatest happiness of the community in question. This is the duty. Things work best when duty is also interest. So we want a political power whose interest is to promote such greatest happiness. Given Bentham's assumption that people act in their own interest, the best supreme power is therefore the people as a whole. Their interest is in the greatest happiness of the greatest number. It is also their duty. Hence by giving power to the people, the proper end of government is promoted. The idea of making the government representative means that we can use people with time and skill, but still control their operations in the general interest, of which the people as a whole are the best ultimate guardians. As Bentham puts it, "the people? what interest have they in being governed badly?"

Among his many practical projects Bentham had a project for the efficient production of monuments. The best representation of a person whom it was desired to remember after their death, he thought, was that very person. He wrote a little pamphlet to this end, called the *Auto-Icon*. Hence after his own death, after he had been publicly dissected to show how dead bodies could be of use in medical research, his skeleton was wrapped and replaced in his clothes and Bentham became his own auto-icon. To this day he sits in London and appears at dinners or other meetings of Benthamites and utilitarians.

Notes

1 Of the various editions of these works, the reader may, for example, consult *Fragment on Government*, eds. J. H. Burns and H. L. A. Hart, with an introduction by Ross Harrison (Cambridge: Cambridge University Press, 1988) and *Introduction to the Principles of*

Morals and Legislation, eds. J. H. Burns and H. L. A. Hart (London: Athlone Press, 1970). References to these works will cite chapter and article, making it easy to locate passages in whichever edition is consulted.

2 *Of Laws in General*, ed. H. L. A. Hart (London: Athlone Press, 1970).

3 *Collected Works*, ed. John Bowring (Edinburgh: William Tate, 1843).

4 *Chrestomathia*, eds. M. J. Smith and W. H. Burston (Oxford: Clarendon Press, 1983).

5 *Constitutional Code*, in *The Collected Works of Jeremy Bentham*, eds. F. Rosen and J. H. Burns (Oxford: Clarendon Press, 1983), ch. 2, art. 1.

6 *Collected Works*, ed. John Bowring, vol. 8, p. 380.

7 Ibid., p. 322.

8 Ibid., p. 198.

9 *Bentham's Political Thought*, ed. B. Parekh (London: Croom Helm, 1973), p. 269.

Chapter 13

G. W. F. Hegel

Stephen Houlgate

G. W. F. Hegel (1770–1831) is one of the most influential (and difficult) of modern philosophers. Indeed, his *Phenomenology of Spirit* (1807) has been described as "one of the few great monuments of philosophical thought."[1] This work is understood by some to put an end to the early modern enquiry into the (apparently) unchanging structure of nature and human cognition, and to inaugurate the era of postmetaphysical, historical, and existential philosophizing – the era of Marx, Kierkegaard, Nietzsche, Heidegger, and Adorno. In my judgment, however, the revolution effected by Hegel's *Phenomenology* is more complex than is sometimes recognized. Hegel's text certainly teaches that human consciousness is social and historical. But it does not simply take us beyond early modern metaphysics and epistemology to a purely historical or existential philosophizing. Rather, it transforms epistemology into phenomenology and serves as the introduction to a new, post-Kantian metaphysics. My aim in this essay will be to examine Hegel's phenomenological enterprise in more detail and to determine precisely how he proposes to reform modern philosophy.[2]

1. Metaphysics Before Kant

Before turning to the *Phenomenology* directly, we must consider Hegel's account of metaphysics before and after Kant. In the Introduction to the *Science of Logic* (1812–16, 1832) Hegel points to what he regards as the fundamental conviction upon which pre-Kantian metaphysics rests: namely, "that what is known of and in things by thought, is alone what is really true in them."[3] There are two sides to this conviction.

First, pre-Kantian metaphysics contends that things are known properly, not by sensuous perception, but by thought that employs pure concepts, such as "substance" and "cause." Second, such metaphysics believes that things do not elude, but are indeed known by, understanding – that pure concepts are not mere metaphors for things, but articulate the true nature of what there is. "This metaphysics believed that . . . thinking in its immanent determinations and the true nature of things form one and the same content" (WL, 1:38; SL, 45).

In the *Encyclopedia of the Philosophical Sciences* (1830), Hegel notes that a similar conviction underlies science and ordinary, everyday consciousness.[4] We all assume that what we understand things to be is indeed what they are. Pre-Kantian metaphysics is distinguished from ordinary consciousness, therefore, not by any fundamentally different attitude towards the world – both regard the world as intelligible – but by the fact that it understands its objects in terms of pure, rather than empirical or imaginative, concepts.

Hegel also notes that objects were regarded by pre-Kantian metaphysics as "*completed, given subjects*" to which concepts or predicates are "applied" by the understanding (EWL, 97 [sec. 30]; EL, 68). Again there are two sides to this idea. First, such metaphysics thought of its objects (including the soul, as well as God and nature) as being distinct from the understanding that knows them. Like ordinary consciousness, metaphysics clearly differentiated between the certainty the mind has of the truth and the truth that is known. Indeed, pre-Kantian metaphysics could be described as the consciousness through pure thought of the objects to which it relates – a description whose significance will become apparent later.[5]

Second, metaphysics proceeded by attributing predicates to its objects in judgments (EWL, 94 [sec. 28]; EL, 66). Such judgments in turn were considered to be *about* those objects and, if correct, to be true *of* them. Truth was thus conceived to lie in the correspondence between our judgments (and their constituent concepts) and what there is – a correspondence which had to be verified by pure reason alone.

In determining whether its judgments were true, Hegel maintains, pre-Kantian metaphysics took for granted that reason had to abide by the laws of formal logic and syllogistic reasoning. It also presupposed that the concepts with which it operated were mutually exclusive – that the soul was either simple or composite, and the universe either finite or infinite. Metaphysics was thus a form of "dogmatism," "because . . . it had to assume that of *two opposed assertions* . . . one must be *true*, and the other false" (EWL, 98 [sec. 32]; EL, 69).

In the *Encyclopedia* Hegel explicitly identifies such pre-Kantian metaphysics with the philosophies of Christian Wolff and the Scholastics (EWL, 106, 383 [sec. 36 Addition, 231]; EL, 76, 299). According to the *Lectures on the History of Philosophy* (delivered in the 1820s), Descartes, Leibniz, and Spinoza also fall within the "period of metaphysics."[6] It would be hard to claim, however, that these philosophers are all completely "metaphysical" in Hegel's sense: Scholastics often denied that God could be adequately understood by human beings, and it is not obvious that Spinoza conceived of substance as a "completed, given subject" distinct from human thought, since he thought of human beings as modes *of* substance itself. But none of these philosophers – with the possible exception of Wolff – is actually reduced to being a metaphysician by Hegel. All Hegel claims is that Leibniz, Wolff, and others are to be considered.

The idea that truth consists in judgments *about* the world – in the correspondence between judgments and the world – would seem to be innocent enough. After all, it overlaps with our ordinary conception of truth. Yet it invites an obvious question: how can we be sure that our concepts do indeed apply to what there is? This question has been posed to metaphysicians (and, indeed, ordinary consciousness) by skeptics throughout history. It is Kant's consideration of this question, however, that interests Hegel most.

2. Kant's Intervention

Kant's principal concern in the *Critique of Pure Reason* (1781, 1787) is with pure concepts, or categories. In that work he argues, famously, that the only way to prove that pure concepts apply to objects is to demonstrate that objects are actually made possible by such concepts. If our concepts are what enable there to be objects in the first place, then those objects must be conceivable through our concepts. Kant argues, however, that we can only prove that our concepts make possible the objects of our experience, not that they are the conditions of objects in themselves. We can demonstrate that an object of experience only emerges for us when what we see and feel is conceived as a quantifiable substance in causal relations to other substances, and that, without being so conceived, what we see and feel would remain an indeterminate mass of sensations. We cannot prove, however, that anything beyond what we experience depends on our concepts for its determinacy or "objecthood."

Kant solves the problem of the correspondence between our concepts and objects through an ingenious reversal of our expectations. He shows, not that our concepts conform to objects, but rather that objects (of experience) necessarily conform to our concepts, because those concepts constitute the conditions which enable what we perceive to be understood and experienced as an object in the first place.[7] His solution still leaves us uncertain, however, whether or not our pure concepts adequately characterize things in themselves.

In Hegel's view, Kant's intervention is vitally important and is "the foundation and point of origin of recent German philosophy" (WL, 1:59; SL, 61). In particular, Hegel praises Kant's conception of objectivity. In ordinary language, Hegel maintains, "to be 'objective' [*objektiv*] is to be present outside us and to come to us from outside through perception" (EWL, 115 [sec. 41 Addition 2]; EL, 82). The trees in my garden are "objectively" real, whereas the images I form in my mind of sunny days spent in the garden are merely "subjective" fancies. It is in this sense that the objects of pre-Kantian metaphysics – God, the soul, the world – are deemed to be objective, even though they are known through pure reason rather than sense perception: they are considered to be independent realities to which our concepts and judgments correspond.

Hegel maintains that Kant conceives of objectivity differently. That which is objective, in Kant's view, is not simply what exists "outside" us or "over against" us, but that which is conceived to be universal and necessary. What is universal in our experience is the structure and unity comprehended by the pure concepts of thought. That which is truly objective, for Kant, is thus the *conceptual* form that is in both the things we experience *and* our own understanding. "Kant called the conceptual [*das Gedankenmäßige*] (the universal and the necessary) objective [*objektiv*]," and, Hegel writes, "he was certainly quite right to do this" (EWL, 115 [sec. 41 Addition 2]; EL, 83).

Hegel is profoundly influenced by this Kantian conception of objectivity. Following Fichte, however, he rejects Kant's conception of the "thing in itself." Kant distinguished between the way things are perceived and understood by us – the realm of "appearance" – and the way things might be in themselves, and claimed that we can only be sure that our concepts condition, and so comprehend the structure of, the former.[8] For Hegel, however, Kant's idea of the "thing in itself" is an utter abstraction generated by thought: "the product of the empty 'I' that makes its own empty self-*identity* into its *object*" (EWL, 120 [sec. 44]; EL, 87). There is no hidden dimension to things beyond their appearance to us; what things are perceived and understood to be is all there is to them.

This is not to say that the things we experience are nothing in themselves and are merely our perceptions ordered in a certain way. This is the conclusion Hegel believes Fichte draws (and, of course, Berkeley). Hegel maintains that the things we experience are something in themselves and exist in their own right, apart from our experience of them. His point, quite simply, is that what they are in themselves is just what we experience them to be: the way things are perceived and understood to be is the way they are.

So, for Hegel, things exist independently of our conceiving of them. Yet he also wants to retain Kant's idea that what is truly objective in things is their universal *conceptual* form. To hold these views together, Hegel must subtly revise Kant's idea of objectivity. He must understand objective conceptual form to have its source not merely in human understanding but in the very fabric of being itself, and so to be an absolute, ontological conceptual order – "*logos*, the reason of that which is" – that informs both human understanding and existing things (WL, 1:30; SL, 39). For Hegel, the legacy of Kant's critical philosophy is thus not merely a transcendental account of the conditions of human experience. It is a new, revised metaphysics in which the truth to be known is no longer simply the world "out there," but the universality and logical form immanent in being and thought.

Note that Hegel does not deny that there is a real world "out there." His point, however, is that the task of metaphysics should not be conceived as that of trying to gain "access" to that world and get it right "about" that world, as if we and the world were simply separate. For Hegel, both the world "out there" and our own understanding share the same universal logical form – though one that is not universally recognized or properly understood – and the task of metaphysics is to comprehend that universal form. Since it is the logical form of both thought and being, that form can be understood purely from *within* thought. Thought can by itself, therefore, understand the nature of being "out there." But, in so doing, thought is not "describing" or forming judgments "about" a distinct realm of being. It is engaged in the activity of understanding *itself*, in the conviction that the structure of its own concepts is the same as the structure of being itself – that the structure of the concept of finitude or substance *is* the structure of finitude or substance itself.

After Kant, metaphysics has thus to become the science of logic. This science differs from pre-Kantian metaphysics because "what we are dealing with in logic is not a thinking *about* [*über*] something which exists independently as a base for our thinking and apart from it . . . ; on the contrary, the necessary forms and self-determinations of thought are the content and the ultimate truth itself" (WL, 1:44; SL, 50). To be more precise, after Kant we recognize that metaphysics has always implicitly been logic – has always tried to understand what there is by clarifying the structure of concepts – even though in its pre-Kantian guise it obscured this fact by taking itself principally to describe God or substance "out there." What changes after Kant, therefore, is not the object to which metaphysics addresses itself, but the conception that metaphysics has of its object and of its relation to it. Metaphysics both before and after Kant has what there *is* – that is to say, *being* – as its object. Before Kant, however, metaphysics is governed by the idea that being is precisely an "object" (*Gegenstand*) about which judgments have to be formulated. After Kant, it is governed by the idea that being is informed by the very same immanent, categorial structure as that found within our own understanding. The consequence of Kant's critical revolution for Hegel is, therefore, not to put an end to metaphysics, but rather to make metaphysics become explicitly what it has always been implicitly: the science of (ontological) logic.

Accordingly, the *Logic*, for Hegel, presents "authentic metaphysics or pure *speculative* philosophy" (WL, 1:16; SL, 27). The categories analyzed in the *Logic* are all forms or ways of being – being determinate, being something, being finite, being mechanical, being chemical, and so on; they are not merely concepts in terms of which we have to understand what is (though they are also that). Hegel's claim in the "doctrine of being" is thus not only, as Robert Pippin argues, that "any being [must] be *characterized* 'contrastively,' in a way that will distinguish it from some other," but also that "*beings* actually oppose and negate each other and, in their opposition and negation, are essentially related."[9] Pippin maintains that this stronger claim "confuses logical with ontological issues": "it appears to claim that a thing's not being something else is a property of it, part of what make[s] it what it is." But, to my mind, there is no "confusion" involved in the ontological interpretation of the *Logic*. Hegel's whole point is that ontology and logic are one and the same enterprise. To maintain, as Pippin does, that we should not "conflate" the structure of intelligibility with the structure of being itself is to fail to recognize that Hegel wishes to transform, not abandon, metaphysics, and leaves us with a "Kantian" Hegel for whom philosophy can never be more than the study of human understanding.

By the way, to claim, with Hegel, that being has an inherent conceptual structure is not to maintain that natural objects, such as stones, have minds and form concepts as we do. Spinoza attributes a mind (albeit very rudimentary) to all things in nature, but Hegel patently does not.[10] His point is simply that all things have an irreducible logical structure articulated by the categories set out in the *Logic*. All things exhibit the structure of being "something," of being "finite," of being "quantifiable" and "reflexive," and of being "mechanical" or "chemical." Even the structures of the "Concept," "judgment," and "syllogism" analyzed in the third part of the *Logic* are understood by Hegel to be universal structures immanent in both being (nature) and human thought. They are not simply ways in which we think, but forms of self-mediation exhibited by existing things themselves.[11]

3. Hegel's Science of Logic

Hegel's post-Kantian metaphysics differs from pre-Kantian metaphysics (as Hegel conceives it) not merely by being explicitly identical with the science of logic, but also by being radically self-critical. Pre-Kantian metaphysics took it for granted that thought was governed by the laws of formal logic and syllogistic (or mathematical) reasoning. It also took for granted certain fundamental distinctions between its concepts, for example, that "infinity is different from finitude, that content is other than form, that the inner is other than the outer, also that mediation is not immediacy" (WL, 1:33; SL, 41). Such concepts were not understood to include one another. The soul was judged to be either simple or composite, therefore, and the world was judged to be either finite or infinite in space and time.

In Hegel's view, such assumptions should not simply be rejected as mistaken, but they cannot be presupposed uncritically at the outset of the science of logic. For Hegel, the spirit of the modern age, embodied above all in the philosophy of Kant, is one of radical *critique*. A post-Kantian science of logic must begin, therefore, by questioning and, indeed, suspending all apparent certainties, including our deepest assumptions about reason. The task of logic is then to determine from scratch, without taking anything for granted, what it is to think and how the basic categories of thought are to be understood (for example, "*whether* such a finite without infinity is something true"; WL, 1:33; SL, 42). In the *Encyclopedia* Hegel places great emphasis on the self-critical character of his new science:

> All . . . presuppositions or assumptions must equally be given up when we enter into the Science, whether they are taken from representation or from thinking; for it is this Science, in which all determinations of this sort must first be investigated. . . . Science should [thus] be preceded by *universal doubt*, i.e. by total *presuppositionlessness*. (EWL, 167–8 [sec. 78]; EL, 124; see also WL, 1:35; SL, 43)

But if logic can take nothing whatsoever for granted about thought and its concepts and rules, how can it ever begin? What is logic to consider? Hegel's answer is clear: logic may start with nothing more concrete than the utterly indeterminate thought of thought's own simple being – the bare thought that thought itself *is*.

That is to say, it begins with the thought of thought itself as nothing but sheer being. The first concept considered in the *Logic* is thus that of "*being*, *pure being*, without any further determination" (WL, 1:82; SL, 82). From this rather inauspicious start Hegel believes all the fundamental concepts of thought can be derived: becoming, determinacy, something, other, finitude, quantity, identity, difference, form, content, necessity, possibility, actuality, and so on – concepts that together constitute the categorial structure of thought (and that also inform, though are not fully understood by, ordinary consciousness).

But how exactly are these concepts, and corresponding ways of being, to be derived? If logic is to take nothing for granted about thought, it may not presuppose the method of any other established science, such as geometry, history, or Aristotelian formal logic. Nor, indeed, can it presuppose a dialectical method: it cannot assume in advance that concepts are to be derived by being contrasted with their opposites or "antitheses" and then "synthesized" with their opposites in a higher "unity." So what is the Hegelian logician to do?

Hegel's answer is that the logician is to do nothing but follow the "immanent development" of the indeterminate concept with which logic begins (WL, 1:17; SL, 28). The logician is not to put forward hypotheses of his own and find reasons to support or refute them, but has simply to think through what is implicit in the initial thought of pure being. Pure thinking proceeds "analytically," Hegel maintains, "in that it simply takes up its object . . . and lets it go its own way [*dieselbe gewährenläßt*], while it simply watches the movement and development of it, so to speak. To this extent philosophizing is wholly passive" (EWL, 390 [sec. 238 Addition]; EL, 305). Of course, the philosopher has to draw out the implications of the concept of being, and in that sense is active. But philosophical activity consists in holding rigorously to what is implied by the concept of being itself, letting that concept develop according to its own immanent logic, and so keeping oneself passive. "When I think," Hegel writes, "I give up my subjective particularity, sink myself in the matter, let thought follow its own course [*lasse das Denken für sich gewähren*]; and I think badly whenever I add something of my own" (EWL, 84 [sec. 24 Addition 2]; EL, 58). In this way, Hegel claims, the logician discovers that the concept of being and all subsequent concepts develop dialectically. Dialectic is thus not a pattern of development imposed on thought by the logician, but the "inwardness of the content [itself], *the dialectic which it possesses in itself*" (WL, 1:50; SL, 54).

But how exactly does the initial, indeterminate thought of being develop dialectically into further determinations? Hegel's account, briefly, is as follows.[12] The first thing to note is that the thought of being with which logic begins is not yet the thought of concrete existence, actuality or nature, but the thought of simple, unspecified immediacy as such. This is the unspecified immediacy that belongs to everything that is, but that does not distinguish one thing from anything else: the simple fact of *being* at all. Such being or immediacy is utterly indeterminate. By virtue of this very indeterminacy, however, the thought of sheer being is quite abstract and empty: "there is *nothing* to be intuited in it." Paradoxically, therefore, the thought of sheer being proves to be indistinguishable from the thought of nothing at all: "being, the indeterminate immediate, is in fact *nothing*, and neither more nor less than *nothing*" (WL, 1:82–3; SL, 82).

Yet, nothing – sheer emptiness and indeterminacy – has its own immediacy for thought. It is sheer and utter nothing, without a trace of being whatsoever: the pure lack of being. But nothing *is* precisely this; it *is* sheer and utter emptiness. "To intuit or think nothing has, therefore, a meaning; both are distinguished and thus nothing *is* (exists) in our intuiting or thinking. . . . Nothing is, therefore, the same determination, or rather absence of determination, and thus altogether the same as, pure *being*" (WL, 1:83; SL, 82).

At the beginning of the *Logic* we think of pure being. But the thought of pure being turns straightaway, through its sheer indeterminacy, into the thought of nothing. Equally, this thought of nothing turns straightaway, because of its simple immediacy, into the thought of simple, immediate being. Each thought is quite distinct from the other: being is being, and nothing is nothing. This difference is not to be overlooked. Nevertheless, the thought of one immediately vanishes into the thought of the other. Indeed, neither can be thought except as immediately disappearing into its other. This vanishing that each is, is named by Hegel "becoming." Pure being and pure nothing turn out, therefore, to be not merely *being* and *nothing*, but the immediate emergence or *becoming* of their opposites: "their truth is . . . this movement of the immediate vanishing of the one into the other: *becoming*, a movement in which both are distinguished, but by a difference which has equally immediately resolved itself" (WL, 1:83; SL, 83).

Hegel's presuppositionless logic has provided its first lesson: that sheer being is actually becoming. The immediacy that characterizes all things is always in flux, always passing away and reemerging. What appears initially to be Parmenides' world of fixed, unchanging being has turned out in fact to be Heraclitus' world of becoming. Moreover, Hegel arrives at this Heraclitean worldview by simply letting the Parmenidean thought of being unfold its own implications: namely, that pure being is not just pure being, but – by virtue of its indeterminacy – pure instability, vanishing and becoming. This is the dialectic at the heart of being, through which being will continue to transform itself in the course of the *Logic* into further, more concrete determinations.

According to Hegel, further reflection reveals that being does not simply vanish into nothing, but proves, through this very movement of disappearing and reappearing, to be both irreducible and inseparable from nothing. Being, understood as inseparable from the purely negative, is named by Hegel "determinate being" or *Dasein*. This is being that only is in *not* being what it is not. Such determinate being, Hegel maintains, has two sides to it: reality and negation. Both are one and the same determinate being, only with the accent differently placed: reality is *being* that *is* in not being what it is not, and negation is being that is in *not* being what it is *not*. "Both are determinate being, but in *reality* as quality with the accent on *being*, the fact is concealed that it contains determinateness and therefore also negation" (WL, 1:118; SL, 111).

Since reality and negation are both aspects of determinate being, the difference between them is one in which determinate being differs from, and relates to, itself. When determinate being is understood to be self-relating in this way, it is understood to have the structure of *something*. To be is thus not just to be, to become, to be real or to be negative (though it is all of these things), but also to be something – to be *self-relating* being, or being with an identity and "selfhood" of its own (WL, 1:123–4; SL, 115–16).

Being "something" also has an affirmative and negative side to it: it is self-relating *being* and self-relating *negation*. As the former it is "something," and as the latter it is what is "other." To be is not just to be something, therefore, but to be something in relation to something else – a relation that eventually leads to the insight that something and something else limit each other and so are finite things. By the end of the second chapter of the *Logic*, the thought of pure being has thus turned dialectically into the thought of finitude. The process whereby finite things cease to be, and give way to other finite things, is understood in turn to constitute the process of *infinity*. Sheer, indeterminate being thus reveals itself to be, not just indeterminate being, but the infinite process of development constituted by real, finite things. The further course of Hegel's logic then reveals these things to have extensive and intensive magnitude, to exercise causality, and to form part of a rational process of mechanical, chemical, organic, and cognitive development – a process disclosed later in Hegel's system to be that of nature and history.

This account of the opening of Hegel's *Logic* has been highly truncated. But it does at least indicate the way in which Hegel proceeds – or, rather, the way in which the concept of pure being transforms *itself* into other concepts. Hegel believes the *Logic* offers a powerful new way to do both logic and ontology. It provides what Kant claimed to provide in the "metaphysical deduction" in the *Critique of Pure Reason*: namely, a derivation of the fundamental categories of thought. It also explains what metaphysicians (such as Spinoza) have tried to explain for centuries: namely, why being takes the form of finite things that come into being, change, and end. In Hegel's view, therefore, the *Logic* provides the definitive, *absolute* knowledge of the structure of thought and being that past philosophers have sought, but failed to attain.

The philosophies of nature and spirit that follow logic in Hegel's system continue his presentation of the categorial structure of thought and being by setting out the categories inherent in (the thought of) space, time and matter and (the thought of) consciousness and historical spirit. Together, Hegel's logic, philosophy of nature and philosophy of spirit constitute his dialectical system of absolute knowledge, speculative philosophy, or reformed, post-Kantian metaphysics.

4. The Need for Phenomenology

Hegel's reformed metaphysics rests upon a new conception of objectivity derived from Kant. We have not yet considered, however, whether Hegel is justified in asserting that thought and being have the same conceptual structure, and that the structure of being is thus the structure that being is *understood* to have.

The immediate justification for Hegel's position stems from his insistence that logic be thoroughly self-critical. At the start of logic, before we have determined fully what it means to think, all we can say is that thought *is*, and is aware that it is. We can say that thought knows itself to be, not consciousness, subjectivity, or "I," but simply being as such. (So, whereas Descartes bases his philosophy on the principle, "I think, therefore I am," Hegel begins from the even more minimal principle, "'thinking,' therefore 'is.'") Now, if we are to take nothing for granted except what we are minimally required to think, we may not begin with the assumption that *being* is anything beyond what *thought* is initially aware of. We may not assume that being stands over against thought or eludes thought, but must take being to be the sheer immediacy of which thought is aware – because that is all that the self-critical suspension of our presuppositions leaves us with. A thoroughly self-critical philosopher has no choice, therefore, but to equate being with what is thought and understood. Any other conception of being – in particular, one that regards being as transcending thought – is simply not warranted by the minimal conception of thought-as-sheer-being from which we must begin.

At the beginning of logic, we do not yet know all that being will turn out to be; but we do know that the structure of being will be the structure of the thought of being: that "the matter [*Sache*] can be for us nothing other than our concepts of it" (WL, 1:25; SL, 36). This is not because we presuppose illegitimately that the divide between the knowing subject and the object can be overcome, but because the self-critical philosopher may not assume that there is such a divide in the first place. From Hegel's point of view, therefore, it is not up to the philosopher to justify to the skeptic the claim that thought can understand what is. It is up to the skeptic to explain why being might possibly diverge from the way it is understood; and Hegel believes the skeptic cannot do this without making assumptions about being and thought that are not available to the self-critical philosopher.

In Hegel's view, therefore, nothing is needed to begin the science of logic except "the resolve [*Entschluß*] . . . that we propose to consider thought as such" (WL, 1:68; SL, 70). We do not need first to prove to the skeptic that thought can understand being. All we need to do is resolve to set aside our preconceptions about thought and being and begin from the least that thought can be: the awareness of itself *as* simple being. Hegel believes that this resolve is required of anyone who proposes to do philosophy in the modern world, because a presuppositionless logic alone fulfills the demand for radical self-criticism issued by Kant. For the modern philosopher, who must now be as self-critical as possible, there is thus no alternative to the presuppositionless science of ontological logic (as the Introduction to Hegel's *Encyclopedia* is designed to show).

The problem is that such a logic will not be regarded as necessary by nonphilosophers who see no need to suspend all their assumptions about the world, but are deeply wedded to everyday beliefs. If such people are to take Hegel's new science of logic seriously, they need to be shown that it is made necessary by those everyday beliefs themselves. The role of the *Phenomenology* is to show them that this is the case. It is thus intended to bring ordinary, nonphilosophical or "natural" consciousness – and those philosophers who still adhere to the basic assumptions of ordinary consciousness – to the standpoint of absolute knowledge.

Hegel recognizes that, without being suitably prepared, ordinary consciousness will find the science of logic problematic. In the *Encyclopedia* he points out that such consciousness is simply not used to thinking abstractly. Ordinary consciousness operates with categories such as "being" or "cause" – it says, for example, that "this leaf *is* green" – but it employs them primarily to understand what it perceives through the senses (EWL, 45 [sec. 3]; EL, 27). It understands "something" to be something visible or tangible, and "causality" to be observable causality. It does not, however, consider the purely logical form of such concepts taken by themselves. Even though "being" is the most fundamental category of consciousness, Hegel notes (anticipating Heidegger), "it never occurs to us to make 'is' the subject matter of our inquiry" (EWL, 85 [sec. 24 Addition 2]; EL, 59).

Consequently, when consciousness is asked to consider Hegel's purely logical account of the categories, it feels as if "the very ground . . . has been pulled from under it," since it is unable to visualize the meaning of those categories (EWL, 45 [sec. 3]; EL, 27). It is told that to be "something" is to be the "negation of negation," but is unable to picture what this might mean, and so complains that Hegel's words are unintelligible. (Schopenhauer's accusation that Hegel's texts are full of "frantic word-combinations in which the mind torments and exhausts itself in vain to conceive something" gives perfect expression to the bewilderment Hegel believes ordinary consciousness is bound to feel on first encountering his logic.)[13]

Of course, ordinary consciousness might have this problem with any philosophy – including pre-Kantian metaphysics – employing pure concepts. Hegel's post-Kantian, ontological logic poses a particular problem for it, however. For ordinary consciousness, as for pre-Kantian metaphysics, there is a clear distinction between the truth or object that is known and consciousness's own certainty of that truth. In the science of logic, by contrast, "the separation of the *object* [*Gegenstand*] from the *certainty of oneself* is completely eliminated [*aufgelöst*]: truth is now equated with this certainty and this certainty with truth" (WL, 1:43; SL, 49). This is because logic understands the truth – the categorial form of things – not merely to be "out there," but to be immanent *in* the very structure of our own understanding and certainty. The claim at the heart of Hegel's logic – that the nature of being can be known purely from within pure thought – thus violates a basic principle of ordinary consciousness and is quite simply beyond its understanding. As Hegel famously puts it, in being asked to take up ontological logic, consciousness feels that it is being "induced by it knows not what, to walk on its head."[14]

So how is ordinary consciousness to be persuaded to take Hegel's "perverse" philosophy seriously? It is not enough simply to assure consciousness that the ordinary view of things is deficient and the new philosophical way of understanding thought and being to be preferred. For, as philosophers from Sextus Empiricus to Fichte have recognized, "*one* bare assurance is worth just as much as another" (PG,

71; PS, 49).[15] Ordinary consciousness is thus not going to consider the assurances made by speculative philosophy to be any more compelling than its own.

If Hegel is to persuade ordinary consciousness (and its many philosophical advocates) to take a serious interest in ontological logic, he cannot simply beg the question against consciousness, but must demonstrate that ordinary consciousness leads *by itself* – without any inducement from philosophy – to the standpoint of absolute knowing. He must provide consciousness with a "ladder" to absolute knowing by showing that consciousness actually constitutes its own ladder to such knowledge (PG, 29; PS, 14–15). Hegel cannot do this by appealing to a drive towards radical self-criticism in ordinary consciousness, which might induce it to suspend its cherished assumptions and take up the project of presuppositionless logic, because, unlike modern philosophical understanding, ordinary consciousness has no such drive. It is characterized, not by the tendency to question itself, but by the *certainty* that its own view of the world is satisfactory (PG, 30; PS, 15). Hegel's task, therefore, is to show that ordinary consciousness's own certainties lead it, in spite of itself, to the standpoint of absolute knowledge. The *Phenomenology* is designed to fulfill this task: its purpose is to "lead the individual from his uneducated standpoint to knowledge" (PG, 31; PS, 16).

The *Phenomenology* may appear to take us beyond metaphysics altogether into a new form of "historical" philosophizing; but its explicit purpose is actually to lead ordinary consciousness to Hegel's new, reformed metaphysics. It thus acts somewhat like Descartes's First Meditation by freeing consciousness from its habitual preconceptions and releasing it to the true understanding of thought and being.[16] The analysis of consciousness in the *Phenomenology* is, however, driven by the dialectic inherent in consciousness's own certainties, not by the strategic activity of a skeptical "I"; and the result, as we have seen, is the bare thought of being as such, not the certainty that *I* exist.

5. The Project of *Phenomenology*

The *Phenomenology* contains many of Hegel's most famous analyses, including those of sense certainty, the master/slave dialectic, and Sophocles' *Antigone*. It does not, however, present Hegel's fully developed philosophy – his systematic account of the categorial structure of being, nature, and history – but serves as the introduction to that philosophy. Its focus is not on the truth as such, but on consciousness and its convictions about itself and the world.

The process of educating consciousness is undertaken by speculative philosophy or absolute knowing itself. Philosophy does not, however, simply force consciousness along a dialectical path that it would not naturally follow. This is because in the *Phenomenology*, as in the *Logic*, philosophy employs no predetermined "dialectical method." The "method" of philosophy, for Hegel, is always to suspend our assumptions about rational procedure and let the matter at hand develop according to its own immanent dialectic: "it can be only the nature of the content itself which spontaneously develops itself in a scientific method of knowing" (WL, 1:16; SL, 27). Accordingly, the phenomenological philosopher must simply "sink [his] freedom in the content, let it move spontaneously of its own nature, . . . and then contemplate this movement" (PG, 56; PS, 36). In the course of his analysis, the philosopher discovers that consciousness develops dialectically, but he does not prescribe or assume in advance that this will be the case.[17]

The development traced in the *Phenomenology* is thus wholly immanent to, not imposed on, ordinary consciousness. But it is immanent to consciousness as consciousness is conceived by the philosopher, not as it is observed by the historian or anthropologist. Philosophy does not examine the concrete activity of people in all its individual and historical detail, but considers certain general "shapes" (*Gestalten*) of consciousness, such as "sense certainty" and the "unhappy consciousness" (PG, 80; PS, 56). These shapes do not exist by themselves, but constitute dimensions of the consciousness of living individuals or actual historical societies. (Hegel's analysis of the French Revolution is, therefore, not a detailed historical study of that event, but a study of the "revolutionary consciousness" informing it.) As both Werner Marx and Ulrich Claesges point out, such general shapes of ordinary consciousness – not natural consciousness as it has actually "developed in history under the 'form of contingency'" – make up the "phenomenal knowledge" that is the subject-matter of the *Phenomenology*.[18]

Hegel uncovers the dialectical development that follows logically from the convictions governing each shape of consciousness, not the historical development that individuals or societies have actually undergone. His belief is that such logical development underlies historical development – the actual course of the French Revolution can therefore be understood to be guided by the logic inherent in revolutionary consciousness – but it is the logical, not the historical, connections between shapes of consciousness in which Hegel is principally interested.[19] His claim, therefore, is that the perspective of absolute knowing is logically entailed by the convictions of ordinary consciousness, even if the majority of ordinary people do not realize this fact and do not regard speculative philosophy as of any importance. Indeed, only in this way can the *Phenomenology* perform its educational function: by showing that, despite the historical indifference or hostility of many ordinary people to speculative philosophy, such philosophy is the logical outcome of all that ordinary consciousness itself holds to be true.

The readers of the *Phenomenology* are intended to be ordinary people (and philosophers tied to ordinary beliefs) who are unmoved by the modern spirit of philosophical self-criticism and need to be persuaded that Hegel's logic is a justified and relevant science. Such people will be firmly immersed in the world of everyday experience. But they cannot be completely bull-headed; they must have some interest in what Hegelian speculative philosophy might disclose about the world and be open to what it may show them about their own everyday beliefs. The *Phenomenology* is thus directed at readers who, although steeped in the certainties of everyday life, share in the openness of mind that characterizes true philosophy itself. Accordingly, the "we" to whom Hegel refers throughout the *Phenomenology* includes the philosopher who analyses consciousness *and* the readers who follow that analysis, and constitutes what we might call the community of the open-minded. What separates the readers of the *Phenomenology* from the philosopher is simply that they have yet to be convinced that the distinction between certainty and truth is eliminable and that the true form of things is immanent in the very structure of thought.

Openness of mind distinguishes the intended readers of the *Phenomenology* from the ordinary consciousness analysed in the text itself. For the principal characteristic of this consciousness is simply the certainty that its way of looking at the world suffices. As we shall see, such consciousness will be forced by its own experience to revise its understanding of its object and to develop into new shapes of consciousness; but it is not actually looking to be educated. Once again, the *Phenomenology* can only perform its function if ordinary consciousness is presented in this way. The point of the *Phenomenology* is to show that ordinary certainties lead logically to the standpoint of philosophy, whether or not ordinary people realize this. To demonstrate this, the philosopher must consider ordinary consciousness at its least open-minded, that is, as quite certain that its worldview is satisfactory. There would be no point to the *Phenomenology*, however, if its readers were similarly closed-minded. They could never be brought to appreciate the logical implications of their own certainties, if they were not, in their very certainty, open to what philosophy may have to say about those certainties. The readers of the *Phenomenology* must thus be prepared to let one shape of consciousness change into another, if such a change is necessitated by the tensions within that shape.

The consciousness of the readers of the *Phenomenology* anticipates the perspective of absolute knowing, but is not absolute knowing in the fullest sense. It shares the readiness of absolute knowing to let the matter at hand develop, but does not yet have the ontological confidence that thought can know the true nature of being from within itself. The philosophical thought that undertakes the phenomenological study of consciousness is not absolute knowing in the fullest sense, either. However, it is absolute knowing that has *suspended* its claim to know the form of being from within thought, rather than open-minded ordinary consciousness that has yet to believe it can make that claim.[20] Philosophy must set aside its ontological convictions, because it cannot simply take its own standpoint for granted in its education of consciousness. The *Phenomenology* does not, therefore, set out a philosophy of consciousness: it is not the study, by pure thought, of what consciousness ultimately *is*. As Kenley Dove remarks, "the *Phenomenology* is *not* an ontology (Hegel's *Logik* may be properly spoken of as his ontology)."[21] The *Phenomenology* is simply a study of the way consciousness experiences itself and the world, a study of consciousness's own multiple certainties. That is to say, it is a logical account of the different ways in which truth *appears* to consciousness, not a presentation of the full truth of either being or consciousness itself. This, indeed, is why Hegel names his study *phenomenology* – the logic of appearance – rather than philosophy.[22]

Hegel calls the consciousness studied in the *Phenomenology* the mere "appearance of knowing" (*Erscheinung des Wissens*) or "phenomenal knowledge" (*das erscheinende Wissen*) (PG, 71–2; PS, 48–9). This is because, as we have just noted, consciousness does not know the innermost truth of being – categorial form – but is conscious of being only as it initially appears to be, that is, as a world of people and things "out there." But Hegel also describes consciousness in this way because the organized shapes of consciousness, culminating in absolute knowing, gradually allow the innermost truth of being to become manifest, or to "appear" in the positive sense of the term. In Hegel's dialectical analysis of consciousness, the initial appearance of things to consciousness thus gives way to the full appearance or disclosure of their truth.

The danger here is that we might misread Hegel as a quasi-Kantian, as if he were saying that consciousness is really only aware of the world as it represents it, and the world in itself – being as such – lies beyond the reach of consciousness. In this case, the role of the *Phenomenology* would be to demonstrate how consciousness, initially restricted to its own representations or ideas of things, breaks out of the circle of its own ideas and touches being. This is not, however, Hegel's position. Hegel takes consciousness to be directly aware of what there is, not merely to be confined to its own representations. But he insists that consciousness is only aware of those aspects of being that are *apparent* from its point of view, and so does not comprehend the full truth of being. Consciousness knows being to stand over against us, but does not bring to mind the universal categorial form immanent in both being and thought. The "appearance" of which consciousness is aware is thus not opposed to being in itself, but encompasses those aspects of being in itself that consciousness can recognize: it is *being* itself as it is *for* consciousness.

According to Hegel, the idea that consciousness is merely aware of its own representations is not one that consciousness itself entertains. In his view, consciousness considers itself to be directly aware of what there is, but is told by epistemological philosophers, such as Locke, Kant, and Reinhold, that it is in fact only conscious of its own representations of being. The "natural idea," referred to at the beginning of the Introduction to the *Phenomenology* – that cognition is a "means" or "instrument" intervening between us and the world, and needing to be examined before being put to work in acquiring knowledge of that world – is not one that natural or ordinary consciousness itself forms, either, but is also advanced by epistemological philosophers.[23]

Hegel claims that this "natural" philosophical idea prevents us from believing that we can ever know the truth, but is in fact a quite unwarranted assumption. It prevents us from believing we can know the truth, by making us think (with Locke and Kant) that we are cut off from what is and immured within the structures of our own cognition, even though we ordinarily regard ourselves as conscious of the world itself. This "natural idea" is an unwarranted assumption, in Hegel's view, because it is grounded neither in the actual experience of ordinary consciousness itself nor in the properly self-critical, philosophical scrutiny of such experience. The Hegelian phenomenologist differs from the pre-Hegelian epistemologist, therefore, by suspending all uncritical philosophical assumptions "about cognition as an *instrument* and as a *medium*" (PG, 70; PS, 47) and simply analysing the certainties of ordinary consciousness itself.[24] The idea that the mind knows only its own representations, but not being itself, is thus simply set aside by Hegel as illegitimate; and phenomenology, accordingly, no longer tries to answer traditional epistemological questions, such as "how can we know that our representations match the world?" This question need no longer be addressed by the phenomenologist, because he is to be the thoroughly self-critical student of ordinary consciousness, who is permitted to take nothing of his own for granted about being, and, as such, has no right to assume at the start of phenomenology that being or the world is anything beyond what consciousness itself is directly aware of. He may not assert (with Kant and Locke), or even suspect (with Nietzsche), that being lies beyond consciousness in any way, nor that it is hidden from consciousness, but must understand being to be simply *that which consciousness is aware of.* Consequently, he has no need to try to establish a "match" between what we are conscious of and what there is. In claiming that consciousness is directly aware of what is, therefore, Hegel is not illegitimately assuming a correspondence between the mind and the world which would need to be proven; he is setting aside as unwarranted – by either common experience or philosophical self-criticism – the assumption that the two could be radically separate.

Note that phenomenology does not altogether dismiss the idea of examining the structure of knowledge, and in that sense does not simply turn its back on pre-Kantian epistemology. But it continues the work of such epistemology by setting aside its assumptions about knowledge, and examining the structure of cognition as consciousness itself describes it – just as Hegel's logic continues the work of ontologists, such as Spinoza, by setting aside their assumptions about being and examining the way being is minimally to be thought. Hegel's *Phenomenology* and *Logic* do not simply break with Kantian and pre-Kantian philosophy, therefore, but transform the two principal strands of that philosophy – epistemology and metaphysics – into two new, radically self-critical, presuppositionless disciplines.

Whereas the *Logic* unfolds the way being is truly to be *thought*, the *Phenomenology* unfolds the way being is experienced by consciousness. From the standpoint of thought, consciousness is aware not of the innermost truth of being – categorial form – but only of being's initial appearance as something "over there." But, according to Hegel, consciousness is nevertheless aware of aspects of what there *is*, not of mere representations of being. Hegel's procedure is to show that consciousness's own experience of being eventually leads it to the standpoint of thought. This procedure involves examining consciousness and asking whether it actually experiences and understands being as it claims it does. Hegel maintains that consciousness in fact never does so and that, as each shape of consciousness becomes aware of the way it actually experiences things, rather than the way it claims to understand them, it comes to be a new shape of consciousness. In this way, he argues, consciousness's own experience leads it to recognize that what it is aware of is not just "over there" after all, but is informed by a categorial structure comprehensible from *within* consciousness – or thought – itself (WL, 1:67–8; SL, 69).

Consciousness's initial experience of being will not be "disproven" in this process. Hegel will not argue that consciousness is simply wrong to think of the world as made up of perceivable things, or self-conscious agents, or forms of social and historical organization. He will argue that the experience of consciousness shows the world not *merely* to be determined in these ways. When consciousness realizes this, it ceases to be mere consciousness of a world over against it, and becomes the thought of what is universal and immanent in that world and in thought (WL, 1:60; SL, 62–3). (Pre-Kantian metaphysics, as we noted above, fails to dissolve the distinction between certainty and truth and so remains the consciousness through pure thought of that to which it relates.)

Consciousness in the *Phenomenology* does not, therefore, move out from its own "representations" to awareness of being "in itself." It moves from the direct consciousness of being itself to the direct thought of being itself. It always remains in touch with what is – and must do so, since "being" is simply that of which consciousness is aware – but it learns to understand more fully and intelligently the being that it has always known. Hegel's logic thus does not set out the structure of a world that lies beyond the realm of common experience; it articulates the immanent categorial form of the very being that consciousness experiences as "out there."[25] The important thing to note, however, is that consciousness is driven onto its clearer awareness or thought of being by its own experience of being, not by any ideas that intrude upon it from an outside authority such as philosophy.

6. The Method of *Phenomenology*

The method of Hegel's *Phenomenology* is given further elaboration in the Introduction. This method entails initially accepting the distinction consciousness draws between its own awareness of the object and the object of which it is aware. Consciousness takes itself to be directly aware of what there *is*; but, for precisely this reason, it takes the object of which it is aware to be real and independent of consciousness (PG, 76; PS, 52). Hegel maintains that this distinction requires consciousness to consider whether its awareness always matches the nature of the object itself. This question might seem to be redundant: for, if the object is nothing but that which consciousness knows, how could there fail to be a correspondence between the object and our knowledge of it? The question is not redundant, however: for, even though consciousness equates the object with what it knows, it also distinguishes its *knowledge* of that object from the *object* known, and thereby opens up the possibility that it may not actually know properly the very object it knows. "The object," Hegel writes, "seems only to be for consciousness in the way that consciousness knows it." But "the *distinction* between the in-itself and knowledge is already present in the very fact that consciousness knows an object at all" (PG, 78; PS, 54). Since consciousness distinguishes in this way between its own knowledge of the object and the object itself, it cannot but ask itself whether these two elements always correspond to one another. Although there is no principle of radical self-criticism in ordinary consciousness, therefore, there is a need to assure ourselves that we do actually understand our object properly. The very structure of our ordinary certainty itself – the fact that we are certain of what is distinct from us – requires that we examine that certainty in order to make certain we are getting things right.

In seeking this assurance, consciousness cannot step outside its own perspective and compare its understanding of the object with the object viewed, as it were, "from nowhere." Consciousness has to consider whether its understanding corresponds to the object as this latter is *for consciousness* itself. The standard or "measure" (*Maßstab*) that consciousness must use to assess the adequacy of its knowledge is thus "what consciousness affirms from within itself as *being-in-itself* or the *True*" (PG, 77; PS, 53). Consciousness is required, by the distinction it draws between its own knowledge and the object itself, to consider whether it properly understands that which it itself regards as its object.

Hegel believes that this is a question consciousness is perfectly capable of answering:

> Consciousness is, on the one hand, consciousness of the object, and, on the other, consciousness of itself; consciousness of what for it is the True, and consciousness of its knowledge of the truth. Since both are *for* the same consciousness, this consciousness is itself their comparison; it is for this same consciousness to know whether its knowledge of the object corresponds to the object or not. (PG, 77–8; PS, 54)

Furthermore, Hegel believes that consciousness invariably discovers that it does not actually understand its own object adequately. The object of consciousness is nothing but that of which it is conscious; but the way consciousness actually understands that object does not always overlap with what it takes or declares its object to be.

To the extent that consciousness's actual understanding or knowledge of its object diverges from what it takes its object to be, "it would seem that consciousness must alter its knowledge to make it conform to the object," that is, to make it consistent with its initial, stated conception of its object (PG, 78; PS, 54). However, the understanding consciousness has reached arises, in Hegel's account, not through any arbitrary fancy of consciousness, but through consciousness's attention to what its own object shows itself to be. That understanding cannot, therefore, simply be rejected or revised because it constitutes *new knowledge of the object itself*; it discloses what the object of consciousness is in truth. What has to be revised, therefore, is the initial conception of the object, since consciousness now recognizes, in light of what it has learned, that that conception was not itself completely adequate and only presented the object as it initially appears to consciousness: "it comes to pass for consciousness that what it previously took to be the *in-itself* is not an *in-itself*, or that it was only an in-itself *for consciousness*" (PG, 78; PS, 54). Accordingly, consciousness now declares itself certain that the object has a new character – disclosed by its experience – and thereby comes to be a new shape of consciousness.

Each subsequent shape of consciousness undertakes a similar examination of its knowledge claims by measuring them against its own distinctive conception of its object, and eventually comes to revise that conception. Throughout the *Phenomenology*, therefore, consciousness continues to try to make certain that it is understanding its object properly; but it does so by measuring its understanding against a standard that constantly changes (PG, 78; PS, 54).

Hegel's analysis continues until consciousness discovers that its understanding of its object does not actually correspond to the stated definition of an object of consciousness at all. An object of consciousness is stated to be something known by consciousness, but standing over against consciousness. Consciousness eventually discovers, however, that it actually understands its object to have one and the same categorial structure as itself, and so not simply to stand over against consciousness after all. At that point, consciousness realizes that it is no longer mere consciousness, but has become thought or absolute knowing.

The dialectical movement through which a new understanding of its object – and so a new object – constantly arises for consciousness is understood by Hegel to constitute the *experience* (*Erfahrung*) of consciousness (PG, 78; PS, 55). This experience is not an historical experience that every individual necessarily makes in his or her own life, but the experience that is logically entailed by the structure of ordinary consciousness itself. It is the experience through which ordinary consciousness is taken, by its own internal logic, from its most primitive shape of sense certainty, through perception, understanding, self-consciousness, reason, spirit, and religion, to philosophy or absolute knowing, but which concrete historical individuals all too often fail to comprehend.

7. Sense Certainty

Hegelian phenomenology continues the project of pre-Kantian epistemology and Kantian transcendental philosophy by presenting a close examination of our several claims to know our world adequately. Hegel differs from his predecessors, however, by setting out the process whereby consciousness examines its own knowledge claims, rather than testing those claims himself. Furthermore, the nature of the examination of knowledge undertaken in the *Phenomenology* differs from those undertaken before. Descartes, Locke, and Kant all understood the mind to be directly aware of its own representations and sought to explain how those representations can be connected to the world (Descartes), or built up (Locke) or synthesized (Kant) into coherent experience. Hegel, by contrast, understands the mind to be directly aware of what there *is*, and so is not concerned to explain how our representations can count as knowledge of anything. He is concerned, rather, to examine the structure of our awareness of what is, and to show that we do not always understand *what we are directly aware of* quite as we initially think we do. Hegel also shows that consciousness is driven by this tension in its own certainty to new and more sophisticated levels of understanding of its object, which eventually culminate in absolute knowing. In contrast to Descartes, Locke, and Kant, therefore, Hegel's analysis of the structure of consciousness shows how consciousness develops, through its own immanent dialectic, into higher forms of itself. He offers an account of consciousness that is both logical-structural *and* dynamic at the same time.

Hegel's account begins with an analysis of the most primitive shape of consciousness: sense certainty.[26] Such certainty has before it the rich and varied content of sensation, but it attends solely to the simple immediacy of what it perceives. That is to say, it registers what it sees and hears, not as red in contrast to green, or as the sound of a bird as opposed to a car, but purely as *this*, of which I am aware here and now. Sense certainty takes itself to be conscious, therefore, of the sheer immediate being of things, not of the ways they relate to one another or are categorized by language: "all that it says about what it knows is just that it *is*; and its truth contains nothing but the sheer *being* of the thing" (PG, 82; PS, 58).

Hegel's examination of sense certainty shows, however, that sense certainty does not actually experience its object quite as it thinks it does. Paradoxically, this is due to the very character it claims for its object. Sense certainty declares that no concept mediates its awareness, but that it is directly conscious of its object – whether it be night, day, a tree or a house – in its undiluted immediacy. It is not conscious of the tree *as* a tree, therefore, but simply as *this*, *here*, *now* before me. In saying this, sense certainty imagines that it is immediately aware of the pure particularity of the thing. But by themselves the terms, "this," "here," and "now," are in fact quite indeterminate. They apply equally to anything we encounter: everything we turn to can be said to be "this," "here," "now." In being conscious of an object – say, a tree – merely as *this*, we are thus not actually attending to the distinctive particularity of that thing after all, but are merely bringing to mind the universal form of presence – of being this, here, now – that all things exhibit. The very way in which sense certainty conceives of its object – as simply *this* – thus denies such certainty precisely what it imagined it was enjoying: direct acquaintance with pure particularity. Sense certainty turns out not actually to be conscious of what it initially took itself to be conscious of.

The logical response to this problem is not for consciousness to abandon its initial understanding of its object altogether, but to modify that understanding slightly. Its object can no longer be thought of simply as *this*, *here*, *now*, because that fails to distinguish it from anything else. Consciousness, however, can still preserve the sense that it is touching the pure particularity of the thing before it by noting that its object is not some general "thisness," but what *I* in particular mean by this – what *this* I, *here*, *now* am immediately aware of. As Hegel puts it, "the force of its [sense certainty's] truth thus lies now in the 'I,' in the immediacy of my *seeing*, *hearing*, and so on" (PG, 86; PS, 61).

But, of course, the same problem arises as before. Sense certainty has before it a particular thing – this tree or this house – but does not think of that thing, in terms of mediating concepts, *as* a tree or *as* a house. Sense certainty thinks of it simply as what *I* am immediately conscious of – as the immediate object of *my* certainty. In so doing, sense certainty believes it has in mind something specific and unique to it: the pure particularity and immediacy of the thing as they are present to the I. But the word "I," taken by itself, is just as indeterminate and universal as the word "this." If, therefore, all I say about the thing before me is that it is what *I* am immediately conscious of, here and now – without specifying who I am or locating myself in space and time – then once again I fail to distinguish it from anything any other subject is aware of. Every subject can say that its object is what *I* am immediately aware of. So what makes my object distinctive, if all I say of it is that it is that of which I am immediately aware? The answer is: nothing. It turns out, therefore, that I am actually conscious of the same thing as everyone else at this level of consciousness: namely, sheer indeterminate immediacy that is for the I, or the universal form of "presence-to-consciousness" as such.

Sense certainty learns in this way that neither the bare consciousness of *this*, nor the equally bare consciousness of what *I* mean by this, affords it the contact with pure, undiluted particularity to which it lays claim. In order to secure such contact, sense certainty subtly has to revise its conception of its object once more. It now declares itself to be aware of what I mean by this to the explicit *exclusion* of what any other subject might mean by this or of what I might mean by this at another time or place. Sense certainty still refuses to categorize or identify its object in any way. Whether the object it has before it is a tree or a house, consciousness focuses solely on the sheer immediate presence of that object and thinks of it simply as *this*, *here*, *now*. But it now holds fast to the object it has in view – say, this tree – and distinguishes it from that which anyone else is aware of, by declaring its object to be what *I* am aware of here and now, *not* what you or you or you are aware of (see PG, 88; PS, 62–3). Hegel maintains, however, that through the very act by which it picks out *this*, not that, as the object of its attention, consciousness reveals that its object cannot be thought of as simple immediacy after all, but must be conceived as a complex unity of different moments.

The problem sense certainty faces is this. It needs to pick out, from amongst a range of things, the particular immediacy constituting its object. It needs to point out to itself (and to others) that *this*, *here*, *now* – not *that* – is what it is immediately aware of. But the very act of pointing or picking out an immediacy – a now – and distinguishing it from other immediacies takes time. Pointing out to ourselves what is there before us *now* thus necessarily moves us on from that now to a subsequent now. What is pointed out, therefore, is, strictly speaking, a now that no longer exists, a now that *has been*. It does not matter how long the now concerned is taken to last – a minute, second, or nanosecond. What matters is that this now has to be pointed out by sense certainty in order to guarantee its distinct particularity, but the process of pointing out takes us beyond the very now that is to be highlighted. The process of pointing – however short or "immediate" it is – always culminates in the now having been pointed out at a later moment. Sense certainty can thus only bring to mind a now that *has been* pointed out – a now that *has been* and so no longer is.

> The *Now* is pointed to, *this Now*. *Now*; it has already ceased to be in the act of pointing to it. The *Now* that is, is another Now than the one pointed to, and we see that the

> Now is just this: to be no more just when it is. The Now, as it is pointed out to us, is a Now that *has been* [*ein gewesenes*], and this is its truth. (PG, 88; PS, 63)

Yet, what is pointed out cannot simply be that which now lies in the past. After all, it is that which *has* indeed been pointed out and so is now present to consciousness. Something *is* indeed picked out *now* by sense certainty, as the object of which it is immediately aware. Nevertheless, as we have just seen, what is pointed out is not something that is simply there *now*, but something that has been *pointed out* and so *has been*.

It is clear that the temporal structure of the object on which sense certainty focuses is complex. What is pointed out *is* present to consciousness *now*; but at the same time it is present to consciousness as also *having been*. Both these thoughts have to be held together. This means that the object of sense certainty cannot be a purely immediate now, but must be a now that stretches back in time and is continuous with previous nows: "The Now, and pointing out the Now, are thus so constituted that neither the one nor the other is something immediate and simple, but a movement which contains various moments" (PG, 89; PS, 63–4). This movement and continuity of the now through time is what sense certainty now experiences its object to be.

Hegel's analysis of sense certainty does not, by the way, depend on the assumption that time is actually divided into discrete units called "nows." His analysis rests on the insight that pointing out what is before us *now*, itself moves us beyond the simple immediacy we wish to point out. The object that sense certainty picks out for itself, therefore, can only be an immediacy – a now – that has a past and so constitutes a complex continuity of different temporal moments – "a Now which is an absolute plurality of Nows" (PG, 89; PS, 64). Similarly, the immediacy of what is *here* can only be pointed out as a "simple complex of many heres," as "a *this* Here which, in fact, is *not* this Here, but a Before and Behind, an Above and Below, a Right and Left" (PG, 89; PS, 64).

The very act through which consciousness tries to hold on to *this* shows consciousness that its object is not actually a simple immediacy after all, but a complex unity of different moments. Such a complex unity is itself immediate in that it *is* what consciousness is now aware of; but it is precisely a complex unity, not pure simplicity or pure particularity. When consciousness accepts this new conception of its object, it ceases being mere sense certainty and becomes a new shape of consciousness: perception.[27]

8. Spirit, Religion, and Absolute Knowing

Hegel's analysis of sense certainty clearly exemplifies the process of self-discovery described in the Introduction to the *Phenomenology*. Consciousness initially takes its object in a certain way, but comes, through experience, to a fuller understanding of that object. In this process, Hegel says, "we learn by experience that we [actually] mean something other than we meant to mean" (PG, 60; PS, 39). Specifically, consciousness learns that its object is in fact not pure immediacy but a concrete object of perception – just as thought, at the beginning of the *Logic*, also recognizes that being is not mere immediacy, but rather determinacy, being-something-in-relation-to-others, and finitude.

This same process of discovery is undergone by every subsequent shape of consciousness in the *Phenomenology*. Perception discovers that its object is not merely a thing with multiple properties, but the concrete expression of invisible, inner force. At this point, perception becomes understanding. Understanding discovers that the inner character of things is not just force, but force governed by law – the same lawfulness that governs understanding itself. Understanding thus finds a dimension of itself in the things it encounters and so becomes *self-consciousness*. Self-consciousness then discovers that the objects to which it relates are not just law-governed objects in nature, but other living, self-conscious beings – self-conscious beings who confirm our own consciousness of ourselves by recognizing us, but whose recognition of us we in turn have to recognize (PG, 145; PS, 111).

In this way, self-consciousness acquires a sense that an individual's identity does not belong to that individual alone, but is constituted by his or her social interaction with others. Self-consciousness comes to regard itself as part of a "unity of different independent self-consciousnesses which, in their opposition, enjoy perfect freedom and independence." That is to say, it begins to think of itself as an "*I* that is *We* and *We* that is *I*" (PG, 145; PS, 110). This social (and historical) unity of different self-consciousnesses is named by Hegel *spirit* (*Geist*) and is understood to constitute the "absolute substance" of those individuals who belong to it.

The relation between the "master" and the "slave" is a social-spiritual one, in that each is tied inextricably to the other: the slave takes his direction from the master, and the master needs the slave to prepare natural objects for his consumption. But the master and slave do not yet acknowledge any common identity or purpose. Their relation is thus not yet a fully spiritual one, but one in which each focuses primarily on himself and his superiority over, or subordination to, the other. Only when there emerges an explicit, shared recognition of a common identity between people, embodied in the laws and institutions of the society they form, does self-consciousness become spirit proper. The basic shape of such spirit, Hegel maintains, is that found in the Greek world depicted in Sophocles' *Antigone*.

At this point the phenomenology of consciousness becomes the phenomenology of *spirit*. Consciousness does not suddenly disappear from Hegel's book, however, but remains an important moment of spirit itself. This is evident from the fact that the spirit Hegel examines remains conscious of itself as spirit. That is to say, it continues to regard its own social, historical, and spiritual character, at least to some extent, as something "over there" – for example, as constituting the world into which individuals are born.

Spiritual consciousness does not, however, just understand itself to be social and historical. It also comes to understand itself as ontologically grounded, as the self-consciousness that being itself – or the "Absolute" – comes to exhibit. The shape of consciousness or spirit that understands itself and "absolute" being in this way is religion, in particular Christianity (PG, 552; PS, 459). In religion, consciousness is not just aware of natural objects or its own social-spiritual character; it understands being as such to become self-conscious in and as human self-consciousness. In this way religious consciousness finds itself included in absolute being, as the very goal and fulfillment of being.

Religious consciousness also finds itself in absolute being in another way, however. For it understands being not just to be nature, but to be God who gives rise to nature and humanity; and it understands God to be infinite, eternal "essence" or reason (*Begriff*) (PG, 558–9; PS, 464–5). For religion, therefore, absolute, "divine" being not only becomes self-conscious in and through human beings, it has the same rational structure as human thought, albeit in an infinite rather than finite form. As Hegel puts it, "the object has the form of *Self* (*Selbst*) in its relation to consciousness." This means that "consciousness knows itself immediately in the object, or is manifest to itself in the object" (PG, 552; PS, 459).

But consciousness still conceives of being, or God, as the "object [*Gegenstand*] of consciousness" (PG, 552; PS, 459), as that which, initially at least, is distinct from human consciousness itself. Yes, God realizes himself (or, rather, itself) *in* humanity; but the process of divine self-realization is understood to be the work of God, not of man. It is conceived of as "the deed of an *alien* [*fremd*] satisfaction." In other words, the power through which divine being develops into human being is understood to reside in divine being alone; the conscious self "does not find it in its *own* action as such" (PG, 573; PS, 477–8).

Religious consciousness changes into absolute knowing, however, when it recognizes that this "power" is actually reason, or the Concept (*Begriff*), that is to be found in both being as such and human consciousness itself. At this point, consciousness ceases to be *consciousness* as such, and becomes thought: for its "object" is no longer simply being "over there," but the universal rational or conceptual structure immanent in being and thought itself (PG, 588–9; PS, 490–1).

The *Phenomenology* culminates, then, in ordinary consciousness becoming aware, not just of its own social, historical, and spiritual character, but of the true nature of being. Consciousness turns, through its own inherent dialectic, into metaphysical thought. The point of the *Phenomenology* is thus not simply to show that consciousness is irreducibly social and historical, but to demonstrate that the metaphysical project of the *Logic* is made necessary by the certainties of ordinary consciousness itself. Post-Hegelian thinkers who would like to uncouple the *Phenomenology* from the *Logic* miss the whole point of Hegel's phenomenological analysis.

The *Phenomenology* also shows, however, that ordinary consciousness could not become absolute knowing without first becoming aware of its social and historical character. There are two reasons for this. First, if consciousness is, as it were, to grow up into mature thought, it must recognize that individuals do not owe their character solely to themselves and their own freedom or perspicacity, but are indebted in various ways to a reality that is greater than they are. As philosophers (and religious believers), they will recognize that they are indebted to the rational development of being itself, insofar as they are simply being that has become self-conscious. According to the *Phenomenology*, however, the first recognition of indebtedness comes with the acknowledgment that our character is constituted by the social and historical (and, of course, natural) relations into which we are born. Understanding that we are products of our society and history, as well as nature, thus proves to be a crucial first step towards understanding that we are produced by the rational drive within the very fabric of being towards self-consciousness.

Second, if consciousness is to become mature thought, it must learn to recognize that being is not just something over against us – a *Gegen-stand* – but is informed by the very same rationality, or categorial structure, that informs our thought. This means that we must come to understand being, not just as being, but as reason; and this in turn means that we must come to see being as having the same *form* as our own thought: the "self-like *form* in which existence is immediately thought" (PG, 589; PS, 491; see PG, 582–3; PS, 485). (As we noted above, this does not mean that natural objects such as stones must be conscious, but that being is intrinsically rational.) We can only understand being properly, therefore, when we learn to recognize a dimension of ourselves in being, that is, when our consciousness of being is at the same time *self-* consciousness. This is why Hegel claims that self-consciousness is "the native realm of truth" (PG, 138; PS, 104). It is not sufficient, however, to be conscious merely of one's individual freedom (or subservience), as the master and the slave are. Consciousness must develop a full understanding of the *universal* character of consciousness – of all that it means to be a conscious self as such. This, Hegel argues, includes discovering that consciousness has a social and historical character and then, later, that it is informed by absolute reason. The absolute knowing that finds its own rational, categorial structure in the very fabric of being thus necessarily knows itself to be a social and historical knowing. This is not to say that absolute knowing is a *relation of consciousness* to the social and historical world into which we are born; such knowing has ceased to be mere consciousness and becomes the pure thought of that which is immanent in thought itself (and in being). Nevertheless, absolute knowing recognizes that its own capacity for immanent self-understanding is socially and historically constituted.[28]

At the end of the *Phenomenology*, both the consciousness that is being examined and the reader of Hegel's text become absolute knowers – knowers released or "absolved" from the "opposition of consciousness" (WL, 1:43; SL, 49) – and so share the perspective of the speculative philosopher. Absolute knowing understands that it (and its science of logic) is made logically necessary by the tensions within ordinary consciousness. But it also understands that it is a social and historical phenomenon. This means two things. On the one hand, absolute knowing recognizes that the science of logic – and, consequently, phenomenology as well – can in fact only be undertaken at a certain point in *history*: namely, once Kant has developed his new concept of objectivity, and the modern spirit of radical self-criticism (promoted by Kant and others) has given rise to the idea of a presuppositionless study of thought and being. On the other hand, absolute knowing recognizes that the categorial development traced in the science of logic – and the development of consciousness set out in phenomenology – is *publicly* determinable, that is, "exoteric, comprehensible, and capable of being learned and appropriated by all" (PG, 20; PS, 7), and not, as Michael Rosen claims, accessible only to some mystical neo-Platonic intuition.[29]

At the start of the science of logic absolute knowing *abstracts* from all it knows (and all we traditionally assume) thought to be and starts from the least that thought can be. It thus begins from the thought of thought, not *as* social and historical (nor *as* made logically necessary by ordinary consciousness), but *as* sheer being. In this way, it is able to provide a rigorously self- critical derivation of the categories that takes for granted as little as possible about thought. Yet absolute knowing recognizes that, in so doing, it is fulfilling a modern *historical* demand. It is thus a knowing freed from the dominance of ordinary consciousness, but still aware of its social and historical character.[30] Indeed, this, to my mind, is the lasting legacy of Hegel's *Phenomenology*: that, far from preventing us from understanding the absolute character of being, the social and historical character of thought is precisely what makes *absolute* understanding possible and necessary. Unfortunately, this is a legacy that all too few post-Hegelians have been willing to inherit.

Notes

1 T. Rockmore, *Before and After Hegel: A Historical Introduction to Hegel's Thought* (Berkeley: University of California Press, 1993), p. 76.

2 For an overview of Hegel's whole system, see J. N. Findlay, *Hegel: A Reexamination* (Oxford: Oxford University Press, 1976), and S. Houlgate, *Freedom, Truth and History: An Introduction to Hegel's Philosophy* (London: Routledge, 1991).

3 G. W. F. Hegel, *Wissenschaft der Logik*, eds. E. Moldenhauer and K. M. Michel, 2 vols. (Frankfurt am Main: Suhrkamp Verlag, 1969), 1:38; G. W. F. Hegel, *Science of Logic*, tr. A. V. Miller (Atlantic Highlands, NJ: Humanities Press, 1989), p. 45. Further references to the *Logic* will be given in the following form: WL, 1:38; SL, 45. Translations throughout this chapter have occasionally been modified. For a fuller account of Hegel's view of metaphysics, see S. Houlgate, *Hegel, Nietzsche and the Criticism of Metaphysics* (Cambridge: Cambridge University Press, 1986), ch. 4.

4 G. W. F. Hegel, *Enzyklopädie der philosophischen Wissenschaft im Grundrisse (1830). Erster Teil: Die Wissenschaft der Logik*, eds. E. Moldenhauer and K. M. Michel (Frankfurt am Main: Suhrkamp Verlag, 1970), p. 93 [sec. 26]; G. W. F. Hegel, *The Encyclopaedia Logic*, tr. T. F. Geraets, W. A. Suchting, and H. S. Harris (Indianapolis: Hackett, 1991), p. 65. Further references to the *Encyclopaedia Logic* will be given in the following form: EWL, 93 [sec. 26]; EL, 65.

5 See Hegel, WL, 1:36, 43; SL, 44, 49, on the connection between pre-Hegelian logic, ordinary consciousness, and the truth/certainty distinction.

6 G. W. F. Hegel, *Vorlesungen über die Geschichte der Philosophie*, eds. E. Moldenhauer and K. M. Michel, 3 vols. (Frankfurt am Main: Suhrkamp Verlag, 1971), 3:122–267; G. W. F. Hegel, *Lectures on the History of Philosophy*, tr. E. S. Haldane and F. H. Simson, 3 vols. [1896] (London: Routledge and Kegan Paul, 1955), 3:217–360.

7 I. Kant, *Critique of Pure Reason*, tr. N. Kemp Smith (London: Macmillan, 1929), p.

126 [B 126].

8 See Kant, *Critique of Pure Reason*, p. 126 [B 126].

9 R. Pippin, *Hegel's Idealism: The Satisfactions of Self-Consciousness* (Cambridge: Cambridge University Press, 1989), p. 188.

10 *A Spinoza Reader*, ed. E. Curley (Princeton: Princeton University Press, 1994), p. 124 [*Ethics*, II, Prop. 13, Schol.]. See Hegel, EWL, 81 [sec. 24 Addition 1]; EL, 56.

11 See, for example, Hegel, WL, 1:45; 2:257; SL, 51, 586, and EWL, 81 [sec. 24]; EL, 56.

12 For a detailed analysis of Hegel's *Logic*, see J. Burbidge, *On Hegel's Logic: Fragments of a Commentary* (Atlantic Highlands, NJ: Humanities Press, 1981).

13 A. Schopenhauer, *The World as Will and Representation* (1819, 1844), tr. E. F. J. Payne, 2 vols. (New York: Dover Publications, 1969), 1:xxiv.

14 G. W. F. Hegel, *Phänomenologie des Geistes*, eds. E. Moldenhauer and K. M. Michel (Frankfurt am Main: Suhrkamp Verlag, 1970), p. 30; G. W. F. Hegel, *Phenomenology of Spirit*, tr. A. V. Miller (Oxford: Oxford University Press, 1977), p. 15. Further references to the *Phenomenology* will be given in the following form: PG, 30; PS, 15. See also M. Forster, *Hegel's Idea of a Phenomenology of Spirit* (Chicago: University of Chicago Press, 1998), pp. 105–6.

15 On Hegel's debt to Sextus Empiricus, see K. Westphal, *Hegel's Epistemological Realism* (Dordrecht: Kluwer, 1989), pp. 10–16, 97–114, and M. Forster, *Hegel's Idea of a Phenomenology of Spirit*, pp. 150–8. On Hegel's debt to Fichte, see, for example, H. S. Harris, *Hegel's Ladder*, 2 vols. (Indianapolis: Hackett, 1997), 1:9–11, 16–17.

16 See Hegel, PG, 73; PS, 50, and J. Hyppolite, *Genesis and Structure of Hegel's Phenomenology of Spirit* (1946), tr. S. Cherniak and J. Heckman (Evanston, Ill.: Northwestern University Press, 1974), p. 48.

17 See K. R. Dove, "Hegel's Phenomenological Method," in *The Phenomenology of Spirit Reader: Critical and Interpretive Essays*, ed. J. Stewart (Albany: SUNY Press, 1998), p. 57: "Hegel's Method is Radically *un*dialectical. It is the experience of consciousness itself which is dialectical and Hegel's *Phenomenology* . . . merely *describes* this dialectical process." See also W. Maker, *Philosophy Without Foundations: Rethinking Hegel* (Albany: SUNY Press, 1994), ch. 5.

18 See W. Marx, *Hegel's Phenomenology of Spirit: Its Point and Purpose*, tr. P. Heath (New York: Harper & Row, 1975), p. 27, and U. Claesges, *Darstellung des erscheinenden Wissens: Systematische Einleitung in Hegel's Phänomenologie des Geistes*, *Hegel Studien* Beiheft 21 (Bonn: Bouvier Verlag, 1981), p. 59.

19 See Marx, *Hegel's Phenomenology of Spirit*, p. 96.

20 Werner Marx writes that absolute knowing "'behaves' towards phenomenal knowledge *as if* it had not yet produced the concept of knowledge" (ibid., p. 91, my italics).

21 Dove, "Hegel's Phenomenological Method," p. 68.

22 On Hegel's debt to J. H. Lambert, Kant, and K. L. Reinhold, who all employed the term "phenomenology" before Hegel, see Harris, *Hegel's Ladder*, 1:16.

23 See Hegel, PG, 68–9; PS, 46–7. Robert Pippin, by contrast, argues that "the assumption that generates a critical skepticism . . . is precisely the assumption that Hegel attributes to natural consciousness" (*Hegel's Idealism*, p. 111).

24 Michael Forster argues – in my view, mistakenly – that Hegel accepts the distinction, drawn by Kant and Reinhold, between consciousness, its representation, and the object. See Forster, *Hegel's Idea of a Phenomenology of Spirit*, pp. 116–18.

25 See, for example, Hegel, EWL, 47–8 [sec. 6]; EL, 28–9.

26 On the precise reasons why Hegel begins with sense certainty, see J. C. Flay, *Hegel's Quest for Certainty* (Albany: SUNY Press, 1984), p. 15.

27 On the parallels between Hegel's immanent critique of sense certainty and Wittgenstein's arguments against a purely private language , see C. Taylor, "The Opening Arguments of the Phenomenology," in *Hegel: A Collection of Critical Essays* (1972), ed. A. MacIntyre (Notre Dame: University of Notre Dame Press, 1976), pp. 151–87, and S. Houlgate, *Hegel, Nietzsche and the Criticism of Metaphysics*, pp. 167–75.

28 For a critique of the claim that absolute knowing is a relation of consciousness to its own intersubjective, historical conditions, see S. Houlgate, "Absolute Knowing Revisited," *The Owl of Minerva* 30 (1998), pp. 51–67.

29 See M. Rosen, *Hegel's Dialectic and its Criticism* (Cambridge: Cambridge University Press, 1982), p. 179.

30 At the end of the *Phenomenology*, therefore, absolute knowing does not (as William Maker appears to suggest) collapse *directly* into the thought of pure being with which the *Logic* begins. Such knowing has been freed from the assumptions of consciousness, but still recognizes the need to suspend all other convictions before beginning the science of logic: "[S]tarting from this determination of pure knowledge [the ultimate, absolute truth of *consciousness*], all that is needed to ensure that the beginning remains immanent in its scientific development is to consider – or rather, *ridding oneself of all other reflections and opinions whatsoever*, simply to take up – what is there before us" (WL, 1:67–8; SL, 68–9, my italics). I agree with Maker, however, that "the Phenomenology does not serve to deduce the concept of science by in any way predetermining or grounding the method, manner or nature of scientific cognition." See Maker, *Philosophy Without Foundations*, pp. 71–4.

Chapter 14

Søren Kierkegaard

C. Stephen Evans

Søren Kierkegaard (1813–55) is universally regarded as one of the most influential thinkers of the nineteenth century, even though much of that influence was not felt until the twentieth century. In many ways, Kierkegaard is a "man for all disciplines," whose writings are important for psychology, theology, and literary theory, as well as philosophy. Much of Kierkegaard's philosophical writings are highly literary in character, so that he is sometimes justly described as a "kind of poet."[1]

Kierkegaard's historical influence has been extensive and diverse. In the middle of the twentieth century, he was probably best known as the "father of existentialism" because of his influence on such writers as Martin Heidegger, Jean Paul Sartre, and Albert Camus, even though each of these writers is in many ways profoundly different from Kierkegaard and even opposed to many aspects of his thought. More recently, Kierkegaard has been avidly discussed by "postmodernists" who see him as breaking with the kind of Enlightenment thinking associated with modernity, especially by challenging various rationalistic epistemologies.[2] Still other philosophers have read Kierkegaard in ways that reflect the subtle thinking about language exhibited by Ludwig Wittgenstein.[3] Many others influenced by Kierkegaard simply resist categorization.

Kierkegaard's importance as a philosopher is sometimes minimized because of his strong religious interests. Heidegger in *Being and Time*, for example, mentions Kierkegaard very rarely, and though he offers praise to Kierkegaard as the person who has gone farthest in analyzing the phenomena of anxiety and vision, the overall picture is of a thinker who does not see things from an "existential" and "ontological" point of view, as does Heidegger himself, because he is not a true philosopher.[4] (Nevertheless, a knowledgeable reader of *Being and Time* cannot help but see the deep influence of Kierkegaard at many points where the influence is not acknowledged, such as Heidegger's analysis of what it means to understand death existentially.)[5] Such attempts to marginalize Kierkegaard, however, surely reflect a post-Enlightenment view of philosophy that is alien to the philosophical tradition in ancient and medieval times, as well as in non-Western cultures. Part of

Kierkegaard's own genius is his sure grasp that philosophy is an activity done by real human beings who are historically situated, and whose philosophizing cannot be divorced from their concerns as humans, including their religious concerns.

1. Is There a Unity to Kierkegaard's Writings?

Kierkegaard's writings are extremely varied in character. Not only do his books vary tremendously; even different passages from the same work may be quite diverse. Some of his writing is highly literary and poetic; some passages have a novelistic quality. Some sections are heavily philosophical; others are quite theological. Many works and passages are devotional or "edifying" in nature. Quite a lot of the writing is highly polemical, directed against philosophers, theologians, church leaders, and established society in "Christendom" generally. Broadly speaking, the writings, or "authorship" as Kierkegaard terms it, can be divided into two streams: a series of "aesthetic" writings attributed to pseudonyms and a series of "religious" writings mostly published under Kierkegaard's own name. The latter series begins with a number of *Edifying* ("Upbuilding" in the Hongs' rather literal translation of the Danish "*opbyggelige*") *Discourses* and continues through such works as *Christian Discourses*, *Works of Love*, *Judge for Yourself*, and *Practice in Christianity*. The former, "aesthetic" series, begins with *Either/Or* and continues with such works as *Fear and Trembling*, *Repetition*, and *Stages on Life's Way*.

In the face of this diversity, it is natural to wonder whether it is helpful to look for any unifying thread or theme, and it is a question that Kierkegaard himself recognizes that readers will ask because of the complexity of the authorship. In *The Point of View for My Work as An Author* Kierkegaard says that the ambiguity or duplicity of the authorship might lead a reader to ask, "Can the phenomenon not be explained in another way, that it is an author who first was an esthetic author and then in the course of years *changed* and became a religious author?"[6] Kierkegaard's own answer to this question is a resounding no. Instead, he makes a protestation or confession, one that he says may be permissible and satisfying to himself as a human being and one that may be required of him as a religious individual: "The content, then, of this little book is: what I in truth am as an author, that I am and was a religious author, that my whole authorship pertains to Christianity, to the issue: 'becoming a Christian', . . . " (23).

In making this protestation, Kierkegaard specifically disavows any special authority or insight, affirming that he must be able to substantiate his claim "in the capacity of a third party, as a reader" (33). He presents as evidence, among other things, the fact that the two types of literature are simultaneous rather than successive, with the *Edifying Discourses* appearing right at the beginning of the authorship in such a way as to accompany the aesthetic works. The most important argument is his claim that, if one assumes he was first (or always) an aesthetic author, the religious writings cannot be explained (30). However, if one assumes his confession is true, and that he was from first to last a religious author, the aesthetic writings can be explained along the following lines.

Since the majority of people in Christendom actually live their lives in aesthetic categories, in order to "reintroduce Christianity into Christendom" it made sense for Kierkegaard to approach his contemporaries on aesthetic grounds, to meet them on their own turf, so to speak (43–4). His hope was that in this way he could eventually get people to reflect on the defining problem of the whole authorship: "becoming a Christian" (31). Clearly, Kierkegaard is right when he says that the ultimate test of this is not his own affirmation, but whether or not this way of reading his texts makes sense of them for the reader. The reader then ultimately must make a judgment.

One might well wonder how Kierkegaard's writings could have general philosophical interest if his primary goal was to be a kind of missionary to a supposedly Christian society. The answer to this question lies in his understanding of the relationship of human existence to Christian faith. As Kierkegaard sees Christianity, it is primarily a way of existence, an answer to the question as to how human life is to be lived. One might say that Christianity is one way of answering the riddle posed by human existence – not a theoretical answer, though it does engage and transform the way an individual thinks about himself or herself and the world, but a practical answer. However, if one misunderstands the question, or worse, fails even to ask the right question, one cannot possibly understand the answer. Hence, Kierkegaard's project of "reintroducing Christianity into Christendom" required him to think deeply about the nature of human existence and the human situation, and his thinking on these subjects has been powerful and influential even on those who do not share his Christian faith.

Critics have often argued that Kierkegaard's confession in *The Point of View* represents a retrospective view, the perspective he wished people to take of his writings after their completion, rather than the intentions he had at the time of writing. To some degree this accusation is correct, and indeed is conceded by Kierkegaard, who says that he did not at the beginning have a clear or precise understanding of what he was doing (76–7). Paradoxically, he says of his project "I certainly am the one who has done it and with reflection has taken every step," though he cannot understand that he now understands so clearly what was not so clear to him at the time he was working it out (77). Kierkegaard himself wishes to say that the unity of the authorship is therefore to be attributed to the role of divine "Governance" (*Styrelse*) in his life.

Of course some readers will be inclined to look for other explanations. Nevertheless, if we bracket the theological explanation, Kierkegaard's description of his life as an author is not in fact all that unusual. Some writers plan a book out and outline everything ahead of time. Others prefer to work things out as they go along, perhaps discovering what they want to say in the process of saying it. If that can be true of an individual book, it certainly can be true of an entire authorship. The fact that Kierkegaard's own understanding of the purpose and unity of his writings evolved as he wrote does not imply that the unity and purpose he claims is illusory.

Some postmodern critics may have a different objection, arguing not that Kierkegaard's claims are suspicious because retrospective, but that the whole notion of a unified "author" is philosophically suspect.[7] However, such postmodern critics, curiously and paradoxically, usually spend a great deal of effort in trying to argue that their view of "authorship" is precisely that of Kierkegaard the author himself.[8] They seem to say that we ought not to think that there is a possibility of a unified authorship, because this was the view of the (unified?) author Kierkegaard. We thus see that it is difficult to engage a human author in a conversation, however complex and polyphonic the author's voice may be, without assuming that there is indeed someone who is speaking with us. In any case, so long as we are allowed to engage the other great philosophers of the past, such as Plato, Aristotle, Descartes, and Kant, in a dialogue, there seems no reason to forbid people from seeking to hear what Kierkegaard has to say as well.

2. Interpreting Kierkegaard and the Question of Truth

Can Kierkegaard make good his claim that a religious reading of his writings makes sense of them as a unified whole? It hardly seems possible that any kind of objective "proof" can be given for such an interpretive question; nor did Kierkegaard think that this could be done. One might conclude from the fact that there is no "method" that can be guaranteed to resolve such a dispute that the dispute is unresolvable, but this is not Kierkegaard's own conclusion.

We here touch on an issue that goes right to the heart of Kierkegaard's epistemology – his views on truth, knowledge, and belief. Kierkegaard himself acknowledges that his authorship is ambiguous and complex and can be read in more than one way. Does this not imply that any "protestation" or "declaration" on his part simply undermines the authorship by resolving its inherent ambiguity? Kierkegaard claims that such an argument "seems very perspicacious, and yet is actually only subtle."[9]

To see why he believes this is so, we must think about Kierkegaard's notion of subjectivity. Kierkegaard is preeminent as a philosopher of subjectivity, but it is crucial to see what role subjectivity plays in his thinking. His philosophy is far from subjectivism. Perhaps the most crucial passage is the famous discussion of "truth as subjectivity" by his pseudonym Johannes Climacus in *Concluding Unscientific Postscript*:

> *When the question about truth is asked objectively, truth is reflected upon objectively as an object to which the knower relates himself. What is reflected upon is not the relation but that what he relates himself to is the truth, the true. If only that to which he relates himself is the truth, the true, then the subject is in the truth. When the question about truth is asked subjectively, the individual's relation is reflected upon subjectively. If only the how of this relation is in truth, the individual is in truth, even if he in this way were to relate himself to untruth.*[10]

This passage does not imply that there is no such thing as objective propositional truth. To the contrary, the possibility that a person who believes what is not true may still be in the truth explicitly presupposes that beliefs may be true or false. The passage claims that when we judge whether a person's *life* is true, the most important question is not the objective truth of the person's beliefs, but the way those beliefs have been appropriated and have transformed the individual's existence.[11]

This claim does not imply, however, that Kierkegaard thinks that true beliefs are unimportant or unattainable for humans.[12] On the contrary, Kierkegaard is convinced that we humans do need the truth, at least the moral and religious truth essential to human life, and can attain it, but only through subjectivity.

> Truly, no more than God allows a species of fish to come into existence in a particular lake unless the plant that is its nourishment is also growing there, no more will God allow the truly concerned person to be ignorant of what he is to believe. That is, the need brings its nourishment along with it, what is sought is in the seeking that seeks it; faith is in the concern over not having faith; love is in the self-concern over not loving. . . . The need brings the nourishment along with it, not *by itself*. . . but by virtue of a divine commandment that joins the two, the need and the nourishment.[13]

Moral and religious truths cannot be grasped by just anyone regardless of the person's degree of emotional maturity and personal concern. Rather, these truths can only be grasped when the seeker's life is qualified with the right kind of passion. This means they cannot be grasped without being appropriated, at least to some degree, and thus we see why a life that is "in the truth" is one that must be characterized not merely by believing the right things, but by the nature of its subjectivity.

Epistemologically, this position is quite different from two others that have dominated Western thinking. On the one hand, the dominant position in modern classical philosophy is to think that if there is objective truth, there must a method that guarantees us objective access to the truth. This is the reasoning that dominated modern philosophy's "classical foundationalist" ideal, with its search for the true method. The history of modern philosophy, both in the great rationalists such as Descartes, Spinoza, and Leibniz, and in empiricists such as Locke, can be seen as a dispute as to the nature of this proper method. This is a dispute that continues through Kant, Hegel, and even into the twentieth century, where both Edmund Husserl and the logical positivists in very different ways sought to make philosophy "scientific" by refining its method.

More recently, some postmodern philosophers, disillusioned by our failure to find such an objective method of reaching truth, have despaired of objective truth altogether.[14] Kierkegaard rejects the premise that both groups hold in common: that if there is objective truth there must be an objective method that guarantees access to that truth.

Kierkegaard holds that there is objective truth. His pseudonym Johannes Climacus affirms that reality or existence is a system for God.[15] However, there can be no existential system for us human beings. Existence itself is in process, as are we existers.

Furthermore, our thinking is always historically situated; we cannot see things from God's point of view, as both Spinoza and Hegel claimed to be able to do. Nevertheless, we are so constituted that when we are personally developed in the right way, developed morally and spiritually through the attainment of what Kierkegaard variously calls "inwardness," "seriousness," and "subjectivity," then truth can be realized in our lives.

Kierkegaard claims that something like this is true for the interpretation of his own work, since that work is concerned with moral and religious questions. The ambiguity in the authorship is genuine. The meaning of the authorship may thus be opaque to the individual who lacks seriousness, and who has no interest in what Kierkegaard calls "dialectical reduplication," which means at least that the person is willing to think about the issues posed in relation to his or her own life (17). To such a "less serious person" the "explanation cannot be imparted" (17). This does not mean, however, that the meaning of the authorship is purely subjective; rather the meaning is there to be grasped by the one with the requisite degree of seriousness. When dealing with moral and religious matters, subjectivity is crucial, not because there is no truth to be grasped, but because the truth that is there to be grasped can only be had through subjectivity.

3. Indirect Communication, Existence, and the Pseudonyms

Kierkegaard's views about truth are closely linked to his theory of communication, a theory that in turn helps to explain the ambiguity or duplicity in his authorship, the fact that though the whole of the authorship has a religious end, some of the writings appear to be aesthetic. Kierkegaard says that his writings have this characteristic because ethical and religious truth must be communicated *indirectly*. His own aesthetic writings embody an attempt to communicate in this way, since Kierkegaard's pseudonyms are not an attempt on his part to conceal his identity. They are more like characters in a novel, personages whom Kierkegaard has created, and who have their own views and voices. Through the use of the pseudonyms Kierkegaard attempts to withdraw from the reader, and thereby to force the reader to think through the possibilities presented for himself or herself in relation to the reader's own life. The theory of indirect communication is most fully developed in *Concluding Unscientific Postscript*, which is itself a pseudonymous book.[16] Some critics have therefore objected that we cannot assume that this theory represents Kierkegaard's own views. However, aside from the fact that *Postscript* has a different status from the other pseudonymous books, since there is a close relation between the pseudonymous author Johannes Climacus and Kierkegaard himself,[17] in this case we have the outlines in Kierkegaard's *Journals and Papers* of a projected lecture course that Kierkegaard himself developed on the subject.[18] It is clear from this outline that the theory of indirect communication in *Postscript* is one that Kierkegaard personally endorses.

The ground of the theory lies in the duality or doubleness of human existence. Human existence for Kierkegaard is a process in which conceived possibilities are actualized or "reduplicated." Mere intellectual understanding of a possibility is never sufficient for the realization of that possibility. "Existing is in relation to thinking just as little something which follows of itself as it is something thoughtless."[19] Intellectual thought has a kind of infinite quality, according to Kierkegaard, in that there is within it no internal principle of closure.[20] A person faced with a decision must reflect on the alternatives, but so long as the person is reflecting, no decision has been made and no action will take place. Even if I conclude intellectually that one alternative is best, it does not follow I will actually seize that alternative. I must still *want* to do what is best. It is always possible for me to postpone the decision and say, "I need to think about this some more." To end the process of reflection, the person must *care* about the action; the person must be willing to say, "I have thought about this long enough; now I must act." The actualization of a possibility is then made possible by what Kierkegaard variously calls passion, subjectivity, or inwardness, leading to the Kierkegaardian dictum, "It is impossible to exist without passion."[21]

Genuine moral and religious understanding therefore requires what Kierkegaard calls a "double reflection." If I am to reduplicate in my life some ethical-religious possibility, it is not enough to understand this possibility abstractly. I must think it through in terms of its implications for my own life. This kind of engaged or existential thinking, which Kierkegaard calls "subjective thinking," though it is not identical with the reduplication that is equivalent to action, requires passion or subjectivity, much as action does. Such passions can then be seen as providing a kind of ability or skill that a person must possess in order to grasp ethical and religious truth.

The individual who wishes to communicate ethical and religious truth must then see that the task involves not just the communication of information, but the communication of this kind of ability.[22] What is communicated is an art, not a science, and the process of communication must itself be seen as an art (I, 272). Such abilities cannot really be directly communicated from one human being to another; with God's help individuals must acquire the requisite passions themselves as they develop their characters. For purely ethical truth, a human being must simply assume the requisite "knowledge" is present. "The ethical must be communicated as an art, simply because everyone knows it" (I, 272). As a result all human communication in this realm must be *indirect.* A human being can never be more than a midwife to another human being, an insight beautifully realized by Socrates, whose maieutic method of teaching required him to question his contemporaries, on the assumption that the truth lies within each person. Of course through this questioning he thereby ironically exposed their pseudo-knowledge and attempted to dispel the illusion that they had knowledge they did not in fact possess.

There is a vast difference, then, between communication of objective knowledge, where subjectivity does not play an essential role, and communication of ethical and religious truth. I can communicate directly to another the results of historical investigation, scientific experiment, or mathematical reasoning, because the understanding of such subjects does not require the "double reflection" by which the possibilities are thought through in relation to the individual's own life. If I wish to communicate about ethical and religious matters, however, I must think not only about the content of the communication, but about how I can assist the other to think through the relevant possibilities in the right way, which in turn requires me to think about how the other can develop the relevant capabilities.

Kierkegaard's pseudonyms are an attempt at this kind of artistic, indirect communication. On the one hand, through the glittering aesthetic quality of these writings, Kierkegaard hopes to engage his readers where they were, so to speak. Though Denmark is a nominally Christian country, he thinks that most people actually "live in esthetic, or, at the most, esthetic-ethical categories."[23] Since people are under the illusion that they are Christians, however, they must be "approached from behind;" the illusion must be dispelled by confronting them with religious questions that are posed in the pseudonymous writings, and before presenting them with the religious answers presented in the nonpseudonymous writings.

There is a sense in which for purely ethical knowledge, God is the only true communicator.[24] Human communicators are purely midwives. However, for religious communication, particularly Christian faith, Kierkegaard says that there is a necessity for direct communication as well: "That there is an element of knowledge is particularly true for Christianity; a knowledge about Christianity must certainly be communicated in advance. But it is only a preliminary" (I, 289). In the end, Christianity also requires the artistic communication of capability, but because of the necessity for preliminary knowledge, the communication is not purely indirect, but "direct-indirect" (I, 308). Christian communication, therefore, is not purely maieutic as is the case for ethical communication, but in the final analysis includes the necessity to bear witness, both in words and deeds.

4. Stages on Life's Way

As noted above, Kierkegaard's pseudonyms are best viewed as characters created by Kierkegaard. Hence, his writings do not simply tell us about ethical and religious issues; as in a good novel, various life-stances are actually incarnated in these characters. The reader does not merely learn information about the aesthetic life or the ethical life, but actually encounters literary versions of those lives. Serious readers will perhaps recognize these life-stances as possibilities reflected in their own lives; the experience of reading Kierkegaard can feel uncomfortably like looking in a mirror and seeing a version of one's own life, often revealing things that a person might prefer to ignore.

Embedded in the authorship as a whole is a kind of map of various stances a person can take towards life. Of course there are countless ways of living a human life and making sense of human existence; nevertheless, Kierkegaard thought that all of these could usefully be viewed as falling under a few basic categories, called sometimes "the stages on life's way" and sometimes the "spheres of existence." Though there are refinements and complications, basically there are three of these stages or spheres: the aesthetic, the ethical, and the religious.

How is it that these can be understood as both stages and spheres? They are stages in the sense that the account is a kind of developmental theory of human existence. All of us humans begin life in the aesthetic stage. There is, however, a natural progression through the ethical to the religious stage for humans who develop properly. But, since human development of this kind is spiritual in character, it is not automatic. One does not become a mature person simply by virtue of physical development. Rather, spiritual growth requires the free participation of the individual. Hence, the various stages can be seen also as spheres which a person can will, rival life-views whose superiority can be disputed.

Some philosophers, such as Alasdair MacIntyre, have thought that Kierkegaard took what might be called an "existentialist" view of these spheres, in which no reasons can be given for a choice of one over the other.[25] Rather, the decision for one kind of life must be seen as a radical choice, an act of will for which no justification can be given.

This is certainly not the way Kierkegaard himself viewed the various spheres of existence. To avoid any question of pseudonymity, one can here look to such nonpseudonymous writings such as *Works of Love* to see the uncompromising way Kierkegaard upholds the superiority of Christianity to poetic or aesthetic views of life. A critic might here object that this simply reflects Kierkegaard's own personal choice, but this ignores the fact that Kierkegaard does not represent such a choice as arbitrary, but constantly gives reasons for the superiority of the ethical over the aesthetic, and the superiority of the religious over the ethical.

Of course, it may be pointed out, a committed aesthete or ethicist may be unconvinced by these arguments. However, it is difficult to see why that is supposed to be a problem. It is hardly surprising that not all of the people who are committed to a view will be convinced by arguments against that view, even if the arguments seem to be good arguments to many other people. That is simply a fact of human life. The fact that Kierkegaard thinks that there are good reasons to move towards the religious life does not imply that he thinks those reasons will be convincing to everyone.

In fact, given his epistemology, it is clear why such reasons will not be convincing to everyone. Kierkegaard has given up on the project of classical foundationalist epistemology, which seeks a foundation of objective certainty which will constitute evidence that would supposedly convince any sane, rational person. Rather, he holds, as we have seen above, that certain kinds of truths can only be grasped by the person who is inwardly developed, and has the "capability" to recognize them. It does not follow from this that the person who has such capabilities does not gain genuine insights. Certainly Kierkegaard does not see such individuals as forming their beliefs and commitments on the basis of arbitrary acts of will.

5. The Spheres of Existence

The aesthetic sphere

What then do the stages or spheres (for brevity I will refer to them using the latter term) look like? The aesthetic sphere is characterized in a number of ways. Perhaps the most illuminating is this: the aesthete lives for the moment. The aesthete seeks to satisfy those urges and impulses that all of us feel. One could say that the aesthete wishes a life of enjoyment or pleasure, but this is not quite right, at least if one thinks of "enjoyment" or "pleasure" as a homogenous, identifiable quality. The aesthete seeks enjoyment in the sense that the aesthete wishes to have his or her momentary desires, whatever those may be, satisfied. But human beings have desires of very different kinds, and part of Kierkegaard's psychological genius is his recognition of the way some individuals can learn to "enjoy" even their own sufferings.

Either/Or Part I presents a fascinating picture of an aesthetic life. The book purports to be the papers of a person known only as A; it includes aphorisms, an essay on Mozart's opera *Don Giovanni*, essays on tragedy and jilted women, and much else besides, culminating in the infamous "Diary of a Seducer," which may or may not have been written by A himself. *Either/Or* Part I reveals a range within the aesthetic life: a continuum of lifestyles ranging, on one extreme, from the life of pure immediate sensuousness symbolized by the story of Don Juan captured by Mozart's opera according to A, to a highly reflective life lived almost solely in the realm of the imagination as illustrated by A himself. The difference is clearly seen in the contrast between the mythical figure of Don Juan, who is supposed to have seduced 1,003 women in Spain alone, and the Seducer who is the author of the "Diary" at the end of the volume. The Seducer deceives just one woman, but he does so through an elaborate scheme. His satisfaction does not really lie in sexual conquest; the actual physical seduction seems valuable to him only as a symbol of his true achievement, which is to seduce in so artful a manner that the woman believes that she is the one who has seduced him.

A is both attractive and frightening. He is intellectually brilliant, witty, and at times very charming. He is also chronically melancholy, or depressed in today's language, and actually seems to revel in his depression. A plausible explanation for this is that A has seen through the problems of the more immediate aesthete. If one actually tried to live like Don Juan, the project would quickly become boring. (Not to mention the likelihood of AIDS for a contemporary Don Juan.) A life of reflective enjoyment seems more sustainable, then. The reflective aesthetic life requires a person to step back in a way and make his or her own life an object of aesthetic appreciation. If I am a reflective aesthete, then I am not only the actor, but in a sense the audience for my life, the play. In this way a person can come to "enjoy" even the sad and tragic elements of life, and the person who is able to do this achieves a certain degree of invulnerability to the storms of life, as the difficulties and sadness simply contribute to the tragedy and provide further aesthetic material. Such an aesthete learns to practice "the art of remembering and forgetting." "No part of life ought to have so much meaning for a person that he cannot forget it at any moment he wants to; on the other hand, every single part of life ought to have so much meaning for a person that he can remember it at any moment."[26] Life then becomes a series of occasions, the source of raw material to be aesthetically refashioned. No commitments, such as those involved in marriage or genuine friendship, can be tolerated, however, as this would compromise the aesthete's ability to play with life.

The ethical sphere

"The ethical" is used in many different ways in Kierkegaard's writings. In such explicitly Christian writings as *Works of Love*, Kierkegaard develops an explicitly Christian ethic grounded in God's command to love thy neighbor as oneself as this is communicated through an authoritative revelation. At other times Kierkegaard speaks of the "ethical-religious" to refer to a type of ethic that is essentially linked to religious existence. However, the term is also used to refer to a sphere that stands as a rival to both the aesthetic and the religious spheres.

Even within Part I of *Either/Or* it is evident that the aesthete struggles with various problems, including boredom as well as depression. The reflective form of the aesthetic life may be more sustainable than the immediate form, but the distancing from actual life this project involves has a price as well. The pseudonymous author of Part II, called B, is a minor public official, Assessor William, who gives a clear critique of the aesthetic life. According to William, the problem with the aesthetic life is that it lacks continuity. The aesthete's life is at best merely a collection of satisfying moments, with nothing to link those moments together so that they become a history. William believes that such a life is ultimately boring and unsatisfying; in fact, he thinks that such a life is meaningless and leads to despair. "There comes a moment in a person's life when immediacy is ripe, so to speak, and when the spirit requires a higher form, when it wants to lay hold of itself as spirit" (II, 188). The spirit does not allow itself to be mocked, and when this spiritual development is repressed, life becomes deeply unsatisfying.

Kierkegaard thinks that there is in fact a kind of boundary zone, a *confinium*, between the aesthetic and the ethical that arises when a person has "seen through" the shallowness of the aesthetic but has not yet committed to the ethical. This boundary area is referred to as *irony*. This kind of irony is not the relative irony by which one individual of supposedly greater sophistication looks down on another individual, but a kind of absolute irony which sees with the author of Ecclesiastes that "all is vanity." It is nice to have homes, good careers, and fame, but even if our temporal desires are satisfied, they cannot bear the weight of making human life meaningful. Irony is a transitional zone that makes possible a move to the ethical life, since the ironist has "seen through" the relative goods that humans tend to absolutize. However, one must remember that spiritual development does not follow automatically from intellectual insight. Irony thus can become a kind of existential life-stance in its own right.

The cure for the problems of the aesthete, according to William, is to become a self. The self is not merely a metaphysical reality, but an ethical achievement, and becoming a self requires choice. The most fundamental choice is simply the choice to choose responsibly; to take choices seriously rather than merely follow aesthetic impulses. Such a choice is the heart of the ethical life: "if one does not choose absolutely, one chooses only for the moment and for that reason can choose something else the next moment" (II, 167). An ethical choice is then equivalent to a commitment, and it is binding commitments that give a person an enduring identity, a self that is more than a collection of moments. Such commitments require ethical passion, passions that are more than aesthetic whims. Such passions endure and can and must be developed.

The superiority of the ethical life over the aesthetic is defended by William on the grounds that the ethical is superior, even on aesthetic grounds. Compare, for example, marriage and the affair as expressions of romantic love. William argues that the element of ethical obligation that grounds marriage is something that love itself desires. Marriage makes it possible for love to have a history, and the permanence it provides is exactly what genuine lovers want: that love should be forever (II, 56). Such a love is ultimately more interesting than a series of meaningless affairs.

The relationship between erotic love and marriage is generalized by William to the whole of the aesthetic life. Just as marriage can and should preserve love, so the ethical life does not annihilate the aesthetic, but preserves it as the set of relative goods that it is: "In the ethical, the personality is brought into a focus in itself; consequently the aesthetic is absolutely excluded or it is excluded as the absolute, but relatively it is continually present" (II, 177).

In *Fear and Trembling* the ethical is contrasted not only with the aesthetic, but also with the religious life. This book, by another pseudonym, Johannes de Silentio, takes as its point of departure the command by God to Abraham to sacrifice his son Isaac in the story of Genesis 22. The book argues that Abraham, as the father of faith, cannot be understood merely in ethical terms. Abraham's ethical obligation as a father is surely to protect his son and not to kill him. If he is right to be willing to sacrifice Isaac, the justification cannot be ethical in character.

In making his case Silentio contrasts the Abraham story with several others in which a parent brings about the death of a child, including Agamemnon's willingness to sacrifice Iphigenia for the sake of the nation, Brutus's impartial sentencing as a judge of his own sons to death, and Jepthah's willingness to fulfill his vow by sacrificing his daughter.[27] Agamemnon, Brutus, and Jepthah embody what Silentio calls "the tragic hero," who is "the beloved son of ethics." It is evident, I think, that this does not mean that these characters' actions are justifiable in terms of some timeless ethical principle, much less that their actions would be ethically approved in society today. Rather, Silentio means that these actions were ethical in the sense of appealing to principles that were universally accepted in their societies. Such appeals to the universal mean that the actions can be understood and rationally justified to the contemporaries of these tragic heroes, who would have approved of the idea that a family responsibility would be trumped by a higher ethical obligation to the state. Abraham's case, however, contains no state or nation for which the family sacrifice is being made. The command by God seems solely to concern Abraham's relation to God; it is a test or trial of his faith or trust in God, and since the test deals with this personal relationship, Abraham's actions cannot be understood in universal or ethical terms.

The religious sphere

"The ethical" in this social sense is contrasted to the religious life which opens itself to something that transcends the rational standards embedded in human institutions and practices. The character of the tragic hero is contrasted by Silentio in *Fear and Trembling* with two religious figures: the knight of infinite resignation and the knight of faith. Infinite resignation is a kind of other-worldly religiousness. If called upon by God to sacrifice a child, the knight of infinite resignation can carry out the act because essentially this person has already sacrificed the finite, temporal world and lives only for the eternal. That Abraham is not merely a knight of infinite resignation is shown by the fact that when God reveals that it is not in fact his will for Abraham to sacrifice Isaac, Abraham is able to receive Isaac back with joy and gladness. "By faith Abraham did not renounce Isaac; but by faith Abraham received Isaac" (49). Faith, Silentio says, makes two movements: it infinitely resigns the finite for the sake of the infinite, but paradoxically, it then receives the finite back again. Infinite resignation makes only the first of these two movements. Faith believes and has hope for this life also.

In *Concluding Unscientific Postscript* the religious life is also described in terms of resignation: to live religiously is to have an absolute relation to the absolute *telos* or end and a relative relation to relative ends.[28] The difficulty is that when we embark on this task we discover that we are already committed to the relative, and must begin by "dying to self." Religious existence is closely linked in *Postscript* to tasks and emotions regarded by many as negative. The initial expression of religiousness is resignation. When a person seriously undertakes this task, it is discovered to require a painful "dying to self." Hence the essential expression of the religious life is suffering.[29] Finally, the person who travels down this road discovers the decisive expression of the religious life: guilt (525–55).

What is it that motivates the move to the religious sphere of existence? In some ways the ethical life sounds much better. The ethical sphere is described as a life of action and victory, while the religious sphere is the sphere of suffering (288). The difference between the two cannot be captured by such conventional identifiers as belief in God or even participation in a religious community, as the ethical characters in Kierkegaard are sincere religious believers and church-goers. It is noteworthy that in Kierkegaard's philosophy as a whole the question of God's existence is not at the center of attention. There is little worry in Kierkegaard that Enlightenment rationalism has undermined belief in God, and no attempt to buttress religious faith by proofs of God's existence. On the contrary, Kierkegaard thinks that doubts about God's existence only arise when it is regarded as a matter that needs to be proved:

> To demonstrate the existence of someone who is present is the most shameless affront, since it is an attempt to make him ridiculous, but the trouble is that one does not even suspect this, that in dead seriousness one regards it as a godly undertaking. How could it occur to anyone to demonstrate that he exists unless one has allowed oneself to ignore him; and now one does it an even more lunatic way by demonstrating his existence right in front of his nose. (543)

If the difference between the religious exister and the ethicist does not revolve around belief in God, then where does it lie? The difference lies rather in the self-confidence of the ethical exister. So long as a person believes that the ethical task of becoming a self is one that can be accomplished by the individual through autonomous choice, then the religious life in the deeper sense is not present. The ground of the religious life is the discovery that the ethical task is not easy to accomplish: that it may in fact be impossible, a point that is already intimated in *Fear and Trembling*, where it is asserted that "an ethic that ignores sin is a completely futile discipline, but if it affirms sin, then it has *eo ipso* exceeded itself."[30]

One might say that the most ethical people, who are of course the most honest people, are the people who recognize most deeply their own shortcomings, who do not see themselves as superior to others but recognize how far short of their own ideals they often come. "As soon as sin emerges, ethics founders precisely on repentance; for repentance is the highest ethical expression, but precisely as such it is the deepest ethical self-contradiction" (98n). The religious life offers hope, then, to those for whom the ethical life has led to a kind of despair. It is for this reason that the figure of Abraham, though he is not a tragic hero to be ethically admired, is so important, since "it is one thing to be admired and another to become a guiding star that saves the anguished" (21). The religious life offers hope for those who are anguished.

In *Concluding Unscientific Postscript*, the pseudonymous author Johannes Climacus distinguishes two types of religiousness. The first type, called "Religiousness A," represents the kind of religious life possible for humans that does not presuppose any transcendent revelation from God. "Of religiousness A one may say that, even if it had not been present in paganism, it could have been because it has only generic human nature as its presupposition."[31] This kind of religiousness is distinguished from a more specific form, called B, that is found in Christianity. In general, religiousness A seems to be a kind of generic religious pathos or concern that lies at the foundation of more specific forms of the religious life, such as Christianity. "One will therefore see how foolish it is when a man without pathos wants to relate himself to the Christian; for before there can be any talk at all of merely being in the situation for becoming aware of it [Christianity], one must first exist in religiousness A" (557). Christianity is distinguished by its dialectical conceptual content, and a person moves from religiousness A to B when the pathos of religiousness A is fused with the conceptual content of Christianity so as to produce a new passion (555).

The difference between religiousness A and B lies chiefly in their attitudes toward human reason and its ability to deal with the suffering and guilt that are the problems of the religious life. Religiousness A can be seen as an energetic struggle with guilt: "The totality of guilt-consciousness in the single individual before God in relation to an eternal happiness is the religious" (554). The notion of an eternal happiness here must not be thought of as a kind of external reward for becoming the kinds of persons we ought to be, but is rather itself the state of being whole. The highest form of the religious life refuses to finitize our guilt in failing to achieve this by taking refuge in penance or some other finite solution. That there is some way that the problem of guilt can be satisfied is for this kind of religiousness only "an obscurely sensed possibility" (472).

The person who turns away from the struggle with guilt to rest in this "obscurely sensed possibility" lives in a kind of limiting zone to the religious life that Johannes Climacus calls "humor." Humor is a kind of boundary area to the religious life, in much the same way that irony is said to be a boundary between the aesthetic and the ethical. The humorist is described as someone who sees the contradiction in life, but is able to smile at what might appear tragic to others because the humorist knows a way out. What underlies the humorist's view seems to be a type of religious insight which implies that despite the gap between our ideals and actuality, in the end all humans do achieve the eternal happiness that is their goal. At times the humorist is described as someone who has a kind of knowledge of Christianity, and thus the humorist may be someone who is taking the Christian promises of redemption and forgiveness as universal truths about the human condition rather than existential possibilities to be appropriated. The genuinely religious figure does not treat such themes as excuses for withdrawal, but continues to struggle energetically with the quest for authentic selfhood that is understood as a quest for a God-relationship and an eternal happiness.

6. Christian Existence: Faith and the Paradox

As we have seen, Christianity is distinguished from religiousness A by virtue of being grounded in a transcendent revelation, a revelation that comes to human beings from outside their own immanent consciousness. For Kierkegaard this means that Christianity is rooted in the particularities of history, with the incarnation of God in Jesus lying at the heart of the matter. He makes no attempt to understand how God could become incarnate in a particular human being; rather he maintains steadfastly that the incarnation is "the absolute paradox," a paradox that human reason is powerless to understand.[32] Historical arguments to prove the divinity of Christ are useless (though history cannot disprove this either).[33] Just as a "capital crime absorbs all the lesser crimes" so in this case the enormous improbability of the incarnation itself makes any problems in the quality of the historical evidence unimportant.[34]

Some critics have thought that Kierkegaard means to say that the incarnation is logically contradictory when he says it is a paradox. However, it is much more plausible that he thinks of a paradox simply as something that reason cannot understand, something that may *appear* contradictory to reason when reason tries to comprehend it, but which the believer at least does not think is a genuine logical contradiction.[35]

Although the paradox is not a formal contradiction, there is a kind of natural tension between human reason and the paradox. Johannes Climacus describes the situation like this: "The understanding certainly cannot think it [the paradox], cannot hit upon it on its own, and if it is proclaimed, the understanding cannot understand it and merely detects that it will likely be its downfall. To that extent, the understanding has strong objections to it" (47). The paradox is a threat to the autonomy of human reason in that it presents itself as "that which thought cannot think" and human reason has within it an imperialistic quality that resists any recognition of limits (37).

Climacus argues, however, that this tension is accompanied by ambivalence. There is a sense in which reason is seeking to discover the very limit that the paradox embodies; the discovery of such a limit would be both a defeat and a victory for human reason. When reason understands this, then it is possible for reason and the paradox to enjoy good relations. What is required is that reason recognize its own limits: "when the understanding and the paradox happily encounter each other in the moment, when the understanding steps aside and the paradox gives itself" (59).

Climacus claims that this "happy relationship" between human understanding and the paradox is made possible by a passion, the passion of faith. The passion of faith is described as a gift, one that is given directly to the disciple by God (62). Without faith, no amount of historical information is sufficient to make a person a disciple; when faith is present almost any amount of historical information is sufficient, so long as the person comes to know God and is transformed by the encounter.[36] Kierkegaard does not, however, think of the gift of faith as something that is given independently of a person's choice. Even the power to choose must in some sense be given by God, but humans must accept the gift and can refuse it. The key element here seems to be the potential disciple's consciousness of sin, a consciousness that implies that the learner lacks the truth and even lacks "the condition" for grasping the truth. Even this insight that the person lacks the truth is made possible by God, but it is a recognition that the person must accept for himself or herself.[37] The person who understands his or her need for God is the person who will accept the gift of faith that God offers.

That there is no necessary conflict between faith in the paradox and reason is shown by the fact that the basic tension and contrast is between faith and *offense* rather than between faith and reason. Offense is the response of the person whose reason is unwilling to recognize its own limits. Johannes Climacus describes offense as similar to the selfish kind of self-love that refuses to love another and thereby cuts itself off from the genuine happiness and fulfillment that love provides. The selfish person who senses what has been lost can be embittered, angry at love. In a similar way, the offended consciousness is a kind of unhappy love, a form of suffering since offense cuts a person off from a kind of healing and fulfillment.

Though it is true that offense is in some sense a natural response on the part of reason, it is important to see that offense is no more rational than faith. Rather, both faith and offense are passions, and passions are not generated simply by reason. The person who is offended may claim that faith is being rejected simply because it fails to measure up to the standards of rationality; this is in fact Kierkegaard's gloss on the attack of some Enlightenment philosophers on religious belief as irrational. However, Johannes Climacus says that the accusations of the offended reason are really an "acoustic illusion," an echo. "Everything it [offense] says about the paradox it has learned from the paradox, even though, making use of an acoustical illusion, it insists that it itself has originated the paradox" (53). The fact of offense is actually a confirmation of the claim of the paradox to be something that reason cannot understand, a sign that the paradox is indeed what it claims to be. Climacus has the paradox address offense, when offense tries to denounce the paradox as unreasonable: "It is just as you say, and the amazing thing is that you think that it is an objection, but the truth in the mouth of a hypocrite is dearer to me than to hear it from an angel and an apostle" (52).

Christian existence is supposed to be a kind of new life, a "higher immediacy" or "immediacy after reflection," and it cannot simply be willed into existence.[38] Rather, as we have seen, it depends on faith which is a gift. Nevertheless, faith requires a decision or "a leap" on the part of the individual. This concept of the leap is often misunderstood. Kierkegaard never talks about "blind leaps" or "a leap into the dark" as in some presentations of existentialism. Rather, the leap is simply his way of designating that faith is discontinuous with what came before, not simply the inevitable development of something already present in a person's past. The leap is the category of decision, and in genuine human decisions, the future is actually formed. Something new comes into being and a person must welcome the new mode of existence.

7. Conclusions: Kierkegaard's Contributions as a Philosopher

As already noted, Kierkegaard did not write philosophy systematically nor did he do philosophy for its own sake. He struggles with philosophical issues in the course of pursuing ethical and religious aims. He writes about traditional questions in metaphysics, epistemology, and ethics, but he does so in the course of thinking about other questions. Perhaps his contributions to philosophy can best be seen in his critique of the great German Idealist G. W. F. Hegel. The encounter with Hegel's thought allowed Kierkegaard to develop themes and insights that have a relevance and importance that transcends the particular dispute.

The dispute with Hegel revolves around the Hegelian claim to have developed a comprehensive system. I have already noted the Kierkegaardian claim that although reality is a system for God, it cannot be so for any finite human being. Kierkegaard's critique of Hegel, again developed in the writings of Johannes Climacus, centers on the beginning and the end of such a system. How does a system of philosophy get started, and how can it be finished?

A genuine system would be presuppositionless, but Climacus argues that human thinking cannot begin in this way.[39] One might think that one could begin in Cartesian style with a universal doubt that would destroy all taken-for-granted assumptions and begin anew. However, Kierkegaard argues that such doubt is impossible, and this is fortunate for humans, since if such a doubt were possible, it would be incurable.[40] Philosophy must be carried out by existing human beings, and such human beings cannot completely divest themselves of their prior beliefs and values. Skepticism is a possible human attitude, but skepticism is itself rooted in a resolution to take a certain attitude towards human existence. Skepticism is not primarily grounded in reasons, and it cannot be overcome simply by reasoning. Nevertheless, the example of skepticism shows that philosophy cannot be divorced from human existence.

The other problem with Hegel's claim to have produced a system, according to Climacus, is that a system must be final and complete to be a system. Human thinking, however, since it is the thinking of existing human beings who are never complete, can never attain this kind of finality. We can and must strive for a truth that is final, but we cannot hope to do more than constantly strive towards it.

Both criticisms reflect a deep sense that philosophy is not a matter of seeing the world *sub specie aeternitatis*, as Spinoza would claim, nor a way that Absolute Spirit comes to think itself, as Hegel would claim. We cannot adopt "the view from nowhere," but must always recognize the situated character of human thinking. This involves not only recognizing the finite and historical character of our thinking, and the ways in which we are conditioned by our culture, but also explicitly coming to terms with the meaning of philosophy for human existers. Kierkegaard thinks that the Hegelian claim that philosophy must "beware of the edifying" is wrong. Human beings have a right to ask what a philosophy means for their existence as human beings; philosophers are in fact giving answers to such questions, even if they try to deny this.

Part of Kierkegaard's genius is his recognition that this admission of finitude does not have to lead to despair, whether that despair be epistemological or existential. Human life is a risky business, and we have no ultimate security or guarantees. Nevertheless, it is possible to venture and commit oneself. The tasks set by human existence are, he thinks, the same in every age. Greater knowledge and technological sophistication does not make it easier or harder to become a self. Becoming a self in the fullest sense requires the development of the passions, the achievement of what might today be called emotional maturity. When Kierkegaard talks about "inwardness" or "subjectivity" he wants to make it clear that the emotions are not always distorting filters that must be removed if the truth about human life is to be grasped, but focusing lenses that enable us to see clearly who we are and why we are here. Through his disciplined reflection on the spheres of human existence, Kierkegaard tries to provide a conceptual map that clarifies the task. In communicating that map in the way that he does, he also tries to make it clear that the possession of the map is never equivalent to the completion of the task.

Notes

1 See Louis Mackey, *Kierkegaard: A Kind of Poet* (Philadelphia: University of Pennsylvania Press, 1971).

2 See Merold Westphal, *Becoming a Self: A Reading of Kierkegaard's "Concluding Unscientific Postscript"* (Indiana: Purdue University Press, 1996) and, in a different vein altogether, Roger Poole, *Kierkegaard: The Indirect Communication* (Charlottesville, Va.: University of Virginia Press, 1993).

3 See Robert Roberts, *Faith, Reason, and History: Rethinking Kierkegaard's "Philosophical Fragments"* (Macon, Ga.: Mercer University Press, 1986) and H. A. Nielsen, *Where the Passion Is: A Reading of Kierkegaard's* Philosophical Fragments (Tallahassee, Fla.: Florida State University Press, 1983).

4 See Martin Heidegger, *Being and Time*, tr. John Macquarrie and Edward Robinson (New York: Harper & Row, 1962), nn to pp. 190, 235, and 338.

5 See Heidegger, *Being and Time*, secs. 49–52, pp. 290–304.

6 Kierkegaard, *The Point of View*, ed. and tr. Howard V. Hong and Edna H. Hong (Princeton, NJ: Princeton University Press, 1998), p. 29.

7 For a good example of this kind of "postmodern" reading of Kierkegaard, see Louis Mackey, *Points of View: Readings of Kierkegaard* (Tallahassee, Fla.: Florida State University Press, 1986). For a critical response to "antirealistic" readings, see my essay, "Realism and Antirealism in Kierkegaard's *Concluding Unscientific Postscript*," in *The Cambridge Companion to Kierkegaard*, eds. Alastair Hannay and Gordon Marino (Cambridge: Cambridge University Press, 1998).

8 For a fine example, see Sylviane Agacinski, *Aparté: Conceptions and Deaths of Søren Kierkegaard*, tr. Kevin Newmark (Tallahassee, Fla.: Florida State University Press, 1988).

9 Kierkegaard, *The Point of View*, p. 34.

10 Kierkegaard, *Concluding Unscientific Postscript*, ed. and tr. Howard V. Hong and Edna H. Hong (Princeton, NJ: Princeton University Press, 1998), p. 199.

11 For a fuller account, see ch. 7 of my *Kierkegaard's "Fragments" and "Postsript": The Religious Philosophy of Johannes Climacus* (Atlantic Highlands, NJ: Humanities Press, 1983).

12 See Merold Westphal, *Becoming a Self*, pp. 114–30 for an excellent discussion of this point.

13 Kierkegaard, *Christian Discourses*, ed. and tr. Howard V. Hong and Edna H. Hong (Princeton, NJ: Princeton University Press, 1997), pp. 244–5.

14 See Richard Rorty, who sees truth as a purely "social transaction" between human knowers, rather than a transaction between knowers and reality. Truth is not an accurate "representation of reality" but simply "those beliefs which are successful in helping

us to do what we want to do." *Philosophy and the Mirror of Nature* (Princeton, NJ: Princeton University Press, 1979), p. 10.

15 Kierkegaard, *Concluding Unscientific Postscript*, p. 118.

16 For an exposition of the account of communication in *Postscript*, see ch. 6 of my *Kierkegaard's "Fragments" and "Postsript."*

17 This close relationship is signaled in *The Point of View*, pp. 31–2.

18 See *Søren Kierkegaard's Journals and Papers*, 7 vols., ed. and tr. Howard V. Hong and Edna H. Hong (Bloomington, Ind.: Indiana University Press, 1967–78), I, pp. 267–308. Subsequent references to this work will cite volume and page numbers.

19 Kierkegaard, *Concluding Unscientific Postscript*, pp. 254–5. (Hong's edition is cited but the translation is mine.)

20 Here and at several other places, I attribute to Kierkegaard ideas found in the writings of Johannes Climacus. I believe these ideas do represent Kierkegaard's own thinking, and that discussing them as those of Climacus, while more precise and strictly accurate, would be pedantic. See *Postscript*, pp. 335–43.

21 *Concluding Unscientific Postscript*, p. 311 (my translation).

22 *Søren Kierkegaard's Journals and Papers*, I, p. 307.

23 Kierkegaard, *The Point of View*, p. 43.

24 *Søren Kierkegaard's Journals and Papers*, I, p. 272.

25 See Alasdair MacIntyre, *After Virtue*, 2nd edn. (Notre Dame, Ind.: University of Notre Dame Press, 1984), pp. 36–50.

26 Kierkegaard, *Either/Or*, 2 vols., ed. and tr. Howard V. Hong and Edna H. Hong (Princeton, NJ: Princeton University Press, 1987), I, p. 293.

27 Kierkegaard, *Fear and Trembling*, ed. and tr. Howard V. Hong and Edna H. Hong (Princeton, NJ: Princeton University Press, 1989), pp. 57–9.

28 This theme is discussed at length in *Concluding Unscientific Postscript*, pp. 387–431.

29 See *Concluding Unscientific Postscript*, pp. 431–525.

30 Kierkegaard, *Fear and Trembling*, pp. 98–9.

31 *Concluding Unscientific Postscript*, p. 559 (Hong's pagination, my translation).

32 Kierkegaard, *Philosophical Fragments*, ed. and tr. Howard V. Hong and Edna H. Hong (Princeton, NJ: Princeton University Press, 1985), title of ch. 3. The language of "paradox" is found more in the pseudonymous works, but the thrust of the idea, that the incarnation is not comprehensible to human reason, is certainly Kierkegaard's own view.

33 Kierkegaard, *Concluding Unscientific Postscript*, pp. 23–34.

34 Kierkegaard, *Philosophical Fragments*, p. 104.

35 For detailed arguments that the paradox is not a formal contradiction, see my *Passionate Reason: Making Sense of Kierkegaard's "Philosophical Fragments"* (Bloomington, Ind.: Indiana University Press, 1992), pp. 96–107, and Merold Westphal's *Becoming a Self*, pp. 180–9.

36 This is the argument of chs. 4 and 5 of *Philosophical Fragments.*

37 Johannes Climacus says that with respect to discovering my own untruth, the "Socratic principle" applies; the individual must learn this for himself or herself. *Philosophical Fragments*, p. 14.

38 *Søren Kierkegaard's Journals and Papers*, II, p. 12.

39 Kierkegaard, *Concluding Unscientific Postscript*, pp. 111–17.

40 On the difficulty of doubting, see *Fear and Trembling*, pp. 5–7. On the impossibility of doubt overcoming itself, see *Postscript*, pp. 111–17 and 335–6.

Chapter 15

Arthur Schopenhauer

Christopher Janaway

Arthur Schopenhauer (1788–1860) was a thinker of fierce independence and self-assurance. Unlike many of his prominent German contemporaries he never had a real academic career, and (from a financially secure position) regarded "university philosophy," especially the leading Hegelian variety, with contempt. His posture as the lone "outsider" makes for a uniqueness of vision, a freedom to be acerbic, and a license to think the unthinkably disturbing. It allows also a kind of luxuriant idiosyncrasy that might have been curbed had Schopenhauer's thought been subjected to the discipline of close debate. But his philosophy was not shaped in that manner: it had arrived more or less fully formed in 1818 with the first edition of *The World as Will and Representation*, published when he was 30 years old. The composition of this book, which Schopenhauer himself compared to a gestation, and which can be traced through the first volume of the Manuscript Remains, seems to have been a particularly solitary and inward process. Had his work received critical attention, there is no doubt that Schopenhauer would have risen to the challenge of debating his doctrines. His command of argument and rhetoric, his writing style and direct manner of expression – among the most powerful in modern philosophy – would have been equal to the task. However, throughout most of his life *The World as Will and Representation* and the rest of his writings were very little read. The period when he exercised most influence on European culture, to a large extent through the arts, began only in the 1850s, not many years before he died.

1. The Character of Schopenhauer's Philosophy

Schopenhauer's broad view of the history of modern philosophy is one with which a present-day audience would be familiar – it is the view that there is a mainstream originating with Descartes and culminating in the great achievements of Kant. Schopenhauer locates himself as continuous with this stream in many ways, but in other respects he is arguably quite discontinuous from it. In his fundamental description of the nature of the world and of the place of humanity within it, Schopenhauer breaks violently with certain remaining inheritances of Christianity, rationalism, and Enlightenment. He is a philosopher of pessimism. He argues that there is no "dignity of man," that rationality is of no especial value, that our essence is a nonrational force that strives towards organic survival and reproduction, that science reveals only a superficial aspect of reality, that perfectibility or even progress is a sham, that our will is never free, that moral doctrines and social institutions can never alter a fundamentally egoistic or malicious character, that there is no "highest good," that the world is the worst of all possible worlds, and that the life of any individual of the human species is full of meaningless unredeemed suffering and not worth living. In these respects Schopenhauer can appear to belong to a slightly later time than the one in which he lived and to anticipate some preoccupations of Nietzsche, Freud, and existentialism. As we shall see, his own need for an ameliorating response to this bleak vision of things gives rise to his distinctive doctrines of aesthetic value and of the denial of the will: states in which the subject of experience becomes, to an extent, detached from individuality and its attendant desires. The core of Schopenhauer's philosophy might be said to lie here, in his struggle to locate value in existence at all. We could call him a descriptive irrationalist, as long as we do not confuse that with methodological irrationalism. Schopenhauer believes fervently in truth and in its discoverability by philosophical reflection. But such reflection reveals that the essence of things and selves is not at all rational.

Let us turn to the continuities Schopenhauer himself claims with the mainstream of modern philosophy as he sees it. In a passage in the second volume of *The World as Will and Representation*, published in 1844, Schopenhauer writes as follows:

> By taking [Descartes's] *cogito ergo sum* as the only thing certain, and provisionally regarding the existence of the world as problematical, the essential and only correct starting-point . . . of all philosophy was really found. This point, indeed, is essentially and of necessity the subjective, our own consciousness. . . . It is thus rightly considered that the philosophy of the moderns starts from Descartes as its father. Not long afterwards, Berkeley went farther along this path, and arrived at idealism proper; in other words, at the knowledge that what is extended in space, and hence the objective, material world in general, exists as such simply and solely in our *representation*, and that it is false and indeed absurd to attribute to it, *as such*, an existence outside all representation and independent of the knowing subject . . . Accordingly, true philosophy must at all costs be idealistic. (W2, 4)[1]

Schopenhauer continues the story by adducing Kant's *transcendental* idealism as the legitimate heir of this post-Cartesian tradition. Kant saw that space, time, and causality comprised the *a priori* necessary *mode and manner* in which objects in the empirical world could be present to a subject (W2, 8). So philosophy proceeds correctly if it starts with consciousness and arrives at the view that empirical reality is the conscious subject's representation, organized according to necessary principles within the subject.

So pervasive are Kant and Kantian terminology in the presentation of Schopenhauer's position that one might almost be forgiven for treating it merely as some would-be derivative or adjunct of his great predecessor's work. But that would be a mistake. To see this, one need only turn to the extended "Criticism of the Kantian Philosophy" which forms the Appendix to volume 1 of *The World as Will and Representation*. Schopenhauer there indeed lauds Kant for three great achievements – the distinction between appearance and thing in itself, the insight that the significance of morality relates to the thing in itself rather than the realm of appearance, and the "complete overthrow of the scholastic philosophy," the Christian metaphysics whose influence he says had continued to affect Descartes and "all his successors down to Kant" (see W1, 417–23). But the greater part of this "Criticism" essay is just what its title suggests: Schopenhauer is severely critical of Kant for many faults, and in most cases puts a very good case against. Nor is it just a matter of disputing details within the Kantian program. There are other aspects of Schopenhauer's larger philosophical enterprise which at best sit uneasily with the idea that he is a Kantian in any straightforward sense, and more plausibly show him to be an underminer or opponent of Kant.

First, Schopenhauer evinces a certain sympathy with empiricism. He always treats Kant's enterprise as a continuation of the work of Berkeley, and also of Locke and Hume (see W1, 418, W2, 19–20). He sometimes expressed an aspiration to be considered a "German Hume." It was partly that he admired Hume's style as an antidote to the inflated verbiage of the prevalent German Idealism, and partly that he found Hume's treatment of religion congenial. To see Hume's true greatness, he said, one must read the *Dialogues concerning Natural Religion* (see W2, 338). Both these factors played a part in Schopenhauer's serious, though unsuccessful, proposal to undertake a translation of Hume into German. (A similar proposal to render Kant into English was also never realized.) But did Schopenhauer's own philosophy have any genuine empiricist tendencies?

At times Schopenhauer enunciates a kind of naturalism, particularly in his later writings. He faults Kant's idealism (along with all idealism) for being "one-sided" and ignoring the material basis of conscious experience: "it is just as true that the knower is a product of matter as that matter is a mere representation of the knower" (W2, 13). Schopenhauer sees the empirical work of "zootomists and physiologists" in the first half of the nineteenth century (see W2, 272) as an important complement to the idealist method which starts from subjective consciousness. We must also look at the human organism empirically and discover which of its functions account for – indeed, which of them *are* – the intellect. Schopenhauer takes it for granted that the representation of the world in human consciousness is a function of the brain. Yet it may be misleading to call his position naturalism. He is by no means a scientific naturalist, because he does not consider scientific explanation ever to be adequate or basic.

A more fundamental aspect of Schopenhauer's philosophical program should alarm both a straightforward Kantian and a scientific naturalist, and that is his claim to reinstate *metaphysics* as a possible enquiry into the nature of the world as it is in itself, indeed as the ultimate form of knowledge which it is the prime task of philosophy to pursue. Following an aspiration broadly similar to those of Leibniz or Spinoza – and already subjected to severe critique by Kant – Schopenhauer proposes to tell us the essence, the true inner nature, of the world and of the self, both considered as *things in themselves.* His central claim is that, in themselves, both world and self are *will.* This claim plays an important role in his castigation of both Leibnizian and Spinozist metaphysical systems as wrongly optimistic descriptions of the nature of things.

Schopenhauer's notion of a true essence, the ultimate "in itself" of things, is combined with a strong view, held from his earliest student days, that the essence must lie in some way hidden behind what is accessible to ordinary empirical consciousness. Here he was influenced by his youthful reading of Plato and of the Hindu Upanishads, the religious text that he most revered throughout his life. For both Plato and Hinduism, that which we ordinarily experience is an illusion or dream, and an extraordinary or heightened consciousness is required to penetrate beyond it. It was always in this spirit, a profoundly un-Kantian spirit, that Schopenhauer approached Kant's distinction between things in themselves and appearances. If he wished to understand the nature of the world as presented to empirical consciousness, it was with the ulterior motive of showing how limited that consciousness was, and how much of the world – its whole essence or nature "in itself" – was left to be explored by philosophical reflection, art, and ineffable mystical experience.

In expounding the nature of Schopenhauer's philosophy we appear now to have an uneasy amalgam between three elements: (1) a transcendental idealist characterization of the world from the point of view of the subject's consciousness, (2) a kind of naturalism about the mind, (3) a metaphysics of the world as it is in itself. How these may be reconciled is no simple question, but Schopenhauer's own answer is, in outline, quite clear. He holds that the metaphysics of the world as it is in itself is the most basic level of description, and can give a satisfactory explanation both of material nature and of subjectivity. When seeking to know the thing in itself, we are, in Schopenhauer's view, seeking to decipher the world, to give it a single graspable "meaning." We would be possession of this meaning if we could understand the inner *essence* of the world. His conviction is that there is a single essence, *will*, from which can be seen to flow the true nature both of the material things that are the objects of experience and of the subject who has that experience.

2. Self as Will, World as Will

We are to discover will as this essence by a process of philosophical reflection that takes its departure from a particular datum of our experience. In our own self-consciousness we are aware of ourselves as acting. This means that we are not just the subject of consciousness required by transcendental idealism, the knowing subject which is a necessary correlate of all experienced objects, but is itself nowhere among them. We are subjects of willed actions, conscious of ourselves as intimately related with the body in action and thereby located in the world. So there is at least one thing – his or her own body – that is both a part of the world of spatio-temporal, causally interacting objective things, and known uniquely and immediately to the subject. Schopenhauer proposes to use this as the "key" to unlock the essence of everything for the philosophical enquirer. The object which is my individual human body, and those movements of it which can be equated with my actions, are phenomena of will. In appearance they are spatio-temporal objects and events, parts of the empirical world; in their inner essence, their nature in itself, revealed to us uniquely in self-consciousness, they are will. Schopenhauer asks us to extend this dual pattern to every other thing and event in the empirical realm. In the case of all those things and events which we can know as appearance but not by the immediate access of self-consciousness, philosophical reflection can lead us to discern one and the same essence underlying them. The whole world in essence is will, every individual thing and event an empirical manifestation of it.

Schopenhauer's conception of will and action is strongly antidualist. "Willing" is not the name of some purely mental event that is antecedent to a bodily movement while not being itself bodily – which is why it can be misleading to translate his word *Wollen* as "volition," since volitions have often been conceived in this mentalistic manner. Rather, for Schopenhauer, willing is the "bodily action" itself (see W1, 100). So, if you like, I am conscious of being the subject of my willed bodily movements, not just of some mental states that bring about physical effects in the world. Part of the physical world, my body, stands uniquely nearer to me as subject than the rest of the world, while yet I also experience even my own body as an "object among objects" (W1, 99). Schopenhauer is impressed that there appears to be no mediation between myself as subject and the willing that I am conscious of as mine. When I act I know without further observation or evidence that I am willing, and what I am willing. From this notion of immediacy he moves to saying that the "inner nature" or "inner essence" (*Wesen*) of my body and its actions is revealed to me directly as *will.*

So my bodily action exhibits a two-sided picture: appearance as spatio-temporal object (or event) and essence as will. The decisive question now is: is my body to be the sole object that I regard in this way? I know that all other things exist as appearance, as spatio-temporal, causally ordered objects for a subject, but unless I opt for a form of solipsism, I should not be content to consider other objects merely as appearance, but should hold that they also have an inner essence. In arguing that I must regard the common essence of everything as will, Schopenhauer relies on a strong, if not clearly argued, assumption that there must be a single answer to the question what the world is. It is as if metaphysics will be fundamentally unsatisfactory and the world robbed of any genuine "meaning," unless we can be assured that at the deepest level there is a single nature within all things. (Another route to this conclusion relies on the proposition that space and time are the principle of individuation. At the level of the thing in itself, which is beyond space and time, there cannot be a plurality of individuals – see section 4 below.)

With this conviction that the same essence must be in everything that appears empirically, Schopenhauer can regard every bodily and organic process as an appearance of will:

> the whole series of actions, and consequently every individual act and likewise its condition, namely the whole body itself which performs it, and therefore also the process through which and in which the body exists, are nothing but the phenomenal appearance of the will, its becoming visible, the *objectivity of the will*. . . . Therefore the parts of the body must correspond completely to the chief demands and desires by which the will manifests itself . . . teeth, gullet, and intestinal canal are objectified hunger; the genitals are objectified sexual impulse; grasping hands and nimble feet correspond to the more indirect strivings of the will which they represent. (W1, 108)

But the scope of "will" is soon much wider than this. Every natural thing, event, kind, or force must be regarded likewise as an expression of the same essence. Schopenhauer argues that scientific explanation is never completely adequate. It always explains events in terms of laws and forces, but ultimately stops short without explaining what they in turn are. So, he alleges, its explanations in terms of gravitation, heat, light, magnetism always rely on what are in effect *qualitates occultae*, obscure qualities. Science tells us *how* the world works, but not *what* it is (W1, 121, 125). It is to metaphysics that we must look if we want to know the true nature of the world itself that appears in all these regular phenomena. And metaphysics tells us that the whole world is will. Here are some examples Schopenhauer gives:

> the force that shoots and vegetates in the plant, indeed the force by which the crystal is formed, the force that turns the magnet to the North Pole . . . the force that appears in the elective affinities of matter as repulsion and attraction, separation and union, and finally even gravitation . . . all these [the reader] will recognize as different only in the phenomenon, but the same according to their inner essence. He will recognize them all as that which is immediately known to him so intimately and better than everything else, and where it appears most distinctly is called *will*. (W1, 110)

How to take all this is another matter. At first it sounds incredibly naive, as if Schopenhauer is asking us to think that crystals want to grow, that the bones in your hand are there because they (or something that existed before they did) want to grasp, that your intestine desires to digest things, and so on. Fortunately, Schopenhauer states that this would be a woeful misunderstanding of his idea (see W1, 105, 111). But then it becomes quite unclear what does mean. We can establish that consciousness and mentality do not pertain to everything that is an instance of will, in Schopenhauer's sense:

> the circumstance of its being accompanied by knowledge, and the determination by motives which is conditioned by this knowledge . . . belongs not to the inner nature of the will, but merely to its most distinct phenomenon as animal and human being. Therefore, if I say that the force which attracts a stone to the earth is of its nature, in

> itself . . . will, then no one will attach to this proposition the absurd meaning that the stone moves itself according to a known motive, because it is thus that the will appears in man. (W1, 105)

Thus to say the world is will is not to say that there is some mind at work inside or outside nature choosing or designing how things are. But, in that case, how can the mindless, unconscious essence of a stone, or of the force which makes it fall, be just exactly what I discover as my own essence when I employ my self-conscious experience of actions determined by mental motives? Schopenhauer never makes this clear.

Nevertheless, certain features of Schopenhauer's thesis that the world is will have interesting and serious consequences for the place of humanity in the world. Everything has to be seen as striving or tending towards some goal, whether temporary, or all-pervasive:

> Everything presses and pushes towards *existence*, if possible towards *organic existence*, i.e., *life*, and then to the highest possible degree thereof. In animal nature, it then becomes obvious that *will to life* [*Wille zum Leben*] is the keynote of its being, its only unchangeable and unconditioned quality. (W2, 350)

But my essence is the same as that of every other thing in the world. And since throughout nature the striving for existence is "blind," not essentially mediated by consciousness, this must apply also to my essence. So what I essentially am is a thing that blindly tends towards living existence. It is crucial to Schopenhauer that I tend by nature not only to preserve my own existence, but to propagate the existence of more living things. For him, reproductive sexuality is as basic to the nature of the human individual as the drive towards continuing his or her own existence. The genitals, he comments, are "the focus of the will" (W1, 330). The whole body is will, including the brain, but the organs of reproduction are where the will to life is seen most plainly for what it is.

Once we regard humanity this way, we have to attribute to ourselves some of the characteristics of the world at large. The will (the world) is itself groundless and has no exterior purpose. It merely, as a brute fact, manifests itself endlessly as individuals which endlessly strive. Nothing in the world strives or tends as it does for any ultimate reason. It is not to fulfil any rational purpose, or because there is a good end-state to be attained, that plants or crystals grow, or that objects gravitate towards the earth. And so it is with humanity. We each exist as an individual organism that blindly and for no good reason "gravitates" towards survival and sexual reproduction. Hence, although rational thought and choice are characteristics of human beings, they are not at the core of the human psyche, and are, Schopenhauer believes, explicable as mere instruments of the more fundamental will to life. Even consciousness, let alone the self-consciousness which was earlier proclaimed the true starting-point for philosophy, must be underlain by a nature that is more fundamental than it. The idea that an unconscious striving constitutes our inner nature clearly looks forward to the work of Freud.

3. Pessimism

Although Schopenhauer was apparently a somewhat gloomy and neurotic man, it is not true that his pessimism has its origin only in his personality. Rather it is integral to his metaphysics of world and self, which knowingly sets itself up as a riposte to theism, pantheism, rationalism, Kant, Hegel, and the mainstream Judeo-Christian tradition of theorizing about the nature of reality. Schopenhauer's metaphysics of the will is designed to teach us that the world and our own existence is without purpose, that there cannot be a highest good, or perfection, or a rational order of things, and that the awfulness of life has to be faced without such comforts. The dominant strain of optimism in Western thought is a "wicked" doctrine, according to Schopenhauer, "a bitter mockery of the sufferings of mankind" (W1, 326). But to counter the mockery he constructs a metaphysics as grand as any in that tradition. Adorno's remark (*Minima Moralia*, 153) that Schopenhauer is the "peevish ancestor of existential philosophy and malicious heir of the great speculators" seems quite appropriate.

One of Schopenhauer's starkest metaphors concerning the will is that it devours itself. Each individual is equally an expression of striving for existence and propagation, but must destroy or inflict pain on other expressions of the same striving. "The will must live on itself, since nothing exists besides it, and it is a hungry will. Hence arise pursuit, hunting, anxiety, and suffering" (W1, 154). Schopenhauer argues that the predicament of the individual willing human being is characterized principally by suffering, unredeemed by any happiness or attainment that possesses genuine value. We strive perpetually, not because we have chosen rationally to do so, but because it is our nature to do so. Whatever we achieve by striving cannot change our very nature, and hence cannot extinguish striving within us. Thus "[the will's] claims are inexhaustible, and every satisfied desire gives birth to a new one." Eating a meal does not switch off one's propensity for hunger, sexual intercourse does not still one's sexual desire forever, success in writing a book, say, or building a skyscraper, or conceiving a child, does not make one cease to be hungry for food, or sex, or knowledge – and so on.

Schopenhauer defines satisfaction as the cessation of striving or willing. As such it is always relative to an episode of willing. If you are hungry, feeling a lack of food, then satisfaction consists in the erasing of that lack. But to feel a lack is already a form of suffering. So every satisfaction is relative to some suffering. More than this, Schopenhauer insists that satisfaction itself is essentially negative:

> We feel pain, not painlessness; care, but not freedom from care; fear, but not safety and security. We feel the desire as we feel hunger and thirst; but as soon as it has been satisfied, it is like the mouthful of food that has been taken, and which ceases to exist for our feelings the moment it is swallowed. (W2, 575)

Even attaining all one's goals for a while does not bring an end to suffering. If one lacks desires and has no ends to strive for, one becomes painfully bored. Any animal's life "swings like a pendulum to and fro between pain and boredom, and these two are in fact its ultimate constituents" (W1, 312).

It is a common belief that happiness consists in attainment of what is willed. But this is an illusion, according to Schopenhauer. Time distorts our interpretation of happiness: "happiness lies always in the future, or else in the past, and the present may be compared to a small dark cloud driven by the wind over a sunny plain" (W2, 573). It is especially concerning future happiness that we are prone to illusion: that it will be somehow radically different from our present state. We should reflect that, when the circumstances we want come about, they will be the present; and in that present we shall begin willing anew. Each present is going to contain a wish or desire that looks ahead to its own resolution, as yet absent. And yet we tend to pursue happiness as if it could be both permanent and all-resolving. The explanation is that the will to life constitutes our very nature.

> There is only one inborn error, and that is the notion that we exist in order to be happy. It is inborn in us, because it coincides with our existence itself, and our whole being [*Wesen*] is only its paraphrase, indeed our body is its monogram. We are nothing more than the will to life, and the successive satisfaction of all our willing is what we think of through the concept of happiness. (W2, 634)

Schopenhauer concludes that the whole of existence for an individual willing being is composed of suffering, since one either wills (which is to suffer from lack), or fails to attain what one wills (which is suffering), or has nothing to will (which is another form of suffering). Punctuating the suffering are brief pockets of satisfaction, but satisfaction is not positively felt, and amounts only to a pause between sufferings. He attaches enormous weight to suffering, to the extent that its very presence invalidates the whole of existence:

> that thousands have lived in happiness and joy would never do away with the anguish and death-agony of one individual; and just as little does my present well-being undo my previous sufferings. Were the evil in the world even a hundred times less than it is, its mere existence would still be sufficient to establish a truth that may be expressed in various ways . . . namely that we have not to be pleased but rather sorry about the existence of the world; that its non-existence would be preferable to its existence; that it is something which at bottom ought not to be. (W2, 576)

This is an extremely pessimistic thought: the occurrence of any suffering at all renders worthless the existence of everything there is.

However, Schopenhauer does not leave us bereft of all remedy. States of genuine value can be attained in human life. There is aesthetic experience, there are morally good impulses, and there is an extreme attitude of self-renunciation or denial of the will which, though rare, shows that existence can ultimately arrive at salvation. Before we discuss these redeeming states, however, we must examine in more detail the ordinary state of empirical consciousness with which Schopenhauer contrasts them.

4. The Principles of Empirical Consciousness

Schopenhauer's account of the organizing principles of ordinary empirical consciousness is best presented in his early doctoral dissertation, *On the Fourfold Root of the Principle of Sufficient Reason*, which he wrote in 1813, and republished in revised, though not in all respects improved, form in 1847. Though *The World as Will and Representation* is the fullest and most inspired encapsulation of his philosophy, a reading of *On the Fourfold Root* can be recommended, especially since Schopenhauer says in *The World as Will and Representation* that he presupposes knowledge of the earlier dissertation.

The theme of the dissertation is the principle of sufficient reason which states *nihil est sine ratione cur potius sit quam non sit* (Nothing is without a ground or reason why it is rather than is not). This principle may concern distinct species of "reason" or "ground," and hence different species of explanation. Schopenhauer seeks to clarify matters by mapping out four distinct kinds of explanatory principle, which he calls the sufficient reason of becoming, the sufficient reason of knowing, the sufficient reason of being, and the sufficient reason of acting. The framework of *On the Fourfold Root* is Kantian. Schopenhauer uses the dichotomy of subject and object, in which objects are the known and the subject is the knower that can never itself be an object of knowledge. What can be known as objects are representations (*Vorstellungen*) which the subject has. Hence the four kinds of explanation in the dissertation concern different classes of representations and the connections between them.

Schopenhauer follows Kant here in describing empirical consciousness as consisting of representations organized by the *a priori* forms of space and time. The empirical content that fills these forms is matter, appearing to the subject as distinct spatio-temporal objects. Schopenhauer's first kind of connection among representations is the *principle of the sufficient reason of becoming* which asserts that every state that appears must have resulted from a change that preceded it. This version of the principle is thus the *law of causality*. Schopenhauer's discussion of causality builds on but also criticizes Kant's, and is the longest and most successful section of *On the Fourfold Root* (see FR, ch. 4). Space and time also yield the distinct explanatory principle which Schopenhauer calls the *principle of the sufficient reason of being*. This is supposed to cover reason-giving in mathematics, and Schopenhauer here relies on Kant's idea that mathematics involves non-empirical, *a priori* intuition of spatial position and temporal succession. Space and time themselves are described as objects or representations for the subject, and the connections in space and time cognized *a priori* are termed relations of "mathematical necessity" (FR, ch. 6)

Schopenhauer holds concepts to be another distinct class of representations. He calls them "representations of representations," regarding them as derivative from perceptual experience by a process of abstraction. Concepts enable the subject to make judgments, and the *principle of the sufficient reason of knowing* states that if a judgment is to express knowledge, it must be related to a ground – which may lie in perception, in inference from another judgment, or in the possibility of experience or thought as such (FR, ch. 5). Finally, Schopenhauer states the *principle of the sufficient reason of acting*, or law of motivation, which says that every act of will is related to a motive which causes it (FR, ch. 7). The subject's own will is the unique object of experience which this form of the principle concerns.

The first general point to take from the dissertation is that all empirical consciousness is constituted by relations among objects of experience, or (equivalently) among representations. Nothing we experience in ordinary objective perception, or in scientific investigation of the world, stands alone within some relation to another representation which is its ground. Secondly, these relations have their origin in the subject. In Kantian fashion, the requirements of the subject's representing to itself a world of objects dictate the various grounding relations that hold between the objects the subject experiences. Schopenhauer's explanation for these relations is ultimately very different from Kant's, however. While for Kant they are the *a priori* necessary conditions of any possible experience, for Schopenhauer they are the modes through which a willing being of a certain organic constitution must filter its experience, if it is to survive and manipulate its environment. The difference is masked by Schopenhauer's presentation (especially in *On the Fourfold Root* where his full metaphysics of the will is not present), but has two very important consequences. First, our understanding of the connections of space, time, causality, and the other forms of explanation is given an instrumental force that it does not have for Kant:

> Sensibility, nerves, brain, just like other parts of the organic being, are only an expression of the will . . . hence the representation that arises through them is also destined to serve the will as means . . . for the maintenance of a being with many different needs. Thus, originally and by its nature, knowledge is completely the servant of the will. (W1, 176)

Secondly, there is left open the implicit possibility – anathema to Kant – of states of conscious experience that need not be governed by the same rules of consciousness. It is this possibility of experiential states which, because they fight free of the bondage of the will, break the Kantian rules and present us with objects shorn of their spatial, temporal, causal, and other modes of connectedness, that Schopenhauer seeks to exploit to the full in his aesthetics and ethics.

The notion of another form of experience that transcends the limitations of empirical consciousness arises early in Schopenhauer's development. In his *Manuscript Remains* it can be found in the conception of the "better consciousness" which he developed in 1813–14, under the influence of Plato and the Upanishads, while struggling to integrate them with his understanding of Kant. What survives in his mature philosophy is the idea that experiences can occur in which the principle of sufficient reason is abandoned.

When considering the divide between these two forms of consciousness, we must pay special attention to *individuality*. The *principium individuationis* or principle of individuation is constituted, for Schopenhauer, by space and time. That is, without space and time there would be no distinct individuals. The empirical world of objects presented in ordinary experience is a spatio-temporal world of individuals. But if there can be an experience in which the ordinary modes of connectedness lapse, then there can be an experience which is not governed by space and time. And that would be an experience in which individuals are no longer distinguished from one another. In our account of Schopenhauer's aesthetics and ethics we shall see how he exploits this basic thought in a number of ways.

5. Art and Aesthetic Value

Schopenhauer has often been well regarded by aestheticians, firstly because of the great significance he assigns to art and aesthetic experience in human life in general, and secondly for the wealth of informed critical judgment he brings to his discussions of the arts. He can be seen as the main prototype of what later became known as aesthetic attitude theory, which held, roughly, that aesthetic value attaches to a certain state of mind in which desires and other interests are wholly suspended and a perceived object can be experienced with pleasure for its own sake. The unifying thought in Schopenhauer's aesthetic theory is that one may have perceptual experience while the will is suspended. Such an occurrence is comparatively rare because the intellect is by nature a tool of the will and not prone to contemplating reality with the objectivity and freedom from desires that aesthetic experience demands. In aesthetic experience one is sunk in contemplation of some object and ceases to impose upon it the usual spatial, temporal and causal connections: "we no longer consider the where, the when, the why, and the whither of things, but simply and solely the *what*" (W1, 178).

Aesthetic experience, whether of nature or of art, is a temporary state of calm will-lessness, from which desire and suffering alike are excluded. This is already to assign it huge value, given Schopenhauer's doctrine of the will and his emphatic view that the life of willing is a merciless round of suffering and boredom. Unique worth resides in aesthetic experience if it has such power to ameliorate, even temporarily, an existence that any of us should otherwise wish to be without. But Schopenhauer's valorization of aesthetic experience does not stop there. He also sees in aesthetic contemplation a cognitive gain and an alteration in one's sense of self. The subject in aesthetic experience becomes unaware of its separateness from that which it experiences: "the person who is involved in this perception is no longer an individual, for in such perception the individual has lost himself; he is *pure* will-less, painless, timeless *subject of knowledge*" (W1, 179). At the same time, the object of the experience is not merely the individual spatio-temporal thing, but a kind of universal, one of the eternal Ideas fixed in nature.

Schopenhauer's conception of Ideas is openly influenced by Plato and he often refers to them as "Platonic Ideas" or "(Platonic) Ideas." They are best regarded as kinds inherent in nature at a level above that of individual spatio-temporal things.

Typical examples are living species and natural forces. They are the regular and universal ways in which the world as will makes itself manifest. Schopenhauer calls them "grades of the will's objectivity" (see, for example, W1, 212) and the "adequate objectivity" of the will (W1, 179), meaning by this that they are the nearest we can come to experiencing reality as it is in itself. One vital divergence from the Platonic original is that Schopenhauerian Ideas are accessible to perception rather than ratiocination. The artist or aesthetic observer sees the universal in the particular, rather than engaging in any particular conceptual thinking. The latter is downgraded in comparison with perception, as it is throughout Schopenhauer's philosophy. "The concept," as he puts it, "is eternally barren and unproductive in art" (W1, 235).

At the same time the heightened perception of will-less aesthetic experience is alleged to be cognitively superior to ordinary empirical perception and indeed to empirical investigation in science. Aesthetic experience achieves greater objectivity because in it the subject casts off the forms of the principle of sufficient reason that ordinarily mediate between the subject and its objects. Schopenhauer's thinking is as follows: individual empirical things are experienced when and only when the subject applies to its representations the *a priori* forms of space, time, and causality. But ordinary empirical knowledge is driven by the will: it consists in brain-processes whose occurrence subserves the ends of the organism. Thus, if the intellect breaks away from its service to the will, it must leave behind the forms of space, time, and causality. And since we experience individual spatio-temporal things only because we impose these forms, a timeless and spaceless experience must have as its object something beyond individual spatio-temporal things. This doctrine of Ideas is clearly the descendant of Schopenhauer's earlier thinking about the "better consciousness." He believes that by freeing one's intellect temporarily from the will one gains a higher form of knowledge, and becomes a pure subject mirroring reality in the most objective possible manner, and leaving behind one's identification with any individual part of the empirical world.

Although he recognizes that nature provides many opportunities for this kind of elevated contemplation, Schopenhauer's main interest is in art, where the spectator's experience is facilitated by the activity of the artist. For Schopenhauer the true artist is a genius, by which he means someone whose intellect – the capacity for perception, not concept-use or reasoning – is abnormally powerful and able to function in greater isolation from the will. The genius can discern the universal in the particular with greater objectivity, as it were on behalf of the rest of us, and convey this insight in perceptible form.

Schopenhauer's writing is informed by a wide knowledge and appreciation of the various arts. He discusses architecture, painting of different genres, sculpture, poetry, and drama. Each art form has Ideas or grades of the will's objectivity which it is especially able to reveal. Schopenhauer accordingly places the arts in a hierarchy. At the lower end architecture, for example, enables us to know the fundamental Ideas of gravity, cohesion, and rigidity. Landscape painting displays Ideas of inanimate nature and the plant world. Other paintings reveal the Ideas of different species of animals, and finally of human beings – but the highest art form, whose speciality is the Idea of humanity in all its complexity, is poetry. At the very pinnacle stands tragedy, which has a special significance for Schopenhauer, since the eternal Idea of humanity which it makes known contains the most profound picture of the misery of our condition. Yet the value of tragedy for Schopenhauer does not lie solely in this knowledge of what he calls "the conflict of the will with itself." He contends that the best tragedies present the hero's will turning away from life and adopting a sublime resignation in the face of suffering – thus exemplifying the attitude which he later argues is the only genuine "salvation."

Schopenhauer's account of music is especially noteworthy and has attracted much attention. He suggests that while the other arts all attempt to stimulate knowledge of Ideas by depicting individual things, music "is as *immediate* an objectification and copy of the whole *will* as the world itself is" (W1, 257). The will expresses itself as the phenomenal world; the same will expresses itself again in music, which bypasses the level of Ideas altogether. Thus Schopenhauer maintains that the appeal of music lies in its copying the patterns of striving and resolution of the will, to which we respond because they resonate with our lives as willing beings. But no personal strivings or sufferings enter into music: "Music does not express this or that particular and definite pleasure, this or that affliction, pain, sorrow, horror, gaiety, merriment, or peace of mind, but joy, pain, sorrow, horror, gaiety, merriment, peace of mind *themselves*, to a certain extent in their abstract nature" (W1, 261). Hence the value of music to the listener may also be that of a will-less calm. Even though it enables us to become better acquainted, objectively, with the behavior of the will, it does so by freeing us for a time from the pressure of our own individual willing and feeling.

6. Ethics

The Fourth Book of *The World as Will and Representation* concerns ethics, taken broadly to include questions about the value of human existence, and what kind of happiness or salvation we may hope for. Schopenhauer gives his views here on the nature of morality and the question of free will and responsibility. However, these views are more cogently stated in his pair of essays, *On the Freedom of the Will* and *On the Basis of Morality*, which he published jointly in 1841 under the title *On the Two Fundamental Problems of Ethics.* Both are fine, powerful essays, and give the most accessible account of Schopenhauer's views on morality and freedom. It is only in *The World as Will and Representation*, however, that his broader conclusions about the human condition and his advocacy of denial of the will are fully presented.

In *On the Freedom of the Will* Schopenhauer gives an elegant case for determinism. He first makes a distinction between freedom to act, which one has when there are no impediments to one's doing what one wills, and freedom to will. The latter raises the really important philosophical question: given that one in fact willed to do such-and-such, could one have willed a different course of action? Schopenhauer suggests that acts of will are caused by a combination of one's permanent unchanging character and motives, which are representations of states of affairs in the world that impinge upon one's character. No act of will could have failed to occur if the same motives and the same character had been present. In this sense there is no free will. Yet the feeling that we are responsible for our actions remains. Schopenhauer tries to account for this by saying that we feel responsible for what we are – for our unchanging, intelligible character, a character which is supposedly what we are beyond the realm of the empirical. If my actions issue from my unchanging essence, he believes I rightly feel responsible, even though I can neither choose nor change what I am. Nietzsche's later notion of *amor fati*, love of fate, seems to revisit the same ground as Schopenhauer's conception of character.

Schopenhauer's theory of morality rests on a set of trenchant criticisms of Kant's ethics. He is mightily unimpressed by the notion of a categorical imperative, seeing it as a relic of the idea that commands are issued by the absolute authority of a divine being. He also questions the way Kant links morality with rationality; other animals for Schopenhauer should be accorded moral status, and the fact that they lack rationality is irrelevant. His own account of morality is comparatively simple, and has been acknowledged as a precursor of the recent renaissance of virtue ethics. The one genuine moral impulse, according to Schopenhauer is compassion (or sympathy, *Mitleid*), which he says is present in each human being in some degree. Individuals governed by compassion apprehend the world and their place in it in a superior way, and they and their actions are good. The impulse of compassion expresses itself in actions which are just or which show *Menschenliebe*, philanthropy or love of humankind. The sole principle of morality is that which encapsulates the virtues of justice and philanthropy, and which states "injure no one, rather help everyone as much as you can" (see BM, 147).

Each individual's character – which for Schopenhauer is inborn and unchanging – has some combination of the ingredients egoism, compassion, and malice. Malice is the impulse to seek another's harm, egoism the impulse towards one's own well-being and the avoidance of harm to oneself. Egoism is the greater part of most characters, according to Schopenhauer, since as manifestations of the will to life we must strive continually to survive and further ourselves. Pure malice is as much an exception as pure compassion, but both impulses must be accepted as facts of human nature. Compassion is the impulse to seek another's well-being and to prevent their suffering, and is grounded in a vision of the world which sets less store than usual on divisions between individuals: the good man, says Schopenhauer, sees everywhere "I once more" (BM, 211). The metaphysical foundation for this is the claim that individuation is not an ultimate truth in the universe, since whatever appears as distinct at the empirical level is, at the level of the "in itself," one and the same will. If individuality is thus illusory, compassion is more profoundly justified than egoism.

The idea that individuality is not metaphysically basic also plays a role in

Schopenhauer's view of life and death. Death is not something to fear, in Schopenhauer's view, since the world-will which expresses itself in this one fleeting individual continues undisturbed; death is "the great opportunity no longer to be I . . . the moment of that liberation from the one-sidedness of an individuality that does not constitute the innermost kernel of our true being" (W2, 507–8). Despite this, Schopenhauer does not approve of suicide, which he regards as a failure to accept life on proper terms. The suicide affirms life, but revolts against the particular sufferings life contains. The contrasting attitude which Schopenhauer advocates is denial of the will to life, an attitude which accepts the state of being alive but acquiesces in the suffering and the non-fulfilment of desires which it brings.

The question arises whether denial of the will to life is, paradoxically, something one can bring about at will. Schopenhauer appears to think not, since he talks of "those in whom the will has turned and denied itself" – as if the will were an agency of its own – and says denial of willing "is not to be forcibly arrived at by intention or design . . . it comes suddenly, as if flying in from without" (W1, 404). There are two routes to this turning of the will. One is the life of what Schopenhauer calls a saint. Such a person has knowledge of the illusoriness of individuation, and his or her individual will is "quieted" thereby. The attitude of saints is one of such overwhelming compassion that they do not seek to further their own ends in distinction from those of others, nor to avoid harm to themselves. The other path leading to the turning of the will is to undergo suffering so great that spontaneously one's will to life gives out, while yet one remains alive. Those in whom the will has turned attain a state which Schopenhauer describes as "resignation, true composure, and complete will-lessness" (W1, 379). He asks us to consider the blissful state of aesthetic contemplation, and then to imagine it prolonged: such, he claims is the state of will-less self-denial that is the only genuine "salvation" for humanity. Since our existence as bodily, striving individuals is one we would have been better without, the only remedy lies in achieving a vision of the world which attaches the lowest possible importance to one's individuality. The resulting state is one Schopenhauer finds hard to describe: it is a kind of knowledge (W1, 410), but it is also "nothingness" (W1, 411). The being in whom the will has turned and denied itself has "overcome the world" and the world as "melted away with the abolished will."

Some of Schopenhauer's criticisms of Kant's ethics appear to look forward to Nietzsche, especially the idea that if we no longer believe in God we should have no place for absolute imperatives or any kind of absolute good. On the other hand, Schopenhauer's defense of morality and his reliance on compassion as its foundation provoke explicit criticism from Nietzsche in turn. Nietzsche was passionately involved with Schopenhauer's philosophy early in his career, and remained fixated by it even as he later attempted to negate it almost in its entirety. We might say that Schopenhauer's philosophy of value, with its heavy emphasis on will-lessness and escaping from individuality and self-affirmation, plays the decisive role in Nietzsche's attempt to revalue the values of morality and of the tradition of philosophical metaphysics.

Notes

1 I use the following abbreviations for Schopenhauer's works: BM, *On the Basis of Morality*, tr. E. F. J. Payne (Oxford: Berghahn Books, 1995); FR, *On the Fourfold Root of the Principle of Sufficient Reason*, tr. E. F. J. Payne (Illinois: Open Court, 1974); FW, *Essay on the Freedom of the Will*, tr. Konstantin Kolenda (Indianapolis, Ind.: Bobbs-Merrill, 1960); W1, W2, *The World as Will and Representation*, 2 vols., tr. E. F. J. Payne (New York: Dover, 1969).

Chapter 16

John Stuart Mill

Wendy Donner and Richard Fumerton

1. Mill's Ethics and Political Philosophy

Like many of his contemporaries in the nineteenth century, Mill did not restrict himself to one specialized field, but made notable and enduring contributions to a number of subjects including political economy, history, psychology, sociology, and literary theory.[1] He also reached beyond the intellectual life. He was a committed social and political activist, who worked for many campaigns including women's suffrage; a politician (as member of the British parliament for Westminster); and a devoted botanist. Though Mill's reputation as a philosopher declined in the early decades of this century, he has in recent years been recognized as a moral and political thinker of the highest stature.

The vicissitudes in the reception of Mill's philosophy are not surprising. The range and complexity of his writings, as well as his willingness to grapple with the messiness of ethical and political issues, can and has frustrated students and scholars. It has even led to the charge that his philosophy lacks coherence. However, as recent reevaluations of Mill's thought have shown, his method of welcoming intricacy as an essential part of cultural and political life provides an appealing and useful tool for understanding and accommodating the diversity of contemporary society. Indeed, a more careful reading of Mill will reveal that his philosophy is both consistent and unified around a progressive view of human nature and a conception of the good that is fundamentally concerned with self-development. This is reflected most clearly in his political philosophy which, I shall suggest, has much in common with current approaches to deliberative democracy. Far from being incoherent, Mill's moral and political philosophy offers a substantive and credible perspective for contemporary students.

1.1 Mill's utilitarianism

The classic source for Mill's elaboration of his theory is the essay *Utilitarianism*, but several other writings, in particular his essays *On Liberty* and *Representative*

Government, as well as parts of the *System of Logic*, must be drawn on for an adequate understanding of his views.[2] While Mill is rightly seen as a major utilitarian philosopher, and as part of the historical line of British empiricist utilitarians, he is also correctly placed as a revisionist thinker, and one who attempts to preserve the tradition of his father James Mill and Jeremy Bentham while liberating it from the confines of the narrower Benthamite version in order to enlarge and sustain it. Whether Mill succeeds in this task of preservation and transformation, or whether this attempt at expansion leads to inconsistency and abandonment of essential utilitarian principles, are matters of continuing and sometimes heated debate.

Mill's utilitarianism begins with his formulation of the principle of utility, which is the supreme or foundational principle of morality in his system. He says that

> The creed which accepts as the foundation of morals, Utility, or the Greatest Happiness Principle, holds that actions are right in proportion as they tend to promote happiness, wrong as they tend to promote the reverse of happiness.[3]

Utilitarianism is classified as a consequentialist moral theory, or as one that evaluates actions in terms of their consequences, that is, whether they produce utility. This is in contradistinction to those nonconsequentialist theories that evaluate actions in terms of some of their intrinsic properties, and which claim that certain sorts of action are right or wrong in themselves and apart from their consequences. Another basic feature or hallmark of utilitarianism is that principles or concepts of the good or intrinsic value are taken to be prior to principles and concepts of right and obligation; obligations thus are grounded on or determined by reference to the good. There are numerous varieties of utilitarianism which arise from different conceptions of the foundational good or value, as well as from different methods of determining obligations by reference to the good. The former cluster of varieties can be classified as hedonist or nonhedonist, while the latter cluster is often classified as act-utilitarian or rule-utilitarian

1.2 *The nature of the good and qualitative hedonism*

Mill shares with his father and Bentham a commitment to a mental-state account of utility; such an account claims that the value to be promoted consists in certain mental states of experience like pleasure, happiness, enjoyment, or well-being. While the appealing and unifying core idea of utilitarianism is the centrality of promoting well-being, there is thus much room for maneuver around the questions of what is the most plausible account of utility or well-being and of what is the best method for promoting this utility. Mill remains true to his roots in classical utilitarianism in espousing a form of hedonism, albeit one that is enlarged and sophisticated. He agrees that the good for humans consists in pleasurable mental states of experience or that states of pleasure, happiness or satisfaction are intrinsically valuable. The principle of utility, as formulated above, is indeed the foundational principle of morality, but in his philosophy this principle is most directly a principle of the good, and one which is also the foundation of all practical reasoning, which is a field much broader than morality, including the other areas of what Mill calls the Art of Life, such as prudence and nobility, but also numerous other moral arts or practical fields such as education and health.[4] This broad status of the principle is clarified when he says: "The utilitarian doctrine is, that happiness is desirable, and the only thing desirable, as an end; all other things being only desirable as means to that end."[5] He expands this meaning in claiming that "pleasure, and freedom from pain, are the only things desirable as ends; and . . . all desirable things (which are as numerous in the utilitarian scheme as in any other scheme) are desirable either for the pleasure inherent in themselves, or as means to the promotion of pleasure and the prevention of pain" (210).

Mill goes on to advance a more sophisticated version of mental-state account than is found in Benthamite quantitative hedonism. Value is still found in states of experience which are pleasurable or satisfying. But Mill was sensitive to objections that Bentham's quantitative hedonism was too narrow in its views about the good-making properties of these states of experience, and he worried that this narrowness made Bentham's theory succumb to the charge that utilitarianism is "a doctrine worthy only of swine" (210). To counter this and other problems, Mill expands the conception of the good at the heart of his theory in two respects: he claims that value resides in complex mental experiences rather than simple sensations of pleasure (as Bentham holds); he claims that the quality (or kind) of these states of experience as well as the quantity or amount are both properly seen as good-making properties which produce their value. So Mill's alternative qualitative hedonism is a complex mental-state account which takes into consideration quality as well as quantity of pleasurable experience in producing a measurement of value.

While Mill's version of the theory is well able to effectively ward off objections that it is a doctrine worthy only of swine, it opens up new lines of criticism by its advocacy of an enlarged concept of utility. Mill is often seen by critics as betraying utilitarianism and hedonism and as propounding a view of value inconsistent with hedonism. While this debate is ongoing and unresolved, I propose that the objections that Mill's qualitative hedonism is inconsistent with hedonism are in fact misguided and stem from the critics' error of conflating and confusing the two quite distinct issues of (1) what things are intrinsically valuable (pleasurable mental states) and (2) what properties of these mental states are productive of their value or are good-making (quantity alone on Bentham's account; quantity and quality on Mill's account). Even after we have taken a position on the first question of what things are intrinsically valuable (hedonistic or nonhedonistic), we still must explore the further question of what properties of those things create or increase their value.

Before I explore further this crucial question, it should be noted that Mill's hedonism is but the starting point for his pursuit of value, and his theory should not be seen as focusing only on evaluations of pleasures. These are the building blocks, and the bulk of Mill's writings are concerned with higher order questions of how to promote human self-development and nurture characters, life plans, projects, and commitments within a liberal culture that provides the sustaining conditions for meaningful human lives. His ethical theory provides the groundwork for his social and political philosophy.

Consider the following seemingly innocuous, even commonsensical, quote from *Utilitarianism*:

> It is quite compatible with the principle of utility to recognize the fact, that some ***kinds*** of pleasure are more desirable and more valuable than others. It would be absurd that while, in estimating all other things, quality is considered as well as quantity, the estimation of pleasures should be supposed to depend on quantity alone. (211)

Yet with this statement Mill makes a decisive break with a central principle of Benthamite quantitative hedonism, and earns for himself the title of revisionary utilitarian. Many sharp criticisms, even condemnations, spring from the claim that we must include quality or kind in the measurement of value. One persistent claim is that Mill does not simply revive and revise hedonism, as I contend, but that he abandons hedonism altogether.

In order to place Mill's perspective on this question in context, it is helpful to consider his version of mental-state account against the backdrop of Bentham's theory. Bentham, we may recall, regards simple sensations of pleasures as the bearers of value, and takes only the quantities of pleasure as productive of value or as being the properties of pleasures in virtue of which the pleasures which have them increase in value. Mill, in contrast, regards both the quantity and the quality (kind) of pleasurable mental states as productive of good. To understand Mill's views, it is important to see that quality is not synonymous with or the same thing as value. It is also important to understand that what utilitarians are trying to promote, or maximize, and so what they must have tools to measure, is value. Value or goodness is produced by quantity and quality, which are for Mill the two fundamental good-making characteristics. Mill's procedure for measuring utility calls upon agents to rank mental experiences on a scale of value by taking into account the properties (quantity and quality) that contribute to this value.

Bentham and Mill both propose methods to measure the value of the pleasurable mental states which are the bearers of value. Bentham's famous (or notorious) felicific calculus is designed to measure the quantity of pleasure or pain, as quantity is the sole good-making property on his account. The calculus works out the amount of each pleasure and pain of each person with a stake in the moral situation, and then balances the quantities of all these pleasures and pains to determine which action will result in the greatest balance of pleasure over pain. Quantity is broken down into two components or dimensions of intensity and duration; the calculus quantifies intensity and duration and integrates them into the scale of value. Since value is a function of quantity, the higher on the scale of quantity each pleasure is placed, the greater is its value. Bentham's scales are cardinal, and so units that can be added and multiplied and aggregated are needed for each dimension.

The drawbacks to this approach are obvious. It is notoriously difficult to defend the ability of agents through introspection accurately to measure these internal properties, much less accurately to do interpersonal comparisons of different persons' experiences. The demands for such rigorous measurement in this field cannot realistically be met, and so Mill's noncardinal and much less demanding scales are far more plausible as an accurate reflection of measurement of value.

The felicific calculus, with its dimensions of intensity and duration, is already a multidimensional procedure. But Mill's proposed alternative measurement procedure has more dimensions to integrate into the central scale of value. Mill's procedure uses the judgments of competent (self-developed) agents. These agents can be thought of as being all adult citizens who have the right to make public choices, and should not be thought of as an elitist subgroup of citizens. In making judgments of value, they must integrate quantity and quality onto the value scale, but, crucially, these scales are much weaker than Bentham's cardinal scales. Recent work on utility theory and social-choice theory has illustrated that there is a wide range of kinds of scale on which utility and value can be measured. Usable scales need not be as strong as Bentham's cardinal scales; scales of utility can be of many different strengths and can measure utility construed in many different ways.[6]

Mill uses the preferences of competent agents who judge certain kinds of pleasurable experiences to be more valuable and who thus place them higher on the scale of value.[7] When Mill says that "the pleasures derived from the higher faculties [are] preferable in kind" (213), he is claiming that intellectual pleasures, for example, can be a kind of pleasure. But he uses a scheme of categorization which is broader than this comment suggests. Millian kinds are also based on causes (causal properties) and phenomenal differences (intentional properties, feeling-tone properties) of pleasures, although Mill's comments on the satisfactions arising from the exercise of the "higher faculties" are sometimes given undue prominence and obscure the more general nature of his classification scheme for kinds.

Mill's bold revisionism in expanding the conception of the good and in proposing the judgments of competent agents as an alternative to the felicific calculus has drawn a good deal of scrutiny, skepticism, and sharp critique. In this chapter I have space only to sketch out some lines of criticism and some possible replies and rejoinders.

One persistent objection is that the introduction of quality (kind) as a good-making property is an abandonment of or is inconsistent with hedonism. The historical critic F. H. Bradley puts this objection succinctly: "If you are to prefer a higher pleasure to a lower without reference to quantity – then there is an end altogether of the principle which puts the measure in the surplus of pleasure to the whole sentient creation."[8] But if we recall our earlier discussion about misdirected criticisms based upon conflation of separate issues, we can see that this objection is off target. Hedonism holds that pleasurable states are good and are the only things that are good (issue 1). However, hedonists can disagree (as do Mill and Bentham), over the issue of which properties of pleasurable states contribute to its overall value (issue 2). Bradley's objection simply begs the question in assuming without argument that the only legitimate form of hedonism is quantitative hedonism.

Another persistent objection is to all forms of hedonism. This objection, put simply, challenges the notion that *only* happiness is intrinsically good, and claims to the contrary that value pluralism is the correct doctrine. According to value pluralism, other things can be considered as valuable in themselves, apart from any relation to human well-being. While the list of other intrinsically valuable things may vary, usually virtue and knowledge are featured prominently on it.

Mill draws upon his moral psychology of associationism to reply to this line of thought. In effect, Mill claims that through psychological association virtue becomes part of our happiness or a component of happiness. Although initially we desire virtue as a means to happiness, through psychological association virtue becomes pleasurable and so a component of happiness. Virtue is pleasurable especially when a person has developed and exercises the moral and intellectual "higher" capacities and so it becomes not just a means to but a part of happiness.[9]

Is Mill correct in asserting that virtue and knowledge must have this link to happiness? For the claims of value pluralism to be convincing, a contrary case must be made that virtue and knowledge are valuable *apart from* this relationship to human happiness. Critics who claim that happiness is not the sole thing which is good in itself usually point to these other examples without making the extensive positive case for the claim that they are good in themselves. A closer scrutiny of the case for knowledge as intrinsically valuable may serve to point to the counter-objections of hedonism to this example.

If knowledge is valuable in itself, then it must be so valuable even in cases in which it has no link to happiness, as well as in cases in which it is the cause of suffering, even great suffering. Critics of value pluralism can argue that the example of the knowledge which led to the creation of weapons of mass destruction such as the atomic and nuclear bombs provides a powerful challenge to the claim that knowledge is good in itself. The horror of Hiroshima should give us pause. The reply that we do not know to what good consequences this knowledge will lead in the future is self-defeating, since this is a line of thought which appeals to well-being and undermines the objection to hedonism. Value pluralism must convince us that knowledge is a good *even if* it leads only to horrific suffering. Reflection on this example may well incline us to the conclusion that Mill's arguments are the stronger. Other similar examples can be brought in by Millians. The massive human destruction of the life-sustaining environment, including a rapid increase in the rate of species extinctions due to human intervention, as well as alarming levels of toxins and pollution of air, water, and soil, and ozone depletion and global warming, could not have occurred without scientific and technological knowledge. Is this to be valued? Mill's claim that there must be links to well-being to make the case for the value of knowledge is bolstered by such counterexamples to value pluralism.

1.3 Moral principles, obligation, and rights

The principle of utility, the ultimate principle of utilitarianism, is a principle of the good underlying all of our practical reasoning. But this principle also provides grounding for concepts and principles of duty and obligation, including those justice principles concerned with rights. It is now time to turn our attention to different positions which have been adopted on the question of the best role for the principle of utility to play in making decisions about obligations and rights. Just as utilitarians can advocate different positions on the issue of the nature of the good, so they can also differ over the question of the relation of the principle of utility to secondary rules of obligations. Discussions of the last few decades have tended to frame these debates by categorizing positions as act-utilitarian or rule-utilitarian. These are not rules that Mill himself used and it is questionable whether he would have been comfortable aligning himself with either of these perspectives, or whether these perspectives capture his intent. But as these terms and categories dominate the literature, it is well to begin by setting them out. Although there is a vast literature on these questions, this literature can obscure the underlying substantive issue at stake. The underlying substantive issue is the strength of the moral rules in Mill's system – they must be strong enough to avoid being easily overturned, yet not so strong that they are rigidly adhered to when reflection might lead us to the conclusion that it would be better not to follow them in certain extreme circumstances.

Act-utilitarians claim that moral agents decide what is right or wrong by examining the consequences of doing a particular act in a particular situation. This is a case-by-case methodology. Rule-utilitarians claim that moral agents perform their obligations by following general moral rules. These are the rules Mill refers to as secondary moral principles, such as the rule prohibiting killing. Rule-utilitarians argue that we ought to follow justified moral rules, and rules are justified if they would produce the greatest balance of happiness over suffering if they were generally adhered to by moral agents. Rule-utilitarians argue that we should adhere to such a rule even if on a particular occasion adherence to the rule would not lead to the best consequences. This is often seen as separating out rule-utilitarians from act-utilitarians, because the case-by-case methodology of act-utilitarians would sometimes incline act-utilitarians to break the rule on this particular occasion and follow the course of action which would lead to the best consequences in this setting. Rule-utilitarians argue that agents should follow generally useful rules because there is the danger of undermining confidence that moral rules will be respected if agents are encouraged to break rules on particular occasions. Trust in the institution of moral rules and respect for such rules must be upheld. But it should also be remembered that both act- and rule-utilitarians turn to the principle of utility to ground their decisions.

Mill has been interpreted as both an act- and a rule-utilitarian.[10] But the problem with firmly placing him in either of these camps is that, while his theory has a strong and central place for secondary moral principles which should be generally adhered to, there are also, according to Mill, cases in which a direct appeal should be made to the principle of utility, and at least some forms of rule-utilitarianism do not allow this. Mill also encourages direct appeal to the principle in cases when we are considering moral reform, that is, when we think that a currently accepted rule should be changed. Mill says: "The corollaries from the principle of utility, like the precepts of every practical art, admit of indefinite improvement, and in a progressive state of the human mind, their improvement is perpetually going on."[11]

As Fred Berger argues, Mill held a "strategy conception of rules," which proposes that "in *practical* deliberations, we should follow useful rules in determining our moral duties, except in extreme or special circumstances where a great deal is at stake, in which case we determine what morality requires by appeal to the consequences of the act."[12] Mill's perspective on secondary moral rules is a model of balance, in which agents deliberate and reflectively balance considerations about whether to follow generally useful rules or consider whether to appeal directly to the principle of utility.

There is an important substantive issue at stake, one which could provide fodder for an objection to utilitarianism if it is not resolved. This objection to utilitarianism claims that the theory permits or sanctions examples of injustice which are at odds with the moral intuitions of reflective moral agents. A classic example, adapted from H. J. McCloskey by Roger Crisp, is the following:

> A town in the Wild West has been plagued by a series of violent crimes. The sheriff is confronted by a deputation led by the mayor. The deputation tells him that, unless he hangs the vagrant he has in his jail, whom the whole town believes to be the criminal, there will without doubt be a terrible riot, in which many people will be killed or maimed. This vagrant has no friends or family. The sheriff knows he is innocent.[13]

Crisp goes on to raise the question whether "by breaking the normal rules of justice that people should be given fair trial, and that those known to be innocent should not be punished, he could produce the best outcome."[14] Crisp says that Mill would reject this line of reasoning and keep the rule because of the bad consequences of breaking the rule. In this case, "the sheriff's ploy may be discovered," but his more general point is that "it is just not clear in practice whether, in any particular case, one might maximize by breaking the rule."[15] So ignorance and uncertainty about future outcomes should lead us to follow rules. There are other considerations that could also be brought in here to argue for rule adherence. For example, pandering to the mob instincts at work could have disturbing consequences.

This line of thought backs up the utilitarian case for following rules and thus helps in answering the objection. But Mill's particular brand of utilitarianism has a further response to those not satisfied. Mill's theory, unlike Bentham's, accords a central place to rights which protect vital interests – and this is a far more secure rebuff to those who claim that utilitarianism sanctions injustice.

Mill's moral philosophy has a complex structure. This structure is explained in some detail in *Utilitarianism* in a chapter entitled "On the Connexion between Justice and Utility." Since the principle of utility is a general principle of the good, or of "expediency" as Mill sometimes calls it, we must first mark off rules of morality or obligation from the broader class of general promotion of good.[16] As David Lyons has explained with great clarity, Mill here conceptually links moral obligation and punishment and has "a model based on coercive social rules."[17] Lyons continues:

> These considerations suggest that Mill had a view something like this. To call an act wrong is to imply that guilt feelings, and perhaps other sanctions, would be warranted against it. But sanctions assume coercive rules. *To show an act wrong, therefore, is to show that a coercive rule against it would be justified.* The justification of a coercive social rule establishes a moral obligation, breach of which is wrong.[18]

And so Mill's justification of utilitarian moral rules of obligation takes into account the cost of setting up and enforcing a coercive moral rule; such costs include the sanctions tied to breaking the rule as well as the restrictions on the freedom of following it.

So Mill's moral theory thus separates out rules of obligation from rules of general promotion of good in all areas of practical reasoning. But Mill also distinguishes a subgroup of rules of obligation – moral rules of justice which defend rights. He says that rules of justice "involve the idea of a personal right – a claim on the part of one or more individuals."[19] He defines a right as follows:

> When we call anything a person's right, we mean that he has a valid claim on society to protect him in the possession of it, either by the force of law, or by that of education and opinion. If he has what we consider a sufficient claim, on whatever account, to have something guaranteed to him by society, we say that he has a right to it. (250)

Mill's utilitarian justification for rights follows. He claims that "if the objector goes on to ask why it ought, I can give him no other reason than general utility." The justification is based on "the extraordinarily important and impressive kind of utility which is conceived" (250–1). Mill names the right to security and the right to liberty (including liberty of self-development) as the two most basic rights. He emphasizes that justice and utility are not in conflict, for rules of justice must be grounded on utility (255).

Since rights are defined as involving claims which are guaranteed protection, and since they protect the most vital human interests, rights claims ward off the casual trade-offs permitting some people's important interests being overturned to promote other people's moderately important interests. So the example from Crisp has a ready and strong reply from Mill. Since rights are defined as involving claims which are effectively guaranteed by social institutions, they cannot be sacrificed for small gains in utility to others, even large numbers of others.

1.4 Development and self-development

Let us return to Mill's method for measuring value which uses the preference rankings of those who are competently acquainted with the relevant satisfactions. These "competent agents" who have undergone a process of development and self-development are not an elitist subgroup of members of society. Rather, they are all adult members of society who have been socialized and nurtured by their society to develop and exercise their human excellences. While many sorts of society may serve to foster such human capacities, Mill's extensive writings on these questions are focused on these processes in Western democratic liberal societies. (It should be noted that "liberal" in this context covers a wide spectrum of social and political formations and includes social democratic societies.)

Like many other classical and contemporary liberals, Mill holds firmly to the belief that education and socialization are at the heart of the projects of creating and sustaining members of society who are prepared for their role as democratic citizens. The same education and socialization process also positions people to lead good lives, a precondition of which, according to modern liberals, is that people are "free to form, revise, and act on our plans of life."[20] The modern liberal John Rawls puts the point that Mill's utilitarianism is a comprehensive moral doctrine, in which "the principle of utility . . . is usually said to hold for all kinds of subjects ranging from the conduct of individuals and personal relations to the organization of society as a whole."[21] Mill's moral doctrine is indeed comprehensive in this sense, and he holds a unified view of the socialization and educative processes that develop the capacities which are the preconditions for nurturing the character traits that go along with the ability to choose good and meaningful lives, as well as to cooperate with other citizens in promoting the common good in the public realm.

Mill's more familiar writings such as *Utilitarianism* and *On Liberty* rely upon extensive background writings which lay out and explore his views on these educative processes of development and self-development. Mill's procedure for measuring the value of enjoyments, projects, characters, and life plans is also comprehensive, and his claim is that if self-developed agents judge certain enjoyments or projects to be more valuable, then these judgments have the best chance of being correct in the long term. While individual autonomy in value choices is strongly protected in the private realm (a realm characterized not just in terms of space, but also in terms of interests),[22] in the public realm democratic procedures govern social choices.

Thus a lot rests on the educative and socialization procedures. The process of development in childhood is the first stage of the education and socialization of competent agents. In the process of development the generic human intellectual, affective and moral capacities are nurtured. Developed and self-developed agents are the pivot of the theory since their judgments and preferences provide the best indicators of the value of enjoyments. Mill argues that the most valuable enjoyments are those which involve the development and exercise of the generic human capacities developed in childhood. Mill wrote extensively on the theory of character formation, using his associationist theory of psychology as a basis from which to argue that education should be planned to develop and encourage the character traits that would promote the most utility if they were manifested in a community.[23]

Mill sees affective development, or the development of feelings, as the foundation for all forms of development. Here he follows Hume in regarding morality as the realm of feeling as well as thought. He traces his own well-known "mental crisis," a serious bout of depression, to the absence of internal culture and the lack of nurturing of feeling in his own education. He corrected this imbalance in his own philosophy and theory of socialization and was careful always to find a proper place for internal culture.[24] He found strong links with the writings of Romantic poets such as Wordsworth and Shelley.[25] This proper place for the feelings does not lead Mill to ignore intellectual culture, and he is well-known for his emphasis on the value of intellectual enjoyments and mental development. The process of moral development educates children to connect sympathetically to others and to enjoy their happiness. He claims that this feeling of sympathy and connection is firmly rooted in human nature.[26] Mill rejects the conception of moral agents as rational and self-interested only. He is always careful to balance our intellectual/individualist side with our moral/social side and to deplore the creation of a hierarchy among them. Mill claims that moral development must always accompany mental development, and this has important implications for his conception of self-development as well as for his liberal political philosophy (215–16).

When children reach adulthood the process of development continues as one of self-development. In self-development, the higher-order capacities of individuality, autonomy, sociality, and cooperativeness are built up on the groundwork of the generic human capacities. The higher-order capacities must also be balanced. The core liberal capacity of autonomy is the ability to reflect on, choose, endorse, and revise the character, relationships, projects, and life plans most reflective of our nature. Individuality is the capacity to discover and explore the range of our abilities and talents. While Mill does not believe that individuals have fixed essences, there is a range of potential characters and plans of life most in harmony with our individuality and our happiness is augmented by building on this basis.

Mill is well-known for his defense of individuality and freedom in *On Liberty*, but Millian individuals are deeply rooted in their social and cultural contexts and are not anomic and atomistic (233). But Millian individualism is characterized by a concern that the focus of value be the individual and not social groupings. In his view value is located in each individual member of a community and the value of a community flows from the value of its individual members. So individual rights cannot easily be overturned in the name of communal values. Millian autonomous individuals are self-determining creators and controllers of their lives, and their choices and life plans reflect their particularity. Thus the intricate balance of individual/social continues.

All this has profound implications for Mill's form of liberalism, for since a certain threshold level of self-development is needed in order to create a good life, to deny someone the opportunity of self-development is to violate some of their most vital interests – and thus their basic rights. Since almost all have the potential to realize self-development, it is the social context and institutions and circumstances which have a large influence in determining whether this potential does develop. According to Mill's moral and political philosophy, people have the right to liberty of self-development, and their rights are violated if their society actively bars them, or does not take action to provide the means to develop and exercise their human capacities. So Mill's liberalism has a strong egalitarian flavor. This egalitarianism emerges strongly in his democratic theory.

1.5 Democracy, deliberation, and self-development

In a study of the historical transitions of liberal political philosophy, critic C. B. Macpherson notes the shift in point of view from Bentham and James Mill to John Stuart Mill. Mill's father was primarily interested in the function of democracy in protecting the interests of citizens, but John Stuart Mill, because of his enlarged conceptions of human nature and of the good, had far greater hopes for the prospects of democracy. Macpherson says:

> But he saw something even more important to be protected, namely, the chances of improvement of mankind. So his emphasis was not on the mere holding operation, but on what democracy could contribute to human development. Mill's model of democracy is a moral model . . . it has a moral vision of the possibility of the improvement of mankind, and of a free and equal society not yet achieved. A democratic system is valued as a means to that improvement – a necessary though not a sufficient means; and a democratic society is seen as both a result of that improvement and a means to further improvement. The improvement that is expected is an increase in the amount of personal self-development of all the members of a society.[27]

Macpherson here points to the heart of Mill's vision. The principle of utility governs and lays out the goal of all of the practical moral arts, including political philosophy. Mill's conception of human nature, which accords a central place for the development and exercise of our human capacities, leads naturally to a normative view of the art of politics, in which democratic theory is organized around its relation to the promotion of good. Thus Mill sets out the central criterion of good government as "the degree in which it tends to increase the sum of good qualities in the governed, collectively and individually; since, besides that their well-being is the sole object of government, their good qualities supply the moving force which works the machinery." One of the roles of government is to act as an "agency of national education." A test of good governments is "the degree in which they promote the general mental advancement of the community, including under that phrase advancement in intellect, in virtue, and in practical activity and efficiency."[28]

The further development and exercise of human excellences is an ongoing project, and Mill sees active participation in the political and social life of the community as one of the main avenues for these activities. Mill's essay *On Liberty* is primarily concerned with his arguments for liberty in the sphere of life in which our actions do not harm others in the sense of violating their rights. But many passages in the essay are eloquent calls for an increase in public debate and discussion which Mill sees as being important means for the exercise of our mental and moral capacities as well as for increasing the chances that correct public choices will be made.[29]

A major theme of *Representative Government* as well is the developmental impact of political and social participation and activity, and Mill highlights the benefits of such commitments, claiming that they lead to a situation in which "the whole public are made, to a certain extent, participants in the government, and sharers in the instruction and mental exercise derivable from it."[30] But he warns:

> Where this school of public spirit does not exist, scarcely any sense is entertained that private persons . . . owe any duties to society, except to obey the laws and submit to the government. There is no unselfish sentiment of identification with the public. Every thought or feeling, either of interest or of duty, is absorbed in the individual and in the family. The man never thinks of any collective interest, of any objects to be pursued jointly with others, but only in competition with them . . . Thus even private morality suffers, while public is actually extinct.[31]

This warning applies to our own age as well. Mill's vision has not yet come to be realized, and democratic theorists at the end of the twentieth century are grappling with the dilemmas of democratic systems which have not lived up to their ideals. Much of the life seems to be drained out of the ideal of democratic participation on which Mill pinned his hopes. The attainment of universal suffrage for which he fought all his life has been turned, according to many commentators, into an exercise in which citizen participation is limited to voting. Mill never intended democratic participation to stop at the exercise of casting a ballot. Moreover, Mill saw the vote as being a trust in which citizens have the responsibility to vote for the common good rather than their own narrow self-interest – yet this is not how the vote is usually seen. The welcome diversity of perspectives has also led to new dilemmas as pluralism of contemporary societies leads inevitably to moral disagreement. Contemporary political theorists Amy Guttmann and Dennis Thompson are among the thinkers calling for a revitalized view of political life which places moral considerations at the center, which is deliberative in its emphasis on public reasoning and rational debate, and which is just in its search for reciprocity in which citizens "seek fair terms of social cooperation for their own sake."[32] This revitalization project can look for inspiration to Mill's vision of self-development and a deliberative and participatory democracy.

2. Mill's Metaphysics and Epistemology

In many ways it makes sense to see Mill's metaphysics and epistemology as the culmination of British Empiricism and a natural transition to the logical positivism of the early twentieth century. While this view is entirely plausible, I'll conclude by suggesting that some crucial aspects of Mill's thought might even hint at much more recent trends towards naturalizing and externalizing epistemology.

In all of his major works Mill carefully tried to work out a radical foundationalism and an equally radical reductionist program that would allow one to employ inductive reasoning to move from non-inferential knowledge of phenomena to the world of common sense and science. If Mill's metaphysics and epistemology does not have as honored a place in the pantheon of great works by the modern philosophers, it is only because he rarely displays the kind of originality or rhetorical flair that so characterized such figures as Descartes, Berkeley, and Hume. Indeed, it is clear that Mill himself thought that he was largely building and refining the ideas of others. His restriction of epistemic foundations to mental phenomena (modifications of the mind) of which we are directly aware was a theme that consistently ran through many of his immediate predecessors and contemporaries. His analysis of causation and his insistence that only induction could advance one beyond the phenomenologically given to any genuinely new knowledge were elaborations (albeit often much more sophisticated elaborations) of ideas introduced by Hume. Even the reduction of propositions describing the physical world to propositions describing "the permanent possibilities of sensation" was already hinted at (albeit not as explicitly or consistently) by Berkeley. Where Mill is most original, he is often least plausible. His apparent endorsement of induction as the source of even elementary knowledge of arithmetic and geometric truths, for example, isolates him from even his most staunch fellow empiricists.

Still, to characterize Mill only as someone primarily interested in developing the views of others is radically to understate his contributions to metaphysics and epistemology. Although he often did not anticipate many of the critical problems that were to beset the reductionist programs of the positivists, he took the views of the British empiricists to the point at which others could begin to see clearly some of the enormous obstacles those views must surmount. That transition from the sketch of interesting new and original ideas to clearly worked out views whose vulnerability becomes exposed was an enormously important development in the history of philosophy. Nor should one downplay the significance of his role as critic of other philosophers. *An Examination of Sir William Hamilton's Philosophy*[33] is a work truly impressive not only as a vehicle through which Mill developed his own views, but as a tribute to the often highly sophisticated theories of philosophers who through the many accidents of history have not survived as dominant figures, but whose work is often every bit as sophisticated as that of present-day metaphysicians and epistemologists.

In the space available here I could not even try to evaluate critically all of Mill's epistemological, metaphysical, and logical views. *A System of Logic* alone is a work that engages a vast array of problems, from issues concerning the foundations of knowledge, to the metaphysics of causation, and ultimately even to the metaphysical underpinnings of value judgments. I will, however, try to present and evaluate some of the main theses which I think are most importantly associated with Mill. And I'll begin with what I take to be the driving and unifying force behind most everything else he argues: Mill's views about the foundations of knowledge and the epistemic principles available to take one beyond those foundations to justified belief in the propositions endorsed by common sense.

2.1 *Mill's epistemology*

Like almost all of his predecessors and contemporaries, Mill thought it obvious that some form of foundationalism was true:

> Truths are known to us in two ways: some are known directly, and of themselves; some through the medium of other truths. The former are the subject of Intuition, or Consciousness; the latter, of Inference. The truths known by intuition are the original premises from which all others are inferred. Our assent to the conclusion being grounded on the truth of the premises, we never could arrive at any knowledge by reasoning, unless something could be known antecedently to all reasoning.[34]

Firmly in the tradition of his fellow British empiricists Mill also seemed to think that it was simply obvious that the data of which we are directly and immediately aware are the contents of mind – sensations, ideas, sentiments, beliefs, and the like. Propositions describing the occurrence of the "phenomena" are the truths that can be known non-inferentially and that constitute the foundations of all other knowledge. There is but one means of moving beyond knowledge of what we apprehend directly to knowledge of truths describing what is not before consciousness, and that is through inductive reasoning. Since inductive reasoning always requires awareness of correlations among the occurrences of various phenomena, Mill, like Hume before him, was convinced that we could never really reach any conclusions that take us beyond the realm of the phenomenal. Unlike Hume (more like Berkeley), Mill thought that he could reconcile this conclusion with common sense – if we understand properly the content of ordinary everyday beliefs, we'll find that there is a sense in which such beliefs never really *require* us to advance beyond complicated claims about the *kind* of phenomena with which we are directly acquainted. We'll have much more to say shortly about Mill's attempts to reconstruct the content of ordinary beliefs so as to make them amenable to inductive proof.

Initially, there might seem to be nothing very interesting or original about the truths Mill identifies as foundational. One is, however, immediately taken aback to find that the examples Mill gives of truths known immediately include not only descriptions of *present* conscious states, but also descriptions of *past* conscious states: "Examples of truths known to us by immediate consciousness, are our own bodily sensations and mental feelings. I know directly, and of my own knowledge, that I was vexed yesterday or that I am hungry to-day" (3). One might initially put this down to carelessness but it seems clear that Mill did not think that one's knowledge of one's own past conscious states through memory was *inferential* knowledge – or, if it was inferential knowledge, it clearly constituted an exception to his otherwise exceptionless principle that all inferential knowledge required inductive reasoning. His most extensive discussion of the epistemic status of phenomenal truths presented to us through memory is in a long footnote in EWH, from which I here quote: "Our belief in the veracity of Memory is evidently ultimate; no reason can be given for it which does not presuppose the belief, and assume it to be well grounded."[35] Perhaps, to reassure himself that he is not out on a limb here, Mill does claim that all of his predecessors who attempted to secure knowledge from a foundation consisting of truths about sensation, also "gave" themselves memory-based knowledge of their immediate phenomenal past (210n). But philosophy is one field in which there simply is no safety in numbers, and it is worth exploring the issues raised here in more detail, for they invite questions that threaten to undermine Mill's entire project.

There are, it seems, only two real possibilities. Either (1) Mill thought that through memory one could know directly and immediately at least some truths about the past, or (2) he recognized that there is a sense in which truths about the past are implicitly inferred from present memory "experience," but where the nondeductive principle sanctioning the inference is known directly (through intuition). If (1) is true, Mill is in danger of losing any clear criteria to characterize foundational knowledge. On the other hand, (2) is simply incompatible with the entire thrust of an epistemology that allows only inductive reasoning as a legitimate epistemic tool for advancing knowledge. Let me elaborate.

Although Mill sometimes seems to eschew introspection as a way of determining what can or cannot be known directly, there are a number of passages in which he does seem to identify what is directly known through consciousness with what cannot be doubted or what cannot be believed falsely. He recognizes, of course, that there is enormous debate about such questions as whether we can apprehend directly physical objects and their properties – this is one of the primary themes discussed in connection with Hamilton's philosophy. And he certainly doesn't think that one can decide that issue simply by paying close phenomenological attention to the character (the intentional character) of one's sensory states and the beliefs to which they give rise. But here he is primarily concerned with confusion that is likely to beset the philosopher who has become so accustomed to various associations of phenomena built up from earliest experience that the philosopher cannot separate in thought that which involves inference from that which does not. Mill does seem to think that we can identify that which is *truly* given (non-inferentially) to consciousness with that about which we cannot be mistaken: "Consciousness, in the sense usually attached to it by philosophers, – consciousness of the mind's own feelings and operations, cannot, as our author truly says, be disbelieved" (172). Here Mill certainly seems to be implying that the mark of what is truly presented directly to consciousness (in a way that affords us direct, non-inferential knowledge) is that there is no possibility of doubt concerning its existence. The impossibility of doubt isn't the same thing as the impossibility of error, but again in this context (and the tradition in which this locution is used), one might reasonably infer that for Mill the given in consciousness is the truth-maker for a proposition that can be infallibly believed.

But here one wonders how Mill can possibly recover in the *foundations* of knowledge his experiential past. Philosophers have worked hard through fanciful thought experiments involving illusion, hallucination, dreams, and the like, to convince us that sensory experience is never an infallible source of knowledge about the external world, but it takes almost no effort at all to convince even the most philosophically unsophisticated that memory, even memory of what seems to be the relatively immediate past, is fallible. Once we allow in the foundations of knowledge *one* sort of fallible belief – belief in the past prompted by present memory – it's hard to see how one can maintain a *principled* objection to those philosophers who claim to know directly certain truths about the physical world where the occasion of such knowledge is the occurrence of sensory states that give rise to (fallible) beliefs about the external world. To be sure a sensory state can occur in the absence of the physical object we take to be its cause, but then a memory experience "of" a past sensory state S can occur in the absence of the sensory state S we take to be its cause.

If including beliefs about the past in the foundations of knowledge threatens to open the floodgates to spurious claims of direct knowledge, option (2) discussed above threatens to open the floodgates to unwanted nondeductive principles of reasoning that go well beyond Mill's treasured principle of induction. Within the framework of traditional foundationalism Mill is, of course, right in suggesting that there is no possibility of *reasoning* to the conclusion that memory is generally reliable.[36] Any such argument must appeal to evidence, and in the passing of a moment, that evidence will be "lost" to the past. Its "recovery" will involve relying on memory. It is particularly obvious that an *inductive* justification of the reliability of memory is a nonstarter. It is the essence of inductive reasoning that the person who employs it reaches a conclusion based on *past* observed correlations among phenomena. But to get that knowledge of past correlations, one cannot avoid relying on memory.

It is to Mill's great credit that he realizes the enormity of the problem here and that he doesn't try to hide it.[37] But understanding that one faces a problem and having a solution to that problem consistent with the system of philosophy one defends are not the same. In the end, Mill seems resigned to arguing that we simply have no choice but to concede that memory gives us knowledge of the past. We *need* to make such an assumption if we are to have any chance of knowing anything beyond the momentary, fleeting, contents of our minds. But skeptics have never been much impressed with the philosopher's plaintive appeals to what is needed in order to get the knowledge we would *like* to have. Descartes needed knowledge of a nondeceiving God, Berkeley may have needed a God to keep in existence a world unperceived by finite minds, and Mill needed knowledge of past experiences. But what has philosophical need got to do with what one is philosophically entitled to claim? Mill knows perfectly well that there are all kinds of philosophers convinced that his attempts to regain knowledge of the external world by performing inductions on the phenomena will itself be doomed to failure. If he were to conclude that he does so fail, would he also give himself whatever epistemic principles were needed to convert beliefs in material objects prompted by sensory states into knowledge?

2.2 *Mill on our knowledge of the external world*

How does Mill rescue justified belief in the physical world from a stark foundation that consists solely of knowledge of present and past experiential states and a view of reasoning that recognizes only induction as a means of projecting past correlations among phenomena into the future? The solution, Mill argues, is to understand clearly the content of beliefs about the physical world. Such beliefs should be understood as beliefs in "the permanent possibility of sensations." Just as earlier representative realists wanted to construe the secondary qualities of objects (the sourness of the lemon, for example as "in" the lemon) only as powers to produce certain sensations under certain conditions, so Mill wants to reduce all claims about the physical world to claims about the existence of permanent powers to affect sentient beings in certain ways under certain conditions.

Now the above crude sketch of the view still suggests two importantly different, though closely related, theories. On the one view, as Mill describes it:

> External things exist, and have an inmost nature, but their inmost nature is inaccessible to our faculties. We know it not, and can assert nothing of it with a meaning. Of the ultimate Realities, as such, we know the existence, and nothing more. But the impressions which these Realities make on us – the sensations they excite, the similitudes, groupings, and successions of those sensations, or, to sum up all this in a common though improper expression, the *representations* generated in our minds by the action of the Things themselves – these we may know, and these are all that we can know respecting them.[38]

This is essentially the last attempt by Hylas to rescue an intelligible concept of material object before his complete capitulation to Philonous' (Berkeley's) idealism. Such a view would certainly have a claim to being one according to which the concept of a physical object just is the concept of a permanent possibility or power of producing sensations of various sorts. In the language of contemporary predicate logic, claims about the existence of physical objects are existential claims whose variables range over objects other than sensations, but whose predicate expressions are exhausted by causal descriptions of the ways in which those objects affect sentient beings. So on such a view to assert that there exists something rectangular and brown might be to assert that there exists that which could (lawfully) cause in a subject the visual sensation of seeming to see something rectangular and brown and is such that if it were causing such a sensation and the subject were to have the kinesthetic sensation of initiating a certain grasping motion, and if conditions of perception were normal then it would also produce the tactile sensation of seeming to feel something rectangular, and . . . The analysis trails off in this way to indicate that there is an indefinitely complex array of possible sensations that could and would be produced under the relevant conditions.

It is important to recognize that Mill has no principled objection to the intelligibility of the above view. It is, however, probably not the understanding he wanted of permanent possibilities of sensations. Mill describes a version of what he calls the doctrine of the Relativity of Knowledge with which he is clearly sympathetic:

> the sensations which, in common parlance, we are said to receive from objects, are not only all that we can possibly know of the objects, but are all that we have any ground

> for believing to exist. What we term an object is but a complex conception made up by the laws of association, out of the ideas of various sensations which we are accustomed to receive simultaneously. There is nothing real in the process but these sensations. They do not, indeed, accompany or succeed one another at random; they are held together by a law, that is, they occur in fixed groups, and a fixed order of succession; but we have no evidence of anything which, not being itself a sensation, is a substratum or hidden cause of sensations. (8)

If Mill were endorsing this view, then his identification of material (physical) objects with the permanent possibilities of sensations is his attempt to formulate one of the earliest and clearest versions of reductive phenomenalism. Reductive phenomenalism is best understood as the view that assertions about the physical world are equivalent in meaning to indefinitely complex subjunctive conditionals that make assertions about what sensations would follow others. That Mill can most naturally be read as a phenomenalist is evidenced by passages such as this:

> I believe that Calcutta exists, though I do not perceive it, and that it would still exist if every percipient inhabitant were suddenly to leave the place, or be struck dead. But when I analyse the belief, all I find in it is, that were these events to take place, the Permanent Possibility of Sensation which I call Calcutta would still remain; that if I were suddenly transported to the banks of the Hoogly, I should still have the sensations which, if now present, would lead me to affirm that Calcutta exists here and now. (253)

As I indicated above, the two views – (1) physical objects understood as potential causes (unknown as to their nonrelational character) of various sensations, and (2) physical object claims understood as complex conditional claims about what sensations a subject would have were he to have certain others – are strikingly similar. Both rely crucially on subjunctive or counterfactual conditionals describing the sensations a subject would have under certain conditions. However, (1) commits the theorist to the existence of something other than sensations; (2) does not. But it is precisely for that reason that despite the valiant efforts of twentieth-century positivists, reductive phenomenalism wilted before devastating objections. The first and most obvious problem, the one labeled by R. M. Chisholm the problem of perceptual relativity,[39] virtually cries out to be noticed in Mill's various characterizations of the permanent possibilities. For the reductive analysis to work, for Mill to secure a meaning for physical object claims that allows one to establish such claims *solely* through correlations discovered among sensations, the antecedents and consequents of the subjunctive conditionals must make reference to nothing other than sensations. And here the phenomenalist's critic simply waits patiently for the phenomenalistic analysis to be offered. Mill's crude analysis of his belief about Calcutta clearly fails the test of a successful phenomenal translation. If he were transported to the banks of the Hoogly he would have various sensations. Perhaps he would, but our *translation* of what we believe into phenomenal language must replace reference to the *physical* location, the banks of the Hoogly, with a purely phenomenal description of experience. But how would that translation proceed? If I were to have the sensations of floating through the air and have the sensations of seeming to see a river and if I were to have the tactile sensations of ground beneath me, then I would have . . . But this isn't going to work. There are indefinitely many real and imaginable places that are visually indistinguishable from various places along the banks of the Hoogly. Moreover, as Chisholm pointed out, what sensations a subject would have even if one could "fix" the subject's relevant "location" (again, the phenomenalist must do without referring to *physical* space or *physical* spatial relations) would depend on the state of the subject's *physical* organs of sense. Blind people wouldn't have any visual sensations were they on the banks of the Hoogly. A person whose entire body has been anesthetized would have no kinesthetic or tactile sensations. And one can't revise one's conditionals so as to take account of the absence of these physical conditions without violating the phenomenalist's commitment to fully reducing talk about the physical world to complex talk of phenomena.

Wilfred Sellars presented an argument against phenomenalism which in many ways was quite similar to Chisholm's.[40] Sellars stressed that subjunctives of the sort used in a phenomenalist's analysis of the meaning of physical object claims assert lawful connections between their antecedents and their consequents. To be sure the antecedent might be only a nonredundant part of some complex condition that is lawfully sufficient for the antecedent, but given the phenomenalist's *ontological* commitments the other conditions presupposed must themselves be purely phenomenal. But, Sellars argued, there simply are no laws of nature correlating sensations. Mill was a Humean about laws of nature. Laws assert only exceptionless correlations among phenomena.[41] But ask yourself whether you can describe any universal truths describing sequences of sensations. Is it true that whenever anyone seems to see a table and seems to reach out and touch it, that person seems to feel one? No it isn't. Dreams, illusions, hallucinations, and people with anesthetized hands testify to the fact there is no genuinely lawful connection between these sensations. Can't we "save" the regularity by making the relevant description of the related sensations complicated enough? Do it, the phenomenalist's critic insists. There are too many causally relevant *physical* conditions of perception to allow one to construct genuine lawful regularities in the world of phenomena, and for that reason the antecedents of subjunctive conditionals used by the phenomenalist must make reference to normal or standard conditions of perception where such reference can only be construed as implicit acknowledgment of a world different from, but causally relevant to, sensation.

Given the limits of space, I won't try to defend Mill against these enormously powerful objections. I would, however, argue that he might have been better off had he construed the permanent possibility of sensations in the first of the two ways identified earlier. Provided that he could come up with an inductive argument for the principle that everything has a cause (something he claims he can do – SL, Bk. III, ch. V) he wouldn't necessarily encounter insurmountable epistemological problems by allowing in to his metaphysics entities whose sole function was to plug nomological holes in "gappy" correlations among sensations. Furthermore, he would have had a much more natural way of attempting to secure meaning for "bare" existential claims about physical objects, claims which provide no "setting" for the actual and possible sensations described by the relevant counterfactuals. How would a phenomenalist, for example, understand the bare existential claim that there exists *something somewhere* in the universe that is brown? If a subject were to have the visual experiences we would associate with canvassing the entire infinite universe, would that subject eventually have the visual experience of seeming to see something brown? Hardly. How would one successfully distinguish *phenomenologically* covering the universe from moving around in slow circles in empty space. With Hylas's model of matter as the thing unknowable in itself but the potential cause of sensations, one has a solution, at least, to *this* problem. The analysis of what is clearly a nonhypothetical claim begins with the existential claim that there does exists some x which (lawfully) could produce the relevant sensations and which would produce certain others under normal (perhaps statistically defined) conditions.[42]

2.3 *Mill's "reduction" of deductive reasoning to inductive reasoning*

Mill's *A System of Logic* is not nearly as valuable today as a work in logic as it is a work in metaphysics and epistemology. Modern predicate logic has supplanted Mill's now outdated categorizations of argument kinds. Still, the work contains many intriguing suggestions. The most startling is that *all* genuine reasoning is inductive reasoning. What's more, Mill seems to argue that all inductive reasoning is itself inference from particulars to particulars.[43] When we conclude that all metal expands when heated after observing individual pieces of metal expand when heated, the universal conclusion is just our way of marking the fact that for any *particular* metal we heat next, it will expand. Of course, one needs only to state the thesis clearly in order to see that it is in danger of becoming merely verbal. One hasn't avoided a universal conclusion by thinking of the conclusion sanctioned by the inductive evidence as one about *all* particular unexamined and future pieces of metal that have been heated. There is good reason to think that Mill believed that universal generalizations were themselves just conjunctions of particular propositions. That all men are mortal is equivalent to that Jones is a man and that Smith is a man and . . . And so on until we have named *all* of the men. Of course the fact that we need to add this last part with the italicized "all" indicates why the proposed translation must fail (as a meaning analysis). But in any event, if Mill believed that general propositions were themselves conjunctions of particular propositions, his claim that all reasoning is from particulars to particulars immediately becomes less mysterious.

If Mill's claim that inductive reasoning always takes one from particulars to particulars is itself at best misleading, his further thesis that syllogistic reasoning is not genuine reasoning at all is even more puzzling. When we conclude based on the premises that all men are mortal and that John is a man that John is mortal, it certainly looks as if we are engaged in genuine deductive (not inductive) reasoning. Mill, however, tries to convince us that the general proposition in the syllogism is just a kind of reminder that you have, or at least have had, at your disposal an array of particular propositions which would allow one to infer inductively that John is mortal. The conclusion about John is a conclusion based on "forgotten facts" about particular men dying (127).

Construed literally as an attempt to reduce deductive reasoning to inductive reasoning, the above seems just wrong. There is a relation of entailment between the premises of a syllogism and its conclusion which we can "see" and which we can use to draw out of a universal claim various consequences. Deductively valid arguments are simply not disguised inductive arguments. But Mill is probably not really trying to make a point of *logic*. His concern is better construed as one of *epistemology*. If one is to know something about John's dying, Mill is arguing, no argument whose premises describe universal truths about the mortality of man will capture the structure of the *evidence* upon which one bases one's conclusion. One's justification for believing the conclusion of an argument based on its premises is never any better than one's justification for believing the premises, and the epistemologist's task is to lay bare the structure of the evidence upon which one relies in reaching a conclusion. In this context Mill's claim becomes relatively straightforward. If he's right, one's evidence for believing that all men are mortal consists of observations of correlations between particular individuals being men and those men eventually dying. Knowledge of those particulars allows one in a sense to infer the universal proposition that all men are mortal, but if Mill's earlier claim is also true, then the intermediate universal conclusion is just our way of reminding ourselves that whatever particular conclusion we next draw about the mortality of some particular man will be inductively supported. We can now see how Mill might argue that it would be more *perspicuous* to represent the relevant reasoning as an inductive argument that proceeds directly from observed men dying to the conclusion about John's mortality. Furthermore, if Mill's views discussed in the previous section were correct (they are not) and there is no way of knowing *any* general truth other than through inductive reasoning, then this reconstruction of all reasoning as moving inductively from evidence describing correlations among particulars to conclusions projecting those correlations in the case of new particulars would seem quite plausible.

2.4 Mill on the ground of inductive reasoning

It is perhaps fitting that we conclude by briefly examining Mill's views on the *ground* of inductive reasoning. As we have seen, Mill seems almost obsessed with construing *all* reasoning as implicit inductive reasoning. But why should one suppose that inductive reasoning itself is legitimate? What grounds do we have for supposing that the premises of an inductive argument make probable its conclusion? Why should we assume that just because we have always found F's followed by G's that the next F we find will also likely be G? Mill is sensitive to the fact that this question needs to be answered, but it is not at all easy to make sense of the answer (or answers) he gives.

On the face of it, Mill seems to offer the straightforward, if counterintuitive, suggestion that we justify our reliance on induction by *inductively* establishing that induction is reliable. But he gets off to a bad start by first putting the point in terms of an assumption or axiom that inductive reasoning requires. Mill claims that whenever we reason inductively, we take as an axiom that the future will resemble the past in relevant respects, or that nature is *uniform* in relevant respects (201). At one point, he even seems to suggest that if we take this assumption as an implicit premise we can transform inductive arguments into syllogistic deductively valid arguments. Instead of reasoning from observations of *F*'s which have been *G*'s to the conclusion that the next *F* will be *G*, we can make explicit the premise that if observed *F*'s have all been *G*'s, that indicates that there is uniformity in nature with respect to *F*'s being *G*. That premise, taken together with our observation of *F*'s which are *G*, will allow us to *deduce* that the next *F* we observe is a *G*.

You will recall from the previous section, however, that Mill believes it is a kind of illusion to suppose that we can really advance our knowledge through any sort of syllogistic reasoning, and so it is not surprising that he later makes clear that one isn't really getting anywhere by trying to transform inductive arguments into deductively valid syllogisms (374–5). The major premise does no epistemic work – the argument is only as good as is the inference from observed *F*'s being *G* to particular conclusions about unobserved *F*'s being *G*.

The whole discussion is complicated by the fact that Mill sometimes seems to run together the question of how we justify our belief that inductive reasoning is legitimate with the quite different question of how we can justify our belief in the law of causality, the principle that everything that happens has a cause, where causation is understood in terms of Humean constant conjunction. The principle that the universe is deterministic is a contingent proposition that *can* plausibly be regarded as itself the conclusion of an inductive argument. Mill's famous methods of discovering causal connections sometimes seem to presuppose the principle of determinism. So, for example, if we discover that the only common denominator to events preceding an event of kind *B* is an event of kind *A*, then we can deduce from the principle that everything has a cause and a crude regularity theory of causation, that *A* is the cause of *B*. But that reasoning is only as strong as is the conclusion that everything has a cause. Mill construes the inductive reasoning that supports the law of causation as a relatively straightforward, if ultimately implausible, argument from success. As we examine carefully one kind of phenomenon after another, Mill argues, we find again and again (through induction) that we can subsume the phenomenon under universal laws. We simply project such success in the cases in which we have yet failed to look, or look hard enough, to find the exceptionless regularities. It is interesting to speculate as to how Mill would react to the relatively sanguine reaction of most contemporary physicists to the conclusion that there exists fundamental indeterminacy at the quantum level.

However we evaluate Mill's claim that the thesis of determinism is inductively confirmed, we are still left without an answer as to how we could establish that inductive reasoning is legitimate. The relevant truth we need to know is that the premises of an inductive argument do indeed make probable its conclusion How can we use induction to confirm that proposition? It is tempting to suggest that in a confused way Mill's discussion of this issue was a harbinger of contemporary internalism/externalism disputes in epistemology. Contemporary externalists, such as reliabilists, argue that a method of forming beliefs results in justified beliefs if, as a matter of contingent fact, the belief-forming process is reliable when it comes to producing true beliefs (conditionally, if the belief-forming process is belief-dependent, that is, takes as input beliefs; unconditionally, if the belief-forming process is belief-independent, that is, takes as input stimuli other than beliefs).[44] There is no one way to define the internalism/externalism debate.[45] Externalists are sometimes defined in terms of their rejection of that tradition in epistemology which takes the factors that constitute a person's having justified beliefs as states that are "internal" to the person (states of mind, for example). But just as important, externalists are associated with rejecting the claim that a person's having a justified belief always involves that person's having introspective access (or potential access) to the fact that they have such justification. This sort of *access* internalism threatens vicious regress and should, I think, be rejected even by traditional foundationalists. But there is another form of access internalism that I take to be much more plausible, a view that I call *inferential* access internalism. The inferential access internalist argues that in order to infer justifiably some proposition *P* from another, *E*, one must be justified in believing that *E* confirms *P* (that there is an evidential connection between *E* and *P*). Paradigm externalists in epistemology virtually all reject this view. They argue that one can form a justified belief in *P* by inferring it from *E* without one's having any beliefs (justified or not) about the legitimacy of the form of reasoning one is employing. The reliabilist, for example, would argue that it is enough that the form of reasoning be (conditionally) reliable.

I have argued elsewhere that once one rejects inferential access internalism (for example, once one accepts something like a reliabilist account of justified belief), there is no objection in principle to using a reliable belief-forming process in order to discover that that very process is indeed reliable.[46] Indeed, contemporary externalist accounts of justification and knowledge allow one a way of making sense of the recommendation that we "naturalize" epistemology. On one interpretation, the enjoinder to naturalize epistemology is just the suggestion that we study knowledge and justified belief using the very scientific methods that we use to study any other phenomena. And if a view like reliabilism is true, why shouldn't we use the methods of empirical science to study the methods of empirical science? If inductive reasoning is generally reliable, then its output beliefs are justified. If one wants to find out whether or not inductive reasoning is reliable one can simply remember (assuming that memory is reliable) past successful uses of inductive reasoning in order to conclude inductively that induction is reliable. This suggestion would, of course, strike someone like Hume as being almost comical. The idea that one could use a method of reasoning to ascertain whether or not it was reliable seems pathetically question-begging. But Hume wasn't an externalist about justification. Hume wanted some sort of direct and immediate access to the legitimacy of inductive reasoning, and without such access he was convinced that we would be unable to satisfy the philosophical demands of reason with respect to grounding appropriately our reliance on induction.

For some reason Mill didn't seem bothered by the idea that there is no viable alternative to using inductive reasoning to establish its own legitimacy. He couldn't bring himself to introduce a faculty of "intuition," the purpose of which was to allow us to see that inductive reasoning was reliable. And it is perhaps small wonder that a philosopher who couldn't convince himself that we can just see by the light of reason that 2 + 2 = 4, wouldn't be able to convince himself that we can just "see" the truth of the far more complicated principle of induction. But if anyone should have been sensitive to the charge that he was begging the question in using induction to ground induction it should have been Mill. Such a charge lay at the heart of his complaint that syllogistic reasoning could hardly be thought of as a (non-question-begging) way of increasing our knowledge. In the end, though, perhaps all we can do is speculate that one of the pivotal philosophical figures closing out the nineteenth century would have been far more comfortable in the company of late twentieth-century epistemologists who, through their externalist analyses of epistemic concepts, took a radical naturalistic turn in epistemology. Coming full circle to the issues raised at the start of this paper, Mill could take fundamental belief-forming processes such as memory and induction to need no further "ground" than that provided by a *nature* that cooperates so as to ensure that the beliefs produced in this way are usually true. On the other hand, if Mill were vulnerable to the seduction of contemporary naturalistic approaches to epistemology, it is not clear what would motivate him to labor so hard in an effort to restrict available legitimate belief-forming processes to just introspection, memory, and induction.

Notes

1 The first part of this chapter, "Mill's Ethics and Political Philosophy," is by Wendy Donner; the second part, "Mill's Metaphysics and Epistemology," is by Richard Fumerton.

2 All page references to Mill's writings are to *The Collected Works of John Stuart Mill*, 33 vols., gen. ed. John M. Robson (Toronto: University of Toronto Press, 1963–91), unless otherwise noted. Hereafter *Collected Works* is cited as CW.

3 J. S. Mill, *Utilitarianism*, CW, X, 210.

4 J. S. Mill, *Logic*, CW, VIII, 831–952.

5 J. S. Mill, *Utilitarianism*, CW, X, 234.

6 For a full discussion of these matters, see James Griffin, *Well-Being* (Oxford: Clarendon Press, 1986), pp. 75–124.

7 J. S. Mill, *Utilitarianism*, CW, X, 211.

8 F. H. Bradley, *Ethical Studies*, 2nd edn. (London: Oxford University Press, 1962), pp. 119.

9 J. S. Mill, *Utilitarianism*, CW, X, 235.

10 Commentators continue to be divided on this question. For example, L. W. Sumner has vehemently claimed that the act-utilitarian "interpretation of Mill is certainly mistaken; indeed, given its currency, it is surprising just how little textual support there is for it." On the other hand, Roger Crisp even more recently offers a sustained defense of an act-utilitarian interpretation of Mill. See L. W. Sumner, "The Good and the Right," in Wesley E. Cooper, Kai Nielsen, and Steven C. Patten, eds., *New Essays on John Stuart Mill and Utilitarianism, Canadian Journal of Philosophy*, supplementary vol. 5, 1979, p. 102; Roger Crisp, *Mill on Utilitarianism* (London: Routledge, 1997), pp. 102–33.

11 J. S. Mill, *Utilitarianism*, CW, X, 224.

12 Fred Berger, *Happiness Justice, and Freedom: The Moral and Political Philosophy of John Stuart Mill* (Berkeley: University of California Press, 1984), pp. 66–7.

13 Adapted from H. J. McCloskey, "An Examination of Restricted Utilitarianism," *Philosophical Review* 66 (1957), pp. 466–85. Roger Crisp, *Mill on Utilitarianism*, p. 118.

14 Roger Crisp, *Mill on Utilitarianism*, p. 118.

15 Ibid., p. 118.

16 J. S. Mill, *Utilitarianism*, CW, X, 246.

17 David Lyons, "Mill's Theory of Morality," in *Rights, Welfare, and Mill's Moral Theory* (Oxford: Clarendon Press, 1994), p. 54.

18 Ibid., p. 55.

19 J. S. Mill, *Utilitarianism*, CW, X, 247.

20 Will Kymlicka, *Contemporary Political Philosophy: An Introduction* (Oxford: Clarendon Press, 1990), p. 209.

21 John Rawls, *Political Liberalism* (New York: Columbia University Press, 1993), p. 13.

22 Mill's *On Liberty* is a sustained argument for the importance of such liberty. See CW, VIII, 213–310.

23 J. S. Mill, *A System of Logic*, CW, VII, 869–70.

24 J. S. Mill, *Autobiography*, CW, I, 147.

25 Michele Green, "Sympathy and Self-Interest: The Crisis in Mill's Mental History," *Utilitas* 2 (1989), pp. 259–77.

26 J. S. Mill, *Utilitarianism*, CW, X, 231.

27 C. B. Macpherson, *The Life and Times of Liberal Democracy* (Oxford: Oxford University Press, 1977), p. 47.

28 J. S. Mill, *Representative Government*, CW, XIX, 390–3.

29 J. S. Mill, *On Liberty*, CW, VIII, 243.

30 J. S. Mill, *Representative Government*, CW, XIX, 436.

31 Ibid., p. 412. However, in *Subjection of Women* Mill argues for the educative powers of just family relations when he claims that the family should be a "school of sympathy in equality." See CW, II, 295. See also Maria Morales, *Perfect Equality: John Stuart Mill on Well-Constituted Communities* (Lanham, Md.: Rowman & Littlefield, 1996).

32 Amy Guttmann and Dennis Thompson, *Democracy and Disagreement* (Cambridge, Mass.: Belknap Press, 1996).

33 J. S. Mill, *An Examination of Sir William Hamilton's Philosophy* (London: Longmans, Green and Co., 1889).

34 J. S. Mill, *A System of Logic* (London: Longmans, Green and Co., 1906), p. 3.

35 J. S. Mill, *An Examination of Sir William Hamilton's Philosophy*, p. 209.

36 As we will see later, in connection with Mill's inductive justification of induction, cer-

tain externalist approaches to knowledge of reliable belief-forming processes might actually allow one to use the very process one is investigating in order to certify its reliability.

37 The same cannot be said for a great many of Mill's predecessors and contemporaries. Often it seemed that either they didn't realize the threat of skepticism with respect to the past, or they realized it and chose to ignore it.

38 J. S. Mill, *An Examination of Sir William Hamilton's Philosophy*, pp. 9–10.

39 Roderick M. Chisholm, "The Problem of Empiricism," *Journal of Philosophy* 45 (1948), pp. 512–17.

40 Wilfred Sellars, "Phenomenalism," in *Science, Perception and Reality* (London: Routledge and Kegan Paul, 1963).

41 Of course, they don't really assert only exceptionless correlations among phenomena. To this day, regularity theorists like Mill are plagued by the problem of distinguishing lawful from accidental regularities. In the few places where Mill addresses this problem, he simply turns to the subjunctive conditional in explaining the difference. The fundamental problem for a regularity theorist, however, is to specify the truth conditions for contingent subjunctive conditionals without invoking the concept of law we are trying to analyze using subjunctives.

42 For a full defense of this sort of view, see Richard Fumerton, *Metaphysical and Epistemological Problems of Perception* (Lincoln: University of Nebraska Press, 1985), chs. 4–6.

43 J. S. Mill, *A System of Logic*, p. 126.

44 The best and clearest statement of such a view is still, arguably, found in Alvin Goldman, "What is Justified Belief?" in *Justification and Knowledge*, ed. George Pappas (Dordrecht: Reidel, 1979), pp. 1–23.

45 For a detailed discussion of importantly different versions of the internalism/externalism debate, see Richard Fumerton, *Metaepistemology and Skepticism* (Lanham, Md.: Rowman and Littlefield, 1995).

46 The theme runs through much of *Metaepistemology and Skepticism* (ibid.), but is developed most thoroughly in ch. 6.

Chapter 17

Karl Marx

Terrell Carver

Leszek Kolakowski opens his three-volume study *Main Currents of Marxism* with the statement "Karl Marx was a German philosopher."[1] All the terms in this apparently factual proposition are highly contestable. Drawing out these issues will help us to locate Marx intellectually in relation to philosophical ideas, both of his time and ours, and to identify and evaluate his contributions and insights.

1. Marx and Engels

Perhaps most surprisingly, it is not even clear that Karl Marx, in relation to philosophy, was one person or two. He was in association for almost forty years (from around 1844 until his death) with Friedrich Engels (1820–95). For many years this partnership was taken to be sacrosanct, giving Engels an interpretive imprimatur over Marx's ideas, published works, and manuscripts. Indeed Engels was not only Marx's first biographer but also the original biographer of the partnership itself. His multiple roles as popularizer, editor, and eventually literary executor became a full-time occupation during the 12 years by which he outlived Marx. In his lifetime Marx was certainly in intimate correspondence with Engels, and almost wholly in financial dependence upon his resources and goodwill. However, they wrote only three major works together (of which two were published at the time in the 1840s, and one many years later from manuscript). Marx himself acknowledged Engels's own works very generously though not extensively in his published writings, though these were major works that Engels wrote and published before the partnership was underway.

These joint biographical details would not be of great importance, had Engels not published very famous works on philosophical issues in later life. These were produced from the mid-1870s onwards, when Marx was ill and no longer publishing, and Engels continued writing on these subjects through the 1880s. Moreover

Engels's extensive notebooks were posthumously published after the turn of the century, and all these works became best-selling classics of Marxism. There is no doubt that from the 1870s onwards, the hitherto little-noticed Marx was in fact read by both the wider public and the academic audience through the lens of Engels's ideas. Only recently has this orthodoxy been rigorously and extensively questioned, and the case put forward that the two writers had fundamental – if unacknowledged – differences in perspective on topics of philosophical interest.

One view is that there are really two positions here that students of philosophy should understand and study: Marx's, and Engels's. This at least is usefully opposite to the preceding view, that there was only one set of ideas involved, and that Marx and Engels could not – and should not – be separated for analytical purposes. In between the two extremes just stated, there are numerous way-stations of similarity and difference that can be argued. To argue for the middle ground, however, Marx and Engels have in principle to be separable, and that is the position adopted for this account.[2]

2. German Politics

Of course there was no "Germany" in 1818, when Marx was born in Trier in the Rhineland, nor did this political entity really exist until the unifying imperial constitution of 1871. To identify Marx as German-speaking is certainly accurate, though he also spoke French and English with accented fluency, and published major works in both those languages. He lived more of his life (about 35 years) in England as an exile and nonreturner than he did in any of the German states (about 30 years). While he was not an economic emigrant, as were so many of his compatriots at this time, he never seems to have felt any great loss in leaving the Rhineland (voluntarily, for Paris and Brussels) in his early twenties. For someone with this background and outlook, and who additionally scorned nationalism, and both practiced and preached internationalism from the earliest stages of his career, it seems odd and misleading to label him "German" in some defining way.

Even on the philosophical side the modifier "German" will hardly do. While encyclopedically knowledgeable about philosophy in German, such as the works of Hegel, and of Kant (an object of Hegelian critique), Marx had a thoroughly classical and scholastic background in "the greats," most particularly Aristotle. His doctoral dissertation, submitted to the University of Jena by post in 1841, was on Democritus and Epicurus. While reckoning correctly that he would never get academic employment (for political reasons), he had little difficulty intellectually in adapting to journalism and freelance criticism as a lifelong vocation. The difficulties for him were economic, in that he was always poor; personal, in that he felt his wife Jenny and children (three surviving, of six infants) suffered greatly; and political, in that his plans and projects never came to anything like fruition.

3. Philosophy and Philosophers

All the issues traced so far have an important bearing on how, if at all, Marx was ever a "philosopher." There is no doubt that from the 1870s onwards, Marxism was taken to have a critical bearing on previous philosophies and on philosophy itself, as previously conceptualized. As noted above, Marxism was a way of viewing Marx through Engels's eyes, and so the philosophical ideas that Engels published himself become relevant, as does his own conception of philosophy, and – conceivably – of himself as philosopher. In terms of a broad characterization it can be said that Engels saw his own work, and Marx's work as he interpreted it, as producing a convergence of science and philosophy, in particular reconciling the certainties propounded in contemporary physical science with the apparent uncertainties of human historical actions and development. Engels's model for this was the encyclopedic systematizing philosophy of Hegel, purged of its philosophical idealism and refounded on a materialism of matter-in-motion.

The extent to which the specific tenets of this view were endorsed by Marx explicitly, or were implicitly reflected in his own works, is controversial and possibly undecidable, as Marx in his own authorial voice was never more than gnomic about philosophical matters and about philosophy as a vocation. Thus it may be that Engels merely drew out what Marx intended to say, or indeed shared as an outlook. Alternatively, it may be that what Marx actually had to say in his own works was really rather different from what Engels said in his, and that for Marx, when he was alive, this difference was not a real problem.

For purposes of this exposition it seems sensible to run the clock forwards from Marx's early career, avoiding hindsight and teleology. This approach relies on textual scholarship and on contextual information unavailable until the mid-twentieth century, and on approaches to biography and history, as well as to philosophy and politics, that were similarly unavailable to commentators before the 1960s. Marx would never have been famous as a "philosopher" or anything else, had not Engels and Marxism established him indelibly in the intellectual firmament. However, it does not follow that later writers and readers must view him in just those Engelsian terms, nor does it follow that his early career – unknown or undervalued in traditional Marxist accounts – has to remain in just that subordinate position.

It has been very difficult for orthodoxy in Marxism either to appreciate the "early Marx" at all, or to reconcile what is there with the later writings, which Engels praised as masterworks of science on a par with Darwin's, and as revolutions in philosophy surpassing Hegel's. It is even possible today to see the Marx, who is most significant for philosophy, as the "early Marx," and indeed to argue this in various contrasting ways. It is still an open question how these interpretations of the "early Marx" relate to his later publications and manuscripts, and to what extent the later works have a similar or contrasting significance for present-day philosophical studies.

4. Early Marx

It is readily apparent from Marx's writings of the 1840s that he scorned traditional conceptions of philosophy as an activity, and traditional conceptions of the philosopher as an intellectual figure. It is thus an interesting question how and why he himself managed to contribute substantially to philosophy in the mid- and later twentieth century, and to enter, in spite of himself, into the pantheon of major influences on philosophical thinking. Biographically it is important to recognize that by 1842 Marx was already radicalized in politics as a liberal constitutionalist and economic radical, as that is when he began writing articles for a Rhenish newspaper about agricultural poverty and rural hardship.

"Radicalized" is not too strong a word to use for this kind of outlook in those days, as advocates of even the formal democracy of widespread voting, never mind any notion of economic redistribution, were generally proscribed and indeed persecuted. Marx's career as a thoughtful reporter and then local editor only flourished because of a brief liberalization in official censorship, and the window of opportunity to express even moderate opinions concerning political and economic reform swiftly closed in 1843. Marx had previously been a student in legal and historical studies at the universities of Bonn and Berlin, moving in left-wing circles that criticized contemporary governments in the German states for a lack of constitutional checks on monarchical powers and of guaranteed rights for free expression, civil association, and political participation.

How then does philosophy enter the picture? Precisely because of the reactionary character of the Prussian and other German regimes of the period, in particular the prohibitions on advocacy for wider rights of civil participation in politics, such political agitation as could be undertaken was necessarily somewhat coded and restricted in its audience. On the one hand, religion and philosophy were acceptable subjects for academic debate within political limits, and on the other hand, it was therefore possible to stretch those limits in speech and in print. This could be undertaken, provided that writers and audiences were academically insulated from any question of popular agitation, and provided that the language through which this argumentation was conducted was merely puzzling to the censor, rather than openly seditious.

For nationalistic as well as intellectual reasons, Hegel's voluminous philosophical writings were well established in the academic and political culture of German universities, and in those writings Hegel had clearly incorporated a philosophy of history and a history of philosophy as appropriate ways for a philosopher to write. He had also written a philosophy of the state and politics, and further writings were published and edited posthumously as a set of standard works. This is to say that Hegel's work had incorporated very specific views on political history and ideas, and on the place of philosophy in public life, and that these subjects – in a contemporary, not just historical sense – were well in the philosophical mainstream.

The question of the day in the later 1830s and early 1840s was the extent to which Hegelianism was merely tracing out the conclusions of the master, or was instead a creative appropriation of his method, which might indeed lead to new or even contrary truths. For rulers in the German states, as well as for ordinary Christians and religious intellectuals, the status of scripture and doctrine was crucial, both for individual salvation and for state authority. When the Hegelian David Friedrich Strauss published his *Das Leben Jesu* (Life of Jesus) in 1835, philosophical speculation met the new historical methodologies pioneered in German universities. Strauss aimed to find the worthy truths embedded in the imperfect texts of the Gospels, which were inevitably marked by a more primitive culture, and then to rescue them from such apparently corrosive skepticism, by reinterpreting them as moments in the dialectical development of humanity.

In one way Strauss was completely unsuccessful, in that for many radicals this skepticism was unstoppable and atheism was an inevitable conclusion, as it was for Marx and Engels. Politically this rejection of Christianity was seditious by definition, and even where tolerated, atheism reduced any holders or advocates of such views to a very low status of citizenship, if any at all. In another way Strauss was too successful, in that he seemed to indicate that philosophers could move the world of politics and struggle by following a Hegelian method of conceptual analysis that purported to find "the real" in the "the rational" and "the rational" in "the real." Thus in a politically charged context, Marx tackled Hegel's *Philosophie des Rechts* (Philosophy of Law) precisely to work out for himself what was valuable in Hegel's method – given his own radical project of encouraging constitutionalism – and what could be rescued from Hegel's substantive views. In terms of the latter Marx found Hegel insufficiently sympathetic to the logic of widespread suffrage and democratic institutions, and in terms of the former, he found him overly abstract and suspiciously ethereal. Nonetheless, it was clear to Marx that Hegelians thought they could do things with words. The question was how to use words effectively to create political change.

Thus Marx arrived at a critique of "Young Hegelian" philosophy and politics. This critique is interesting not merely for the substantive points Marx was able to make on both counts, but also for his engagement with the practical linkages between ideas and action, particularly when action was largely proscribed and politics confined to a world of philosophical ideas. As a radical journalist he was already on the edge of a political "underground," and after 1843 he was involved with suspect agitational groups of radical liberals and class-conscious socialists, working among like-minded émigrés in the German-speaking communities of Paris and Brussels. In his view philosophers and philosophy, as traditionally conceptualized, would never move the world:

> The weapon of criticism cannot, of course, replace criticism by weapons, material force must be overthrown by material force; but theory also becomes a material force as soon as it has gripped the masses. Theory is capable of gripping the masses as soon as it demonstrates ad hominem, and it demonstrates ad hominem as soon as it becomes radical.[3]

This is not so much a political philosophy as a reconceptualization of philosophy as radical engagement with mass action. This is not bizarre, as arguably the curtailment of feudalism and the introduction of representative government – as in France in the preceding century – were themselves important instances of philosophical ideas (of nascent liberalism) put into action, and this was indeed Marx's model. Following on from this position, Marx launched excoriating critiques of left-wing philosophers whose radicalism, in his view, remained in the realm of mere ideas and therefore lacked engagement with the realities of political struggle. Chief amongst these objects of criticism was Ludwig Feuerbach, though Marx's now famous "Theses on Feuerbach" of 1845 were not published until the 1880s by Engels, who saw them as an early development of the particular kind of materialism he attributed to Marx. In the 1960s, however, when far more early texts by Marx had become available, and when the philosophical context of Engelsian dialectics was no longer unchallenged as a perspective on Marx, the "Theses on Feuerbach" were reedited from the manuscript, and reinterpreted as a masterpiece.

5. Theses on Feuerbach

In 1843 Feuerbach published three influential works in quick succession: the second edition of *Das Wesen des Christenthums* (The Essence of Christianity), "*Vorläufige Thesen zur Reformation der Philosophie*," ("Preliminary Theses on the Reform of Philosophy"), and "*Grundsätze der Philosophie der Zukunft*" ("Foundations of the Philosophy of the Future"). In these texts, which were not completely consistent with each other, he went a stage further than Strauss in attacking religion, moving from textual and historical criticism of Christianity to an anthropological retheorization of the relationship between humans and divinity altogether. Using a "transformative" method of reversing "subject and object," rather than a dialectical method of conceptual development through contradiction, he argued that the realm of spiritual beings was itself a human construction. Moreover he argued that the religious world mirrored the activities that humans necessarily engaged in as a species in their physiological and social interchange with nature. The mysticism of the "heavenly" realm was therefore resolved into an explanatory history of "alienation." This was a projection of the human "essence" into a superfluous realm of concepts, both religious and, in the case of a quasi-religious Hegelian pantheism, philosophical. Transformation would involve the reclaiming of this essence, a process of "practice" subsumed within Feuerbachian "humanism," but only very vaguely defined.

Marx's overall complaint about Feuerbach was trenchantly put in 1843: "Feuerbach's aphorisms seem to me incorrect only in one respect, that he refers too much to nature and too little to politics. This latter is the only means by which present philosophy can become a reality."[4] Countering Feuerbach, Marx produced his own eleven aphorisms, tackling such philosophical staples as materialism, idealism, humanity, nature, society, activity, change, philosophy, and philosophers.[5] These

"Theses" are extraordinary for the highly compressed but startling way in which Marx reconceptualized the human social world, including why and how it should be represented by intellectuals, even touching importantly, though implicitly, on language and truth. While Marx's text is ambiguous and aphoristic, that in itself aligns it today with styles of philosophy that celebrate a hermeneutic encounter between reader and text, and promote the validity of individual "readings" that develop philosophical richness through their very diversity.

Marx's opening criticism of Feuerbach was that he viewed the world as mind contemplating matter, and in that way merely reproduced the defects of "hitherto existing materialism" and empiricist epistemologies. As David McLellan comments, "for Feuerbach, nature was what gave immediate truth to the senses, whereas for Marx nature was no static reality but something constantly changing itself through the mediation of men."[6] Balancing this objection to materialism, Marx praised idealism for developing the "active side," that is, breaking away from philosophy as pure epistemological contemplation by mind of material objects, and instead making philosophy a narrative of historical and conceptual development. Idealism, of course, had developed this only "abstractly," whereas Marx proposed an ambitious finesse of the mind/matter dichotomy – both are effectively involved in "'practical-critical'" human activity. Human practice is both the way the world is viewed, and the way the world is made, that is, making sense of the world is a purposive and constitutive activity (not mere "contemplation"), and the world as objects and humans is itself crucially formed by human practice.

This redefinition of philosophy was elliptically denominated by Marx as a "new" materialism, to distinguish it from Feuerbach's version of the "old" one, but Marx's text was much more critical of preceding philosophies than it was definitional for a new one, no doubt precisely because philosophy as an activity was so suspect. The "new" materialism was very much one of human conscious activity and a transcendence of the mind/body dichotomy, though deducing this from Marx's aphorisms means that the terms and implications of this view are much less than clear. Still, this is a very revolutionary conception in philosophy. Marx, of course, also intended it to be revolutionary in practical and political senses.

It follows, then, that truth is not a theoretical but a practical question, as Marx said in the second of his "Theses on Feuerbach": "Man must prove the truth, i.e. the reality and power, the this-worldliness of his thinking in practice. The dispute over the reality or non-reality of thinking that is isolated from practice is a purely scholastic question." It also follows that truth is not something that individuals arrive at or something that is held as such in individual minds, but rather something that is socially achieved as both human circumstances and humans themselves change through "revolutionary practice." Having correctly resolved "the religious world into its secular basis," Feuerbach then failed to see that the secular basis itself has cleavages and self-contradictions which must be understood and revolutionized. And within that secular basis Marx could see little point in Feuerbach's faith in "the essence of man," arguing instead that what humans have in common that is of practical significance is not some abstraction supposedly held within each human individual, but rather "the ensemble of . . . social relations" as they develop historically.

Moreover the abstract and "isolated" human individual employed as a figure in Feuerbach's philosophy, was, in Marx's view, a social product and therefore a historically contingent reflection of contemporary social relationships. Feuerbach's "contemplative materialism" was thus rooted in the civil or "bourgeois" society of his time precisely because of the way in which individuals were conceptualized philosophically as minds gazing abstractly at matter, and because their supposed "essence" was ascribed to them as some ahistorical and unchanging generality "which unites the many individuals in a natural way." In conclusion Marx famously redefined what philosophers should do, and hence what philosophy should be: "The philosophers have only interpreted the world, in various ways; the point is to change it."

This could be very close to Ludwig Wittgenstein's parable of philosophers as flies in fly-bottles. Or it could be something very different and very confused. As with the *Philosophical Investigations*, what readers get out of such fragmentary yet stimulating aperçus depends on what they bring to them and what they intend to do next.[7] Marx's own next step was to team up with Engels in a critical politics aimed at the German-speaking community of radical intellectuals, presumably on the theory that what they said could be seriously counter to the politics that the two were beginning to pursue. This was a politics of liberal constitutional reform, pushing further on the redistribution of private property and the cooperative reorganization of industry than many liberals dared or wanted to go. In parallel with the critique of philosophy came a critique of utopian and religious forms of socialism, in favor of a socialization of productive resources in land and capital, and an egalitarian programme of distribution to eliminate urban and rural poverty.

The radical philosophers that Marx and Engels had in their sights had various philosophical and political differences, but from the perspective of *Die deutsche Ideologie* (*The German Ideology*), the manuscript work drafted by the two for publication (which came only posthumously in 1926), the various differences mattered less than the similarities that were up for critique. These were their unclarity on the relationship between their words and the actions they advocated, and more crucially their failure to divorce themselves clearly from idealist philosophy as a discourse and from pious idealism as a politics.

6. The German Ideology

The German Ideology began to achieve a certain currency in philosophical circles in the 1930s, though it was taken seriously by orthodox Marxists only because it promised to use an empirical method and to begin a new science. By the 1960s, however, the continuities in argument between it and the preceding early works had become an object of interest, and so the text, at least the opening section (sometimes known as "Feuerbach: Opposition of the Idealist and Materialist Outlooks") then stimulated considerable comment. As a text it is uniquely puzzling and ultimately indeterminate. It is mostly in Engels's handwriting, though as he often acted as an amanuensis for Marx (whose handwriting was notoriously poor), it is unclear whether Engels was speaking for himself (for Marx to comment on), or whether he was recording Marx's thoughts on paper, or whether he was writing down a jointly produced and agreed text.

Moreover the large manuscript leaves of *The German Ideology* are divided into two columns, which are separately and discontinuously filled with writing (also doodles and caricatures). There are considerable crossings-out and redrafted passages, unexplained starts and stops in several discussions, and in sum, no definitive way of organizing the thoughts as a smooth text. Any arrangement of this material can be challenged as editorially rather than authorially inspired (even straightforward reproduction of the text as it stands on the leaves). And it is unclear throughout how exactly authorship is to be understood, as, for instance, in some places there is evidence, through inserted text, that debate and contradiction could have been a feature of the compositional process. There is a certain temptation to argue that *The German Ideology* is nearly meaningless as it is left to us, or at least that what we read is necessarily imbued with editorial intentions and predilections.

The saving grace is that no matter how you read it, *The German Ideology* contains passages as intellectually stimulating and potentially revolutionary as the "Theses on Feuerbach" – it is just that the usual discourses of commentary and interpretation have to be heavily qualified or modified in view of the textual considerations just discussed. The political thrust of the work is the claim that what passes for revolutionary agitation in the German states is parochial and mystifying, and not at all the world-historic discourse that Hegelians, both "Old" and "Young," seemed to think they were producing. Both groups were said to share the same fault, not unknown today, of considering "conceptions, thoughts, ideas, in fact all the products of consciousness" as entities with an existence independent of human activities. The difference between "Old" and "Young" Hegelians was merely that the former declared these ideas to be "the true bonds of human society" while the latter saw them as "real chains." The politics of the "Old" Hegelians was therefore simply reactionary, while that of the "Young" Hegelians was a fantasy: a mere demand "to change consciousness . . . to interpret reality in another way," fighting phrases with phrases in nugatory "philosophic criticism." From this political context, *The German Ideology* then sets out a program that occupied Marx for the rest of his life: inquiring into "the connection of German philosophy with German reality," the relation of political criticism to "material surroundings."[8]

In a few short paragraphs *The German Ideology* radically reorients philosophical inquiry by radically reorienting what it is to be human, to produce ideas, and to inquire into them. There is no truck with philosophical synchrony in terms of "what it is to be human," that is, *The German Ideology* rejects any abstract definition of humanity in favor of a historical one: "Men can be distinguished from animals by consciousness, by religion or anything else you like. They themselves begin to distinguish themselves from animals as soon as they begin to produce their means of subsistence." On the one hand this is a definitional account, hypothesizing what has happened in the history of humanity to divide human consciousness and activities from animal ones. On the other hand, *The German Ideology* sketches a historical anthropology that is clearly recognizable and can be researched empirically, a task the authors set for themselves (CW, 5:31).

Perhaps even more important, *The German Ideology* theorizes consciousness and the production of ideas at any time as necessarily and intimately related to the production of "actual material life": "This mode of production must not be considered simply as being the reproduction of the physical existence of the individuals. Rather it is a definite form of activity of these individuals, a definite form of expressing their life, a definite mode of life" (CW, 5:31). This redefinition of humans, and of human consciousness, is nonreductive, in that the concept of production widens out from subsistence towards the economic and technological, rather than closes in towards the biological and physical "basics." However, what counts as other than productive, and so less crucial as a determinant of the "nature of individuals" and of their mutual relationships, is therefore necessarily less than analytically sharp.

The remainder of this philosophically original opening to *The German Ideology* elaborates a scheme of historical development, employing concepts of productive forces, division of labor, social relations within and between nations, and most importantly property relationships, leading ultimately to modern industrial societies based on capital. While the concept of ideology had a tortuous history prior to *The German Ideology*, and while its use in that text and by Marx and Engels elsewhere has famously raised interesting philosophical issues concerning truth and science, it is nonetheless reasonably clear in this early polemical context that it was supposed to capture the supposedly "upside-down" perspective of German idealism. Idealism was said to have a method of descending "from heaven to earth," that is, working from ideas to realities, whereas the text argues for ascending "from earth to heaven," that is, working from "real, active men" and showing how their ideas are "reflexes and echoes" of their "life-process." This is said to remove the independence ascribed by idealists to the realm of "[m]orality, religion, metaphysics" when they wrote as if these ideas developed in and through themselves such that humanity then progressed or developed along corresponding lines (CW, 5:36–7).

The German Ideology puts matters the other way round: "men, developing their material production and their material intercourse, alter, along with this their actual world, also their thinking and the products of their thinking" (CW, 5:37). These ideas, referred to by Marx as an "outlook," were developed in similar formulations most notably in the *Manifest der kommunitischen Partei* (*Communist Manifesto*) of 1848 and the "*Vorwort*" to *Zur kritik der politischen Ökonomie* ("Preface" to *A Contribution to the Critique of Political Economy*) of 1859, and then employed in the historical researches incorporated into the first volume of *Das Kapital* (*Capital*) (1867), and also in the contemporary political analysis undertaken by Marx in *Der achtzehnte Brumaire des Louis Bonapartes* (*The Eighteenth Brumaire of Louis Bonaparte*) (1852).

The German Ideology then takes up the political consequences of adopting this outlook, intriguingly defining "the practical materialist" as "the communist," and tackling the subject of "liberation" as the revolutionary goal. This is the overthrow of the circumstances in which "man's own deed becomes an alien power opposed to him, which enslaves him instead of being controlled by him." These circumstances have arisen historically with the division of labor, which eventually results in societies in which "each man has a particular, exclusive sphere of activity, which is forced upon him and from which he cannot escape." Drawing on manuscripts composed by Marx the previous year (1844) in Paris, *The German Ideology* summarizes what has become known since the 1960s as Marx's theory of alienation or estrangement: "This fixation of social activity, this consolidation of what we ourselves produce into a material power above us, growing out of our control, thwarting our expectations, bringing to naught our calculations, is one of the chief factors in historical development up till now" (CW, 5:38–9, 47–8). While *The German Ideology* is somewhat snide about the term "estrangement" as rather too temptingly philosophical (for those fighting phrases with phrases), it is clear that the phenomena discussed in the "early manuscripts" of 1844, and then through Marx's later career, are all rather similar and similarly understood, most notably in the "fetishism of commodities" section that closes the first chapter of *Capital*, vol. 1.

In terms of revolutionary action and liberation from humanity's self-produced oppressions, *The German Ideology* is hard-hittingly explicit: there must be a great increase in productive power, the great mass of humanity must be rendered "propertyless," and this must happen on a world scale: "Empirically, communism is only possible as the act of the dominant peoples 'all at once' and simultaneously, which presupposes the universal development of productive forces" and of the world market through competition. True to the opening critique of the "Young" Hegelians as "German ideologists," the political conclusion here is that "Communism is for us not a state of affairs . . . an ideal to which reality [will] have to adjust itself. We call communism the real movement which abolishes the present state of things." This movement is identified with the political activity of the proletariat, the mass of propertyless workers – the utterly precarious position of "labor-power on a mass scale cut off from capital" . . . "an existence of individuals which is directly linked up with world history" (CW, 5:48–9).

Whether this linkage is a purely experiential and ultimately contingent one, or whether there is some supposition, as in the earlier writings of 1843 and 1844, that the proletariat is the ultimate representation of human suffering and human potential, is never resolved in *The German Ideology*, nor in the subsequent texts which outline this long-term political perspective. The political context of philosophical politics of the 1840s was such that Marx clearly wanted to avoid sounding like just another philosopher with yet another abstract conception of "man," yet to make his empirical, historical, and hypothetical claims he needed a set of necessarily abstract conceptions such that his empirical evidence and allusions would make sense and carry conviction, particularly as a rhetoric of action: "This manner of approach is not devoid of premises . . . Its premises are men, not in any fantastic isolation and fixity, but in their actual, empirically perceptible process of development under definite conditions. As soon as this active life-process is described, history ceases to be a collection of dead facts, as it is with the empiricists (themselves still abstract), or an imagined activity of imagined subjects, as with the idealists." For philosophers today as then, the conclusion here is quite startling: "When the reality is described, a self-sufficient philosophy loses its medium of existence. At the best its place can only be taken by a summing-up of the most general results, abstractions which are derived from the observation of the historical development of men" (CW, 5:37).

7. Marx and Marxism

This result left Marx with twin problems: the further depiction of "reality" – as an "ensemble" of developing productive and social relationships on a global scale – and the linkage between that at least somewhat intellectual project and the international proletarian politics that would abolish both the rigid division of labor for individual workers and the class-divisions of modern commercial societies. There is considerable philosophical interest in the finer points of his successive works and manuscripts, particularly the discussions of the commodity and its fetishism in *Capital*, vol. 1, together with his definitional and empirical claims concerning human labor and labor-power, value-in-exchange, and capital as a self-expanding behavioral dynamic. However, it has to be said that Marx's originality and importance for philosophy in the most general sense lies in raising, rather than solving, the problems connected with an inherently politicized project for liberating humanity.

Until the 1960s Marx was almost universally associated only with the Marxist and later Soviet philosophy of dialectical materialism, and with historical materialism, its particular application. While neither term was used by Engels, he laid the groundwork for these conceptions in his landmark and very widely read works *Herrn Eugen Dührings Umwälzung der Wissenschaft* (*Anti-Dühring*), *Socialisme utopique et socialisme scientifique* (*Socialism: Utopian and Scientific*), *Ludwig Feuerbach und der Ausgang der klassischen deutschen Philosophie* (*Ludwig Feuerbach and the End of Classical German Philosophy*), and the posthumously published manuscripts known as *Dialektik und Natur* (*Dialectics of Nature*). These works were written as expositions of the ideas of Karl Marx, supplemented by Engels in the role of "junior partner." The materialism involved was said to be an inversion of idealism, and compatible with the matter-in-motion materialism that Engels attributed to the physical sciences of his day. The dialectics attributed by Engels to Marx rested on three "laws": interpenetration of opposites, negation of the negation, and the transformation of quantity into quality.[9]

Since Engels's death in 1895 questions have repeatedly been raised as to whether, or to what extent, his overarching philosophy of "nature, history, and thought" represents either what Marx was getting at all along, or what he came to believe in his later works. Leaving that issue aside and treating these ideas as a philosophy, it is evident that this philosophy tackles virtually all the problems that philosophers like to raise in dichotomies that they like to use: mind/matter, determinism/freedom, nature/humanity. Serious engagement with these issues within that framework was hampered by the overtly politicized character of Engels's discourse, in that for many Marxists and adherents of Soviet communism, the political outlook itself defeated any important doubts they might have held about the philosophies involved, and for anti-Marxists or other philosophers anxious to avoid the dangers of that kind of politics, or the difficulties inherent in any philosophy that was politicized at all, it was easy if not essential to ignore these writings or to dismiss them as crude or worse.

By the 1960s, however, the intellectual and political situation concerning Marxism was developing in more interesting ways. Louis Althusser's *For Marx* put a structuralist gloss on the mechanistic certainties of dialectics, in that Engels's notorious doctrine of economic "determination in the last instance"[10] became a theory of "overdetermination," through which "ideological apparatuses" were allowed considerable efficacity in politics, but were said still to be determined within an economic frame.[11] This theorizing attracted considerable attention because it arose on the "Left" in the "West," and because it was a philosophy that prioritized "structure" over individual will in forming and reproducing social subjects. This approach developed a notion of individuals as "bearers" (*Träger*) of the defining features of, say, capitalist society, as Marx had mentioned in *Capital*, vol. 1.[12] Althusser worked to resist romantic and unexplored notions of individual uniqueness and defining autonomy, and so to put liberal "humanism" very pointedly under critique.

With the discovery and wide circulation of the "early Marx" in the 1960s, and subsequent reinterpretation and revaluation of his thought in that light, the Marxist tradition of dialectics has waned, surviving notably in "Hegelian" interpretations of Marx, but not so much in philosophical expositions of such an interpretive framework in the first place. Bertell Ollman's philosophy of internal relations comes the closest to doing both, though this version of Hegelianism has had little more impact on "mainstream" philosophy than any other.[13] Much the same can be said of Aristotelian interpretations of Marx, such as Scott Meikle's, though the perspective is fresher, because it is rather unexpected, given Hegel's prominence as an intellectual and political force in Marx's formative years, and because of the apparent paucity of clues or reasons for finding commonalties between Aristotle and Marx.[14] However, in the wider circles of philosophy there have been three important developments to which work on Marx has substantially contributed. These are theories of ethics and justice, "analytical Marxism" as an intellectual discipline, and postmodern theories of representation.

8. Morality and Justice

Marx's hostility to, and profound interest in, philosophy and its political effects was mirrored in his negative attitude to morality, mentioned in *The German Ideology*, and also to justice, discussed in *Capital*, vol. 1. Are morality and justice merely ideological or epiphenomenal conceptions, inherently reflective of an inverted and mystifying notion of human action and social reality? If so, what are the implications in terms of political discourse and tactics? Or, are there new theories of ethics and justice that can be discerned in Marx that are consistent with his dismissive comments? One angle on this was that Marx was confused and so no coherent position is available. By contrast, those who claimed that at least some consistency was available in Marx, or could be analytically reconstructed, argued in two ways: either that he mistakenly (and dangerously) dismissed important considerations of ethics and justice in the usual sense by rejecting contemporary theories, or that he actually generated new and distinctive ethical and metaethical views that are of interest to moral philosophers and theorists of justice.

In relation to morality, Marx was certainly opposed to a moralizing politics (whether of reform or revolution) in which ideals, however abstractly justified, were set up as goals to which everyone should conform. He was particularly hard on religious conceptions of socialism, in this regard, as well as on the more rarefied forms of socialism incorporating idealist philosophies. In relation to justice, he famously expounded the apparently just exchange of value between laborers offering labor-power at a price adequate for its reproduction, and employers offering wages to meet that value in monetary terms. In accounting then for profits, Marx argued that the expansion of value relative to the original transaction was "a piece of good luck" for capitalists. This was because human labor, so he maintained, has a peculiar capacity to generate more value than is represented by its cost of reproduction. Leaving aside the definitional or empirical plausibility of that particular argument, we can focus instead on Marx's comment that this was "by no means an injustice towards the seller."[15] While equating mere justice with the surface transactions of the capitalist mode of production, Marx also wrote movingly and at length about exploitation in *Capital*, not least in implying that any product in society, therefore any surplus product, can only come from workers, and that those who control and enjoy this surplus – without working – are exploiters and worse: "The greater part of the yearly accruing surplus production, which is embezzled from the English workers without any equivalent being given in return, is thus used as capital."[16]

This seems to imply a view that something like a theory of ethics is operative in Marx's thinking, in that otherwise there really would be no justification for arguing so strongly that exploitation should be overthrown. Such comments as Marx endorses in terms that look like distributive justice are again merely indicative rather than philosophically informative: "From each according to his abilities, to each according to his needs," in the *Communist Manifesto*, and repeated in the *Randglossen zum Programm der deutschen Arbeiterpartei* (*Critique of the Gotha Program*). R. G. Peffer has done the best job in summarizing the various philosophical issues that arose in that debate, and also in constructing positions that Marx might indeed have held in ethics and moral philosophy. These are positions such that his dismissive comments about morality and justice, on the one hand, and his disdain for mere moralizing and facile notions of fairness, on the other hand, both make the best possible sense.[17] As usual, Marx's readers are stuck with an essential contradiction: his reconceptualization of philosophy as politics was philosophically very well grounded and very fully informed, yet not itself very philosophical or friendly to philosophers.

9. Analytical Marxism

"Analytical Marxism" arose in the 1970s with an agenda to set this to rights. Rather than an ad hoc group created by a debate, the individuals involved formed themselves self-consciously as an international seminar and generated a short prospectus. Announcing a "new paradigm," they eschewed "dogmatic or purely exegetical" studies, as well as "the increasingly discredited methods and presuppositions" of "Marxist thought." Instead, they proposed to use "the tools of non-Marxist social science and philosophy," so that "what is true and important in Marxism will be more firmly established."[18] This approach has the obvious advantage of looking outwards from Marx to larger and more contemporary issues, though it also has the less apparent disadvantage of relying rather uncritically on "social science and philosophy," indeed on some of the very concepts and methodologies that are trenchantly criticized in Marx's own work and elsewhere. As with any academic group there are considerable differences between the various individuals involved in terms of approach and subject matter. Broadly speaking, the movement divides into two: those concerned with the "theory of history" in a rigorously reconceptualized form, and those concerned with more abstract and historically limited inquiries using explanatory models of individual and social choice.

G. A. Cohen's *Karl Marx's Theory of History: A Defence* was a landmark effort to extract theoretically precise propositions and explanatory hypotheses from works such as the "Preface" to *A Contribution to the Critique of Political Economy*, tracing out the "primacy" of the economic "base" (as forces of production) over "relations of production" (as the economic structure) and then over further "superstructural" ideas and beliefs.[19] In his text Marx presented both a general model for all societies and also a detailed picture within this for capitalist society, though he himself termed this merely a "guide" for his studies, and used an ambiguous array of mixed metaphors. He then turned to an outline of historical transitions from one "mode of production" to another: primitive to classical to feudal to modern. By following Cohen's explication of the theory, other historians have researched a variety of these transitions in different geographical contexts, and proved the utility, if not the "truth," of this way of explaining historical change.[20] For Cohen, though, his engagement with Marx was not in the end a defense, as he concluded that he had put the best possible construction on Marx's thoughts, and that unfortunately even in that form, the propositions were false or flawed.[21] That conclusion, of course, was based on views of explanation and truth that are possibly alien to what Marx was doing, whether in his now famous "Preface" or elsewhere in his work.

The more abstractly inclined "rational choice Marxists," notably Jon Elster and John Roemer, have covered virtually the whole of Marx's social theory, subjecting it to a fierce critique founded on (highly contestable) notions of methodological individualism as the only sure explanatory basis for social science.[22] This, of course, presumes that Marx was either attempting to write social science himself, though rather unsatisfactorily from the present perspective, or that whatever he was doing, the most accessible framework for social scientists to adopt when reading him is the one which they accept. This effectively cuts off contemporary social science, and philosophy of social science, from a critical perspective on the very things that arguably Marx was keen to promote in his own time, or from a critical perspective that today's readers can derive from Marx's intriguing reconceptualizations of philosophy as an activity, and humanity as a historical subject. While Marx is credited for setting up conceptions of alienation and exploitation in class-divided societies which social scientists today should recognize, he is then "improved" through the use of a strategic-interaction perspective and game-theoretic analysis. By presupposing an autonomous and self-interested individual, these perspectives reflect in large measure the very social presuppositions of commercial and capitalist societies that Marx was concerned to undermine, and which analytical Marxists are not always concerned to question very deeply.

10. Construction and Representation

Thus far philosophical appropriations of Marx have generally begun where he did, with concepts of "material" production and reproduction in human life, economic activities, and corresponding social and political relationships. However, the linkages can be reversed in a certain sense, both for political and philosophical reasons. After the communist and socialist political failures of the 1920s in Western Europe, and the political struggles and subsequent authoritarian turns in the "East," doubts about a politics of economic determinism began to circulate, notably in the "Frankfurt School" and, independently of this, in the writings of Antonio Gramsci in Italy. An explanation for current reversals, on these views, must take the "social and political superstructure" seriously as a causal and structural determinant of action (or the lack of it). This led to more exploratory and eclectic modes of theorizing and to writings arguably rather closer to Marx's own political interventions than to his "guiding" propositions and presumptions, at least as Engels read them in his rather more deterministic and reductionist discussions. Philosophically the issues involved are not very challenging, as multidimensional and interpretive explanatory narratives, giving due weight to individuality, on the one hand, and the formative pressures of society, on the other hand, seem unexceptionable. The overall strategy of political engagement with class politics, however, is starkly at odds with more conventional views of philosophy as above politics altogether, or covertly or overtly identified with other political outlooks, such as liberalism or Catholicism, for example.

The "linguistic turn" in philosophy, according to which language is thought to construct the human social world for individuals, rather than to be a reflection of the world as perceived by individuals, provided a significant bridge between philosophies that were "Marx-identified" and those that were not. The move away from economic (or, ambiguously, "material") reductionism undertaken by the Frankfurt School and by Gramsci, can thus be read into philosophies of social construction through "representation," that is, the creation of intersubjective meaning as text. Text in this hermeneutic understanding is not limited to written language but can include images, "body-language," or architecture, for example – anything which can be "read" as having meaning. Meaning is further not restricted to an author's intent, say, but is rather located in readers, whose views may very well differ.

These views pose considerable challenges for foundational ontologies and epistemologies – theories as to what the world must be like before anything can count as knowledge – because the certainties traditionally claimed in foundational philosophies are simply dissolved into the contestable consensus(es) held within and between different and ultimately unpredictable human linguistic communities. Communities, on this understanding, are merely sites where representations of "self" and "other" are generated, and concomitant power-relations are continually generated and subverted. The "identities" available to individuals, on this view, are not instances of natural or naturalized features of body or culture, such as sex or ethnicity, but rather conceptualizations that are "performed" by individuals as repeated citations of what they "are," that is, one is what one does, though of course one cannot do this entirely as one pleases.

On this view, then, even social class is a performance and therefore individually and historically contingent, though rather than negating a politics of class struggle, it sets the stage for generating one through representation and intervention – precisely what Marx aimed to do in his political career. It certainly dissolves any foundational claims for a mechanically explanatory base/superstructure theory of society and social change, and indeed it provides no assurance as to what constitutes development or progress, or even process in history. It is thus rather difficult to square this view with almost any reading of, say, Marx's "Preface" to *A Contribution to the Critique of Political Economy.* By the same token, though, it opens up a reading of most of Marx's other works as a political rhetoric aimed at a mass audience. Ernesto Laclau and Chantal Mouffe caused consternation by espousing these kinds of claims, and thereby initiating a debate on "post-Marxism."[23] They also announced their adherence to "radical democracy," a pluralist but action-oriented view that socialism has to be made rather than awaited, and that it should be highly democratic. Arguably this is very close to the politics that Marx himself pursued, but it may also prove to be just as unsuccessful in the foreseeable future, as it was in Marx's lifetime.

Less politically ambitious but notable from the philosophical perspective are recent rereadings of Marx in this "representational" vein by the "situationist" Guy de Bord and by the academic philosopher Jean Baudrillard. Both utilize a considerable element of word-play, irony, fun, and extravagance, tending to the unintelligible or gnomic. In the manner of the "Young" Hegelians, de Bord parodies the form of Marx's "Theses on Feuerbach," but takes his text mostly from *Capital*, vol. 1, which he reinterprets. For Marx's emphasis on commodities as material goods and services, de Bord substitutes "the spectacle," defined as "the image of the ruling economy," and therefore a "social relation among people, mediated by images." Rewriting the opening of Marx's masterwork, de Bord writes: "In societies where modern conditions of production prevail, all of life presents itself as an immense accumulation of spectacles. Everything that was directly lived has moved away into a representation."[24]

From de Bord's text of 1967 it is a fairly short step to Baudrillard's writings of the 1970s and onwards, suggesting that capitalism has transmogrified into a "hyperreality" in which the circulation of commodities, as conceptualized by Marx, is no longer the important alienating feature and political determinant of society. Instead Baudrillard draws attention to the circulation of "signs" (which stand for commodities) and to the production of "simulacra" (copies without originals). Simulacra are fictive images or narrative fictions generated in the economy, especially as entertainment, but are far from innocuous. They normalize fantasies as acceptable and valuable, and conversely they devalue and distance realities that economic interests in capitalist societies find unpalatable, disruptive or unmarketable.[25] Some of the inspiration for this view derives from Marx's writings on the "fetishism of commodities" in *Capital*, vol. 1, but departs drastically from his views on value, surplus-value and labor-power as an underlying and destructive dynamic within the capitalist system of production and exchange. This has the virtue of posing value and exchange as philosophical problems of the utmost interest and urgency, as well as pushing hermeneutic theories of meaning and representation out into the realm of popular culture and news media where politics is really practiced. It has the vice of lending itself to charges of covert elitism and academic diffuseness.

11. Feminism and Marx

Feminist philosophers have found considerable interest in Marx, though at first glance he is not a promising resource. Politically he had no overt engagement with feminism in his career, and textually his references to women, and to what are often construed as feminist issues, are few and far between. While some feminists have found orthodox or structuralist readings of Marx's economic and historical theorization useful as a model, they have consequently often found it difficult to fill in the theory, tending either to choose one factor (sexual or economic) over the other, or to elaborate a "dual systems" approach, taking both factors into account as sources for, and explanations of, women's oppression and exploitation. Engels addressed the "woman question" directly in *Der Ursprung der Familie, des Privateigenthums und des Staats* (*The Origin of the Family, Private Property and the State*), published in 1884, but the extent to which this work represents Marx's own views, or is consistent with Marx's own work, is of course highly debatable. There is no doubt that Engels, at least, proposed a theory that professed to combine "material" production and sexual reproduction. The former factor relies on the reductionism and determinism of his reading of Marx (about which many feminist philosophers would have been unhappy on methodological grounds), and the latter factor incorporates a considerable element of now suspect anthropological prehistory and recently debunked Darwinian views of sexual selection.[26]

In terms of contemporary industrial societies, some feminist philosophers have debated the relationship between unpaid domestic labor, on the one hand, and the use of paid exploited labor to generate surplus value in the economy, on the other, with particular reference to the maintenance as well as the reproduction of the labor force. Other feminist philosophers have pursued postmodern readings of Marx as a philosopher of representation, singularly important in tracing out the mechanisms through which women's oppression and exploitation are maintained and enforced, largely though not wholly through the economic system, and the way that this is normalized through the transmission of culture. While feminists have had to read Marx somewhat "against the grain," a good deal of the attraction has been the politicized character and philosophical sophistication of his social theory.[27]

12. Conclusion

Some philosophers today would deny that Marx was a philosopher at all, arguing perhaps that his subject matter belongs elsewhere, such as sociology or economics, or that his methods are inappropriate or invalid, either because they are Hegelian-dialectical or Continental-hermeneutic. A few would argue that he could possibly count as a philosopher in so far as he fulfills what they consider to be the definitional requirements for the role, but only in occasional texts and passages. These might be discourses on the social character of humanity, at one extreme, or tracing out a formal logic of rational choice and unintended consequences, at another. A very few might suggest that his redefinition of philosophy as an engagement with mass movements in order to realize a true realm of freedom, where freedom is defined specifically in terms of the production and distribution of material goods and services, is precisely where philosophy should be, but simply has not yet arrived. Certain texts by Marx are undoubtedly important sites of philosophical engagement, and any question as to whether he is really a philosopher or not merely points to the need that many contemporary philosophers feel to engage with his writings, and the necessary conclusion that to ignore or dismiss them puts any philosopher at peril.

Notes

1 Leszek Kolakowski, *Main Currents of Marxism*, vol. 1: *The Founders*, tr. P. S. Falla (Oxford: Clarendon Press, 1978), p. 1.

2 For a full-length study arguing substantial differences, see Terrell Carver, *Marx and Engels: The Intellectual Relationship* (Brighton/Bloomington, Ind.: Wheatsheaf Books/Indiana University Press, 1983); for a critique of this position, see S. H. Rigby, "Engels after Marx: History," in *Engels after Marx*, eds. Manfred Steger and Terrell Carver (University Park, Penn./Manchester: Pennsylvania State University Press/Manchester University Press, 1999).

3 Karl Marx, "Critique of Hegel's Philosophy of Law: Introduction," in *Karl Marx and Frederick Engels, Collected Works* (hereafter CW), vol. 3 (Lawrence & Wishart, London, 1975), p. 182.
4 Karl Marx, letter to Arnold Ruge, March 13, 1843, in CW, vol. 1 (1975), p. 400.
5 Karl Marx, "Theses on Feuerbach," in CW, vol. 5 (1976), pp. 3–5.
6 David McLellan, *The Young Hegelians and Karl Marx* (Basingstoke: Macmillan Press, 1980), p. 114.
7 Ludwig Wittgenstein, *Philosophical Investigations*, tr. G. E. M. Anscombe, 2nd edn. (Oxford: Blackwell, 1958 repr.).
8 Karl Marx and Frederick Engels, *The German Ideology*, in CW, vol. 5, pp. 27–30.
9 Frederick Engels, *Dialectics of Nature*, in CW, vol. 25 (1987), pp. 356–7.
10 Frederick Engels, letter to J. Bloch, September 21–2, 1890, in Karl Marx and Frederick Engels, *Selected Correspondence*, tr. I Lasker, ed. S. Ryazanskaya, 2nd edn. (Moscow: Progress Publishers, 1965), p. 417.
11 Louis Althusser, *For Marx*, tr. Ben Brewster (London: Allen Lane, 1969).
12 Karl Marx, *Capital*, vol. 1, tr. Ben Fowkes (Harmondsworth: Penguin Books, 1976 repr.), p. 179.
13 Bertell Ollman, *Dialectical Investigations* (New York/London: Routledge, 1993).
14 Scott Meikle, *Essentialism in the Thought of Karl Marx* (, London: Duckworth, 1985).
15 Marx, *Capital*, p. 301.
16 Marx, *Capital*, pp. 344–5, 761.
17 R. G. Peffer, *Marxism, Morality and Social Justice* (Princeton: Princeton University Press, 1990).
18 Series prospectus for "Studies in Marxism and Social Theory," eds. G. A. Cohen, Jon Elster, and John Roemer, as published facing title page in Jon Elster, *Making Sense of Marx* (Cambridge/Paris: Cambridge University Press/Editions de la Maison des Sciences de l'Homme, 1985).
19 G. A. Cohen, *Karl Marx's Theory of History: A Defence* (Oxford: Oxford University Press, 1978).
20 Robert Brenner, "Bourgeois Revolution and Transition to Capitalism," in *The First Modern Society*, eds. A. L. Beier, David Cannadine, and James M. Rosenheim (Cambridge: Cambridge University Press, 1989), pp. 271–304.
21 G. A. Cohen, *History, Labour and Freedom: Themes from Marx* (Oxford: Clarendon Press, 1988).
22 For a collection of defining articles and critiques, see Terrell Carver and Paul Thomas, eds., *Rational Choice Marxism* (Basingstoke/University Park, Penn.: Macmillan/Pennsylvania State University Press, 1995).
23 Ernesto Laclau and Chantal Mouffe, *Hegemony and Socialist Strategy: Towards a Radical Democratic Politics*, tr. Winston Moore and Paul Cammack (London: Verso, 1985).
24 Guy de Bord, *Society of the Spectacle* (Detroit, Black & Red, 1983), secs. 1, 4, 14.
25 Jean Baudrillard, *Selected Writings*, ed. Mark Poster (Cambridge: Polity Press, 1988).
26 See Janet Sayers, Mary Evans, and Nanneke Redclift, eds., *Engels Revisited: New Feminist Essays* (London: Tavistock, 1987).
27 See Michèle Barrett, *Women's Oppression Today: The Marxist/Feminist Encounter*, rev. edn. (London: Verso, 1988).

Chapter 18

Friedrich Nietzsche

Richard Schacht

With the same justice and injustice with which Descartes is commonly deemed "the father of modern philosophy," and Kant its apogee, Nietzsche may be accorded the same honors in the instance of "postmodern philosophy." He also is often taken to have had even more to do with the demise of its "modern" predecessor than with the more notorious "death of God." Yet Nietzsche's relationship to the "modern tradition" in philosophy is complex, and is far from being one of unqualified opposition; while his relationship to much that is said and done under the banner of "postmodernism" in philosophy and neighboring precincts is debatable, and in any event is far from being one of obvious and complete accord. In some respects his thinking is deeply akin to that of Hume, for example, and to that of Spinoza as well, as he himself recognized; and, like both of them, he is far from hostile to some of the most significant traits and insights of the thought of Descartes, Kant, and even Hegel.

There is an important sense, however, in which Nietzsche marks and makes a strong and deliberate break with elements of the "modern tradition" associated for good reasons with Descartes and Kant, requiring a fundamental reconsideration both of the character and prospects of philosophical inquiry and of many of the matters with which it may concern itself. If this tradition may be taken to be characterized by a preoccupation with Cartesian ambitions relating to the attainability and attainment of a kind of knowledge that would be certain, grounded in self-evidence, and immune to rational doubt and rejection, and that would settle the Big Questions decisively (and satisfyingly) and put both the sciences and those other cognitive disciplines concerned with normative matters on a firm footing (whether this preoccupation takes the form of efforts to advance or limit or attack these ambitions), then Nietzsche did turn away from it, and did seek to move beyond it in favor of a differently oriented "philosophy of the future." And if this tradition is conceived as revolving around Enlightenment values, truth-claims, and confidences with respect to what can be expected of nature, humanity, history, and inquiry, by way of their advancement or rational reconstruction and vindication, then he turned away from that as well – even though he remained committed to the importance (although not the sufficiency) of a radicalized and "dis-illusioned" version of "free-spirited" enlightenment to the end of his productive life.

Nietzsche was a harsh critic of philosophers and philosophy previously and in his own time, and would also no doubt have been quite critical of subsequent developments on both sides of the English Channel in the century following his death in 1900 – including much of what has been done by those who have paid homage to him. Some have taken his critical stance to be so sweeping that it is tantamount to a repudiation of philosophy itself, either heralding its end (as those who themselves are so minded would see him) or demonstrating his irrelevance to it (in the eyes of those who identify with the Western tradition and contemporary mainstream of the discipline). And it is true enough that he was a philosopher neither by training nor by profession, with academic credentials only in the significantly different discipline of classical philology (in his case, the study of the Greek, Latin, and Middle Eastern languages and literatures). Like so many of his predecessors among those we now regard as significant figures in the history of philosophy prior to Kant, he never held a professorship in philosophy, even though (like Descartes and Hume) he at one point did aspire to such a position, and (unlike most) did hold a professorship in the discipline in which he was educated, for ten years, at the Swiss university of Basel.

It also is quite true that Nietzsche refused to conform to the norms of publication, writing, and argumentation characteristic of professional philosophy in his day and ours, and indeed went very much his own way both in his framing of the issues with which he dealt and in the manner in which he sought to deal with them. And it is further true that his unconventional writings include not only many efforts of an overtly "literary" character (from aphorisms and poems to *Thus Spoke Zarathustra*), but also a great deal of commentary on writers, events of the day, cultural and political developments, social and psychological phenomena, artistic and musical matters, and many other things one seldom encounters in the philosophical literature. He therefore made it easy for others to see him as something other than a philosopher, whatever one might think he was, and whatever one might think of it.

Yet for the last dozen years of his short productive life (prior to his terminal collapse in early 1889, at the age of only 44), Nietzsche considered himself to be a philosopher more than anything else, attempting to reform or transform philosophy from what it long had been and had become into what he believed it could and should be. He gave *Beyond Good and Evil* the subtitle "Prelude to a Philosophy of the Future"; and he sought to show in his practice as well as to proclaim by his preaching what the "new philosophers" he heralded would do. Indeed, few figures in the history of modern philosophy rival Nietzsche in the importance he attached to philosophy in human life; and he was no less concerned to transform it into the kind of inquiry he believed to be so greatly needed as he was to expose and counter the harmful consequences of philosophy gone astray (as he believed it had to a very considerable extent from Socrates onward). He has come to be associated in recent years with the effort to "deconstruct" many of the basic concepts and ideas central to our thinking about meaning and mattering, the problematic character of which tended to go unrecognized even among philosophers; but while this is appropriate enough as far as it goes, he deserves to be associated no less importantly with the effort to "reconstruct" the conceptual means of proceeding to reinterpret and revalue the many things requiring to be reconsidered in the aftermath of such "deconstruction."

Nietzsche's association with this recent philosophical fashion is the result of only one of the more recent appropriations of him that have so complicated his reception and interpretation in the course of the century following his death. At the time of his collapse, he was (to his great distress) almost completely ignored, not only by academic philosophers but by virtually everyone else as well, and had been reduced for some years to publishing his books (in runs of just a few hundred copies, of which few were sold) at his own expense, out of his dwindling assets and minuscule pension from Basel. During the decade of invalid illness preceding his death, however, his writings began to attract somewhat more attention (in part owing to his discovery by a growing number of artists, writers, and other intellectuals, and in part in consequence of the efforts of his sister and care-taker to market his work and reputation); and by the end of the First World War he had become something of a posthumous intellectual celebrity. Even philosophers were beginning to take notice, particularly among the early figures associated with the newly emerging developments of the day: *Existenzphilosophie* (existential philosophy), *Lebensphilosophie* (the philosophy of organic life in general, and life of the human sort in particular), the newly emerging "philosophical anthropology," and the "critical theory" of the Frankfurt School in particular.

But then came Mussolini and Hitler, both of whom Nietzsche's sister courted and managed to attract to her version of her brother's thought; and his celebrity soon turned to notoriety in the eyes of most of the rest of the civilized world, as he was appropriated by the Nazis and Fascists. The lingering effects of this travesty continue to impede efforts to understand his thinking, and even to gain him a serious hearing. His assimilation to French and popularized versions of "existentialism" after the Second World War complicated the situation further, both because of the oversimplification and distortion of his thought in another direction that this involved and encouraged, and because this did little to persuade mainstream Anglo-American philosophers that he deserved to be taken seriously after all.

The problem was compounded further in more recent years, for similar reasons, when he was appropriated and accordingly reinterpreted by existentialism's poststructuralist successors. The fact that he could be and was also given alternative interpretations as a Germanic cousin of the American pragmatists and as a proto-analytic philosopher, for all his unconventionality and rhetorical excesses, makes the entire interpretive situation even more confusing. Whether or not the diverse interpretability of the world in general is without limit, and whether or not Nietzsche held this to be the case, it would seem to come close to the truth with respect to his thought itself. The account to be given of his thought here, therefore, cannot be claimed to reflect the general consensus of interpretive opinion, because there is no such consensus (and in all likelihood never will be).

One reason for this state of affairs is that Nietzsche did not write treatises systematically working out clearly articulated positions on various philosophical issues in a once-and-for-all way. He largely abandoned the monograph form after his first few works, in favor of a more aphoristic style of reflection seldom running to more than a page and often of just a few lines, organized in ways that seldom amount to a comprehensive treatment of a topic or even an extended line of thought. He also returned to the same or similar topics repeatedly in different volumes, exploring them in different ways and often to seemingly different effect, leaving it to the reader to try to figure out what to make of them both individually and collectively. Moreover, his productive life came to an abrupt and early end, when he was only 44, and had been devoting his efforts to philosophical reflection for too short a time. And during the last decade of his productive life, after his early retirement from Basel, he lived an unsettled nomadic life, in chronically poor health, while undergoing an extraordinary intellectual development, for the most part on his own. His writings frequently have a provisional and enigmatic character even when his language is at its most emphatic; for experimentation with terms, concepts, metaphors, analyses, explanations, interpretations, theories, and styles were his stock in trade. And, to complicate things even further, he kept voluminous notebooks, surpassing his published writings in length, and constituting an enormous *Nachlass* the significance of which is endlessly debatable. Add to this that he was much given to polemics, metaphor, and the delights of rhetoric, and it is only too easy to see why the interpretation of Nietzsche's philosophical thought is as vexing and contentious as it is fascinating and rewarding.[1]

1. Life

Friedrich Wilhelm Nietzsche was born to the Lutheran pastor of the little village of Röcken in Saxony (midway between Leipzig and Berlin in what is now eastern Germany) and his wife on October 15, 1844, the first of their two children.[2] His sister Elisabeth, to whom he came to be intimately bonded, was born two years later. Both grandfathers had also been Lutheran pastors; and the immediate and extended family, like the communities in which the young Fritz spent his early life, were both pious and deeply conservative. Nietzsche's father, although severe and melancholy, played the organ in the ancient village church in addition to preaching; and Nietzsche's love of music as well as his own melancholic tendencies may well have been paternally inspired. His father died very early of a brain injury and subsequent complications, however, in 1849, obliging the family to relocate to the nearby town of Naumburg, where Nietzsche spent his childhood. It was there that his lifelong loves of literature and of music both took root; and by the time he was in his teens he was an avid reader, writer, pianist, and youthful composer. His intellectual prowess earned him a scholarship to the nearby prestigious classics-oriented academy Schulpforta, which he could not otherwise have attended; and there he distinguished himself in his studies, while also continuing to cultivate his musical and compositional talents.

The young Nietzsche began his higher education at the university at Bonn, contemplating the possibility of following his father's footsteps into the ministry as well as pursuing either literary or compositional studies. Languages and literatures won out, and he transferred to Leipzig to pursue their study, abandoning theology; but he continued to devote considerable time and effort both to piano and to composition, not only for piano but also for piano and voice and even for larger ensembles. He largely abandoned composition in his late twenties, around the time that his academic career began in earnest; but his interest in and love of music remained central both to his personal life and to his thought, and he continued to play the piano even into his final years.

It was in Leipzig, as a student, that Nietzsche became acquainted both with the work of Arthur Schopenhauer and with Richard Wagner in person, then midway through the meteoric rise that carried him to the heights of accomplishment, fame, and controversy in the worlds of opera and music. Schopenhauer's *The World as Will and Representation*, which Nietzsche happened upon in a used book store, changed the direction of his intellectual life, planting the seeds of thought and challenge that eventually summoned him to philosophy. Through his passionate but rigorously and persuasively argued case for a pessimism bordering on nihilism, Schopenhauer had thrown down a gauntlet that Nietzsche had to pick up. He was determined to find some way to a life-affirming alternative to Schopenhauer's life-rejecting pessimism without denying Schopenhauer's fundamental premises, which Nietzsche subsequently summed up in terms of the "death of God." In Wagner, who shared his early enthusiasm for Schopenhauer, Nietzsche initially thought that he had found the fountainhead of a post-Christian cultural rebirth both of tragedy and of a tragically-inspired life-affirmation, as well as a musical genius to whose advancement he was prepared to commit the prestige of his academic position and his budding talents as a writer and thinker. It was not long before he became increasingly disillusioned with both of them, and eventually searingly critical of both of them; but they remained of the utmost significance for him throughout his life – both because of their brilliance and because they were at once (as he himself knew so well) so compellingly and so dangerously seductive.

Central European academics in Nietzsche's time rarely were called to professorships until relatively late in life, after years of subprofessorial academic subsistence following the completion of their second doctorates. Nietzsche seemed so clearly destined for great things in the discipline of classical philology that he was called to a philology professorship at Basel when he was only 24, and before his first doctorate had even been awarded. He remained there for ten years, after which his increasingly debilitating health problems – some of which had long plagued him, others of which were acquired during his service as a volunteer medical orderly during the Franco-Prussian War of 1870 – compelled him to resign; but by that time it had also become clear both to him and to his colleagues that he was profoundly ill-suited both to the institution and to the academic discipline of classical philology.

During his decade at Basel, Nietzsche's relationship with Wagner evolved from intimacy to estrangement; while his intellectual orientation shifted from philology to philosophy. His only significant publications during this period were one monograph, *The Birth of Tragedy* (1872), inspired by and dealing with both the Greeks and Wagner; the four essays later published as *Untimely Meditations* (*David Strauss, the Confessor and Writer*; *On the Uses and Disadvantages of History for Life*; *Schopenhauer as Educator*; and *Richard Wagner in Bayreuth*; 1873–6), dealing with various intellectual and cultural developments that he considered in need of analysis and commentary; and a volume of aphorisms on a broad range of these and other topics that is now the first volume of *Human, All Too Human* (1878), much in the spirit of Voltaire (to whom it was dedicated) and other radical Enlightenment thinkers and writers.

In the mere ten more years that remained to Nietzsche before his collapse (which in all likelihood was of syphilitic origin, his near-celibacy notwithstanding), he never had a permanent residence, residing in boarding houses in Switzerland, Italy, and France while seeking relief from his incessantly tormenting ailments, and environments in which he could think and write. It was during this final decade, and under these circumstances, that he wrote all the rest of the work through which he has come to rank among the most important figures in the history of modern philosophy. (He lingered on for another eleven years of invalid insanity following his collapse, finally dying in Weimar – where his sister had brought him, to be on display and expire in the company of the remains of Goethe and Schiller – on August 25, 1900.)

During the two years following his retirement from Basel Nietzsche published two more installments of aphorisms that became the second volume of *Human, All Too Human* (1879 and 1880), and two other such volumes in what he called his "Free Spirit" series: *Daybreak* (1881) and the first four-part version of *The Gay Science* (1882). The next three years (1883–5) saw the completion and appearance of but a single work: his extraordinary literary-philosophical experiment *Thus Spoke Zarathustra*. Only three years remained before his collapse; and it was during those three years that he wrote all of the other works that make up the greater part of his philosophical legacy – *Beyond Good and Evil* (1886), a fifth "book" of a new edition of *The Gay Science* and *On the Genealogy of Morals* (1887), and *Twilight of the Idols*, *The Case of Wagner*, *The Antichrist* and *Ecce Homo* (all in 1888).[3] During these three final productive years, moreover, he also wrote new prefaces to all of his pre-*Zarathustra* works, became his own publisher,[4] carried on a great deal of correspondence, and filled numerous notebooks with jottings, reflections, and revisions of such material on a great many topics, only some of which was incorporated into the works he published during these last years.[5]

2. Philosophy

Nietzsche drove himself with such urgency, as he was driven to philosophy in the first place, out of an intense and profound concern with the crisis he believed threatened the very future of humanity, which he came to characterize in terms of "the death of God" and "the advent of nihilism." He was convinced that the interpretive and evaluative foundations of our entire Western culture and civilization were eroding, as traditional ways of thinking about ourselves and the world and about meaning and value were losing their capacity to convince and sustain us; that neither other cultures nor modern science nor the resources of reason and the arts nor the recourses of ideology, nationalism or other such would-be substitutes for religion were capable of filling the void; and that, unless a new sort of thinking could show the way out of and beyond this predicament, the human prospect would be bleak indeed.

Schopenhauer had in effect posed the same basic challenge starkly; but Nietzsche was determined to try to find some way of avoiding his profoundly pessimistic conclusion and its life-negating implications. Wagner initially seemed to him to be on the track of a solution, through a rebirth of a new tragic culture akin to that of the Greeks by way of a new wave of tragic musical art; but Nietzsche soon became first disillusioned with this pseudo-solution and then convinced that it posed a grave danger, diminishing rather than enhancing our capacity to discover and embrace a genuinely viable way of rendering life worth living and affirming. The "philosophy of the future" to which he conceived his efforts as a "prelude" and introduction might not itself be paradigmatic of the "enhanced" sort of life in question; but it could at least serve to reorient our thinking in a manner conducive to its ascertainment and attainment. And so he strove to discover and show the way, in the hope that he would be joined or at least followed by like-minded "new philosophers" in the kind of *fröhlich-Wissenschaftliche* inquiry he sought to inaugurate, of which his book of that title (*The Gay Science*) is an early instance.

Philosophy, Nietzsche came to recognize, has always been both an interpretive and an evaluative affair, covertly if not self-consciously and avowedly. His own kind of philosophy is very overtly just such an activity, involving both the examination and assessment of prevailing interpretations and evaluations, and the attempt to come up with alternatives to them, even improving upon them. His interpretive efforts revolve around the project of a naturalistic (postreligious, postmetaphysical) reinterpretation of human life, setting the stage for his "revaluation of values" and for the associated project of the development of a naturalistic reconceptualization of value and valuation. His "genealogy of morals" is but a preliminary part of this far more ambitious pair of projects, even if one that he believes contributes significantly not only to the comprehension of moral and normative phenomena but also to the emancipation from the grip of a certain sort of "moral" perspective that has long distorted philosophical thinking, both interpretively and evaluatively.

His insistence upon the interpretive and evaluative character of all thinking notwithstanding, however, Nietzsche was far from supposing that this requires the abandonment of all cognitive aspirations and of the very notions of truth and knowledge. Absoluteness, finality, completeness, and certainty must indeed be abandoned as attainable or even meaningful goals or criteria of "genuine" truth and knowledge; and if these notions are to have a future, they must be reinterpreted in ways better attuned to the actual character of human language, thought, and experience in the kind of circumstances and world in which we find ourselves. But this, for Nietzsche, opens the way for their rehabilitation and for the preservation of the ideas and ideals of cognitive endeavor, comprehension, truthfulness, and intellectual conscience – in philosophy, in science, and in many other human contexts. It is only if truth and knowledge are conceived and defined in certain ways – ways for which he believes there to be all-too-human explanations – that they warrant the negative verdicts he sometimes articulates, which actually are directed at those construals of these notions, rather than these very notions themselves.

This understanding itself, however, which eludes so many of his readers and interpreters, cost him some pains and took him some time to achieve. It was bound up with the considerable time and effort it required to emancipate himself from the longstanding metaphysical distinction between appearances and some sort of underlying "true world" that had found its latest incarnation in the Kantian (and Schopenhauerian) "phenomena–noumena" distinction, and indeed from the very notion of the "thing in itself," and further to reconceive the relation between appearance and reality along with both terms of this relation. A like task of overcoming and rethinking, not unrelated to this one, was required with respect to value, before Nietzsche could grasp the outlines of an affirmative alternative to nihilism "beyond good and evil" as well as beyond "the death of God."

Nietzsche was no less severely critical of the philosophical tradition than he was of most forms of traditional religion, and for somewhat similar reasons. In the philosophical flight into metaphysics and yearning for absolutes, he discerns the same sort of all-too-human tendencies that he detects in leaps of religious faith and commitment. He also finds philosophers all too often to be much too ready to indulge in wishful thinking, take things for granted, rationalize, deceive themselves, and sacrifice intellectual integrity for the sake of some value they hold dear. He faults them less for their principles, however, than for their failure to be true to them; and less for their determination to think things through and to comprehend them than for their failure to do so well enough, clearly enough, and deeply enough. His kind of philosophy therefore builds upon what he considers to be the best of the tradition, rather than repudiating it altogether.

So, for Nietzsche, critical analysis is the first order of business; and he prided himself in excelling at it. But its purpose, for him, is to prepare the way for interpretations yielding greater insight and comprehension, and for assessments not only in terms immediately appropriate to the context of the matter under consideration but also with respect to any stakes involved relating to the quality of human life. His kind of philosophy also calls for taking account of and bringing to bear all relevant available forms of knowledge – scientific, historical, linguistic, sociological, psychological, practical – and the perspectives as well as the sorts of sophistication they afford; and indeed this is one of the most important meanings of his idea of "perspectivism."

3. Religion

Nietzsche's generally critical stance in relation to religion manifests itself most vividly in his hostility to Judeo-Christianity, culminating in his late polemic *The Antichrist* (the title of which might better be rendered as *The Antichristian*, since Nietzsche's German title is *Der Antichrist*, and "*Christ*" in German usually means "Christian," and his main target in the book is Pauline Christianity rather than Jesus). His fundamental objection to it is not the dubiousness of its theology or the weakness of arguments for the existence of God and the immortality of the soul, but rather its devaluation of this life and this world (in favor of God's purported kind of reality and the life to come) and its debasement of everything conducive to the flourishing and enhancement of this life in this world. Under the influence of its teachings and evaluations, people have come to think and feel that if there is no God (and no God-given meaning and no hereafter in which divine justice prevails), then nothing matters.

Nietzsche considers this to be a truly terrible "crime against life" that has set the stage for the advent of nihilism, and so for a crisis that could turn into a catastrophe, if the demise of this faith results in an epidemic of despair that could doom humanity. What is objectionable about most forms of religion, on his view, is not their falsity per se but their detrimental impact upon human life. He argues that they tend to feed upon and foster weakness, sickliness, life-weariness, resentment, and self-abnegation, poisoning the wellsprings of vitality and creativity in the process. He therefore declares war upon Christianity in particular and upon all life-negating and life-diminishing religions more generally, both interpretively (through their theologies) and evaluatively (*Der Antichrist* was presented as the "First Book" of a projected multivolume *Revaluation of All Values*), in an attempt to break the grip of religious modes of thinking and valuation, and to prepare the way for more truthful and life-affirming and life-enhancing alternatives. His primary strategy is to expose the misguided reasons and ulterior motives underlying and contributing to the emergence and acceptance of the former, and to show that "God or bust" (that is, faith or despair) is a false dichotomy. Recognizing that the "God-hypothesis" cannot be directly refuted once and for all, he attempts instead to subvert it decisively by depriving it of all credibility.

It should be observed, however, that Nietzsche is differently disposed toward forms of religion that turn out to affect people with certain sorts of needs and limitations in a manner more conducive to their flourishing, or at least to their optimal attainable well-being (offering Buddhism and even the religiousness of Jesus himself as cases in point). Indeed, he goes even further, admiring both the Apollinian and the Dionysian forms of religiousness of the early Greeks, and coming close to envisioning and even commending a new quasi-Dionysian, neo-pagan kind of religiousness centering upon the affirmation and celebration of life and that about it which does or can make it estimable and worth living. Here too, as in the case of his critique of Judeo-Christianity, what is ultimately decisive for Nietzsche in his assessment of forms of religion is not their truth-value or epistemic plausibility as belief-systems, but rather their impact upon the quality of the lives of those whose lives they do or might touch and affect.

In speaking of "the death of God," Nietzsche has in mind a number of things. One is the demise of belief-systems featuring something like the "God-hypothesis," and of modes of interpretation and evaluation that turn out to be unable to stand on their own in the absence of such beliefs. Another is of religions as ways of life and forms of thought and experience, which may once have flourished as cultural phenomena but which likewise have died out or are in the process of doing so. And another is the demise of ways of thinking involving the postulation of absolutes of one sort or another that have served as God-substitutes for interpretive or evaluative purposes, as in the case of those who in effect absolutize and divinize metaphysical, moral, historical or other such principles on the basis of which they understand the meaning of their lives or of human life more generally.

Nietzsche's fundamental point about "the death of God" is that at this juncture all such recourses are on the wane, and that we are past the point at which we may hope and expect to come up with something comparably capable of filling the God-role. Whether this is the beginning of the end or the end of the beginning for humanity is the great question it poses, with the "advent of nihilism" as the all-too-natural withdrawal-symptom of this "event." As a philosophical crisis, however, it was Nietzsche's point of departure and challenge – and one that he welcomed. And he took it to call for a radical reconsideration of life and the world, of human existence and knowledge, and of value and morality as well.

4. Truth and Knowledge

Nietzsche came to philosophy neither through a study of the history of philosophy nor through a systematic education in the central problems of philosophy as they had been conceived by classical modern philosophers from Descartes to Kant. He came to it rather through a deepening concern with problems of value and human self-understanding to which his attention was initially drawn by his comparative cultural and literary studies, and by his own experiences and attempts to make sense of life without the aid of traditional modes of interpretation and evaluation that he could no longer take seriously. But this concern eventually led him to think extensively – if also unconventionally – about many of the kinds of problems in which philosophers have long been centrally interested. Like many others both before and after him, for example, he came to recognize that he could not do justice to the matters of greatest interest to him without coming to grips with questions relating to the nature and scope of truth and knowledge; and his way of doing so has come to be of growing interest, as well as the object of no little confusion and misunderstanding (to which his manner of expressing himself has certainly contributed).

Nietzsche makes much of the point that, in dealing with truth and knowledge, one is confronted with certain sorts of *human affairs*; and he contends that our understanding of them is likely to be either superficial or erroneous – as it long has been in the history of philosophy as well as among the unsophisticated – if they are not recognized to be so and dealt with accordingly. Philosophers have tended to treat the elements of our conscious life as a set of processes, relations, and activities altogether different from those occurring in the world of nature; and he regards this as a mistake. It is only if human life is "translated back into nature," at least initially, that we and our various activities and capacities – those relating to thought and cognition included – can be properly understood. But Nietzsche considers it no less important to understand them and ourselves *socially* as well. For it is in this context that the human intellect has arisen and taken shape, and that the linguistic medium and various practices associated with all human thinking and knowing have developed and are sustained and acquired.

Initially and still for the most part, on Nietzsche's view, this involves the establishment and transmission of linguistic conventions guided by pragmatic considerations. When we replace ordinary language with scientific terms and theories, we only produce more sophisticated versions of the same basic kind of conventional-pragmatic schematization of our relations to what transpires in the world with which we find ourselves confronted. The "truth" of scientific thinking, like that of the more ordinary ways of thinking with which we operate, is basically a matter of its *effectiveness*, to which simplification, abstraction, the use of fictions, and transmogrification all contribute, mooting the very idea of exactness of representation. One facet of this effectiveness relates to the extension of our capacity to control and exploit courses of events. The other pertains to the furthering of our ability to reduce the bewildering profusion of phenomena to a semblance of order and simplicity.

What human knowledge in general therefore basically amounts to, for Nietzsche, is the assimilation of our relations to our environing world to conceptual schemes in the construction of which our constitutions, circumstances, and practical needs have played major roles. This leads him to characterize truth as a kind of error, and knowledge as a kind of fiction, at least in relation to the traditional model of truth as the precise correspondence of thought to being, and of knowledge as justified true belief; for that model, on his view, is a myth. All humanly meaningful truth has a contingently relational character that requires to be differently understood, and all humanly possible knowledge has a perspectivally interpretive and provisional character that has to be reckoned with.

Yet Nietzsche does not take the upshot of these reflections to be either that there is nothing to be comprehended or that we are incapable of comprehending it any better than ordinary language and common sense equip anyone to do. He readily allows that the sciences enable us to expand our comprehension of a great many things in some respects, even while narrowing or distorting it in others; but that is not all. He further suggests that our ability to shift perspectives, in ways including but not limited to those opened up by the sciences, can enable us to come to understand a good deal about ourselves and our world after all. Aspects of human culture and of human life and human nature more generally, as well as at least something about the kind of world in which we find ourselves and what goes on in it, are among the things he takes to be commonly misinterpreted, and to admit of more adequate comprehension in this way. Indeed, he even considers the range of attainable comprehension to extend into the areas of value and morality.

It is this sort of inquiry and reflection that Nietzsche pursues under the banner of *fröhliche Wissenschaft* and commends to the "philosophers of the future." The road to comprehension is no royal one, leading directly and with certainty to its goal. It is not even a single road, but rather a variety of often rough and round-about paths, leading to various vantage points from which different aspects of life and the world become discernible. They include scientific inquiry, historical investigation, psychological analysis, and reflection upon various forms of human conduct, endeavor, attainment, pathology, and much else that we may observe and experience. The results of such thinking may not measure up to certain standards of truth and knowledge reflecting the preconceptions, convictions or longings of some philosophers; and it is not to be supposed to be anything like the meaning or goal of human existence. But Nietzsche attaches great importance to its attainment – notwithstanding the avowedly problematic character of the "value for life" of their pursuit under various human circumstances – at least for those like himself, whose "will to power" expresses itself as a "will to comprehend," and perhaps also as a means to the enhancement of human life.

5. The World and Life

What Nietzsche seeks to reinterpret and comprehend, more truthfully and with more justice than he thinks his predecessors had, is first and foremost our human reality, both as it is and as it might become. To that end, he attempts to achieve a better understanding than theirs of the world of which we are a part, since its nature must be supposed to be reflected in our own, however human life may have become transmuted in the course of human events. The world in which we find ourselves and of which we are a part is the only reality of which he considers it meaningful to speak, in opposition to those who have envisioned or postulated a higher reality or "true world" transcending it.

While he began by accepting Schopenhauer's idea that the world and life are fundamentally manifestations of a basic active principle Schopenhauer calls "will," Nietzsche soon became convinced that this view, too, is objectionably metaphysical. It is debatable to what extent he may be considered to have developed and committed himself to an alternative interpretation amounting to something like a philosophical cosmology; but he certainly did experiment with language suggestive of an interpretation of this world that is suggestive of a worldview having affinities with the modern scientific understanding of it in terms of energy or force. He does not simply accept that account as it stands, however, believing it to be possible to improve upon it. In doing so, he seeks to make more comprehensible both the basic character of life and the world and their rich diversity of phenomena – which in turn would then lend credence to the interpretation he offers.

That interpretation is cast in terms of a fundamental disposition he suggests to characterize all force at all levels of its organization, which he calls "will to power." He takes this disposition to be so basic that even the phenomenon of "becoming" is owing to it. This world is a world of dynamic quanta which by their very nature are interrelated and interrelating, in ways best understood in terms of power-relations. Power is, as it were, the name of the game; and the disposition to engage in such relations makes sense not only of the reality of change but also of both organization and disorganization in the world, and so of this world's pervasive general character and of the occurrence of various forms of organization and interacting systems of such functional unities within it. The state of the world at any point, on this interpretation, is a function of whatever such systems and relations happen to obtain, which will be forever changing, even though the game played by the world with itself remains forever the same.

Nietzsche presents this interpretation only tentatively in his published writings, but on a number of occasions in them expresses what appears to be at least a clear provisional commitment to it. In his notebooks he discusses it much more extensively, experimenting with various ways of formulating it and elaborating upon it. He certainly appears to have considered it superior to the various other world-interpretations he discusses – materialistic as well as idealistic, and scientific as well as metaphysical and religious – and to be at least a candidate for serious consideration. It enables sense to be made of the undeniable reality of creatures and structures of considerable complexity in the world, despite the absence of any God who might ordain them, or of any "true world of Being" that might engender them. It even enables one to dispense with the dubious idea of immutable "laws of nature" somehow written into the very nature of things that would explain them and what goes on within and among them. And it sets the stage for a philosophical biology, psychology, and sociology suggested by Nietzsche to be both plausible and fruitful.

The conception of power figuring in this interpretation should not be understood too simplistically. The varieties of power are many, and the "will to power" of which he speaks is not to be reduced to the idea of any particular sort of attempt to attain any one of them. The general theme Nietzsche discerns throughout the whole wealth of phenomena taken to be its expressions is not mere assertion and domination or assimilation as such. Rather, it might most appropriately be construed in terms of the idea of a disposition to *ordering transformation* in one way or another; and "power" for Nietzsche is fundamentally a matter of the imposition of some pattern of "ordering relations" upon forces not previously subject to them.

The idea that "the more things change, the more they remain the same" in this respect is one version of what Nietzsche may have had in mind in proclaiming a notion to which he clearly attached great importance, but the meaning and point of which are much debated: the notion of "the eternal recurrence." Another version, to which he also commits himself, is the idea that there is an unending alternation between extremes of order and disorder in the world. In both cases the notion vividly conveys his rejection of the idea that the world is developing or moving in a linear manner, from some absolute beginning toward some pre-established final goal or end-state. A further version, to which he gestures on several occasions in published writings (in *Zarathustra* in particular) and with which he at least experiments in his notebooks, is the idea that all events recur eternally, in sequence and down to the last detail. This version may have been meant less as a cosmological theory than as a kind of test of one's ability to affirm life and the world under what Nietzsche regarded as the most challenging of suppositions; for if one were able to do so even if faced with that prospect, then one would be past susceptibility to Schopenhauerian disillusionment and pessimism, and would have the resources required for the overcoming of nihilism. If one has the ability to live joyfully and affirmatively without any hope that life and the world will ever have a significantly different character – or even a different character at all – than they already do, one will have the qualities characteristic of that higher, postnihilistic humanity of which the "overman" stands as Nietzsche's symbol.

6. Value

It should already be clear that Nietzsche was intensely concerned with the problem of value – about the nature of value, the "revaluation" of things traditionally or commonly supposed to be of value, and about the kinds of value that remain or become available to us after the "death of God." His early writings reflect this concern, even before he developed the vocabulary in which to express and pursue it; but it was above all his dawning recognition of the threat and danger of nihilism, as the devaluation and abandonment of all prevailing and discernible values, that compelled him to take up the problem and raise it to the top of his philosophical agenda. And this in turn led him to seek a new fundamental standard or locus of value, by reference to which it might be possible to revalue rather than merely devalue all previous values – and perhaps to be able to proceed beyond the genealogy and deconstruction of such values to what he came to call "value-creation."

If (as Nietzsche supposes) there is nothing beyond this life in this world that even could (let alone should) serve as such a standard or locus, then the only intellectually respectable alternative to nihilism – beyond mere conventionalism or subjectivism that are but a step away from it – seemed to him to be to consider whether something about the basic character of this world and this life might serve. And this in fact turns out to be the case; for Nietzsche grounds his new conception and standard of value in his interpretation of their fundamental character in terms of "will to power." It is in these terms that he suggests life is to be both comprehended and *justified*; and it is also in these terms that he proposes to conceive both of the nature of value and of the basis of his "revaluation" and "rank-ordering" of values and human possibilities. Indeed, it is even in these terms that he understands the very phenomena of valuation and value-creation.

Life, as Nietzsche construes it, is an array of processes expressing this basic disposition; and there is nothing external to it by reference to which its value might be measured or even conceived. Value is internal to it, and must be understood in terms of its fundamental character; and thus value, in the final analysis, can only be "value for life." But this deceptively simple formulation turns out to mask enormous complexity in the case of something as richly variegated as *human* life. Nietzsche articulates his position concerning value in two different even if ultimately connected ways, along both "naturalistic" and "artistic" lines. They often are taken to be at odds with each other; but they actually are complementary rather than contradictory, each serving to bring out an important and fundamental aspect of the phenomenon of value as he understands it. Together they yield his notion of the "enhancement of life," which has both quantitative and qualitative dimensions, and which in our case has both physiological roots and cultural expressions, mediated by social and psychological relations and processes. They involve both the cultivation and organization of power relations and their transfiguration, rendering appropriate the language not only of growth and development but also of creation. Quality is taken to depend crucially upon quantity and vitality, but not to be identical with them.

It is to such transfiguration, coming about through the creative sublimation of an abundance of organized energy, rather than to its mere incrementation as such, that Nietzsche attaches the greatest significance. But he is also attentive to considerations pertaining to the manner of such transfiguration, and in particular to its internal and external dynamics; for it is of the greatest importance not only what its short-term impact may be but also whether in the longer run and in a larger way it is "life-enhancing" or detrimental to the flourishing and enhancement of life as a more-than-merely-natural affair. His "revaluation of values" and "rank-ordering of values" are intended to be carried out with such considerations in mind. And his conception of "the overman" as "the meaning of the earth" is meant to be emblematic of this reorientation of evaluative thinking, centering neither upon the basic character nor the mere preservation of life as such, but rather upon its artistically-modeled enhancement. The "overman" is the apotheosis of the "higher humanity" Nietzsche discerns as a human possibility and occasional piecemeal human reality, representing a transformation of life beyond the level of robust but insipid animality, and also beyond that of ordinary all-too-human humanity. And its hallmark is neither knowledge nor morality nor mere health or strength by themselves, but rather *creativity*.

Creating, for Nietzsche, is not peculiar to the arts, conceived as something distinct from the rest of life, even if the arts have served as a kind of special preserve for its cultivation and expressions. It is intimately related, on his view, both to "willing" and to "esteeming"; for they are all aspects of the same process, through which life transforms itself and endows itself with value. Life attains value through its creativity; and its creativity also engenders values of more specific sorts, through our creations and their esteeming. This is the phenomenon of what Nietzsche calls "value-creation," which he considers to be life raised to its highest potency, expressing itself at once self-transformatively and self-affirmatively.

The value with which human existence and "the earth" are in this way endowed is itself "created," and is nothing apart from human life and creative activity. Yet it is no merely apparent (but illusory) value for this reason in Nietzsche's eyes, and is no small value either. It is as real as this higher humanity itself is or may come to be. The creation of values is more than the bestowal of value upon something one creates; for it is even more importantly an *attainment* of value. And the imbuing of life and the world with value in this manner is for him the highest of all forms of "will to power," through which it achieves its own vindication, and becomes something more than mere pointless striving and suffering, all sound and fury signifying nothing – even if there is no tribunal external to it before which that vindication can be appreciated or even conceived.

7. Human Nature

Human life differs in many important respects from other forms of life, as well as exhibiting a remarkable degree of variation; and those are salient points to which Nietzsche is highly attentive. Yet another salient point about it is that, its distinctiveness notwithstanding, "the type 'man'" began as and remains a biological reality, originating in this world among and in relation to other life-forms, rather than in some higher reality transcending it. We are indeed "the no-longer-merely-animal animal"; but this, for Nietzsche, can only be owing to the manner in which humanity has developed, and must be comprehended accordingly. "Translating our humanity back into nature" thus is one of the most important tasks of Nietzsche's philosophical-anthropological reinterpretation of our human reality, even if reading our humanity back out of nature again, in a manner doing justice to the developmental emergence of that humanity, is another. We do ourselves no favor to mythologize our origins and fictionalize our status; for we thereby do not do justice to ourselves, and render ourselves vulnerable to a nihilistic self-depreciation in the aftermath of the disillusionment that would be all too likely to follow upon enlightenment.

One of the most common misunderstandings of ourselves, which it is one of Nietzsche's central concerns to overcome, involves conceiving of the human mind or spirit as something separate and distinct from the body, rather than as "something about the body" (as he has Zarathustra put it), developed under certain social conditions and in the context of an interplay of physiological, psychological, cultural, and educational variables. Another involves failing to grasp and take seriously that our human nature is not some unchanging, timeless reality, but rather is the product of a long evolutionary and historical development (with much that is all-too-human about it). And yet another is that human nature is not something uniform in all of us, but rather has both a plasticity about it and a degree of variation in our endowments that can and does lead human beings to turn out very differently indeed, in many respects.

Viewed in the perspective of the general norms of vitality and flourishing animality, our humanity might be regarded as a multifaceted result of a variety of things that *went wrong* or that required drastic measures in the course of our development. Indeed, Nietzsche suggests, we may be the "sickliest" and "most endangered species" as a consequence, with the eventual outcome very much in doubt. Yet for all that, he is far from advocating or even desiring a return to some more "healthily natural" state; for that would mean sacrificing what makes us "the most interesting animal," and precluding the possibility of any further enhancement of life that might also enhance its worth. It is as if nature were making a unique experiment in us. In our social and conscious life, a complex alternative manner of existence to those characteristic of other creatures has emerged. The conditions imposed by social life played an important role in the breakdown of our former instinct-structure, as well as in the filling of the void that was left. It was under those conditions, on Nietzsche's view, that consciousness, powers of thought and expression, conscience, responsibility, and the whole panoply of our psychology came about and took shape. Human spirituality and mentality were born, and the genealogy of the soul began.

Thus Nietzsche is far from denying that there is anything to the ideas of the spirit, mind, and soul; but he maintains that they must be understood as shorthand for our spiritual, mental, and experiential lives, which in turn must be construed as developments of and out of protohuman and subsequent biological and social phenomena. Even consciousness and rationality are held fundamentally to be products of our social existence and circumstances (including the necessity of communication and so the medium of language) in conjunction with our practical needs and abilities. Our personal identities, too, are suggested to have originated socially, through our being held responsible for our conduct over time. And while fundamentally a fiction, such socially engendered and reinforced self-identification has the consequence that, as it sinks in, we cease to be creatures of the moment, and actually begin to become such "selves," for all practical (human) purposes, even if not metaphysically.

But this is not the end of the story of our humanity. While the imposition of personal identities on human beings is fundamentally a socialization-phenomenon, Nietzsche suggests that it prepares the way for a possible further development transcending this outcome. A genuine measure of individual "sovereignty" or autonomy, self-mastery and self-direction become humanly possible, rendering those attaining it capable of living "beyond good and evil" and dispensing with the social straitjacket without lapsing into impulsiveness and barbarity. The foundation is thus laid for the emergence of what Nietzsche calls a "higher" type of human being, transcending these lesser ways of being human.

The attainment of that "higher spirituality" in which Nietzsche's "higher humanity" culminates involves not the eradication or repression of the basic drives with which we are endowed, but rather their *sublimation*. These drives may be short-sightedly selfish and even brutal and destructive in their rudimentary forms and expressions; but on his view they are indispensable to flourishing vitality and supply the impetus to all higher spirituality and culture, through which alone human life can transform itself into something worthy of esteem. Their sublimation is the key both to the emergence of all higher culture and to a participation in the life of such culture that admits of ever further enhancement and enrichment, thereby funding the "value creation" that affords a viable alternative to nihilism. Those who for whatever reasons do not rise to a life of this sort (the human "herd"), remaining rather in the "lowlands" of all-too-human mediocrity, both dismay Nietzsche and worry him. He may have underestimated the extent to which such "higher humanity" is attainable by human beings generally; but he surely does well to underscore the difficulty of doing so – which may well have the consequence that, for better or for worse, it will never become the human rule.

Nietzsche is often taken to have unduly and even insidiously excluded great segments of humanity even from potential candidacy for higher humanity, including women and minorities generally (as well as the white male members of a good many ethnic groups), not only statistically but for reasons relating to their purportedly inferior basic natures. And one can certainly find numerous passages in which he says things that would seem to warrant this conclusion, particularly with respect to women. A careful and through reading of him shows that his views on these matters are neither as simplistic nor as easily dismissed as one might suppose; but they undeniably do leave a good deal to be desired. His thinking on this matter was undoubtedly influenced by his Larmarckian belief in the heritability of acquired characteristics, which allowed him to suppose that cultural patterns could become ingrained in whatever it is (the mechanism was not known) that determines trait inheritance. The general state of understanding of heredity in his time was such that it is not surprising that he went astray in a number of such respects precisely in his attempt to pay more attention to human biology, physiology, and evolution than philosophers previously had.

What is perhaps more important, however, is Nietzsche's commitment to a kind of philosophical anthropology that calls for provisional rather than dogmatic conclusions on all such matters, and for continual reconsideration and revision in the light of both critical reflection and new understanding deriving from empirical investigations in the various sciences. If we have good reasons for thinking that he is mistaken in some of the things he says with respect to either our shared or our differing natures, we also have good reasons for supposing that he, too, eventually would come to have second thoughts about them.

On Nietzsche's reinterpretation of our humanity, neither human life in general nor human lives in particular have intrinsic value rendering them worthy of reverence, respect or even perpetuation merely as such. The only value human beings have relates to what they represent and may bring about; and this is a function of characteristics they do not all possess in equal measure, as well as of what is made of them. Nor does Nietzsche shrink from the consequence that this warrants not only competition and differentiation but also exploitation. But the *forms* of competition and exploitation he has in mind, when he goes beyond observing that they are basic to life to commending them, are those the flourishing and advancement of *culture* require, rather than those which merely serve the specific interests or satisfy the desires of particular individuals. His entire conception of "higher humanity" is related directly and intimately to his conception of culture and its significance. Human life is crucially transfigured when it makes the transition to this plane of activity and experience; and that transfiguration is of such importance to Nietzsche's proffered solution to the problem of nihilism that he embraces its implications for the revaluation of values.

8. Morality

Nietzsche was preoccupied with the problem of morality throughout the whole of his philosophical life. He calls himself an "immoralist"; but he adopts this misleading label to convey his opposition to a certain type of conventional morality that is commonly taken to be identical with morality itself, and to a kind of moral theory that reinforces that claim by ruling out anything of a different sort as a morality at all. He often refers to that type of morality as "herd animal morality"; and his basic point actually is that that sort of morality deserves neither to be taken for granted nor taken as the paradigm of what a morality should be. Indeed, he further maintains that there is a good deal that is wrong with it, and that there is much to be said for a different way of thinking about morality and for different moralities in at least a good many human contexts.

Nietzsche's moral philosophy is part analysis, part critique, and part normative theory, and by no means reduces either to his "genealogy of morals" (which is but one of the sorts of analysis with which it merely begins) or to the contents of Zarathustra's exhortations in *Thus Spoke Zarathustra*. He considers it to be imperative, in setting out to do moral philosophy, to arrive at a proper understanding of the ways in which moralities function in human life, and of how they have come to do so and have evolved, regardless of whether they are in any sense either "true" or authorized or even beneficial, to everyone or even to their adherents. He readily allows that various moralities do exist and have existed; and he makes much of the fact that they have long played very significant roles in human affairs and even in the course of the emergence and development of our humanity. Traditional moralities, he observes, are fundamentally social phenomena, reflecting the attitudes, needs, fears, circumstances, and other such features of various human cultures, societies, communities, or groups within them.

A dynamic that has been fateful for the history of morality in the Western world and that is of particular interest to Nietzsche is that which he frames in terms of the clash of "master" and "slave" moralities, in the course of which the latter eventually attained the upper hand, with the result that the kind of morality he takes to have become dominant in the modern world is a "herd" morality with a strong "slavish" hue. ("Master morality" is in the first instance affirmative of things associated with the distinctive qualities of a dominant group, and is only secondarily dismissive of things contrasting with them. "Slave morality" by contrast is suggested to be prompted fundamentally by resentment and reaction against the dominant group and everything associated with its dominance on the part of a dominated group, and so to begin with a negation, with its affirmations then being secondary and derivative.)

Whatever their origins and symptomatic significance, Nietzsche observes that moralities tend to reflect underlying valuations and to promote their acceptance by those whose lives they touch. Under the spell of such norms and values, people live differently than they otherwise might – not only if they were to be entirely amoral or pre-moral, but also if they were to embrace differing normative and evaluative schemes. The morality that has come to prevail reflects and reinforces a number of these value-determinations; and Nietzsche's most fundamental objections to it concern their detrimental impact upon the quality of human life and lives, not only in the case of exceptions to the human rule to whose potential it is very ill-suited, but even in the case of many others for whom alternative versions of "herd morality" would be considerably healthier and more conducive to their flourishing.

Nietzsche is concerned not merely to come to terms with past and present moralities, but moreover to look beyond them. He attempts to achieve a reorientation of the manner in which morality is understood that would serve to place it on a new footing. Owing to the constitutional and circumstantial differences among human beings, he contends, different manners of life are properly prescribable for various human types, with associated differing moralities. The result is the idea that morality is best thought of in the plural, and as conditional and delimited in scope rather than categorical and universal: different morals are warranted in some human contexts and for some human beings, while being inappropriate or even detrimental in other contexts and for others.

But Nietzsche ultimately asks more of moralities than that they simply answer to the "conditions of life" of various types of human beings. For it is to human life as a broader phenomenon that he would refer them, the strengthening and enhancement of which they are to serve, indirectly if not directly. A particular sort of morality may be warranted for human beings of some type in some context not simply because it answers to their needs, but rather (and more importantly) because it serves to maximize their contribution in one way or another to human worth. And he does not at all suppose that the kind of "higher morality" that would be appropriate for certain exceptions to the human rule under certain conditions would be equally appropriate either for all humankind or even for other equally (but differently) exceptional human beings. Morals, for Nietzsche, are better customized than universalized.

Further, Nietzsche's "higher moralities" are not to be conceived on the model of the sort of thing he calls "master moralities," even if the latter may be considered as preliminary versions and instances of the former; for just as Nietzschean "higher humanity" differs markedly in its more developed forms from the robust but bar-

baric humanity of his "master" types, the moralities associated with each differ accordingly. Such "higher" moralities do not or would not enjoin or even simply license exceptions to the human rule to assert their own individuality, or to act in accordance with whatever desires or impulses they may have. On the contrary, Nietzsche stresses the function of this sort of morality as a form of *discipline*, in the service of values the pursuit of which transfigures them. Its prescriptions, proscriptions, and standards reflect the requirements of the pursuit of some sort of enriched, strengthened, refined, and more creative form of life. (If there is anything that Nietzsche takes to characterize moralities generally, it is that they all have to do with self-restraint; and this applies to those he terms "higher" no less than to those he deems "herd" phenomena.)

This unconventional higher type of morality would seem to be modeled on the more familiar idea of the "morality" of the artist, whose only law is that called for by the kind of creativity attempted and by the tasks undertaken in its pursuit. Self-overcoming, self-mastery, self-cultivation, and self-direction in the employment of one's powers, along with the "loftiness of soul" they make possible, characterize both Nietzsche's higher type of human being and the correspondingly higher type of morality associated with that distinctive human possibility. And this is only fitting, since at this level, for Nietzsche, human life becomes something like art, while art and the lessons learned from it merge into life, in the flourishing of culture. For this, in the final analysis, is what Nietzsche's vision of a mature, sustainable, and affirmable humanity comes down to: the ongoing transformation of merely biological and social existence into an ever-expanding array of cultural expressions of human ability, through the sublimation of merely natural drives into a higher spirituality characterized by a wealth of forms of creative activity.

9. Conclusion

Nietzsche is severely critical of religion, morality, science, traditional values, and many of our most cherished beliefs about our society and ourselves. Yet there may never have been a philosopher whose thought is more profoundly affirmative in its basic thrust: affirmative of this life in this world, of the promise humanity represents, of the future that lies open to us, and of philosophy as the key not only to their comprehension but also to their realization. His deepest concern is to show that neither the "death of God," nor the demise of all faiths predicated upon otherworldly hopes or this-worldly optimisms, gives the last word to nihilism; and to find a way beyond it without recourse once again to illusion vulnerable to disillusionment.

Nietzsche's philosophy is a stock-taking of all that we have been and are, and of all that we have both to deal with and to work with. And it is also an extraordinary attempt to proceed to do what we can with what we've got, with respect to the twin tasks of interpretation and evaluation, in the service of both the comprehension and the enhancement of life. Nietzsche certainly is not the first or the last philosopher to have had such concerns and ambitions; but there are few either before or since whose thought is as seminal, who so richly reward continuing attention, and who remain at once so untimely and so timely.[6]

Notes

1 The now-standard German-language edition of Nietzsche's writings is the *Kritische Gesamtausgabe: Werke*, also available in a paperback version, *Sämtliche Werke: Kritische Studienausgabe*, both edited by Giorgio Colli and Mazzino Montinari, and published (in many volumes) by de Gruyter (Berlin).

2 For more detail on Nietzsche's life than can be provided here, and for a variety of differing treatments including attention to his general intellectual and philosophical as well as personal biography, see Ronald Hayman's *Nietzsche: A Critical Life* (New York: Oxford University Press, 1980), R. J. Hollingdale's *Nietzsche: The Man and His Philosophy*, rev. edn. (Cambridge: Cambridge University Press, 1999), and Walter Kaufmann's *Nietzsche: Philosopher, Psychologist, Antichrist*, 4th edn. (Princeton: Princeton University Press, 1974).

3 Early translations of Nietzsche's writings into English generally leave a good deal to be desired. Walter Kaufmann and R. J. Hollingdale, both intellectually and in some instances collaboratively, produced translations of most of the works he published or completed for publication that for many years were commonly considered to be the best available. While other translations of many of these works have been published in recent years and continue to be made, the Kaufmann and Hollingdale translations remain the most widely used, and are at least among the best available.

4 See William Schaberg's *The Nietzsche Canon* (Chicago: University of Chicago Press, 1995) for a detailed account of Nietzsche's early publication history.

5 A sampling of this material from his notebooks of 1883–8 may be found in a compilation made and published under Nietzsche's name after his collapse by his sister under the title *Der Wille Zur Macht* or *The Will to Power* (published in various versions in 1901, 1904, and 1910–11), tr. Walter Kaufmann and R. J. Hollingdale (New York: Vintage, 1967).

6 For a more extended introduction to Nietzsche, see my *Making Sense of Nietzsche* (Urbana: University of Illinois Press, 1995); and for a much more extensive examination of his philosophical thinking on such topics as truth and knowledge, life and the world, human nature, value and values, morality and art, see my *Nietzsche* (London: Routledge & Kegan Paul, 1983). Other recent studies of Nietzsche deserving of attention include Alexander Nehamas's *Nietzsche: Life as Literature* (Cambridge, Mass.: Harvard University Press, 1985), Maudemarie Clark's *Nietzsche on Truth and Philosophy* (Cambridge: Cambridge University Press, 1990), and Peter Poellner's *Nietzsche and Metaphysics* (Oxford: Oxford University Press, 1995). For a fairly extensive bibliography through 1995, see my *Making Sense of Nietzsche*.

Select Bibliography

In addition to the works cited in the "List of Contributors" section, the following titles are recommended for those who wish to pursue a more advanced study of the history of modern philosophy.

Scientific Background

Hall, A. Rupert. *The Revolution in Science, 1500–1750.* London: Longman, 1983.

Merz, John Theodore. *A History of European Scientific Thought in the Nineteenth Century.* 2 vols. New York: Dover, 1965.

Westfall, Richard. *Construction of Modern Science: Mechanisms and Mechanics.* Cambridge: Cambridge University Press, 1977

——. *Never at Rest: A Biography of Isaac Newton.* Cambridge: Cambridge University Press, 1980.

General Surveys

Beck, Lewis White. *Early German Philosophy: Kant and His Predecessors.* Cambridge, Mass.: Harvard University Press, 1969.

Beiser, Frederick C. *The Fate of Reason: German Philosophy from Kant to Fichte.* Cambridge, Mass.: Harvard University Press, 1987.

Cassirer, Ernst. *The Philosophy of Enlightenment.* Princeton: Princeton University Press, 1951.

Garber, D. and Ayers, M., eds. *The Cambridge History of Seventeenth-Century Philosophy.* Cambridge: Cambridge University Press, 1998.

Löwith, Karl. *From Hegel to Nietzsche: The Revolution in Nineteenth-Century Thought*, tr. David E. Green. New York: Columbia University Press, 1991.

Mandelbaum, Maurice. *History, Man, & Reason: A Study in Nineteenth-Century Thought.* Baltimore: Johns Hopkins University Press, 1971.

McLellan, David. *The Young Hegelians and Karl Marx.* London: Macmillan, 1969.
Stephen, Leslie. *History of English Thought in the Eighteenth Century.* New York: Peter Kemp, 1949.

Works on Individual Philosophers

Ariew, Roger. *Descartes and the Last Scholastics.* Ithaca: Cornell University Press, 1999.
Ayers, Michael. *Locke.* 2 vols. London: Routledge, 1991.
Cassirer, Ernst. *Kant's Life and Thought*, tr. James Haden. New Haven: Yale University Press, 1981.
Cranston, Maurice. *Jean-Jacques* [vol. 1]. New York: Norton, 1983.
——. *The Noble Savage* [vol. 2]. Chicago: The University of Chicago Press, 1991.
——. *The Solitary Self* [vol. 3]. Chicago: The University of Chicago Press, 1997.
Gaukroger, Stephen. *Descartes: An Intellectual Biography.* Oxford: Oxford University Press, 1995.
Griswold, Charles L. *Adam Smith and the Virtues of Enlightenment.* Cambridge: Cambridge University Press, 1999.
Harris, H. S. *Hegel's Development.* 2 vols. Oxford: Oxford University Press, 1972/1983.
Hollingdale, R. J. *Nietzsche: The Man and His Philosophy.* Cambridge: Cambridge University Press, 1999.
Kirmmse, Bruce H. *Kierkegaard in Golden Age Denmark.* Bloomington: Indiana University Press, 1990.
Livingston, Donald W. *Hume's Philosophy of Common Life.* Chicago: University of Chicago Press, 1984.
Luce, A. A. *Berkeley and Malebranche: A Study in the Origin of Berkeley's Thought.* Oxford: Oxford University Press, 1934.
Magee, Bryan. *The Philosophy of Schopenhauer.* Oxford: Oxford University Press, 1983.
Martinich, A. P. *Hobbes: A Biography.* Cambridge: Cambridge University Press, 1999.
McLellan, David. *Karl Marx: His Life and Thought.* London: Macmillan, 1973.
Miller, James. *Rousseau: Dreamer of Democracy.* New Haven: Yale University Press edition, 1984.
Nadler, Steven. *Spinoza: A Life.* Cambridge: Cambridge University Press, 1999.
Sleigh, R. C., Jr. *Leibniz and Arnauld.* New Haven: Yale University Press, 1990.
Stephen, Leslie. *The English Utilitarians.* 3 vols. New York: Peter Kemp, 1950. (Vol. 1: Jeremy Bentham; vol. 2: James Mill; vol. 3: J. S. Mill.)
Wartofsky, Marx. *Feuerbach.* Cambridge: Cambridge University Press, 1977.
Wilson, Catherine. *Leibniz's Metaphysics: A Historical and Comparative Study.* Princeton: Princeton University Press, 1989.
Yirimyahu, Yovel. *Spinoza and Other Heretics: The Marrano of Reason.* Princeton: Princeton University Press, 1991.
Zagorin, Perez. *Francis Bacon.* Princeton: Princeton University Press, 1998.

Edited Series

The Blackwell Philosopher Dictionaries are an invaluable resource for detailed information about conceptual vocabulary, social and cultural background, and personal biography, as well as comprehensive coverage of the philosophers' writings. The following volumes have appeared on figures of the modern period (all Blackwell Publishers, Oxford):

Caygill, Howard. *A Kant Dictionary*. 1995.
Cottingham, John. *A Descartes Dictionary*. 1993.
Dent, N. J. H. *A Rousseau Dictionary*. 1992.
Inwood, Michael. *A Hegel Dictionary*. 1992.
Yolton, John W. *A Locke Dictionary*. 1993.

The Cambridge Companions to Philosophy series (Cambridge University Press) features collections of scholarly essays on all the important thinkers of the modern period. These volumes are especially useful for their in-depth treatment of all the major aspects of a thinker's life and work.

Index